Criminal
Behavior
Systems

A TYPOLOGY

Criminal Behavior Systems

A TYPOLOGY

MARSHALL B. CLINARD
University of Wisconsin

AND

RICHARD QUINNEY
New York University

HOLT, RINEHART AND WINSTON, INC. · New York · Chicago · San Francisco · Atlanta · Dallas
Montreal · Toronto · London

To Ruth and Valerie

PREFACE

Our basic purpose has been to present the student of criminology with a broad survey of recently accumulated knowledge concerning the various forms of criminal behavior. We feel that continued progress in criminology will largely depend on the study of *types* of crime. One of the most significant recent developments in criminology has been research based on the realization that crime covers a wide and diverse range of phenomena.

In order to present these forms of criminal behavior systematically, the book contains (1) a discussion of the construction of types of crime, (2) the formulation and utilization of a typology of crime based on criminal behavior systems, and (3) the presentation of some of the most important research on types of crime.

We propose eight types of criminal behavior systems. The construction of our typology is based on such sociological criteria as the criminal career of the offender, group support of the criminal behavior, correspondence between criminal behavior and legitimate behavior patterns, and societal reaction. We have called the types (1) violent personal crime, (2) occasional property crime, (3) occupational crime, (4) political crime, (5) public order crime, (6) conventional crime, (7) organized crime, and (8) professional crime. These eight criminal behavior systems provide the basic framework for the presentation of the research and writings on the types of crime.

Each criminal behavior system is preceded by a discussion of the characteristics of the type. A selected bibliography, which follows this discussion, provides a guide for further reading on the particular system.

Each research study has been carefully chosen from the standpoint of research design and theoretical orientation. Wherever possible, the studies were selected on the basis of empirical investigation and sociological orientation. The selections vary according to their particular level of analysis. Some are devoted almost entirely to the offender and his behavior, some to an analysis of the social structure which generates crime, and others are primarily concerned with the criminal law and society's reaction to the crime. Several of the articles were prepared especially for this book, and they appear here for the first time.

We believe that *Criminal Behavior Systems* will prove useful in several ways. First of all, it should provide the principal or supplementary reading for the undergraduate course in criminology. Secondly, it may serve as reading for discussion in graduate courses and seminars in this field. Thirdly, it should be of value to criminologists in formulating their own theories and research. Fourthly, the examination of types of crime and the reporting of research may be useful to personnel in the field of corrections. Whatever its use, we hope that our book will make the student of criminology aware of the importance of studying the various forms of criminal behavior.

We are indebted to the criminologists who have devoted much time and effort to research and who have given us permission to include their works in our book. Without such research, the presentation and analysis of criminal behavior systems would not be possible.

May 1967   *Marshall B. Clinard*

Richard Quinney

CONTENTS

Criminal
Behavior
Systems

A TYPOLOGY

CHAPTER 1

Types of Crime

The goal of a science is to accumulate and systematize knowledge of the natural world. Using established methods accompanied by a particular view of reality, science conceptually orders empirical phenomena. Science is a search for the recurrent and uniform. In eliminating the unique and irrelevant, science attempts to understand that which can be expressed in general terms.

The scientific study of human behavior assumes that the basic criteria of science can be utilized. In the search for generalizations, human behavior is studied as a process or as a sequence of events in which certain phenomena are related to other phenomena. Such generalizations, when eventually achieved, are usually stated in terms of probabilities.

In the study of human behavior there is an attempt to order the diversified world of discrete phenomena. This task is often accomplished through the development of classifications. The categorizing of observations into classes or types provides a means by which concrete occurrences can be ordered and compared. As an abstraction, a type necessarily deviates from reality in that it accentuates a group of attributes which are relevant to a particular analysis. A type consists of characteristics which have empirical referents, although they may not be experienced directly in the form of a given type.

An important scientific typology, for example, was created by the great Swedish botanist Linnaeus two centuries ago when he developed the modern scientific classification of plants and animals. The use of typologies is common today not only in botany, but in zoology, geography, geology, and other physical sciences. Similarly, in the area of human behavior, the scientist attempts to derive types, whether they be types of social organization, occupational types, or types of deviants. The use of types in the ordering of the diversities of observed phenomena has been instrumental in the development of the social sciences.[1]

Types not only reduce phenomena to more systematic observation; they also assist in the formulation of hypotheses and serve as guides for research. The construction of types may lead to theoretical formulation. The constructed type, in fact, as Hempel notes, can serve as a theoretical system in itself by "(a) specifying a list of characteristics with which the theory is to deal, (b) formulating a set of hypotheses in terms of those characteristics, (c) giving those characteristics an empirical interpretation, and (d) as a long-range objective, incorporating the theoretical system as a 'special case' into a more comprehensive theory."[2]

Thus, the construction of types from a broad range of phenomena is a necessary stage in the development of specific theories; it also offers the possibility of formulating a comprehensive theory for the explanation of all the phenomena under observation. It is unlikely that an adequate comprehensive theory of behavior can be readily formulated and verified directly from a heterogeneous mass of phenomena. Type construction may be regarded as a necessary preliminary stage in the development of general theory.

It should be noted that technically, while not always followed in practice, a distinction may be made between a classification (consisting of classes) and a typology (consisting of types).[3] A strict classification is composed of a set of variables or attributes which are linked to form a number of logically possible combinations. Typologies are classifications, which, in addition, attempt to specify the ways in which attributes or variables are empirically connected.

A constructed type, then, drawing upon McKinney's recent analysis of typology, is a "purposive, planned selection, abstraction, combination, and (sometimes) accentuation of a set of criteria with empirical referents that serves as a basis for comparison of empirical cases."[4]

[1] The construction of types in social science has been discussed, among other places, in John C. McKinney, "Constructive Typology and Social Research," in John T. Doby (ed.), An Introduction to Social Research, Harrisburg, Pa.: The Stackpole Company, 1954, Chap. 7; Don Martindale, "Sociological Theory and the Ideal Type," in Llewellyn Gross (ed.), Symposium on Sociological Theory, New York: Harper & Row, Publishers, 1959, pp. 57–91; Howard Becker, Through Values to Social Interpretation, Durham, N.C.: Duke University Press, 1950, Chap. 2.

[2] Carl G. Hempel, "Typological Methods in the Natural and the Social Sciences," Proceedings, American Philosophical Association, Eastern Division, Philadelphia: University of Pennsylvania Press, Pt. I, 1952. p. 84.

[3] This distinction has been made and used in criminology in Clarence Schrag, "A Preliminary Criminal Typology," Pacific Sociological Review, 4 (Spring 1961), pp. 11–16. Schrag's usage follows Carl G. Hempel, Science, Language, and Human Rights, American Philosophical Association, Eastern Division, Philadelphia: University of Pennsylvania Press, 1952, Pt. 2.

[4] John C. McKinney, Constructive Typology and Social Theory, New York: Appleton-Century-Crofts, Inc., 1966, pp. 3, 203.

CLASSIFICATIONS AND TYPOLOGIES IN CRIMINOLOGY

A diverse and wide range of behaviors is included in the category of crime. The one characteristic which all the behaviors have in common is that they have been defined as criminal by recognized political authority. Much of the work in criminology has been concerned with crime in general. Because of the increasing realization, however, that crime refers to a great variety of behaviors, criminologists have in recent years turned their attention to the study of particular types of crime. Thus, criminologists are now giving greater attention to the identification, classification, and description of types of criminal behavior.

Moreover, efforts are being made to delineate categories of crime and criminal behavior which are homogeneous with respect to a specific explanation. In criminology, considering the wide range of phenomena subsumed under the concept of crime, an adequate general theory may be formulated only after specific theories at lower levels of explanation have been formulated and verified for specific orders of crime. Figure 1 illustrates the likely path of theory construction in criminology.[5]

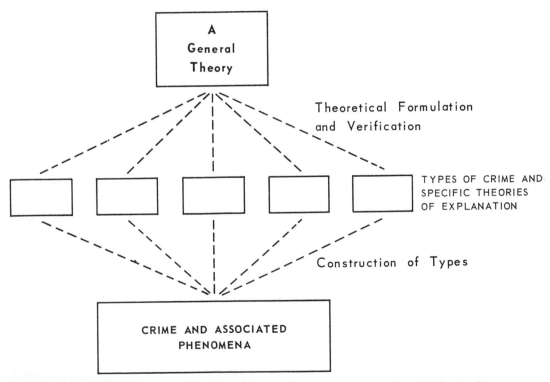

TYPOLOGY AND THEORY CONSTRUCTION
IN CRIMINOLOGY

An adequate explanation of criminal behavior should show not only how the explanation applies to all crime but how it should be modified to explain certain types.

5 This strategy has been followed in Melvin L. De Fleur and Richard Quinney, "A Reformulation of Sutherland's Differential Association Theory and a Strategy for Empirical Verification," *Journal of Research in Crime and Delinquency*, 3 (January 1965), pp. 1–22.

For the purposes of understanding and controlling criminal behavior, definitive generalizations are needed regarding criminal behavior as a whole, with specifications of the general theory applied to particular criminal behaviors. The relation between the general theory and the particular criminal behaviors is analogous to the relation between a germ theory of disease and the particular germs which cause particular diseases. . . . Continued efforts should be made to state valid generalizations regarding criminal behavior as a whole, and continued efforts should be made to explain particular criminal behaviors. . . . Just as the germ theory of disease does not explain all diseases, so it is possible that no one theory of criminal behavior will explain all criminal behavior. In that case, it will be desirable to define the areas to which any theory applies, so that the several theories are co-ordinate and, when taken together, explain all criminal behavior.[6]

Criminologists in the past have constructed and utilized various kinds of classifications and typologies of crime and criminals. The task, however, has not been an easy one. The most commonly used classifications and typologies have been the legalistic, individualistic, and social.

LEGALISTIC CLASSIFICATIONS

The oldest and still the most frequently used forms of classification are based on the legal definition of the offense. A familiar legalistic classification is in terms of the *seriousness* of the offense as indicated by the kind of punishment provided for the behavior. The most serious offenses are called felonies and are usually punishable by confinement in a state prison or by death. The less serious offenses are called misdemeanors and are usually punishable by fines or by confinement in a local jail. As a classification of crime this is not very useful and is ambiguous because it is difficult to make clear-cut distinctions between the two major types of offenses. For example, many criminal acts which are classified as felonies in one state are classified as misdemeanors in other states. There is also the fact that the form of punishment prescribed for a given offense changes from time to time.

It is common also to identify the criminal act (or the criminal) in terms of a *legal category*. Thus, criminals are referred to as murderers, burglars, robbers, embezzlers, and rapists in terms of specific offenses defined in the criminal code. The category of crimes against the person includes such illegal acts as murder, assault, and rape; crimes against property include burglary, larceny, forgery, and automobile theft; and crimes against public order consist of such behavior as prostitution, gambling, drunkenness, disturbing the peace, and the use of narcotics. This method of classifying criminals suffers from a number of disadvantages.[7] For example, (1) it tells nothing about the person and the circumstances associated

---

[6] Edwin H. Sutherland and Donald R. Cressey, *Principles of Criminology*, 7th ed., Philadelphia: J. B. Lippincott Company, 1966, p. 74.

[7] For a good discussion and evaluation of various criminal classification systems, see Richard R. Korn and Lloyd W. McCorkle, *Criminology and Penology*, New York: Holt, Rinehart and Winston, Inc., 1959, pp. 142–156.

with the offense; nor does it consider the social context of the criminal act, as in the case of rape or the theft of an auto. (2) It creates a false impression of specialization by implying that criminals confine themselves to the kind of crime for which they happen to be caught or convicted. (3) It is a common practice in order to secure easy convictions to allow offenders to receive a reduced sentence by "plea copping" or pleading guilty to a lesser charge which may have only a slight resemblance to the original charge or offense. (4) Because the legal definition of a criminal act varies according to time and place, the legal classification of crime presents problems for comparative analysis. The legal title of a criminal act perhaps better serves as an indication of public policy rather than as a description of a type of crime. (5) Finally, most important of all, the use of legal categories in a classification assumes that offenders with a certain legal label, such as burglars, robbers, auto thieves, and rapists, are all of the same type or are a product of a similar process. Such legal classifications do not identify theoretically significant types.

There have been a number of attempts to overcome some of the problems of legalistic classifications, while still utilizing the legal categories. Although the categories of crime defined in the criminal law may not be appropriate for sociological purposes, they may nevertheless be used in various ways in forming types of crime. One possibility is that types may be defined *within* specific legal categories. For example, burglars, depending upon their mode of operation, could be divided into housebreakers, safecrackers, professional burglars, and amateur burglars. Another possibility is that legal categories may be *combined*. Criminologists who favor the strategy of defining types according to legal categories claim that the procedure is desirable because official data concerned with criminal histories exist in terms of legal nomenclature and because the criminal code contains specific, operational definitions of criminal behavior.

Roebuck has constructed a typology based on arrest records derived from a sample of 1155 prison inmates in the District of Columbia reformatory.[8] On the basis of arrest patterns, Roebuck postulates four main types of careers: the single arrest pattern, the multiple pattern, the mixed pattern, and no pattern. The single pattern refers to those situations in which an individual is arrested three or more times for one type of crime such as narcotic violations or burglaries. The multiple pattern refers to those situations in which an individual presents two or more patterns. The mixed pattern refers to those situations in which an individual is arrested three or more times but no single pattern emerges. The fourth type, no pattern, refers to those situations in which an individual is arrested fewer than three times. Employing this scheme, thirteen different patterns of crime emerge: single robbery, single narcotics, single numbers game, single burglary, single sex offense, single auto theft, single confidence game, single forgery, double pattern (larceny and burglary), double pattern (assault and drunkenness), triple pattern

[8] Julian B. Roebuck, "The Negro Numbers Man as a Criminal Type: The Construction and Application of a Typology," *Journal of Criminal Law, Criminology and Police Science*, 54 (March 1963), pp. 48–60. Also see Roebuck and Mervyn L. Cadwallader, "The Negro Armed Robber as a Criminal Type: The Construction and Application of a Typology," *Pacific Sociological Review*, 4 (Spring 1961), pp. 21–26; Roebuck, "The Negro Drug Addict as an Offender Type." *Journal of Criminal Law, Criminology and Police Science*, 53 (March 1962), pp. 36–43; Roebuck and Ronald Johnson, "The Negro Drinker and Assaulter as a Criminal Type," *Crime and Delinquency*, 8 (January 1962), pp. 21–23. Roebuck and Johnson, "The Jack-of-all-Trades Offender," *Crime and Delinquency*, 8 (April 1962), pp. 172–181; Roebuck, *Criminal Typology: The Legalistic, Physical-Constitutional-Hereditary, Psychological-Psychiatric and Sociological Approaches*, Springfield, Ill.: Charles C Thomas, Publisher, 1967.

(larceny, assault, and drunkenness), mixed patterns, and no patterns. His typology includes such offender types as "Negro drinkers and assaulters," "Negro drug addicts," "Negro armed robbers," and "Negro jack-of-all-trades offenders."

While typologies such as this have been useful in pointing out the error of using a single arrest to type an offender and suggesting instead career patterns, they have a number of limitations. One has been the tendency to categorize offenders by race, as a Negro or Caucasian armed robber, which may not be an especially meaningful distinction. Moreover, such inductively derived typologies could mount up indefinitely by this method of using arrests.

Another possibility regarding the use of legal categories is that sociological types may be constructed which cut across some of the behaviors included in a number of legal categories. Cressey, for example, included within "criminal violation of financial trust" some of the behaviors officially handled as forgery, confidence game, embezzlement, and larceny by bailee.[9] As practical as these procedures of using various legal classifications appear, they have largely resulted in innumerable unrelated categories of crime lacking a common frame of reference. They have not generated integrated typological schemes.

An important problem remains in the construction of legal typologies of crime. The problem is in respect to the controversy over what behaviors and what persons should be regarded as criminal.[10] This controversy is relevant to the construction of typologies of crime. Posed in question form: At what stage of the criminal defining process should persons and behaviors be regarded as criminal? Is it at the stage of official detection, at the stage of official adjudication, or at the stage of official disposition? Or, to state the extreme, should a typology of crime include persons and behaviors irrespective of official legal action? Even if the criterion of official legal action is dropped in the construction of a typology, there is still the problem of how long a person remains a criminal after he violates the criminal law. This last problem aside, the selection of the stage of legal action which is going to be used in defining the persons and behavior to be included in a typology of crime depends upon the purpose of the typology and the kinds of research problems that are anticipated.

INDIVIDUALISTIC CLASSIFICATIONS

In contrast to the various legal classifications and typologies, which emphasize the overt act, have been schemes based on certain attributes of individuals.

Several Italian criminologists who rejected the legal definitions of crime over seventy-five years ago were instrumental in turning the attention of criminologists to classification and to the use of criteria other than those found in the criminal law.[11] The early criminologists of the Italian or positivist school delimited types of offenders in terms of a heterogeneous collection of personal attributes. Lombroso (1835–1909), for example, identified, to his satisfaction at least, a "born criminal" with a unique, inferior physique. Later, Lombroso recognized other

---

[9] Donald R. Cressey, *Other People's Money*, New York: The Free Press of Glencoe, 1953.
[10] See Paul W. Tappan, "Who Is the Criminal?" *American Sociological Review*, 12 (February 1947), pp. 96–102.
[11] See Hermann Mannheim, *Pioneers in Criminology*, London: Stevens & Sons, Ltd., 1960, especially Chaps. 1 and 19.

types of criminals, including (1) the insane criminal, (2) the criminal by passion, and (3) the occasional criminal, a type which emphasized the social aspects of the offender as well as individualistic characteristics.

Garofalo (1852–1934), an Italian jurist, maintained that criminals are characterized by psychological anomalies. He divided these defectives into four categories: (1) typical criminals, or murderers who kill for enjoyment, (2) violent criminals, (3) criminals deficient in pity and probity, and (4) lascivious criminals. In a not too different fashion, Ferri (1856–1929) distinguished between five types of criminals, namely, (1) the insane, (2) the born, (3) the habitual, (4) the occasional, and (5) the passionate.

With reference to individualistic factors, offenders have been divided according to their sex, age, rural-urban background, and other personal attributes. Sex is not a meaningful criterion for classification for, with the exception of prostitution, women in the Western world now commit as wide a variety of offenses as men, although not as frequently. It is increasingly difficult to distinguish clearly among offenders merely upon the basis of sex. Likewise, age is a somewhat meaningless classification because all types of crime are committed by persons of varying ages. Offenders committing the most overt serious crimes, however, are more frequently under twenty-five years of age, while the so-called white collar crimes of business and professional persons are committed by older persons. Classification of offenders by age has little merit, for the criminal development of an offender may have little relation to his age. An offender can be considered developed criminally if he has unfavorable attitudes toward laws, property, and the police, professional knowledge of techniques to commit crimes and avoid prosecution, and a framework of rationalizations to support his conduct. These qualities may be present in a teenage offender and be comparatively absent in a middle-aged one.

Clinical psychologists and psychiatrists have attempted to classify criminal offenders by utilizing either a single personality trait or a syndrome or grouping of traits. Accordingly, criminal offenders have been grouped according to whether they are "immature," "emotionally insecure," "dependent," "hostile," "antisocial," "nonconformists," or "aggressive." Sometimes a single trait has been used to apply to a variety of criminal careers differing in both the nature and the seriousness of the activity. Consequently, personality trait syndromes by themselves have little meaning for distinguishing either types of criminal careers or the behavior of criminals from noncriminals who also may have these traits.

The individualistic approach to criminal classification employs the questionable assumption that individuals with particular personal characteristics commit certain types of crime. In addition, the individualistic approach implies that persons with these characteristics specialize in particular offenses. Finally, while individualistic classifications may have limited diagnostic possibilities for treatment, they have little utility for the construction of sociological theories of criminal behavior.

TYPOLOGIES BASED ON SOCIAL BEHAVIOR SYSTEMS

The division of criminal behavior into social behavior typologies consists of more than merely dividing the phenomena of crime into "classes." The construction of types consists of the formation of a *configuration* or *pattern of variables linked in* specified ways. Classifications of crime are typologies when they are composed of constructed types rather than classes of phenomena.

If crime is to be studied as a social phenomenon, it is necessary to delineate types of criminal behavior according to the social context of the criminal offender and the criminal act. A number of such types have been developed. Two European criminologists of the last century, Mayhew and Moreau, proposed criminal types based on the way in which crime is related to the various *activities* of the criminal. Mayhew distinguished between professional criminals, who earn their living through criminal activity, and accidental offenders, who commit criminal acts as a result of unanticipated circumstances. Moreau added one other type of criminal to Mayhew's types. Recognizing that many of the criminals who commit crimes against the person cannot be included in either of Mayhew's types, Moreau designated the "habitual criminal" as one who continues to commit criminal acts for such diverse reasons as a deficiency in intelligence and lack of self-control.

Lindesmith and Dunham, with an awareness of the Mayhew-Moreau criminal types, devised a continuum of criminal behavior ranging from the *individualized criminal* to the *social criminal*.[12] The criminal acts of the individualized criminal are committed for diverse and personal reasons, with the behavior finding little cultural support. The criminal behaviors of the social criminal, on the other hand, are supported and prescribed by group norms. The social criminal through his criminal behavior achieves status and recognition within a group. In addition, while the social criminal uses means which are illegitimate, the goals he seeks, such as economic gain and security, are valued by the broader culture. The types of criminals found between the extremes share in varying degrees the characteristics of one or the other polar types. In the individualized category is the situational or accidental criminal, for example, a murderer who prior to the crime was a law-abiding person. In the social category is the professional criminal, such as the racketeer or the confidence man. Lindesmith and Dunham also employ a third type, *habitual-situational*. This type is utilized to classify all those criminals who actually are not professional, but are more than situational or accidental offenders. This type of criminal is described as the offender who, while not a professional, is constantly in trouble with the legal authorities, committing in a somewhat fortuitous and free-wheeling manner such crimes as robbery and larceny, intermixed with legitimate economic activities. A slum juvenile delinquent might be described as *habitual-situational*. This trichotomy, while consisting of rather broad categories, does not, however, appear to be exhaustive. For instance, as Lindesmith and Dunham themselves suggest, white collar crime committed by persons in the upper socio-economic groups, does not seem to fit in any one of the three categories. It is not a situational or accidental crime, since in many cases the individual criminal may have committed the crime continuously over a lifetime. It is not a professional crime, for in many cases (such as embezzlement) the offender may be a situational criminal. Also, it is not a habitual-situational crime, for Lindesmith and Dunham definitely describe this type as being overt in nature, and white collar crime is characterized by anything but overtness. More important, research subsequent to the development of this typology has indicated considerable group and

[12] Alfred R. Lindesmith and H. Warren Dunham, "Some Principles of Criminal Typology," *Social Forces*, 19 (March 1941), pp. 307–314.

social factors in such offenses as murder, aggravated assault, and forcible rape which they had tended to regard as of the individual type.

Another scheme with a somewhat different inflection has been developed by Gibbons and Garrity.[13] They suggest that a significant difference between criminals is the chronological age at which the offender is defined by society as a criminal. They express these differences as a dichotomy: (1) that group of offenders defined as criminals from the time of their first criminal act, and (2) that group of offenders not defined as criminal until late in life, though committing criminal acts early in life. Gibbons and Garrity understand this dichotomous scheme to differentiate respectively between the criminal whose total life orientation is guided by criminal groups, and the criminal whose life orientation is largely guided and reinforced by noncriminal groups.

While it may be true that the chronological age at which the offender is labeled a criminal is an excellent predictor of the criminal patterns of the offender, in terms of constructing a typology this information is of little value, since it is simpler to use the actual behavior patterns, which are accessible, to type the offenders rather than causal indicators of these patterns. For a typology is not a predictive device; rather it is a device employed to order and describe parsimoniously data from which potential predictive statements are generated.

A number of criminologists have stressed the vocational aspects of certain forms of crime. They have seen that some crimes are committed by persons who pursue criminal behavior as a career. Reckless has suggested three criminal careers: ordinary, organized, and professional.[14] As career crimes, these three types of crime are similar in that they usually involve property offenses for the purpose of gain; the criminals tend to specialize in particular violations; the commission of the offenses requires various degrees of skill and experience; crime is pursued as a way of life; and career criminals continue in crime for a long period of time, possibly for a lifetime. In terms of differences among the career types, ordinary criminals represent the lowest rank of career crime. They engage in conventional crimes, such as robbery, larceny, and burglary, which require limited skill. Ordinary criminals lack the organization to avoid arrest and conviction. Organized criminals, on the other hand, through a high degree of organization are able, without being detected or convicted, to specialize in activity which can be operated as a large-scale business. Force, violence, intimidation, and bribery are used to gain and maintain control over economic activity. Special types of organized crime include various forms of racketeering, control of gambling and prostitution, and the distribution of narcotics. Professional criminals, as the third type of career criminals, are highly skilled and are thus able to obtain considerable amounts of money without being detected. Because of organization and contact with other professional criminals, these offenders are able to escape conviction. Professional criminals specialize in offenses which require skill rather than violence, such as confidence games, pickpocketing, shoplifting, sneak thievery, and counterfeiting. While this distinction is important and largely valid insofar as it goes, it is limited to those who make an occupation or career out of crime. Many persons who commit illegal acts are not career criminals.

[13] Don C. Gibbons and Donald L. Garrity, "Some Suggestions for the Development of Etiological and Treatment Theory in Criminology," *Social Forces*, 38 (October 1963), pp. 51–58.
[14] Walter C. Reckless, *The Crime Problem*, 3d ed., New York: Appleton-Century-Crofts, Inc., 1961, Chaps. 9 and 10.

Using a more comprehensive typology by emphasizing the career patterning of offenders, Clinard has developed a classification based on a continuum of criminal behavior systems.[15] At one extreme is the noncareer offender and at the other the career offender. The criminal types constructed in the typology vary according to such characteristics as the social roles of the offender, the degree of identification with crime, conception of the self, pattern of association with others, progression in crime, and the degree to which criminal behavior has become part of the life organization of the person. Based on these criteria, he has ranged criminal behavior along a continuum, with subtypes under each, of the criminally insane, extreme sex deviate, occasional offender, prostitute and homosexual, habitual petty offender, white collar criminal, ordinary criminal career, organized criminal, and professional criminal.

A significant typology of criminal offenders has been constructed by Gibbons in terms of offense patterns, self-image, normative orientation, and other social psychological characteristics.[16] Types, to Gibbons, are primarily role-careers in which identifiable changes occur in different offender types.

There are some criminal patterns in which role-performance is begun and terminated in a single illegal act, and there are others in which involvement in the deviant role continues over several decades or more, as in the instance of professional criminals. Some delinquent roles lead to adult criminality, whereas other delinquent roles are terminal ones, for they do not normally precede or lead to involvement in adult deviation. In turn, some criminal roles have their genesis in juvenile delinquent behavior, whereas certain other forms of adult criminality develop in adulthood and are not presaged by delinquent careers. Then, too, some role-careers involve more changes in the component episodes of the pattern than do others. Semiprofessional property offenders are one illustration. This pattern begins at the onset of minor delinquent acts in early adolescence. Such a career line frequently leads to more serious forms of delinquency with advancing age: repeated police contacts, commitment to juvenile institutions, "graduation" into adult forms of illegal activity, and more contacts with law enforcement and correctional agencies. Over this lengthy developmental sequence, the social-psychological characteristics of offenders also change. For example, the degree of hostility toward policemen and correctional agents exhibited by the adult semiprofessional criminal is likely to be considerably greater than the antagonism demonstrated by the same person at an early age. The same comment could be made regarding changes in self-image, attitudes, and other matters.[17]

A uniform frame of reference employing the criteria of "definitional dimensions" and "background dimensions" is used by Gibbons. The definitional dimen-

[15] Marshall B. Clinard, *Sociology of Deviant Behavior*, rev. ed., New York: Holt, Rinehart and Winston, Inc., 1963, Chap. 8.

[16] Don C. Gibbons, *Changing the Lawbreaker: The Treatment of Delinquents and Criminals*, Englewood Cliffs, N.J.: Prentice-Hall, Inc., 1965. He also sets up a program of treatment for each type.

[17] Gibbons, pp. 51–52.

sions consist of: (1) the nature of the offense behavior, (2) the interactional setting with others in which the offense takes place, (3) self-concept of the offender, (4) attitudes toward society and agencies of social control such as the police, and (5) the steps in the role career of the offender. There are four aspects of the "background dimensions" of each type: (1) social class, (2) family background, (3) peer group associations, and (4) contact with defining agencies such as the police, courts, and prisons.

On this basis Gibbons sets up fifteen adult types and nine juvenile types.

Adult Types	*Juvenile Types*
Professional thief	Predatory gang delinquent
Professional "heavy" criminal	Conflict gang delinquent
Semiprofessional property criminal	Casual gang delinquent
Property offender—"one-time loser"	Casual delinquent,
Automobile thief—"joyrider"	nongang member
Naive check forger	Automobile thief—"joyrider"
White-collar criminal	Drug user—heroin
Professional "fringe" violator	Overly aggressive delinquent
Embezzler	Female delinquent
Personal offender—"one-time loser"	"Behavior problem" delinquent[18]
"Psychopathic" assaultist	
Violent sex offender	
Nonviolent sex offender—	
nonviolent "rapo"	
Nonviolent sex offender—	
statutory rape	
Narcotic addict—heroin	

Gibbons provides a description of each type. Unfortunately, some of his types are not sharply delineated and tend to overlap or be unclear as to their specific characteristics. Other types depart from an essentially general group and cultural frame of reference and present a largely individualistic psychological orientation which is somewhat contradictory to the overall frame of reference.

A somewhat different typology has been developed by Cavan, which gives principal consideration to the public reaction to crime and the criminal's reaction to the public.[19] In an analysis of the interaction between the public and the criminal, seven types of criminal behavior are constructed: (1) criminal contraculture (professional crime, robbery, burglary), (2) extreme underconformity (for example, occasional drunkenness), (3) minor underconformity (for example, embezzlement), (4) "average" conformity (minor pilfering), (5) minor overconformity (exactness in obeying laws and moral codes), (6) extreme overconformity (attempts to reform society by persuasion and legal means), and (7) ideological contraculture (strenuous efforts to remodel society, possibly through the use of illegal means). Because societal reaction is crucial to the criminal's self-concept and subsequent behavior, it is an important variable to be included in a typology of crime.

An indication of the importance of the typological approach in modern crimi-

[18] Gibbons, Chap. 3.
[19] Ruth Shonle Cavan, *Criminology*, 3d ed., New York: Thomas Y. Crowell Company, 1962, Chap. 3.

nology can be seen in the attention devoted to the subject in some recent criminology textbooks. Bloch and Geis, for example, give considerable attention to types of criminal behavior systems and to the social and cultural structure in which criminal behavior systems arise.[20] Their types of criminal behavior systems include professional criminals, organized crime, homicides and assaults, sexual offenders, property offenders, white collar offenders, juvenile delinquents, and petty and miscellaneous offenders.

PRINCIPLES OF CRIMINAL TYPOLOGY

Ideally, a typology of crime should be constructed on the basis of a general, underlying theory of crime. No matter how implicit, some assumptions are always present concerning the nature and etiology of crime. In addition, the particular selection of characteristics and variables which ultimately determine the types in the system is guided by the interests of the criminologist. In other words, the purpose at hand determines how the typology is to be constructed. For example, if the purpose of the typology is to view crime in terms of public reaction, then one set of characteristics will be used. Likewise, another purpose will require a different typology. Also, the level of explanation desired by the criminologist will play a part in the particular selection of characteristics in the typology.

General characteristics for the construction of typologies can be developed in the course of criminological research. With the use of such a technique as factor analysis, for example, common characteristics of offenders can be found.[21] These dimensions in turn can be used in the construction of a typological system. Typologies can also be constructed through the use of findings from other research studies of various kinds of crime and delinquency.[22] Once such typologies are constructed, and with the addition of terms, concepts, and postulates, typologies can serve as axiomatic theories whereby further statements regarding types of crime can be deduced.[23]

Related to the selection of characteristics underlying typologies is the problem of the phenomena to be included in the typology. There has been the tendency in criminology, especially in the development of typologies, to avoid distinguishing between the subclasses of phenomena included in the study of crime. The phenomena associated with crime include *criminal behavior, the criminal,* and *criminality.* These phenomena represent the areas of study in criminology.[24] Criminal behavior refers to the behavioral aspects of the violation of the law and the crimi-

[20] Herbert A. Bloch and Gilbert Geis, *Man, Crime, and Society,* New York: Random House, Inc., 1962.

[21] Employed on the ecological level in Calvin F. Schmid, "Urban Crime Areas: Part I," *American Sociological Review,* 25 (August 1960), pp. 527–542.

[22] Don C. Gibbons and Donald L. Garrity, "Definition and Analysis of Certain Criminal Types," *Journal of Criminal Law, Criminology and Police Science,* 53 (March 1962), pp. 27–35; and John W. Kinch, "Continuities in the Study of Delinquent Types," *Journal of Criminal Law, Criminology and Police Science,* 53 (September 1962), pp. 323–328.

[23] Schrag, p. 16.

[24] Various views on this subject are presented in Austin T. Turk, "Prospects for Theories of Criminal Behavior," *Journal of Criminal Law, Criminology and Police Science,* 55 (December 1964), pp. 454–461; Clarence R. Jeffery, "The Structure of American Criminological Thinking," *Journal of Criminal Law, Criminology and Police Science,* 46 (January–February 1956), pp. 658–672; Marvin E. Wolfgang, "Criminology and Criminologists," *Journal of Criminal Law, Criminology and Police Science,* 54 (June 1963), pp. 155–162.

nal refers to the person who violates the law. Criminality refers to the official status conferred upon behavior and persons by authorities within a political unit. There is, thus, the possibility of constructing separate typologies of criminal behavior, criminals and criminality.

The distinction between criminal behavior, the criminal, and criminality is crucial in the attempt to construct types in criminology. Typologies will differ markedly from one another according to the particular phenomena upon which they are based. For example, if a typology is based on criminals, the emphasis will be on such matters as life histories of offenders, self-conceptions, attitudes, and social background factors. On the other hand, if the objective is a typology of criminal behavior, attention will be focused on such matters as the mode of operation, the overt criminal act, the situation in which the offense occurs, opportunities to commit crime, subcultural norms, relationships between offenders, and structural aspects of the larger society. A typology based on criminality would consist of characteristics that relate to the conditions and processes by which persons and behaviors become defined as criminal. In addition, a typology might be constructed which would combine the three classes of phenomena associated with crime. Such a typology would consider the fact that persons and behaviors with certain characteristics are more likely to be defined as criminal than are persons and behaviors with other characteristics.

Other problems connected with underlying principles in the construction of criminal typologies can be described briefly as follows: (1) Multidimensional typologies: It is conceivable that any number of characteristics could be used in the construction of a criminal typology. In the construction of any typology, decisions must be made regarding the number of characteristics to be included and the kind of measurement to be used. (2) Exhaustiveness: There is the question of whether or not a typology should include the entire universe of crime or should be limited in scope. (3) Homogeneity of types: An objective of a typology may be the division of crime into types such that the types are homogeneous, that is, so that the behaviors within a given type are subject to a single explanation. This objective is related to the level of abstraction of both the types and the theories to explain the types. (4) Types and behavior systems: Types of crime do not necessarily represent behavior systems. Since some types of crime may not be systematic in that they do not consist of, among other things, social relationships and cultural norms, not all types can be studied as behavior systems. (5) Juvenile delinquency: While minors and adults are handled differently before the law, many of the offenses of juveniles are behaviorally the same as those of adults. Therefore, in constructing types, there may be little reason to create separate types for minors and adults. It may be more realistic and theoretically sound to integrate various forms of juvenile delinquency into typologies of crime.

Whatever the basis of typological construction, the trend in criminology is clearly toward further study of types of crime. In the development of typologies we cannot, however, expect to achieve a typological system which can be agreed upon by all criminologists as being the most desirable. To be certain, there will be classifications which will at various times be more popular than others. But there are a number of reasons why we cannot look forward to a single typology in criminology.

First, as already mentioned, typologies differ according to the purposes which they are to serve. Since there will continue to be a multitude of purposes, including levels of analysis and degrees of generality, there will be a number of typologies. Second, there is the fact that crime is relative. That is, the definitions of crime change from time to time and from place to place. Therefore, the behaviors and persons to be included in a typology will vary according to time and place. It may be that future typologies will be developed which will include the crimes of other historical periods. Third, theory within criminology will continue to develop. As this happens, typologies will be altered. Finally, theories, theoretical frameworks, and the related typologies will change as the orientations of criminologists change. Inevitably, as with all intellectual trends, the interests of criminologists will be attuned to the developments in the larger society.

A TYPOLOGY OF CRIME

In the approach to typological construction used in this book, types of crime are constructed according to *systems* of criminal behavior. As heuristic devices, types are necessarily constructed as "systems." McKinney has noted, "The constructed type is a special kind of concept in that it consists of a set of characteristics wherein the relations between the characteristics are held constant for the purposes at hand. Hence, the type is a pragmatically constructed 'system.' "[25] Criminal behavior systems are constructed types that serve as a means by which concrete occurrences can be compared and understood within a system of characteristics that underlie the types.

Accordingly, eight types of criminal behavior are constructed:
1. Violent personal crime
2. Occasional property crime
3. Occupational crime
4. Political crime
5. Public order crime
6. Conventional crime
7. Organized crime
8. Professional crime

The typological construction is based upon four characteristics: (1) the criminal career of the offender, (2) the extent to which the behavior has group support, (3) correspondence between criminal behavior and legitimate behavior patterns, and (4) societal reaction.

1. *Criminal Career of the Offender:* The extent to which criminal behavior is a part of the offender's career. Includes conception of self, identification with crime, progression in crime, and the degree to which criminal behavior has become a part of the life organization of the offender.

2. *Group Support of Criminal Behavior:* The extent to which the offender's criminal behavior is supported by the norms of the group or groups to which he belongs. Includes the differential association of the offender with criminal and noncriminal norms, the social roles of the offender, and the integration of the offender into social groups.

3. *Correspondence between Criminal Behavior and Legitimate Behavior Patterns:* The extent to which the type of criminal behavior is consistent with legitimate patterns of behavior in the society. Includes the degree to which the criminal

[25] McKinney, *Constructive Typology and Social Theory*, p. 7.

behavior corresponds to the valued goals and means that are regarded as legitimate by the dominant power segments of society. Includes the extent of conflict between value systems.

4. *Societal Reaction:* The extent to which society reacts to the criminal behavior. Includes the various forms of informal reaction, such as disapproval and censure, and the forms of official reaction, such as enforcement of law, prosecution, conviction, and sentencing.

The types of criminal behavior systems in the typology are shown in the following table. Eight distinct patterns of crime are delineated in relation to the four characteristics. The career continuum is used to order the criminal behavior systems. The ranking of the criminal behavior systems on each continuum is based on available research evidence.

There are undoubtedly other ways of dividing crime into types along the career continuum in reference to group support of criminal behavior, correspondence between criminal behavior and legitimate behavior patterns, and societal reaction. The behaviors and associated phenomena that run along the continua have been, for our purposes, abstracted and segmented into eight distinct types. The typology serves the purpose of allowing us to present existing research on various forms of crime.

The eight types of criminal behavior systems which we have constructed may be summarized as follows:

1. *Violent Personal Crime:* Includes such forms of criminal activity as murder, assault, and forcible rape. The offenders do not conceive of themselves as criminals. They are often persons without previous records, but because of certain circumstances commit a personal offense. The offenses are not directly supported by any group, though there may be subcultural definitions which are favorable to the general use of violence. The behaviors are in sharp contrast to the middle class values of the society. There is a strong reaction to the offenses.

2. *Occasional Property Crime:* Includes some auto theft, shoplifting, check forgery, and vandalism. The offenders do not usually conceive of themselves as criminals and are able to rationalize their criminal behavior. They are usually committed to the general goals of society and find little support for their behavior in group norms. The offenses are in violation of the values of private property. Societal reaction often involves arrest, especially for the offender who already has a criminal record.

3. *Occupational Crime:* Includes embezzlement, fraudulent sales, false advertising, price fixing, fee-splitting, black market activity, prescription violation, and antitrust violation. Violators do not conceive of themselves as criminals and rationalize their behavior as being merely a part of their daily work. Their behavior may be tolerated by their peers. They accept conventional values and attempt to seek a greater share of the rewards in the conventional world. The illegal behavior corresponds to the social and economic philosophy of the achievement of ends in the society. Because such crime is committed by persons in high status positions and the violation of law is often complex and not highly visible, there is little reaction from the public when these violations occur.

4. *Political Crime:* Includes treason, sedition, espionage, sabotage, military draft violations, war collaboration, radicalism and the various other forms of protest which may be defined as criminal. The offenders occasionally violate the law when they feel that illegal activity is essential in achieving necessary changes in society.

TYPOLOGY OF CRIMINAL BEHAVIOR SYSTEMS

CLASSIFICATION CHARACTERISTICS	1 VIOLENT PERSONAL CRIME	2 OCCASIONAL PROPERTY CRIME	3 OCCUPATIONAL CRIME	4 POLITICAL CRIME
Criminal Career of the Offender	LOW Crime not part of offender's career; usually does not conceive of self as criminal	LOW Little or no criminal self-concept; does not identify with crime	LOW No criminal self-concept; occasionally violates the law; part of one's legitimate work; accepts conventional values of society	LOW Usually no criminal self-concept; violates the law out of conscience; attempts to change society or correct perceived injustices; desire for a better society
Group Support of Criminal Behavior	LOW Little or no group support, offenses committed for personal reasons; some support in subcultural norms	LOW Little group support; individual offenses	MEDIUM Some groups may tolerate offenses; offender integrated in groups	HIGH Group support; association with persons of same values; behavior reinforced by group
Correspondence between Criminal Behavior and Legitimate Behavior Patterns	LOW Violation of values on life and personal safety	LOW Violation of value on private property	HIGH Behavior corresponds to pursual of business activity; "sharp" practices respected; "buyer beware" philosophy; hands off policy	MEDIUM Some toleration of protest and dissent, short of revolution; dissent periodically regarded as a threat (in times of national unrest)
Societal Reaction	HIGH Capital punishment; long imprisonment	MEDIUM Arrest; jail; short imprisonment, probation	LOW Indifference; monetary penalties, revocation of license to practice, seizure of product or injunction	HIGH Strong disapproval; regarded as threat to society; prison
Legal Categories of Crime	Murder, assault, forcible rape, child molesting	Some auto theft, shoplifting, check forgery, vandalism	Embezzlement, fraudulent sales, false advertising, fee-splitting, violation of labor practice laws, antitrust violations, black market activity, prescription violation	Treason, sedition, espionage, sabotage, radicalism, military draft violations, war collaboration, various protests defined as criminal

5	6	7	8
PUBLIC ORDER CRIME	CONVENTIONAL CRIME	ORGANIZED CRIME	PROFESSIONAL CRIME
MEDIUM Confused self-concept; vacillation in identification with crime	MEDIUM Income supplemented through crimes of gain; often a youthful activity; vacillation in self-concept; partial commitment to a criminal subculture	HIGH Crime pursued as a livelihood; criminal self-concept; progression in crime; isolation from larger society	HIGH Crime pursued as a livelihood; criminal self-concept; status in the world of crime; commitment to world of professional criminals
MEDIUM Partial support for behavior from some groups; considerable association with other offenders	HIGH Behavior supported by group norms; status achieved in groups; principal association with other offenders	HIGH Business associations in crime; behavior prescribed by the groups; integration of the person into the group	HIGH Associations primarily with other offenders; status gained in criminal offenses; behavior prescribed by group norms
MEDIUM Some forms required by legitimate society; some are economic activities	MEDIUM Consistent with goals on economic success; inconsistent with sanctity of private property; behavior not consistent with expectations of adolescence and young adulthood	MEDIUM Illegal services received by legitimate society; economic risk values; large-scale control also employed in legitimate society	MEDIUM Engaged in an occupation; skill respected; survival because of cooperation from legitimate society; law-abiding persons often accomplices
MEDIUM Arrest; jail; prison; probation	HIGH Arrest; jail; probation; institutionalization; parole; rehabilitation	MEDIUM Considerable public toleration; arrest and sentence when detected; often not visible to society; immunity through politicians and law officers	MEDIUM Rarely strong societal reaction, most cases "fixed"
Drunkenness, vagrancy, disorderly conduct, prostitution, homosexuality, gambling, traffic violation, drug addiction	Robbery, larceny, burglary, gang theft	Racketeering, organized prostitution and commercialized vice, control of drug traffic, organized gambling	Confidence games, shoplifting, pickpocketing, forgery, counterfeiting

The offenders are committed to the larger society or to an order which they are trying to bring about. Their behavior is prescribed and supported by their own groups. Democratic societies are based on the right to petition, yet societal reaction is strong when such behavior is regarded as a threat to the society.

5. *Public Order Crime:* Includes drunkenness, vagrancy, disorderly conduct, prostitution, homosexuality, traffic violation, and drug addiction. The violators may conceive of themselves as criminals when they are repeatedly defined as criminals by others. They may vacillate between criminal values and the values of a larger social order. They may associate with other offenders. There is some correspondence between the illegal behavior of public order offenders and legitimate patterns. Some of the forms of public order crime (for example, prostitution) are desired by parts of the legitimate society. Other forms (for example, drunkenness and vagrancy) are regarded as merely representative of "failure" in the existing economic system. There may be informal punitive reaction as well as arrest and limited incarceration.

6. *Conventional Crime:* Includes robbery, larceny, burglary, and gang theft. The offenders pursue crime as a part-time career, usually supplementing a legitimate income through crimes of gain. Many juvenile gang members may be beginning a career in illegal activity. While there may be some identification with the larger society, there is likely to be greater commitment to a criminal subculture. There is usually association with other offenders. The behavior corresponds to the goals of economic success; but there is public reaction to the behavior because the value on the sanctity of private property is violated.

7. *Organized Crime:* Includes racketeering, organized prostitution, organized gambling, and control of narcotics. The offenders pursue crime as a livelihood. In the lower echelons they conceive of themselves as criminals, associate primarily with other criminals, and are isolated from a larger social order. In the top levels the individuals associate as well with persons of legitimate society and often reside in the better residential areas. There is considerable correspondence between the illegal activities of organized crime and legitimate society. The principles of large-scale enterprise are shared by legitimate society. Illegal services desired by legitimate society are provided by organized crime. The public tolerates organized crime, partly because of the desired services it provides and partly because of the difficulty in dealing with its operation.

8. *Professional Crime:* Includes confidence games, shoplifting, pickpocketing, forgery, and counterfeiting. Professional criminals pursue crime as a livelihood and as a way of life. They conceive of themselves as criminals, associate with other criminals, and have high status in the world of crime. They are usually isolated from the larger society and are committed to a career of crime. There is some correspondence between professional crime and dominant behavior patterns in that professional criminals are, after all, engaged in full-time employment. Also, law-abiding persons are sometimes involved as accomplices in an attempt to obtain money in a quick and easy manner. Societal reaction is not usually strong. Many cases of professional crime are "fixed" in the course of legal processing.

ORGANIZATION OF THE BOOK

The organization of this book follows the typology developed above. Each of the chapters represents one of the criminal behavior systems of the typology. There is a discussion of the particular type of criminal behavior system at the beginning of each chapter. Characteristics of the type and previous research and writing on the type are discussed. The chapters include a selected bibliography for each type of crime. Following the discussion of each criminal behavior system are research selections which are related to each type of crime. Each selection is preceded by a brief comment on the research.

CHAPTER 2

Violent
Personal
Crime

Personal crimes involving violence include acts in which physical injury is inflicted, primarily criminal homicide, aggravated assault, and forcible rape, as well as attempts to inflict such injury. Kidnapping involves the element of physical force, and child molesting on occasion also involves the use of force and personal violence. Armed robbery involves violence because of the element of force, such as a gun, knife, or threat of violence in obtaining money.

The use of violence and the reaction of society to it can be viewed in an even wider perspective. The use of personal violence has played an important part in human history from riots to war.

Not all violence transgresses legal norms, but legal sanctions proscribing many types of violence reflect a general societal opposition to violence, the historical concern with it, and the need to regulate its expression. Murder, rape, aggravated assault, armed robbery, and kidnapping are obvious examples of criminal violence. Labor riots, race riots, lynching mobs, fights among delinquent gangs, and attacks by organized criminal syndicates are all forms of collective violence that have punctuated the history of social change.[1]

This chapter, however, will deal chiefly with criminal homicide, aggravated assault, and forcible rape, inasmuch as there is significant research on these offenses. Child molesting will be included, although the research is limited. Robbery will not be included as a violent personal crime, primarily because the behavior is generally associated with a career of theft and will thus be discussed as a type of conventional crime. The legal aspects of the crimes discussed here need clarification in order to understand clearly the explanation of this type of crime. The type of criminal homicide which will be referred to here as "murder" consists of murder, first or second degree, and nonnegligent manslaughter, excluding justifiable homicide or attempts or assaults to kill, and includes negligent manslaughter other than manslaughter arising from motor vehicles. Murder is the unlawful killing of a human being with malice aforethought. Malice aforethought represents a "guilty mind" but not necessarily premeditation and planning. In many parts of the United States there are degrees of murder, first and second degree, a legal situation which affects the length of sentence. Manslaughter is unlawful or criminal homicide without malice aforethought, that is, without a state of mind which makes a killer a murderer. It covers a wide range of acts, the most serious of which result in accidental death. A person might attack another without the intention of causing death or severe bodily harm but death may be the outcome. The unlawful killing is in a sudden heat or anger and without premeditation. The element of provocation by the victim is often considered an element in manslaughter. All such manslaughter is termed voluntary or nonnegligent manslaughter. Involuntary manslaughter is death arising from unintentional killing, primarily from negligence, that is, death attributable to the negligence of some person other than the victim. In research studies of criminal homicide, deaths arising from negligence in motor vehicle accidents are often excluded.[2]

In general, murder and aggravated assault are similar, for both involve the use of physical force to settle an argument or a dispute. In aggravated assault there is an attempt to cause a person injury or even deprive him of his life. Nearly all murders thus represent some form of aggravated assault, the chief difference being that the victim died. In fact, serious assaults are invariably considered felonies as they cover such behavior as an attempt to inflict severe injury or to kill, including assault with a deadly weapon, assault to commit murder or assault by shooting, cutting, stabbing, maiming, and so forth. Whether the behavior results in injury or is only an attempt to cause injury, it is still aggravated assault. In most cases it is probably the element of chance, rapid transportation of the injured party, and effective medical treatment that prevents the offense from sliding over into criminal homicide by the death of one of the parties.

Forcible rape, the act of having unlawful sexual intercourse with a woman

[1] Marvin Wolfgang, "A Preface to Violence," *The Annals*, 364 (March 1966), p. 2.
[2] Marvin Wolfgang, *Patterns in Criminal Homicide*, Philadelphia: University of Pennsylvania Press, 1958.

against her will, is to be distinguished from statutory rape, or sexual intercourse with a female under a specific age, generally sixteen or eighteen, with or without consent. Although the actual percentage is not known, it appears that forcible rape constitutes only a small proportion of all arrests and prosecutions for "rape." Most arrests for rape are for statutory rape. In the United States, rape involves sexual intercourse accompanied by force and against the woman's consent. If she consents to the intercourse, although the consent may be reluctantly given, and although there may be some force used to obtain it, the offense is generally not rape. In England, on the other hand, the woman's consent is no defense if it is obtained by force.

Violence is generally not associated with child molesting. It is included in this section because violence is generally thought to be associated with it, and does sometimes occur. In one study, for example, no violence was associated with 76 percent of the cases.[3] Four percent of the offenders used verbal threats, 17 percent used force only in order to gain compliance, and only 3 percent inflicted actual physical violence upon the child. Child molesting involves statutory rape, indecent liberties, homosexual contacts, and indecent exposure with a child, usually under the age of fourteen. Individuals who engage in such acts may be charged under a variety of statutes, which may be designated more generally as disorderly conduct or contributing to the delinquency of a minor.

CRIMINAL CAREER OF THE OFFENDER

Murderers, assaulters, and forcible rapists generally do not have criminal careers. A few persons are exceptions in using actual or threatened violence in the form of assault and even homicide as part of their careers in crime. They are organized criminal offenders who will be discussed in a later chapter.

Most murderers and assaulters do not conceive of themselves as being real "criminals"; they seldom identify with crime, and criminal behavior is not a significant part of their life organizations. To most of these offenders a criminal is one who steals. The situation is different with forcible rapists, since they are reported by some to have a fairly extensive criminal record for other offenses, particularly against property.

Persons who commit assault are unlikely to be involved in other types of crime. In a St. Louis study the majority of the offenders had no prior arrest records, and relatively few were for crimes against the person.[4] Two thirds of the cases in the age bracket of 20–34, however, had a prior arrest record. Contrary to general belief, Negro assaulters were no more likely than others to have had a prior arrest record. In another St. Louis sample of 88 male offenders, it was found that persons arrested for crimes of violence are rarely arrested for crimes against property and that the reverse holds equally true for property offenders.[5]

A Philadelphia study of criminal homicides indicated something of the same

---

[3] Charles McCaghy, "Child Molesters: A Study of Their Careers as Deviants," unpublished Ph. D. dissertation, University of Wisconsin, 1966.

[4] David J. Pittman and William Handy, "Patterns in Criminal Aggravated Assault," *Journal of Criminal Law, Criminology and Police Science*, 55 (December 1964), pp. 462–470.

[5] Richard A. Peterson, David J. Pittman, and Patricia O'Neal, "Stabilities in Deviance: A Study of Assaultive and Non-Assaultive Offenders," *Journal of Criminal Law, Criminology and Police Science*, 53 (March 1962), pp. 44–49.

general pattern, 66 percent having been previously arrested for offenses against the person, (48 percent for aggravated assault) and 34 percent for property and other offenses.[6] Of those offenders with an arrest record, a larger proportion had a record of aggravated assault involving wife beating and fighting than all types of property offenses combined. In a Wisconsin study, it was found that about half (46.7 percent) of ninety-six Wisconsin prisoners serving time for murder had never been arrested before, whereas only one in three of the sex offenders and only one in eleven of the property offenders had such a record.[7]

A London study of "crimes of violence" found that the vast majority (eight in ten) of London offenders convicted for a violent offense were convicted for the first time for this type of offense. In fact, the study concluded that "the analysis of crimes of violence according to their factual substance shows that most of the crime is not committed by criminals for criminal purposes but is rather the outcome of patterns of social behavior among certain strata of society."[8] A considerable proportion (nearly half), however, had been convicted of petty offenses, larceny, malicious damage, drunkenness, and, in some instances, breaking and entering.[9] The previous offense history was lowest, however, among those whose offenses arose from a family dispute.

Many of those involved in rape appear to have had a record of arrests for criminal offenses. One study of 1292 forcible rape offenders in Philadelphia showed that 50 percent of them had a past arrest record, and there was no difference in the extent of this past record between Negro and white offenders.[10] Only 20 percent of those with a past arrest record, however, had previously committed a crime against the person, with Negroes far outnumbering the whites in this respect. Approximately one in ten (9 percent) had committed rape in the past. Another study has shown that by the age of twenty-six, 87 percent of forcible rapists had been convicted of some crime; two thirds had been convicted of a felony, half of them nonsex offenses. For slightly more than half, the forcible rape was their first sex offense, and for about one quarter, their second. A substantial number had a record of juvenile offenses, 22 percent of the sample, but only 5 percent for sex offenses.[11] In another study aggressive sex offenders showed few sex offenses but many nonsex offenses, a ratio quite different from that of other sex offenders.[12]

GROUP SUPPORT OF CRIMINAL BEHAVIOR

The general cultural and subcultural pattern seems to determine the frequency of crimes of violence. Acceptance of the use of violence varies from country to country, region to region, and state to state. It also varies by neighborhood within a city, by social class, occupation, race, sex, and age.[13]

[6] Wolfgang, Patterns in Criminal Homicide, p. 178.
[7] John L. Gillin, The Wisconsin Prisoner, Madison: The University of Wisconsin Press, 1946.
[8] F. H. McClintock, Crimes of Violence, New York: St. Martin's Press, Inc., 1963, p. 57.
[9] McClintock, p. 57.
[10] Menachem Amir, "Patterns of Forcible Rape," unpublished Ph.D. dissertation, University of Pennsylvania, 1965.
[11] Paul H. Gebhard, John H. Gagnon, Wardell B. Pomeroy, and Cornelia V. Christenson, Sex Offenders: An Analysis of Types, New York: Harper & Row, Publishers, 1965, pp. 192–194.
[12] Albert Ellis and Ralph Brancale, The Psychology of Sex Offenders, Springfield, Ill.: Charles C Thomas, Publisher, 1965.
[13] Ronald H. Beattie and John P. Kenney, "Aggressive Crimes," The Annals, 365 (March 1966), pp. 73–85.

In general, homicide is associated with the degree of urban and industrial development of a country, although there are exceptions; for example, Great Britain, Sweden, and Canada have quite low rates of criminal homicide, Finland has one of the highest rates in the world,[14] and Ceylon has a high rate in Asia.[15] One study of criminal homicide and assault in Puerto Rico indicated that the high rates of these crimes in such Latin cultures are related to personal insult or honor. In other words, in some cultures the individual may be expected to attack the offender in cases of personal vilification or marital triangles.[16] Today among tribal peoples in most of Africa, homicides occur within an institutional setting which defines the social relationships between the killer and the victim.[17] These relationships tend to differ from Western societies; for example, a woman might kill her children rather than her husband in a domestic quarrel. Likewise, altercations over money are rare, but fear of witches or land disputes may be more common reasons for homicide.

The importance of the cultural definitions in criminal homicide was revealed several decades ago when wide regional differences in the United States were found.[18] Even today southern homicide rates are considerably higher than those in other regions. This difference is due to the fact that cultural definitions demand personal violence in certain situations and that weapons are more frequently carried in some areas than in others. One study showed that, contrary to the general pattern of other offenses, murder and aggravated assault are negatively correlated with most socio-economic variables whether they occur in rural, urban, or standard metropolitan statistical areas.[19] "Offenses against the person regardless of the population area may become institutonalized and perceived by people in these structures as the most appropriate solutions to interpersonal problems."[20]

Murder and assault rates also vary a great deal by ethnic, racial, and class groups. A study of victims and slayers in Philadelphia, between 1948 and 1952, indicated the role of group factors in defining the use of violence, or what Wolfgang has termed the "subculture of violence."[21] Murder was found to be highest among Negroes, males, those in the age group 20–24 and 30–34, from the lower social classes, and related to certain occupations. The rate among the Negroes was found to be four times that of the whites, indicating the role of subculture and the isolat-

[14] Veli Verkko, *Homicides and Suicides in Finland and Their Dependence on National Character*, Copenhagen: G. E. C. Gads Forlag, 1951.
[15] Richard Quinney, "Suicide, Homicide, and Economic Development," *Social Forces*, 43 (March 1965), pp. 401–406. Also see Jacqueline and Murray Straus, "Suicide, Homicide, and Social Structure in Ceylon," *American Journal of Sociology*, 58 (March 1953), pp. 461–469 and Arthur Wood, "Murder, Suicide, and Economic Crime in Ceylon," *American Sociological Review*, 26 (October 1961), pp. 744–753.
[16] Jaime Toro-Calder, "Personal Crimes in Puerto Rico," unpublished M. A. thesis, University of Wisconsin, 1950.
[17] Paul Bohannan, *African Homicide and Suicide*, Princeton, N.J.: Princeton University Press, 1960.
[18] H. C. Brearley, *Homicide in the United States*, Chapel Hill: University of North Carolina Press, 1932.
[19] Richard Quinney, "Structural Characteristics, Population Areas, and Crime Rates in the United States," *Journal of Criminal Law, Criminology and Police Science*, 57 (March 1966), pp. 45–52.
[20] Quinney, "Structural Characteristics . . . the United States," p. 49.
[21] Wolfgang, *Patterns in Criminal Homicide*. For a summary, also see "A Sociological Analysis of Criminal Homicide," *Federal Probation*, 25 (March 1961), pp. 48–55 and F. Ferracuti and M. E. Wolfgang, "Design for a Proposed Study of Violence," *British Journal of Criminology*, 3 (April 1963), pp. 377–388. Also see Wolfgang and Ferracuti, *The Subculture of Violence: Towards an Integrated Theory in Criminology*, London, Tavistock Publications, 1967.

ing effects of segregation from the general norms of society. The highest rate, in fact, was reported among recent Negro migrants to the city. In Wolfgang's study, nine out of ten criminal homicides were in lower-class occupations, laborers, for example, committing far more criminal homicides than did clerks.

An indication of the importance of subcultural factors in criminal homicides is the fact that of 489 cases in Houston, Texas, over 87 percent occurred in four areas, not far apart, located in certain slum areas near the center of the city.[22] For the most part, other areas within the city had no criminal homicides at all. Nearly all the homicides occurred in areas populated chiefly by Negroes and Spanish-Americans. In more than 70 percent of the cases the victim and the murderer lived less than two miles apart, and in 32.8 percent of the cases they lived in the same house or block. The conflicts which gave rise to the disputes were chiefly between members of the same social group, and in 87 percent of the cases the murderer and his victim had known each other before. Similarly, criminal homicides and other crimes of violence in London were found to be concentrated in slum areas where violence is used to settle domestic disputes and neighborhood quarrels.[23] Some indication of the relationship between criminal homicides and the pattern of life in certain areas of the city is suggested by the fact that 65 percent of all criminal homicides in Philadelphia occur during weekends, particularly on Saturday night.[24]

A London study of crimes of violence, primarily assault, found that the majority of the offenders were unskilled or were casually employed.[25] The higher clerical and professional workers accounted for no more than five percent of the total. Of those involved in a sample group of assaulters four fifths of the offenders, as well as a like percentage of the victims, were from the working class. "The general neighborhood context is one populated by lower socio-economic groups, especially Negroes of this class."[26] The social background of a sample of London persons convicted of assault was not much different from those convicted of criminal homicide; both tended to have a lower class slum background.[27] As with criminal homicides, most aggravated assaults occur on weekends and late at night. The spontaneous nature of the offense is indicated by the fact that most injuries are inflicted by a knife, which is generally the most accessible weapon. Likewise, assaultive offenders who were members of juvenile gangs appear to have developed, as a result of social influences, a higher degree of dependence on the use of force than do property offenders.[28] The gangs to which a group of assaultive offenders belonged, for example, had as their prime interests gang fighting and rolling drunks whereas theft was the prime activity of the gangs to which nonassaultive offenders belonged.

Organized criminal groups may use force to maintain internal discipline and to restrain competition from outside groups. Such violence in organized crime is the product of a "series of cultural situations and sequential adaptations of individuals to these situations."[29] Individuals in this type of crime grow up in slum areas hospitable to violence. They learn in adolescent gangs the value of violence in

[22] Henry Allen Bullock, "Urban Homicide in Theory and Fact," Journal of Criminal Law, Criminology and Police Science, 45 (January–February 1955), pp. 565–575.

[23] McClintock.

[24] Wolfgang, Patterns in Criminal Homicide, pp. 106–107.

[25] McClintock, pp. 131–132.

[26] Pittman and Handy, p. 469.

[27] McClintock, pp. 131–132.

[28] Peterson, Pittman, and O'Neal, p. 47.

[29] Gilbert Geis, "Violence and Organized Crime," The Annals, 364 (March 1966), p. 94.

settling disputes and enforcing demands. The delinquent gang of the slum produces the adult "gangster," frequently with a long criminal record, who may use
strong-arm methods and be employed by organized criminal groups for this purpose.

Aggressive sex offenders are generally responding to culturally based patterns
of aggression and situational factors. Forcible rape is generally commited by a
young unmarried male, aged 15 to 25, who comes from the lower class.[30] In a
Philadelphia study, 90 percent of the offenders from both races belonged to the
lower part of the occupational scale. Approximately four in ten were from
the lower class; if the lower middle is added, the figure is six in ten.
One third were from the lowest part of the lower class. Another study of a sample
of forcible rapists showed that this behavior is related to the more aggressive patterns
of the lower class, particularly in sexual matters.[31] Offenders of the lower class
are those whose behavior included unnecessary violence; for sex to be gratifying it must be accompanied by physical violence or threats. Others came from
patterns of gang delinquency where boys with other delinquent records simply wish
to have sex relations without considering the wishes of the female. "They are not
sadistic—they simply want to have coitus and the females' wishes are of no particular consequence. They are not hostile toward females, but look upon them
solely as sexual objects whose role in life is to provide sexual pleasure. If a woman
is recalcitrant and will not fulfill her role, a man may have to use force, threat,
weapons, or anything else at his disposal."[32] The Kinsey report showed that lower
class males had considerably more frequent premarital sex experiences and were
likely to restrict their sexual contacts to the more direct form of sexual union
rather than petting and other practices.[33] Moreover, lower class males are likely
to look with disgust on the indirect sexual gratification practices of the higher
classes.

The role of group factors is also shown by the fact that areas with high rates of
forcible rape have been found to correspond to areas having a high rate of
crimes against the person generally.[34] These slum areas in Philadelphia where
Negroes were living had the highest rates of forcible rape. The proportion of Negro
offenders was four times that of the general population, as was the proportion of
Negro victims. The role of group and subcultural factors in forcible rape is also
indicated by the high prevalence of multiple rapes in which the victim was raped
by more than one male. Of the 646 cases of forcible rape in the Philadelphia
study, 43 percent were multiple rapes.[35] Altogether 912 offenders, or 71 percent of
the total offenders, were involved in multiple-rape cases. Group factors were also
indicated by the fact that Negro offenders were more likely to be involved in a
group rape, the group rape was generally an intraracial affair, and the older the
offender the less likely was he to participate in group rape.

The Gusii, a large African tribe in Zambia, are an example of how cultural approval can be given to make forcible rape an accepted form of sex relations for unmarried males.[36] Even the normal forms of sexual intercourse among the married

[30] Amir.
[31] Gebhard, Gagnon, Pomeroy, and Christenson.
[32] Gebhard, Gagnon, Pomeroy, and Christenson, p. 200.
[33] Alfred C. Kinsey, Wardell B. Pomeroy, and Clyde E. Martin, *Sexual Behavior in the Human Male*, Philadelphia: W. B. Saunders Company, 1948.
[34] Amir.
[35] Amir.
[36] Robert A. Levine, "Gusii Sex Offenses: A Study in Social Control," *American Anthropologist*, 61 (December 1959), pp. 696–990.

involve the use of male force and female resistance with an emphasis on the pain inflicted by the male upon the female. This aggressive pattern of sexual behavior is not entirely pretense, but represents an extension in marriage of the sexual patterns developed among unmarried Gusii young men because of their sexual frustrations based on restrictions on interclan sexual contacts, the sexual contacts and provocative behavior of the girls, and the high bride payments which postpone marriage.

A sample of child molesters showed that they generally had low socioeconomic status.[37] Three fourths of them were employed in unskilled and semiskilled occupations. It is likely that subcultural definitions of sex behavior of this economic and social level affect the possibility of sex molestation of children.

SITUATIONAL INTERACTION AND THE USE OF VIOLENCE. Most murder and aggravated assault represent a response, growing out of social interaction between one or more parties, in which a situation comes to be defined as requiring the use of violence. Generally in order for such an act to take place, all parties must come to perceive the situation as one requiring violence. If only one responds in a dispute, it is not likely to become violent; likewise, if only one of the disputants is accustomed to the use of violence, and the other is not, the dispute is likely to end only in a verbal argument. On the other hand, when a cultural norm is defined as calling for violence by a person in social interplay with another who harbors the same response, serious altercations, fist fights, physical assaults with weapons, and violent domestic quarrels, all of which may end in murder, may result. In the process of an argument, A and B both define the initial situation as a serious threat, B then threatens A physically, A threatens B, and B then threatens A. By circular reaction, the situation can then rapidly build up to a climax in which one takes serious overt action, partly because of fear. Consequently, the victim, by being a contributor to the circular reaction of an argument increasing in its physical intensity, may precipitate his own injury or death.

Violence may result from a single argument or dispute. Other cases may result from a series of arguments, extending sometimes over a period of years, between husband and wife, lovers, neighbors, or fellow employees. Increasingly, verbalization in these arguments has declined, while emotional reactions have increased, until, in a final argument, a climax is built up, and with the use of a weapon one of the parties is injured or killed.

Because of the interplay between two parties which generally exists in a dispute leading to violence, the victim often "causes" his own death or serious injury. Wolfgang's Philadelphia study showed that more than one in four criminal homicides were precipitated by the victim, in that the victim first showed or used a deadly weapon or struck a blow in an altercation.[38] Victim-precipitated homicides were found to be significantly associated with Negroes, victim-offender relationships involving male victims of female offenders, mate slaying, alcohol in the homicide situation, or in the victim, and victims with a previous record of assault or arrest. Other homicides, not included in this figure, involved the infidelity of a mate or a lover, failure of the victim to pay a debt, use of vile names by the victim in such a manner that the victim contributes to the homicide. Even in robbery the behavior of the victim may incite the robber to kill.

[37] McCaghy.
[38] Wolfgang, *Patterns in Criminal Homicide*, p. 252. Also see T. P. Morris and Louis Blom-Cooper, *A Calendar of Murder*, London: M. Joseph, 1964.

A period of social interaction between the parties takes place before any aggravated assault. In fact, Pittman and Handy, in their St. Louis study, reported that 70.5 percent of the 241 cases studied had been preceded by verbal arguments.[39] Such quarrels included primarily family arguments, but there were also disputes arising in a tavern, as well as other places. Disputes arose primarily from persons of similar age group, sex, and race.

Sex relations generally may be preceded by interplay between two persons, each responding to cues from the other person. The use of force or threat in sexual relations is affected by a number of factors.[40] In the first place, a sexually aroused female may be ambivalent toward sex relations when excited, thus confusing her male partner about the use of more forcible persuasion. Second, some females, particularly those of the lower class, may actually wish to be overpowered and treated roughly in sex relations. Third, some may wish to justify their own conduct by encouraging force by the male partner. Fourth, the male may interpret the lack of strong verbal or physical resistance by the female as acquiescence to his use of some force.

The victim of forcible rape often appears to have much to do with the fact that she is raped. Amir found that 19 percent of the forcible rapes in his Philadelphia study were victim-precipitated in the sense that the "victims actually, or so it was interpreted by the offender, agreed to sexual relations but retracted before the actual act or did not resist strongly enough when the suggestion was made by the offender or offenders."[41] The role of the victim was also crucial when she entered a situation in which sexual stimulation was pervasive or made what could be interpreted as an invitation to sex relations. In over half the rapes the victims displayed submissive behavior. Moreover, 19 percent of the victims had an arrest record and 56 percent of them had been charged with some sort of sexual offense.

PERSONAL RELATIONSHIPS IN VIOLENT CRIME.   Many studies have indicated that close relationships generally existed between the offender and the victim of violence. Criminal homicides and aggravated assaults result from domestic quarrels, altercations, jealousies, and arguments over money or property. Most of the offender-victim relationships have been intimate, close, and frequent, primarily involving family members and close friends. The major exception is the small proportion of such crimes occurring in connection with other crimes like robbery. A study of 713 New Jersey murders classified according to victim-offender relationships and the situations in which the murders took place found that less than one fourth committed murder in connection with another crime.[42] The largest group (about two-thirds) of the murders grew out of some altercation with male acquaintances, sex rivals, relatives, or mistresses. Wolfgang's Philadelphia study found that approximately a third of 588 male and female criminal homicides resulted from general altercations. Family and domestic quarrels accounted for 14 percent, jealousy 12 percent, altercation over money 11 per cent, and robbery, contrary to popular impression, only 7 percent.[43] Close friends and relatives accounted for over half (59 percent) of all homicides and four fifths of the women victims. In 28 percent

[39] Pittman and Handy, p. 467.
[40] Gebhard, Gagnon, Pomeroy, and Christenson, pp. 177–179.
[41] Amir, p. 611.
[42] E. Frankel, "One Thousand Murderers," Journal of Criminal Law, Criminology and Police Science, 29 (1938–1939), pp. 687–688.
[43] Wolfgang, Patterns in Criminal Homicide, p. 191.

of the cases the victim was a close friend of the murderer, in 25 percent a family relative, in 14 percent an acquaintance. In only one out of eight murders was the victim a stranger. As contrasted with men, a much larger proportion of women generally kill someone in their own families. It was concluded that when a woman committed a homicide, the victim was more likely to be her mate, and when a man was killed by a woman, he was most likely to be killed by his wife.[44] A study of Wisconsin prisoners charged with murder also disclosed a large percentage of cases with a previous history of difficulties with the victim. Two thirds of the Wisconsin murders grew out of a long-standing or an immediate quarrel, and most of the others were connected with some crime. Many of the Wisconsin murders studied involved situations in which the marital situation was most important, and some grow out of disputes between farmers or some similar controversy.[45]

Studies in countries with different cultures have also revealed the significance of personal contacts in criminal homicide. A Danish study revealed that the murderer's victim was a relative or an acquaintance in nine out of ten cases and that strangers were seldom the victims.[46] Similarly, an Indian study has indicated that most murders occur within the same caste and frequently involve husband and wife.[47] Nearly 80 percent of all homicides in a London study and "murderous assaults" (an English category of attempted murder) were committed against relatives or victims well known to the attacker. Half the offenses arose from family strife, that is, the offender and the victim belonged to the same family. If there are added close associates, with whom the person lived or worked, the proportion committed by persons intimately associated with their victims increased to 60 percent. A further 20 percent were committed against friends and acquaintances. Arrests in 1960 in London showed that crimes of violence, 90 percent involving felonious assaults, tended to occur in the family or between persons who were well known to each other in the neighborhood.[48] More specifically, 13.1 percent involved a family relative, 15 percent a relationship with friends or neighbors of some duration, 15.1 percent acquaintances, and 6.4 percent a business or similar relationship. In 43.1 percent the relationship was slight, and 7.3 percent involved the police. This study concluded that homicides or murderous assaults on police, on strangers in the street, or those associated with sexual attack, are rare.

> The main conclusion is that the vast majority of offenses were committed in the poorer areas of London among working-class people. This was predominantly so in the cases of domestic strife and neighborhood quarrels, but even in the attacks and fights in public houses, cafes and streets the victims were involved in fights or attacked by other working-class people in the same neighborhood. Social status is to some extent reflected in the occupation of the victim and it was found that more than two-thirds of the victims were either casual or general laborers, or factory workers or in some other unskilled employment, or wives of people so employed.[49]

[44] Wolfgang, *Patterns in Criminal Homicide*, p. 325.
[45] Gillin, p. 60.
[46] Kaare Svalastoga, "Homicide and Social Contact in Denmark," *American Journal of Sociology*, 62 (July 1956), pp. 37–41.
[47] Edwin D. Driver, "Interaction and Criminal Homicide in India," *Social Forces*, 40 (December 1961), pp. 153–158.
[48] McClintock, pp. 238, 248.
[49] McClintock, pp. 44–45.

CORRESPONDENCE BETWEEN CRIMINAL BEHAVIOR AND LEGITIMATE BEHAVIOR PATTERNS

All violence is by no means harmful to a society. As Coser has pointed out, violence in a society may perform a usual function.[50] It may help groups of individuals in a society to achieve certain goals which are otherwise difficult for them to achieve. The resort to violence may serve as danger signals of political and economic dislocation in a society, and it may serve as a catalyst to change, as in the case of the excessive use of violence to curb Civil Rights demonstrations in the South in 1965.

Middle and upper class persons are likely to define certain situations as trivial which among persons of the lower class or certain ethnic groups may precipitate a serious personal dispute leading to the use of force. Moreover, middle class norms prohibiting violence often clash with the norms of the lower class which require violence in certain situations. All of this is what Wolfgang has termed the "subculture of violence," in the sense that certain persons, because of their normative definitions, come to interpret some situations as requiring violence.

> The significance of a jostle, a slightly derogatory remark, or the appearance of a weapon in the hands of an adversary are stimuli differentially perceived and interpreted by Negroes and whites, males and females. . . . A male is usually expected to defend the name and honor of his mother, the virtue of womanhood (even though his female companion for the evening may be an entirely new acquaintance and/or a prostitute), and to accept no derogation about his race (even from a member of his own race), his age, or his masculinity. Quick resort to physical combat as a measure of daring, courage, or defense of status appears to be a cultural expectation, especially for lower socio-economic class males of both races.[51]

The greater the degree of integration of the individual into a subculture of violence, in terms of expected reactions to certain types of stimuli and the importance of human life, the more likely that he will resort to violence in a dispute or to gain a sexual objective. "Subcultures of violence" refer to certain areas such as slums, certain ethnic or racial groups, the lower class, and certain occupations. Child rearing practices and peer group associations which employ violence are part of this subculture. "Ready access to weapons may become essential for protection against others in this milieu who respond in similarly violent ways, and the carrying of knives or other protective devices becomes a common symbol of willingness to participate in and to expect violence, and to be ready for its retaliation."[52]

The middle and upper socioeconomic groups in society have codified legal rules that prohibit the use of violence. The middle class denunciation of violence is in part an attempt to discourage attacks against established political power.[53]

---

[50] Lewis A. Coser, "Some Social Functions of Violence," *The Annals,* 364 (March 1966), pp. 8–18.

[51] Wolfgang, *Patterns in Criminal Homicide,* pp. 188–189.

[52] Marvin E. Wolfgang, "A Sociological Analysis of Criminal Homicide," *Federal Probation,* 25 (March 1961), p. 55.

[53] Wolfgang, "A Preface to Violence," p. 3.

These criminal laws do not recognize the separate existence of subcultural norms among certain groups which recognize the use of force to settle disputes as legitimate. These same groups would, however, generally not approve of murder, but at the same time in sanctioning violence which may lead to murder there is an inconsistency in their value system.

SOCIETAL REACTION

Middle and upper class persons react strongly to the use of violence as seen in the severe legal penalties for murder, manslaughter, forcible rape, and child molesting. In the United States, murder can carry with it the death penalty in 38 out of 50 states, despite the fact that the murderer sociologically is often far less a "criminal" than are other offenders. Likewise, manslaughter, forcible rape, and child molesting usually are punished by an unusually long period of imprisonment. Penalties for sex offenses with females who are underage are much more harsh than laws prohibiting essentially the same offense with adults. Many are subject to long indefinite confinement under various sex deviate laws. In fact, the severe penalties for child molesting result in many offenders being unwilling to accept full responsibility for their offenses.[54] Forcible rape carries the death penalty in three states, while fifteen other states punish it with either death or life imprisonment.[55]

Such offenses are punished severely not because they constitute a serious threat to the larger political and economic order. Rather, the punishment is severe because of the injury to the individual. Severe punishment is thought to work as a deterrent, helps to avoid retaliation by relatives and friends of the victims, and also serves to reinstate the religious beliefs held by many in the larger society about the sanctity of life and the sexual conduct of individuals.

SELECTED BIBLIOGRAPHY

1. Amir, Menachem., "Patterns of Forcible Rape," unpublished Ph.D. dissertation, University of Pennsylvania, 1965.
2. Beattie, Ronald H., and John Kenney, "Aggressive Crimes," *The Annals*, 364 (March 1966), pp. 73–85.
3. Bedau, Hugo Adam (ed.), *The Death Penalty in America*, Chicago: Aldine Publishing Co., 1964.
4. Bloch, Herbert A., and Gilbert Geis, "Homicide and Assaults," in their *Man, Crime, and Society*, New York: Random House, Inc., 1962, Chap. 10.
5. Bohannan, Paul, *African Homicide and Suicide*, Princeton, N.J.: Princeton University Press, 1960.
6. Brearley, H. S., *Homicide in the United States*, Chapel Hill: University of North Carolina Press, 1932.
7. Bromage, Kenneth G., and Harry V. Ball, "A Study of Juvenile 'Battery' Cases," *Alpha Kappa Deltan*, 28 (Spring 1958), pp. 18–24.
8. Bullock, Henry Allen, "Urban Homicide in Theory and Fact," *Journal of*

---

[54] McCaghy.
[55] Leonard D. Savitz, "A Study in Capital Punishment," *Journal of Criminal Law, Criminology and Police Science*, 49 (November–December, 1958), pp. 338–341, and Hugo Adam Bedau, (ed.), *The Death Penalty in America*, Chicago: Aldine Publishing Co., 1964.

Criminal Law, Criminology and Police Science, 45 (January–February 1955), pp. 565–575.

9. Coser, Lewis A., "Some Social Functions of Violence," The Annals, 364 (March 1966), pp. 8–18.

10. Driver, Edwin D., "Interaction and Criminal Homicide in India," Social Forces, 40 (December 1961), pp. 153–158.

11. Ellis, Albert, and Ralph Brancale, The Psychology of Sex Offenders, Springfield, Ill., Charles C Thomas, Publisher, 1965.

12. Fitch, J. H., "Men Convicted of Sexual Offenses against Children," British Journal of Criminology, 3 (July 1962), pp. 18–37.

13. Frankel, E., "One Thousand Murderers," Journal of Criminal Law, Criminology and Police Science, 29 (1938–1939), pp. 687–688.

14. Gebhard, Paul H., John H. Gagnon, Wardell B. Pomeroy, and Cornelia V. Christenson, Sex Offenders: An Analysis of Types, New York: Harper & Row, Publishers, 1965, pp. 192–194.

15. Geis, Gilbert, "Violence and Organized Crime," The Annals, 364 (March 1966), pp. 86–96.

16. Gibbins, T. C. N., and A. Walker, "Violent Cruelty to Children," British Journal of Delinquency, 6 (April 1956), pp. 260–277.

17. Gillin, John L., "Murder as a Sociological Phenomenon," The Annals, 248 (November 1952), pp. 20–25.

18. ———, The Wisconsin Prisoner, Madison: The University of Wisconsin Press, 1946.

19. Gold, Martin, "Suicide, Homicide, and the Socialization of Aggression," American Journal of Sociology, 63 (May 1958), pp. 651–661.

20. Kinsey, Alfred C., Wardell B. Pomeroy, and Clyde E. Martin, Sexual Behavior in the Human Male, Philadelphia: W. B. Saunders Company, 1948.

21. Levine, Robert A., "Gusii Sex Offenses: A Study in Social Control," American Anthropologist, 61 (December 1959), pp. 696–990.

22. McCaghy, Charles, "Child Molesters: A Study of Their Careers as Deviants," unpublished Ph.D. dissertation, University of Wisconsin, 1966.

23. McClintock, F. H., Crimes of Violence, New York: St. Martin's Press, Inc., 1963.

24. Morris, T. P., and Louis Blom-Cooper, A Calendar of Murder, London: M. Joseph, 1964.

25. Peterson, Richard A., David J. Pittman, and Patricia O'Neal, "Stabilities in Deviance: A Study of Assaultive and Non-Assaultive Offenders," Journal of Criminal Law, Criminology and Police Science, 53 (March 1962), pp. 44–49.

26. Pettigrew, Thomas F., and Rosalind B. Spier, "Ecological Pattern of Negro Homicide," American Journal of Sociology, 67 (May 1962), pp. 621–629.

27. Pittman, David J., and William Handy, "Patterns in Criminal Aggravated Assault," Journal of Criminal Law, Criminology and Police Science, 55 (December 1964), pp. 462–470.

28. Quinney, Richard, "Structural Characteristics, Population Areas, and Crime Rates in the United States," Journal of Criminal Law, Criminology and Police Science, 57 (March 1966), pp. 45–52.

29. ———, "Suicide, Homicide, and Economic Development," Social Forces, 43 (March 1965), pp. 401–406.

30. Roebuck, Julian, and Ronald Johnson, "The Negro Drinker and Assaulter as a Criminal Type," *Crime and Delinquency*, 3 (January 1962), pp. 21–33.

31. Savitz, Leonard D., "A Study in Capital Punishment," *Journal of Criminal Law, Criminology and Police Science*, 49 (November–December, 1958), pp. 338–341.

32. Straus, Jacqueline and Murray, "Suicide, Homicide, and Social Structure in Ceylon, "*American Journal of Sociology*, 48 (March 1953), pp. 461–469.

33. Svalastoga, Kaare, "Homicide and Social Contact in Denmark," *American Journal of Sociology*, 62 (July 1956), pp. 37–41.

34. Toro-Calder, Jaime, "Personal Crimes in Puerto Rico," unpublished M.A. thesis, University of Wisconsin, 1950.

35. Verkko, Veli, *Homicides and Suicides in Finland and Their Dependence on National Character*, Copenhagen: G. E. C. Gads Forlag, 1951.

36. Wattenberg, William W., and John B. Moir, "A Phenomenon in Search of a Cause," *Journal of Criminal Law, Criminology and Police Science*, 48 (May–June 1957), pp. 54–58.

37. Wolfgang, Marvin E., "Husband-Wife Homicides," *Journal of Social Therapy*, 2 (1956), pp. 263–271.

38. ———, *Patterns in Criminal Homicide*, Philadelphia: University of Pennsylvania Press, 1958.

39. ———, "A Preface to Violence," *The Annals*, 364 (March 1966), pp. 1–8.

40. ———, "A Sociological Analysis of Criminal Homicide," *Federal Probation*, XXV (March 1961), pp. 48–56.

41. ———, "Victim Precipitated Criminal Homicide," *Journal of Criminal Law, Criminology and Police Science*, 48 (May–June 1957), pp. 1–11.

42. ———, and Franco Ferracuti, *The Subculture of Violence: Towards an Integrated Theory in Criminology*, London: Tavistock Publications, 1967.

43. Wood, Arthur, "Murder, Suicide, and Economic Crime in Ceylon," *American Sociological Review*, 26 (October 1961), pp. 744–753.

VICTIM-PRECIPITATED CRIMINAL HOMICIDE*

Marvin E. Wolfgang

In a study of criminal homicide in Philadelphia, Wolfgang found that the victim precipitated the act of homicide in one out of four cases of recorded homicide. Homicide, thus, often results from an intense interaction in which the victim first initiates physical action against the subsequent slayer. It is often merely chance which determines who will be the victim and who will be the

* Reprinted by special permission of the author and the Journal of Criminal Law, Criminology and Police Science, Copyright © 1958 by the Northwestern University School of Law, Volume 48, Number 1, May–June, 1957, pp. 1–11.

offender. In this article, victim-precipitated homicides are compared with nonvictim homicides. Significant differences exist between the two types of homicide.

In many crimes, especially in criminal homicide, the victim is often a major contributor to the criminal act. Except in cases in which the victim is an innocent bystander and is killed in lieu of an intended victim, or in cases in which a pure accident is involved, the victim may be one of the major precipitating causes of his own demise.

Various theories of social interaction, particularly in social psychology, have established the framework for the present discussion. In criminological literature, however, probably von Hentig in *The Criminal and His Victim*, has provided the most useful theoretical basis for analysis of the victim-offender relationship. In Chapter XII, entitled "The Contribution of the Victim to the Genesis of Crime," the author discusses this "duet frame of crime" and suggests that homicide is particularly amenable to analysis.[1] In *Penal Philosophy*, Tarde[2] frequently attacks the "legislative mistake" of concentrating too much on premeditation and paying too little attention to motives which indicate an important interrelationship between victim and offender. And in one of his satirical essays, "On Murder Considered as One of the Fine Arts," Thomas De Quincey[3] shows cognizance of the idea that sometimes the victim is a would-be murderer. Garofalo,[4] too, noted that the victim may provoke another individual into attack, and though the provocation be slight, if perceived by an egoistic attacker it may be sufficient to result in homicide.

Besides these theoretical concepts, the law of homicide has long recognized provocation by the victim as a possible reason for mitigation of the offense from murder to manslaughter, or from criminal to excusable homicide. In order that such reduction occur, there are four prerequisites.[5]

(1) There must have been adequate provocation.

(2) The killing must have been in the heat of passion.

(3) The killing must have followed the provocation before there had been a reasonable opportunity for the passion to cool.

(4) A causal connection must exist between provocation, the heat of passion, and the homicidal act. Such, for example, are: adultery, seduction of the offender's juvenile daughter, rape of the offender's wife or close relative, etc.

Finally (4), a causal connection must exist between provocation, the heat of passion, and the homicidal act. Perkins claims that "the adequate provocation must have engendered the heat of passion, and the heat of passion must have been the cause of the act which resulted in death."[6]

DEFINITION AND ILLUSTRATION

The term *victim-precipitated* is applied to those criminal homicides in which the vic-

[1] Von Hentig, Hans, *The Criminal and His Victim*, New Haven: Yale University Press, 1948, pp. 388–385.
[2] Tarde, Gabriel, *Penal Philosophy*, Boston: Little, Brown and Company, 1912, p. 466.
[3] De Quincey, Thomas, "On Murder Considered as One of the Fine Arts," *The Arts of Cheating, Swindling, and Murder*, Edward Bulwer-Lytton, and Douglas Jerrold and Thomas De Quincey, New York: The Arnold Co., 1925, p. 153.
[4] Garofalo, Baron Raffaele, *Criminology*, Boston: Little, Brown, and Company, 1941, p. 373.
[5] For an excellent discussion of the rule of provocation, from which these four requirements are taken, see: Rollin M. Perkins, "The Law of Homicide," *Journal of Criminal Law and Criminology* (March–April, 1946), 36: 412–427; and Herbert Wechsler and Jerome Michael, *A Rationale of the Law of Homicide*, pp. 1280–1282. A general review of the rule of provocation, both in this country and abroad, may be found in The Royal Commission on Capital Punishment, *1949–1952 Report*. Appendix II, pp. 453–458.
[6] *Ibid.*, p. 425. The term "cause" is here used in a legal and not a psychological sense.

tim is a direct, positive precipitator in the crime. The role of the victim is characterized by his having been the first in the homicide drama to use physical force directed against his subsequent slayer. The victim-precipitated cases are those in which the victim was the first to show and use a deadly weapon, to strike a blow in an altercation—in short, the first to commence the interplay or resort to physical violence.

In seeking to identify the victim-precipitated cases recorded in police files it has not been possible always to determine whether the homicides strictly parallel legal interpretations. In general, there appears to be much similarity. In a few cases included under the present definition, the nature of the provocation is such that it would not legally serve to mitigate the offender's responsibility. In these cases the victim was threatened in a robbery, and either attempted to prevent the robbery, failed to take the robber seriously, or in some other fashion irritated, frightened, or alarmed the felon by physical force so that the robber, either by accident or compulsion, killed the victim. Infidelity of a mate or lover, failure to pay a debt, use of vile names by the victim, obviously means that he played an important role in inciting the offender to overt action in order to seek revenge, to win an argument, or to defend himself. However, mutual quarrels and wordy altercations do not constitute sufficient provocation under law, and they are not included in the meaning of victim-precipitated homicide.

Below are sketched several typical cases to illustrate the pattern of these homicides. Primary demonstration of physical force by the victim, supplemented by scurrilous language, characterizes the most common victim-precipitated homicides. All of these slayings were listed by the Philadelphia Police as criminal homicides, none of the offenders was exonerated by a coroner's inquest, and all the offenders were tried in criminal court.

A husband accused his wife of giving money to another man, and while she was making breakfast, he attacked her with a milk bottle, then a brick, and finally a piece of concrete block. Having had a butcher knife in hand, she stabbed him during the fight.

A husband threatened to kill his wife on several occasions. In this instance, he attacked her with a pair of scissors, dropped them, and grabbed a butcher knife from the kitchen. In the ensuing struggle that ended on their bed, he fell on the knife.

In an argument over a business transaction, the victim first fired several shots at his adversary, who in turn fatally returned the fire.

The victim was the aggressor in a fight, having struck his enemy several times. Friends tried to interfere, but the victim persisted. Finally, the offender retaliated with blows, causing the victim to fall and hit his head on the sidewalk, as a result of which he died.

A husband had beaten his wife on several occasions. In the present instance, she insisted that he take her to the hospital. He refused, and a violent quarrel followed, during which he slapped her several times, and she concluded by stabbing him.

During a lovers' quarrel, the male (victim) hit his mistress and threw a can of kerosene at her. She retaliated by throwing the liquid on him, and then tossed a lighted match in his direction. He died from the burns.

A drunken husband, beating his wife in their kitchen, gave her a butcher knife and dared her to use it on him. She claimed that if he should strike her once more, she would use the knife, whereupon he slapped her in the face and she fatally stabbed him.

A victim became incensed when his eventual slayer asked for money which the victim owed him. The victim grabbed a hatchet and started in the direction of his creditor, who pulled out a knife and stabbed him.

A victim attempted to commit sodomy with his girl friend, who refused his overtures. He struck her several times on the side of her head with his fists before she grabbed a butcher knife and cut him fatally.

A drunken victim with knife in hand approached his slayer during a quarrel. The slayer showed a gun, and the victim dared him to shoot. He did.

During an argument in which a male called a female many vile names, she tried to telephone the police. But he grabbed the phone from her hands, knocked her down, kicked her, and hit her with a tire gauge. She ran to the kitchen, grabbed a butcher knife, and stabbed him in the stomach.

THE PHILADELPHIA STUDY

Empirical data for analysis of victim-precipitated homicides were collected from the files of the Homicide Squad of the Philadelphia Police Department, and include 588 consecutive cases of criminal homicide which occurred between January 1, 1948 and December 31, 1952. Because more than one person was sometimes involved in the slaying of a single victim, there was a total of 621 offenders responsible for the killing of 588 victims. The present study is part of a much larger work that analyzes criminal homicide in greater detail. Such material that is relevant to victim-precipitation is included in the present analysis. The 588 criminal homicides provide sufficient background information to establish much about the nature of the victim-offender relationship. Of these cases, 150, or 26 percent, have been designated, on the basis of the previously stated definition, as VP cases.[7] The remaining 438, therefore, have been designated as non-VP cases.

Thorough study of police files, theoretical discussions of the victim's contribution, and previous analysis of criminal homicide suggest that there may be important differences between VP and non-VP cases. The chi-square test has been used to test the significance in proportions between VP and

[7] In order to facilitate reading of the following sections, the victim-precipitated cases are referred to simply as VP cases or VP homicides. Those homicides in which the victim was not a direct precipitator are referred to as non-VP cases.

non-VP homicides and a series of variables. Hence, any spurious association which is just due to chance has been reduced to a minimum by application of this test, and significant differences of distributions are revealed. Where any expected class frequency of less than five existed, the test was not applied; and in each tested association, a correction for continuity was used, although the difference resulting without it was only slight. In this study a value of P less than .05, or the 5 percent level of significance, is used as the minimal level of significant association. Throughout the subsequent discussion, the term *significant* in italics is used to indicate that a chi-square test of significance of association has been made and that the value of P less than .05 has been found. The discussion that follows (with respect to race, sex, age, etc.) reveals some interesting differences and similarities between the two. (Table 1.)

Race. Because Negroes and males have been shown by their high rates of homicide, assaults against the person, etc., to be more criminally aggressive than whites and females, it may be inferred that there are more Negroes and males among VP victims than among non-VP victims. The data confirm this inference. Nearly 80 percent of VP cases compared to 70 percent of non-VP cases involve Negroes, a proportional difference that results in a *significant* association between race and VP homicide.

Sex. As victims, males comprise 94 percent of VP homicides, but only 72 percent of non-VP homicides, showing a *significant* association between sex of the victim and VP homicide.

Since females have been shown by their low rates of homicide, assaults against the person, etc., to be less criminally aggressive than males, and since females are less likely to precipitate their own victimization than males, we should expect more female *offenders* among VP homicides than among non-VP homicides. Such is the case, for the

Table 1.
VICTIM-PRECIPITATED AND NON-VICTIM-PRECIPITATED
CRIMINAL HOMICIDE BY SELECTED VARIABLES
PHILADELPHIA, 1948–1952

	TOTAL VICTIMS		VICTIM-PRECIPITATED		NON-VICTIM-PRECIPITATED	
	Number	*Percent of Total*	*Number*	*Percent of Total*	*Number*	*Percent of Total*
Race and Sex of Victim						
Both Races	588	100.0	150	100.0	438	100.0
Male	449	76.4	141	94.0	308	70.3
Female	139	23.6	9	6.0	130	29.7
Negro	427	72.6	119	79.3	308	70.3
Male	331	56.3	111	74.0	220	50.2
Female	96	16.3	8	5.3	88	20.1
White	161	27.4	31	20.7	130	29.7
Male	118	20.1	30	20.0	88	20.1
Female	43	7.3	1	0.7	42	9.6
Age of Victim						
Under 15	28	4.8	0	—	28	6.4
15–19	25	4.3	7	4.7	18	4.1
20–24	59	10.0	18	12.0	41	9.4
25–29	93	15.8	17	11.3	76	17.3
30–34	88	15.0	20	13.3	68	15.5
35–39	75	12.8	25	16.7	50	11.4
40–44	57	9.7	23	15.3	34	7.8
45–49	43	7.3	13	8.7	30	6.8
50–54	48	8.2	11	7.3	37	8.5
55–59	26	4.4	6	4.0	20	4.6
60–64	18	3.1	7	4.7	11	2.5
65 and over	28	4.7	3	2.0	25	5.7
Total	588	100.0	150	100.0	438	100.0
Method						
Stabbing	228	38.8	81	54.0	147	33.6
Shooting	194	33.0	39	26.0	155	35.4
Beating	128	21.8	26	17.3	102	23.3
Other	38	6.4	4	2.7	34	7.7
Total	588	100.0	150	100.0	438	100.0
Place						
Home	301	51.2	80	53.3	221	50.5
Not Home	287	48.8	70	46.7	217	49.5
Total	588	100.0	150	100.0	438	100.0
Interpersonal Relationship						
Relatively close friend	155	28.2	46	30.7	109	27.3
Family relationship	136	24.7	38	25.3	98	24.5
(Spouse)	(100)	(73.5)	(33)	(86.8)	(67)	(68.4)
(Other)	(36)	(26.5)	(5)	(13.2)	(31)	(31.6)
Acquaintance	74	13.5	20	13.3	54	13.5
Stranger	67	12.2	16	10.7	51	12.8

Table 1. continued

	TOTAL VICTIMS		VICTIM-PRECIPITATED		NON-VICTIM-PRECIPITATED	
	Number	Percent of Total	Number	Percent of Total	Number	Percent of Total
Paramour, Mistress, Prostitute	54	9.8	15	10.0	39	9.8
Sex rival	22	4.0	6	4.0	16	4.0
Enemy	16	2.9	6	4.0	10	2.5
Paramour of Offender's mate	11	2.0	1	.7	10	2.5
Felon or police officer	6	1.1	1	.7	5	1.3
Innocent bystander	6	1.1	—	—	6	1.5
Homosexual partner	3	.6	1	.7	2	.5
Total	550	100.0	150	100.0	400	100.0
Presence of alcohol during Offense						
Present	374	63.6	111	74.0	263	60.0
Not Present	214	36.4	39	26.0	175	40.0
Total	588	100.0	150	100.0	438	100.0
Presence of alcohol in the victim						
Present	310	52.7	104	69.3	206	47.0
Not Present	278	47.3	46	30.7	232	53.0
Total	588	100.0	150	100.0	438	100.0
Previous arrest record of victim						
Previous arrest record	277	47.3	93	62.0	184	42.0
Offenses against the person	150	25.5 (54.2)	56	37.3 (60.2)	94	21.4 (50.1)
Other offenses only	127	21.6 (45.8)	37	24.7 (39.8)	90	20.5 (49.9)
No previous arrest record	311	52.7	57	38.0	254	58.0
Total	588	100.0	150	100.0	438	100.0
Previous arrest record of Offender						
Previous arrest record	400	64.4	81	54.0	319	67.7
Offenses against the person	264	42.5 (66.0)	49	32.7 (60.5)	215	45.6 (67.4)
Other offenses only	136	21.8 (34.0)	32	21.3 (39.5)	104	22.1 (32.6)
No previous arrest record	221	35.6	69	(46.0)	152	32.3
Total	621	100.0	150	100.0	471	100.0

comparative data reveal that females are twice as frequently offenders in VP slayings (29 percent) as they are in non-VP slayings (14 percent)—a proportional difference which is also highly *significant*.

The number of white female offenders (16) in this study is too small to permit statistical analysis, but the tendency among both Negro and white females as separate groups is toward a much higher proportion among VP than among non-VP offenders. As noted above, analysis of Negro and white females as a combined group does result in the finding of a *significant* association between female offenders and VP homicide.

Age. The age distributions of victims and offenders in VP and non-VP homicides are strikingly similar; study of the data suggests that age has no apparent effect on VP homicide. The median age of VP victims is 33.3 years, while that of non-VP victims is 31.2 years.

Methods. In general, there is a *significant* association between method used to inflict death and VP homicide. Because Negroes and females comprise a larger proportion of offenders in VP cases, and because previous analysis has shown that stabbings occurred more often than any of the other methods of inflicting death,[8] it is implied that the frequency of homicides by stabbing is greater among VP than among non-VP cases. The data support such an implication and reveal that homicides by stabbing account for 54 percent of the VP cases but only 34 percent of non-VP cases, a difference which is *significant*. The distribution of shootings, beatings, and "other" methods of inflicting death among the VP and non-VP cases shows no significant differences. The high frequency of stabbings among VP homicides appears to result from an almost equal reduction in each of the remaining methods; yet the lower proportions in each of these three other categories among VP cases are not separately very different from the proportions among non-VP cases.

Place and Motive. There is no important difference between VP and non-VP homicides with respect to a home/not-home dichotomy, nor with respect to motives listed by the police. Slightly over half of both VP and non-VP slayings occurred in the home. General altercations (43 percent) and domestic quarrels (20 percent) rank highest among VP cases, as they do among non-VP cases (32 and 12 percent), although with lower frequency. Combined, these two motives account for a slightly larger share of the VP cases (3 out of 5) than of the non-VP cases (2 out of 5).

Victim-offender Relationships.[9]   Intra-racial slayings predominate in both groups, but inter-racial homicides comprise a larger share of VP cases (8 percent) than they do of non-VP cases (5 percent). Although VP cases make up one-fourth of all criminal homicides, they account for over one-third (35 percent) of all inter-racial slayings. Thus it appears that a homicide which crosses race lines is often likely to be one in which the slayer was provoked to assault by the victim. The association between inter-racial slayings and VP homicides, however, is not statistically significant.

Homicides involving victims and offenders of opposite sex (regardless of which sex is the victim or which is the offender) occur with about the same frequency among VP cases (34 percent) as among non-VP cases (37 percent). But a *significant* difference between VP and non-VP cases does emerge when determination of the sex of the victim, relative to the sex of his specific slayer, is taken into account. Of all criminal homicides for which the sex of both victim and offender is known, 88 involve a male victim and a female offender; and of these 88 cases, 43 are VP homicides. Thus, it may be said that 43, or 29 percent, of the 150 VP homicides, compared to 45, or only 11 percent, of the 400 non-VP homicides, are males slain by females.

It seems highly desirable, in view of these findings, that the police thoroughly investigate every possibility of strong provocation by the male victim when he is slain by a female—and particularly, as noted below, if the female is his wife, which is also a strong possibility. It is, of course, the further responsibility of defense counsel, prosecuting attorney, and subsequently the court, to determine whether such provocation was sufficient either to reduce or to eliminate culpability altogether.

The proportion that Negro male/Negro

---

[8] Of 588 victims, 228, or 39 percent, were stabbed; 194, or 33 percent, were shot; 128, or 22 percent were beaten; and 38, or 6 percent, were killed by other methods.

[9] Only 550 victim-offender relationships are identified since 38 of the 588 criminal homicides are classified as unsolved, or those in which the perpetrator is unknown.

male[10] and white male/white male homicides constitute among VP cases (45 and 13 percent) is similar to the proportion these same relationships constitute among non-VP cases (41 and 14 percent). The important contribution of the Negro male as a victim-precipitator is indicated by the fact that Negro male/Negro female homicides are, proportionately, nearly three times as frequent among VP cases (25 percent) as they are among non-VP cases (9 percent). It is apparent, therefore, that Negroes and males not only are the groups most likely to make positive and direct contributions to the genesis of their own victimization, but that, in particular, Negro males more frequently provoke females of their own race to slay them than they do members of their own sex and race.

For both VP and non-VP groups, close friends, relatives, and acquaintances are the major types of specific relationships between victims and offenders. Combined, these three relationships constitute 69 percent of the VP homicides and 65 percent of the non-VP cases. Victims are relatives of their slayers in one-fourth of both types of homicide. But of 38 family slayings among VP cases, 33 are husband-wife killings; while of 98 family slayings among non-VP cases, only 67 are husband-wife killings. This proportional difference results in a *significant* association between mate slayings and VP homicide.

Finally, of VP mate slayings, 28 victims are husbands and only 5 are wives; but of non-VP mate slayings, only 19 victims are husbands while 48 are wives. Thus there is a *significant* association between husbands who are victims in mate slayings and VP homicide. This fact, namely, that *significantly* more husbands than wives are victims in VP mate slayings—means that (1) husbands actually may provoke their wives more often than wives provoke their husbands to assault their respective mates; or,

10 The diagonal line represents "killed by." Thus, Negro male/Negro male means a Negro male killed by a Negro male; the victim precedes the offender.

(2) assuming that provocation by wives is as intense and equally frequent, or even more frequent, than provocation by husbands, then husbands may not receive and define provocation stimuli with as great or as violent a reaction as do wives; or (3) husbands may have a greater felt sense of guilt in a marital conflict for one reason or another, and receive verbal insults and overt physical assaults without retaliation as a form of compensatory punishment; or, (4) husbands may withdraw more often than wives from the scene of marital conflict, and thus eliminate, for the time being, a violent overt reaction to their wives' provocation. Clearly, this is only a suggestive, not an exhaustive, list of probable explanations. In any case, we are left with the undeniable fact that husbands more often than wives are major, precipitating factors in their own homicidal deaths.

Alcohol. In the larger work of which this study is a part, the previous discovery of an association between the presence of alcohol in the homicide situation and Negro male offenders, combined with knowledge of the important contribution Negro males make to their own victimization, suggests an association (by transitivity) between VP homicide and the presence of alcohol. Moreover, whether alcohol is present in the victim or offender, lowered inhibitions due to ingestion of alcohol may cause an individual to give vent more freely to pent up frustrations, tensions, and emotional conflicts that have either built up over a prolonged period of time or that arise within an immediate emotional crisis. The data do in fact confirm the suggested hypothesis above and reveal a *significant* association between VP homicide and alcohol in the homicide situation. Comparison of VP to non-VP cases with respect to the presence of alcohol in the homicide situation (alcohol present in either the victim, offender, or both), reveals that alcohol was present in 74 percent of the VP cases and in 60 percent of the non-VP cases. The proportional difference results in a *signifi-*

cant association between alcohol and VP homicide. It should be noted that the association is not necessarily a causal one, or that a causal relationship is not proved by the association.

Because the present analysis is concerned primarily with the contribution of the victim to the homicide, it is necessary to determine whether an association exists between VP homicide and presence of alcohol in the victim. No association was found to exist between VP homicide and alcohol in the offender. But victims had been drinking immediately prior to their death in more VP cases (69 percent) than in non-VP cases (47 percent). A positive and *significant* relationship is, therefore, clearly established between victims who had been drinking and who precipitated their own death. In many of these cases the victim was intoxicated, or nearly so, and lost control of his own defensive powers. He frequently was a victim with no intent to harm anyone maliciously, but who, nonetheless, struck his friend, acquaintance, or wife, who later became his assailant. Impulsive, aggressive, and often dangerously violent, the victim was the first to slap, punch, stab, or in some other manner commit an assault. Perhaps the presence of alcohol in this kind of homicide victim played no small part in his taking this first and major physical step toward victimization. Perhaps if he had not been drinking he would have been less violent, less ready to plunge into an assaultive stage of interaction. Or, if the presence of alcohol had no causal relation to his being the first to assault, perhaps it reduced his facility to combat successfully, to defend himself from retaliatory assault and, hence, contributed in this way to his death.

Previous Arrest Record. The victim-precipitator is the first actor in the homicide drama to display and to use a deadly weapon; and the description of him thus far infers that he is in some respects an offender in reverse. Because he is the first to assume an aggressive role, he probably has engaged

previously in similar but less serious physical assaults. On the basis of these assumptions several meaningful hypotheses were established and tested. Each hypothesis is supported by empirical data, which in some cases reach the level of statistical significance accepted by this study; and in other cases indicate strong associations in directions suggested by the hypotheses. A summary of each hypothesis with its collated data follows:

(1) In VP cases, the victim is more likely than the offender to have a previous arrest, or police, record. The data show that 62 percent of the victims and 54 percent of the offenders in VP cases have a previous record.

(2) A higher proportion of VP victims than non-VP victims have a previous police record. Comparison reveals that 62 percent of VP victims but only ~~only~~ 42 percent of non-VP victims have a previous record. The association between VP victims and previous arrest record is a *significant* one.

(3) With respect to the percentage having a previous arrest record, VP victims are more similar to non-VP offenders than to non-VP victims. Examination of the data reveals no significant difference between VP victims and non-VP offenders with a previous record. This lack of a significant difference is very meaningful and confirms the validity of the proposition above. While 62 percent of VP victims have a police record, 68 percent of non-VP offenders have such a record, and we have already noted in (2) above that only 42 percent of non-VP victims have a record. Thus, the existence of a statistically *significant* difference between VP victims and non-VP victims and the *lack* of a statistically significant difference between VP victims and non-VP offenders indicate that the victim of VP homicide is quite similar to the offender in non-VP homicide—and that the VP victim more closely resembles the non-VP offender than the non-VP victim.

(4) A higher proportion of VP victims than of non-VP victims have a record of

offenses against the person. The data show a *significant* association between VP victims and a previous record of offenses against the person, for 37 percent of VP victims and only 21 percent of non-VP victims have a record of such offenses.

(5) Also with respect to the percentage having a previous arrest of offenses against the person, VP victims are more similar to non-VP offenders than non-VP victims. Analysis of the data indicates support for this assumption, for we have observed that the difference between VP victims (37 percent) and non-VP victims (21 percent) is *significant*; this difference is almost twice as great as the difference between VP victims (37 percent) and non-VP offenders (46 percent), and this latter difference is not significant. The general tendency again is for victims in VP homicides to resemble offenders in non-VP homicides.

(6) A lower proportion of VP offenders have a previous arrest record than do non-VP offenders. The data also tend to support this hypothesis, for 54 percent of offenders in VP cases, compared to 68 percent of offenders in non-VP cases have a previous police record.

In general, the rank order of recidivism —defined in terms of having a previous arrest record and of having a previous record of assaults—for victims and offenders involved in the two types of homicide is shown in Table 2.

than the present situation, or which afforded him greater opportunity to defer attacks made upon him. It is known officially that over one-third of them assaulted others previously. It is not known how many formerly provoked others to assault them. In any case, the circumstances leading up to the present crime in which he plays the role of victim are probably not foreign to him since he has, in many cases, participated in similar encounters before this, his last episode.

SUMMARY

Criminal homicide usually involves intense personal interaction in which the victim's behavior is often an important factor. As Porterfield has recently pointed out, "the intensity of interaction between the murderer and his victim may vary from complete non-participation on the part of the victim to almost perfect cooperation with the killer in the process of getting killed. . . . It is amazing to note the large number of would-be murderers who become the victim."[11] By defining a VP homicide in terms of the victim's direct, immediate, and positive contribution to his own death, manifested by his being the first to make a physical assault, it has been possible to identify 150 VP cases.

Comparison of this VP group with non-VP cases reveals *significantly* higher proportions of the following characteristics among

Table 2.

	PERCENT WITH PREVIOUS ARREST RECORD	PERCENT WITH PREVIOUS RECORD OF ASSAULT
(1) Offenders in non-VP Homicide	68	46
(2) Victims in VP Homicide	62	37
(3) Offenders in VP Homicide	54	33
(4) Victims in non-VP Homicide	42	21

Because he is the initial aggressor and has provoked his subsequent slayer into killing him, this particular type of victim (VP) is likely to have engaged previously in physical assaults which were either less provoking

VP homicide:

[11] Porterfield, Austin L. and Talbert, Robert H., *Mid-Century Crime in Our Culture: Personality and Crime in the Cultural Patterns of American States*, Fort Worth: Leo Potishman Foundation, 1954, pp. 47–48.

(1) Negro victims;

(2) Negro offenders;

(3) male victims;

(4) female offenders;

(5) stabbings;

(6) victim-offender relationship involving male victims of female offenders;

(7) mate slayings;

(8) husbands who are victims in mate slayings;

(9) alcohol in the homicide situation;

(10) alcohol in the victim;

(11) victims with a previous arrest record;

(12) victims with a previous arrest record of assault.

In addition, VP homicides have slightly higher proportions than non-VP homicides of altercations and domestic quarrels, interracial slayings, victims who are close friends, relatives, or acquaintances of their slayers.

Empirical evidence analyzed in the present study lends support to, and measurement of, von Hentig's theoretical contention that "there are cases in which they (victim and offender) are reversed and in the long chain of causative forces the victim assumes the role of a determinant."[12]

In many cases the victim has most of the major characteristics of an offender; in some cases two potential offenders come together in a homicide situation and it is probably often only chance which results in one becoming a victim and the other an offender. At any rate, connotations of a victim as a weak and passive individual, seeking to withdraw from an assaultive situation, and of an offender as a brutal, strong, and overly aggressive person seeking out his victim, are not always correct. Societal attitudes are generally positive toward the victim and negative toward the offender, who is often feared as a violent and dangerous threat to others when not exonerated. However, data in the present study—especially that of previous arrest record—mitigate, destroy, or reverse these connotations of victim-offender roles in one out of every four criminal homicides.

[12] Von Hentig, op. cit., p. 383.

PATTERNS IN CRIMINAL AGGRAVATED ASSAULT*

David J. Pittman and William Handy

In this study patterns of criminal aggravated assault are analyzed in terms of the time of the offense, location and season of the year, weapon, reporting, injury, police processing, alcohol involvement, victim-offender relationship, and prior arrest record. A comparison of homicide and aggravated assault reveals that the patterns for the two crimes are similar. In terms of the behavior involved, there is only a thin line of difference between homicide and assault.

* Reprinted by special permission of the authors and the *Journal of Criminal Law, Criminology and Police Science*, Copyright © 1964 by the Northwestern University School of Law, Volume 55, Number 4, December 1964, pp. 462–470.

No crimes are considered more serious than homicide and aggravated assault, for homicide deprives an individual of his life, and aggravated assault is an attempt to deprive an individual of his life or to cause him serious injury.

The act of homicide has been analyzed in numerous studies, the most complete of these being Wolfgang's *Patterns in Criminal Homicide*.[1] In his study, Wolfgang formulated a series of hypotheses concerning the nature of acts of homicide, tested them through the use of police homicide data, and thereby established the "patterns" in criminal homicide.

As far as can be discerned no study of Wolfgang's type has been made of the crime of aggravated assault. The lack of such a study is remarkable, for often the line dividing aggravated assault from homicide is so thin that a factor such as the speed of an ambulance carrying the victim to the hospital will determine whether the crime will be aggravated assault or homicide. The purpose of this study is to analyze the crime of aggravated assault and to attempt to establish its "patterns," as Wolfgang did for homicide, by testing where possible Wolfgang's homicide hypotheses against acts of aggravated assaults.

The Federal Bureau of Investigation classifies the crime of aggravated assault as "assault with intent to kill or for the purpose of inflicting severe bodily injury by shooting, cutting, stabbing, maiming, poisoning, scalding, or by the use of acids, explosives, or other means."[2] In November, 1960, the FBI added a supplement to this definition by stating that aggravated assault was "an unlawful attack by one person upon another for the purpose of inflicting severe bodily injury accompanied by the use of a weapon or other means likely to produce death or great bodily harm. Attempts should be included since it is not necessary that any injury result from an aggravated assault."[3] The following guides were also given in this supplement: "Careful consideration of the following factors should clarify the classification of an aggravated assault. (1) The seriousness of the injury. (2) The type of weapon used or the use made of an object as a weapon. (3) The intent of the assailant to cause serious injury."[4] Furthermore all these factors should be weighed before the crime is classified as an aggravated assault.

Even with this clarification of the definition of aggravated assault, the crime remains one of the most difficult to classify. According to the Department of Justice of the State of California:

Aggravated assault is an offense which is very difficult to classify. There has been a growth in the number of aggravated assaults reported over the years, but there does not seem to be a corresponding growth in the number of felonious assaults prosecuted. This would suggest that because of the relationship of the parties or the conditions under which the assaults occurred, many altercations, largely domestic quarrels, characterized in reports as aggravated assaults, do not seem to fall in the general area of felonious assault. There is a need to have a sub-classifying of this type of offense in order to arrive at a true picture of assault.[5]

This statement was prepared before the supplement in the FBI definition and clearly states one of the many reasons for the refinement. However, other factors which are impossible to regulate by a clarification in definition will adversely affect the proper classification of aggravated assaults; the way in which the police officer fills out a report form and the difference of interpretation held by two clerks who classify these acts may cause variance. Such factors will have to be overlooked in this study, and the police classification of the crime will be accepted.

By popular definition, the crime of ag-

[1] Marvin E. Wolfgang, *Patterns in Criminal Homicide,* Philadelphia: University of Pennsylvania Press, 1958.
[2] FBI, *Uniform Crime Report* 29 (1960).
[3] FBI, *Uniform Crime Reporting—Aggravated Assaults* (Supp. Nov. 1960).
[4] *Ibid.*
[5] California Department of Justice, Bureau of Criminal Statistics, *Crime in California* 18 (1958).

gravated assault is known as "attempted murder," "assault with intent to kill," "assault with intent to do great bodily harm" or just "assault." All of these terms might be thought of as subclassifications of the act, for they all more or less describe the purpose of the offender.

STUDY METHOD

The study group was composed of a random sample of 25 per cent of the 965 crimes classified by the St. Louis Metropolitan Police Department as aggravated assault for the period January 1, 1961, to December 31, 1961. Sampled cases totaled 241. Copies of the offense reports for each sampled case were obtained as well as the arrest records of the offender and the victim involved in the act. The information concerning the crime contained in offense reports was considered adequate, and the arrest records were also considered sufficient. Records such as those concerning the individual's prison, parole, and psychiatric status were unavailable, and the addresses of the individuals were not current and were difficult to determine. The collected data were analyzed in terms of a set of formulated hypotheses concerned with the variable of time, location and season of year, weapon, reporting, injury, police processing, alcohol involvement, victim-offender relationship, and arrest records.

In a few cases there were multiple offenders or victims. Generally, the additional offender or victim will not be considered, and the act will be analyzed as one crime, the emphasis being on the act and not on the individuals involved. In certain analyses, however, all offenders and all victims must be considered, and this accounts for the variable number of cases.

RESULTS

I. Time. During week days, interaction among people is limited by their work, and there is less leisure time than on the weekends. For this reason, it was hypothesized that the majority of the acts of aggravated assault would occur between 6:00 P.M. Friday and 6:00 A.M. Monday.

As shown in Table 1, 132 of the 241 acts occurred during the hypothesized time. The period between 10:00 P.M. and 11:00 P.M. contained more acts than any other hour. More aggravated assaults occurred on Saturday than on any other day of the week, with Friday and Sunday following in that order. The hours between 4:00 P.M. and 3:00 A.M. were those during which the largest number of acts occurred, confirming the view of the police that this period has the largest num-

Table 1.

DAY AND TIME OF OCCURRENCE OF AGGRAVATED ASSAULT CASES

	MID-NIGHT– 6:00 A.M.	6:00 A.M.– NOON	NOON– 6:00 P.M.	6:00 P.M.– MID-NIGHT	TOTAL	PER CENT
Sunday	15	5	5	10	35	14.5
Monday	1	2	7	11	21	8.6
Tuesday	5	4	5	10	24	10.0
Wednesday	7	1	8	8	24	10.0
Thursday	5	0	6	10	21	8.6
Friday	10	5	5	24	44	18.4
Saturday	22	6	11	33	72	29.9
Total	65	23	47	106	241	
Per cent	27.0	9.6	19.5	43.9	100.0	100.0

ber of all types of crime, since they reach their climax under the cover of darkness.

Our second hypothesis concerning time factor was that the majority of the acts would occur between 8:00 P.M. on a given evening and 4:00 A.M. the following morning. This hypothesis was accepted. As shown in Table 2, the number of acts is the

Table 2.
TIME OF OCCURRENCE

8:00 P.M.–4:00 A.M.	4:00 A.M.–NOON	NOON–8:00 P.M.	TOTAL
140	31	70	241

Mean no. for 8-hour period = 80.3.

greatest between 8:00 P.M. and 4:00 A.M., the period of darkness and more interaction. Aggravated assaults decline sharply during the next eight hours, when most people are sleeping and then going to work. The number begins to rise again between noon and 8 P.M., as interaction after the working day slowly increases, and finally reaches its climax between 10:00 and 11:00 P.M. in the evening.

II. Location and Season of the Year. Criminal aggravated assaults may occur in a wide variety of places, but it was hypothesized that place of occurrence would be related to the season of the year, victim-offender relationship, and sex status. First, it was hypothesized that the largest number of acts would occur on public streets, rather than in taverns or bars, residences, or other places. This hypothesis was accepted (Table 3).

Also it was expected that more acts would occur during the winter than during other seasons. Summer months for St. Louis were defined as June, July, August, and September,[6] while winter months were defined as November, December, January, and February. Table 3 shows that 87 acts occurred during the four summer months,

[6] In St. Louis, the month of September is regarded as a summer month.

Table 3.
PLACE OF OCCURRENCE BY MONTH

	STREET	TAVERN OR BAR	RESIDENCE	OTHER	TOTAL	PER CENT
Jan.	5	2	10	2	19	7.9
Feb.	12	2	6	1	21	8.7
March	10	3	3	0	16	6.6
April	11	1	6	1	19	7.9
May	8	1	7	2	18	7.5
June	9	2	6	0	17	7.1
July	7	5	12	0	24	10.0
Aug.	10	2	10	2	24	10.0
Sept.	10	1	8	3	22	9.1
Oct.	9	0	9	1	19	7.9
Nov.	13	4	6	0	23	9.5
Dec.	6	4	8	1	19	7.9
Total	110	27	91	13	241	100.0
Per cent	45.6	11.2	37.8	5.4	100.0	

while 82 occurred during the winter months. Thus, this hypothesis was rejected.

In relation to location and season of year, it was hypothesized that during the winter months, a greater number of acts would occur indoors as against the summer, when the larger number would occur outdoors. For this testing, summer was defined as April through September, and winter as October through March, so that all of the acts might be included. This hypothesis was also rejected (see Table 4).

Table 4.
PLACE OF OCCURRENCE BY SEASON

	SUMMER	WINTER	TOTAL
Indoors	55	55	110
Outdoors	61	57	118
Total	116	112	228*

* For remaining 13 acts, location indoors or outdoors not assigned.

It was thought that since females spend the majority of their time indoors, the acts in which they were offenders would be likely to occur indoors, and this hypothesis was accepted (Table 5).

Table 5.
PLACE OF OCCURRENCE BY SEX OF OFFENDER

	FEMALE	MALE	TOTAL
Indoors	41	75	116
Outdoors	18	107	125
Total	59	182	241

Chi sq. = 14.27; P < .001. All cases assigned to outdoors-indoors categories.

Since related persons tend to have most of their interaction within their own home, it was hypothesized that if the offender and victim were related, the act of assault would take place within a residence. As shown in Table 6, the hypothesis was accepted.

Table 6.
PLACE OF OCCURRENCE BY KIN RELATIONSHIP

	KIN	NOT KIN	TOTAL
In Residence	42	49	91
Not in Residence	5	145	150
Total	47	194	241

Chi sq. = 66.13; P < .001.

III. *Weapon.* In choosing a weapon for assault, offender's choice is almost unlimited, and any given weapon may be used in a variety of ways. A gun, for instance, may be employed as a firearm or as a club. The offender may choose one of the more common weapons, such as a gun or knife, or some unique concoction such as a curtain rod, bottle, meat cleaver, shovel, or can opener.

It was hypothesized that a knife, being readily accessible, would be used in more instances than any other weapon. In 126 of the 241 cases, the offender did choose a knife; guns were used in only 39 cases. Per-

sonal force (fists, feet, or any part of the body, but without the use of a weapon), although certainly more accessible than a knife, was used in only 14 cases, perhaps because the offender is more certain of inflicting injury upon his victim with a knife than with his own striking power. The remaining 62 cases involved weapons ranging from sharp instruments to fire, lye, and vases.

It was further hypothesized that, proportionately, white offenders would use personal force to a greater extent than would Negro offenders. The fact that in Negro neighborhoods, weapons for self defense are commonly carried[7] gave rise to this proposition. The hypothesis was accepted (Table 7).

Table 7.
TYPE OF FORCE BY RACE OF OFFENDER

	WHITE OFFENDER	NEGRO OFFENDER	TOTAL
Personal Force	6	7	13
Weapon	36	189	225
Total	42	196	238*

Chi sq. = 7.72; P < .01.
* Three unknown.

It was hypothesized that white females would use guns more frequently than other weapons, since guns require less strength to use and are "cleaner" than other weapons. This hypothesis was rejected, as no white female offender selected a gun, while four of them chose knives. Apparently the accessibility of knives and the lack of knowledge about guns took precedence over other factors.

IV. *Reporting.* There are numerous ways in which a case of aggravated assault may become known to the police. The crime may be reported by the victim, the offender,

[7] E.g., Schultz, *Why the Negro Carries Weapons*, 53 J. Crim. L., C & P.S. 476 (1962).

a witness, a hospital, or a physician, or it may be observed by the police. The hypothesis that the victim would report the crime in the majority of cases proved acceptable, for such was the case in 146 of the 241 acts. In only 10 cases did the offender report his own crime, while in 41 cases a witness reported the act. In 16 cases the police observed the crime or its consequences, in 23 cases they were called by medical authorities, and in five cases by a relative of the victim. Acts in progress observed by the police were usually those occurring on a street where a crowd had gathered. In those cases in which a relative notified police, much time had elapsed since the act.

V. *Injury*. In the act of aggravated assault, the offender or the victim may be wounded, and the degree of injury varies. Although the extent of injury does determine, in some cases, whether or not the crime is classified as aggravated assault, it does not necessarily determine which party is the victim and which the offender. Sometimes the offender may be seriously wounded, and the victim only slightly injured, if at all.

In all of the sampled cases, the victim was wounded to some degree, and only when he refused medical attention was he not conveyed to a hospital. As was hypothesized, in more than half the cases, the victim was seriously wounded, while the offender was not (Table 8). Seriously wounded was defined as being incapacitated to the extent to require hospitalization.

VI. *Police Processing*. Aggravated assault is generally a distinct crime; in other words, usually no other Index Crime is involved, since the assault follows some type of verbal argument. In only three of the 241 cases was another Index Crime involved—in all cases robbery. In these cases, the police reports contained information which led authorities to believe that robbery was an afterthought, with assault the primary motive of the offenders.

Table 8.
SERIOUSNESS OF WOUND BY VICTIM AND OFFENDER

	SERIOUSLY WOUNDED	NOT SERIOUSLY WOUNDED	TOTAL
Victim	134	117	251
Offender	35	222	257
Total	169	339	508*

Chi sq. = 90.47; P < .001.
* More than one offender or victim in 22 cases studied.

Sometimes, both the victim and the offender are charged by the police with aggravated assault. Both were charged in 10 of the sampled cases. In the remaining 231 cases, the victim was charged with either suspicion of affray or suspicion of peace disturbance. The charging of the victim with one of these counts was a police practice at the time of the study, and the charge was deleted only when it was ascertained that the victim was in no way responsible for the attack upon himself. Witnesses were often charged with affray or peace disturbance, depending on their role in the act. Clearance by arrest of aggravated assault cases is generally high, being surpassed only by homicide. In this sample, 77.2 per cent of the cases were cleared by arrest.

Elapsed time following a crime before the offender is apprehended is of importance to the police, for the longer the time lapse, the less the chance the police will arrest the offender. For aggravated assault, it was believed that the offender would usually be apprehended within an hour after the act, and such proved to be the case (Table 9). Of course a number of offenders were apprehended at the scene of the crime.

In 193 of the 241 cases, the identity of

Table 9.
LENGTH OF TIME BETWEEN THE ACT AND APPREHENSION OF THE OFFENDER

TIME ELAPSED	NUMBER ARRESTED	PERCENTAGE
0.1 hour	116	62.3
1–5 hours	28	15.1
5–24 hours	19	10.2
Over 24 hours	23	12.4
Total	186	100.0

the offender was known to either the offender, the witness, or the police. This number corresponds closely with the number of clearances by arrest; in only seven cases was the offender not apprehended when his identity was known.

It was hypothesized that more female than male offenders would be apprehended, since a female would be less able to avoid arrest by escape, more likely to be known to the offender, a witness, or police, and less likely to take part in a street attack. The hypothesis was accepted (Table 10).

Table 10.
CLEARANCE BY SEX

	ARRESTED	NOT ARRESTED	TOTAL
Female Offender	60	2	62
Male Offender	126	50	176
Total	186	52	238*

Chi sq. = 17.03; P < .001.
* Three unknown.

We hypothesized that a Negro offender would be more likely to be arrested than a white one, for the former would have less means at his disposal to avoid arrest and detection. The competing hypothesis would be that significantly fewer Negroes than whites would be arrested, in accordance with a popular belief in certain segments of the society that the police ignore Negro personal crimes of violence. Table 11 shows that both hypotheses were rejected. Where Negroes were the offenders, 79 per cent of

Table 11.
CLEARANCE BY RACE

	ARRESTED	NOT ARRESTED	TOTAL
Negro Offender	155	41	196
White Offender	31	11	42
Total	186	52	238*

Chi sq. = .56; P < .50. Association not significant.
*Three unknown.

the cases were cleared by arrest; the comparable figure for whites was 74 per cent. This is not a statistically significant difference.

VII. *Alcohol Involvement.* It was hypothesized that prior alcohol ingestion by both the offender and the victim would be common in acts of aggravated assault. It was found, however, that alcohol ingestion was present in only slightly more than one-quarter (57 offenders and 58 victims) of all the cases. This, however, may be a consequence of either the inability to detect the presence of prior alcohol ingestion or the failure to report it. But in 41 cases the offender and victim had been drinking together prior to the crime. To discern the role of alcohol ingestion in aggravated assault, one would need more complete information than police records provide.

VIII. *The Relationship of Offender and Victim.* Prior to the act of aggravated assault, the offender and victim have generally been in interaction with each other. Verbal arguments (181 of 241 cases) usually precede the aggression. These quarrels may range from domestic incidents to tavern disputes over who was to sit on which bar stool. On the surface the quarrels appear to have little rationality. They must be understood in terms of the social and psychological mechanisms which the offenders and victims have developed to handle their aggressive impulses.

Furthermore, aggravated assault most

often involves only one offender and one victim—in this sample, 219 cases of 241. In eight cases there was one offender and a multiplicity of victims, in 11 cases more than one offender but one victim, and in only three cases a multiplicity of both.

Since it was expected that there would be few interracial assaults (in this sample only 10 cases, of which only one was cross-sex and cross-race lines), it was hypothesized that if the offender and victim were of the same race, they would be of the same sex. Table 12 shows that the hypothesis was rejected.

Table 12.

RACE AND SEX RELATION OF OFFENDER AND VICTIM

	SAME RACE	DIFFERENT RACE	TOTAL
Same Sex	135	9	144
Different Sex	93	1	94
Total	228	10	238*

Chi sq. = 3.65; P < .10. Association not significant.

* Three unknown.

Persons of the same age group are most likely to interact with each other, and for this reason it was hypothesized that the victim and offender would be within the same age category. The categories adopted were under 20, 20–34, 35–49, and 50+. The assumption was true in 146 of the 241 cases. Where offender and victim were in the same age category, there were more cases in the 20–34 age group than in any other single group. Also, more offenders and more victims, considered apart, were in the 20–34 group than in any other single age group (Table 13).

In 106 of the cases, the offender was older than the victim, while in 92 cases the victim was older. In 23 cases, they were of the same age, and in the remaining 20 cases the age of the offender was unknown.

It was expected that the majority of both offenders and victims would be im-

Table 13.

AGES OF OFFENDERS AND VICTIMS

	UNDER 20	20–34	35–49	50+	NOT IN SAME AGE GROUP
Both Offender and Victim	22	75	33	16	77*
Offender only	35	105	71	30	—
Victim only	28	91	59	35	—

* Remainder unknown.

migrants to St. Louis. This assumption was checked by ascertaining the place of birth of the arrestees. Of the offenders, 71 per cent were born outside St. Louis, and of the victims 62 per cent were born outside the city.

Of the known offenders (237), 139 were Negro males, while 118 of the victims were Negro males; the hypothesis was thus validated that in cases involving Negro male offenders, the majority of victims would be Negro males.

Of the 252 victims, 218 (86.5 per cent) were married, while only 143 (60.3 per cent) of the 237 offenders were married. This is a statistically significant difference between the two groups in reference to marital status. In cases involving spouses, only, the wife was the victim in 21 cases, while the husband was the victim in the remaining 15.

It was expected that blue collar workers would be involved in more acts of aggravated assault than their white collar counterparts—a belief confirmed by the data. Two hundred twelve of the 252 victims and 229 of the 237 offenders were blue collar workers. A housewife was considered to be a blue collar worker if her husband's socioeconomic status was blue collar.

It was hypothesized that a female, being more likely to have interaction with a male to whom she was related than with an unrelated male, would commit aggravated assault against a male to whom she was related more frequently than would a male attack a female to whom he was related. Table 14 indicates that this hypothesis was rejected.

Table 14.
KINSHIP RELATIONSHIP OF MALE AND FEMALE OFFENDER AND VICTIM

	NOT RELATED	RELATED	TOTAL
Male Attacks Female	21	72	93
Female Attacks Male	15	30	45
Total	36	102	138

Chi sq. = 1.82; P < .20. Association not significant.

In cases involving a male and a female not legally related, it was hypothesized that prior to the assault the two would have had a relationship of common law marriage, sexual intimacy, or dating. Table 15 sup-

Table 15.
RELATION OF MALE AND FEMALE OFFENDER AND VICTIM

	MALE ATTACKS FEMALE	FEMALE ATTACKS MALE	TOTAL
Former Close Relation	9	16	25
No Former Relation	16	9	25
Total	25	25	50

Chi sq. = 3.92; P < .05.

ports the hypothesis in cases involving a female attacking a male, but not in cases of a male attacking a female. This finding indicates that the female is more likely than a male to aggress against one with whom there is some intimate relationship.

Inter-racial assault was an uncommon occurrence in this sample. Only 10 of the 241 cases involved an offender and victim of different race. It was hypothesized that in an inter-racial assault, a white person would most likely be the victim. This hypothesis was accepted (Table 16).

Only a small number (22 cases) of the victims had previous arrests for Index

Table 16.
INTER-RACIAL ASSAULTS

	WHITE OFFENDER	NEGRO OFFENDER	TOTAL
White Victim	40	8	48
Negro Victim	2	188	190
Total	42	196	238

Chi sq. = 178.19; P < .001.

Crimes. Most offenders, however, had previous criminal records (Table 17), with the

Table 17.
PRIOR ARREST RECORD OF OFFENDERS AND VICTIMS

	OFFENDERS	VICTIMS	TOTAL
Prior Arrest Record	156	121	277
No Prior Arrest Record	92	131	223
Total	248	252	500

Chi sq. = 11.21; P < .001.

prior arrest most frequently being for peace disturbance. The record, however, does not indicate whether this prior act was a slight scuffle or affray or a reduced charge from a more serious offense. At least 37 of the offenders had at least one previous arrest on an assault charge.

It was hypothesized that Negro offenders would be no more likely to have prior arrest records than white offenders; this belief was confirmed (Table 18).

Table 18.
PRIOR ARREST RECORD OF OFFENDERS BY RACE

	NEGRO OFFENDER	WHITE OFFENDER	TOTAL
Prior Arrest Record	128	28	156
No Prior Arrest Record	68	24	92
Total	196	52	248*

Chi sq. = 2.32; P < .20. Association not significant.
* Remainder unknown.

The last hypothesis was that there would be no correlation between the age of the offender and presence of a prior arrest record. Using the age categories previously cited, it was found that the age category 20–34, into which the largest number of offenders fell, had a higher percentage of prior records than did other groups, but the percentage did not sharply increase or decrease with a change in age. Forty-six per cent of the offenders under 20, 62 per cent of those 20–34, 48 per cent of those 35–49, and 57 per cent of those 50 or over had prior arrest records.

AGGRAVATED ASSAULT, THE TYPICAL PATTERN

The patterns in aggravated assault are based on a random sample of 241 acts in 1961 drawn from the cases reported to the St. Louis Metropolitan Police Department. From the analysis presented here, it is possible to state the expected pattern of aggravated assault in the "typical" case.

An act of aggravated assault is more likely to occur on a weekend than during the week, specifically between 6:00 P.M. Friday and 6:00 A.M. Monday, with peak frequency on Saturday, between 10:00 P.M. and 11:00 P.M. While the event shows little likelihood of being more frequent in the four summer months considered together than in the winter, this type of assault peaks in the months of July and August.

The crime will occur on a public street, or, secondly, in a residence. If a female is the offender, the act will occur indoors, if a male offender, outdoors. When offender and victim are related, the act will more likely occur in a residence than elsewhere. The general neighborhood context is one populated by lower socioeconomic groups —especially Negroes of this class.

The weapon used by both men and women will in most cases be a knife, with a gun the second choice. In acts involving white offenders, personal force will be used more often than in those involving Negro offenders.

Generally, the act will be reported to the police by the victim. The victim will be wounded seriously enough to require hospitalization, but the offender will not. More than 75 per cent of the aggravated assault cases will be cleared by arrest within one hour after the crime occurs. A Negro is no more likely to be arrested for his crime than is a white.

These records indicate that neither the offender nor the victim will be under the influence of alcohol, nor will they have been drinking together, and neither will be a user of drugs.

The aggravated assault will be preceded by a verbal argument, most likely centering around a domestic quarrel.

The offender and victim will be of the same race and of the same sex; there will be only one offender and one victim, and both will have been born outside of the city in which the crime occurs. Both will be of the same age group, usually between the ages of 20 and 35, with the offender being older. The victim will more often be married than the offender, but both will be blue collar workers. A female offender is more likely to be related to her male victim than is the male offender to his female victim. Females assault males with whom they have had a previous close relationship (such as dating, sexual intimacy, or common law marriage); but this not the case with males assaulting females.

Negro offenders are no more likely than their white counterparts to have a prior arrest record. Offenders in the age bracket 20–34 will in the majority of cases have a prior arrest record.

AGGRAVATED ASSAULT COMPARED TO CRIMINAL HOMICIDE

Despite the lack of sociological studies of aggravated assault, it was believed that this offense had many similarities to homicide.

A comparison of the findings in this study with those of Wolfgang[8] for criminal homicide reveals more similarities than differences, even though the two studies represent different time periods, cities, and police departments.

1. *Time.* For both aggravated assault and homicide, occurrences were higher on Saturdays, with the time of day being most frequently late evening and early morning hours; for homicide, between 8:00 P.M. and 2:00 A.M., and for aggravated assault, between 4:00 P.M. and 3:00 A.M. The next highest time for both acts were the hours immediately following the highest period.

2. *Location.* Both crimes occurred more often on a public street than in any other location, with residences second. Summer months accounted for a higher percentage of crimes in both cases, but to a greater extent for homicides. In winter these crimes occurred indoors. Females committed both acts more often indoors than outdoors. If the victim and offender were related, the crime most likely occurred in a residence. Both types of acts usually took place in a lower class, Negro neighborhood.

3. *Weapon.* The weapon most often used differed between homicide and aggravated assault; a pistol or revolver was most common in homicides, while a knife was most common in assaults. White females used a revolver or pistol most often in homicide, while they used a knife most often in assault.

4. *Police Processing.* No other Index Crime was involved in the majority of both crimes, and there was a high cleanup rate for both, although it was higher for homicides. The offender in both crimes was arrested within a short time of committing the act, and he was known to either witnesses or police. Clearance was higher for females and Negroes than for males and whites in both homicide and assault.

5. *Alcohol Involvement.* The ingestion of alcohol was more common in homicide than in assault, as was a drinking episode between offender and victim prior to the crime.

6. *Situational Context.* Verbal arguments preceded both crimes, but alcohol was involved in the arguments in homicide situations more often than in aggravated assault cases.

7. *Offender-Victim Relationship.* For both crimes, the victim and offender were typically of the same age, sex, and race. There were most often only one victim and one offender. Negro males were disproportionately involved in both types of crime. The participants in both acts were usually married, blue collar workers, and the victims of inter-racial assaults were white more often than Negroes. In acts of homicide, a wife attacked her husband more often than a husband attacked his wife, while the reverse was the case in aggravated assaults.

8. *Prior Arrest Records.* For both homicide and aggravated assault, the majority of the victims had no prior arrest record, while the majority of the offenders did. For homicide offenders, two-thirds had a prior record of a crime against the person, while for aggravated assault the number of offenders having this type of record, if one excepts peace disturbance, was negligible.

This comparison of findings concerning acts of homicide and aggravated assault indicates that the pattern for the two crimes is quite similar. Both acts, of course, are reflections of population subgroupings which tend to externalize their aggression when confronted with conflict situations.

[8] *Op. cit. supra* note 1.

INTERACTION AND CRIMINAL HOMICIDE IN INDIA*

Edwin D. Driver

*Criminal homicide in India, as in Western countries,
usually involves interaction between kinsmen or close
associates of the same sex, religion, and caste. When the
customary social devices to solve disputes over sexual
relations, property, and living arrangements fail, enmity
increases and finally culminates in homicide.*

Several studies of criminal homicide in the United States and Europe have found that criminals and their victims are generally homogeneous with respect to sex and personal relations. Berg and Fox found that 66 percent of 200 male convicts in Michigan had chosen as victims persons of their own sex.[1] The study of 500 male and female murderers in Alabama by Harlan indicates that victims were of the same sex in 59.8 percent, of the same race in 92.8 percent, and of the same sex and race in 56.6 percent of the cases.[2] Approximately the same degree of homogeneity is found for Texas[3] and North Carolina cases.[4] These characteristics of homicide are also noted by Sutherland[5] and other students of criminology.[6]

Further, victims are usually kinsmen or close associates rather than strangers. In 87 percent of 489 homicides studied by Bullock, criminals and their victims had had intimate, face-to-face relations.[7] The results of Svalastoga's investigation of 172 Danish victims are similar: 57.0 percent were kinsmen; 30.8 percent were close associates; and only 12.2 percent were strangers.[8] East's study of 200 sane and 300 insane murderers in England revealed that only 16.5 percent chose strangers as victims.[9] According to of the former and 6.5 percent of the latter the Royal Commission on Capital Punishment, spouses, parents, and lovers constituted 45 percent of the persons killed by the 1210 persons convicted of murder and sentenced to death in England and Wales from 1900 to 1949.[10] Of the 588 victims in Wolfgang's analysis of Philadelphia cases, 136 were kinsmen, of which 100 were wives or husbands.[11] On the basis of German

[1] Irving A. Berg and Vernon Fox, "Factors in Homicides Committed by 200 Males," *Journal of Social Psychology*, 26 (August 1947), p. 115.

[2] Howard Harlan, "Five Hundred Homicides," *Journal of Criminal Law and Criminology*, 40 (March–April 1950), p. 744.

[3] Henry A. Bullock, "Urban Homicide in Theory and Practice," *Journal of Criminal Law, Criminology and Police Science*, 45 (January–February 1955), p. 570.

[4] Harold Garfinkel, "Research Notes on Inter- and Intra-Racial Homicides," *Social Forces*, 27 (May 1949), p. 370.

[5] Edwin H. Sutherland, *Principles of Criminology* (New York: Lippincott, 1947), p. 25.

[6] See the studies cited by Marvin E. Wolfgang, *Patterns of Criminal Homicide* (Philadelphia: University of Pennsylvania Press, 1958), pp. 222–237.

[7] Bullock, op. cit., p. 572.

[8] Kaare Svalastoga, "Homicide and Social Contact in Denmark," *American Journal of Sociology*, 62 (July 1956), p. 40.

[9] W. Norwood East, *Medical Aspects of Crime* (London: J. and A. Churchill, 1939), p. 369.

[10] Royal Commission on Capital Punishment, *1949–1953 Report* (London: H. M. Stationery Office, 1953), pp. 304–305.

[11] Wolfgang, op. cit., pp. 212–213.

* Reprinted from *Social Forces*, 40 (December 1961), pp. 153–158, by permission of the author and the publisher.

statistics, von Hentig likewise shows that spouses are prominent among the victims.[12]

OBJECTIVES AND DATA

The aim of this paper is to describe the kinds of interaction which characterize homicide in India, a country that is mainly rural and which has a complex religious and caste structure. Consideration is given to the degree of homogeneity between criminals and their victims with respect to religion, caste, sex, and the extent to which they are kinsmen or close associates rather than strangers. The second objective is to describe the kinds of "motives" which, in the opinion of the judge in each trial, brought about the acts of homicide. Data for this study were obtained from the 1946–1956 official records of two courts of sessions which have jurisdiction over 4,000,000 persons in Central India. The study is limited to the 144 convictions for murder during the above-named years. Approximately 34 percent of the persons charged with this act are subsequently convicted.[13] In India, murder is an act of commission or omission by a person who has the knowledge and the intent that his act will cause death or such bodily injury as will result in the death of another.[14] It is punishable by death, but if it is proved that the act was due to sudden or grave provocation of the offender by the victim, then the sessions court may sentence the offender to life imprisonment and recommend to the Provincial Government a further reduction in the penalty.[15] Because of this circumstance, the judge, irrespective of the jury's finding of murder with or without premeditation, will carefully weigh all evidence in order to form an opinion about the offender's motive.

FINDINGS

Homogeneity and Social Relationship. Our data show a high degree of homogeneity between criminals and their victims in the matter of religion, caste, and sex. In 136 of the 144 cases (94.5 percent), as indicated by Table 1, they were of the same

Table 1.

RELATION OF RELIGION OF CRIMINAL TO RELIGION OF VICTIM

	CRIMINAL	VICTIM	FREQUENCY Number	FREQUENCY Percent
Homogeneity	Hindu	Hindu	127	88.2
	Muslim	Muslim	8	5.6
	Sikh	Sikh	1	0.65
Heterogeneity	Hindu	Muslim	3	2.1
	Muslim	Hindu	4	2.8
	Christian	Hindu	1	0.65
Total			144	100.0

religion. However, the tendency of offenders to select as victims members of their own religion is more pronounced among Hindus (97.7 percent) than Muslims (66.7 percent).

In view of the fact that most of the 25 castes in our study may be found living adjacent to one another, it is quite significant that 83.7 percent of murders are of an intracaste character. This percentage as well as that for religious homogeneity is, of course, in part attributable to the frequency of kinsmen among victims. For the individual castes (Table 2) the degree of homogeneity ranges from 66.7 percent in the case of Telis to 100.0 percent in the case of Brahmins, Dhimars, Lodhis, and Powars.

There is also a high degree of homogeneity (70.8 percent) between criminals and their victims with respect to sex but, as indicated by Table 3, this results from both

[12] Hans von Hentig, *The Criminal and His Victim* (New Haven: Yale University Press, 1948), p. 392.

[13] Government of Madhya Pradesh, *Report on Judicial Administration, 1953* (Nagpur, India: Government Printing Office, 1956), p. 6.

[14] Noshirvan H. Jhabvala, *The Indian Penal Code, Ninth Edition* (Bombay: C. Jamnadas, 1957), pp. 154–161.

[15] *Ibid.*

Table 2.
RELATION OF CASTE OF CRIMINAL TO CASTE OF VICTIM

CASTE OF VICTIM (1)	CASTE OF CRIMINAL										
	Brahmin (2)	Dhimar (3)	Lodhi (4)	Kosthi (5)	Kunbi (6)	Kalar (7)	Powar (8)	Teli (9)	Mahar (10)	Other* (11)	Total† (12)
1. Brahmin	2	—	—	—	—	—	—	—	—	—	2
2. Dhimar	—	3	—	—	—	—	—	—	—	—	3
3. Lodhi	—	—	5	—	—	—	—	2	—	—	7
4. Kosthi	—	—	—	15	—	—	—	—	—	2	17
5. Kunbi	—	—	—	—	9	1	—	—	—	2	12
6. Kalar	—	—	—	—	—	8	—	—	—	—	8
7. Powar	—	—	—	—	—	—	3	—	—	—	3
8. Teli	—	—	—	—	—	—	—	6	2	1	9
9. Mahar	—	—	—	1	—	—	—	—	20	—	21
10. Other*	—	—	—	—	3	—	—	1	2	16	22
11. Total†	2	3	5	16	12	9	3	9	24	21	104
12. Identical victims by number	2	3	5	15	9	8	3	6	20	16	87
13. Identical victims by percent	100.0	100.0	100.0	93.8	75.0	88.8	100.0	66.7	83.3	76.2	83.7

* Includes: Mali, Gaoli, Telanga, Maratha, Sonar, Mehtar, Gowari, Pasi, Agarwal, Thakur, Kohari, Merar, Mochi, Dhanagar, Kachi, and Gond (a tribal group).
† Of the 130 cases in which Hindus were offenders, only 104 gave the caste of both criminal and victim.

Table 3.
RELATION OF SEX OF CRIMINAL TO SEX OF VICTIM

	CRIMINAL	VICTIM	FREQUENCY	
			Number	Per cent
Homogeneity	Male	Male	97	67.3
	Female	Female	5	3.5
Heterogeneity	Male	Female	38	26.4
	Female	Male	4	2.8
Total			144	100.0

the way that males select victims and the fact that only 6.3 percent of the murderers are female. This small representation of females, in comparison with Western homicides,[16] may be associated with the statuses that women in India usually occupy.[17] They are expected to manage the household, care for the children, respect the authority of their spouses, and leave the management of business matters as well as the settlement of disputes to their male relatives.[18] The few women who have activities outside of the home are usually assisting their husbands in cultivation or other economic pursuits, and participating in religious and other ceremonial activities. Males, on the other hand, frequently participate in various kinds of interpersonal relations which may evoke strong tensions.

[16] See the data cited by Wolfgang, op. cit., pp. 46–64.

[17] An excellent discussion of the relationship of criminality to the status of women in Western societies is provided by Otto Pollak, The Criminality of Women (Philadelphia: University of Pennsylvania Press, 1950).

[18] D. N. Mazumdar, "About Women in Patrilocal Societies in South Asia," in A. Apadorai (ed.), The Status of Women in South Asia (Bombay: Orient Longmans, 1954), pp. 57–64.

In addition to its low incidence, female homicide is distinguished by the type of victim chosen. Kinsmen constitute 77.7 percent of their victims but only 43.8 percent of those of male offenders. Of the nine female offenders, two killed their children and attempted suicide, claiming that their lives were intolerable because of their husbands' liaisons with neighboring women and public embarrassment by their husbands when they complained of the liaisons. In four cases illegitimate children were the victims of widowed women who resided with their husbands' kinfolk. It seems from the testimony of witnesses and the judge's opinion in these cases that illegitimacy rather than infanticide is the grave offense. The woman experiences a strong sense of shame and is ostracized by the kinfolk. Further, she and the man responsible for the pregnancy, and all of their kinfolk are excommunicated by the caste group. Readmission to the group is possible only if the woman severs her connection with the infant and then persuades her kin and those of the man to give a dinner for the caste and perform other purificatory rituals.[19] In a society organized upon the basis of kinship and caste, ostracism and excommunication are equivalent to social death. Under these circumstances, in the absence of adoptive parents, the court views infanticide as a reasonable action:

The accused had to dispose of her child in this manner merely to avoid the contempt of her relatives and acquaintances towards her and that child. She is an illiterate labourer, and saw no other means for her and that child to face, and live in, the world and her stratum of society. She is young, and having been a widow for about 4½ years, fell a victim to her natural passions. . . . She had not remarried during that period, and the future of her only son might possibly have been one of the considerations. I recommend her case to

the Provincial Government for a substantial remission of her sentence.[20]

The remaining three victims of female homicide were: (1) a paramour who broke his promise of marriage, (2) a husband whose wife thought that she could "bring him under her thumb" by putting dhatura (a deadly poison) in his food, and (3) a female neighbor who was a participant in an interfamily feud.

In general, irrespective of the sex of the criminal, victims are seldom strangers but rather kinsmen or close associates, i.e., neighbors, friends, sweethearts, or co-workers. Of the total victims, 70 were kinsmen, 61 were close associates, and only 13 were strangers. Of the strangers 10 were killed while attempting to thwart the commission of a crime, and they constitute over one-half the persons thus killed.

Motives. Our previous discussion of the kinds of victims selected by female offenders throws some light on the court's view of the motives of offenders. In our cases of male offenders homicide is likewise viewed as the product of considerable provocation rather than a sudden impulse, mental aberration, or the influence of intoxicants. Except for homicides associated with the commission of other crimes and those resulting from street brawls, the act is the culmination of growing enmity between the actor and his victim. The friendly, affectionate relationship which initially existed is transformed into a hostile one when the actor correctly or incorrectly perceives of the victim as a violator of important social norms. It is the view of the court that hostility increased and finally took the form of physical aggression after personal appeals, mediation by community leaders, legal threats, and other social devices failed to resolve the dispute.

The major situations which motivated male offenders to attack their victims were: public embarrassment; sexual infidelity, tres-

[19] Crown vs. Mst. Sayatra, Sessions Trial Number 5 of 1948, State of Madhya Pradesh. Similar practices are reported for Ceylon by Bryce Ryan, Caste in Modern Ceylon (New Brunswick: Rutgers University Press, 1953), pp. 247–248.

[20] Crown vs. Mst. Manki, Sessions Trial Number 34 of 1948, State of Madhya Pradesh.

pass or rivalry, and other transgressions of norms governing heterosexual relations; disputes over the ownership or use of property, especially agricultural land and products; abuse or neglect of a child, sister, wife, or mother; and the refusal of a wife or her kin to accept the living arrangements provided by the husband. Most frequently, homicide occurred after the victim refused to apologize for or to desist from actions which were publicly embarrassing. Of major importance in this regard were habitual disobedience or other inappropriate conduct by the wife and derogatory references to the offender, his kin, or caste by neighbors. Next in importance as a motive for homicide are transgressions against norms governing heterosexual relations. In 22 cases there was either sexual infidelity, real or suspected, on the part of a wife or paramour, or sexual trespass or rivalry by kinsmen or close associates of the offender. A distinction between infidelity and trespass may seem unnecessary because where infidelity exists, there is usually a third party (rival or trespasser). In our cases, the difference lies in the fact that in trespass the offender attacks the third party rather than his beloved. It is evident from a comparison of column 2 with column 3 (Table 4) that offenders are just as prone to kill their loved ones as rivals or trespassers. In addition to these 22 cases there are several others (column 4) where various kinds of disparity between actual and ideal heterosexual relations, as perceived by the offender, motivated the aggressive act.

Third in frequency are disputes over property. The striking feature of the 25 cases in this category is that most of them were bona fide disputes between kinsmen or neighbors in the sense that property rights were not clearly defined because of either changes in the tenancy laws or the failure to adequately demarcate land boundaries. Other disputes centered around the purchase, use, or sale of implements and produce, and the obligations of kinsmen to render financial assistance. The remaining situations which apparently motivated the homicides are distributed as follows: nine disputes over the failure of a wife to reside with her husband; six instances where the offender was aggrieved by the persistent abuse or neglect of primary kin by other kinsmen or neighbors; and 13 miscellaneous acts.

Table 4.

STATUS OF THE VICTIM AND COURT'S JUDGMENT OF OFFENDERS' MOTIVE

		COURT'S JUDGMENT OF OFFENDER'S MOTIVE									
		SEXUAL				Dispute over Prop-					
		Tres-		Dispute over Living	Abuse or Neglect	erty Use, Owner-	Public Embar-	Rob- bery or Other	Physi- cal		
Status of the Victim	Infidel- ity	pass or Rivalry	Other	Arrange- ment	of Primary Kin	ship, etc.	rass- ment	Crime	Assault	Other	Total
(1)	(2)	(3)	(4)	(5)	(6)	(7)	(8)	(9)	(10)	(11)	(12)
A. *Kinsmen**											
a. Primaries											
1. Wife	9	—	1	3	1	—	6	—	—	4	24
2. Husband	—	—	1	—	—	—	—	—	—	1	2
3. Father	—	—	—	—	1	2	—	—	—	—	3
4. Mother	—	—	—	1	—	1	—	—	—	—	2
5. Son	—	—	—	—	—	—	2	—	—	—	2
6. Daughter	—	—	—	—	—	—	4	—	—	1	5

7. "Bhau" (brother)	—	1	—	—	—	9	—	—	—	1	6
b. Collaterals											
8. "Culata" (father's brother)	—	—	—	—	1	4	—	—	—	—	5
9. "Mama" (mother's brother)	—	1	—	—	—	1	—	—	—	—	2
10. "Culat bhau" (father's brother's son)	—	1	2	—	—	—	—	—	—	—	3
c. Affines											
11. "Sala" (wife's brother)	—	—	—	—	—	—	2	1	—	—	3
12. "Bhauji" (sister's husband)	—	—	—	—	2	—	—	—	—	—	2
13. "Sali" (wife's sister)	—	—	1	—	—	—	—	1	—	—	2
14. Others†	—	—	—	2	1	1	1	—	—	1	6
15. Total	9	3	5	6	6	15	15	2	1	8	70
B. *Close Associates*											
16. Sweetheart, paramour	2	—	1	—	—	—	—	—	—	—	3
17. Paramour's husband	—	—	3	—	—	—	—	—	—	—	3
18. Wife's paramour	—	4	—	—	—	—	—	—	—	1	5
19. Friend	—	1	—	—	—	—	1	—	3	—	5
20. Neighbor	—	2	—	—	4	10	16	3	3	—	38
21. Employer, employee, co-worker	—	1	—	—	—	—	2	2	—	2	7
22. Total	2	8	4	—	4	10	19	5	6	3	61
C. *Strangers*											
23. Constable	—	—	—	—	—	—	—	7	—	—	7
24. Other	—	—	—	—	—	—	—	3	1	2	6
25. Total	0	0	0	0	0	0	0	10	1	2	13
26. Grand Total	11	11	9	6	10	25	34	17	8	13	144

* The terms in quotation marks are in Marathi, the major language of the area included in this study. For a complete list of kinship terms for India, see: G. S. Ghurye, *Family and Kin in Indo-European Culture*, London: Oxford University Press, 1955.
† Includes one of each of the following: "bhabi" (brother's wife); "sasura" (wife's father); "sasu" (wife's mother); "sadu" (wife's sister's husband); "mausa" (wife's sister's son); and "juvai" (daughter's huband).

SUMMARY

Criminal homicide in India, as in Western countries, usually involves interaction between kinsmen or close associates rather than strangers and between persons of the same sex, religion, and caste. The affectionate or friendly relationship which has existed between them may be altered by an act on the part of one which is interpreted by the other as a violation of the norms governing sexual conduct, the use or ownership of property, terms of reference, treatment of primary kin, residence of the wife, and other important matters. When the customary devices employed to resolve disputes fail, enmity increases and finally culminates in homicide.

PATTERNS OF FORCIBLE RAPE*

Menachem Amir

Reported below are the results from a study of
646 cases of forcible rape in Philadelphia. In an analysis
of the patterns of forcible rape and the characteristics of
the rape situation, a number of common misconceptions about
the crime of rape are refuted. On the basis of a sociological
interpretation, Amir views forcible rape in its broader social
and cultural setting.

The primary purpose of this work has been to explore the nature and disclose the patterns of forcible rapes among 646 cases that occurred in Philadelphia, from January 1, 1958 to December 31, 1958, and from January 1, 1960 to December 31, 1960. The material presented is based on an empirical study of cases found in the files of the Morals Squad of the Philadelphia Police Department, where all complaints about rapes are recorded and centrally filed.

The emphasis in this study has not been on the psychological dynamics of the offenders and their victims but on their social characteristics, social relationships, and on the act itself, that is, on the *modus operandi* of the crime and the situations in which rape is likely to occur. The patterns which emerged were derived from information about the 646 victims and 1292 offenders who were involved in 370 cases of single-rape, 105 pair-rape, and 171 group-rape events. Patterns were sought regarding race, age, marital status, and employment differences, as well as seasonal and other temporal patterns, spatial patterns, the relation between forcible rape and the presence of alcohol and the previous arrest record of *victims* and *offenders*. In the analysis of the *modus operandi* a search for patterns made regarding the initial interaction and meeting place of offender and victim, the place of the offense, the planning of the crime, the methods used to subdue the vic-

* This selection, prepared especially for this book, is published here for the first time. Amir prepared it from his "Patterns of Forcible Rape," unpublished Ph.D. dissertation, University of Pennsylvania, 1965.

tim, the degree of violence in the rape event, the sexual humiliation to which the victim was subjected (other than forced intercourse), and the degree of the victim's resistance. Further questions were raised regarding rape during the commission of another felony, the interpersonal relationship between victim and offender, victim-precipitated rape, and unsolved cases of rape. Finally, all of these aspects were related to the phenomenon of group rape and to leadership functions in such situations.

The orientation toward these problems was empirical and the method used was that of phenomenological inquiry. While the study was approached from a sociological viewpoint, that is, crime as a socioculturally learned behavior committed within socioculturally defined situations, it was not guided by a specific theoretical system for explaining the offense studied. Nor did it attempt to find causes of and specific explanations for the offense. Rather, the purpose was to learn about the characteristics of the offense, the offender(s), and the victim(s). The associations were tested primarily by the Chi-square test of significance.

In order to provide a perspective and a basis for comparison with the patterns found in this study a review of the existing reports and studies of forcible rape was made along with a survey of other works believed to be relevant to the various aspects of the present research. No other study of forcible rape is known which deals with the number of variables included in the present study.[1] Some variables touched upon here are either new to research on sex crimes in

general or new to studies of forcible rape in particular.[2]

Crime statistics and studies which present crude rates of offenses and offenders and tell nothing about the victim can be criticized.[3] Finally, most previous studies, although alluding to the necessity of studying both victim and offender, still treat them separately. The present work examines "victims and offenders separately as distinct units but also as mutually interacting participants."[4]

OFFENDERS AND VICTIMS

The following is a summary of the major significant findings which emerged from the study.

Race. A significant association was found between forcible rape and the race of both victims and offenders. Negroes exceed whites both among victims and offenders, in absolute numbers as well as in terms of their proportion in the general population. Negroes have four times their expected number of victims, and the proportion of Negro offenders was four times greater than their proportion in the general population of Philadelphia. Sellin's[5] concept of "potential population" was used—that is, the members of each race whose age and sex is such that they could be an offender or a victim, respectively, and from which the involvement

[1] The phenomenological method used in Wolfgang's study of criminal homicide served as a model for the present study. M. E. Wolfgang, *Patterns in Criminal Homicide*, Philadelphia: University of Pennsylvania Press, 1958. Mohr and associates, *Pedophilia and Exhibitionism*, appeared while this study was being written and represents another, although more limited, example of this approach to the study of sex offenses. —J. W. Mohr, R. E. Turner, and M. B. Jerry, *Pedophilia and Exhibitionism*, Toronto: University of Toronto Press, 1964.

[2] For the growing list of other phenomenological studies, not mentioned before, in which the offense is the prime target of analysis, see I. Chein and others, *The Road to H*, New York: Basic Books, 1964; M. O. Cameron, *The Booster and the Snitch: Department Store Shoplifting*, New York: The Free Press of Glencoe, 1964; F. H. St. Martin's Press, Inc., 1963; F. H. McClintock and E. Gibson, *Robbery in London*, New York: St. Martin's Press, Inc., 1961; J. M. Martin, *Juvenile Vandalism*, Springfield, Ill.: Charles C Thomas, 1961; and A. L. Wood, *Crime and Aggression in Changing Ceylon*, Transactions of the American Philosophical Society, N. S., 51 (December 1961), Pt. 8.

[3] Wolfgang, p. 319.

[4] Wolfgang, p. 319.

[5] T. Sellin, "The Significance of Records of Crime," *Law Quarterly Review*, 67 (1951), pp. 496–504.

of the participants can be presumed. When specific rates by age and sex were calculated on the basis of the "potential" population of each race, it was found that the rates for the Negro women who were rape victims (on the basis of total Negro female population) is almost 12 times higher than that of the white women who were victims (on the basis of white female population). Similarly, for offenders, when the rates were computed on the basis of male population in each racial group, the proportion of Negro offenders was 12 times greater than that of white offenders. Furthermore, when the rates were figured on the basis of "potential" race populations, the rates for Negro offenders turned out to be 3 times greater than that of Negro victims. The data on racial differences reveals that forcible rape is mainly an *intraracial* event, that is, it occurs primarily between members of the same race. Moreover, forcible rape occurred *significantly* more often between Negroes than between whites.

Age. A *significant* association existed between age and forcible rape, the age group 15–25 years having the highest rates among offenders and among victims. In examining the relative ages of the offender(s) and the victim(s), it was found that the higher the age of the offender, the more likely it was that the victim would be in a lower age group. When the differences were broken down further by race, it appeared that, regardless of the population basis, the top "risk" age group for Negro and white offenders is the same (15 to 19 and 20 to 25 years of age), but the rates for Negroes in these age levels are higher than for whites. For each age group, however, the rates show a greater proportion of Negro than of white males involved in forcible rape.

The age pattern for victims was found to be somewhat different from that of offenders; for victims there is a wider range of "critical" age groups. Both races had a high proportion of victims between the ages of 10 to 14 and 15 to 19 years, with the Negro victim rates exceeding that of the white

victims in these age groups, as well as in all other age groups. Examination of age differences according to race of victim and offender showed that offenders and victims were generally of similar age levels in Negro and white intraracial rapes. In interracial rapes, however, Negro offenders tend to be at least ten years younger than their white victims.

Marital Status. Both offenders and victims were generally found to be unmarried. The highest rates for victims were in the "dependent" category, that is, below marriageable age. Negro victims showed a greater concentration in the "single" and "dependent" groups than did white victims, who were, however, concentrated also in these groups. Negro offenders differ from their Negro victims in their marital status only in the "married" and "separated" categories, where Negro victims have higher rates than that of their Negro offenders. An attempt was made to check Von Hentig's[6] demographic explanation of forcible rape, which is that a disturbed sex ratio for unmarried persons aged 19 to 49 years resulting in a surplus of males, leads to rape as a solution to their problem of securing sexual partners. It was found that the marital demographic structure of Philadelphia cannot explain the extent to which males, especially Negroes, resort to forcible rape. The same applied when marital status, age, and sex ratio were analyzed together.

Occupation. Examination of the occupational status of the offenders indicated that 90 percent of the offenders of both races belonged to the lower part of the occupational scale: from skilled workers down to the retired and unemployed. The rate of Negro offenders in the unemployed category was twice as high as the rate of unemployed Negroes in Philadelphia at that time, and five times as high as that of white offenders

---

[6] H. Von Hentig, "The Sex Ratio," *Social Forces,* 30 (1951), pp. 443–449.

when the semiskilled, unskilled, and un-employed categories were combined.

Time of the Year. Although the number of forcible rapes tended to increase during the hot summer months, there was no significant association either with the season or with the month of the year. While Negro intraracial rapes were spread all over the year, white intraracial rape events showed a more consistent increase during the summer, which was found also to be the season when multiple rapes were most apt to occur.

Day and Hour. Forcible rape was found to be significantly associated with days of the week. It was found that the highest concentration of rapes (53 percent) was on weekends. A study of the distribution of forcible rapes by hours of the day found top "risk" hours to be between 8:00 P.M. and 2:00 A.M. Almost half of all the rape events occurred during these hours.

Spatial Distribution. In the analysis of the ecology of forcible rape in various areas of Philadelphia, a correspondence was found between high rates of crime against the person and the rates of forcible rape. Moreover, those police districts where Negroes are concentrated were also the areas where the rates of forcible rapes were highest. A check was made to determine whether the offender(s) lived in the vicinity of the victim(s) or of the offense. In the majority of cases (82 percent) of the offenders and victims lived in the same area, while in 68 percent a *neighborhood triangle* was observed, that is, offenders lived in the vicinity of victim and offense. Also observed are the pattern of *residence mobility triangle*, that is, instances in which the site of the crime was in the area of the residence of the offender but not of the victim. A new concept used in this study was that of *crime mobility triangle*. In 4 percent of the cases the offenders lived in the vicinity of the victims, while the crime was committed outside the boundaries of their residential area. When correlating these

ecological patterns with the race and age factors, it was found that forcible rape was an intraracial event between victims and offenders who were at the same age level and who were ecologically bound, that is, victims and offenders lived in the same area, which tended to be also the area of the offense. This was especially true for Negro intraracial rapes.

Alcohol. Previous studies which have examined the relationship between the use of alcohol and rape have failed to examine the relation of alcohol to the victim. While alcohol was found only in one third of all the rape events, in 63 percent of the 217 cases in which alcohol was present, it was present in both the victim and the offender. The presence of alcohol in the rape situation appeared to be *significantly* associated with whites, both victims and offenders, and with the Negro victim when she had consumed alcohol before the offense. Alcohol was frequently found to be present in the victim, offender, or both in white intraracial rape events.

Alcohol is a factor found to be strongly related to violence used in the rape situation, especially when present in the offender only. In terms of race, drinking Negro victims or the offenders were involved most often in violent rapes. Also, alcohol was found to be *significantly* associated with sexual humiliation forced upon a drinking victim. Finally, weekend rapes were found to be *significantly* associated with the presence of alcohol in either the victim, the offender, or both. As an explanation, we offered (as did Wolfgang in his homicide study[7]) the fact that Friday brings "payday" and with it the greater purchase of alcohol and the more intense social and leisure activities.

Criminal Record. Unlike those considered in other reports and studies, a relatively high proportion of rapists in Philadelphia (50 percent) had previous arrest records. Con-

[7] Wolfgang, pp. 142–143.

trary to past impressions, it was found that there are almost no differences between the races, for offenders or victims, in terms of police or arrest record, although Negro offenders had a *significantly* higher proportion of two or more offenses in their past than white offenders. When cases of persistence in violating the law were examined, it was found that over 50 percent of those who had an arrest record as adults also had a record as juveniles.

Analysis of the type of previous offenses committed by the offenders revealed that only 20 percent of those who had a past arrest record had previously committed a crime against the person, with Negro offenders outnumbering the whites in this respect. Among offenders with criminal records, 9 percent had committed rape in the past, and 4 percent had been arrested before for a sexual offense other than rape. When examining the continuity and persistence of offenses from juvenile to adult age, it was found that the highest proportion was in offenses against the person. Adults arrested for rape were found less likely to be first offenders than adults arrested for other types of offenses.

The analysis of victims' criminal records revealed that 19 percent of victims had an arrest record, the highest proportion of these arrests being for sexual misconduct. It was observed that 56 percent of the victims who had an arrest record had been charged with some sort of sexual offense. These offenses included juvenile misconduct, which often has a sexual connotation.

Another type of "record" was explored: the victim's "bad" reputation in the local community. It was found that 128, or 20 percent of the 646 victims, had such reputations, with a *significantly* higher proportion of Negro victims having such a reputation. The assumption was made, and later confirmed, that a "bad" reputation, together with other factors such as ecological proximity, was a factor in what was termed "victim-precipitated" forcible rape.

CHARACTERISTICS OF THE RAPE SITUATION

The analysis of the *modus operandi* was made in terms of processes and characteristics of the rape situation, that is, sequences and conjunctures of events which enter into the perpetration of the offense. Six phases were distinguished according to offender's behavior, victim's reaction, and situational factors which finally set the stage for the rape event.

Offender's Behavior. Phase one was concerned with the initial interaction between victim and offender, and the relevant problems are their place of meeting and the degree of planning of the offense. It was found that the most frequent meeting places were the street, and the residence of the victims or offenders or place of sojourn. In one third of the cases, the offender met the victim at, and committed the offense in, the victim's home or place of sojourn. Such was especially the case in intraracial rape events.

On the basis of description of the event by the victim and the offender, three degrees of planning were distinguished and analyzed for their relationships to some pertinent variables. The analysis revealed that 71 percent of the rapes were planned. Most planned events were intraracial events when the meeting place was one of the participants' residence or when the rape was a group affair. Explosive rapes were characterized as being single interracial rapes, with the street as the meeting place.

The location of the offense is *significantly* associated with the place of initial meeting. Thus, when the meeting place was outside the participants' residence or place of sojourn, this is also where the offense took place. Movement of the crime scene was mainly from outdoors to inside. The automobile, which was already found to be a vehicle of crime commission, was revealed to be the location of the offense in only 15 percent of the cases, and more often when white offenders were involved in the offense. A *significant* association was also found between the location of the rape in the participants' place of residence and use of violence in the commission of the offense, as well as the subjection of the victim to sexually humiliating practices.

Next, attention was turned to various aspects in the actual commission of the offense: nonphysical methods used to manipulate the victim into submission, the degrees of violence used against her, and the sexual humiliation and its content which she was forced to endure. Nonphysical methods included verbal coercion and intimidation by means of a physical object to force the victim into submission. Nonphysical aggression was used in the majority of cases (87 percent), with Negroes in *significant* proportion using both forms of intimidation against their Negro victims. The differences between intra- and interracial events in this respect were not found to be statistically significant.

Degrees of violence were classified into three main groups: roughness, beatings (brutal and nonbrutal), and choking. In 15 percent of the 646 rapes, no force was used. Of the cases in which force was used, 29 percent took the form of roughness, twenty-five percent were nonbrutal beatings, twenty percent were brutal beatings, and 12 percent involved choking the victim. Violence, especially in its extreme forms, was found to be *significantly* associated with Negro intraracial events and with cases in which the offender was Negro and the victim white. Also, a *significant* association was found between multiple rape and the use of force in the rape situation and between the latter and the outside as the place of rape. Multiple rape and the "outside" as the place of the offense were found to be *significantly* associated, too.

It was not merely to forced intercourse that the female was subjected in rape, but also to various forms of sexual practices usually defined as sexual deviations. It was found that sexual humiliation existed in 27 percent of all rape cases, especially in the forms of fellatio, cunnilingus, or both, or in the form of repeated intercourse. Sexual humiliation was found to be *significantly* associated with white intraracial rapes, where the victims were subjected most frequently to fellatio and pederasty, and with Negro intraracial rapes where Negro victims were forced more often to repeated intercourse by their Negro assaulters. Sexual humiliation was found also to be *significantly* associated with multiplicity of offenders and with the presence of alcohol in the rape situation, especially when it had been consumed by the offender only or by both the offender and the victim. In these cases sexual humiliation appeared mainly in the form of fellatio.

Victim's Reaction. The behavior of the victim, that is, whether she resisted the offender, was, and still is, the cornerstone in determining for legal purposes whether or not the offender is guilty of forcible rape. The issue of "consent" and the questioning of it in the court rest on determining the presence or absence of resistance. This problematic dimension of victim behavior is therefore analyzed here. The varieties of victim behavior have been divided into three groups: submission, resistance, and fight. The analysis revealed that in over half of the rapes the victims displayed only submissive behavior; in 173, or 27 percent, victims resisted the offender; and in 116, or 18 percent, victims put up a strong fight against their attackers. In both intra- and interracial rapes Negro and white victims displayed the same proportion of these forms of behavior. The highest proportion of the instances of submissive behavior were cases in which the victim was white and the offender Negro. These cases included almost all felony-rape events—in most of which the victim was older than her attacker. The younger the age, the more submissive was the victim; the most submissive victims were those aged 10 to 14 years. In the adult age (victims aged 30 and over), victims showed *significantly* more resistance. Victims who were 10 or more years younger or older than the offenders were more submissive, while those who were nearly the same age as their assailants (not more than five years younger or, older) displayed the highest proportion of fighting behavior. Victims tended to fight more when they were more intimidated in the initial encounter with the offender, or when force was used against them by the offenders. As expected, the presence of alcohol in the victim diminished her capacity to resist, and her behavior was found to be mainly submissive in such cases.

Multiple Rape. The phenomenon of multiple rape has been given special attention in this study; a tentative theory was suggested which emphasizes the role of the leader. The leader was analyzed in the framework of the structural-functional school of sociology, while the content of the leader's role was borrowed from Redl's[8] theory of the "central" person and his function as an "initiator" and/or "magical" seducer. The various aspects of the offense discussed before were then collated with the phenomena of multiple rape, particularly with leadership functions. Multiple-rape situations were divided into pair rape, in which two offenders rape one victim; and group rapes, in which three or more males rape one victim. Of the 646 cases of forcible rape, 276 cases, or 43 percent, were multiple rapes. Of these cases, 105 were pair rapes and 171 were group rapes. Of 1292 offenders, 210, or 16 percent, were involved in pair rapes and 712, or 55 percent, participated in group rapes. Altogether, 912 offenders, or 71 percent, of the 1292 offenders were involved in multiple-rape events.

The analysis of multiple rapes revealed the following characteristics: more white than Negro offenders participated in pair rape and more Negro than white offenders were involved in group rape. Multiple-rape situations were found to be mainly an intraracial affair, with no differences in proportions between Negro and white intraracial

events. The older the offender, the less likely he is to participate in group rape; all of the offenders of ages 10 to 14 participated either in pair rape or group rape. The highest proportion of pair rape or group rape was perpetrated by offenders between the ages of 14 and 19. Like all other kinds of rape, group rapes were found to be characterized by victims being in the same age level as the offenders. Group rape shows a tendency to occur more often on weekends in the evening as well as late at night, and a tendency to be associated with the presence of alcohol. In group rape alcohol was more likely to be present, especially in the victim only, while in pair rape it was more often present only in the offender who was the leader.

A *significant* proportion of participants in multiple rape had a previous arrest record either for offenses against the person, for sex offenses other than rape, or for forcible rape. This was true for pair-rape leaders, as compared to their partners, but not for group-rape leaders *vis-à-vis* their followers. The homogeneity of the dyad is established for this as well as for other variables.

Turning to the *modus operandi* in multiple-rape situations, it was observed that multiple-rape offenders in such situations are most likely to attack victims who live in their area (*neighborhood* or *delinquency triangles*). The initial interaction between the victim and the offenders usually occurred first in the street, and there also the rape took place. There was little "mobility of crime scene" in multiple-rape situations. Multiple rapes, especially group rapes, were found to be planned events. Pair rapes also tended to be planned, but in a lesser proportion. Compared to group rapes, pair rapes showed a high proportion of cases of explosiveness or partial planning.

Is it necessary to intimidate the victim of a multiple rape or is the sheer number of attackers enough to frighten her into submission so that only slight coercion is necessary? Transforming these questions into specific hypotheses, it was found that multiple-rape situations, especially group rapes, are characterized by coercion, while there was

[8] F. Redl, "Group Emotion and Leadership," *Psychiatry*, 5 (1942), pp. 573–596.

more use of intimidation in pair-rape events. The leader was found to be the initiator of the manipulating acts, that is, he was the first to tempt or to intimidate the victim into submission.

A *significant* association existed between violence and multiple rapes, especially group rapes. Group-rape and pair-rape events are also characterized by the greater use of non-brutal beatings. Extreme violence and brutality characterize the single-rape events, since the lone offender must constantly subdue the victim and does not have the help of others. The leader in pair and group rapes was more violent than his followers, and he was also the one to initiate the beatings. Group rapes are also characterized by tormenting the victim with perverted sexual practices, especially in the form of repeated intercourse. Testing the theory of "magical seduction" it was found that only the pair-rape leader inflicted sexual humiliation upon the victim, and especially in the forms of fellatio, cunnilingus, or both.

Is the leader responsible for both "magical seduction" and "initial action," or can he abstain from one of them and still be the leader of the group offense? When the association between these leadership functions was tested, it was found that both are significantly associated, that is, those who first attacked the victim were also the first to rape her. However, "magical seduction" was found to be the more important role of the leader. Introducing another leadership function, that of "commanding" and organizing the situation, it was found that in group rape the "true" leader was the one who performed all three functions. If the three functions were not performed by the same person, however, the one who first raped the victim was also likely to be the one who commanded the event.

The futility of resistance and fight by the group-rape victim is revealed by the fact that in group-rape situations the victim was more submissive or resisted the offender but was less inclined to put up a strong fight. Pair-rape victims showed no definite pattern in this respect. For many variables pair rapes

and group rapes show some variations from the cluster of patterns which distinguished the multiple-rape situations. It was mainly the pair rape which varied from the typical multiple-rape situations portrayed in this study. It was found that in many instances pair rape resembled single rape more than group rape. Thus, it may be better to see pair rapes not as a form of group event but rather as a form of criminal "partnership."

Rape in Connection with Other Crimes.
In 76 cases, or 4 percent, of the 646 rape events, a felony in the form of burglary or robbery was committed in addition to the rape. These cases were mainly single rapes, and especially Negro intraracial rapes. A special trait of felony rape is the age disparity between victim and offender; in more than half of these cases the offender was at least ten years younger than the victim, and a higher proportion of the felony-rape cases in which the offender was Negro and the victim white exhibited the age disparity. Examination of the previous records of felony-rapists showed them to be more often recidivists than the offenders in rape generally. Felony rapes also were characterized by a greater proportion of cases in which sexual humiliation was inflicted upon the victim. Because of the age differences between victim and offenders, it was expected and, indeed, generally found that victims of felony rapes were more inclined to be submissive than victims of rape.

Acquaintance with the Victim. Almost half (48 percent) of the identified victim-offenders were known to each other to the extent to constitute a "primary" relationship. When the types of primary contacts were further divided into "acquaintanceship" and more "intimate" contacts, the former constituted 34 percent and the latter contributed 14 percent of all types of victim-offender relationships. A detailed analysis of victim-offender relationships revealed that when primary relationships existed, a relatively large proportion of cases involved Negro victims whose assailants were their

close neighbors, or victims who were drinking acquaintances of their white assaulters.
As expected, Negro intraracial events involved mainly close neighbors. White intraracial events occurred mainly between acquaintances who established their relations
just before the offense. Acquaintanceships
were formed mainly between victims and
offenders who were at the same age level.
Neighbors met initially in one of the participants' residences, where the rape also
took place. The automobile was the place
of rape for those who were intimate. Although nonphysical means of coercion in its
light forms were used between acquaintances,
the closer the relationship was between
victim and offender the greater was the use
of physical force against the victim, and
neighbors and acquaintances were found to
be the most dangerous people so far as brutal
rape was concerned.

A greater proportion of multiple than
single rape was found to take place between
strangers. In general, the analysis of the
interpersonal relations between victim and
offender lent support to rejecting the myth
of the offender who attacks victims unknown to him. But equally rejected is the
notion that rape is generally an affair between, or is a result of intimate relations between, victims and offenders.

After discussing the psychological approach to victim proneness and victim selection, it was found more fruitful to deal with
vulnerable (risky) *situations* rather than
with psychological concepts like "victim
proneness." Those factors were noted which
emerged in *significant* proportions as constituents of such situations. It is probable
that women entering these risk situations
will more likely become victims of rape regardless of their own psychological characteristics. The following were the main features of vulnerable situations in which rape
occurred: victims and offenders of single-
and multiple-rape events were either of the
same race or age or both; victims of felony
rape tended to be at least 10 years older
than the assailants; offenders, Negro and
white, lived as neighbors or acquaintances

in the same area as victims of their own race
and age level—which was also the area where
the crime was committed; offenders and victims of the same race and age level met
during the summer months, mainly on weekends and/or during the evening and night
hours, in places which allowed or encouraged the development of an acquaintanceship, or relations between neighbors; alcohol
was present in both white offender and white
victim, or in white offender and Negro victim, or in the victim only, especially when
her assailant was white; Negro victims
having a "bad" reputation lived in the
neighborhood of their Negro attackers;
groups of offenders who planned the rape
of victims of their own race lived in the same
vicinity; victims and offenders were neighbors
of the same race and age, between whom primary relations existed; victims and offenders
established drinking relations just prior to the
offense; a drinking victim was accosted in the
street by a stranger, usually of her own race.

Victim-Precipitated Rape. The term "victim-precipitated," initiated by Wolfgang in
his study of homicide,[9] was introduced to
refer to those rape cases in which the victim actually (or so it was interpreted by
the offender) agreed to sexual relations, but
retracted before the actual act or did not
resist strongly enough when the suggestion
was made by the offender. The term applies also to cases in which the vulnerable
victim enters situations charged with sexuality, especially when she uses what could
be interpreted as indecent language and
gestures or makes what could be taken as an
invitation to sexual relations. After establishing the theoretical and legal basis, the Philadelphia data revealed several significant factors associated with the 122 victim-precipitated rapes, which comprised 19 percent of
all forcible rapes studied. These factors are
white victims; white intraracial rapes; alcohol in the rape situation, particularly in the
victim or in both offender and victim;
victims with a bad reputation; victims who

[9] Wolfgang, pp. 245–269.

live in residential proximity to the offender(s) and/or to the area of the offense; victims who meet their offenders in a bar, picnic, or party; victims who were raped outside their or the offenders' home or place of sojourn; the subjection of victims to sexual humiliation; and victims who were in "primary" relationships with the offenders but who were not their relatives.

Unsolved Rape Cases. Two types of "unsolved" cases were distinguished: the "undetected," those cases in which the police could not attribute the recorded offense to any identifiable offender(s); and the "vanished," those cases about which the police have some information on suspected, identified, or alleged offenders but in which suspects are still at large. In 124, or 19 percent, of the cases the offenders were classified as "undetected" and in 24, or 4 percent, as "vanished." Together they represent 148, or 23 percent, "unsolved" cases. Of 1292 offenders, 405, or 33 percent, were classified as undetected and 40, or 34 percent, as undiscovered offenders. In unsolved cases of rape in Philadelphia there was a higher proportion of Negro offenders involved in Negro intraracial rape than in solved cases; a higher average age among the offenders than among offenders in general; a higher proportion of explosive types of rape; a higher proportion of cases in which alcohol was present in the victim only or in the offender only; a higher proportion of single-rape situations; and a higher proportion where there was delay by the victim or others in reporting the offense to the police, especially because of fear of the offender or an inability to describe him adequately.

A SOCIOLOGICAL INTERPRETATION OF FORCIBLE RAPE

The present study maintained that an act, like criminal behavior, is a patterned and structured event. In this connection, the study made assumptions based on a sociological theory of behavior, in general, including that of deviant and criminal behavior:[10]

(1) roles represent a way of behaving in social situations, regulated by normative definitions and expectations;

(2) roles are learned through, and supported by, group definitions; some roles are products of family socialization, some are peer-group products, and both may be class or ethnically bound;

(3) roles describe only part rather than the entire behavior or personality system of the person; thus

(4) a specific role may be part of the role-set, that is, being a juvenile gang member may involve being a rapist;

(5) one plays criminal and noncriminal roles as part of his role set

(6) some roles are fairly stable (professional criminal), while others represent only temporary patterns of behavior

Since roles are normative and group-bound, the reason must be found for the concentration of forcible rape within certain groups which were found to be exceptionally heavily represented in the present study: adolescent and young adults and members of lower class groups, especially Negroes.

Subculture of Violence and Forcible Rape.

A broader phenomenological approach has been adopted for the present study. It calls for "uncovering of recurring patterns in which particular groups of people are found to commit a particular type of crime in particular types of circumstances."[11] The clinical psychiatric and psychological approach does not explain rape, especially the epidemiology of the offense. Such an approach

[10] Any good textbook in sociology will provide a definition and description of the concept. For an analysis and a summary of the literature see R. H. Turner, "Role Taking: Process Versus Conformity," in A. M. Rose (ed.), *Human Behavior and Social Processes,* Boston: Houghton Mifflin Company, 1962, pp. 20–41. For a summary of role theory in relation to criminal typology see Don C. Gibbons, *Changing the Lawbreaker,* Englewood Cliffs, N.J.: Prentice-Hall, Inc., 1965, pp. 43–48.

[11] B. Wootton, *Crime and Criminal Law,* London: Stevens & Sons, Ltd., 1963, p. 23.

does not explain the differential distribution and patterns of the crime and those involved[12] in terms of variations among groups in their cultural norms and social conditions.[13] Because the highest rates of the offenses studied occurred among relatively homogeneous groups, it is therefore assumed that these groups, situated in a subculture,[14] hold a particular set of conduct norms which emphasize and condone aggressive behavior, and have also the least "resistance potential"[15] toward aggressive sexual behavior. Thus, under special circumstances, violence, including sexual violence toward women, is more likely to occur. Furthermore, it is contended that members of these subcultures are more likely to react aggressively than nonmembers. Hence, individual differences in aggressive behavior may also reflect different degrees of integration with the subculture rather than only personality differences of a pathological nature.[16]

It is not contended, however, that there is a subculture of rape. Rather, there exists a subculture of violence. Rape is therefore only an epiphenomenon occurring under special circumstances. Members of these groups are not constrained by their subculture to rape whenever the group demands. However, they are influenced by the group and accept, more readily than nonmembers, the idea of the offense and the justification of the act before and after its commission. They are also more apt to view certain situations as appropriate for rape. This study, along with Wolfgang's study of criminal homicide[17] conducted in the same area, shows that the rates for forcible rape are highest among Negro[18] males (591.25), as compared to whites (41.9) and adolescents ages 15 to 19 (521) and young adults ages 20 to 24 (332) and those who are maritally unattached and belong to the lower socioeconomic class.

Again by increasing the specificity of race spatial arrangements, it was found that of the total 885 offenders who lived in the vicinity of their victims and of the crime, 92 percent were Negroes who assailed Negro victims. Among the 704 Negro offenders who attacked Negro victims, 79 percent showed this pattern. The ecological factor is introduced to enhance the argument of subculture interpretation of forcible rape. Residential proximity serves to maintain and strengthen the idea of interaction between those who are differentially associated[19] in terms of being members of the

[12] E. Durkheim, *Suicide*, translated by J. A. Spaulding and G. Simpson, New York: The Free Press of Glencoe, 1951. On the empirical approach, see H. C. Selvin, "Durkheim's 'Suicide' and Problems of Empirical Research," *American Journal of Sociology*, 63 (1958), pp. 607–619.
[13] This sociological approach also assumes variations in cultural integration; variations in social integration; malintegration between cultural and social structure; variations in the integration of conventional and deviant values, as well as in difference in the manner with which individual members are integrated into their groups. See H. D. Stein and R. S. Cloward (eds.), *Social Perspectives on Behavior*, New York: The Free Press of Glencoe, 1958, pp. 478–481.
[14] On the meaning and problems of subculture see D. J. Bordua, "Delinquent Subcultures: Sociological Interpretation of Gang Delinquency," *The Annals*, 338 (1961), pp. 119–136; D. J. Bordua, *Sociological Theories and Their Implication for Juvenile Delinquency*, Washington, D.C.: Department of Health, Education, and Welfare, 1960, No. 2; J. F. Short, Jr., "The Sociological Context of Delinquency," *Crime and Delinquency*, 6 (1960), pp. 365–375.
[15] Thorsten Sellin, *Culture Conflict and Crime*, Social Science Research Council Bulletin, 41 (1938) p. 34.
[16] F. Ferracuti and M. E. Wolfgang, "The Prediction of Violent Behavior," *Corrective Psychiatry and Journal of Social Therapy*, 10 (1964), pp. 289–301, at p. 293.
[17] Wolfgang, pp. 245–269.
[18] The description is centered on the Negro group because of the higher proportion of Negroes in this study. No claims are made that the white offender is different from the Negro offender in terms of "inherent criminality." What is important, and therefore emphasized, is a "social fact": the overrepresentation of the Negro as a group in this sample. See M. E. Wolfgang, *Crime and Race: Conceptions and Misconceptions*, New York: Institute of Human Relations Press, Pamphlet Series No. 6, 1964.
[19] On the theory of differential association and criticism see: D. Glaser, "The Differential-Association Theory of Crime," in Rose, Chap. 22, pp. 425–443.

same race and of being on the same age level. The assumption of subculture gains support because it is within the neighborhood that favorable attitudes toward violence and the use of violence are learned in "a process of differential learning, associated or identification."[20]

The data on previous arrest records, when used cautiously, may allow one to accept the assumption that such a record to a large extent reflects the development of a potential for aggressive reaction to situations, where such reactions are learned and supported by the normative system and the peer-group interaction.[21] The analysis of the data showed that 49 percent of all offenders had an arrest record for crime against the person. Among Negro offenders, 49 percent had such a record. Negroes had a higher proportion of records for two or more offenses, and as a group had a higher proportion of persistent offenders (54 percent of the cases).

The concept of subculture assumes, among other things, that criminality is learned in a sociocultural framework, with the ecological factor an important asset for such learning. Moreover, the sociological theory of lower class criminality contends that the process of learning and maintaining criminal behavior occurs primarily in the peer group or gang.[22] This study indicates that of 646 rape cases, 276 were group rape events. Moreover, group rapes were predominantly intraracial events.

The results suggest one of the mechanisms by which the individual is integrated into and maintains membership with the subculture. The peer group serves also as an exposing and defining agency for situations in which sexual violence is called for, thus making them less chance events, but rather planned and organized. In this study

a relatively small percentage of the rape events was precisely planned or organized.

Studies of Negro delinquents indicate the lower class origin of such girls[23] and their intensive involvement in the life of the male-dominated peer group. It seems that the girls from these studies contribute to the dynamics of the male peer group, especially to its activities in the sexual realm.[24] It was also found that in 58 percent the victims were not strangers to their assailants and in 25 percent they were actually neighbors or close friends. These results lead to the assumption that both victims and offenders are members of the same subculture.

The existence of subcultures of aggression and violence and its ecological distribution is well documented in criminological literature.[25] Also documented are the high rates of aggressive and violent crimes among young males located in the lower class sectors of the American social structure;[26] especially notable are the rates among lower class Negro men in their adolescence and early adulthood.[27]

Studies in socialization show that lower class boys learn overt and direct aggressive

[20] Ferracuti and Wolfgang, "The Prediction of Violent Behavior," p. 296.
[21] F. E. Hartung, Crime, Law and Society, Detroit: Wayne University Press, 1965, p. 74.
[22] The data also show that 19 percent of the victims had a prior arrest record, especially of sexual misconduct, and 20 percent had a "bad" reputation, that is, promiscuity.
[23] J. C. Ball and N. Logan, "Early Sexual Behavior of Lower Class Delinquent Girls," Journal of Criminal Law, Criminology and Police Science, 51 (1960), pp. 209–214, and see summary of the literature there.
[24] See K. Hanson, Rebels in the Streets: The Story of New York's Girl Gangs, Englewood Cliffs, N.J.: Prentice-Hall, Inc. 1964; H. E. Salisbury, The Shook-up Generation, New York: Harper & Row, Publishers, 1958; J. F. Short, Jr., and F. L. Strodtbeck, "A Strategy of Utilizing Research Dilemmas: A Case from the Study of Parenthood in a Street Corner Gang," Sociological Inquiry, 22 (1962), pp. 185–202.
[25] For a recent documentation see F. Ferracuti and M. Wolfgang, "Design for a Proposed Study on Violence," British Journal of Criminology, 3 (1963), pp. 377–388.
[26] Any of the recent textbooks will serve as a reference.
[27] See L. D. Savitz, "Crime and the Negro: A Critical Review of the Literature," Philadelphia Department of Sociology, Temple University, 1962, Chaps. III, VII; Wolfgang, Crime and Race: Conceptions and Misconceptions, pp. 29–32.

attitudes and conduct in their families,[28] as well as from peers.[29] As a result of these processes of socialization, the subculture becomes part of their perceptual and motivational structure. They become sensitive and habitually responsive to its expectations and definitions of situations.[30] Under these conditions, aggressive and exploitative behavior toward women become part of the normative systems of those members who do not conceive such behavior as wrong or as a deviation from the normal.[31] Moreover, the pressure of certain stimuli (special situations) precipitates the potential violence and sexual aggression that exist in each of them, which leads them to see many situations as opportunities for sexual conquest.

Subculture: The Sex Aspect. The general impression gained from the literature[32] is that lower class people tend to show more freedom in sexual experimentation, which starts earlier in their lives. The men tend to exploit promiscuous girls in order to establish status within their peer group.[33]

Patterns of cultural learning of aggressive sex behavior produce selective perception of, and kinds of interaction with, women, which may partially explain the over representation of lower class Negroes in this sample. The Negro lower class subculture embodies all the characteristics of a lower class subculture but has some of its features in a more pronounced form. The Negro subculture is characterized by the revolving of life around some basic "focal concerns,"[34] which include a search for thrills[35] through aggressive actions and sexual exploits. The emphasis is given by males to masculinity, and their need to display and defend it[36] through brief and transitory relations with women.[37] Such needs, and the subsequent concern with sex, stems from growing up in a family in which the mother is dominant and the father has a marginal position.[38] Moreover, because the lower

---

[28] For a summary on the socialization of aggression and sex drives in the lower class, see L. Berkowitz, *Aggression: A Social Psychological Analysis*, New York: McGraw-Hill Book Company, Inc., 1962, Chap. 10. See bibliography there.

[29] See bibliography in Ferracuti and Wolfgang.

[30] Wolfgang, *Patterns in Criminal Homicide*, p. 329.

[31] See, for instance, A. J. Reiss, "Sex Offenses: The Marginal Status of the Adolescent," *Law and Contemporary Problems*, 25 (1960), pp. 309–334, which provides a good summary of the literature on this aspect of lower class subcultures.

[32] W. Breed, "Sex Class and Socialization in Dating," *Marriage and Family Living*, 18 (1956), pp. 137–144; E. B. Crook, "Sexual Delinquency in Relation to Cultural Infiltration," *Sociology and Social Research*, 19 (1934), pp. 44–45; Crook, "Cultural Marginality in Sexual Delinquency," *American Journal of Sociology*, 39 (1934), pp. 493–500; A. B. Hollingshead, *Elmtown's Youth*, New York: Science Editions, Inc., 1961, pp. 110, 416–424; A. C. Kinsey, et al., *Sexual Behavior in the Human Male*, Philadelphia: W. B. Saunders Company, 1948, pp. 497–516, 549–562; L. J. Neiman, "Peer Groups and Attitudes toward the Female Role," *Social Problems*, 2 (1959), pp. 104–110; M. Rabban, "Sex Identification in Young Children in Two Diverse Social Groups," *Genetic Psychological Monographs*, 42 (1950), pp. 91–158; C. Vincent, *Unmarried Mothers*, New York: The Free Press of Glencoe, 1961; W. T. Whyte, "A Slum Sex Code," *American Journal of Sociology*, 49 (1943), pp. 24–31; F. G. Wood, *Cultural Values of American Ethnic Groups*, New York: Harper & Row, Publishers, 1956.

[33] Hollingshead, pp. 412–416; A. J. Reiss, "Sex Offenses: The Marginal Status of the Adolescent," *Law and Contemporary Problems*, 25 (1960), pp. 309–334; W. T. Whyte, "A Slum Sex Code," *American Journal of Sociology*, 49 (1943), pp. 24–31.

[34] W. B. Miller, "Lower Class Culture as a Generating Milieu of Gang Delinquency," *Journal of Social Issues*, 24 (1958), pp. 5–19.

[35] Miller, p. 14. Also S. M. Miller and F. Riessman, "The Working Class Subculture: A New View," *Social Problems*, 9 (1961), pp. 86–97, 95.

[36] Miller and L. Rainwater, *And the Poor Get Children*, Chicago: Quadrangle Books, Inc., 1960, p. 69.

[37] H. J. Gans, *The Urban Villagers*, New York: The Free Press of Glencoe, 1962, Chap. 11, p. 246.

[38] J. Dollard, *Caste and Class in a Southern Town*, New Haven, Conn.: Yale University Press, 1937, p. 276; For a historical account of this phenomenon see E. F. Frazier, *The Negro Family in the United States*, Chicago University of Chicago Press, 1934. For the results of such family structure see Gans, Chap. 11; A. Kardiner and S. L. Ovesey, *The Mark of Oppression*, New York: W. W. Norton & Company, Inc., 1951; Miller, p. 5–19, p. 9.

class subculture stresses male dominance outside the family circle it allows women to enter relationships with men mainly via sex and in situations of an episodic and instrumental nature.[39]

Among lower class Negroes there has usually been found permissiveness in sexual socialization and control,[40] early sexual experience among boys and girls,[41] promiscuous behavior of girls, and the use of sex by boys for achieving status and as an indication of masculinity. For girls sex provides prestige and a way to enter the boys' peer groups.[42]

Subculture: The Age Factor. The analysis in the present study reveals that most of those who are involved in the crime of rape are adolescents and young adults. Hence, sexual aggression should be considered also in the perspective of age. It can be assumed that the natural developmental processes *together* with the manner in which the lower class subculture[43] handles them,

partially explains the extent to which these age groups resort to sexual aggression. Sexual experimentation usually takes place in the peer groups,[44] and in the lower class it involves promiscuous relations with girls who are targets for such exploits.[45] These lower class patterns are part of the general pattern of delinquency;[46] and they are aided by the availability of "marked" girls in the milieu, who are not themselves devoid of aggressive sexuality.[47] The sexual conduct of adolescents partially reflects the general aggressiveness which prevails in other aspects of the subculture.[48]

SUMMARY

The study was able to refute some of the misconceptions surrounding the crime of rape. The following is a list of some of the *myths* which were challenged by the findings of the study.[49]

(1) *Negro men are more likely to attack*

[39] M. Brenman, "Urban Lower Class Negro Girls," *Psychiatry*, 6 (1943), pp. 307–324; J. F. Short, Jr., F. L. Strodtbeck, and D. C. Cartwright, "A Strategy of Utilizing Research Dilemmas: A Case from the Study of Parenthood in Street-Corner Gangs," *Sociological Inquiry*, 22 (1962), pp. 185–192.
[40] A. T. Childers, "Some Notes on Sexual Mores among Negro Children," *American Journal of Orthopsychiatry*, 6 (1936), pp. 442–446; A. Davis and R. J. Havighurst, "Social Class and Color Differences in Child Rearing," *The American Sociological Review*, 11 (1946), pp. 298–712; E. F. Frazier, "Negro Sexuality," in Albert Ellis and Albert Arbanel, eds., *Encyclopedia of Sexual Behavior*, Vol. II, New York: Hawthorn, 1961, pp. 769–775; E. F. Frazier, "Sex Morality among Negroes," *Religious Education*, 23 (1943), pp. 447–450.
[41] Childers, Davis and Havighurst, pp. 298–712; L. B. Haman and B. Schoffner, "Sex Life of Unmarried Men," *American Journal of Sociology*, 52 (1946), pp. 501–507; W. B. Miller, "Implications of Lower Class Culture for Social Work," *Social Service Review*, 33 (1959), pp. 219–236.
[42] J. F. Short, Jr., and F. L. Strodtbeck, "Values and Gang Delinquency," *American Journal of Sociology*, 69 (1963), pp. 109–128.
[43] On the general problems of adolescence and sexual development see P. Blos, *The Adolescent Personality: A Study of Individual Behavior*, New

York: Appleton-Century-Crofts, Inc., 1941. Of the classical works concerned with psychosexuality and the reaction-ego defense of youth see A. Freud, *The Ego Mechanisms of Defense*, New York: International Universities Press, Inc., 1946.
[44] H. A. Bloch and A. Neiderhoffer, *The Gang*, New York: Philosophical Library, Inc., 1958; *California Sexual Deviation Research* (final report), Sacramento: State of California, Department of Mental Hygiene, March, 1954, pp. 122–136; Hollingshead, pp. 110–142, 421. Also, M. and C. W. Sherif, *Reference Groups*, New York: Harper & Row, Publishers, 1964. This source contains extensive references on this phenomenon among lower class delinquents, pp. 57–67. On the general problem of youth culture in America, see T. Parsons, "Youth in the Context of American Society," *Daedalus*, 91 (1962), pp. 97–123.
[45] Miller, "Lower Class Culture as a Generating Milieu of Gang Delinquency," p. 5–19; Reiss, pp. 312–314; Whyte, pp. 24–31.
[46] J. C. N., Gibbens, "Sexual Behavior of Young Criminals," *Journal of Mental Science*, 103 (1957), pp. 527–540; also note 44.
[47] Reiss, pp. 312–314; Whyte, pp. 24–31.
[48] Miller, "Implications of Lower Class Culture for Social Work," pp. 219–236; S. Wheeler, "Sex Offenses: A Sociological Critique," *Law and Contemporary Problems*, 25 (1960), p. 276; Short, Strodtbeck, and Cartwright, pp. 185–192.
[49] For one good discussion of the problem with an attempt to disprove it by statistics see G. J. Falk, "The Public Image of the Sex Offender," *Mental Hygiene*, 48 (1964), pp. 612–620.

white women than Negro women. Rape, it was found, is an intraracial event, especially between Negro men and women.

(2) *Rape is symptomatic of a demographic structural strain due to sex-marital status imbalance in the social structure.* This theory was refuted, along with the derivative assumption about age-sex imbalance which might exist within the general populations.

(3) *Rape is a hot-season crime.* Rape was found not to be particularly associated with the summer months, but spread over all seasons and months of the year. The "thermic law of delinquency" is not confirmed by the present study.

(4) *Rape usually occurs between total strangers.* This assumption was challenged by the analysis of several variables. First, rape in a sizable proportion of cases is ecologically bound—that is, it occurs between males and females who live in the same area—a fact that allowed victim and offender some knowledge of each other. In more than one third of the cases studied they knew each other as close neighbors or as acquaintances. Second, offenders and victims frequently met in the home or place of sojourn of either one of them, and the offense also occurred in that place.

(5) *Rape is associated with drinking.* In two thirds of the cases alcohol was absent from the rape situation.

(6) *Rape victims are innocent persons.* One fifth of the victims had a police record, especially for sexual misconduct. Another 20 percent had "bad" reputations.

(7) *Rape is predominantly an explosive act.* In almost three quarters of the cases rape was found to be a planned event, especially when the meeting place was in the residence of one of the participants or when the rape was a group affair.

(8) *Rape takes place in a dead-end street or dark alley.* A significant association was found to occur between the place where the victim and offender initially met each other (especially when the meeting was in the residence of one of the participants) and the place of rape.

(9) *Rape is always a violent crime in which brutality is inflicted upon the victim.* In a large number of cases (87 percent) only temptation and verbal coercion were used initially to subdue the victim; in 15 percent no physical force was used at all against the victim; and in almost 50 percent of the cases when force—in one degree or another—was used, the victim was only manhandled.

(10) *The law is always justified in rigidly demanding the victim's resistance or some form of "genuine" nonconsent on her part in order to establish later that rape occurred.* The folk and literary expression which cast doubt on the prevalence of resistance, and hence on the assumption on which this demand is based, are found equally convincing. As it is commonly believed that almost no woman wants to be deprived of her sexual self-determination, it was surprising to find that over 50 percent of the victims failed to resist their attackers in any way. Race, age, and special circumstances were given as explanations for this result, but it seems that the law should give these factors more consideration.

(11) *Rape is a one-to-one forced sexual relationship.* Among our cases, over two fifths (43 percent) were found to be multiple-rape cases. The possibilities which are open for sociological and criminological studies are numerous, and it is hoped that someone will investigate them.

(12) *Victims are not responsible for their victimization either consciously or by*

default. The proportion of rape events precipitated by the victim and the characteristics of such rape events refute this claim and open the door for fruitful studies which might be made in the field of "victimology."

CHILD MOLESTERS: A STUDY OF THEIR CAREERS AS DEVIANTS*

Charles H. McCaghy

This study tests four major hypotheses concerning careers of 181 persons convicted of sex offenses against children. The sample was divided into three categories of interaction according to the extent to which the offender's life pattern involved children. These three groups differed significantly in the amount of coercion used in the child molesting, the context of the offense encounter, and the form of sexual contact. Verbalized motives were also studied in connection with their relation to offenses, societal reaction, and the motives offenders attributed to others.

Although various forms of sexual behavior are punishable by criminal law, the severity of sanctions is based on criteria which include the degree of consent between participants, the nature of the participants or objects, the nature of the sexual act, and the setting in which the act occurs.[1] Child molesters, because of the nature of the participants in their offenses, are singled out as objects of special legal and psychiatric concern in the United States.

The legal concern over child molesting is best illustrated by the existence of "statutory rape" laws forbidding consensual intercourse with underaged females. Penalties under these laws are harsher than under laws prohibiting essentially the same offense with adults: adultery, fornication, and lewd cohabitation. Such concern is also evident from statutes in many states which provide increased penalties when a child is involved in offenses categorized as ordinary rape, indecent liberties, homosexual contacts, and indecent exposure. In other words, the criminal codes in the United States reflect a greater concern over sexual contacts with children than over similar illicit contacts with adults.

Legal action against child molesting is not restricted to relatively severe penal sanctions, however. In twenty-six states plus the District of Columbia, there have been enacted "sexual psychopath statutes" under which sex offenders, contingent upon psychiatric examination, may be sentenced to

[1] Stanton Wheeler, "Sex Offenses: A Sociological Critique," *Law and Contemporary Problems*, 25 (1960), pp. 258–259.

* This selection, written especially for this book, is published here for the first time. McCaghy prepared it from his "Child Molesters: A Study of Their Careers as Deviants," unpublished Ph.D. dissertation, University of Wisconsin, 1966.

indefinite periods of "treatment."[2] Of course, these laws are also applicable to sex offenders other than child molesters; but it should be noted that psychiatrists have especially singled out molesters as likely to be suffering from mental disorder. For example, London and Caprio define child molesting as a "serious medico-legal problem," while Guttmacher and Weihoffen tell us there is probably no other "group of criminal offenders with which the court can get more help in arriving at proper disposition through a complete psychiatric evaluation."[3] The Group for the Advancement of Psychiatry has specifically listed "age disparity" (relations between a child and an adult) as one of the criteria of mental disorder where a sexual offense is involved.[4]

Thus psychiatrists, whose ostensible task is to deal with the mentally disordered, view with suspicion persons who have used children as sexual objects. And psychiatric interest in molesters is not merely academic: states having sexual psychopath laws rely upon psychiatric judgments as to whether an individual molester is "normal" and should be sentenced under the usual criminal code, or whether he is "mentally disordered" and should be committed for an indefinite period of psychiatric treatment.

Despite psychiatrists' claims of knowledge about molesters, however, until recently there have been no systematic studies

distinguishing among different types of molesters; and in the several existing empirical and clinical studies of molesters, no attempt has been made to account for the variety of forms child molesting assumes.[5] Despite the unique legal and psychiatric stigmas which attach to child molesters, previous studies have not explored the impact of societal reaction upon these offenders.

The present sociological study will (1) demonstrate that neither molesters nor their offenses are homogeneous entities and that a typology of molesters, incorporating the characteristics of their offenses, may be feasible and (2) test hypotheses concerning relationships between societal reaction against deviance and the ways in which molesters verbally cope with that reaction.

The first task of this study was to test whether there were any relationships between characteristics of the offenders and their offenses. We assumed, first, that children might have other than sexual meanings for some molesters. The sense of "meaning" here is similar to Shibutani's concept of sentiment:

A sentiment is one type of meaning—an organized disposition to act toward a personification upon which some kind of value is placed. To hate someone is to be prepared to act in an aggressive or defensive manner toward him. . . . Sentiments may be defined behav-

[2] For a discussion of the provisions of these laws, see Alan H. Swanson, "Sexual Psychopath Statutes: Summary and Analysis," Journal of Criminal Law, Criminology and Police Science, 51 (1960), pp. 215–236.
[3] Louis S. London and Frank S. Caprio, Sexual Deviations, Washington, D.C.: Linacre Press, 1950, p. 606; and Manfred S. Guttmacher and Henry Weihoffen, Psychiatry and the Law, New York: W. W. Norton & Company, Inc., 1952, p. 115.
[4] Group for the Advancement of Psychiatry, Psychiatrically Deviated Sex Offenders, Report No. 9, May 1949, Revised February 1950, Topeka, Kans.: Committee on Forensic Psychiatry of the Group for the Advancement of Psychiatry, p. 2. Thomas J. Meyers provides the precise age range of the victim for purposes of diagnosis: below fourteen. "Psychiatric Examination of the Sexual Psychopath," Journal of Criminal Law, Criminology and Police Science, 56 (1965), p. 28.

[5] Some of the current studies which have focused on statistical data include Paul H. Gebhard, et al., Sex Offenders, New York: Harper & Row, Publishers 1965, passim; Louise V. Frisbie and Ernest H. Dondis, Recidivism among Treated Sex Offenders, California Mental Health Research Monograph No. 5, Sacramento: State of California Department of Mental Hygiene, 1965; and J. W. Mohr, R. E. Turner, and M. B. Jerry, Pedophilia and Exhibitionism, Toronto: University of Toronto Press, 1965. Primarily clinical observations of child molesters will be found in Bernard C. Glueck, Jr., "Psychodynamic Patterns in the Sex Offenders, New York: Julian Press, Inc., 1954, 1–21; V. Hartman, "Some Observations of Group Psychotherapy with Paedophiles," Canadian Journal of Corrections, 3 (1961), pp. 492–499; Benjamin Karpman, The Sexual Offender and His Offenses, New York: Julian Press, Inc., 1954, passim; and P. G. Thomson, "Sexual Deviation," Canadian Medical Association Journal, 80 (1959), pp. 381–389.

ioristically not so much in terms of any particular act but through their organization. The various movements are directed toward a goal, but diverse means are selected to achieve it depending upon the circumstances.[6]

Individuals can thus view children in many different ways which will be reflected in their general behavior patterns toward them. When child molesting occurs, the meaning children have for the offender should be reflected in the offense situation. In symbolic interactionist terms, some adults see children as "significant others" whose judgments and appreciation are crucial for the adults' self-concepts. Such adults would not jeopardize their self-concepts by committing acts which would detract from the children's regard for them. We suggested, therefore, that among molesters who regard children as significant others, the offense would be of a nature not likely to alienate or harm the child.

Since this study dealt with persons officially labeled as child molesters, their own statements concerning the meaning which children had for them prior to the offense might well be biased. Thus, for research purposes, "meaning" was measured by the range of interaction which adults had with children: the extent to which their life patterns were occupied by contacts with children. The rationale here was that individuals whose occupational and leisure activities involved contacts with children would be more likely to value the opinions of children than would individuals whose contacts were minimal or limited to their own offspring. The hypothesis tested was: *The range of molesters' interaction with children is related to the characteristics of their molesting behavior.*

The second hypothesis examined the manner in which molesters accounted for their behavior in the face of societal reaction.[7] When behavior conforms to the ex-

pectations of one's group, it will not be questioned; but when an act does not conform to expectations, inquiries will be made of the actor. The motives verbalized at this point are not necessarily "real motives," yet neither may they be merely rationalizations or attempts at *ex post facto* justification. When a person expresses motives for his past behavior, he is supplying socially available answers in an attempt to convince others and himself of the propriety of his actions. Motives justifying deviant behavior are not invented by the individual but already exist within the language of society. The motives are for him, at least, socially acceptable justifications for his past behavior and may, as such, serve equally well for present and future conduct.

Previous sociological studies illustrate the point we are making here. Studies by Cressey, Sykes and Matza, Becker, and Jackman, O'Toole, and Geis reveal that deviants do not necessarily possess values contrary to those of conventional society but, rather, learn socially available motives which are instrumental in decreasing the effectiveness of social control.[8]

While the deviant is interested in justifying his actions to others, the explanation he offers must also make sense to himself. An individual looks upon himself as a particular kind of person capable of acting in many ways and in many roles; the motives he expresses must be compatible with his conception of who he is and what roles he believes to be his. In the face of societal reaction, he may find that motives previously intelligible to him are not consistent or even "correct" for explaining his behavior because he cannot conceive of himself as de-

---

[6] Tamotsu Shibutani, *Society and Personality* (Englewood Cliffs, N.J.: Prentice-Hall, Inc., 1961), pp. 332–333.

[7] The following discussion draws upon comments on vocabularies of motive by Hans Gerth and C. Wright Mills, *Character and Social Structure,*

New York: Harcourt, Brace & World, Inc., 1953, pp. 114–119.

[8] Donald R. Cressey, *Other People's Money,* New York: The Free Press of Glencoe, 1953, pp. 93–138; Gresham M. Sykes and David Matza, "Techniques of Neutralization: A Theory of Delinquency," *American Sociological Review,* 22 (1957), pp. 664–670; Howard S. Becker, *Outsiders,* New York: The Free Press of Glencoe, 1963, pp. 72–78; and Norman R. Jackman, Richard O'Toole, and Gilbert Geis, "The Self-Image of the Prostitute," *Sociological Quarterly,* 4 (1963), p. 150–161.

liberately playing that role.[9] If deviants draw upon socially available motives in explaining their offenses, we would expect that as their behavior departs more and more from social expectations, it will become increasingly difficult for them to offer motives that will be acceptable to themselves and to others. In the light of these assumptions the following hypothesis was tested: *Verbalized motives are related to the degree to which molesting offenses deviate from sexual norms.*

The third hypothesis was concerned with societal reaction to molesting in relation to changes in verbalized motives over time. When molesters enter the legal process, they discover that their explanations for their behavior do not free them from sanctions: some molesters are found to need psychiatric treatment, some are sentenced to prison under the ordinary criminal code, and still others are placed on probation. These alternative forms of societal reaction may not only create different incentives to change motives but also differentially provide molesters with new motives. The hypothesis tested was: *Changes in verbalized motives are related to the type of societal reaction experienced.*

The last hypothesis represented an attempt to discover whether a sense of identification existed between the individual molester and other molesters. The concept of identification used here does not refer to actual membership in a group of child molesters, nor does it imply that the individual is necessarily seeking status within a "world" of child molesters. Instead, it concerns the degree to which molesters perceive that they share a common point of view with other molesters. Do molesters perceive other molesters as acting with motives similar to their own, or do they consider their own motives to be unique?

Verbalized motives serve a two fold purpose: just as a person's own motives place his behavior into a meaningful context for him, the motives he imputes to others make their behavior comprehensible to him. The individual assigns motives both to himself and to others to facilitate social intercourse. The very fact that a molester has been labeled deviant makes it likely that he will experience ambivalent feelings with regard to his identity. If he denies his offense or claims he had no control over his actions, it would be inconsistent for him to identify with other individuals who molest. On the other hand, if he offers an explanation which renders his own behavior "understandable" under the circumstances, he may extend the same motives to others, even to the point of justifying molesters' behavior in general. The hypothesis tested was: *Motives verbalized by molesters differ from the motives they attribute to other molesters.*

RESEARCH PROCEDURES

Characteristics of the Sample. For purposes of this research, a child molester was defined as a male, eighteen years or older, who had been convicted of an offense in which the genitals of a child (thirteen years or younger) were exposed or manipulated by the adult, or in which the adult had the child view or manipulate his (the adult's) genitals. In selecting a sample of molesters, it was necessary to consider the probability that not all molesters would have been convicted under a statute directly applying to molesting offenses. Frequently the charge on which a criminal is found guilty is the result of a "bargaining" procedure.[10] Therefore, the sample was drawn by investigating the records of persons convicted under all

[9] Donald R. Cressey applies this notion to persons conceiving themselves as "kleptomaniacs": "Role Theory, Differential Association, and Compulsive Crimes," in *Human Behavior and Social Processes*, Arnold M. Rose (ed.), Boston: Houghton Mifflin Company, 1962, pp. 460–461.

[10] Donald J. Newman, "Pleading Guilty for Considerations: A Study of Bargaining Justice," *Journal of Criminal Law, Criminology and Police Science*, 46 (1956), pp. 780–790; and David Sudnow, "Normal Crimes: Sociological Features of the Penal Code in a Public Defender Office," *Social Problems*, 12 (1965), pp. 255–276.

statutes, ranging from disorderly conduct to rape, which might logically be applicable when convicting a child molester. To obtain as complete a sample as possible, persons placed on probation as well as those incarcerated were included.

The sample consisted of the following: (1) all molesters incarcerated in Wisconsin state correctional institutions during February 1964; (2) all molesters on probation in Dane County, Wisconsin, during February 1964; and (3) all molesters on probation in Milwaukee County, Wisconsin, during April 1964. The sample totaled 181 subjects, of whom 124 were incarcerated and 57 were on probation.

Subjects were generally of low socio-economic status: the usual employment of 74 percent was in unskilled and semiskilled occupations; their mean education was 8.6 years. Fourteen percent resided in places of under 2500 population while 59 percent resided in cities of over 100,000. The mean ages of the subjects and of their victims were 37.3 and 9.0 years, respectively.

Data Collection. Data for this research were obtained from two sources: official records and interviews. The official records provided background information on the subjects as well as details of the molesting offenses of which they had been convicted. In terms of the variables investigated, the records assisted in classifying subjects according to their range of interaction with children, provided data on the characteristics of the molesting behavior, and indicated the motives which convicted molesters expressed to correctional personnel.

The interviews followed a semistructured format similar to the "focused interview" described by Merton, Fiske, and Kendall.[11] The principal goals of the interviews were to complete information on the subjects' range of interaction with children

[11] Robert K. Merton, Marjorie Fiske, and Patricia L. Kendall, *The Focused Interview,* New York: Free Press of Glencoe, 1956.

prior to their offenses, to ascertain their current motives for the offenses, and to discover their impressions of the motives of other molesters. One hundred fifty-eight of the 181 subjects were interviewed on a voluntary basis.

Space does not permit a detailed analysis of the data sources; suffice it to say that the author was aware of the deficiencies of official records as sources of data but that he was reasonably satisfied that in the great majority of cases these records were remarkably complete and accurate. Although there were no objective checks, it was also believed that a high degree of rapport was obtained in all but a few interview situations.

*INTERACTION
WITH CHILDREN
AND CIRCUMSTANCES
OF OFFENSE*

The range of molesters' interaction with children was related to the characteristics of their molesting behavior. On the basis of information from official records and interviews, the sample of molesters was divided into three categories according to their range of interaction with children: (1) *minimal*—60 subjects who had little or no previous contact with children; (2) *limited*—103 subjects who resided with children, who had contacts with relatives' children, or who interacted with children in the immediate neighborhood; and (3) *high*—18 subjects whose life pattern involved many contacts with children outside their own home and immediate neighborhood.

These categories of molesters were compared on four characteristics of their offenses: (1) familiarity of victims; (2) amount of coercion used; (3) context of the offense encounter; and (4) form of sexual contact. The resultant distributions all took the direction anticipated and chi-square tests revealed that all were signifi-

cantly different from chance distributions
(p < .05).[12]

Familiarity of Victims. Consistent with
other studies, the present investigation
found that most molesters (68 percent)
were at least casually acquainted with their
victims.[13] However, 50 percent of the minimal interaction offenders molested strangers, compared to only 11 percent of the
high interaction offenders. Twenty-five percent of the victims of limited interaction
molesters were strangers, while 49 percent
were known because they resided in the
molester's residence (they were usually but
not always related).

Subjects who molested relatives or non-
relatives within the same residence were
not generally involved with children; in the
majority of cases their victims were the only
children with whom they had any extended
contact. On the other hand, high interaction molesters often appeared to distinguish
between the roles of "authority over" and
"sexual partner of" children. The majority
of their victims, while well known to the
offenders, were not their charges (pupils,
daughters, and so forth).

Amount of Coercion. In this study, as in
others, it was found that molesting offenses
were generally not accompanied by overt
coercion.[14] In 76 percent of the cases there
was no evidence of any type of coercion:

4 percent of the subjects used verbal threats;
17 percent used force only in order to gain
compliance; and 3 percent inflicted actual
physical violence upon the child. As anticipated, no high interaction molester used
any form of coercion, whereas over one
third of the minimal interaction subjects
did so. In all cases in which the child was
harmed, the offenders were minimal interaction molesters. Limited interaction molesters used coercion in one fifth of their offenses.

Sociologists have suggested that the use
of physical force to attain goals is a way
of life for some segments of society, that
the physically aggressive individual is the
product of a normative system supporting
violence.[15] Although it has been suggested
that such a system is most likely to be
found among the lower social classes, our
data failed to reveal a significant relationship between occupational level and
amount of coercion employed in molesting
offenses.

Another variable found to be related
to use of coercion was the familiarity of
the victim: while offenses involving strangers and casual acquaintances were characterized by coercion in one third of the
cases, coercion was used against close acquaintances and victims residing in the
molester's household in only 14 and 15 percent of the cases, respectively.[16]

Context of the Encounter. "Context" refers to the nature of the interaction between
adult and child immediately preceding the
offense: (1) sexual only—this encounter

---

[12] The criterion set for rejecting hypotheses was a
level of significance less than .05. Hereafter, the
term "related" will be used only when the chi-
square value for the distribution of variables
meets that criterion.

[13] Gebhard *et al.*, pp. 773–775; Mohr *et al.*, p. 28;
R. W. Bowling, "The Sex Offender and Law
Enforcement," *Federal Probation*, 14 (1950),
p. 14; *Final Report: Research Project for the
Study and Treatment of Persons Convicted of
Crimes Involving Sexual Aberrations, June 1952
to June 1955*, Bernard C. Glueck, Director, New
York: n. p., n. d., p. 295; and *Report of the
Governor's Study Commission on the Deviated
Criminal Sex Offender*, Lansing, Mich.: n. p.,
n. d., pp. 31 and 215.

[14] *Final Report*, pp. 293–295; and Gebhard *et al.*,
pp. 38 and 820.

[15] Walter B. Miller, "Lower Class Culture as a
Generating Milieu of Gang Delinquency," *Journal of Social Issues*, 14 (1958), pp. 5–19; and
Martin Gold, "Suicide, Homicide, and the Socialization of Aggression," *American Journal of
Sociology*, 63 (1958), pp. 651–661. For discussions of the relationship between social class
and the use of violence in sex offenses, see
Wheeler, pp. 276–277, and Leon F. Fannin, "A
Study of the Social Class Affiliation and Societal
Reaction to Convicted Sex and Non-Sex Offenders," unpublished Ph.D. dissertation, University
of Wisconsin, 1962, pp. 175–181.

[16] Cf. Gebhard *et al.*, pp. 149, 774–775, and 817.

is best described as spontaneous: the adult approached the child and immediately commenced the sexual act; there was no evidence of preliminary nonsexual interaction; (2) enticement—this includes cases in which the adult interacted with his victim only long enough to lure him into a situation conducive to molesting; (3) nonsexual —this category includes cases in which the molesting occurred during the course of nonsexual interaction with the child; the preoffense interaction ostensibly did *not* occur solely for the purpose of deceiving the child, as in the second category. For the total sample, the context of the molesting encounter was categorized as sexual only, enticement, and nonsexual in 23, 28, and 49 percent of the cases, respectively. As anticipated, the offenses of high interaction molesters were generally preceded by nonsexual interaction: 83 percent compared to 48 and 39 percent for the limited and minimal interaction molesters. No high interaction molester committed his offense without some prior interaction with his victim, even if it were solely for the purpose of enticement, whereas minimal and limited interaction molesters made sexual contacts without any preliminary interaction in 25 and 26 percent of their cases, respectively.[17]

Form of Sexual Contact. The offenses of high interaction molesters were limited primarily to acts involving manipulation of the genitals, of or by the victim or both. Such contacts characterized 78 percent of the high interaction molesters' offenses and accounted for 42 and 31 percent of the minimal and limited interaction molesters' offenses. Offenses involving genital-genital contacts and "perversions" (fellatio, cunnilingus, genital-anal contacts, and so forth)

---

[17] While space limitations do not permit an examination of the role of the victim in these offenses, there is evidence that in sex offenses involving children the distinction between "victimized" and "victimizer" is frequently a tenuous one. Gebhard *et al.*, pp. 792–797, 812; *Final Report*, p. 296; and Karpman, pp. 67–70.

were found in these proportions: high interactions—22 percent; limited interaction—63 percent; and minimal interaction—44 percent. Residual percentages concern cases in which the adults simply exposed themselves to the children.

Form of sexual contact was also related to the familiarity of the victim. When victims, both related and unrelated to the molesters, lived in the same residence as the molesters, 73 percent of the offenses involved genital-genital contacts or perversions. For close acquaintances residing apart, these types of contacts accounted for 54 percent of the offenses; for casual acquaintances and strangers, 43 percent.

CIRCUMSTANCES OF OFFENSE AND VERBALIZED MOTIVES

We have suggested that molesters, when called to account for their behavior, draw upon socially available explanations, explanations which are differentially available according to the extent to which their behavior departs from normative expectations. To test this hypothesis we tried to discover whether relationships existed between the characteristics of molesters' offenses and the types of explanations they gave to officials *after* being found guilty. It was anticipated that as molesters' behavior departed from sexual role expectations in terms of the victims' age, amount of coercion used, form of sexual contact, and sex of the victims, there would be a tendency for them either to deny that molesting had occurred or to admit the offenses but deny responsibility for it because of loss of rationality: they were "too drunk" to know what they were doing; "everything went blank"; and so on. These "motives of denial," accounting for 47 percent of all motives, differ from other motives in which molesters simply admit their offenses, share the blame with the victims, or point to conditions (other than loss of rationality) which contributed to the behavior, such as trouble in the family, and so forth.

The data used to test the hypothesis concerning motives were those recorded in official records by social workers, probation officers, and, in a few instances, psychiatrists, who questioned molesters shortly after conviction and sentencing. Since convicted offenders had little to gain at this point by denying their offenses (except the maintenance of their self-concepts), it was assumed that such motives represented the extent of acceptance of their role in the behavior rather than attempts to gain concessions. Since there was a theoretical reason to believe that prior "labeling" procedures might alter self-concepts, only those offenders who had not been previously arrested for a molesting offense were included in the investigation.[18]

Verbalized motives were found not to be related to the degree to which molesting offenses deviated from sexual norms. Significant relationships were found in testing subhypotheses in only two of four instances.

Age of Victims. While the distribution of victims' ages and types of motives was in the direction anticipated, the distribution was not significantly different from chance: 55 percent of the molesters of younger victims (ages two to nine) compared to 40 percent of those with older victims (ages ten to thirteen) used motives of denial. The lack of a significant difference was due in part to the fact that molesters of younger victims often relied upon explanations involving children's sexual curiosity and "accidents" in which victims came upon the adults while they were bathing or urinating. Such themes did not occur among molesters of older victims, who emphasized their victims' sexual sophistication: "I knew she had been broken in a long time ago because

[18] Edwin M. Lemert, *Social Pathology*, New York: McGraw-Hill Book Company, Inc., 1951, pp. 73–78; Mary Owen Cameron, *The Booster and the Snitch*, New York: The Free Press of Glencoe, 1964, pp. 159–170; and Becker, pp. 31–39. Our data revealed, however, no significant differences between motives of 129 "first-time" molesters and 42 subjects who had been previously arrested for molesting.

I have seen her in a station wagon in the yard playing hanky-panky."

Amount of Coercion. As anticipated, a significant relationship existed between the use of coercion and types of motives: molesters accused of employing threats, force, and violence expressed motives of denial in 68 percent of their cases, whereas such motives were used by only 40 percent of molesters involved in noncoercive offenses.

Form of Sexual Contact. It was anticipated that molesters who engaged in legally more serious offenses would use motives of denial more frequently than those who simply exposed themselves or limited the offense to caressing and fondling. However, motives of denial were used in the following percentages of cases: exposure, 50; manipulation, 52; genital-genital, 52; and perversions, 33. This distribution did not differ significantly from chance.

Sex of Victims. While 53 percent of those who molested females used motives of denial, only 25 percent of those who molested males did so. This distribution differed significantly from chance but in a direction opposite that anticipated. It had been assumed that since homosexual contacts represent a greater departure from sexual role expectations, homosexual molesters would tend to rely on motives divorcing themselves from their offenses. Molesters of boys, however, were often very candid; 58 percent simply admitted their offenses without any elaboration. Furthermore, they were more likely than molesters of girls to admit to officials that although this was their first arrest for molesting, they had engaged in homosexual behavior for some time, either with children, with adults, or with both. An admittedly extreme example was the subject who claimed at least eighty homosexual contacts with young boys without a single arrest.

It appears that many homosexual molesters have previously accepted a homosexual role, which in itself represents a drastic departure from the sexual norms of conventional society. Being accused of molesting does not constitute a threat to their present self-concepts as sexual deviants. Since deviant sexual behavior is already a way of life for them, they do not feel compelled to deny responsibility for the molesting offense. This interpretation was lent support during the author's interviews with these molesters. Many considered themselves to be first of all homosexuals. Their contact with a person under the age of fourteen was, to them, unfortunate and perhaps accidental, but only secondary to their basic sexual behavior patterns. Since they were already at odds with approved sexual norms, the molesting offense did not result in any need for serious self-examination.

CHANGES IN MOTIVES

The third hypothesis concerned whether changes in verbalized motives were related to the type of societal reaction which molesters experienced. Changes were measured by comparing motives recorded in official records with the motives expressed to the author during his interviews with 158 subjects.[19] The types of societal reaction considered possibly related to changes in verbalized motives were (1) types of correctional supervision—probation and incarceration, and (2) amount of exposure to psychiatric therapy.

Probation and Incarceration. While it was not the purpose of this study to evaluate the relative effectiveness of incarceration and probation in changing attitudes, there were three reasons for anticipating that probationers would be less likely than incarcerated molesters to change their verbal interpretations of their offenses: (1) the probationary situation generates no urgency to re-evaluate one's motives, an urgency which

can develop under conditions of incarceration where release may seem to depend upon the presentation of oneself to treatment staff and parole boards; (2) probationers remain in essentially the same milieu they have always known, while incarcerated offenders must daily face the tangible consequences of being labeled deviant; (3) the prison setting, with its contacts with treatment staff and with other inmates, is more likely to expose individuals to new motives for past behavior.

Although the distribution of motive changes was in the direction anticipated (half the incarcerated sample changed their motives whereas only a third of the probationary sample did so), the Chi-square of the distribution was not significant at the .05 level. While it was discovered that probationers changed their motives more often than expected, it was also determined that of those who did, 36 percent changed *away from* acceptance of responsibility for the behavior to claims that the offenses had never occurred or that they were not responsible for their actions. In other words, probationers who originally accepted responsibility for their offenses now expressed disbelief that they were even capable of the behavior. This type of change accounted for only 2 percent of the incarcerated sample's revisions.

A recurrent theme of detachment from the offense was also apparent during interviews with probationers; even those who took full responsibility for their offenses wished to "forget." The offense was "all over" or they did not "care to think about it." Such remarks rarely came from incarcerated molesters.

Therapy. As mentioned earlier, psychiatrists view the child molester as an especially appropriate subject for their discipline. In Wisconsin psychiatrists have an instrument, the Wisconsin Sex Crimes Law,[20] to

---

[19] The interviewed portion of the sample consists of 115 subjects who were incarcerated and 43 on probation.

[20] *Wisconsin Statutes* (1958), 959.15. Fifty-seven percent of the subjects in the total sample were convicted under this law.

implement treatment of such offenders. The State Welfare Department maintains control over persons convicted under the law "as long as in its judgment such control is necessary for the protection of the public." For the offender, the indeterminate aspect of the law can be a compelling feature: he may be released sooner than under any other arrangement, but he may also be detained for years longer than would be permitted under a prison sentence imposed in accordance with the ordinary criminal code.

Assuming that most molesters are interested in terminating their stay as soon as possible, they may quickly perceive the importance of treatment sessions toward that end. As one psychiatrist involved in this program succinctly stated:

It is mandatory for those under the sex deviate facility to respond to some form of treatment as a condition of their release. This provides an incentive that is not present in the usual manipulation for parole on the part of those committed under the criminal code.[21]

Thus provided with "incentive," an offender must perceive how to "respond" to treatment. Since the treatment staff's contact with offenders is generally limited to treatment sessions, it is here that their evaluation of the offender's progress takes place. The molester's problem becomes how to express himself in a manner that will convince staff members that he is making progress toward his release date. He will first discover that his original motives are generally inappropriate for this purpose:

Many sex offenders dismiss their behavior as being entirely the product of overindulgence in alcohol. Sometimes the offense is denied in its entirety both to the authorities and to themselves. More often attempts are made to rationalize deviant behavior by claims that the patient was seduced by sexually aggressive, precocious young boys or girls. Given the personality limitations of our patients and the impact of the prison milieu, there is need for

immediately creating a climate of acceptance which at the same time discourages rationalizations, denial, and projection.[22]

Thus, in the face of the urgency created by the indeterminate sentence, molesters find their previous motives completely unacceptable to the persons influential in terminating that sentence. They have no alternative but to embark, within the therapy setting, upon a search for new explanations to replace the old.

In order to test whether a relationship existed between changes in motives and exposure to psychiatric therapy, our sample was dichotomized into categories representing the number of sessions attended. Subjects classified under "many" sessions had attended at least eleven individual or twenty-one group therapy sessions, while those classified under "few" had attended either fewer sessions or none at all. As anticipated, molesters with many sessions exhibited significantly more changes in motives (56 percent) than did those with few sessions (27 percent).

The influence of therapy was also evident in the *kinds* of changes made. During interviews, the author often found subjects expressing motives not represented in the official records. While official records usually reported such motives as denial, intoxication, and cooperative victims, the new motives included references to early childhood experiences, psychiatric terminology, and personal inadequacies. These kinds of motives, hereafter referred to as "insight motives," accounted for 84 percent of the changes among molesters who had attended many therapy sessions and only 26 percent among those who had attended few.

Although psychiatrists connected with treatment programs are aware of this tendency on the part of their charges to adopt any vocabulary to which they are exposed, they attribute it to offenders' "inadequa-

[21] Harold F. Uehling, "Group Therapy Turns Repression into Expression for Prison Inmates," *Federal Probation*, 26 (1962), p. 47.

[22] Asher R. Pacht, Seymour L. Halleck, and John C. Ehrmann, "Psychiatric Treatment of the Sex Offender," *Current Psychiatric Therapies*, Jules H. Masserman (ed.), New York: Grune & Stratton, Inc., 1962, II, p. 176.

cies" and "passivity."[23] A perhaps more relevant explanation may lie in the structure of the treatment policy itself. Changes in verbalized motives occur because such changes are a condition of release. Molesters must reject old, unacceptable motives and discover those which are "acceptable," that is, those of which the staff approves. Furthermore, the psychiatric orientation of treatment sessions provides the direction which these new motives will take. For example:

I just wanted to be a kid again. This was from my unconscious mind, of course. I never had sex play when I was a child and I just wanted to be young and like them again.

I was still fighting my father for the affection of my mother. It is due to a confusion of the Oedipus complex—a retaliation against the mother.

It is questionable whether motives generated under such conditions are any more "real" than previous ones; they still represent attempts to explain behavior in terms understandable to the actor and to those who demand an explanation, in this case the treatment staff. It appears that offenders even come to accept such motives as satisfactory explanations, which will be more apparent when we see how insight motives are related to perceptions of other molesters.

PERCEPTIONS OF OTHER MOLESTERS

The final hypothesis, stating that molesters do not attribute to other molesters motives similar to their own, was not rejected: of 121 subjects admitting their offenses, only 36 percent (significantly less than half) assigned others the same motives they claimed for themselves. The motives most frequently attributed to others were insight motives, such as "Back in their childhood they were pampered by their mother or they didn't play with kids their own age." This type of explanation accounted for 35 percent of all attributed motives. In 27 percent

of the cases subjects either claimed they did not know why others molested or stated that they could not generalize. Twenty-four percent felt that child molesters were mentally disordered ("nuts," "off their rocker," and so forth); the residual categories included such motives as blaming the victims, getting "kicks," and affection for the victims.

Though molesters generally did not perceive of themselves as sharing common motives with other molesters, there was a significant relationship between the types of motives they verbalized and the types they attributed to others. Of those who explained their own behavior in terms of insight motives, 77 percent attributed similar motives to others and only 18 percent attributed no motive or mental disorder. Among subjects who denied either the offense or responsibility for it, no motive and mental disorder accounted for 77 percent of the attributed motives.

This relationship between types of verbalized and attributed motives can be summed up in the principle that deviants identify with other deviants to the extent that they associate themselves with their own deviant behavior. Simply because society labels an individual a deviant does not mean that he will accept that status. Indeed, he may react with militant zeal against the very group to which he has been relegated.[24] One molester who denied his offense said of other molesters:

There is something wrong with them in their upstairs. I look down on them. I don't want to associate with them and I don't associate with them.

One who claimed he was "too drunk" to know what he was doing stated:

If the guy isn't drinking there is something out of balance. He's sick; there is something wrong upstairs. If somebody touched my kid I'd kill the son-of-a-bitch.

23 Pacht et al., pp. 175–176 and 177–178.

24 This reaction is similar to the "negative chauvinism" of Jews suggested by Kurt Lewin, *Resolving Social Conflicts*, New York: Harper & Row, Publishers, 1948, pp. 188–193.

In accepting his deviant role, an offender concurs with society's judgment of him. The changes in self-concept which an individual undergoes in this process are undoubtedly complex and subject to modification through time, but the process appears to include the phenomenon of closure,[25] which operates to narrow the possible perceptions of other similar deviants. Certain explanations of others' behavior are not likely to be used because they would reflect unfavorably upon the speaker as well. On the other hand, explanations found personally satisfactory (in this case insight motives) can be extended to others, if only in the spirit of sympathy:

Before this happened I didn't think much of them, but now I know they've got the same problem I've got.

Thus psychiatric treatment, which makes it difficult for molesters to dissociate themselves from their offenses, also provides them with something they previously lacked: a sense of common identity, or, at least, of mutual sympathy.

TOWARD A TYPOLOGY OF CHILD MOLESTERS

Students of criminal behavior have long been aware of the futility of studying criminals as a homogeneous group, since offenders may have little in common except their violation of the criminal code. Researchers have thus been interested in classifying offenders into small homogeneous units which can be profitably investigated. As a result of this interest, several typologies have been developed for both theoretical and treatment purposes.[26] Within such typologies, the child molester is generally lumped together with certain other offenders. For example, Gibbons includes molesters with *all* exhibitionists and incestuous offenders under the rubric of "nonviolent sex offender, 'rapo.' "[27] Although such a "type" does have the benefit of parsimony, it definitely sacrifices completeness for conciseness. When Gibbons refers to the "nonviolent" character of an offense he is obviously aware that violence usually does *not* occur in such offenses. However, force or violence occurred in 20 percent of the cases in the present sample. Differentiating between violent and nonviolent molesters might prove crucial for treatment purposes; yet these violent offenders do not logically fit any of the other categories Gibbons has provided.

Recently there have been two attempts to differentiate various types of molesters.[28] Mohr divides them into three age groups: the adolescent group, fifteen to twenty-four; the middle-aged group, twenty-five to forty-four; and the senescent group, forty-five and over. Each group, according to the author, possesses certain common psychosocial characteristics which should be considered when making a disposition. While Mohr's study is often provocative, his typology is extremely broad and in no way accounts for the wide diversity of forms which molesting behavior may assume. Furthermore, his sample is very selective: fifty-five persons recommended by the court for psychiatric treatment on an outpatient basis. There is some question whether it is representative of incarcerated molesters. The existence of bias is suggested by the fact that unskilled and semiskilled occupations account for only 38 percent of the sample, whereas for other studies, including our own, this figure is at least 70 percent.[29]

Gebhard's investigation is more thorough and is ostensibly representative of incarcerated molesters. By "inspection" Gebhard divided into nine "varieties" sex of-

[25] Edwin M. Lemert, "An Isolation and Closure Theory of Naive Check Forgery," *Journal of Criminal Law, Criminology and Police Science*, 44 (1953), pp. 296–307.

[26] For a complete discussion and bibliography of existing typologies, see Don C. Gibbons, *Changing the Lawbreaker* (Englewood Cliffs, N.J.: Prentice-Hall, Inc., 1965), pp. 21–128.

[27] Gibbons, pp. 119–121.

[28] Mohr et al., and Gebhard et al., *passim*.

[29] *Final Report*, p. 290; and Gebhard et al., p. 51.

fenders whose victims were under twelve.[30] Since we cannot describe the typology in detail here, suffice it to say that it too fails to incorporate the circumstances of offense situations; moreover, there is a possibility of a high degree of overlap between types.

Regardless of weaknesses in Mohr's and Gebhard's typologies, they are valuable if only in indicating that child molesters are not a homogeneous lot. The research discussed here served essentially the same purpose but also showed that molesters' involvement with children is related to the characteristics of molesting offenses. This relationship failed to account for the *total* variation in offense characteristics, however. While we found that the high interaction molester commits his offense against victims with whom he is familiar, does not use coercion, molests during the course of initially nonsexual interaction, and limits the sexual contact to manipulation, it cannot be said that the converse generally applies to minimal interaction molesters. The findings of this study suggest that one type of molester has been isolated but that other types remain virtually unaccounted for. Armed with our inspection of the data plus the results of factor analysis, we tentatively suggest six types of molesters who appear to be relatively distinct from one another with regard to several characteristics, only the most prominent of which are mentioned here: (1) high interaction molester (whose characteristics have been described above); (2) incestuous molester (whose victim is related and living in his residence); (3) asocial molester (whose molesting offense is but one segment of a lawbreaking career); (4) senile molester (whose older age and low educational level distinguish him from other molesters); (5) career molester (whose current offense does not represent his only arrest for molesting); and (6) spontaneous-aggressive molester (whose offense characteristics are opposite those of the high interaction molester).

[30] Gebhard et al., pp. 73–81, 151–153, 225–229, and 294–296.

CONCLUSIONS

This study investigated a sample of persons convicted of sexual contacts with children to determine, among other things, whether the meaning children have for molesters (measured by individual molesters' range of interaction with them) accounts for the various characteristics molesting behavior assumes. There was also an interest in testing hypotheses about the impact upon molesters of societal reaction.

The discovery of significant relationships between range of interaction with children and four characteristics of molesting offenses renders questionable the usefulness of a unitary typological approach to molesters, either for causal analysis or in providing a diagnostic framework for correctional purposes. Even if we assume that molesters are generally characterized by "immaturity" and "compulsiveness," this assumption scarcely tells us anything about most acts of molesting, which are typically episodic and situationally confined. Any coherent theory of deviant sexual behavior cannot be limited to an analysis of what is "wrong" with the offender. Criminal behavior is more than a function of "immaturity" or "compulsiveness": any criminal act involves a particular type of person, a particular type of offense, and a particular time and place. In short, we need to formulate more homogeneous units out of the many diversities existing among molesters and their offenses. This research has indicated that such a typology may be feasible.

The child molester is extremely resistant to accepting full responsibility for his offense. This is consistent with both the severe societal reaction against molesting and the existence of motives which society provides for mitigating the rigidity of criminal law. If he does not deny his offense, the typical molester uses motives which magnify aspects of the law which, even in conventional society, are open to debate.

Doubts expressed about the criminal character of behavior committed while the actor is intoxicated or when the "victim" is a willing participant are hardly limited to child molesters.

One exception is the career homosexual who has wholly internalized the self-concept of a sexual deviant. A consequence of this internalization is that he is less concerned than others with justifying his behavior as a molester, a fact which suggests that the homosexual molester might be more likely to recidivate, since societal reaction against his sexual practices does not threaten his established self-concept.[31]

Society's attempts to alter molester's motives are on the whole successful. Under conditions in which accepting responsibility for the offense is a prerequisite for release, molesters come to embrace new, and presumably socially acceptable, explanations for their conduct. At the same time, they become tolerant of and sympathetic toward other molesters.

Because there has been no controlled systematic study to date indicating that compulsory treatment of child molesters prevents recidivism, some important questions must be raised for correctional personnel: (1) Is compulsory psychiatric treatment any more effective in preventing repetition of molesting than either incarceration or probation alone? It can be argued that the latter

alternatives, by pointing out the social inappropriateness of initial motives, are just as efficient as the treatment system, which forces the offender to discover new motives. (2) Despite the treatment staff's precautions, may not the new motives which molesters acquire serve as justifications for future offenses? Glasser, for example, contends that psychiatric therapy in correctional institutions often serves only to remove responsibility for behavior from the individual to unconscious conflicts, and so on.[32] Such treatment would certainly be ineffective in preventing recidivism. (3) Many not forcing the molester to accept his deviant role lead to a more systematized career of molesting than existed prior to treatment? Such role-acceptance might have self-fulfilling consequences: what might have been but episodic instances in the offender's life pattern may come to assume major proportions and molesting become a perceived behavior alternative to a greater degree than ever before.[33]

We ask these questions not in the spirit of criticism but to call attention to areas where research could profitably be focused. Only through a systematic search for the answers will we learn whether sex offenders such as child molesters warrant special legal and psychiatric concern.

[31] Limited evidence bears this out. A California study of recidivism among psychiatrically treated offenders indicates that cumulative rates for homosexual "pedophiles" are about twice those of the heterosexuals. Frisbie and Dondis, pp. 95–100.

[32] William Glasser, "Reality Psychiatry: An Effective Treatment for Delinquents," Reference Bulletin No. 24, San Diego County Probation Department, 1962.

[33] For a theoretical discussion of how labeling a deviant may serve to maintain a behavior pattern, see Thomas J. Scheff, "The Role of the Mentally Ill and the Dynamics of Mental Disorder: A Research Framework," Sociometry, 26 (1963), pp. 436–453.

CHAPTER 3

Occasional
Property
Crime

The characteristics of a fully developed criminal career include identification with crime and a conception of the self as a criminal. There is group support for criminal activity in the form of extensive association with other criminals and with criminal norms and activities. Criminality progresses to the use of more complex techniques and frequent offenses, and ultimately crime may become a sole means of livelihood. Those who have careers in crime generally engage in some type of theft of property or money.

Occasional property criminals are the opposite of career criminals. While they may commit offenses similar in type to those committed by career criminals, they do so only infrequently and irregularly. Likewise, things may be taken, checks forged, and autos stolen, but rather crudely. It has been estimated that three fourths of all check forgeries, for example, are committed by persons with no previous patterns of such behavior and an even larger proportion of shoplifting is committed by noncareer offenders. Similarly, the destruction of property through vandalism is a sporadic offense; one could hardly visualize a person making a career out of vandalism.

CRIMINAL CAREER OF THE OFFENDER

Many property offenders commit only an occasional theft of some kind. Such criminal behavior is incidental to their way of life. The offenses are so rare that such offenders in no way make a living out of crime and they do not play criminal roles.

Occasional property offenders do not identify with crime or conceive of themselves as criminals. Their offenses show little sophistication in the techniques of crime. Most of them have little real knowledge about criminal activities or of the criminal argot or vocabulary of crime.

Occasional shoplifters or pilferers, for example, as contrasted with boosters or professional shoplifters, do not, in general, define themselves as being criminals. Generally they are largely "respectable" employed persons or "respectable" housewives.[1] Similarly, a study of occasional or naive check forgers showed that they do not conceive of themselves as being criminals. As Lemert pointed out, forgery for them "emerges as behavior which is out of character or 'other than usual' for the persons involved."[2]

Nonprofessional shoplifters largely steal for their own purposes. Naive check forgers commit such offenses where other alternatives are blocked in the face of a financial problem. The offense is a product of certain difficult social situations in which the offender finds himself, a certain degree of social isolation, and a process of "closure" or "constriction of behavior alternatives subjectively held as available to the forger."[3]

Likewise, a large proportion of youths who commit vandalism are likely to be noncriminal in orientation. The fact that often nothing is stolen during acts of vandalism tends to reinforce the vandal's conception of himself merely as a prankster and not a young delinquent or criminal.[4]

A similar lack of criminal career characteristics has been noted in a study of young rural offenders who commit simple, occasional property offenses.[5] It was found that (1) their criminal behavior did not start early in their life, (2) they exhibited little progressive knowledge of criminal techniques and crime in general, (3) crime was not the sole means of livelihood, and (4) they did not conceive of themselves as criminals. The rural offenders did not identify with crime, rather they considered themselves as "reckless" and unattached to traditional ways. They were mobile, referred to their behavior as "fast," and engaged in occasional criminal activity as an adventure.

Of particular significance among occasional offenders is their ability to rationalize their criminal behavior. Department store pilferers, for example, tend

[1] Mary Owen Cameron, *The Booster and the Snitch: Department Store Shoplifting*, New York: The Free Press of Glencoe, 1964.
[2] Edwin M. Lemert, "An Isolation of Closure Theory of Naive Check Forgery," *Journal of Criminal Law, Criminology and Police Science*, 44 (October 1953), p. 300.
[3] Lemert, p. 289.
[4] Marshall B. Clinard and Andrew L. Wade, "Toward the Delineation of Vandalism as a Sub-Type in Juvenile Delinquency," *Journal of Criminal Law, Criminology, and Police Science*, 48 (January–February 1958), pp. 493–499.
[5] Marshall B. Clinard, "Rural Criminal Offenders," *American Journal of Sociology*, 50 (July 1944), pp. 38–45.

to take relatively inexpensive items of merchandise just a little above the level of that which they would purchase so that their acts, according to their views, although somewhat reprehensible, are not really criminal acts. Other rationalizations include the thought that "department stores are rich" or that many other persons also steal small items.[6]

GROUP SUPPORT OF CRIMINAL BEHAVIOR

The occasional property offender generally has little group support for his criminal behavior. He is usually unacquainted with a criminal culture or with criminal techniques. In fact, the concept of "naive" check forgery implies that such forgeries were committed by persons "with no previous contact and interaction with criminals."[7] This type of offender generally does not come from an area with a high delinquency rate. Similarly, most pilferers have had no present or sustained contact with a criminal subculture. In Cameron's study, approximately 92 percent of the women who were officially charged with shoplifting had never been convicted of an offense.[8] Some may have had such associations when they were younger, however.

In acts of vandalism several persons are usually associated, but what takes place is more the result of the collective interaction of the moment than a product of a criminal subculture or a subculture of vandalism.[9] Juvenile vandalism is largely spontaneous, unplanned behavior.

Group support of criminal behavior appears to be relatively unimportant in the activities of rural offenders who commit occasional acts of forgery, larceny, burglary, and auto theft. The rural offenders in Clinard's study had little contact with previous criminal patterns. The offenders only occasionally associated with groups in town, and group associations were minimal in regard to criminal behavior. The group associations lacked cohesion or continuity and existed more or less on a chance basis.

> We couldn't thresh for a couple of days, and so I went to town the next day and ran across some boys, and they asked me if I wanted to go to a celebration with them. I said I didn't care, for I couldn't haul bundles because it rained. And that is how it started. They wrote some checks out that day. Then we went to another one the next day, and then I got started to write some. Well, I never did know how to write a check, for they wrote most of them and cashed them, too, for I was a little bit scared to cash them. Then after a while I thought it was a pretty good idea of getting a little money on the side, so I wrote two or three and tried it out myself and they cashed them every time.[10]

[6] The extent to which the size of the victim organization may play a role in rationalization for the offender is indicated in public attitudes toward stealing from large organizations, cf. Erwin O. Smigel, "Public Attitudes toward Stealing as Related to the Size of the Victim Organization," *American Sociological Review*, 21 (June 1956), pp. 320–327.
[7] Lemert, p. 297.
[8] Cameron, p. 110.
[9] Andrew L. Wade, "Social Processes in the Act of Juvenile Vandalism," prepared paper in this volume.
[10] Clinard, p. 41.

Perhaps one reason why some occasional crimes need relatively little group support is that they are fairly easy to commit in the sense that few skills are employed. This suggests the relative unimportance of criminal associations in crimes of this type. Most persons in their everyday lives have occasion to cash personal checks. Likewise, the present day mass display of merchandise in stores makes training in theft largely unnecessary. Similarly, most acts of vandalism require little sophisticated knowledge. To some who illegally "borrow" an automobile it involves no more than driving away an unlocked car.

CORRESPONDENCE BETWEEN CRIMINAL BEHAVIOR AND LEGITIMATE BEHAVIOR PATTERNS

Occasional property offenders find little support for their criminal behavior in the legitimate behavior patterns of the society. In general, all of the offenses represent a violation of the values placed on private property. The offenders in most cases are attempting to obtain something which they consider to be necessary and important, but due to circumstances are unable to obtain through legitimate channels.

Occasional property offenders tend to be committed to the general goals of society. Naive check forgers "appear to have acquired normal attitudes and habits of law observance."[11] Department store pilferers are "respectable" citizens with little or no contact with criminal groups.[12] Juveniles involved in automobile theft, as found in a study in Detroit, come from favored neighborhoods.[13]

On the other hand, the extent to which occasional property crime represents a rejection of legitimate behavior patterns, as incorporated in middle class norms, is open to question. Much destruction of property through vandalism seems to occur as a way of challenging the complex of values associated with the emphasis placed on private property in our society. Yet, vandalism in many cases appears to be an attempt merely to derive "kicks" from the destruction of property or just to have some fun. Increasing evidence indicates that middle class legitimate behavior patterns are not internalized by all persons and groups and that many law violators are involved in a world of their own which is relatively isolated from the behavior patterns of the dominant power segments of society.[14] Others, however, feel that both delinquent and middle class legal norms are internalized and that delinquency is a product of the delinquent's relations with an inconsistent and vulnerable legal code.[15]

The "swastika incidents" that occurred in various parts of the world during the winter of 1959–1960 illustrate the way in which the same acts may have diverse meanings for the offenders. In a study of swastika daubings and related vandalistic activities, Stein and Martin suggested that two distinct types of behaviors were occurring.[16] Some of the acts represented outright hostility toward Jews, the behavior

[11] Lemert, p. 300.
[12] Cameron, p. xii.
[13] William E. Wattenberg and James Balistrieri, "Automobile Theft: A 'Favored-Group' Delinquency," *American Journal of Sociology*, 57 (May 1952), pp. 575–579.
[14] Cf. Bertram Spiller, "Delinquency and Middle Class Goals," *Journal of Criminal Law, Criminology and Police Science*, 56 (December 1965), pp. 463–478.
[15] See David Matza, *Delinquency and Drift*, New York: John Wiley & Sons, Inc., 1964.
[16] Herman D. Stein and John M. Martin, "Swastika Offenders: Variations in Etiology, Behavior and Psycho-Social Characteristics," *Social Problems*, 10 (Spring 1962), pp. 23–31.

definitely being anti-Semitic in character. On the other hand, similar acts were pursued as a part of play activity, representing only a desire for fun and excitement. Thus, although the offenses were on the surface similar, they differed markedly in the motivation of the offenders. As with all the forms of property offenses, the behaviors which may become defined as criminal are pursued for a variety of reasons, with variations occurring according to the location of the participants in the social structure. The caution to the criminologist is that in the study of criminal behavior care must be taken not to impute his own motives and values to those which underlie the behavior of the offenders.

SOCIETAL REACTION

The societal reaction toward occasional crime often is not severe, inasmuch as the offender is unlikely to have any, or at most a minor, previous record. Consequently, the charge is often likely to be dismissed or the offender placed on probation or given a suspended sentence.

In most cases the illegal behavior is carried out in isolation from the supporting values of a criminal subculture or group, and largely in a system of noncriminal relationships. The criminal behavior of the occasional offender is likely to be unstable and when confronted with legal action in the form of an arrest, which defines the behavior as actually being "criminal," the offender is usually deterred from continuing such activity.

The effect of this societal reaction generally holds true whether it is shoplifting, simple check forgery, or vandalism. Persons can behave, for example, as thieves without defining themselves as thieves. Arrests by store detectives or the police are crucial in helping to redefine a shoplifter's conception of his behavior as being merely "antisocial" or "bad," to being "criminal." As Cameron has stated, "Because the adult pilferer does not think of himself, prior to arrest, as a thief and can conceive of no group support for himself in that role, his arrest forces him to reject the role."[17] Considerable leniency is thus allowed the occasional property offender by law enforcement and judicial agencies because of the fact that such offenders are not likely to progress into a career of crime.

Another element in the moderate reaction to occasional property crime is the fact that the offenders often come from the same classes that are responsible for the enforcement of the law. In many localities the offenders are an integral part of the community. In most communities much criminal behavior of residents is ignored by the local law enforcement agencies. In a study of a rural community, Esselstyn observed that a great deal of discretion operated in the enforcement of the law and that the local sheriff interpreted the law according to the overall interests of the community.[18] The primary functions of the sheriff were to conserve the peace and to provide for the public safety. Reporting of some offenses might have actually threatened those functions. The public also knew of many offenses which were not reported for a variety of reasons. Official reaction to these offenses is increased only when the offenses are engaged in by a large number of persons to such an extent that the behavior becomes a nuisance to the community or

[17] Cameron, p. 165.
[18] T. C. Esselstyn, "The Social Role of the County Sheriff," Journal of Criminal Law, Criminology and Police Science, 44 (July–August 1953), pp. 177–184.

exceeds what is regarded as normal for the community. Through legal agencies, communities are able to establish and make viable the limits to which they will tolerate certain forms and amounts of human behavior.

SELECTED BIBLIOGRAPHY

1. Cameron, Mary Owen, *The Booster and the Snitch: Department Store Shoplifting*, New York: The Free Press, 1964.
2. Clinard, Marshall B., "Rural Criminal Offenders," *American Journal of Sociology*, 50 (July 1944), pp. 38–45.
3. Ehrlich, Howard J., "The Swastika Epidemic of 1959–1960: Anti-Semitism and Community Characteristics," *Social Problems*, 9 (Winter 1962), pp. 264–272.
4. Lemert, Edwin M., "An Isolation of Closure Theory of Naive Check Forgery," *Journal of Criminal Law, Criminology and Police Science*, 44 (September–October 1953), pp. 296–307.
5. Martin, John M., *Juvenile Vandalism*, Springfield, Ill.: Charles C Thomas, Publisher, 1961.
6. Robin, Gerald D., "Patterns of Department Store Shoplifting," *Crime and Delinquency*, 9 (April 1963), pp. 163–172.
7. Savitz, Leonard, "Automobile Theft," *Journal of Criminal Law, Criminology and Police Science*, 50 (July–August 1959), pp. 132–145.
8. Schepses, Erwin, "Boys Who Steal Cars," *Federal Probation*, 25 (March 1961), pp. 56–62.
9. Stein, Herman D., and John M. Martin, "Swastika Offenders: Variations in Etiology, Behavior and Psycho-Social Characteristics," *Social Problems*, 10 (Spring 1962), pp. 23–31.
10. Wade, Andrew L., "Toward the Delineation of Vandalism as a Sub-Type of Juvenile Delinquency," *Journal of Criminal Law, Criminology and Police Science*, 48 (January–February 1958), pp. 493–499.
11. Wattenberg, William E., and James Balistrieri, "Automobile Theft: A 'Favored-Group' Delinquency," *American Journal of Sociology*, 57 (May 1952), pp. 575–579.

SOCIAL PROCESSES IN THE ACT OF JUVENILE VANDALISM*

Andrew L. Wade

Most of the literature on vandalism has described the characteristics of participants and the types of destructive acts. When thus examined, vandalism has usually been assumed to be delib-

* This selection, written especially for this book, is published here for the first time.

*erate and vindictive. This selection presents juvenile vandalism as
spontaneous, unplanned behavior. It is analyzed within the sociopsychological framework of the social act. Vandalism as a behavioral act is thus seen to have a series of stages in its processual
development. The situational contexts from which it emerges are
discussed and pressures for participation are delineated. The
participant's self-image is also described.*

Because of the prevalence of destructive acts by juveniles, a number of studies have recently been directed toward the understanding of vandalism.[1] Most have treated vandalism from the standpoint of a deliberate and wanton act, often vindictive in nature. A few have suggested that much could be gained by a typological approach to such behavior.[2] The need for so-called "theories of the middle range" in the field of delinquency research has been predicated upon this typological emphasis with the added belief that these interpretations would in turn lead to more effective prevention programs.[3]

While vandalism has been distinguished as a type within the spectrum of deviant juvenile behavior, how the activity comes into being and is consummated has received scant attention. The impression has often been left that it is a deliberate act while in actuality much property destruction by juveniles is a spontaneous outgrowth of group interaction having social, cultural and ecological determinants.[4] The imperative need would seem to be for research into the processual development of the act. This kind of emphasis could lend insight to a segment of deviant behavior which needs illumination if the motivational elements are to be understood.

Although the social processes underlying vandalism as behavior are of importance, they cannot be appreciated without an examination of the concept of self held by the participant and his definition of the act. As Blumer points out, the important datum is not the attitude behind the act but the process of definition by the individual or group of the act or the contemplated act.[5] Supposedly, the boy who has defined himself as a "prankster" and the act

[1] See John M. Martin, *Juvenile Vandalism: A Study of Its Nature and Prevention*, Springfield, Ill.: Charles C Thomas, Publisher, 1961; Nathan Goldman, "A Socio-Psychological Study of School Vandalism," Syracuse, N.Y.: Syracuse University Research Institute, *Final Report*, July 31, 1959 (Mimeographed); David Caplovitz and Candace Rogers, *Swastika 1960: The Epidemic of Anti-Semitic Vandalism in America*, New York: Anti-Defamation League of B'nai B'rith, 1961; *Why the Swastika? A Study of Young American Vandals*, New York: Institute of Human Relations Press, January 1962; Martin Deutsch, "The 1960 Swastika-Smearings: Analysis of the Apprehended Youth," *Merrill-Palmer Quarterly of Behavior and Development*, 8 (April 1962), pp. 1–22; Howard J. Ehrlich, "The Swastika Epidemic of 1959–1960: Anti-Semitism and Community Characteristics," *Social Problems*, 9 (Winter 1962), pp. 264–272; Herman D. Stein and John M. Martin, "Swastika Offender: Variations in Etiology, Behavior and Psycho-Social Characteristics," *Social Problems*, 10 (Summer 1962), pp. 56–70; William Bates, "Caste, Class and Vandalism," *Social Problems*, 9 (Spring 1962), pp. 349–353; and William Bates and Thomas McJunkins, "Vandalism and Status Differences," *Pacific Sociological Review*, 2 (Fall 1962), pp. 89–92.

[2] Martin, Chaps. III and IV; Marshall B. Clinard and Andrew L. Wade, "Toward the Delineation of Vandalism as a Sub-Type in Juvenile Delinquency," *Journal of Criminal Law, Criminology and Police Science*, 48 (January–February 1958), pp. 493–499; and William Cress and James R. Shofner, "A Comparative Study of Family Characteristics among Two Groups of Juvenile Offenders, Auto Thieves and Vandals," unpublished M.S. thesis, Raymond A. Kent School of Social Work, University of Louisville, 1961.

[3] For example, Don C. Gibbons, *Changing the Lawbreaker: The Treatment of Delinquents and Criminals*, Englewood Cliffs, N.J.: Prentice-Hall, Inc., 1965.

[4] See the articles by Ehrlich, Bates, and Bates and McJunkins.

[5] Herbert Blumer, "Attitudes and the Social Act," *Social Problems*, 3 (October 1955), pp. 59–65. Also see S. Frank Miyamoto, "The Social Act: Re-examination of a Concept," *Pacific Sociological Review*, 2 (Fall 1959), pp. 51–55.

of vandalism as "having fun" would be more likely to engage in property destruction. Such participation becomes possible because of acceptable definitions of self and of the act itself. Furthermore, since vandalism is more often a group form of behavior, the peer group norms would seem more pressing or demanding a higher loyalty than society's expectations of conformity to its standards.[6]

This paper is thus concerned with research into the above-mentioned neglected areas with the emphasis upon vandalism as a spontaneous social act. A brief appraisal is first made of various elements deemed usually present in order for property destruction to take place. They are thought of as interrelated variables and believed to be of considerable importance to an analysis of the processes leading to the commission of vandalism. The behavior in vandalism includes many acts of destruction:

Studies of the complaints made by citizens and public officials reveal that hardly any property is safe from this form of aggression. Schools are often the object of attack by vandals. Windows are broken; records, books, desks, typewriters, supplies, and other equipment are stolen or destroyed. Public property of all types appears to offer peculiar allurement to children bent on destruction. Parks, playgrounds, highway signs, and markers are frequently defaced or destroyed. Trees, shrubs, flowers, benches, and other equipment suffer in like manner. Autoists are constantly reporting the slashing or releasing of air from tires, broken windows, stolen accessories. Golf clubs complain that benches, markers, flags, even expensive and difficult-to-replace putting greens are defaced, broken or uprooted. Libraries report the theft and destruction of books and other equipment. Railroads complain of and demand protection from the destruction of freight car seals, theft of property, wilful and deliberate throwing of stones at passenger car windows, tampering with rails and switches. Vacant houses are always the particular delight of children seeking outlets for destructive instincts; windows are broken, plumbing and hardware stolen, destroyed, or rendered unusable. Gasoline operators report pumps and other service equipment stolen, broken, or destroyed. Theater managers, frequently in the "better" neighborhoods, complain of the slashing of seats, wilful damaging of toilet facilities, even the burning of rugs, carpets, etc.[7]

METHOD OF STUDY

The data in this study are from interviews with 50 boys from 13 to 17 years of age who had been referred to the Kansas City, Missouri, Police Department's Youth Bureau or to the Jackson County Juvenile Court in that city for the act of vandalism. They were interviewed by the author, then a research fellow with Community Studies, Inc., as soon as possible after the act occurred. The interviews lasted from three quarters of an hour to about an hour and a half, depending on the level of rapport established as well as on the fluency of the adolescent interviewed. In all cases the subjects were assured that the information furnished would be held in strict confidence and would not reach the police, the juvenile court, or the probation officer.

There was no way to verify the boy's story as to what "really did happen" other than by an inspection of the arresting officer's report or possibly by a talk with the boy's probation officer. In some cases a subject's account would be checked with that given by his companions in the same act of vandalism. There were a number of such instances. However, there was no reason to doubt the general truthfulness of the subjects. None expressed unwillingness to talk about vandalism as a social act. Since all of the interviews were conducted by a person in a nonofficial capacity and in private except in three instances, it is reasonable to assume that the adolescent had little to gain from not giving an accurate account of what happened. Furthermore, the fact that most of them were willing to talk about

[6] Gresham M. Sykes and David Matza, "Techniques of Neutralization: A Theory of Delinquency," *American Sociological Review*, 22 (December 1957), p. 669.

[7] J. P. Murphy, "The Answer to Vandalism May Be Found at Home," *Federal Probation*, 18 (March 1954), pp. 8–10. This issue of *Federal Probation* contains a symposium on vandalism.

this type of behavior rather than about the offenses for which they were then on probation, in detention, or committed to the institution, was in itself indicative of the general indifference with which vandalism was often regarded by many of these juveniles.

THE SETTING FOR VANDALISM

When conformity with peer group pressures takes the form of participation in an act of vandalism, the social interaction is complex. First of all, several norms function in the action. They help determine when the behavior is to take place, which are the "proper" objects to be vandalized, who are the "acceptable" victims to suffer from the destructive actions, and what situations are "acceptable" for the behavior. The participant's self-image is also of prime importance. This includes his definition of the act of vandalism as essentially a "prank" or a "good joke" on the victim or victims. Certain rationalizations are utilized to make possible this self definition. These tend to neutralize any guilt feelings present as a consequence of the internalization of the cultural norms governing the sanctity and worth of personal and public property. Also included are the overall attitudes the adolescent has toward himself, toward juvenile behavior in general, and toward the reactions of peers to deviant behavior in particular.

The *situational and cultural variables* cited above are functionally interrelated with the values and norms of the boys' effective reference system. This system is, in turn, related to the class system within which he received his basic socialization. As a part of the overall socialization pattern, the influence of the adolescent subculture is also important to the process of socialization.

In addition to the above variables, there are certain *functional variables* operating. These are actually analytical concepts but are utilized in this study as variables. One of these has been designated as the "oppor-

tunity structure."[8] This is a situation which, when present, makes possible the fulfillment of a deviant act. In the context of vandalism an obvious opportunity structure would be the time of Halloween itself, a time when such acts are more or less expected and tolerated by the community at large. Other obvious opportunity structures would be such situations as abandoned houses with broken windows, buildings under construction where doors are left unlocked and water pipes and electrical wires exposed, or a closed school building in a secluded area.

Another analytical concept employed here as a variable has been described elsewhere as the "learning structure."[9] In some of the more complicated forms of criminal activity, such as pickpocketing and confidence games, an elaborate set of techniques or body of knowledge must be mastered prior to the commission of the act if results are to be successful. The underlying assumption is that regardless of how often an opportunity structure may occur, its potentialities are not recognized and exploited unless the actor has learned to identify such situations as containing intrinsic rewards he has been trained to seek.

This generalization may also be applied to the act of vandalism. However, the learning structure variable is probably not as imposing as in other forms of delinquent behavior such as the act of "hot-wiring" an automobile for the purpose of "joy riding." On the other hand, some indirect learning does take place even in vandalism. This occurs through the recitation of Halloween escapades and similar destructive acts by parents and adults in the presence of children or by juveniles telling one another of exploits involving vandalism.

There is a third variable present in the interaction underlying participation in an act of property destruction, the "operating

[8] Richard A. Cloward, "Illegitimate Means, Anomie and Deviant Behavior," *American Sociological Review*, 24 (April 1959), p. 168.

[9] Cloward, p. 168.

invention."[10] This is primarily a behavioral innovation assuring the fulfillment of the potential behavior possible within the limits established by the institutional norms. The act of vandalism may be regarded as an operating invention within the normative structure of the gang or deviant peer group. The particular institutional norms involved in this context are those of solidary relations and internal competition among members for status. When the whole group engages in property destruction, it does so with the expectation that its activities will be solidary. The participant in vandalism responsible for suggesting or instigating the activity and its direction does so in the hope of raising his status in the eyes of his fellow participants. Obviously, the act must fall within the normative structure of the group in order to function as an acceptable status-conferring device for the innovator.[11] The fact that the overwhelming percentage of teenagers think it vitally important to act the way other people (their peers) expect[12] makes the possibilities of status-conferring actions by the adolescent seem almost limitless. Any hesitancy on his part to participate in what may seem to him a nonacceptable or delinquent act is generally overcome by the neutralization or rationalization techniques he learns from his peers and which help him to reconcile pressures of the peer group and the normative standards of society.[13]

STAGES IN THE ACT OF VANDALISM

The variables discussed above imply that participation in an act of property destruction is far more complicated than the simple decision so often assumed. There is an involved set of processes underlying this decision which move from one stage to another until the act of vandalism takes place. Viewed in terms of the broader perspective of deviant behavior, these processes constitute the most perplexing issue in the contemporary theory of deviant behavior.[14] Vandalism as a social act may be thought of as a sequence of behavior which has some meaning in terms of a goal or end result.[15] This sequence implies a series of steps or stages which are considered herein as social processes. An act of vandalism may be (1) a deliberately planned event, (2) one that takes place fortuitously as part of a larger social action, such as the play situation, or (3) one that functions as a catalyst for a series of unplanned additional acts as the element of mutual excitation takes hold of the participants. Since the deliberately planned act is rare, the emphasis here is upon vandalism as spontaneous deviant acts.

Structuring the Act. Participation in any social activity usually involves an evaluation by the actor of the imminent action in light of how his reference group will regard the act. If this group is "deviant-prone," delinquent behavior is more likely to occur than if the reverse is true. On the other hand, one's reference group may be "deviant-opposed" but the enveloping situation fraught with deviant opportunity structures. For this person to choose the deviant opportunity suggests the intervention of an additional variable, perhaps the rejection of the reference group itself. In some instances, the choice may involve the substitution of the authority of another reference group:

Each situation presents its own variety of problems. A boy out on a window-breaking spree "for fun" may assess the relative weight of conflicting directives: "My mother (or teacher) says this is not the thing to do, but

---

[10] Robert Dubin, "Deviant Behavior and Social Structure: Continuities in Social Theory," *American Sociological Review*, 24 (April 1959), p. 152.
[11] Dubin, p. 153.
[12] H. H. Remmers and D. H. Radler, *The American Teenager*, Indianapolis: The Bobbs-Merrill Company, Inc., 1957, p. 254.
[13] Sykes and Matza, p. 669.

[14] Cf. Clarence Ray Jeffrey, "An Integrated Theory of Crime and Criminal Behavior," *Journal of Criminal Law, Criminology and Police Science*, 49 (March–April 1959), pp. 533–552.
[15] Theodore M. Newcomb, *Social Psychology*, New York: Holt, Rinehart and Winston, Inc., 1950, p. 77.

hell, she's only a woman. The kids in my gang say to do it, so I guess I better."[16]

How pressure is applied on the motivational system of the actor will vary as the function of the kind of pattern with which he is expected to conform. The resulting behavior is itself a function of the nature of the situation in which the individual finds himself.

In an act of vandalism there are usually five stages: (1) waiting for something to turn up, (2) removal of uncertainty: the exploratory gesture, (3) mutual conversion, (4) joint elaboration of the act, (5) aftermath and retrospect.

Stage I: "Waiting for something to turn up." Preliminary to the act is the situation from which the suggestion or innovating behavior develops. Much of the juvenile's free time outside school and in other unsupervised contexts is spent in unstructured situations. This free time is characterized by him as "messing around." What is often interpreted as aimless activity by the untrained observer and even the participants themselves has in actuality a subtle pattern. Much of it centers about and emanates from a particular location serving a vital function in the emotional life of the adolescent.[17] These are the kinds of situations utilized by the innovator. The actors are poised, ready for an action-provoking suggestion. As one boy defined a similar situation:

Well, we were all at the cafe; we didn't have anything to do. We were all sitting, talking. When we didn't have anything else to do, we'd go over there to the cafe and sit down. The guys who were old enough would play the pinball machine.

"An opportunity structure" is present. The aimless talk and "bull sessions" provide the chance for gossip. The talk concerns what other juveniles have done and the escapades of their contemporaries. Such talk might never get started if these seemingly purposeless get-togethers did not occur. One interviewee summed up the situation when he said, "Things get around, boy to boy."

The *play situation* is another general type of context out of which vandalism may develop. The destructive activity may itself be a form of play or it may be a spontaneous outgrowth of the play situation. The two forms are often inextricably bound together by the nature of the play activity itself. The following account illustrates how vandalism may take the form of a play activity:

There were these lights in the apartment house; they stand on a stand, have a bulb (globe) on the outside. There were three others besides me; we'd been messing around. We went walking around—went down, got a cup of coffee. We came up; we broke that light bulb. Gene picked it up and threw it on the sidewalk. He just acted like he was bowling and threw.

Vandalism as play generally takes the shape of a *game of skill*. As such, either the quantity or the quality of the destruction is stressed. The following account shows how the quantity aspect is emphasized, although not originally intended as the goal of the play activity:

The first time we did vandalism, me and my brother and another boy down at the garage, we were smoking and playing cards. They had some old cars in the back; we played around there. We cleaned them out one day. Swept out the broken glass—busted windshields—rolled down the windows so we wouldn't cut ourselves. This one guy threw a whiskey bottle up on the roof; threw another. It hit the side of the window. We just started throwing at the windows. When we were through, we had broken twenty-seven of them. We saw who could break out the most. There wasn't anything else to do. We finally got tired and just left. They didn't catch us until the next day. We returned to see what had happened; we were out there playing cards and smoking again.

16 William C. Kvaraceus and Walter B. Miller, *Delinquent Behavior: Culture and the Individual*, Washington, D.C.: National Education Association, 1959, pp. 112 f.
17 Herbert A. Bloch and Arthur Niederhoffer, *The Gang: A Study in Adolescent Behavior*, New York: Philosophical Library, Inc., 1958, p. 178.

On other occasions the destruction is subordinate. What primarily counts is one's ability to hit a target with a BB gun, pellet gun, a stone, or some other object. The target chosen is something easily broken since a hit is more visible or audible. A competitive situation ensues with destruction resulting:

About seven years ago I was shooting out switch lights on a rail road track with an air rifle. There were three of us, and each of us had guns. We were looking for pigeons. One of them said, "See that switch light up there?" He shot and missed it, and the other boy shot and missed it. I shot and missed it. So we kept on shooting until we hit it.

Oh, I broke out a few windows—see who was the straighter shot. I had a pellet pistol. See, we'd aim for the center. If you hit the center, then the window wouldn't break, only have a little hole with some small cracks. We tried to shoot through the same hole.

Once the spirit of destructive activity takes hold, massive destruction may result and the "game" quality of the activity heightens. There is a spontaneous eruption of wholesale vandalism:

This last July my parents were out of town. Me and these other kids went on a hay ride. We got home about eleven o'clock. Well, we were walking around; we were going to stay up all night—just something to keep us awake. We went out and broke windows and ran—just for excitement. We would just walk by and someone would pick up a rock and throw it and everyone would start running. We broke about fifty windows. We went around all night till it got light. We ended up walking quite a ways from our neighborhood.

As the interview data show, vandalism is sometimes the inadvertent result of ordinary play activity. Sometimes it may even be an accidental result. For example, several boys gained entry to a feed mill one weekend in order to play tag on the stacks of feed bags. The original objective soon changed as a number of motorized forklifts were discovered, and the boys began having fun driving them. The resulting destruction was rationalized as accidental:

Some of us drove the lifts. I found out I couldn't drive, so I didn't drive after about five minutes. I rode with someone else. (Did any of the guys deliberately drive into the feed bags?) They weren't doing that on purpose; sometimes they'd hit them but never on purpose. We didn't know how to drive. They were piled in huge stacks. You'd try to turn around or something; you know the back wheels are supposed to turn. They'd spin too fast; we'd hit the sack. We didn't do all the damage anyway. We weren't the first ones in there.

Stage II: Removal of Uncertainty (the Exploratory Gesture). The unstructured situation as the general context from which vandalism may develop undergoes a significant change when an action-provoking suggestion is made by one of the actors. It is generally in the form of an "exploratory gesture."[18] This is a suggestion, sometimes cautiously, sometimes boldly, broached to effect action from a group. It functions to change the ongoing interaction and to interject a focus to the interest and conversation of the hangers-on. The prevailing boredom begins to disappear as interest develops in the exploratory gesture:

We were just sitting on the corner talking. Each boy had a different idea, but this boy had a funny idea. He told of wanting to break a window—of about a big crash. I didn't want to do it; I told him that a couple of times. But he called me "chicken." Like the Y (another place where he had committed vandalism), just riding around thinking of something to do—get an idea in their heads about causing trouble.

At times the exploratory gesture meets with little or no resistance. This is usually the case when the suggestion involves a play activity having a decided element of excitement. The original suggestion may not be that the group do property damage but that it participate in an activity challenging individual daring. The resulting vandalism is often a by-product of the situation but may also become the substitute activity:

18 Albert K. Cohen, *Delinquent Boys: The Culture of the Gang,* New York: The Free Press of Glencoe, 1955, p. 26.

This one guy came up to us and said, "Let's go down to the bottom (basement) of Hilliard's (a local new car dealer) and drive around the cars." So we went and started driving around. I think it was on a Saturday. One of the salesmen came down and chased us out. We went down to this cafe and played the pinball machine. I was telling about it, so one of the guys got the bright idea that we go back there. We drove them around, scratched some of them.

The exploratory gesture may also be in the form of an overt act. In this case the act is an event of vandalism. It may be deliberate or spur-of-the-moment behavior. The episode is taken as a cue by others to commit similar ones, and a series of destructive acts may result. The following interviews illustrate this cue-taking sequence of behavior:

Well, me and a couple of boy friends and a girl got in a car we had taken. We were going to stay there that night. She asked me if I had a knife. I said, "Yeah." So she started cutting up the upholstery, ceiling and everything. After she quit cutting up, Joe got out of the car and went to the drugstore. I locked the door and wouldn't let him back in. So Raymond kicked out the window on the right side of the driver's seat. So Joe put his foot through the same window. Then I bent up the gear shift—took out the speedometer. Joe, he took the glove compartment, took it all apart. If I'd known she was going to cut it up, I wouldn't have given her the knife. I just took it away from her and started cutting up myself. So did Joe and Raymond. I cut up the driver's seat. We didn't want to go home that night—just wanted to stay out.

Obviously, the exploratory gesture that the group participate in an act of vandalism may be rejected. No attempt is made here to determine why, when, or how such a suggestion is refused further elaboration. However, the following section has implicit propositions considered as suggestive clues to an explanation of why some adolescents will engage in vandalism while others shy away from such behavior.

Stage III: Mutual Conversion. In most instances vandalism is a group type of activity.

Some degree of agreement, therefore, must be present among the prospective participants in order for the act to materialize. Prefacing this agreement is a period of mutual exploration as discussed above. As a stage in the ongoing sequence of the act, it may be very incidental and of short duration. On the other hand, a series of exploratory gestures may be made and discarded over a relatively long period of time before the process of "mutual conversion" to the idea takes place. The acceptability of an idea to oneself depends upon its acceptability to others. "Converting the other is part of the process of converting oneself."[19]

A number of pressures operate, causing the individual to accede to the implications of the exploratory gesture. In general, these challenge or threaten the person's self-concept as an acceptable peer. One of the most obvious is the dare to commit the act of vandalism. It functions as a device to measure the boy's courage and manliness before the critical audience of his peers. This form of mutual conversion is illustrated below:

I came home from doing three lawns, ate dinner. These boys waited for me till I ate dinner. This boy had some BB's and said, "Why don't you get your gun?" So I got the gun and we walked down the street. Just pointed the gun at it and shot the window. Well, when we started, I thought we were just going over to Larry's house to play cards or mess around. No reason to pick that house (to shoot the window). I think they said, "Bet you can't hit that window." It was just about eight by ten inches. After shooting the window we ran.

There are occasions when the dare involves a particularly danger-charged challenge. But one may enhance his status within the peer group if he accepts the dare even though the chances of getting away with the act are negligible. As an example:

Ronny was stupid for kicking that neon sign in front of the funeral parlor. He knew he was going to get caught. I wouldn't have done it. The cops were standing down the street not

19 Cohen, p. 61.

more than ten feet away. He was going along; anything he saw he was hitting. One of the boys dared him to do it. Then we tried to run, and we didn't make it.

Usually, the dare is reinforced by an epithet in current vogue among juveniles. The one most often used is "chicken." Whether applied in earnest or in jest, this appellation is taken seriously by the adolescent. It is a threat to his status in the eyes of his peers, especially when it is an overt challenge to test his courage. If the pressure toward conformity is too great, he will react as he thinks others in this reference group would react to a similar challenge. An inner struggle results between what he knows to be the right response in keeping with the internalized norms of the larger social system and the demands of loyalty to the peer group or friendship clique.[20] If he sacrifices the demands of larger society for those of the smaller social group, he does so at the risk of violating the law. When the decision is made in favor of the peer group, the process of mutual conversion has taken place.

Continued peer pressure to conform for the promise of psychological rewards, primarily that of being an accepted member of a favored group, will be too much for some juveniles. They eventually accede, and the act of property destruction is consummated:

One of the kids I ran around with and I were walking around one night, and we came to the Motor Company. He just picked up a rock and threw it. He didn't tell me he was going to do it. Those were $150 windows, something like that. He picked up a nice, big, juicy rock. He came back and said, "Now it's your chance." Of course, the guys I ran around with, they call you "chicken." One guy dares another—calls him "chicken." Some guys can't take that. I took it as long as I could until I got into it. They said if you want to belong to our club, you got to break a window. We broke about eight windows that night. Usually it started by someone calling you "chicken." If you get in the gang, you got to break a window if you want to get in our club. So we stopped, found some rocks, and

20 Sykes and Matza, p. 669.

threw them. Happened in a minute and sped off. We thought it was kind of funny.

It is obvious from the story that there is a tendency on the part of these boys to minimize the damage they have done and to excuse their participation in such acts on the basis of an inability to face the scorn of peers if they refuse to commit vandalism. The very fact they do eventually submit to the pressure is indicative of the importance of being accepted as a worthy peer. However, occasionally a boy will find himself included in an act of vandalism without his prior consent. The conversion stage of the act is circumvented as is the preliminary stage of the exploratory gesture. Loyalty to friends prevents him from "ratting" on them:

Yeah, one of my friends got me in some vandalism. Put a cherry bomb in a toilet stool. We were taking boxing then. A kid came in there where I was, told me all about it. We left and came back there. Police picked us up. He threw the cherry bomb in the toilet stool; I guess to have fun. I was with him when they picked him up. A lady knew he was in the rest room—she suspected him anyway. She called the cops on him. Blew it all to bits. They didn't have any proof that he did it, but he did it. I didn't say anything about it to him, I just said he was crazy (to have done that). I asked him why he came in there (into the gym). He said, "Be quiet, I'll tell you about it." He said, "Let's leave." I said I was fixing to leave. So we left anyway.

The time that it takes before the conversion process reaches fulfillment is dependent upon many factors. The more obvious of these is the seriousness of the proposed action as defined by the prospective participants. Many juveniles who already have a history of delinquencies such as theft are not likely to consider vandalism as a particularly serious offense. Little mutual exploration is necessary preliminary to participation in property destruction by these boys. On the other hand, some juveniles might define vandalism as "kid stuff." No amount of inducement short of financial reward or release from boredom would effect conversion to the idea.

But most probably for these boys property destruction would be an incidental and initial phase to the "breaking and entering" of a business establishment for the purpose of burglary.

The mutual conversion process is also effected more quickly in a group in which the configuration of past experiences of the interacting individuals is very similar or strongly related. Little exploration of feelings of fellow members of a delinquent group need be made when past natural histories of their careers indicate predispositions to any behavior hinting of excitement, danger, and even malice.

Parsons[21] indicates still another factor in his discussion of the effect of the uncertainty of alter's reaction to the exploratory gesture. This uncertainty tends to create an indefiniteness in the requirements of the normative pattern, which in turn influences the interactive relationship between alter and ego. As a consequence, the time necessary for the conversion process to be completed will be affected by how quickly the uncertainty is removed as to how alter or alters will react to ego's suggestions. A case in point is the Halloween situation. There is less indefiniteness at this time than at others during the year relative to property destruction. Not only is there more definite expectation as to how alter will react to an exploratory gesture, but the conversion process is more quickly consummated. The unstructuredness of the situation is soon removed because the uncertainty as to what the normative pattern itself requires is less than at other times.

Stage IV: Joint Elaboration of the Act. In this stage of the social act there is likely to be large-scale property destruction. There is a spontaneous eruption of wholesale vandalism once the spirit of the activity takes hold of the participants. For example, breaking one window may lead to extensive damage to others. Occasionally, the participants be-

come so stimulated by the first few acts of destruction that a veritable orgy of vandalism takes place.

One time . . . four or five of us went to an apartment just being built, took a whole wall of cement down. We took a chisel and knocked down hundreds of cinder blocks, just mischievous. We went to old houses, broke windows . . . In one house we found a big Victrola. We threw it down the stairs, we pushed down the bannister, we broke the chandelier. We didn't steal anything, just broke things . . . I had to do it so they wouldn't call me chicken.[22]

It was indicated in the previous section dealing with the conversion stage in the act of vandalism that the tolerance threshold of some adolescents is much lower than that of others. The effects of family and class socialization patterns need to be temporarily removed in order for some of these boys to participate in such an act. Pressure from peers to conform also makes this condition possible. The pressuring takes place within a group situation in which members interact with each other and upon each other in both direct and indirect ways. Mutual testing with exploratory gestures takes place. Calling each other's bluff through the use of epithets is often the device to complete the process of securing conformity from the individual.

Contributing to the elaboration of an act of vandalism is the element of *mutual excitation.* The play situation is often responsible for generating this type of excitement. This is especially true if there is a competitive event involved. Such a situation may develop into a destructive race between contestants to see who can do the most or the best damage. Underlying the event is a kind of "group psychological intoxication."[23] One participant's behavior serves as the model for another's. Present is a "be-

21 Talcott Parsons, *The Social System*, New York: The Free Press of Glencoe, 1951, p. 278.

22 Benjamin Fine, *1,000,000 Delinquents*, Cleveland: The World Publishing Company, 1955, pp. 36 f.

23 This is a term suggested by Dr. Fritz Redl and quoted in Martha M. Eliot, "What Is Vandalism?" *Federal Probation*, 18 (March 1954), p. 4.

havioral contagion" denoted by the spontaneous pickup or imitation by the other
individuals of a behavior initiated by one
member of the group.

In analyzing collective behavior, Blumer
has suggested the term "circular reaction."[24]
By this is meant a type of interstimulation
in which the response of one individual
tends to produce the stimulation for another. When the stimulation is reflected
back to the first person, it is reinforced.
This is the general result in a group contagion situation. Social psychological research has shown that in a situation of
stress where the members of a group have
a common need or mood, the most impulsive person—the one who first reacts in a
manner representative of the shared feeling
—is most likely to evoke a chain of contagion.[25] There are, of course, varying individual thresholds for participation in such
group reactions.

The functional nature of mutual excitation or group contagion is of particular importance in vandalism. A primary function
of this element is the tendency for the individual to lose his feeling of self-identity
in the prevailing group interaction. This
temporary loss of identity is especially significant because it helps make possible his
participation in vandalism and any resulting
elaboration of the act. The very fact that
property destruction is generally a group act
functions to reduce individual feelings of
fear and guilt. The dilution of such feeling
in the peer association operates as a sort of
"guilt insurance."[26] The peer group inadvertently furnishes a sense of security in

numbers which functions to reduce feelings
of individuality and responsibility. The belief is present that when the act is committed by a group, the authorities will find
it difficult, if not impossible, to single out
the specific instigators.

This *feeling of security* is enhanced by
the additional belief that vandalism is one
of the less serious delinquencies. Particularly
is this the case when the adolescent interprets his destructive behavior as a prank
or "just being mischievous." This interpretation also functions as a rationalization of
the activity and as an attempt to neutralize
whatever guilt feelings he may have from
participation in vandalism.

There is still another result of the functional nature of the element of mutual excitation. The apparent loss of individuality
and responsibility obtained from anonymity
operates to bring into the group interaction
patterns the more cautious individuals.
When this occurs, the range of anonymity
is further expanded. An *impression of uni-
versality* is created, giving the appearance
of group solidarity. On some occasions, especially when the participating group is
large, there will be found on the fringes of
the group action the supportive individuals
who cannot be stampeded into actual participation in the act. Although they do not oppose the group, they tend to draw the line at
joining in the "fun." However, these persons
are not averse to enjoying the ensuing action.
The ultimate effect of these "fringers" is to
add to the already created impression of uni-
versality, the impression that everyone is "in
on the act."[27]

The resulting destructive behavior is ex-
temporaneous. The participants are precipitated into it by the fast-rising events of the
situation over which they have had little
control. Once the action begins, apparently
little can be done to prevent it from gathering momentum. The interview data tend to
show that few, if any, of the participants

24 Herbert Blumer, "Collective Behavior," *New Outline of the Principles of Sociology*, Alfred McClung Lee (ed.), New York: Barnes & Noble, Inc., 1951, p. 170.
25 Harold H. Kelley and John W. Thibaut, "Experimental Studies of Group Problem Solving and Processes," *Handbook of Social Psychology*, Gardner Lindzey (ed.), Reading, Mass.: Addison-Wesley Publishing Company, Inc., 1954, II, p. 752.
26 Herbert A. Bloch and Frank T. Flynn, *Delinquency: The Juvenile Offender in America Today*, New York: Random House, Inc., 1956, p. 198.
27 Roger W. Brown, "Mass Phenomena," in Gardner Lindzey (ed.), *Handbook of Social Psychology*, Reading, Mass.: Addison-Wesley Publishing Company, Inc., 1954, p. 847.

offered strong objections to engaging in vandalism. Group pressure and mutual excitation combined to smother any protestations which arose. Not until the destruction was completed or the participants were chased from the scene did the activity halt.

Stage V: Aftermath and Retrospect. The fifth stage is of particular importance in terms of the meaning of the acts to the participant. The motive for the act will largely determine the evaluation the actor makes of the destructive behavior. The fact that nothing is stolen during most acts of vandalism tends to reinforce the vandal's conception of himself as merely a prankster and not a delinquent. In fact, this would appear to indicate that vandalism is nonutilitarian. Actually, many acts do have some meaning and utility for the participants even though not defined explicitly by them. Some property destruction appears to function for the adolescent as a protest against his ill-defined social role and ambiguous status in the social structure. Other meanings are more specific. If a boy has suffered frustration, he may express his resentment by a revengeful act of destruction:

Well, he accused us of stealing some stuff out of his joint. He didn't come right out and say it was us, but the way he talked he made it sound like it, particularly us. We were kidding him about an old rifle he had in there, about ninety years old. And he wanted $15 for it, and the stock on it was all cracked up and everything. And we kept kidding his mother— she's in there (the store) with him—and we kept kidding her. And old Gay (the store owner) himself came over there and started raising the devil, blowing off steam and everything. We didn't like it too well. We left and came back later. I told him (his companion), "Let's go down and break those windows." He said, "Okay," and we went down there and picked up some rocks along the way. We got down there and stood in front of the place till there weren't any cars very close to us, and we threw the rocks and ran.

If a boy is apprehended in the act, the destructive activity will still give him considerable satisfaction. This may be so because he has the feeling of group solidarity and support for his actions:

The cops hauled us in a couple of times out at Cow Town (a teenage dance hall hangout). I kicked in a sign at a funeral home. See, we were all drunk up there (at Cow Town), starting trouble, and they kicked us out. We were all mad. One of my buddies was ahead of me and was going to kick the sign. I ran ahead of him and beat him to it. The cops came running out, chasing us, and we took off down the street. They got Clyde, he was coming out behind us and he was drunk. The cops caught some of us. Boy, when they started chasing us, some of them (his companions) got sober awful quick! They could hardly run, weaving down the street. They took us down to the station in the paddy wagon. What was funny (laugh), we got down to the station, and Clyde raised his head and said, "Make a run for it, boys, I'll hold them off." Boy, we laughed and laughed!

When the act embodies a certain amount of satisfaction, the delight is keen enough for the participants to gloat over what has happened to the victim's property. As one boy described the aftermath of such an act, "Sometimes they do that (vandalism) just before somebody comes out; and when they come out, they will be behind the house killing themselves laughing." This malicious enjoyment of the victim's distress and anger is further illustrated in the following:

We went over to this one girl's house we didn't like. We threw rotten eggs all over the porch, inside the door—everywhere. Boy, did it stink around there! We went by the next day and said, "What happened?" The windows on the second floor were all up, the house and the lawn all covered. She said, "You know what happened." "Prove it," I said. Boy, did it stink! About 300 eggs we used. That place was an odorous mess! After that (the night of the vandalism) we retired to a friendly drugstore, had a couple of malts; went home to bed. Terrific!

Whatever guilt may be felt is usually neutralized by the convenient *rationalizations* motivating the behavior. Such rationalizations may or may not represent the "real" reason: they do reconcile the conflict between legal norms and the acts of vandalism. *Prejudice* is one source of these rationalizations. Both the majority and the minority groups engaging in such behavior find justification for it in prejudice. As an example:

The neighborhood was old and filled with all kinds of people . . . Mexicans and niggers came and everything changed. Niggers and an Indian family lived next door to us and we fought them all the time because we didn't like niggers. The boys would break their windows, holler in their doors, and throw tin cans into their house . . .[28]

The minority's justification for vandalism is usually interpreted as a protest against the prejudice and discrimination shown toward it by the majority group. For example, testimony before the Senate subcommittee investigating juvenile delinquency revealed that in Denver three or four significant gangs which were identified by the police as causing a great deal of vandalism were Spanish-American boys.[29] A study of vandalism in that city some time ago tended to substantiate this view.[30] The investigating committee found a similar situation when it met in Boston.[31] It has also been maintained that much of the vandalism participated in by the Puerto Rican youth of New York City is due to ethnic prejudice shown them by the majority group.[32]

The act is also justified under the rationalization that "they had it coming to them." This is designated by Sykes and Matza as a technique of neutralization labeled "the denial of the victim."[33] The boy insists that what he has done is justifiable in the light of the circumstances. For example, the damage committed is regarded as a form of *rightful retaliation* or punishment:

I know of some friends of mine who went over to school and we decided to break some of Mr. X's windows for the simple reason that we absolutely despise this teacher. There were about four or five of us.

Many windows are broken in our school. In one room in particular in which one unpopular teacher holds classes, about twenty-five panes a year have to be replaced. The vandals believe that this is a way to "get back at" a teacher.[34]

Goldman has also pointed out that additional attitudes such as *boredom* and desire for *status achievement* motivate students to damage school buildings.[35] Such vandalism is generally motivated by feelings of frustration as a result of the child's academic position in the classroom, his status among his peers, and his relationships with his teachers.

In his *retrospective view of the act*, the participant sometimes redefines his behavior from the original definition of "fun" to a negative one. There are indications of mixed feelings on the part of these boys as they look back upon such behavior. It is a mixture of rebellion, guilt, and malicious delight. This process of redefinition and revision of self attitudes has been designated by Faris as the "retrospective act."[36] Usu-

---

[28] Clifford R. Shaw and Henry D. McKay, *Social Factors in Juvenile Delinquency: Report on the Causes of Crime*, National Commission on Law Observance and Enforcement, Vol. II; Washington, D.C.: Government Printing Office, 1931, p. 117.
[29] Subcommittee of the Senate Committee on the Judiciary, *Interim Report, Juvenile Delinquency*, 83d Cong., 2d Sess., 1954, p. 48.
[30] Raymond Gordon, "Vandalism," Letters to the Editor, *Federal Probation*, 18 (September 1954), p. 50.
[31] *Interim Report*, p. 59.
[32] Helen L. Witmer (ed.), *Parents and Delinquency*, Department of Health, Education and Welfare, Social Security Administration, Children's Bureau; Washington, D.C.: Government Printing Office, 1954, pp. 9 f.

[33] Sykes and Matza, p. 668.
[34] These two accounts are taken from the exploratory study by Nathan Goldman, "Attitudes towards Vandalism: A Preliminary Report of Research," revision of a paper presented at the annual meetings of the American Sociological Association in Seattle, Wash., August 29, 1958, p. 9. (Dittoed.)
[35] Goldman, pp. 8–12.
[36] Ellsworth Faris, "The Retrospective Act," *Journal of Educational Sociology*, 14 (October 1950), pp. 82 and 87.

ally, the apprehension and detention experiences are significant in fostering this change in the definition of the act: "But at the time we thought it was fun until the police came and then that was all."

Another element causing a change in the original definition of the act is the realization that it caused "trouble." This is interpreted in personal terms, that is, being brought down to the police station or to the juvenile court or being involved in a disagreeable family situation. Comments such as these are indicative: "We didn't think about getting caught; we were thinking about having fun. I'm sorry I did it—more trouble than it was fun." "It didn't seem like then that it would amount to this much." "I didn't think it would cause so much trouble."

Although the primary aspect of the guilt is that of apprehension, there is also present a feeling that this kind of behavior might have resulted in something more serious, such as an injury. It is particularly true in cases where damage was done to automobiles by throwing rocks or using slingshots. Attitudes expressive of such guilt feelings are: "I could have hurt someone in the car." "It's bad; it could have caused an accident."

Further indicative of the guilt which some held concerning their behavior is a feeling of relief at having been apprehended. This tends to represent how effectively the conventional norms are internalized. The internalization, although not complete enough to forestall deviation from property norms, was still effective enough to provoke guilt feelings. It also led to the realization that vandalism was contrary to parental expectations and "good sense":

First place, we shouldn't have been over there. Second place, one of us might have got killed. Third place, I'm glad we got caught because we'd do more damage and more damage—be hard on our parents. Fourth place, that was an awful place to go play in, the (feed) mill.

Also present on occasion in the retrospective assessment of the act is the boy's conclusion that vandalism is "senseless." To some extent this represents a feeling of shame with the implication that one's behavior should have reason and utilitarian ends to it. Inherent is the idea that one ought to have good sense to think ahead and weigh the consequences of the act. It also represents a certain amount of chagrin at not having met expectations internalized relative to evaluating consequences before acting.

Although there are these feelings of guilt and shame at having been a participant in vandalism, some express a malicious delight at having been a party to the act. This is especially true if the victim is known to the individual and has been defined in negative terms. In some instances it is an attempt to justify the act to oneself.

By engaging in this kind of retrospective activity the vandal is taking the role of the other. In doing so, a changed conception of self begins to form. It is also conceivable that this same process helps to inhibit certain forms of vandalism as well as encourage still other types.[37] However, whether or not such a redefinition takes place will greatly depend upon the individual's "normative reference group." This is especially true of the deviant's choice of behavior responses to begin with in the interactional process.[38]

Since the individual gets much of his self-definition from the way others treat him and talk to him, the roles of law enforcement authorities and other significant adults are important in effecting the retrospective act on the part of the juvenile vandal with the end result of a changed self-image. As mentioned above, his apprehension often leads the boy to re-evalu-

[37] Tamotsu Shibutani, Society and Personality: An Interactionist Approach to Social Psychology, Englewood Cliffs, N.J.: Prentice-Hall, Inc., 1961, pp. 70–79, for a discussion of the blockage of social acts and resulting secondary adjustments.

[38] Albert K. Cohen, "The Study of Social Disorganization and Deviant Behavior," Sociology Today: Problems and Prospects, Robert K. Merton, et al. (eds.), New York: Basic Books, Inc., 1959, pp. 468–473.

ate the act. This re-evaluation in terms of guilt or shame is probably more true in the case of the boy who has never been arrested before than of the adolescent who is a familiar face to authorities. The adolescent's peers, who also function as significant others, are also highly important in fostering his self-conception, as well as revising it to conform with their perceived expectations of him. Obviously, much depends upon how significantly the actor has identified himself with the normative reference group in question.[39]

SELF-IMAGE

The juvenile's conception of the act of vandalism is a clue to his self-image. If he construes the event as "just a joke" or "just having fun," it implies that he thinks of himself as a "prankster" and not specifically as a delinquent. This construction, however, does not also exclude a conception of his actions as "bad" or "wrong" since concurrently he is able to deny responsibility for his actions by a favorable definition of the situation as an acceptable one for vandalism. This denial of responsibility functions to reduce the disapproval of self and others as a restraining influence.[40]

The interview data bear out the vandal's self-definition of being a prankster. Also included on occasion are elements suggesting that this self-image is flexible when the juvenile frames the act from the standpoint of the evaluator rather than the participant. A person who commits property destruction is thus considered "mean" or "ornery." On the other hand, in his efforts to protect his self-image as that of "prankster" or "mischievous" boy, the juvenile will resort to various rationalizations. These include the idea that there are no "good" boys but only "lucky" ones who have never been caught, that the possessions of certain persons or at

particular places are appropriate or acceptable targets for vandalism, and that those who disapprove of such acts are hypocrites and even deviants in disguise.

CONCLUSIONS

In this study juvenile vandalism has been analyzed by viewing it as a social act. Because each behavioral act has a career and is built up in a succession of responses,[41] using this approach has the advantage of bringing into focus the social processes growing out of group interaction. It also emphasizes the definitions held by the actor of himself and of the behavioral act; the two are found to be functionally interrelated.

Within such a framework vandalism is revealed to be spontaneous behavior and the outgrowth of the social situations in which group interaction takes place. There is an observable movement as a result of this interaction. The initial inertia begins to give way as a series of successive interactional responses change the emotional climate of the social situation. Each interactive response builds upon the preceding until a focus develops and a solidary relationship results among the participants.

The act of vandalism functions as a means of ensuring group solidarity. Conformity to the peer group occurs because involvement tends to satisfy the adolescent's need dispositions for status, recognition, and response. Identification with societal property norms becomes subordinate to the demands of the peer group. The adolescent will thus participate in acts of property destruction in order not to appear "chicken." In other words, he can through this involvement maintain a satisfying self-definition and avoid becoming a marginal member of the group. Even though he may recognize the act to be "wrong" or "delinquent," he finds some comfort through the guilt-assuaging rationalizations present in the subculture of the peer group.

[39] Martin R. Haskell, "Toward a Reference Group Theory of Juvenile Delinquency," *Social Problems*, 8 (Winter 1960–1961), pp. 220–230.

[40] Sykes and Matza, p. 667.

[41] Shibutani, pp. 69 f.

Further research is needed in this important area of changing self-definitions. The preceding study pointed out that these redefinitions have a definite relationship to the situational context. The arrest experience is only one such context within which this redefinition takes place. Obviously, there are other significant situations effecting such change. It may occur at the time the participant is involved in a social act, such as, for example, when the boy is with a group on the verge or in the process of committing vandalism.

How easily the redefinition of self takes place may have a real relationship to the ease with which positive changes in treatment programs can be actuated. It may also have important bearing on efforts to formulate a typology of deviants when one of the important elements in the classification is the development within the behavior system of the individual's self-concept.[42]

[42] Cf. John W. Kinch, "Self-Conceptions of Types of Delinquents," *Sociological Inquiry*, 32 (Spring 1962), pp. 228–234.

AN INTERPRETATION OF SHOPLIFTING*

Mary Owen Cameron

There are two major groups of shoplifters: the commercial shoplifters ("boosters") and the pilferers ("snitches"). Boosters are similar to other professional thieves in that they are part of a criminal subculture. Pilferers, on the other hand, have little or no contact with criminal groups. Pilferers do not, for the most part, steal out of the desperation of poverty, nor are they, contrary to popular misconception, kleptomaniacs. In addition, most adult noncommercial pilferers do not conceive of themselves as thieves. In the selection below Dr. Cameron summarizes and interprets the findings from her study of shoplifting in a large department store in Chicago.

From the data already presented, two points are fairly clear: shoplifting is a frequent crime; and most shoplifters are noncommercial pilferers.

Most shoplifting, including pilfering, appears to be chronic, habitual or systematic behavior. In substantiating this generalization, it may be well to summarize the evidence.

Sixty-one per cent of women in the store sample had more than one stolen object in their possession when arrested.

Only about 5–10 percent of women detected in shoplifting are reported to have, when arrested, merchandise in their possession for which they had purchase receipts. It seems probable that a considerable section of the other 90–95 percent were in the store intending to shoplift rather than to buy.

Most pilferers are reported by store detectives to have developed techniques for getting rid of price tags and other incriminating evidence; to have planned ways of evading detection; to have come to the store equipped with receptacles for stolen merchandise; to be alert to potential followers. With these evidences of sophistication in technique it appears impossible to think of these pilferers as impulsive, accidental, or adventitious thieves.

There may or may not exist in any considerable number a third group of shoplifters consisting of impulsive persons who are overcome either by an unexpected urge to steal or by an unpremeditated desire for a particular object. Occasional souvenir hunters are arrested by store police, but store protection personnel do not believe that these people rcprcscnt any important section of shoplifters either in numbers or certainly in their contribution to inventory shrinkage. Economically and residentially the data show that people who steal one object before being apprehended are not different from other shoplifters.

Another generalization arising from the data presented is that most pilferers appear to have no present or sustained contact with a criminal subculture. Evidence on this point takes five forms.

(1) Ratios for the small selection sample of prosecuted shoplifters for whom prior records were obtained from the Police Department showed, when extrapolated to apply to the Court sample of adult women, that about 90 percent of women who were officially charged with shoplifting had probably never before been convicted of any offense. Store data show that a maximum of 2 percent of all women and 12 percent of all men who were apprehended for shoplifting had a prior criminal record with either private or public police in Chicago.

(2) Socioeconomic data on pilferers showed them to be mainly "respectable" employed persons or equally "respectable" housewives.

(3) The residences of the Lakeside Company pilferers in the city were not concentrated in slum areas, and neither were the residences of a sample of 407 white women whose addresses were obtained from the Court records and who had received "token" sentences or probation. Of this group, about 90 percent (see No. 1) were persons who had probably never before been convicted of crime. Their residential distribution in Chicago was approximately that of the Lost and Found claimants of the Lakeside Company, a measure presumed to be representative of typical shoppers in that store.

(4) The small value of the merchandise taken by pilferers implies that it could hardly have been stolen for sale to "fences" through recognized criminal channels. About 50 percent of the women charged with shoplifting in the Court sample had been charged with stealing merchandise worth less than $14.95, and 15 percent of the total had stolen less than $5.00 worth of merchandise. The actual median price tag values of merchandise stolen by persons arrested in the store were $6.74 for adult women and $8.30 for adult men.

(5) Finally, the attitude of pilferers toward arrest may be cited as evidence of absence of contact with a criminal subculture. In witnessing unobserved by the accused person, as the writer did, interrogations of arrested shoplifters, ignorance on the part of arrested pilferers of both criminal folkways and the actions of law enforcing agencies was only too obvious. Pilferers had no knowledge of arrest procedures, and they had clearly given little or no forethought to the consequences of their arrest. They appeared to have thought about being "caught," but not about being *arrested*. Not understanding that they would be searched, for example, many attempted to give fictitious names (for a woman, usually her maiden name) while at the same time carrying a billfold or pocketbook with complete

identification papers. (They did not realize that arrest implied search.) They consistently offered to pay for the stolen merchandise, failing to understand that they had been arrested and that the merchandise stolen had been impounded as evidence of theft and could not be bought by the thief. They frequently signed a waiver against suit of the store immediately after arrest—tantamount to a confession of guilt—but having signed the waiver, they talked threateningly about suit. (The waiver is simple in appearance, saying that there has been no damage, physical or otherwise, at the hands of store personnel, and detailing possible physical damage. The "otherwise," of course, is the waiver against all suit.) Not infrequently pilferers confessed some of their past thefts to store detectives, detailing the time, place, and objects stolen. Some of these past thefts had been memorable events arousing and continuing to arouse strong feelings of guilt.

These data seem to establish the fact that there exists a substantial number of persons who systematically steal merchandise, usually for their own use, and who are not in contact with a specific criminal subculture.

Although these persons were not, then, in association with law-violating groups, it is, however, possible and even probable that they had such associations in the past. Adult pilferers who work alone may have begun their careers as group juvenile delinquents, although not necessarily lower-class delinquents. It is apparent from the data that a large number of young people in Chicago practice shoplifting and presumably learn attitudes and rationalizations favorable to shoplifting and techniques for shoplifting in contact with other adolescents. There is a steady and marked relationship between increasing chronological age and the proportions of shoplifters arrested without companions or accomplices. For women, especially, the number of cases is sufficient to establish a trend, namely a steady and increasing proportion of persons arrested "alone" for each 5-year period between the ages of 15 and 65. The increase of those alone when arrested is most marked between the ages of 15 and 25. Year by year, there is an increase from the ages of 9 to 19 of the proportion of shoplifters alone when arrested. In five-year intervals, the range in the proportion "with others" when arrested runs from 100 percent for those less than 9 years to 0 percent for those above 65 years of age. If indeed shoplifting is a form of criminal behavior in which the techniques and supporting attitudes are learned in the companionship of others, one would expect to find decreasing evidence of companionship as age increases, for at the younger age levels more people would be in the initial stages of the learning process. This is found, and found regularly and strikingly, in the proportion in which it would be expected. But the evidence on the question is certainly incomplete. As far as the data show, it is theoretically possible that the "group shoplifters" who are mainly juvenile may have ceased shoplifting on reaching maturity and a wholly different segment of people began shoplifting in their mature years. It seems more reasonable, however, to suppose that at least an important proportion of the juvenile pilferers either continued to shoplift or later restarted shoplifting.

Adult systematic or habitual pilferers, then, appear to be mainly "respectable" people not in contact with a criminal subculture and showing no special knowledge of the adult criminal world. Although of adult age, pilferers' behavior when apprehended and their excuses for theft appear to be similar to the excuses of the juvenile group. The writer's impression was that in attempting to explain away their thefts, adult pilferers were using the lies, rationalizations, and alibis characteristic of children caught in acts considered reprehensible by adults. They were not realistically facing the different problem of being an arrested adult.

A further generalization from the data

on shoplifting is that adult pilferers do not appear to be compulsive, neurotic personalities. Material bearing on the relationship of personality structure to shoplifting is as follows:

(1) Shoplifting is not frequently associated with psychoses of sufficient intensity to warrant commitment to a mental hospital. Only 12 of 873, or 1.4 percent, of women charged in the Court were committed to mental institutions; of the 1153 people in the store sample, only 4 were committed, a rather smaller proportion, it would seem, than would be found in an unselected cross section of the population.

(2) Shoplifters were not found in psychiatric examination to have any consistent psychoneurotic patterns. Of the 873 women in the Court sample, 57 were recommended by the judges for psychiatric examination. Positive findings were recorded for 55. Of these, 12 were committed to mental institutions. Of the remaining 43, 8 were found to be suffering from involutional disturbances and this was the most frequent finding. No other single diagnosis was made for more than six cases. Thus we can say that no particular trend of personality aberration was recorded as characteristic of any considerable number of women shoplifters.

(3) Neither store arrests nor official charges indicate a tendency for shoplifting rates of women to increase during the ages (45–50) when menopause most frequently occurs.

(4) Among pilferers who are apprehended and interrogated by the store police but set free without formal charge, there is very little or no recidivism. This point, to be discussed later, is important in several respects and is relatively well established by the data of this study. The figures presented here on recidivism are in most respects more complete than "official" figures which are usually used. They include: (1) official figures of arrest by the Chicago Police Department for some cases; (2) the outcome of trial for a larger number of cases—an outcome, it has been established, based largely on known prior arrests; (3) the private arrest records cooperatively kept by the association for store protection maintained by ten downtown department stores in Chicago.

If shoplifting were a form of compulsive, neurotic, or irrational behavior (kleptomania), a very high rate of recidivism among pilferers would have been found. Few persons arrested for shoplifting ever receive the psychiatric attention necessary to alleviate deep-rooted personality disturbances. Yet, once arrested, interrogated, and in their own perspective, perhaps humiliated, pilferers apparently stop pilfering. The rate of recidivism is amazingly low. The reward of shoplifting, whatever it is, is not worth the cost to reputation and self-esteem. Pilfering is not for all, or almost all, shoplifters a basic neurotic manifestation in the sense that alcoholism or other compulsive behaviors seem to be. Even at great cost to their status and apparent comfort, alcoholics continue drinking. No compulsive neurotic ceases his neurotic behavior merely because he is told to do so no matter how forcibly he is told, but apparently shoplifting is a form of behavior which the person can govern apart from the general control of whatever psychoneurotic tendencies he may have.

It can be argued, and it may be a valid argument, that having been blocked from theft, emotionally disturbed persons merely find other ways of expressing hostile, antisocial, or compulsive behavior. Nevertheless if the focus of attention is on shoplifting specifically or even on criminality in general, the concrete direction taken by pathological impulses and the apparent modifiability of these directions is a matter of considerable practical importance. The housewife who has (hypothetically) had shoplifting as an outlet for hostility and finds after arrest that this outlet is now possible only at a greater risk to her reputation, self-esteem, and personal freedom than she is prepared to take, may turn to nagging her husband or she may develop an ulcer. To the psychotherapist whose goal is general personality adjustment, perhaps no essential change has been made. In the eyes of the law, the sociologist, or the store owner, however, the change has been very important, and the mechanism through which this change has been made needs to be understood as completely as possible.

SHOPLIFTING IN RELATION TO A THEORY OF CRIMINAL BEHAVIOR

In the interpretation of the causes of crime, sociologists have generally accepted some direct or modified form of cultural determinism. Psychologists have stressed crime as a symptom of deeper emotional disturbance stemming from unmet needs in infancy and childhood or from uninhibited "id" impulses or similar sources deeply imbedded in the personality structure of the criminal.

The most widely accepted sociological viewpoint on the general sources of crime was placed directly by Sutherland when he constructed his theory of "differential association," stating:

Criminal behavior is learned . . . in interaction with other persons in a process of communication. . . . The principal part of the learning . . . occurs within intimate personal groups. . . . A person becomes delinquent because of an excess of definitions favorable to the violation of the law over definitions unfavorable to the violation of the law.[1]

Alexander and Staub give an equally direct statement of the psychoanalytical position.

Within the innermost nucleus of the personality . . . it is impossible to differentiate normal from criminal impulses. The human being enters the world as a criminal, i.e., socially not adjusted. During the first years of his life the human individual preserves his criminality to the fullest degree. . . . The criminal carries out in his actions his natural, unbridled, instinctual drives; he acts as the child would act if he could. The repressed,

and therefore unconscious criminality of the normal man finds a few socially harmless outlets, like the dream and phantasy life, neurotic symptoms and also some transitional forms of behavior which are harmless. . . . The only difference between the criminal and the normal individual is that the normal man partially controls his criminal drives and finds outlets for them in socially harmless activities.[2]

The material on pilfering presented here constitutes an exception to narrowly defined cultural determinism, for in this study there have been isolated a substantial number of people who appear to be chronic, systematic thieves in the sense that their thefts are not unique, impulsive acts, but involve intent and planning and seem to be carried out with some frequency, regularity and sophistication; yet for these people there is no evidence of present association with a criminal subculture, and there is, in fact, considerable evidence that there is no such association. Within the scope of this study there was no opportunity to discover whether or not individual pilferers had been associated with a delinquent subculture in the past. My own conjecture is that most of them had. In support of this belief may be cited the skills and techniques employed in shoplifting and the irresponsible and naive behavior of the arrested pilferers. The decreasing number of pilferers who were known to be "with others" at the time of arrest as the age of arrested pilferers increased also is relevant. It seems probable that having learned the arts and crafts of shoplifting from juvenile contemporaries, some adults continue pilfering by themselves and continue feeling that although they are adults they are, in fact, acting as naughty children and not really "criminal." Shoplifting thus appears to be the only crime in otherwise "blameless" lives. Adult pilferers are respectable people who carry on their criminal behavior clandestinely and surreptitiously.

The data on pilferers, then, appear to

[1] Sutherland, Edwin H., *Principles of Criminology* (Philadelphia, 1947), p. 4.

[2] Alexander, Franz and Hugo Staub, *The Criminal, the Judge and the Public: A Psychological Analysis* (New York), pp. 34–35.

support the general psychiatric interpretation of crime presented earlier in the words of Alexander and Staub. Shoplifters act as children "would if they could." According to the data assembled here, pilferers do act like children, and a very large proportion of them are children. There is, however, more to the story than mere immaturity, either chronological or psychological. Pilfering is not just acting out unbridled, hostile "id" impulses. To understand pilfering we must know why hostile impulses are acted out by the very specific means of stealing merchandise from stores rather than by violence, crying, cringing or other possible outlets for hostile instinctual drives. Alexander and Staub's explanation is (and is intended to be) a general explanation of adult misbehavior. As such it can be an acceptable base on which to work. But the criminologist's question (and the storekeeper's as well) is "Why this particular outlet? Why shoplifting?"

Many psychiatrically oriented writers have attempted fairly specific explanations of pilfering. These explanations are uniformly disappointing because they are based on conjecture rather than evidence. Benjamin Karpman, Maslow and Mittlemann, and David Abrahamsen, among others, have stressed the belief that shoplifting belongs among the compulsive neurotic acts characteristic of sexually deprived and/or extremely hostile people.

The conditions grouped under the heading of manias are characterized by the fact that the patient engages in acts that are unlawful, in spite of the fact that he is reluctant to commit them and knows that he thereby runs the danger of arrest and punishment. Such patients behave and act well and apparently normally when they are not engaged in these activities. . . . The objects stolen are either not of much use to these individuals, or they do not have to be obtained through theft. . . . Sometimes a person steals objects which have a sexual significance for him. . . .[3]

[3] Maslow, A. H. and Bela Mittlemann, *Principles of Abnormal Psychology* (New York, 1941), p. 394.

Abrahamsen in his *Crime and the Human Mind* says,

We are apt to be satisfied when it appears that a crime has been committed because of apparent gain, but this is not always the real motive. Indeed in delving into the causes of certain types of stealing, such as shoplifting . . . one finds motives which are beyond any comprehension of the culprit. One may find that stealing, which takes the form of a kleptomania, is an expression of a disguised wish for sexual intercourse. . . .

In interpreting what takes place unconsciously in the mind of a pyromaniac or a kleptomaniac, one may say that desires of the id and a desire for punishment alternate, the obsessional neurosis acting as a defense against aggressive impulses. The conflict is internalized while the person's superego keeps the conflict back, with the result that he has to act out his inclination. Deep in the unconscious is a forbidden wish such as a sexual one.[4]

"The true kleptomaniac," says Karpman "belongs in the impulse-ridden and compulsive group. Female kleptomaniacs are believed to be sexually unsatisfied women with tremendous hostility."[5]

In several important respects the data in this study seem to be at variance with these psychological interpretations: (a) There are no data yet established to support the belief that shoplifting is particularly characteristic of women beyond the expected numbers implied in their presence as shoppers in places where shoplifting arrests are made. (b) The psychiatric data from Court cases present nothing to indicate the association of any substantial number of shoplifters with any recognized type of personality deviation. (c) The data show that pilferers generally take objects which are useful as status symbols rather than sexual symbols. (d) The data also indicate that once arrested, pilferers cease shoplifting. This fact is totally inconsistent with the interpretation of shoplifting as "compulsive." "There is never a repeat arrest of an

[4] Abrahamsen, David. *Crime and the Human Mind* (New York, 1944), pp. 21, 107.
[5] Karpman, Benjamin, *The Sexual Offender and His Offenses* (New York, 1954), p. 138.

individual who seemed to realize his problems," said Edwards,[6] writing as an experienced store detective.

To find a case of "kleptomania," Edwards searched his memory from the early part of his more than 20 years of experience in store protection.

Probably the most typical case of kleptomania first came to my attention shortly after entering protection work.

It was reported to me that an exceptionally well and expensively dressed, distinguished and matronly-appearing woman had been observed to steal several inexpensive articles. On two other occasions she had attempted to secure refunds on items for which she had no sales check; they were taken from her and the refund refused. She made no further claim for them, so instructions were given to the operators to apprehend her the next time she lifted anything regardless of the price.

Within a few days she was caught stealing items with a value of about $12.00. She admitted previous thefts and gave assurance that it would never occur again. She was advised to discuss her problem with her husband, a man of prominence.

Several months later she was again apprehended shoplifting. On this occasion she dropped to her knees and begged and pleaded that her husband should not be called. Anything would be promised to avoid it. He was called.

The husband was critical of the fact that he had not been notified of the first episode because he had subsequently been embarrassed when she had taken something from the home of friends. I was blamed for his embarrassment over this, but after some discussion the couple left to visit a psychiatrist.

Some time later I learned that the same woman had been taken to court for shoplifting in another store but that was not her last experience.

Some months elapsed and she was once more apprehended, and again was taken to court. Her psychiatrist appeared in court at the time of this trial, and informed the judge that the

defendant had refused to cooperate with his efforts at treatment and had been sent to a sanitarium by her husband. While there she had pilfered articles from the rooms of other patients which caused her dismissal.

I credit the judge with a wise decision. He continued the case for one year with the stipulation that she was to cooperate with the doctor; that if she failed to do so he was to report to the court, her case would then be advanced on the docket, and she would be sentenced to serve a year's term. The doctor gave a favorable report and she was discharged when the case was finally heard a year later.

I chanced to meet this woman once since. She was in the store with a friend but stopped to assure me that she had overcome her problems and would never again meet me under the previous circumstances. This last meeting was many years ago and I am confident that if she had been in any trouble since, that is, in our city, I would have heard of it.[7]

Although neither conventional sociological explanations of career criminality nor explanations of shoplifting as a consequence of psychological disturbance seem to fit the data, some hypotheses, however, can be put forward which do fit the research data. These hypotheses can be rephrased in more general terms, and the relationship of the findings on pilfering to other research data discussed.

EXPLANATION OF PILFERING

It seems probable that most adult pilferers start their careers as children or adolescents in groups where the techniques of successful pilfering are learned from other more experienced children. Later as group activity is abandoned some of the group members continue the practices they learned as adolescents. The lavish displays of merchandise which department stores exhibit to encourage "impulse buying" are, for the experienced pilferer, there for the taking.

Adult women pilferers, generally belonging to families of rather modest income, enter department stores with a strong sense

[6] Edwards, Loren, *Shoplifting and Shrinkage Protection for Stores.* (Springfield, Ill., 1958), p. 135.

[7] *Ibid.*, pp. 52–53.

of the limitations of their household budgets. They do not steal merchandise which they can rationalize purchasing: household supplies, husband's clothes; children's wear. But beautiful and luxury goods for their personal use can be purchased legitimately only if some other member of the family is deprived. Although pilferers often have guilt feelings about their thefts, it still seems to them less wrong to steal from a rich store than to take from the family budget. Pilferers seem to be, thus, narcissistic individuals in that they steal for their own personal use, but, on the other hand, they do not use the limited family income for their own luxury goods.

Pilferers differ in one outstanding respect, at least, from other thieves: They generally do not think of themselves as thieves. In fact, even when arrested, they resist strongly being pushed to admit their behavior is theft. This became very clear as I observed a number of interrogations of shoplifters by the store detective staff, and it was supported in conversations with the detectives who drew on their own wider experience. It is quite often difficult for the store staff to convince the arrested person that he has actually been arrested, even when the detectives show their licenses and badges. Again and again store police explain to pilferers that they are under arrest as thieves, that they will, in the normal course of events, be taken in a police van to jail, held in jail until bond is raised, and tried in a court before a judge and sentenced. Much of the interview time of store detectives is devoted to establishing this point; in making the pilferer understand that what happens to him from the time of his arrest is a legal question, but it is still a question for decision, first of all, by the store staff.

Store detectives use the naivete of pilferers as an assistance in arrest procedures while the pilferer is in the presence of legitimate customers on the floor of the store. The most tactful approach possible is used. The store detective will say, for example, "I represent the store office, and I'm afraid

the office will have to see what's in your shopping bag. Would you care to come with me, please?" If the pilferer protests, the detective adds, "You wouldn't want to be embarrassed in front of all these people, would you? In the office we can talk things over in private."

Edwards states that the method of making an arrest is important in preventing excitement and even disorder.

A gentle approach will usually disarm any shoplifter, amateur or professional, while a rough seizure or loud accusation may immediately put him on the defensive. At other times it may result in a nervous or hysterical condition accompanied by an involuntary discharge which may be embarrassing to both the arrestor and the arrested.[8]

Inbau adds the thought that the gentle approach is helpful too in forestalling suits for false arrest.

The finesse with which defendant accosts plaintiff is a definite factor also affecting the temper with which the court approaches a case. The defendant acting in good faith with probable cause, whose attitude is quiet, non-threatening, and deferential to the plaintiff's feelings can weather an honest mistake much more cheaply than otherwise. At the most it may induce a court to find there was no imprisonment at all. At the least, it will relieve defendant of punitive damages and reduce the amount of actual damages.[9]

The "deference" of the arresting detective combined with the already existing rationalizations of the pilferer sustain in him the belief that whereas his behavior might be reprehensible, the objects taken were, after all, not of great value; he would be glad to pay for them and be on his way. "Yes, I took the dress," one woman sobbed as she was being closely interrogated, "but that doesn't mean I'm a thief."

Arrest forces the pilferer to think of himself as a thief. The interrogation procedure of the store is specifically and consciously aimed at breaking down any illusions the

[8] *Ibid.*, p. 134.
[9] Inbau, Fred E., "Protection and Recapture of Merchandise from Shoplifters," *Illinois Law Review*, Vol. 46, No. 6. 1952.

shoplifter may have that his behavior is regarded as merely "naughty" or "bad." The
breakdown of illusions is, to the store detective staff, both a goal in itself and a
means of establishing the fact that each
innocent-appearing pilferer is not, in fact, a
professional thief "putting on an act." In
the interrogation the shoplifter is searched
for other stolen merchandise and for identification papers. Pockets and pocketbooks are
thoroughly examined. All papers, letters,
tickets, bills, etc., are read in detail in spite
of considerable protest from the arrested
person. Each person is made to explain
everything he has with him. If suspect items
such as public locker keys, pawn tickets,
etc., are found, he will have to explain very
thoroughly indeed and agree to have the
locker examined and the pawned merchandise seen to avoid formal charge. In
any event, once name, address, and occupation have been established (and for women,
the maiden name and names in other marriages), the file of names and identifying
material of all persons who have, in the past
years, been arrested in any of the State
Street department stores is consulted. The
shoplifter is questioned at length if similarities of names or other identifying data are
encountered.

While identification and prior record are
being checked, store detectives, persons in
charge of refunds, and even experienced sales
clerks may be summoned to look at the
arrested person to determine if he has been
previously suspected of stealing merchandise
or has been noted as behaving suspiciously.

In the course of all this investigation, it
becomes increasingly clear to the pilferer
that he is considered a thief and is in imminent danger of being hauled into court
and publicly exhibited as such. This realization is often accompanied by a dramatic
change in attitudes and by severe emotional
disturbance. Occasionally even hysterical
semiattempts at suicide result.

The professional shoplifter who has been
arrested and knows he is recognized, on the
other hand, behaves quite differently. He

does, of course, make every effort possible
to talk his way out of the situation. But
once he finds that this is impossible, he accepts jail and its inconveniences as a normal
hazard of his trade.

"This is a nightmare," said one woman
pilferer who had been formally charged
with stealing an expensive handbag. "It
can't be happening to me! Why, oh, why
can't I wake up and find that it isn't so,"
she cried later as she waited at a store exit,
accompanied by a city and a store policeman, for the city police van to arrive.
"Whatever will I do? Please make it go
away," she pleaded with the officer. "I'll be
disgraced forever. I can never look anyone
in the face again."

*Pilferers expect no "in-group" support
for their behavior.* As they become aware of
the possible serious consequences of their
arrest (trial, jail, etc.), pilferers obviously
feel isolated from all supporting relationships. Store detectives report that the most
frequent question women ask is, "Will my
husband have to know about this?" Men,
they say, express immediate fear that their
employers will be informed of their arrest
when questions about employment are
raised. Children are apprehensive of parental
reaction. Edwards says,

The composure of juveniles being detained has
never ceased to amaze me, that is, until notified
that they must tell a parent of their misdemeanor. Then the tears flow and pleadings
begin. The interviewer must be firm in his
denial that notification will "kill" the parent,
and he must sell the child on the idea that
any deviation from accepted practice must be
discussed with the person most interested in
his welfare.[10]

Pilferers feel that if their family or friends
learn about their arrest they will be thoroughly disgraced. The fear, shame, and re-
morse expressed by arrested pilferers could
not be other than genuine and a reflection
of their appraisal of the attitudes they believe others will take toward them. One
woman was observed who, thoroughly

[10] Edwards, *op. cit.*, pp. 135–136.

shaken as the realization of her predicament began to appear to her, interrupted her protestations of innocence from time to time, overwhelmed at the thought of how some particular person in her "in-group" would react to her arrest. Her conversation with the interrogator ran somewhat as follows: "I didn't intend to take the dress. I just wanted to see it in daylight. [She had stuffed it into a shopping bag and carried it out of the store.] Oh, what will my husband do? I *did* intend to pay for it. It's all a mistake. Oh, my God, what will my mother say! I'll be glad to pay for it. See, I've got the money with me. Oh, my children! They can't find out I've been *arrested!* I'd never be able to face them again."

Pilferers not only expect no in-group support, but feel that they have literally *no* one to turn to. The problem of being embroiled in a wholly unfamiliar legal situation is obviously not only frightening but unexpected. Apparently they had anticipated being reprimanded; they had not anticipated being searched by a licensed detective, identified, and, on the whole, placed in a position in which the burden of argument for keeping out of jail was theirs.

The contrast in behavior between the pilferer and the recognized and self-admitted thief is striking. The experienced thief either already knows what to do or knows precisely where and how to find out. His emotional reactions may involve anger directed at himself or at features in the situation around him, but he is not at a loss for reactions. He follows the prescribed modes of behavior, and knows, either because of prior experience or through the vicarious experiences of acquaintances, what arrest involves by way of obligations and rights. He has some familiarity with bonding practice and either already has or knows how to find a lawyer who will act for him.

Because the adult pilferer does not think of himself, prior to his arrest, as a thief and can conceive of no in-group support for himself in that role, his arrest forces him to reject the role (at least insofar as department store

shoplifting is concerned). The arrest procedure, even though not followed by prosecution, is in itself sufficient to cause him to redefine his situation. He is, of course, informed that subsequent arrest by any store will be followed by immediate prosecution and probably by a considerable jail sentence. But since this does not act as a deterrent to the self-admitted thief nor could this kind of admonition deter the compulsive neurotic, neither the fear of punishment nor the objective severity of the punishment in itself is the crucial point in relation to the change from criminal to law abiding behavior. Rather the threat to the person's system of values and prestige relationships is involved. Social scientists who have investigated criminal activities which have subcultural support are unanimous in pointing out the persistence of criminal activity: the high rate of recidivism and the resistance to reform shown by law violators. Pilfering seems to be the other side of the coin. Not having the support of a criminal subculture, pilferers are very "reformable" individuals. If the findings of this study are substantiated by studies of other offenses in which the offenders are similarly without support of a criminal subculture, there would be a strong argument in favor of keeping pilferers out of jail lest they receive there the kinds of knowledge and emotional support they need to become "successful" commercial thieves. Crime prevention would seem best achieved by helping the law violators retain their self-image of respectability while making it clear to them that a second offense will really mean disgrace.

Cloward and Ohlin give much weight to this point when discussing juvenile offenders:

The youngster who is motivated by a sense of injustice generally commits his first acts of defiance in a climate of uncertainty and fear of disapproval. The withdrawal of attributions of legitimacy from the dominant social norms is initially tentative and unstable. These first acts are usually minor and often impulsive expressions of resentment against the apparent injustice of the established social order. However, they bring the individual into conflict with the official system and expose him to its arsenal of invidious definitions and punitive sanctions. Members of the conventional community are likely to respond to them with strong efforts at repression, precisely because they recognize the underlying attitude of alienation from the established norms. These early acts of defiance are in effect tentative steps toward the adoption of norms in competition with the official rules. At this stage the deviant needs all the encouragement he can muster to defend his position. He finds these by searching out others who have faced similar experiences and who will support one another in common attitudes of alienation from the official system.[11]

The first offender, whether juvenile or adult, need not search far to find others who have faced similar experiences if he is placed in an institution populated wholly by others who have similarly been arrested.

Generalizing from the data of this study we find:

A. Some forms of criminal behavior can be carried on in isolation from supporting relationships for the activities of the law violator, but in such a noncriminal system of relationships and values, criminal behavior is unstable and ceases when the person finds that to continue the behavior he must define himself as a criminal with the consequent status changes.

1. This means that it is possible for a person to behave as a thief without defining himself as a thief and without seeing his behavior as it will be defined by representatives of the law enforcing culture.

2. On the other hand, it is possible for a person to behave as a thief and to accept himself as a thief when it does not isolate him from his primary group and community contacts. This, of course, is a characteristic of the "booster" and is apparently the common condition in most other kinds of recognized delinquency and crime (burglary, confidence games, robbery, pocketpicking, the "protected" rackets, etc.).

11 Cloward, Richard and Lloyd Ohlin, *Delinquency and Opportunity* (New York, 1960), pp. 126–127.

3. When, however a person is unwilling to accept himself as a thief because it will isolate him from his intimates (he will lose his "respectability"), he will cease stealing. He will cease even though his satisfaction from the crimes has been great, his motivation to continue his theft has been strong, his emotional adjustment weak, his psychological reaction apparently compulsive, or inadequate and infantile, or "he" is a woman suffering from an involutional reaction.

Since most shoplifters do not conceive of themselves as thieves, how do they perceive their own behavior? On this very interesting question the statistical data provide little information. The only clues we have are in the kinds of merchandise taken, which has been commented upon, and from the scattered interview material. Pilferers appear to take merchandise just a little above the level of that which they would buy and they rationalize their thefts so that their behavior can appear to themselves as somewhat reprehensible but not really criminal. They steal, for example, at stores which carry inexpensive lines of merchandise, and even at Lakeside Company, many shoplifters steal from the "budget floor."

Exactly what the rationalizations are, how frequently different types of rationalizations are used could not be determined from the evidence available in this study. An examination of the psychological mechanisms used by pilferers to explain their crimes to themselves and to others would be very interesting.

Pilfering is not the only form of criminal behavior, however, in which processes of rationalization seem to operate in a similar way. Cressey found in his study of embezzlement that

. . . trusted persons become trust violators when they conceive of themselves as having a financial problem which is nonshareable, have the knowledge or awareness that this problem can be secretly resolved by violation of the position of financial trust, and are able to apply to their own conduct in that situation verbalizations which enable them to adjust their conceptions of themselves as users of entrusted funds or property.[12]

Cressey found further,

... most of the trust violators encountered did not so much abandon the folkways of legitimate business behavior as they did restructure the situation in such a way that, from their point of view, they were not abandoning the folkways. Similarly, except for the absconders, the attitudes of the men interviewed were not so much "anti-social" as they were "pro-social" in that the endeavor was to keep from considering themselves as criminals.[13]

Cressey quoted numerous statements of different embezzlers who behaved in a criminal manner without so defining themselves.

I did not plan to keep the money permanently, though I never thought much about just how I was going to get it back.

If the rural depression, which was already bad in that year had ended the next year, I could have replaced the bonds and no one would have known the difference. . . . I have never felt that I was committing a crime.

Maybe it was phony reasoning but I was going to put it [the money] back. . . .

On the embezzlement, in my way of think-

[12] Cressey, Donald, "The Criminal Violation of Financial Trust," *American Sociological Review,* 1950, p. 742.
[13] Cressey, Donald, *The Criminal Violation of Financial Trust.* (unpublished dissertation, Indiana University, 1950), p. 132.

ing, it wasn't embezzlement because I was borrowing it. . . .

I reasoned that I was going to pay it back ($150) in three or four days, and I did pay it back. In a matter of a few days I took some more—it got easier as time went on. From then on it varied. There might be a period of a week or ten days when I'd neither put in nor take out.[14]

Cressey also pointed out that there was a different group of embezzlers, not included in his study, who were, in fact, confidence men or other professional criminals who obtained positions of trust under false pretenses for the purpose of theft. These appear similar to "boosters."

There is unquestionably much in the common culture to support theft, especially petty theft. Most people with whom I have discussed the problem admit to having stolen items of small value. Sutherland found among his university classes that 98 percent of the students were at least "mildly delinquent"[15] and an examination of a part of his original data showed that 20 of 36 (55 percent) of the students admitted shoplifting, chiefly from variety stores. Some of them recorded as rationalization for their thefts that stores were rich and the little they took "would never be missed." It seems likely that this might be a type of rationalization commonly used by pilferers.

[14] *Ibid.,* pp. 85–110.
[15] *Op. cit.,* p. 113.

AN ISOLATION AND CLOSURE THEORY OF NAIVE CHECK FORGERY*

Edwin M. Lemert

Professor Lemert's study of naive check forgery represents one of the first attempts at the delineation and explanation of a type of

* Reprinted by special permission of the author and the *Journal of Criminal Law, Criminology and Police Science,* Copyright © 1953 by the Northwestern University School of Law, Volume 44, Number 3, 1953, pp. 296–307.

criminal behavior. Naive check forgery as a type refers to forgeries committed by persons who have had no previous criminal record and no previous contact and interaction with delinquents and criminals. Naive check forgery is explained in terms of the social isolation of the offender, specific situational factors, and the process of closure.

The research on forgery we report here is inspired by the methodological dissent from older formulations in criminology—formulations which incorporated generalizations covering all crime and all criminals. At the same time our report is a part of that dissent. As such it seeks to build in a cumulative way upon the work of Hall and Sutherland, who have insisted that criminological research will best advance through the study of sociologically defined units of criminal behavior.[1] Over and beyond this, ready justification for the inquiry rests in the paucity of descriptive data available on the crime of forgery itself and the almost complete absence of efforts at its systematic analysis.[2]

In the process of collecting and analyzing our data it soon became apparent that the invocation of many of our more generalized theories of crime provided only minimal insight into the cases which came under our purview. Culture conflict, delinquency area background, emotional conflict and others proved either to be completely irrelevant or non-discriminating theories so far as causation was concerned. While Sutherland's concept of differential association appeared as a necessary factor in the explanation of professional forgery it was found to be unrelated in any important way to the class of forgery cases we chose to consider, namely, naive check forgeries. Hence, a considerable amount of innovating became necessary in order to explain and interpret our research findings. A preliminary of our theoretical formulation was the definition of the behavior unit subsumed under naive check forgery.

In terms of generic or common law, forgery is thought of as the false signing of a legal instrument which creates a liability. This holds even if or when the entire legal instrument is false and only gives the appearance of legality. Thus defined, forgery covers a wide variety of acts, such as forging wills, public documents, sales slips and prescriptions for narcotic drugs. It is not our purpose to propound a theory subsuming all such acts but rather one for check forgeries only. This includes all acts commonly charged as forgery, fictitious checks, issuing checks without sufficient funds, and uttering and passing falsified checks. The theory cannot without further research be applied to forgeries arising out of mail thefts or out of the theft and the raising of money orders.

The concept of naive forgery was devised to indicate forgeries committed by persons who have had no previous criminal record and no previous contact and interaction with delinquents and criminals. It is designed to exclude forgeries which are incidental to the commission of other crimes, and forgeries which are retrogressive or progressive phases of an already established criminal career. Common examples of the types of forgeries eliminated would be those of burglars who come onto a drawer full of

[1] Jerome Hall, *Theft Law and Society*, 1935, Introduction; E. H. Sutherland, *Principles of Criminology*, Revised, 1947, Chapter 13.

[2] While there are incidental data on forgery scattered through the literature on crime we note only two descriptive articles exclusively devoted to forgery: I. A. Berg, *A Comparative Study of Forgery, Journal of Applied Psychology*, 28, 1944; David Maurer, *The Argot of Forgery, American Speech*, December 1941, pp. 243–250: some attempt at the analysis of the forger's behavior will be found in John Gillin, *The Wisconsin Prisoner*, 1949, p. 167; an informal historical treatment of the subject is at hand in Henry T. F. Rhodes, *The Craft of Forgery*, 1934.

checks in burglarizing a business office and often—not too wisely—cash them. We also exclude the forgeries committed by embezzlers, as well as the occasional forgeries of con men, chiefly because they are incidental or alternative techniques by which their crimes are committed. The embezzler is further distinguished from the forger by reason of his being in a position of trust.

The validity of our delimitation of the class of forgeries about which we seek to generalize may be questioned on the grounds that it narrows excessively the universe of crimes and correspondingly decreases the usefulness of our generalizations. The answer to any such question we hold will be found in the nature of the prior records of those convicted of forgery. From the following tabulation we can make several important observations on this point.

Table 1.
PRIOR RECORDS OF 1023 PERSONS CONVICTED FOR FORGERY IN LOS ANGELES COUNTY 1938 AND 1939.

NATURE OF PRIOR RECORD	NUMBER	PERCENT
No prior record	306	29.9
Prior forgery only	189	18.5
Prior forgery plus other crimes	211	20.6
Other crimes only	317	30.9
Total	1023	99.9

First we see that almost one third of the forgers had no prior record whatsoever and almost one half were either in this class or had committed only prior forgeries. In the other two categories there are included substantial numbers of persons convicted on petty theft or grand theft charges which in actuality were forgeries but which for legal reasons were prosecuted otherwise. Also there was a sizeable number of persons whose records involved forgeries plus drunkenness or drunkenness only, which cases we may regard as involving persons essentially without criminal sophistication. Finally

there was a fair number of cases such as those of sex offenders, offenders against family laws, desertions from the armed forces and certain Federal offenses (illegal entry, impersonating an officer) which do not presume criminal associations or learning. Altogether we would be inclined to add another 27 percent of the cases to our general category of naive forgeries, thus raising the total to 75 percent for which our theory is pertinent.

Our theory of naive check forgery as delimited above can be stated in terms of (a) the characteristics of the crime (b) the person (c) the situation (d) the sociopsychological process. The hypothesis in general is that naive check forgery arises at a critical point in a process of social isolation, out of certain types of social situations, and is made possible by the closure or constriction of behavior alternatives subjectively held as available to the forger. We will attempt to show how the four enumerated factors operate both directly and in interaction with one another to produce the crime.

THE CHARACTERISTICS OF CRIME

A number of crimes such as robbery, assault, rape, certain forms of theft and burglary are high visibility crimes in that they are either objectively apparent to others or subjectively perceived by their perpetrators as crimes prior to or at the time they are committed. In contrast to these, check forgeries, especially those committed by first offenders, have low visibility. There is little in the criminal act or in the interaction between the check passer and the person cashing the check to identify it as a crime. Closely related to this special quality of the forgery crime is the fact that while it is formally defined and treated as a felonious or "infamous" crime it is informally held (by the legally untrained public) to be a relatively benign form of crime.[3] The combined effect of these two factors, we will show, facilitates

[3] This inconsistency has a long history. See Henry Rhodes, op. cit., p. 22.

the subjective acceptance of a particular criminal solution to the crisis situation.

THE PERSON

The concept of person is used here simply as a way of delimiting the class of people most likely to commit forgery when situational and sociopsychological factors are present and operate in certain sequence. Generally speaking, forgers tend to be native white in origin, male, and much older than other criminals when they commit their crimes—somewhere in their very late twenties and early thirties. Their intelligence is much higher than that of other criminals and they equal or surpass the general population in the number of years of education they have completed. The occupational classes contributing disproportionately to the population of forgers are clerical, professional, and skilled or craft workers. More particularly, salesmen within the clerical group have a greater-than-expected representation among persons convicted of this crime. Many forgers come from prestigeful, wealthy families in which siblings have achieved considerable social eminence. A large percentage of forgers for many years have been residents of the community in which their crimes are committed. According to comparisons we have made between the past records of forgers and those of burglars and robbers the former are less likely to have a record of juvenile delinquency. From this and the data of our interview sample we are convinced that very few forgers have originated from the so-called "delinquency areas" of their communities.[4]

4 The data for this paper consist of statistical materials compiled on 1023 cases of forgery in Los Angeles County for 1938 and 1939 and a sample of 29 forgers interviewed by the writer at the Los Angeles County Wayside Honor Rancho. Interviews lasted from 45 minutes to two hours. We are indebted to the Los Angeles County Sheriff's department and especially to Captain Harold Stallings for making available facilities and permission to conduct the interviews. In general what

The description of forgers in terms of temperament and personality tendencies is a much more hazardous academic task than their demographic characterization. Nevertheless, we will suggest certain differentials of this sort, chiefly because of their rather uniform occurrence in the interview data. The most obtrusive of these appeared as a distaste or sense of repugnance towards forms of crime other than forgery. In case after case come the unsolicited "I could never hurt anyone," or "I wouldn't have the nerve (or guts) to rob anyone or to steal." While all criminals tend to rationalize their crimes somewhat in the prison situation evidence that we were confronted with real differentials came from other sources, namely, the experience of detectives, who say they seldom if ever have trouble arresting a forger; often they are waiting for the police to come, or they voluntarily give themselves up. Guns are very rarely found in the possession of persons arrested on forgery charges and when they are it is usually a case of some other type of criminal casually turned to check passing. It is also true that inmates of prisons recognize a temperamental difference of forgers, sharply distinguishing them from men in the so-called "heavy rackets."[5]

Detectives who have dealt many years with forgers depict them generally as people who are personally likeable and attractive, who easily ingratiate themselves and who have a facile grasp of the arts of convincing others. They are people who like to live well and fast, being able to con a merchant or "snow a dame under" with equal dispatch. As one burglar (non-forger) put it: "Forgers are guys who like to pretend to be someone they ain't." In addition it has been observed that an element of impulsiveness seems to thread through the behavior of forgers, being detectable even among professionals, who, for example, have expressed to the writer their dislike for

we have said thus far about the population of forgers is corroborated by the findings of I. Berg, op. cit.

5 I. Berg, op. cit.

con games because of the slow "build-up" involved.

Because the observations we record above refer to sophisticated forgers as well as to naive forgers it is difficult to say to what extent such personal tendencies exist in nascent form in the previous histories of forgers and how far they have been the function of the life a forger must necessarily pursue once committed to his check passing. However, it is hard to escape the idea that some sort of precriminal personal differentiae are present in the winsomeness and tempo of behavior shown by persons who resort to check forgery.

In summary at this point it can at least be stated that forgers come from a class of persons we would ordinarily not expect to yield recruits to the criminal population. By definition, of course, naive forgery is a crime of persons who are unacquainted with criminal techniques; but aside from this the persons involved would appear to have acquired normal attitudes and habits of law observance. It follows that naive forgery emerges as behavior which is out of character or "other than usual" for the persons involved. In the act of forging an ephemeral personal reorganization occurs in response to situational interactors which may be recognized as a special symbolic process conceived to cover aspects of motivation, feeling, emotion and the choice of adjustment alternatives. The personal differentiae we have set down here are the original broad limits within which a certain class of situations can impinge upon the person with the possibility of emergent forgery.

THE SOCIAL SITUATION

That the social situation is a dynamic factor in naive check forgery is obvious from even the most cursory reading of case history materials, and it has been commented upon widely by probation officers, judges, social workers and others who have come into contact with forgers. Such contingencies as unemployment, business failure, gambling losses, dishonorable discharge and desertion from the armed forces, alcoholic sprees, family and marital conflict, and separation and divorce all figure prominently in the case histories of naive check forgers. Yet to set down such critical experiences as "causes" of forgery is only indicative and not discriminating, because many people similar in background to naive forgers confronted by similar crises do not seek a solution by forgery. A more discriminating factor was suggested by the unusually high rate of divorce and separation among married forgers and the high incidence of family alienation and repudiation among single forgers. The very high rates of marital disruption for our cases can be seen in Table 2. Even when allowances are made for the somewhat higher divorce rate to be expected

Table 2.

MARITAL STATUS OF 473 PERSONS CONVICTED OF FORGERY AND
53 PERSONS CONVICTED OF GRAND THEFT IN
LOS ANGELES COUNTY 1938.

	FORGERY		GRAND THEFT		LOS ANGELES CITY POPULATION,
	NO.	PERCENT	NO.	PERCENT	PERCENT
Single	118	24.9	16	30.1	30.8
Married	172	36.3	25	47.1	54.9
Divorced, Widowed or Separated	183	38.6	12	22.6	15.3*
Totals	473	99.8	53	99.8	100

* Includes divorced, widowed and "wives not present in home." *United States Census,* 1940, pp. 182, 190, tables 8 and 11.

Table 3.

THE FREQUENCY OF OCCURRENCE OF MEASURES OF SOCIAL ISOLATION
IN 29 CASES OF NAIVE CHECK FORGERY, LOS ANGELES COUNTY 1951.

| CASE NO. | MEASURES OF ISOLATION | | | | | CASE FREQUENCY |
	OCCUPATION	MARITAL	FAMILY	ETHNIC, PHYSICAL, "OTHER"	SUBJECTIVELY FELT ISOLATION	
1	X		X	X		3
2			X	X		2
3	X		X	X		3
4	X			X	X	3
5	X	X				2
6	X	X		X	X	4
7	X			X		2
8	X	X	X			3
9	X			X		2
10		X		X		2
11	X		X		X	3
12	X	X		X	X	4
13			X	X	X	3
14	X	X				2
15	X		X	X		3
16		X	X	X		3
17	X	X			X	3
18	X		X	X	X	4
19		X			X	2
20			X		X	2
21	X	X			X	3
22	X					1
23			X			1
24	X	X	X		X	4
25		X				2
26	X	X				2
27	X		X	X	X	4
28			X	X		2
29	X	X		X		3
Totals	20	14	14	16	13	77

in a middle class group such as our forgers it will be appreciated that the rate remains inordinately high.

Examination of case history documents and our interview materials revealed that the marital breakups of the persons who later became forgers often were exceptionally rough, and usually grossly traumatic experiences, particularly from the view of their subjective impact. The marital ruptures quite frequently were followed by continuous drunkenness, job inefficiency, occu-pational detachment, and occupational mobility, often in decided contrast to the pre-divorce history. This, of course, is not to say that the marital breakups always initiated the social isolation, for in some cases it was a non-marital crisis which led to excessive drinking, sexual promiscuity or loss of earn-ing, which in turn, resulted in separation and divorce. However, in nearly all cases the isolating experiences tended to be progres-sive and mutually reinforcing.

Among the forgers with no marital ex-

periences isolation was perceived as alienation from the paternal family, with the concept of "black sheep" being fairly expressive
of the family status involved. We also noted
among both the single and married forgers
a number of persons who had begun their
adult lives with social status from which
social isolation could be inferred; here we
refer to persons with physical handicaps,
members of ethnic minorities, orphans and
stepchildren, and the occasional homosexual. In all 29 of our interview cases we were
able to find at least one measure of social
isolation and in most of them, multiple
measures.[6] This may be seen in the accompanying table.

Assuming we have established situational
isolation as the more general prerequisite for
the commission of naive check forgery it is
still necessary to factor out more specific situational factors conducive to the crime.
These we believe are found in certain dialectical forms of social behavior, dialectical
in the sense that the person becomes progressively involved in them. These behaviors
are further distinguished in that they make
imperative the possession of money or
money substitutes for their continuance or
fulfillment. They are objective and identifiable and once a person is committed to them
the impetus to "follow through" with them
is implicit. A quick example is that of a
man away from home who falls in with a

[6] Specifically: *occupational isolation was taken as*
unemployment, job instability (some cases had as
many as 20 or 30 different jobs per year) or
conditions of work separating the person from his
customary association; *marital isolation* was taken
as divorce, separation or alienation of spouses;
family isolation was taken as an invidious position in the parental family due to educational,
occupational or economic inadequacy; *ethnic isolation* was taken as isolation due to race or national status, i.e., a rural Negro migrant, a second
generation Portuguese in conflict with parents
and his neighborhood, a Jew who due to bank-
ruptcy and sexual immorality was alienated from
other Jews as well as gentiles; physical and "other"
isolation was that of physically handicapped persons, homosexuals in conflict and the deviants we
mention in the text above; *subjectively felt isolation* was taken as a sense of isolation expressed in
response to direct questions on the subject.

small group of persons who have embarked
upon a two- or three-day or even a week's
period of drinking and carousing. The impetus to continue the pattern gets mutually
reinforced by interaction of the participants,
and tends to have an accelerated beginning,
a climax and a terminus. If midway through
such a spree a participant runs out of money
the pressures immediately become critical to
take such measures as are necessary to preserve the behavior sequence. A similar behavior sequence is perceived in that of the
alcoholic in a bar who reaches a "high
point" in his drinking and runs out of
money. He might go home and get clothes
to pawn or go and borrow money from a
friend or even apply for public relief, but
these alternatives become irrelevant because
of the immediacy of his need for alcohol.
Another example, fairly common during the
late war, is that of the individual who im-
personates a high-ranking army officer or
public official and gets increasingly involved
in a whole set of reciprocal obligations,
which, when his money is exhausted he must
implement with false credit or worthless
checks. Otherwise he must expose himself
or put an end to the whole fraudulent business by leaving town, as he often does.

We encountered several cases in which
forgeries occurred around Christmas time,
and the evidence seems strong that the institutionalized, cumulative social pressures
to engage in buying behavior at this time
(symbolized in newspaper box-scores of the
"number of shopping days left before Christmas" and "getting the Christmas spirit")
were real factors in building up a sense of
crisis leading to forgeries. The sense of social
isolation among the forgers detached from
their families also was intensified during this
holiday period. It was our further impression
that many of the type situations more specifically leading to forgeries—gambling, borrowing and "kiting" to meet debts and business obligations, desertion and escaping authorities, and being the *bon vivant*—tended
to be dialectical, self-enclosed systems of
behavior in the sense that the initial be-

haviors called for "more of the same." While making the possession of money critically necessary they also reinforced or increased the social isolation of the indulgee; many forgers admitted that at the time such behavior was perceived as having a "false structure" to it.

THE SOCIOPSYCHOLOGICAL PROCESS—CLOSURE

Thus far we have spoken of the election of check forgery as a behavior alternative in relation to the general social isolation of the person and in relation to his involvement in collective or institutionalized behavior dialectics directly dependent upon the use of money or symbolic substitutes for money. It is also necessary to note the way in which the sociopsychological processes in the person interact with them to produce check forgeries. The special process is one of closure. This we take to mean a process whereby the tension initiated by a situation is resolved and the configuration (whether of behavior or of mental process) tends to as complete or "closed" a condition as the circumstances permit. The concept denotes a "demand for meaning" as well as a fitting or selection from alternative modes of behavior to resolve a critical situation.[7] As it operates in check forgery it is a total behavioral response, more frequently impulsive and unverbalized than deliberative or narrowly perceptual.

The significant fact to account for in our data was the apparent contradiction of well educated, often gifted, and certainly otherwise law-abiding persons electing a criminal alternative as a solution in this closure process. A second fact to explain is why they selected the particular crime of check forgery. Beginning with the second fact we can say rather simply that the class of per-

sons committing naive check forgery do not have the skills nor are they in a position to carry out or "close on" most other forms of crime. Furthermore, in contrast to many other types of crime no special skills or knowledge are needed in order to manufacture and pass worthless or even forged checks. In thus commenting upon what may be an obvious fact we digress somewhat to discuss the importance of prior learned behavior in commission of this crime.

The first thing to be said in this connection is that forgery (excluding actually imitating other people's signatures) is very simple to perform; it is probably the easiest major crime to commit that we have. Most people in their everyday transactions have occasions to cash personal or payroll checks and hence encounter all the precautions business uses to prevent the making and uttering of bad checks. From this it is arguable that the criminal defense measures adopted by business become in effect an inverted education in the simple essentials of forgery. We can also hold with good reason that in a competitive society which modally creates aggressive temperament they become a challenge to contrive workable evasions of the protective devices. We see this in the resentment shown by "honest" customers at having their checks questioned and in the gamelike characteristics of many of the techniques invented and employed by forgers.

The point we dwell upon here was demonstrated by asking a college class of 25 students to write brief accounts of how they would obtain and pass a bad check if circumstances forced them to do so. The results showed that while the range of ingenuity was wide, nevertheless about the same class of techniques was described as those actually employed by the forgers in our sample. Only one female student was unable to devise a workable scheme. Sources of the ideas in a few cases were listed as radio programs and crime fiction, but most students simply put down "experience with checking account," "experience in retail

[7] See J. F. Brown and D. W. Orr, "The Field Theoretical Approach to Criminology," Jour. of Crim. Psychopathol., 3, 1941, pp. 236–252; Cesar Castillo, Una Teoria gestalgica del delito, Archivo de Medicina Legal, Buenos Aires, 1948, 18, pp. 387–396.

stores," or "just imagination." Quizzing of the naive forgers in our interview group revealed few or none who could trace in retrospect the sources of their specific forgery behavior.

Another reason for the congeniality of the check forgery alternative lies in the previously mentioned facts that while it is formally treated as a serious crime, informally it is held to be a relatively minor offense and indeed in some forms not a legal offense at all. Thus when the situation or special variations in the subjective reactions of the person dissociate the more formal business and legal control symbols from the act it becomes a more attractive or acceptable choice for the crisis-bound individual. It is in this connection that the low social visibility of the crime excludes social clues which otherwise would weight the forgery choice with unpleasant connotations for the self and person considering it.

Even more important than the low social visibility of check forgery in suspending the formal control symbols of this crime is the social isolation of the person. In general we believe from our data that this isolation brings about a real, albeit ephemeral, suspension, abeyance or distortion of the internal aspects of social communication. It led in our forgery cases to an attenuation of what Mead called the "inner forum of thought," and lowered sensitivity to the "generalized others" which might otherwise have produced a rejection or inhibition of the criminal alternative of forgery. The evidence for this came out in strong feelings of unpleasantness immediately following first forgeries, in the tendency for naive check forgers to give themselves up to the police, in great feelings of relief on being arrested, in desires to "pay their debts to society," in extreme puzzlement as to how they "ever could have done it," and in personality dissociations attributing the behavior to "another me," or to a "Dr. Jekyll-Mr. Hyde" complex.

A high degree of tension appeared in practically all of our cases, being manifested as a sense of urgency which also contributed greatly to the disturbance of the subjective aspects of the communication process.[8] In some cases this sense of urgency, as we have shown, arose from commitments to certain types of dialectical social behaviors. In other cases the sense of urgency seemed to arise from special definitions of the social situation. In such cases there appeared to be a heavy discharge of socially unshared or private meanings into the circumstances of the crime. The insurgency of these private meanings into the thought processes seemed clearly to be a function of the social isolation of the person.

Some of these private meanings proved to be specialized extensions of common cultural meanings. Thus, for some of the check forgers ordinary expenditure behavior in our society took on a desperate kind of meaning. Indulgence in clothes, automobiles, housing, and expensive leisure time pursuits seemed to fulfill intricate, specialized sociopsychological functions over and beyond the satisfactions people ordinarily or "modally" receive from buying such things. These people "get the bug," as one detective put it; they become fixated upon some object and spend most if not all of their waking moments scheming how to obtain it. Such fixating, in part a response to high pressure advertising and selling methods, is, we urge, more commonly the reaction of the socially isolated person.

In other cases the tension or sense of urgency felt by the person who resorted to check forgery emerged out of definitions of the situation which were more intimately personal or perhaps interpersonal. In such instances checks or money came to have a special symbolic value apart from any which the culture assigns to them. Thus in a number of cases strong elements of aggression figured in the forgery act, often aggressions

---

[8] It is to be noted that Lottier found a high degree of tension to be a significant factor in embezzlement, which bears many similarities to forgery. Stuart Lottier, "A Tension Theory of Criminal Behavior," *Amer. Sociol. Rev.*, 7, December 1942, pp. 840–848.

against a particular person. In one such case a youthful epileptic man with a well-defined sense of isolation passed an illegal check immediately after quarreling with his father and preparing to leave for another city. While his need for money to travel was urgent, still it is significant that he wrote the check in such a way as to embarrass his father in the local community.

In many cases the impression is strong that forgery of checks becomes a way of punishing "others" or the "self," with banks, department stores, loan companies and material objects taking on very private meanings for the check criminal. While it is not always clear just what these meanings are, nevertheless they constrict the choices of behavior in the situation. In order to satisfy the immediate special subjective needs of the individual, such as aggression against a particular person or organization, he must exploit the situation as it arises, or, in more familiar terminology, "strike while the iron is hot." The several or many legal alternatives which might serve the same function as a bogus check are "out of place" to him, or else the time required to use them causes them to lose their value to him.

The importance of the sense of urgency in narrowing the range of subjectively acceptable means of meeting the forger's crisis was supported in our data by the fact that as a group our forgers were not without resources. They possessed good clothes, jewelry, sporting equipment and other things which could have been pawned or sold; some had families and relatives from whom they might have borrowed money. Some actually had money in the bank at the time the bad check was passed, and some had bonds which could have been cashed to obtain money. Indeed, one of our forgers was a wealthy landowner with large amounts of money on deposit in England and Australia.

CHAPTER 4

Occupational Crime

The concept of white collar crime was introduced in 1939 by Edwin H. Sutherland in his presidential address to the American Sociological Society.[1] In his original formulation, Sutherland used the term to refer to violation of legal codes in the course of occupational activity by persons who are "respectable" and "of high social status." The concept turned the attention of criminologists to the study of offenses which had not been included within the scope of criminology. Traditionally criminologists had studied the conventional offenses, such as murder, robbery, and larceny, largely to the exclusion of those offenses which are in violation of the laws that regulate the numerous occupations.

Sutherland used the term white collar crime to illustrate that persons of high social status commit crimes which must be included in the study of criminal behavior. The concept of white collar crime has thus altered the picture of crime, as

---

[1] Edwin H. Sutherland, "White Collar Criminality," *American Sociological Review*, 5 (February 1940), pp. 1–12.

well as the usual conception of the criminal as lower class and pathological.[2] Yet, while the limitation of the concept to a particular status group may have been historically significant in the reformulation of criminological theory, the terminology does not appear to be appropriate for the research interests of contemporary criminologists. Newman in his critique of white collar crime, for example, suggested that "farmers, repairmen, and others in essentially non-white-collar occupations, could through such illegalities as watering milk for public consumption, making unnecessary 'repairs' on television sets, and so forth, be classified as white collar violators."[3] In his research on wartime black market violations, Clinard included all gasoline station operators and anyone who rented property, irrespective of their social status.[4] Consequently, Quinney has suggested that an expansion of the concept of white collar crime to include all violations which occur in the course of occupational activity—regardless of the social status of the offender— would increase the utility of the concept.[5] Therefore, it seems advisable to change the concept from "white collar crime" to *occupational crime*. While in most instances the terms white collar crime and occupational crime may be used interchangeably, the crucial point is that the behavior to be included in the concept must be directly related to occupations that are regarded as legitimate in the society. Thus, occupational crime can be defined as violation of the legal codes in the course of activity in a legitimate occupation.

Lawbreaking is often divided into two categories: the conventional crimes, such as larceny, burglary, and robbery, which are usually punished under the criminal law; and those violations of law (occupational crimes) which are not usually punished through the use of the criminal law but rather through civil law and administrative law. Punishment by the government through the civil law includes injunctions, treble damage suits, and license suspension suits. Administrative actions include license suspensions, seizure of illegal commodities, monetary payments, and so on.

Research on occupational crime has concentrated on offenses committed by businessmen, politicians, government employees, labor union officials, doctors, and lawyers. Such violations include infringements of law by businessmen and business employers, restraint of trade (through monopoly, illegal rebates, infringements of patents, trademarks, and copyrights), misrepresentation in advertising, unfair labor practices, financial manipulations, and wartime crimes such as black marketeering. Embezzlement is a common form of occupational crime committed by businessmen of various kinds, especially bankers. In developing countries violations by businessmen of the income tax laws, import and export regulations, and currency control measures are often common.

Politicians and government employees commit various occupational offenses, including direct misappropriation of public funds or the illegal acquisition of these funds through padded payrolls, through illegally placing relatives on the payroll, or

[2] Frank E. Hartung, "White Collar Crime: Its Significance for Theory and Practice," *Federal Probation*, 17 (June 1953), pp. 31–36.

[3] Donald J. Newman, "White Collar Crime," *Law and Contemporary Problems*, 23 (Autumn 1958), p. 737.

[4] Marshall B. Clinard, *The Black Market: A Study of White Collar Crime*, New York: Holt, Rinehart and Winston, Inc., 1952.

[5] Richard Quinney, "The Study of White Collar Crime: Toward a Reorientation in Theory and Research," *Journal of Criminal Law, Criminology and Police Science*, 55 (June 1964), pp. 208–214.

through monetary payments from appointees. Their illegal activities are usually more subtle, however. Politicians and government employees may gain financially by furnishing favors to business firms, such as illegal commissions on public contracts, issuance of fraudulent licenses or certificates, and tax exemptions or lower tax evaluations. Labor union officials may engage in such criminal activities as misappropriating or misapplying union funds, defying the government by failure to enforce laws affecting their unions, entering into collusion with employers to the disadvantage of their own union members, or using fraudulent means to maintain control over the union. Doctors may illegally prescribe narcotics, perform illegal abortions, make fraudulent reports or give false testimony in accident cases, and split fees. Fee splitting, wherein a doctor gives part of his fee to the doctor referring the case to him, is illegal in many places in the United States because of the danger that such referrals might be based on the fee rather than on the practitioner's ability. Lawyers engage in such illegal activities as misappropriating funds in receiverships, securing perjured testimony from witnesses, and "ambulance chasing" in various forms, usually to collect fraudulent damage claims arising from an accident. Members of other occupations may also violate the law in various ways.

It can thus be seen that many different kinds of behavior are included in the concept of occupational crime. The concept may be divided into several subtypes of criminal behavior. One suggestion has been that occupational crime may be separated into types, largely on the basis of the nature of employment, according to crimes committed (1) by individuals as individuals, such as lawyers or doctors, (2) by employees against corporations, such as embezzlers, and (3) by policy-making officials for the corporation.[6] From the standpoint of the occupational context, types of occupational crime could also be constructed according to the kind of occupation, the position of the occupation in the occupational structure, the work roles in the occupation, and the institutional nature of the occupation, such as economic, political, industrial, or medical.

CRIMINAL CAREER OF THE OFFENDER

A major characteristic of occupational crime is the way in which the offender conceives of himself. Since the offenses take place in connection with a legitimate occupation and the offender generally regards himself as a respectable citizen, he does not regard himself as a criminal. At most, he regards himself as a "lawbreaker." In this sense his attitude is similar to that of offenders who are convicted of such crimes as statutory rape, nonsupport, or drunken driving. The fact that the offender is a member of a legitimate occupation makes it difficult also for the general public, while not condoning the activities, to conceive of occupational offenders as being real criminals. This attitude is, in turn, reflected in the conception that occupational offenders have of themselves. Although some writers have felt for this reason that occupational criminals are not real criminals, the lack of self-concept as a criminal in criminological studies of lawbreakers can be as significant as the presence of such a self-concept.

The maintenance of a noncriminal self-concept by the offender is one of the essential elements in the process leading to occupational crime. Cressey, in his

6 Herbert A. Bloch and Gilbert Geis, *Man, Crime, and Society*, New York: Random House, Inc., 1962, p. 402.

study of 133 persons imprisoned for violations of trust, found that three interrelated steps were present in all the cases: (1) a nonsharable financial problem, (2) knowledge of how to violate and an awareness that the problem could be secretly resolved by violating their position of trust, and (3) rationalizations about the violations.[7] The violators were able to apply to their own conduct verbalizations which allowed them to adjust their concepts of themselves as trusted persons with their concepts of themselves as users of entrusted funds or property. Potential trust violators defined the situation through rationalizations in terms which enabled them to regard the criminal behavior as essentially noncriminal. It was rationalized that the behavior was merely "borrowing," that it was justified, that it was part of the "general irresponsibility" for which they were not completely accountable, or that it was due to unusual circumstances.

The life organization of the occupational offender is not built around a criminal role. He plays a variety of roles, particularly that of the respected citizen. The fact that respected citizens are criminal seems somewhat paradoxical.

> There is an obvious and basic incongruity involved in the proposition that a community's leaders and more responsible elements are also its criminals. Business leaders and corporation executives by and large play important roles in civic and community affairs. They more often than not constitute an important source of imaginative leadership for community enterprises of all kinds. The very fact of reputable community standing is therefore one of the more confusing and inconsistent aspects of the concept "white collar crime," as the term has been elaborated in American studies.[8]

The reputations of occupational offenders have been observed in several studies. In an examination of the most flagrant cases of price and rationing violations, during World War II, those in which criminal prosecution was instituted, Clinard noted that less than one violator in ten was reported to have had any criminal record.[9] In studies of other occupational offenders, it has been found that the overwhelming majority of the offenders reside in the most desirable areas of the city.[10] The respectability of occupational offenders was observed by a reporter who described the defendants in the 1961 criminal antitrust case in the heavy electrical equipment industry as "middle-class men in Ivy League suits—typical businessmen in appearance, men who would never be taken for lawbreakers."[11] One of the defendants, a General Electric vice-president who was later sentenced to prison, was earning $135,000 a year. His background has been summarized as follows:

[7] Donald R. Cressey, Other People's Money, New York: The Free Press of Glencoe, 1953.
[8] George B. Vold, Theoretical Criminology, New York: Oxford University Press, 1958, pp. 253–254.
[9] Clinard, p. 295.
[10] Frank E. Hartung, "A Study in Law and Social Differentiation, as Exemplified in Violations of the Emergency Price Control Act in the Detroit Wholesale Meat Industry," unpublished Ph.D. dissertation, University of Michigan, 1949, p. 221; and Richard Quinney, "Retail Pharmacy as a Marginal Occupation: A Study of Prescription Violation," unpublished Ph.D. dissertation, University of Wisconsin, 1962, p. 261.
[11] See Gilbert Geis, "White Collar Crime: The Heavy Electrical Equipment Antitrust Cases of 1961," in the present volume.

He had been born in Atlanta and was 46-years-old at the time he was sentenced to jail. He had graduated with a degree in electrical engineering from Georgia Tech, and received an honorary doctorate degree from Sienna College in 1958, was married, and the father of three children. He had served in the Navy during the Second World War, rising to the rank of lieutenant commander, was a director of the Schenectady Boys Club, on the board of trustees of Miss Hall's School, and not without some irony, was a member of Governor Rockefeller's Temporary State Committee on Economic Expansion.[12]

GROUP SUPPORT OF CRIMINAL BEHAVIOR

On the same occasion that he introduced the concept of white collar crime, Sutherland noted the importance of the interpersonal associations of the offender in becoming a white collar criminal. Since that time most of the studies of occupational crime have viewed the behavior in terms of the group attachments of the offender and have explained the behavior according to the principle of differential association, whereby criminal behavior is learned from others who define the behavior favorably and in isolation from those who do not.[13] Lawbreaking can be normative in certain business concerns, for example, and persons, if isolated from other situations, can learn values, motives, rationalizations, and techniques favorable to this type of crime. Several factors isolate businessmen from unfavorable definitions of illegal activity, according to Sutherland. Such agencies of mass communication as the newspaper make conventional crime abhorrent, while treating white collar crime often in comparatively lenient fashion. Furthermore, businessmen are often shielded from severe criticism by government officials, many of whom either were formerly in business or may have accepted political contributions from business sources. In addition, businessmen chiefly associate with other businessmen, both at work and in their social activities, so that the implications of white collar crime are removed from objective scrutiny. Similar conclusions were reached by Lane in his study of the violation of labor relations laws and trade practices laws in a number of manufacturing firms.[14]

In some occupations a man may learn the techniques by which the law can be violated, building up such rationalizations as "business is business," or "good business demands it." This diffusion of illegal practices is spread from a person already in the occupation to new persons, and from one business establishment, political machine, or white collar group to another. The majority of World War II black market violations in the United States by businessmen appear to have had their origins in behavior learned in association with others. Unethical and illegal practices were circulated in the trade as part of a definition of the situation, and rationalizations to support these violations of law were transmitted by this differential association. Types of violations were picked up in conversations with businessmen and from descriptions of violations in trade journals and the press.

[12] Geis.
[13] Edwin H. Sutherland, *White Collar Crime*, New York: Holt, Rinehart and Winston, Inc., 1949.
[14] Robert A. Lane, "Why Business Men Violate the Law," *Journal of Criminal Law, Criminology and Police Science*, 44 (August 1953), pp. 151–165.

Although many forms of occupational crime can be satisfactorily explained by a theory of differential association, it would seem obvious, where there has been continuous and intimate association with unethical and illegal norms and isolation from other norms, this theory as an explanation for *all* cases has several limitations. Many individuals do not engage in these practices, even though they are familiar with the techniques and rationalizations of violation and frequently associate with persons similarly familiar. A businessman could hardly remain in a business any length of time without acquiring a rather complete knowledge of the illegalities involved. Persons appear to accept or reject opportunities for occupational crime according to their orientations toward their roles and their attitudes toward general social values. Some of these factors are negative attitudes toward other persons in general, the relative importance attached to a status symbol of money as compared with law obedience, and the relative importance attached to personal, family, or business reputations.

Some forms of occupational crime are related to the structure of the occupation in which the offender is engaged and in the roles played by the offender within the occupation. The importance of the occupational structure and occupational roles of the offender has been shown by Quinney in a study of prescription violation among retail pharmacists.[15] Because the occupation of retail pharmacy consists of two divergent occupational role expectations, professional and business, pharmacists experience the problem of adapting to one of several "occupational role organizations." The types of occupational role organizations, in turn, differ in the extent to which they produce tendencies toward prescription violation. Pharmacists with an occupational role organization that includes an orientation to the professional role are bound by a system of occupational control which includes guides for the compounding and dispensing of prescriptions. Pharmacists who lack the professional orientation to pharmacy are not bound by the occupational controls. The business-oriented pharmacists are interested in the general business goal of monetary gain. They subscribe to the popular belief in business that self-employment carries with it independence and freedom from control. The professional norms, as incorporated in the prescription laws, exercise little control over the occupational behavior of the pharmacists who are oriented to the business role. Thus, in the study of prescription violation it was found that violations occur more frequently among business pharmacists and least often among professional pharmacists, with professional-business pharmacists and indifferent pharmacists (those not oriented to either role) being intermediate in frequency of violations. It was concluded that prescription violation is related to the structure of the occupation and the "differential orientation" of retail pharmacists to the roles within the occupation.

Occupational crime usually involves some form of organization among the participants. The degree of organization may range from the comparatively simple reciprocal relationships involved in fee splitting among doctors to the more complex procedures involved in the illegal activities of large corporations. In the case of violations within corporations, the violations may not only involve the corporation but may extend to several corporations or subsidiaries. The organization of illegal behavior may be quite informal, as in false advertising, it may be simply organized, although deliberate, as in the case of some wartime black market activities, or it

[15] Richard Quinney, "Occupational Structure and Criminal Behavior: Prescription Violation by Retail Pharmacists," *Social Problems*, 11 (Fall 1963), pp. 179–185.

may be complex and involved, as in the more recent case of electrical company violations in the United States.[16] The selection of a particular form of illegal behavior, as Sutherland has pointed out, may be either on the basis of the smallest danger of detection and difficulty in obtaining proof, on the basis of the firm's capacity to "fix" the case, or even on the basis of the ability to change the law itself.

CORRESPONDENCE BETWEEN CRIMINAL BEHAVIOR AND LEGITIMATE BEHAVIOR PATTERNS

Occupational crime cannot be fully understood without reference to the structure and values of society. The values involved in the regulation of commercial transactions may conflict with those of free enterprise, individualism, or supply and demand. Attitude toward selective obedience to a "good" or "bad" law becomes the key to compliance. "The demand of law arises out of the conflicts in cultures, and because there is conflict in cultures, the law is not effective as a deterrent upon other groups that did not at first demand the law."[17]

One of the most important reasons for the high degree of correspondence between some forms of occupational crime and patterns of legitimate behavior is that many of the activities were not defined as criminal until recent years. While embezzlement was made illegal in the eighteenth century, it was not until the beginning of the nineteenth century that the following behaviors were made illegal in the United States: restraint of trade, false advertising, insolvency of banks due to fraud or negligence of officials, sale of fraudulent securities, and misuse of trademarks. Previously, the philosophy of laissez faire and caveat emptor (let the buyer beware) had dominated the general social, political, and economic thinking in the Western world, prohibiting the development of certain needed legal restrictions regardless of occupation or class. This new legislation directed toward controlling the more powerful economic groups in society grew out of industrialization, the replacement of the entrepreneur by the corporation, and the development of large-scale labor unions. Old conventional colonial laws often were not applicable and in their place were regulatory and administrative laws directed chiefly at the business and professional classes. In addition, organized public feeling about the socially injurious nature of crimes related to occupational activity has developed slowly; and without strong and well-organized public pressure, statutes could not be enacted and enforced against this type of behavior.

Occupational crimes may be thus viewed as violations of laws which are not part of the values of society or of some groups in society.[18] Aubert has pointed out that the concern among sociologists for occupational crime brings into focus a long-neglected relationship between criminal behavior, criminal law, penal sanc-

---

[16] John Herling, The Great Price Conspiracy: The Story of the Antitrust Violations in the Electrical Industry, Washington, D.C.: Robert B. Luce, 1962.

[17] Albert K. Cohen, Alfred Lindesmith, and Karl Schuessler (eds.), The Sutherland Papers, Bloomington: Indiana University Press, 1956, p. 102.

[18] Richard C. Fuller, "Morals and the Criminal Law," Journal of Criminal Law, Criminology and Police Science, 32 (March–April 1942), pp. 624–630; Richard Quinney, "Is Criminal Behavior Deviant Behavior?" British Journal of Criminology, 5 (April 1965), pp. 132–142.

tions, and social structure.[19] In a highly differentiated society the ambivalence of average citizens, businessmen, and lawyers reflects structured conflicts in social roles and the larger social system. Additional studies should give us some idea of the conditions which lead to the definition of behavior as criminal and of the way in which legal norms intersect and are integrated with the norms of other institutional structures.[20] Values, norms, and other aspects of middle and upper class cultures may help explain occupational crime in much the same way that knowledge of the culture of the lower class is necessary to understand conventional crimes.

SOCIETAL REACTION

Occupational crime differs from other crime not only in its unique form of activity but in the toleration and support it receives from the public. In particular, punishments given for occupational offenses almost without exception differ from the punishments given for other offenses. Among the reasons for the public's toleration of occupational crime is the fact that occupational crime is usually more complex and often diffused over a longer period of time than is the case with ordinary crimes, and this fact obscures the essential criminality of the acts. Furthermore, the type of publicity given occupational crimes, as contrasted to the more overt crimes like burglary or larceny, seldom creates much public resentment.

Most statutes outlawing occupational crime differ from conventional criminal laws in five ways: (1) in origin, (2) in determination of responsibility or intent, (3) in philosophy, (4) in enforcement and trial procedures, and (5) in sanctions used to punish violators.[21] Enforcement relies largely on especially created agencies rather than on police and prosecutors. The administrative process of hearing cases, rather than trial procedures, closely approximates the juvenile court procedures. The actions are more often remedial in nature, as in the use of injunctions, rather than the direct punishment of the offender through fine or imprisonment.

In legislation directed at the antisocial behavior of businessmen and others there has been a tendency to enact rather lenient statutes and to enforce them in a similar fashion, showing favoritism to offenders of high social status. Many provide no criminal sanctions, and where sanctions have been included, they have been used hesitantly. Criminal action against a corporation does present a significant problem to the corporation, for even after long litigation often the only results achieved are a modest fine for the corporation or an insignificant sentence for an officer.

Because the legal measures used against occupational offenders differ considerably from the traditional criminal measures used against most other offenders, occupational crime has not been an integral part of criminological theory. To include such violations within criminology, crime must be defined in terms broad enough to cover any crime punishable by the state, regardless of whether the penalty is criminal, administrative, or civil. The concept of occupational crime recognizes that all illegal activity should be studied, regardless of the social class or

[19] Vilhelm Aubert, "White Collar Crime and Social Structure," *American Journal of Sociology*, 58 (November 1952), pp. 263–271.
[20] C. R. Jeffery, "The Structure of American Criminological Thinking," *Journal of Criminal Law, Criminology and Police Science*, 46 (January–February 1956), pp. 658–672.
[21] Newman, p. 738.

legal measures, if meaningful generalizations are to be derived about the nature of criminal behavior.

Without this broad interpretation of "crime," it is not possible to deal analytically with diverse illegal activities which are punishable according to one's occupation and social class. This becomes more apparent when one considers that an apprehended burglar or robber is punished by a jail sentence, a fine, or probation, whereas a doctor may be punished through revocation of his license, a lawyer by disbarment, or a businessman by a government injunction, the levying of civil damages, suspension of license to do business, or, in such cases as the sale of impure foods, the seizure and destruction of the commodity. All these sanctions imply that the behavior is socially injurious, that punishment is involved, and that society is stigmatizing the offender.

The definition of a crime "should not be the spirit of the law for white collar crime and the letter of the law for other crimes, or in other respects be more liberal for one class than for the other."[22] Sutherland stated that unless and until a more inclusive concept of what constitutes crime is used, it would not be possible to deal analytically with illegal activities which are punished according to occupation and social class. "Conviction in the criminal courts is not an adequate criterion since this criterion needs to be supplemented in such a fashion that the crimes of one class are kept consistent with those of another."[23]

Thus, the inclusion of occupational crime in criminology has brought about an alteration of criminological theory. One of the chief contributions of studies of occupational crime is that a pattern of crime can be found to exist outside the popular conceptions and focus of criminological investigations. In this connection Cressey has asked, "Why does a society report the crime it reports, why does it overlook what it overlooks, and how does it go about deciding that it has, in fact, overlooked something?"[24]

SELECTED BIBLIOGRAPHY

1. Aubert, Vilhelm, "White Collar Crime and Social Structure," *American Journal of Sociology*, 58 (November 1952), pp. 263–271.
2. Bloch, Herbert A., and Gilbert Geis, *Man, Crime, and Society*, New York: Random House, Inc., 1962, Chap. 14.
3. Clinard, Marshall B., *The Black Market: A Study of White Collar Crime*, New York: Holt, Rinehart and Winston, Inc., 1952.
4. ———, "Criminological Theories of Violations of Wartime Regulations," *American Sociological Review*, 11 (June 1964), pp. 258–270.
5. Cressey, Donald R., *Other People's Money*, New York: The Free Press of Glencoe, 1953.
6. Geis, Gilbert, "Toward a Delineation of White Collar Offenses," *Sociological Inquiry*, 32 (Spring 1962), pp. 160–171.
7. Hartung, Frank E., "White Collar Crime: Its Significance for Theory and Practice," *Federal Probation*, 17 (June 1953), pp. 31–36.
8. ———, "White Collar Offenses in the Wholesale Meat Industry in Detroit," *American Journal of Sociology*, 56 (July 1950), pp. 25–32.

[22] Sutherland, "White Collar Criminality," p. 5.
[23] Sutherland, "White Collar Criminality," p. 5.
[24] Donald R. Cressey, "Foreword," in Sutherland, *White Collar Crime*, p. xii.

9. Herling, John, *The Great Price Conspiracy: The Story of the Antitrust Violations in the Electrical Industry*, Washington, D.C.: Robert B. Luce, 1962.

10. Lane, Robert A., "Why Business Men Violate the Law," *Journal of Criminal Law, Criminology and Police Science*, 44 (August 1953), pp. 151–165.

11. Mannheim, Hermann, *Comparative Criminology*, Boston: Houghton Mifflin Co., 1965, Chap. 21.

12. Middendorff, Wolf, *Soziologie des Verbrechens*, Düsseldorf-Köln, 1959.

13. Newman, Donald J., "Public Attitudes Toward a Form of White Collar Crime," *Social Problems*, 4 (January 1957), pp. 228–232.

14. ———, "White Collar Crime," *Law and Contemporary Problems*, 23 (Autumn 1951), pp. 735–753.

15. Quinney, Richard, "Occupational Structure and Criminal Behavior: Prescription Violation by Retail Pharmacists," *Social Problems*, 11 (Fall 1963), pp. 179–185.

16. ———, "The Study of White Collar Crime: Toward a Reorientation in Theory and Research," *Journal of Criminal Law, Criminology and Police Science*, 55 (June 1964), pp. 208–214.

17. Schäfer, Herbert, *Grundfragen Der Wirtschaftskriminalität*, Wiesbaden, 1963.

18. Spencer, John C., "White Collar Crime," in *Criminology in Transition*, T. Grygier, H. Jones, and John Spencer (eds.), London: Routledge & Kegan Paul, Ltd., 1965, pp. 233–266.

19. Sutherland, Edwin H., "Crime and Business," *The Annals*, 217 (September 1941), pp. 112–118.

20. ———, "Is White Collar Crime Crime?" *American Sociological Review*, 10 (April 1945), pp. 132–139.

21. ———, "White Collar Criminality," *American Sociological Review*, 5 (February 1940), pp. 1–12.

22. ———, *White Collar Crime*, New York: Holt, Rinehart and Winston, Inc., 1949.

23. Tappan, Paul W., "Who Is the Criminal?" *American Sociological Review*, 12 (February 1947), pp. 96–102.

24. Zirpins, W., and O. Terstegen, *Wirtschaftskriminalität*, Lübeck, 1963.

WHITE COLLAR CRIME: THE HEAVY ELECTRICAL EQUIPMENT ANTITRUST CASES OF 1961*

Gilbert Geis

> The 1961 antitrust conspiracy in the heavy electrical equipment industry permits an opportunity for the re-evaluation of many of the earlier speculations by Sutherland about white collar crime.

* This selection, written especially for this book, is published here for the first time.

*Using evidence gathered from the documents of the hearings, Geis
discusses the techniques of conspiracy, explanations of the
offenses, and the career of an offender. Suggestions are made for
the future study of white collar crime in large corporations.*

An inadvertent bit of humor by a defense
attorney provided one of the major criminological motifs for "the most serious violations of the antitrust laws since the time of
their passage at the turn of the century."[1]
The defendants, including several vice-presidents of the General Electric Corporation
and the Westinghouse Electric Corporation
—the two largest companies in the heavy
electrical equipment industry—stood som-
berly in a federal courtroom in Philadelphia
on February 6, 1961. They were aptly described by a newspaper reporter as "middle-
class men in Ivy League suits—typical business men in appearance, men who would
never be taken for lawbreakers."[2] Several
were deacons or vestrymen of their churches.
One was president of his local chamber of
commerce, another a hospital board member, another chief fund raiser for the community chest, another a bank director, another a director of the taxpayer's association,
another an organizer of the local little league.

The attorney for a General Electric executive attacked the government's demand
for a jail sentence for his client, calling it
"cold-blooded." The lawyer insisted that
government prosecutors did not understand
what it would do to his client, "this fine
man," to be put "behind bars" with "common criminals who have been convicted of
embezzlement and other serious crimes."[3]

The difficulty of defense counsel in considering antitrust violations "serious crimes,"
crimes at least equivalent to embezzling, indicates in part why the 1961 prosecutions
provide such fascinating material for criminological study. Edwin H. Sutherland, who
originated the term "white collar crime" to

categorize offenders such as antitrust violators, had lamented that his pioneering work
was handicapped by the absence of adequate
case histories of corporate offenders. "No
first hand research from this point of view
has ever been reported,"[4] Sutherland noted
and, lacking such data, he proceeded to employ rather prosaic stories of derelictions by
rather unimportant persons in small enterprises upon which to build an interpretative
and theoretical structure for white collar
crime.

To explain corporate offenses and offenders, Sutherland had to rely primarily
upon the criminal biographies of various
large companies, as these were disclosed in
the annals of trial courts and administrative
agencies. In the absence of information
about human offenders, the legal fiction of
corporate humanity, a kind of economic
anthropomorphism, found its way into criminological literature. Factual gaps were filled
by shrewd guesses, definitional and semantic
strategies, and a good deal of extrapolation.
It was as if an attempt were being made to
explain murder by reference only to the
listed rap sheet offenses of a murderer and
the life stories and identification data of several lesser offenders.[5]

Sutherland was writing, of course, before
the antitrust violations in the heavy electri-

---

[1] Judge J. Cullen Ganey in "Application of the
State of California," *Federal Supplement*, 195
(Eastern District, Pennsylvania, 1961), p. 39.
[2] *New York Times*, Feb. 7, 1961.
[3] *New York Times*, Feb. 7, 1961.

[4] Edwin H. Sutherland, *White Collar Crime*, New
York: Holt, Rinehart and Winston, Inc., 1949,
p. 240. Note: "Private enterprise remains extraordinarily private. . . . We know more about the
motives, habits, and most intimate arcana of
primitive peoples in New Guinea . . . than we
do of the denizens of executive suites in Uni-
lever House, Citroen, or General Electric (at least
until a recent Congressional investigation)."—Roy
Lewis and Rosemary Stewart, *The Managers*,
New York: New American Library, 1961, pp.
111–112.
[5] For an elaboration of this point, see Gilbert Geis,
"Toward a Delineation of White-Collar Offenses,"
Sociological Inquiry, 32 (Spring 1962), pp. 160–
171.

cal equipment industry became part of the public record. Though much of the data regarding them is tantalizingly incomplete, unresponsive to fine points of particular criminological concern, the antitrust offenses nonetheless represent extraordinary case studies of white collar crime, that designation which, according to Sutherland, applies to behavior by "a person of high socio-economic status who violates the laws designed to regulate his occupational activities"[6] and "principally refers to business managers and executives."[7] In particular, the antitrust cases provide the researcher with a mass of raw data against which to test and to refine earlier hunches and hypotheses regarding white collar crime.

FACTS OF THE ANTITRUST VIOLATIONS

The most notable characteristic of the 1961 antitrust conspiracy was its willful and blatant nature. These were not complex acts only doubtfully in violation of a highly complicated statute. They were flagrant criminal offenses, patently in contradiction to the letter and the spirit of the Sherman Antitrust Act of 1890, which forbade price-fixing arrangements as restraints upon free trade.[8]

The details of the conspiracy must be drawn together from diverse secondhand sources because the grand jury hearings upon which the criminal indictments were based were not made public. The decision to keep

the records closed was reached on the ground that the traditional secrecy of grand jury proceedings took precedence over public interest in obtaining information about the conspiracy and over the interest of different purchasers in acquiring background data upon which to base civil suits against the offending corporations for allegedly fraudulent sales.[9]

The federal government had initiated the grand jury probes in mid-1959, apparently after receiving complaints from officials of the Tennessee Valley Authority concerning identical bids they were getting from manufacturers of highly technical electrical equipment, even though the bids were submitted in sealed envelopes.[10] Four grand juries were ultimately convened and subpoenaed 196 persons, some of whom obviously revealed the intimate details of the price-fixing procedures. A package of twenty indictments was handed down, involving 45 individual defendants and 29 corporations. Almost all of the corporate defendants pleaded guilty; the company officials tended to enter pleas of nolo contendere (no contest) which, in this case, might reasonably be taken to indicate that they did not see much likelihood of escaping conviction.

The pleas negated the necessity for a public trial and for public knowledge of the precise machinations involved in the offenses. At the sentencing hearing, fines amounting to $1,924,500 were levied against the defendants, $1,787,000 falling upon the corporations and $137,000 upon different individuals. The major fines were set against General Electric ($437,500) and Westing-

---

[6] Edwin H. Sutherland in Vernon C. Branham and Samuel B. Kutash, Encyclopedia of Criminology, New York: Philosophical Library, Inc., 1949, p. 511.

[7] Sutherland, White Collar Crime, p. 9, fn. 7.

[8] United States Statutes, 26 (1890), p. 209; United States Code, 15 (1958), pp. 1, 2. See also William L. Letwin, "Congress and the Sherman Antitrust Law, 1887–1890," University of Chicago Law Review, 23 (Winter 1956), pp. 221–258, and Paul E. Hadlick, Criminal Prosecutions under the Sherman Anti-Trust Act, Washington, D.C.: Ransdell, 1939. The best interpretation of American antitrust law is A. D. Neale, Antitrust Laws of the United States, New York: Cambridge University Press, 1960.

[9] Note: "Release of the Grand Jury Minutes in the National Deposition Program of the Electrical Equipment Cases," University of Pennsylvania Law Review, 112 (June 1964), pp. 1133–1145.

[10] John Herling, The Great Price Conspiracy, Washington, D.C.: Robert B. Luce, 1962, pp. 1–12; John G. Fuller, The Gentleman Conspirators, New York: Grove Press, Inc., 1962, pp. 7–11. See also Myron W. Watkins, "Electrical Equipment Antitrust Cases—Their Implications for Government and Business," University of Chicago Law Review, 29 (August 1961), pp. 97–110.

house ($372,500). Much more eye-catching were the jail terms of thirty days imposed upon seven defendants, of whom four were vice-presidents, two were division managers, and one was a sales manager.

The defendants sentenced to jail were handled essentially the same as other offenders with similar dispositions. They were handcuffed in pairs in the back seat of an automobile on their way to the Montgomery County Jail in Norristown, Pennsylvania, fingerprinted on entry, and dressed in the standard blue denim uniforms. During their stay, they were described as "model prisoners," and several were transferred to the prison farm. The remainder, working an eight-hour day for 30 cents, earned recognition from the warden as "the most intelligent prisoners" he had had during the year on a project concerned with organizing prison records. None of the seven men had visitors during the Wednesday and Saturday periods reserved for visiting; all indicated a desire not to be seen by their families or friends.[11]

Good behavior earned the men a 5-day reduction in their sentence. Toward the end of the year, the remaining defendants, who had been placed on probation, were released from that status, despite the strong protests of government officials. The judge, the same man who had imposed the original sentences, explained his action by noting that he "didn't think that this was the type of offense that probation lent itself readily to or was designed for." Supervision was seen as meaningless for men with such past records and such little likelihood of recidivism, particularly since the probation office was already "clogged to the gunwales" with cases.[12]

The major economic consequences to the corporations arose from civil suits for treble damages filed against them as pro-vided in the antitrust laws. The original fines were, of course, negligible: For General Electric, a half-million dollar loss was no more unsettling than a $3 parking fine would be to a man with an income of $175,-000 a year. Throughout the early stages of negotiations over the damage suits, General Electric maintained that it would resist such actions on grounds which are noteworthy as an indication of the source and the content of the rationale that underlay the self-justification of individual participants in the price-fixing conspiracy:

We believe that the purchasers of electrical apparatus have received fair value by any reasonable standard. The prices which they have paid during the past years were appropriate to value received and reasonable as compared with the general trends of prices in the economy, the price trends for similar equipment and the price trends for materials, salaries, and wages. The foresight of the electrical utilities and the design and manufacturing skills of companies such as General Electric have kept electricity one of today's greatest bargains.[13]

By 1962, General Electric was granting that settlements totaling between $45 and $50 million would have to be arranged to satisfy claimants.[14] Municipalities and other purchasers of heavy electrical equipment were taking the period of lowest prices, when they assumed the price-rigging was least effective, using these prices as "legitimate," and calculating higher payments as products of the price conspiracy.[15] The initial G.E. estimate soon proved as untenable as its original thesis regarding value received. A mid-1964 calculation showed that 90 percent of some 1800 claims had been settled for a total of $160 million,[16] but General Electric could derive some solace from the fact that most of these payments would be tax-deductible.[17]

11 United Press International, Feb. 16, 1961; New York Times, Feb. 25, 1961.
12 Telephone interview with Judge Ganey, Philadelphia, Aug. 31, 1964; New York Times, Dec. 20, 1961.

13 New York Times, Feb. 7, 1961.
14 New York Times, July 27, 1962.
15 New York Times, March 14, 1961.
16 New York Times, Apr. 29, 1964. Regarding Westinghouse see Wall Street Journal, Sept. 3, 1964.
17 Wall Street Journal, July 27, 1964.

TECHNIQUES
OF THE CONSPIRACY

The modus operandi for the antitrust violations shows clearly the awareness of the participants that their behavior was such that it had better be carried on as secretly as possible. Some comparison might be made between the antitrust offenses and other forms of fraud occurring in lower economic classes. It was one of Sutherland's most telling contentions that neither the method by which a crime is committed nor the manner in which it is handled by public agencies alters the essential criminal nature of the act and the criminal status of the perpetrator.[18] Selling faucet water on a street corner to a blind man who is led to believe that the product is specially prepared to relieve his ailment is seen as no different from selling a $50 million turbine to a city which is laboring under the misapprehension that it is purchasing the product at the best price possible from closed competitive bidding. The same may by said in regard to methods of treatment. Tuberculosis, for example, remains tuberculosis and its victim a tubercular whether the condition is treated in a sanitarium or whether it is ignored or even condoned by public authorities. So too with crime. As Miss Stein might have said: A crime is a crime is a crime.

Like most reasonably adept and optimistic criminals, the antitrust violators had hoped to escape apprehension. "I didn't expect to get caught and I went to great lengths to conceal my activities so that I wouldn't get caught," one of them said.[19] Another went into some detail concerning the techniques of concealment:

[18] Edwin H. Sutherland, "White-Collar Criminality," *American Sociological Review*, 5 (February 1940), pp. 1–12.
[19] Senate Committee on the Judiciary, Subcommittee on Antitrust and Monopoly, 87th Cong., 2d Sess., 1961, "Administered Prices," *Hearings*, Pts. 27 and 28. Unless otherwise indicated, subsequent data and quotations are taken from these documents. Space considerations do not permit citation to the precise pages.

. . . it was considered discreet to not be too obvious and to minimize telephone calls, to use plain envelopes if mailing material to each other, not to be seen together on traveling, and so forth. . . . not to leave wastepaper, of which there was a lot, strewn around a room when leaving.

The plans themselves, while there were some slight variations over time and in terms of different participants, were essentially similar. The offenders hid behind a camouflage of fictitious names and conspiratorial codes. The attendance roster for the meetings was known as the "Christmas card list" and the gatherings, interestingly enough, as "choir practice."[20] The offenders used public telephones for much of their communication, and they met either at trade association conventions, where their relationship would appear reasonable, or at sites selected for their anonymity. It is quite noteworthy, in this respect, that while some of the men filed false travel claims, so as to mislead their superiors regarding the city they had visited, they never asked for expense money to places more distant than those they had actually gone to—on the theory, apparently, that whatever else was occurring, it would not do to cheat the company.

At the meetings, negotiations centered about the establishment of a "reasonable" division of the market for the various products. Generally, participating companies were allocated essentially that part of the market which they had previously garnered. If Company A, for instance, had under competitive conditions secured 20 percent of the available business, then agreement might be reached that it would be given the opportunity to submit the lowest bid on 20 percent of the new contracts. A low price would be established, and the remainder of the companies would bid at approximately equivalent, though higher, levels. It some-

[20] The quotation is from an excellent two-part article by Richard Austin Smith, "The Incredible Electrical Conspiracy," *Fortune*, 63 (April 1961), pp. 132–137, and 63 (May 1961), 161–164, which is reproduced in *Hearings*, Pt. 27, pp. 17094–17105 and 17172–17182.

times happened, however, that because of
things such as company reputation, or available servicing arrangements, the final contract
was awarded to a firm which had not submitted the lowest bid. For this, among other
reasons, debate among the conspirators was
often acrimonious about the proper division
of spoils, about alleged failures to observe
previous agreements, and about other intra-
mural matters. Sometimes, depending upon
the contract, the conspirators would draw
lots to determine who would submit the
lowest bid; at other times the appropriate
arrangement would be determined under a
rotating system conspiratorially referred to
as the "phase of the moon."

EXPLANATIONS
OF THE CONSPIRACY

Attempts to understand the reasons for and
the general significance of the price-fixing
conspiracy have been numerous. They include re-examinations of the antitrust laws[21]
as well as denunciations of the corporate
ethos and the general pattern of American
life and American values. For example,
"This is the challenge of the grim outcome
in Philadelphia. Can corporations outgrow
the idea that employes must produce, whatever the moral cost, or lose their prerequisites? Is it possible to create a business ethic
favoring honesty even at the expense of
profit? Can our society get away from its
pervasive attitude that a little cheating is
harmless? The electrical cases raise those
questions not only in the antitrust field, but
in others, especially taxation. And they are
questions not only for large corporations and
not only for business but for all of us."[22]

A not inconsiderable number of the defendants took the line that their behavior,
while technically criminal, had really served
a worthwhile purpose by "stabilizing prices"

[21] See, for instance, Leland Hazard, "Are Big
Businessmen Crooks?" *Atlantic*, 208 (November
1961), pp. 57–61.
[22] Anthony Lewis, *New York Times*, Feb. 12,
1961.

(a much-favored phrase of the conspirators).
This altruistic interpretation almost invariably was combined with an attempted
distinction among illegal, criminal, and immoral acts, with the offender expressing the
view that what he had done might have
been designated by the statutes as criminal,
but either he was unaware of such a designation or he thought it unreasonable that acts
with admirable consequences should be considered criminal. The testimony of a Westinghouse executive during hearings by the
Senate Subcommittee on Antitrust and
Monopoly clearly illustrates this point of
view:

Committee Attorney: Did you know that these
meetings with competitors were illegal?

Witness: Illegal? Yes, but not criminal. I
didn't find that out until I read the indictment. . . . I assumed that criminal action
meant damaging someone, and we did not do
that. . . . I thought that we were more or less
working on a survival basis in order to try to
make enough to keep our plant and our employees.

This theme was repeated in essentially
similar language by a number of witnesses.
"It is against the law," an official of the Ingersoll-Rand Corporation granted, but he
added: "I do not know that it is against
public welfare because I am not certain that
the consumer was actually injured by this
operation." A Carrier Corporation executive
testified that he was "reasonably in doubt"
that the price-fixing meetings violated the
antitrust law. "Certainly, we were in a gray
area. I think the degree of violation, if you
can speak of it that way, is what was in
doubt." Another offender said: "We were
not meeting for the purpose of getting the
most that traffic could bear. It was to get a
value for our product." Some of these views
are gathered together in a statement by a
former sales manager of the I-T-E Circuit
Breaker Company:

One faces a decision, I guess, at such times,
about how far to go with company instructions, and since the spirit of such meetings
only appeared to be correcting a horrible price

level situation, that there was not an attempt to actually damage customers, charge excessive prices, there was no personal gain in it for me, the company did not seem actually to be defrauding, corporate statements can evidence the fact that there have been poor profits during all these years. . . . So I guess morally it did not seem quite so bad as might be inferred by the definition of the activity itself.

For the most part, personal explanations for the acts were sought in the structure of corporate pressures rather than in the avarice or lack of law-abiding character of the men involved. The defendants almost invariably testified that they came new to a job, found price-fixing an established way of life, and simply entered into it as they did into other aspects of their job. This explanatory scheme fit into a pattern that Senator Philip A. Hart of Michigan, during the subcommittee hearings, labeled *imbued fraud*.[23]

There was considerable agreement concerning the precise method in which the men initially became involved in price-fixing. "My first actual experience was back in the 1930's," a General Electric official said. "I was taken there by my boss . . . to sit down and price a job." An Ingersoll-Rand executive said: "[My superior] took me to a meeting to introduce me to some of our competitors, none of whom I had met before, and at that meeting pricing of condensers was discussed with the competitors." Essentially the same comment is repeated by witness after witness. "I found it this way when I was introduced to competitive discussion and just drifted into it," a Carrier Corporation man noted. A General Electric officer echoed this point: "Every direct supervisor that I had directed me to meet with competition. . . . It had become so common and gone on for so many years that I think we lost sight of the fact that it was illegal. Price-fixing, whether or not recognized as

illegal by the offenders, was clearly an integral part of their jobs. "Meeting with competitors was just one of the many facets of responsibility that was delegated to me," one witness testified, while an Allis-Chalmers executive responded to the question: "Why did you go to the meetings?" with the observation: "I thought it was part of my duty to do so."

What might have happened to the men if, for reasons of conscience or perhaps through a fear of the possible consequences, they had objected to the "duty" to participate in price-fixing schemes? This point was raised only by the General Electric employees, perhaps because they alone had some actual evidence upon which to base their speculations. In 1946, General Electric had first issued a directive, number 20.5, which spelled out the company's policy against price-fixing, in terms stronger than those found in the antitrust laws. A considerable number of the executives believed, in the words of one, that the directive was only for "public consumption," and not to be taken seriously. One man, however, refused to engage in price-fixing after he had initialed the document forbidding it. A witness explained to the Senate subcommittee what followed:

[My superior] told me, "This fellow is a fine fellow, he is capable in every respect except he was not broad enough for his job, that he was so religious that he thought in spite of what his superiors said, he thought having signed that, that he should not do any of this and he is getting us in trouble with competition.

The man who succeeded the troublesome official, one of the defendants in the Philadelphia hearing, said that he had been told that he "would be expected to do otherwise" and that this "was why I was offered that promotion to Philadelphia because this man would not do it." At the same time, however, the General Electric witnesses specified clearly that it was not their jobs with the company that would be in jeopardy if they failed to price-fix, but rather the particular assignment they had. "If I didn't do

23 Analysis of the relationship between occupational norms and legal violations could represent a fruitful line of inquiry. See Richard Quinney, "The Study of White Collar Crime: Toward a Reorientation in Theory and Research," *Journal of Criminal Law, Criminology and Police Science*, 55 (June 1964), pp. 208–214.

it, I felt that somebody else would," said one, with an obvious note of self-justification. "I would be removed and somebody else would do it."

Westinghouse and General Electric differed considerably in their reactions to the exposure of the offenses, with Westinghouse electing to retain in its employ persons involved in the conspiracy, and General Electric deciding to dismiss the employees who had been before the court. The reasoning of the companies throws light both on the case and on the relationship between antitrust offenses and the more traditionally viewed forms of criminal behavior.

Westinghouse put forward four justifications for its retention decision. First, it declared, the men involved had not sought personal aggrandizement: "While their actions cannot in any way be condoned, these men did not act for personal gain, but in the belief, misguided though it may have been, that they were furthering the company's interest. Second, "the punishment incurred by them already was harsh" and "no further penalties would serve any useful purpose." Third, "each of these individuals is in every sense a reputable citizen, a respected and valuable member of the community and of high moral character." Fourth, there was virtually no likelihood that the individuals would repeat their offense.[24]

General Electric's punitive line toward its employees was justified on the ground that the men had violated not only federal law but also a basic company policy, and that they therefore deserved severe punishment. The company's action met with something less than wholehearted acclaim; rather, it was often interpreted as an attempt to scapegoat particular individuals for what was essentially the responsibility of the corporate enterprise and its top executives. "I do not understand the holier-than-thou attitude in GE when your directions came from very high at the top," Senator Kefauver said during his committee's hearings, while Senator John A. Carroll of Colorado expressed his view through a leading question: "Do you think you were thrown to the wolves to ease the public relations situation . . . that has developed since these indictments?" he asked a discharged General Electric employee. The witness thought that he had.

Perhaps most striking is the fact that though many offenders quite clearly stressed the likely consequences for them if they failed to conform to price-fixing expectations, not one hinted at the benefits he might expect, the personal and professional rewards, from participation in the criminal conspiracy. It remained for the sentencing judge and two top General Electric executives to deliver the harshest denunciations of the personal motives and qualities of the conspirators to be put forth during the case:

The statement of Judge J. Cullen Ganey, read prior to imposing sentence, received widespread attention. In it he sharply criticized the corporations as the major culprits, but he also pictured the defendants in a light other than that they chose to shed upon themselves in their subsequent discussions of the offenses:

. . . they were torn between conscience and an approved corporate policy, with the rewarding objective of promotion, comfortable security, and large salaries. They were the organization or company man, the conformist who goes along with his superiors and finds balm for his conscience in additional comforts and security of his place in the corporate set-up.[25]

The repeated emphasis on "comfort" and "security" constitutes the basic element of Judge Ganey's view of the motivations of the offenders. Stress on passive acquiescence occurs in remarks by two General Electric executives viewing the derelictions of their subordinates. Robert Paxton, the retired company president, called antitrust agreements "monkey business" and denounced in vitriolic terms one of his former superiors who, when Paxton first joined General Electric, had put him to work attempting

[24] Sharon (Pa.) *Herald*, Feb. 6, 1961.

[25] *New York Times*, Feb. 7, 1961.

to secure a bid on a contract that had already been prearranged by a price-fixing agreement. Ralph Cordiner, the president and board chairman of General Electric, thought that the antitrust offenses were motivated by drives for easily acquired power. Cordiner's statement is noteworthy for its dismissal of the explanations of the offenders as "rationalizations":

One reason for the offenses was a desire to be "Mr. Transformer" or "Mr. Switchgear"* . . . and to have influence over a larger segment of the industry. . . . The second was that it was an indolent, lazy way to do business. When you get all through with the rationalizations, you have to come back to one or the other of these conclusions.

There were other explanations as well. One truculent offender, the 68-year-old president of a smaller company who had been spared a jail sentence only because of his age and the illness of his wife, categorically denied the illegality of his behavior. "We did not fix prices," he said. "I can't agree with you. I am telling you that all we did was recover costs." Some persons blamed the system of decentralization in the larger companies, which they said placed a heavy burden to produce profit on each of the relatively autonomous divisions, particularly when bonuses—"incentive compensation" —were at stake, while others maintained that the "dog-eat-dog" business conditions in the heavy electrical equipment industry were responsible for the violations. Perhaps the simplest explanation came from a General Electric executive. "I think," he said, "the boys could resist everything but temptation."

PORTRAIT OF AN OFFENDER

The highest paid executive to be given a jail sentence was a General Electric vice-president, earning $135,000 a year—about

*Earlier, a witness had quoted his superior as saying: "I have the industry under my thumb. They will do just about as I ask them." This man, the witness said, "was known as Mr. Switchgear in the industry."

$2600 every week. The details of his career and his participation in the conspiracy provide additional insight into the operations of white-collar crime and white-collar criminals.

The General Electric vice-president was one of a disproportionate number of Southerners involved in the antitrust violations. He had been born in Atlanta and was 46 years old at the time he was sentenced to jail. He had graduated with a degree in electrical engineering from Georgia Tech, and received an honorary doctorate degree from Sienna College in 1958, was married, and the father of three children. He had served in the Navy during the Second World War, rising to the rank of lieutenant commander, was a director of the Schenectady Boy's Club, on the board of trustees of Miss Hall's School, and, not without some irony, was a member of Governor Rockefeller's Temporary State Committee on Economic Expansion.[26]

Almost immediately after his sentencing, he issued a statement to the press, noting that he was to serve a jail term "for conduct which has been interpreted as being in conflict with the complex antitrust laws." He commented that "General Electric, Schenectady, and its people have undergone many ordeals together and we have not only survived them, but have come out stronger, more vigorous, more alive than ever. We shall again." Then he voiced his appreciation for "the letters and calls from people all over the country, the community, the shops, and the offices . . . expressing confidence and support."[27]

The vice-president was neither so sentimental about his company nor so certain about the complexity of the antitrust regulations when he appeared before the Kefauver committee five months later. "I don't get mad, Senator," he said at one point, referring to his behavior during a meeting with competitors, but he took another line

[26] *New York Times*, Feb. 7, 1961.
[27] *Schenectady Union-Star*, Feb. 10, 1961.

when he attempted to explain why he was no longer associated with General Electric:

. . . when I got out of being a guest of the Government for 30 days, I had found out that we were not to be paid while we were there,* and I got, frankly, madder than hell. . . .

Previously, he had been mentioned as a possible president of General Electric, described by the then president, as "an exceptionally eager and promising individual." Employed by the company shortly after graduation from college, he had risen dramatically through the managerial ranks, and passed that point, described by a higher executive, "where the man, if his work has been sufficiently promising, has an opportunity to step across the barrier out of his function into the field of general management." In 1946, he had his first contact with price-fixing, being introduced to competitors by his superior and told that he "should be the one to contact them as far as power transformers were concerned in the future."

The meetings that he attended ran a rather erratic course, with numerous squabbles between the participants. Continual efforts had to be made to keep knowledge of the meetings from "the manufacturing people, the engineers, and especially the lawyers," but this was achieved, the witness tried to convince the Kefauver committee, because commercial transactions remained unquestioned by managerial personnel so long as they showed a reasonable profit. The price-fixing meetings continued from 1946 until 1949. At that time, a federal investigation of licensing and cross-patent activities in the transformer industry sent the conspirators scurrying for shelter. "The iron curtain was completely down" for a year, and sales people at General Electric were forbidden to attend gatherings of the National Electrical Manufacturers' Association, where they had traditionally connived with competitors.

Meetings resumed, however, when the witness's superior, described by him as "a great communicator, a great philosopher,

and, frankly, a great believer in stabilities of prices," decided that "the market was getting in chaotic condition" and that they "had better go out and see what could be done about it." He was told to keep knowledge of the meetings from Robert Paxton, "an Adam Smith advocate," then the plant works manager, because Paxton "don't understand these things."

Promoted to general manager in 1954, the witness was called to New York by the president of General Electric and told specifically, possibly in part because he had a reputation of being "a bad boy," to comply with the company policy and with the antitrust laws, and to see that his subordinates did so too. This instruction lasted as long as it took him to get from New York back to Massachusetts, where his superior there told him: "Now, keep on doing the way that you have been doing but just . . . be sensible about it and use your head on the subject." The price-fixing meetings therefore continued unabated, particularly as market conditions were aggravated by overproduction which had taken place during the Korean War. In the late 1950s foreign competition entered the picture, and lower bids from abroad often forced the American firms to give up on particular price-fixing attempts.

In 1957, the witness was promoted to vice-president, and again brought to New York for a lecture from the company president on the evils of price-fixing. This time, his "air cover gone"—he now had to report directly to top management—he decided to abandon altogether his involvement in price-fixing. He returned to his plant and issued stringent orders to his subordinates that they were no longer to attend meetings with competitors. Not surprisingly, since he himself had rarely obeyed such injunctions, neither did the sales persons in his division.

The witness was interrogated closely about his moral feelings regarding criminal behavior. He fumbled most of the questions, avoiding answering them directly, but ultimately came to the point of saying that the consequences visited upon him represented the major reason for a re-evaluation

---

* A matter of some $11,000 for the jail term.

of his actions. He would not behave in the same manner again because of what "I have been through and what I have done to my family." He was also vexed with the treatment he had received from the newspapers: "They have never laid off a second. They have used some terms which I don't think are necessary—they don't use the term price fixing. It is always price rigging or trying to make it as sensational as possible."[28] The taint of a jail sentence, he said, had the effect of making people "start looking at the moral values a little bit." Senator Hart drew the following conclusions from the witness's comments:

Hart: This was what I was wondering about, whether absent the introduction of this element of fear, there would have been any re-examination of the moral implications.

Witness: I wonder, Senator. That is a pretty tough one to answer.

Hart: If I understand you correctly, you have already answered it. . . . After the fear, there came the moral re-evaluation.

Nevertheless, the former General Electric vice-president viewed his situation rather philosophically. Regarding his resignation from the company, it was "the way the ball has bounced." He hoped that he would have "the opportunity to continue in American industry and do a job," and he wished some of the other men who had been dismissed a lot of good luck. "I want to leave the company with no bitterness and go out and see if I can't start a new venture along the right lines." Eight days later, he accepted a job as assistant to the president in charge of product research in a large corporation located outside Philadelphia.[29] Slightly more

than a month after that, he was named president of the company, at a salary reported to be somewhat less than the $74,000 yearly received by his predecessor.[30]

A SUMMING UP

The antitrust violations in the heavy electrical industry permit a re-evaluation of many of the earlier speculations about white collar crime. The price-fixing behavior, flagrant in nature, was clearly in violation of the criminal provisions of the Sherman Act of 1890, which had been aimed at furthering "industrial liberty." Rather, the price-fixing arrangements represented attempts at "corporate socialism," and in the words of Senator Kefauver to a subcommittee witness:

It makes a complete mockery not only of how we have always lived and what we have believed in and have laws to protect, but what you were doing was to make a complete mockery of the carefully worded laws of the Government of the United States, ordinances of the cities, rules of the REA's [Rural Electrification Administration], with reference to sealed secret bids in order to get competition.

The facts of the antitrust conspiracy would seem clearly to resolve in the affirmative debate concerning the criminal nature and the relevance for criminological study of such forms of white collar crime,[31] though warnings regarding an indefinite and unwarranted extension of the designation "crime" to all acts abhorrent to academic criminologists must remain in force.[32] Many

---

[28] A contrary view is expressed in Note, "Increasing Community Control over Corporate Crime—A Problem in the Law of Sanctions," *Yale Law Journal*, 71 (December 1961), footnoted material pp. 287–289. It has been pointed out that Time Magazine (Feb. 17, 1961, pp. 64 ff.) reported the conspiracy in its "Business" section, whereas it normally presents crime news under a special heading of its own.—Donald R. Taft and Ralph W. England, Jr., *Criminology*, 4th ed., New York: The Macmillan Company, 1964, p. 203.

[29] *New York Times*, May 12, 1961.

[30] *New York Times*, June 23, 1961.

[31] See Edwin H. Sutherland, "Is 'White Collar Crime' Crime?" *American Sociological Review*, 10 (April 1945), pp. 132–139. Note: "It may be hoped that the Philadelphia electric cases have helped to dispel this misapprehension. . . . It should now be clear that a deliberate or conscious violation of the antitrust laws . . . is a serious offense against society which is as criminal as any other act that injures many in order to profit a few. Conspiracy to violate the antitrust laws is economic racketeering. Those who are apprehended in such acts are, and will be treated as criminals."—Lee Loevinger, "Recent Developments in Antitrust Enforcement," Antitrust Section, American Bar Association, 18 (1961), p. 102.

[32] Paul W. Tappan, "Who Is the Criminal?" *American Sociological Review*, 12 (February 1947), pp. 96–102.

of Sutherland's ideas concerning the behavior of corporate offenders also receive substantiation. His stress on learning and associational patterns as important elements in the genesis of the violations receives strong support.[33] So too does his emphasis on national trade conventions as the sites of corporate criminal conspiracies.[34]

Others of Sutherland's views appear to require overhaul. His belief, for example, that "those who are responsible for the system of criminal justice are afraid to antagonize businessmen"[35] seems less than totally true in terms of the electrical industry prosecutions. Sutherland's thesis that "the customary pleas of the executives of the corporation . . . that they were ignorant of and not responsible for the action of the special department . . . is akin to the alibi of the ordinary criminal and need not be taken seriously"[36] also seems to be a rather injudicious blanket condemnation. The accuracy of the statement for the antitrust conspiracy must remain moot, but it would seem important that traditional safeguards concerning guilty knowledge as a basic ingredient in criminal responsibility be accorded great respect.[37] Nor, in terms of the antitrust data, does Sutherland appear altogether correct in his view that "the public agencies of communication, which continually define ordinary violations of the criminal code in a very critical manner, do not make similar definitions of white collar crime."[38]

Various analytical schemes and theoretical statements in criminology and related fields provide some insight into elements of the price-fixing conspiracy. Galbraith's caustic observation regarding the traditional academic view of corporate price-fixing arrangements represents a worthwhile point of departure:

Restraints on competition and the free movement of prices, the principal source of uncertainty to business firms, have been principally deplored by university professors on lifelong appointments. Such security of tenure is deemed essential for fruitful and unremitting thought.[39]

It seems apparent, looking at the antitrust offenses in this light, that the attractiveness of a secure market arrangement represented a major ingredient drawing corporate officers to the price-fixing violations. The elimination of competition meant the avoidance of uncertainty, the formalization and predictability of outcome, the minimization of risks. It is, of course, this incentive which accounts for much of human activity, be it deviant or "normal," and this tendency that Weber found so pronounced in bureaucracies in their move from vital but erratic beginnings to more staid and more comfortable middle and old age.[40]

For the conspirators there had necessarily to be a conjunction of factors before they could participate in the violations. First, of course, they had to perceive that there would be gains accruing from their behavior. Such gains might be personal and professional, in terms of corporate advancement toward prestige and power, and they might be vocational, in terms of a more expedient and secure method of carrying out assigned tasks. The offenders also apparently

---

[33] Sutherland, *White Collar Crime*, pp. 234–257.
[34] Sutherland, p. 70.
[35] Sutherland, p. 10.
[36] Sutherland, p. 54.
[37] For an excellent presentation, see Sanford H. Kadish, "Some Observations on the Use of Criminal Sanctions in Enforcing Economic Regulations," *University of Chicago Law Review*, 30 (Spring 1963), pp. 423–449. See also Richard A. Whiting, "Antitrust and the Corporate Executive," *Virginia Law Review*, 47 (October 1961), pp. 929–987.
[38] Sutherland, *White Collar Crime*, p. 247.

[39] John Kenneth Galbraith, *The Affluent Society*, Boston: Houghton Mifflin Company, 1958, p. 84. See also Richard Hofstadter, "Antitrust in America," *Commentary*, 38 (August 1964), pp. 47–53. An executive of one corporation is said to have remarked regarding the collusive antitrust arrangements: "It is the only way business can be run. It's free enterprise." Quoted by Mr. Justice Clark to Antitrust Section, American Bar Association, St. Louis, Aug. 8, 1961, p. 4.
[40] Max Weber, *The Theory of Social and Economic Organization*, translated by A. M. Henderson and Talcott Parsons, New York: Oxford University Press, 1947, pp. 367–373.

had to be able to neutralize or rationalize their behavior in a manner in keeping with their image of themselves as law-abiding, decent, and respectable persons.[41] The ebb and flow of the price-fixing conspiracy also clearly indicates the relationship, often overlooked in explanations of criminal behavior, between extrinsic conditions and illegal acts. When the market behaved in a manner the executives thought satisfactory, or when enforcement agencies seemed particularly threatening, the conspiracy desisted. When market conditions deteriorated, while corporate pressures for achieving attractive profit-and-loss statements remained constant, and enforcement activity abated, the price-fixing agreements flourished.

More than anything else, however, a

41 See Donald R. Cressey, *Other People's Money*, New York: The Free Press of Glencoe, 1953; Gresham M. Sykes and David Matza, "Techniques of Neutralization: A Theory of Delinquency," *American Sociological Review*, 22 (December 1957), pp. 664–670.

plunge into the elaborate documentation of the antitrust cases of 1961, as well as an attempt to relate them to other segments of criminological work, points up the considerable need for more and better monographic field studies of law violators and of systems of criminal behavior, these to be followed by attempts to establish theoretical guidelines and to review and refine current interpretative viewpoints. There have probably been no more than a dozen, if that many, full-length studies of types of criminal (not delinquent) behavior in the past decade. The need for such work seems overriding, and the 1961 antitrust cases represent but one of a number of instances, whether in the field of white collar crime, organized crime, sex offenses, personal or property crimes, or similar areas of concern, where we are still faced with a less than adequate supply of basic and comparative material upon which to base valid and useful theoretical statements.

THE BLACK MARKET*

Marshall B. Clinard

Regulations during World War II made it illegal to charge more than a fixed price for nearly all commodities. Several types of black market violations developed as a result of the laws which controlled the pricing and rationing of commodities. Several possible explanations of black market violations are considered in the following selection. Also discussed is the role of the government in the enforcement of economic controls.

Profiteering by some businessmen and the securing of unfair advantages by many civilians have probably characterized all wars. Even Washington is said to have wished

that he could have hanged some of the men who made excessive profits from sales to his ragged soldiers. In the Civil War, the Spanish-American War, and World War I

* Reprinted from *The Black Market*, New York: Holt, Rinehart and Winston, Inc., 1952, pp. 1–2, 15–16, 27, 293–310, 324–329, by permission of the author and publisher.

there were stories of men who enriched themselves at the expense of others. Much of this activity was not illegal, however, since there were few clearly defined wartime restrictions prohibiting the sale of commodities above a certain price. While people generally frowned on such behavior, they seldom had any laws with penalties to prevent it.

With the coming of World War II all this changed. Drastic regulations were issued making it against the law to charge more than a certain fixed price for nearly all commodities, and for the first time in American history there was compulsory rationing of certain goods by the government. As a result, this country was swept with a new type of danger, as serious a threat to our political, social, and economic welfare as major military reverses. This insidious new attack on the home front came in the form of what was called a "black market," a term previously almost unknown in this country but one which developed rapidly in significance. The actual origin of this term is not quite clear, although it appears to have been identified with "black" to indicate illegal activities occurring under conditions of great secrecy.[1]

Whatever the origin of the term might be, the black market and what it signified became a great wartime interest in this country, involving attempts to circumvent economic controls set up by the government to guarantee more adequate and equal distribution of certain essential goods and

to prevent inflation. In general, these controls concerned the allocation of scarce industrial materials, the regulation of prices and rents, and the distribution by rationing of vital commodities in scarce supply. These regulations were in effect not only in this country but in all those at war, regardless of the form of government. Great Britain, for example, instituted price controls at the outbreak of war in 1939 and extended these controls in 1941, while rationing was begun in 1940. Such controls helped to make available the maximum amount of materials necessary for conducting total war.[2]

The black market covered a wide range of activities, with price or rationing violations occurring in almost all commodities, from heavy industrial materials to items such as clothing, gasoline, shoes, sugar, potatoes, onions, cigarettes, and alcoholic beverages, involving mainly manufacturers, wholesalers, and retailers, but in the case of rationing, sometimes consumers.[3] There

[1] The Columbia Encyclopedia does not include the term as a part of American speech, and the Encyclopedia Americana first listed it in the Annual of 1944. "The etymology of the term [black market], as of the continental marché noir which already flourished in World War I, is doubtless to be sought in comparable expressions denoting forbidden activities carried on in dark secrecy to escape detection and punishment, e.g., 'black bourse,' 'black mass,' 'black hand.' "—Britannica Book of the Year 1944, p. 112. The term "black marketeer" did not appear until 1945 in Webster's or in Funk and Wagnalls' Dictionary, or in H. L. Mencken's The American Language (New York: Alfred A. Knopf, Inc., 1945), in which it was stated in Supplement 1 (p. 360) that it carried a disparaging significance.

[2] Black marketing in Europe after World War II was chiefly on an individual basis but had much wider ramifications than ever was the situation in the United States. In Germany, for example, Germans and the occupation troops sold cigarettes, coffee, foodstuffs, and the like at prices far above those set by the authorities concerned. In addition, occupation scrip was frequently sold at any price from ten to twenty times the legal rate. Further, there was a great deal of direct barter, particularly among the peasants, who withheld foodstuffs from the market, and either sold them for reichsmarks at high rates, or, much more frequently, insisted on the direct bartering of radios, sewing machines, rugs, and other things, in exchange for foodstuffs. There was some currency manipulation. Reichsmarks were traded for occupation francs, Swiss francs, pounds, and the like. Except for the barest necessities of life the black market was all-pervasive.

[3] The majority of violations of price regulations were by the seller rather than the buyer, for a buyer for ultimate consumption could not ordinarily be a violator and a violation ordinarily originated with the seller. Price violations by the buyer, in those regulations prohibiting such behavior, were derivative in the sense that the seller ordinarily, but not always, initiated the transaction. Even assuming the purchaser to be a willing buyer, if he paid a price above ceiling he had to pass on the overcharge, provided he was not the ultimate consumer and did not wish to sell at a loss.

were also violations of rent regulations by landlords. Black market violations consisted of several types of activities: (1) over-ceiling price violations, (2) evasive price violations, (3) rationing violations (including the theft and counterfeiting of ration currency), (4) violations of rent ceilings, and (5) record-keeping and reporting violations.

A black market of immense proportions engulfed our country in a relatively short period of time. The very extent of wartime controls permitted latitude for great variety in types of violations, and the evasive nature of many of the violations is indicative of the ingenuity of those businessmen and others who engaged in the black market. The absence of previous experience with such wartime regulatory measures restricting the economic life of the entire population, moreover, indicates that patterns of violation developed in a relatively short period of time, which seriously hampered the government in an effective and immediate control of the black market.

EXPLANATIONS
OF THE BLACK MARKET

The Black Market Cannot Be Attributed to Gangster and Shady Elements in Business. There was the common assumption that the black market was due primarily to the entrance of shady or gangster elements into American business. This public misconception about the black market seems to have arisen from the publicity program directed at arousing the country in a melodramatic fashion to the dangers of violations of price and rationing controls.[4] Such views have not been entirely confined to these sources, for a postwar study dealing with the relation of World War II to social disorganization surmises, but with no supporting evidence, that "certain wartime crimes, particularly those involving black market operations, may have been carried on by the criminal or quasi-criminal groups who normally would be engaged in more conventional criminal activities. Such behavior may merely represent the transfer of activity away from the traditional offenses, particularly those against property, toward activities which offer immediate return in wartime."[5]

One enforcement official, however, has stated: "I had thought, when I got into enforcement activities, and I think most people would, when we speak of violators and enforcement, we think of a racketeer. That has not been our experience. After all, who has the goods to sell? It is the person who customarily is in the line of supply."[6] A former OPA administrator, writing on the black market in 1946, had this to say about the violators:

Criminal racketeers of the gangster variety have relatively little place in the wholesale chiseling now going on. They do not control our slaughterhouses, lumber mills, textile centers, and automobile agencies, nor do they have any interest in our retail stores and railroads. Current racketeering is largely in the hands of men and women with whom we have always done business.[7]

Even the meat black market, which was widely thought of as primarily a gangster racket, with hijacking and sales through "blind pigs" as in the prohibition era, was found to have been largely a product of ordinary business channels, although the number of nonfederally inspected meat slaughterers increased considerably during the war. In 1946 there was a significant ex-

[4] Statements were made that organized racketeers were engaging in black market activities, and there were numerous magazine and newspaper articles, as well as motion-picture shorts, describing such cases. For example, the following statement about the meat black market was released by the Office of War Information and appeared in the Washington *Post*, March 5, 1943: "Another source of supply, the OWI said, is the rustler who rides the range at night, shooting animals where he finds them, dressing them on the spot and driving away with the carcasses in a truck."

[5] Francis E. Merrill, *Social Problems on the Home Front* (New York: Harper & Row, Publishers, 1948), p. 181.
[6] *Hearings before the Senate Banking and Currency Committee on Senate Resolution 2,028*, Seventy-ninth Congress, Second Session, II, p. 1679.
[7] Leon Henderson, "How Black Is Our Market?" *Atlantic Monthly*, July 1946, p. 46.

change of communications between the general counsel of the National Independent Meat Packers Association and the government official in charge of enforcing meat regulations, in which the government official stated: "My point was, if you read my testimony, that the black market consists of numerous violations, none of them committed by the Capone type conspirator or meat bootlegger, but rather by established members of industry, including members of your association and the American Meat Institute."[8] Hartung, after studying the meat black market in Detroit, concluded:

First and most important, the meat black market was not a clandestine criminal organization parasitic upon the industry. It did not hijack meat at various stages in the normal flow and sell it through blind pigs known to fortunate customers. It was most definitely not an excrescence upon the industry composed of racketeers coming from various criminal fields, or perhaps surviving from the prohibition era. Had this been the case, effective detective work could have uncovered it, and OPA would indeed have been remiss in not doing so.

Of the thousands of meat black marketeers proceeded against criminally, civilly, and administratively, the writer knows of none who were gangsters. Of the several hundred defendants in the Detroit area, only two had a previous criminal record, but neither of these could in any way have been regarded as a gangster. Neither of the convictions was for activities related to meat, and both had been committed outside of Michigan some years previously. Actually, then, the violations in this industry were committed by persons more or less well established in the different levels, from slaughterers to wholesalers and retailers. And the violations ranged from hardly more than traditional sharp practices to the most studied and deliberate attempts at conspiracy.[9]

In examining those price and rationing cases where criminal prosecution was instituted, which constituted a sample of flagrant cases, we find that less than one violator in ten was reported to have had any criminal record.[10] Those with criminal records probably represented chiefly thieves and counterfeiters of ration currency. Only somewhere between one in two and one in three persons sentenced for more than one year were known to have had previous institutional commitments.[11] Since these figures included dealers who violated the rationing provisions, as well as those professional criminals who stole or counterfeited the currency and the relatively few persons who were prosecuted for price and rent violations, the proportion of the last-named group who had a criminal record was probably even smaller. In fact, as has been pointed out elsewhere, one reason for the small number of prosecutions for price violations was that few of those violators had previous records of criminal behavior, thus making the possibility of conviction, or imprisonment, difficult. Among those persons with criminal records who violated the price regulations were some liquor dealers with a record of violation during the prohibition period. One case of this type represented a violation of the price ceilings on whiskey, and the offender was sentenced to the federal prisons for twenty-four months and fined $10,000. He had been engaged in bootlegging from 1926 to 1932, both as a liquor runner and a moonshine dealer. He operated five liquor stores in a fairly large southern city, and his black market profits were estimated at $30,979.

A somewhat different explanation, but with the same implication, was that those businessmen who engaged in the black market were chiefly either shady operators before the war or new elements, but not

---

[8] *Hearings before the Senate Committee on Banking and Currency*, 1946 Extension of the Emergency Price Control and Stabilization Acts of 1942, as Amended, Seventy-ninth Congress, Second Session, Pt. II, 1247.

[9] Frank E. Hartung, "A Study in Law and Social Differentiation: As Exemplified in Violations of the Emergency Price Control Act of 1942 and the Second War Powers Act, in the Detroit Meat Industry." Unpublished Ph.D. Dissertation, University of Michigan, Ann Arbor, Michigan, 1949, pp. 159–160.

[10] Unpublished OPA Enforcement Department data.

[11] Information furnished by the Federal Bureau of Prisons. In 1945, 45.5 percent; 1946, 38.8 percent; and 1947, 46.5 percent.

gangsters, entering business during the war. While it is true that some new businesses, for example, entered the meat and apparel black market, they constituted a relatively small proportion of the total business in the country. With few exceptions, businessmen and writers in various journals of business stated flatly that regular business was primarily responsible for the black market: "The big trouble in foods is that black markets are usually operated by regular merchants through regular channels of trade."[12] Statements of government enforcement officials, and an analysis of black market cases, furnish further proof of this contention. While not definitely proving that the persons either were respectable or had always lived in these areas, in one particular study, where a tabulation was made of the residence of meat black market offenders, it was found that more than 80 percent lived in the most desirable areas of the city.[13]

Black Market Not Restricted to Certain Commodities or Business Areas. Many persons believed that the black market was characteristic of certain commodities such as meat and gasoline, or fields of business, but a survey of violations has indicated that the black market was not the outgrowth of unique conditions of any particular industry, the peculiar injustice of certain regulations, the squeeze at a particular level of trade, or the conditions prevailing in certain parts of the country. There were black markets in all types of commodities. Our analysis has shown that extensive violations occurred in at least twenty-one major commodity groups and in many minor ones, and in all sections of business. Farmers, packers, manufacturers, wholesalers, retailers, large and small companies—all participated in the black market and each one took his particular share of illegal profits. It is possible that the producers' and whole-

salers' violations were the more flagrant insofar as their violations were subsequently reflected in the retailers' dealings with the consumer. Still the relative seriousness of violations cannot be definitely established empirically.

Black Market Primarily Due to Certain Cultural and Ethical Definitions in Business. If the black market cannot, therefore, be attributed to certain elements in our society, or as so many individuals flaunting the law, to what can we attribute such wholesale disregard of the law at the very time one should expect patriotic compliance? Certainly the situation out of which this black market arose was complex. While the problem was primarily one of social and cultural factors, as the discussion will show, also involved were problems of economics and the relation of government to business. Before going into the matter in more detail, however, it is important to understand how these activities spread, for this was one of the underlying causes of the black market.

Most black market violations appear to have their origin in behavior learned in association from others, unethical and illegal practices being conveyed in the trade as part of a definition of the situation and rationalizations to support these violations of law being similarly transmitted by this differential association.[14] This type of learning must be regarded as a pull between unethical forces favorable to black market violations on the one hand and the forces leading to legal behavior. The same process of acquiring criminal behavior operates among businessmen as it does among ordinary criminals who learn how to steal, make counterfeit ration currency, and dispose of it. Such a theory does not explain all viola-

---

12 "Ceiling-Price Gyps," *Business Week*, June 26, 1943, p. 72.
13 Hartung, "A Study in Law and Social Differentiation," p. 221.

14 By differential association is meant a person's contact with various cultural definitions. While the term usually refers to deviant or illegal cultural definitions, it actually signifies a relation between law-abiding norms and norms of disobedience to law and ethics. Also see Edwin H. Sutherland, *White Collar Crime*, New York: Dryden Press, 1949, Chap. XIV.

tions, however, and, as will be indicated later, other factors had an effect on such differential association.

Both the extensiveness of the black market and the kinds of violations indicate primarily subcultural transmission. Basically the black market appears to have been related to many practices current among certain elements in business during peacetime. Some of the black market represented "normal" business procedures which were outlawed by the government, while others represented unethical and illegal behavior which the government attempted to deal with during peacetime on a limited scale and whose extensiveness was probably accentuated by the opportunities afforded by the war. Among the practices that might be termed "normal" during peacetime were tie-in sales of certain commodities, the giving of excessive discounts or kickbacks to favored customers, and a certain amount of quality deterioration in products, particularly through upgrading.

. . . Some types of illegal practices current in peacetime are revealed in the reports of the Federal Trade Commission, which was established in 1914 to deal with unfair methods of competition in industry. There are many cases of false and misleading advertising, misbranding of commodities as to quality, purity, origin, source, attributes, or nature of manufacture, and their sale under names and circumstances which deceive the public. Many other violations come under such activities as procuring the business or trade secrets of competitors by espionage or by bribing their employees; making false and disparaging statements respecting competitors' products and business; conspiring to maintain uniform selling prices, terms, and conditions of sale through the use of a patent licensing system or combinations or agreements to fix, maintain, or depress prices; giving products misleading names in order to give them a value to the consumer which they would not otherwise possess; and shipping products at market prices to customers or prospective customers or to the customers or prospec-

tive customers of competitors without an order and then inducing or attempting by various means to induce the consignees to accept and purchase such consignments.[15] Sutherland found in his study that among the common illegal practices in business were violations of the antitrust laws and the fair labor practices laws, false advertising, illegal rebates, violation of trademark laws, the giving of illegal bonuses and commissions to officers and favored stockholders, "wash sales" of stocks and manipulation of the market to sell company securities, and false income tax returns.[16]

In some instances during the war almost the entire industry engaged in violations of particular types, as, for example, the lumber industry in the South and the poultry industry in the Delmarva Peninsula, "where a very high proportion of the business was transacted in flagrant and intentional violation."[17]

Many types of black market violations were picked up from conversations of businessmen and descriptions of violations appearing in trade newspapers and the general press. In most cases there was a remarkable similarity in the nature of the violations, particularly in certain evasive practices in the meat black market and the side payments in used-car violations. The extensiveness of the relations with the professional criminals in the gasoline black market indicates that knowledge of how to obtain illegal ration currency was acquired, in part, from other gasoline dealers. In some black market activities the pattern of violation was diffused from the supplier to the purchasing concern. In others there was actual collusion between buyer and seller. In still other cases large concerns diffused the violations among their subsidiaries. Competitors

[15] See the annual reports of the Federal Trade Commission.

[16] Sutherland, White Collar Crime.

[17] Harvey C. Mansfield and Associates, A Short History of OPA, General Publication of the Historical Reports on War Administration, Office of Price Administration, Washington, D.C.: Government Printing Office, 1947, p. 256.

copied illegal practices not necessarily to stay in business but rather to take advantage of the additional profits afforded. The following cases illustrate, at least in part, the explanation of the violations through differential association.

1. An established commission agent in meat sales, who, as far as is known, up to that time had never participated in the black market, received a long-distance telephone call from a meat dealer in another part of the country. According to the telephone conversation, the latter asked how conditions were and "I told him that conditions were miserable and I was having a difficult time and I wished to goodness he would give me some meat to sell. At that time I said, 'I understand that you have been shipping some meat into ——.'" At this the meat dealer laughed and said, "So, you did wake up! How would you like to handle some meat?" The proposition was then outlined calling for shipments invoiced at ceiling prices. Cash side payments were to be secured in —— and instructions were given that no checks were to be taken or any receipts given for the cash. A contact man was to pick up the cash.

2. In a flagrant violation, scrap metal, essential to the armed services, was upgraded by the inclusion of tin cans and then sold as No. 1 scrap. The owners of this concern, which operated in several states, specifically instructed their employees to include tin cans in the material invoiced. They, moreover, instructed the employees in the manner of handling such scrap so that the tin cans would be concealed in the bundle and would not be visible upon inspection.

3. During 1942 two eastern tire salesmen were instrumental in organizing a state-wide ring which purchased, received, and transferred new rubber tires and tubes without exchanging rationing certificates. In this case the two principal defendants arranged a meeting with retail tire dealers, who later became involved also, and explained the method that they were using to transfer tires without surrendering rationing or replenishment certificates and advised them that they could get any tires they needed. The plan was to have signed blank bill-heads on printed stationery to be used as "sign-offs," giving the impression that the principals were bona fide agents when acquiring tires in large metropolitan centers.

The tires were then sold to the retailers at a cash profit and then resold by the latter mostly in bulk sales. No certificates were to be used in transferring these tires, and no accurate records were to be kept of the transactions, since it was suggested that the retailers bill these tires to "phony" individuals or to defunct garages which had been out of business for many years. The eventual tire ring involved a large number of dealers in scattered cities and towns who disposed of thousands of tires through this illegal device.[18]

Many violations indicated such great ingenuity that they undoubtedly represented the assistance given by lawyers and others who helped work out a method of getting around or violating the regulations. Reports from informed persons indicated that advisers were hired by business concerns, or legal advice was sought, in order to discover just how close one could come to breaking a regulation without being subject to prosecution.[19] Numerous amendments to the various regulations, which were often the subject of ridicule by the press and various business interests, became necessary when ways and means of getting around them were devised.

Evidence of both consensus and organized behavior among certain business interests further supports the view that the black market was primarily a product of differential association. Examples of such organized behavior on the part of some businessmen were their planned violations, attitudes toward enforcement personnel, lack of condemnation for violators, reluctance to inform on black market violators, and their general failure to offer real support to the government program. Many black market offenses involved a close-knit

18 Cases from unpublished Enforcement Department case material.
19 Some attorneys were hired away from the OPA for this purpose. In most cases the attorney did not actually participate in a trial involving the OPA, which would have been contrary to the federal statutes prohibiting a former government employee from appearing against the government for a period of two years. This did not, however, deter such individuals from working behind the scenes in some law firms.

chain of relationships between various levels of activity, for example, manufacturers, wholesalers, and retailers in textiles and apparel. Some activities tied together parent company and subsidiary. Other violations were organized on an extensive geographical basis, as in a used-car conspiracy, for example, which involved thirty-one persons centering around southern Illinois, the entire state of Kentucky, and Detroit. This conspiracy involved picking up used cars and redistributing them at over-ceiling sales throughout the country. In another case a postwar black market in wholesale food was operated out of a small Wisconsin city with a hotel room in New York as the eastern office of operation. Practically all dealings of the company were in the black market, including the sale of corn syrups, dextrose, butter and eggs, poultry and meats, and about 800 carloads of cheese. Payments were made in bills of small denominations to an agent who kept the room continuously in a New York hotel where these illegal payments were made.

There was also consensus among certain sections of business that the OPA enforcement staff was stupid and inefficient. Interviews, for example, with wholesale food dealers found most of them in agreement on this point of stupidity and inefficiency. Whether investigators displayed these characteristics is irrelevant here, for it would be difficult for potential violators to be objective. Certainly there was little indication that these people wanted, or tried to get, more intelligent and better trained enforcement officials.

If you give them more supplies the enforcing end will take care of itself. They need more enforcement officers that are of the intelligent type. A lot that they have now are qualified to join the Gestapo. Too many assume you're dishonest before they start.—Eastern grocery dealer.

I might abolish it [the OPA] entirely—now I'm not saying I would but I might—it sure needs a good overhauling. I'd cut the payroll to one third. Put more efficient men in charge. I had 14 coops of chickens marked hens and

springs and the OPA man comes along and he looked at them and he said, "Are you sure those hens are not springs?" He didn't know hens from springs. Now you know he shouldn't have been trying to tell us how to run the chicken business if he didn't know hens from springs! I think it's wrong to have a twenty-eight-year-old lawyer who has just graduated from college come in trying to tell you how to run your business.—Midwestern poultry dealer.[20]

Although there were some instances where businessmen offered to help police their trades, a study of the testimony of representatives of business organizations before congressional committees, as well as of interviews with businessmen, indicates that nearly all statements were directed at the weakening of enforcement or in favor of outright repeal of the entire program because of its "failure." Conversations with the man on the street, discussions in the trade press, even the attitudes of many newspapers were such as to convince many a businessman that his fellows, as well as a majority of the public, shared his disrespect for the OPA. There is little evidence to indicate that leading representatives of many business trades made speeches or used other means to appeal for real compliance in their trades. Most efforts were directed at attacks on the OPA or toward achieving greater liberality in the regulations. When food wholesalers were asked what they would do to help enforce regulations, the following replies were typical:

Lady, it can't be done, not if they put a whole army of people to work. You are not going to get me to propose anything. I wouldn't be connected with that OPA, because it just isn't doing any good. In the first world war we just let supply and demand take care of the situation and we got along all right.—Midwestern meat dealer.

I wouldn't have any [suggestions] to give you. Before I'd take a job with the OPA I'd retire. There are too many parasites in the government now. You are doing your best to put me down on that question but no matter how you word it I won't offer any suggestions on how

20 Cases taken from interviews, "Opinion Survey of Food Wholesalers," conducted for the OPA.

to enforce something I don't believe in.— Midwestern grocery dealer.

I'm not in favor of the OPA regulations so I wouldn't want to make any suggestions as to how to force people to comply. But understand this: as long as there are OPA regulations I'll abide by them. [*Question:* Couldn't you suppose that you were in favor of them? Couldn't you make some suggestions under these circumstances?] No. It'd be too much of a strain on my imagination!—Midwestern grocery dealer.[21]

Some businessmen also displayed considerable consensus about black market violators, for there is little indication that many of them regarded such people, or, in fact, any violators of wartime regulations, as persons who had lost much face or prestige. At the height of the meat or apparel black market, for example, large sections of these trades stuck together. Nothing better illustrates the degree of organization and consensus among businessmen than their reluctance to testify against each other. One southwestern fresh fruit and vegetable dealer described it this way: "When a merchant buys, we tell him of all the over-ceiling fellows that we know about—but we don't report them to the OPA."[22] A Pittsburgh case illustrates this reluctance to inform on another businessman engaging in black market operations. After a local distributor of frozen meat and poultry had received a bill for a carload of poultry which he was expecting, he was approached by a black marketeer who had somehow learned of the shipment and offered him $3000, plus the price of the poultry itself, if he would make this carload over to him. Although the poultry dealer refused the offer, saying he "couldn't look at his own face in the mirror" if he did such a thing, since his own son was "over there fighting for us," he did not report the offer, nor could he be persuaded by the OPA to reveal the name of the man who had approached him.[23]

Despite numerous rationalizations and protestations, the tradition of not testifying against others was effective. As one OPA official well familiar with this practice put it, "they will not directly tattle on their competitors." There were occasional cases of informing against particularly bad chiselers and newcomers, but in general, when they were faced with the problem of punishing certain persons in order to clear up a particularly bad black market situation, it was extremely difficult to persuade businessmen to testify. Even persons being milked by numerous violations of suppliers in the form of upgrading and tie-ins with worthless commodities would rarely testify. While undoubtedly some of this reluctance, particularly among retailers, involved the fear of being cut off from supplies, this explanation does not sufficiently account for the degree of this solidarity. Some businessmen felt that the trade would disapprove of behavior which might undermine a solid front against the government as well as interfere with supplies. In one criminal case in 1944 involving one of the leading wholesale liquor dealers of a large city, the government maintained that he was charging over-ceiling prices and engaging in extensive tie-in sales. Although this had been admitted by retailers to the investigators, not a single one in a long parade of retailers on the witness stand confirmed such violations.[24] This was true even where they were not having direct business dealings with the suspected offenders. Realization that the

---

21 *Ibid.*

22 "Opinion Survey of Food Wholesalers." This behavior was certainly not true of all businessmen, as the OPA received numerous complaints of violations.

23 From OPA Information Department data.

24 It appears that if business concerns had been sufficiently well organized or had been particularly inclined to exert collective pressure upon their suppliers they could have forced compliance with the regulations. This is indicated by the fact, which was frequently heard, that many large concerns, particularly chains, forced compliance by their suppliers on the ground that they would not pay over-ceiling prices for the commodities they obtained. The small merchant, however, unless organized, had difficulty in exerting such control.

OPA was a legal agency and part of the government of the United States was a disconcerting thought which many an associate of a businessman helped him to overcome.[25] To speak with only those sharing similar attitudes served to reinforce a belief and did not bring it out into the light of logical scrutiny.

Most of the sellers subject to controls were businessmen unaccustomed to such outside interference in the operation of their businesses, and in many instances resentful of it on principle. Moreover, the vast majority of them were respected members of their community. They were not professional criminals —on the contrary, they were regarded and regarded themselves as staunch supporters of the constituted order. Since the regulations being enforced often set new and unusual restrictions on customary practices, violations of these restrictions did not in themselves seem heinous offenses, either to the violators or to the public generally. . . . Firms in trouble frequently found influential friends and character witnesses to intercede for them.[26]

Criticisms of Differential Association as a Complete Explanation of the Black Market. While it is likely that most cases of violations of price and rationing regulations, where there had been continuous and intimate association with unethical and illegal differential norms and at the same time some isolation from other norms, can be satisfactorily explained by a theory of differential association, there are several limitations in such a general theory as an explanation for *all* cases.[27] Such a theory does not adequately explain why some individuals who were familiar with the techniques and the rationalizations of black market violations, and were frequently associated with

[25] In fact, to counteract the misconception that the OPA was something different from other agencies of the government, nearly all OPA materials, such as stationery, legal notices, as well as many of the forms used in enforcement cases, employed the phrase "The United States Government."
[26] Mansfield, *op. cit.*, p. 257.
[27] Sutherland, for example, has suggested differential association as a universal explanation of all white collar crime. See his *White Collar Crime*, Chap. XIV.

persons similarly familiar, did not engage in such practices. It is doubtful whether any businessman could participate in a given line of business for any length of time, either in peacetime or in wartime, without acquiring a rather complete knowledge of the illegal practices in his trade. This was particularly true of black market practices as a subject of much general conversation at this time. Certainly besides talking with competitors and customers a businessman had ample opportunity to read of techniques of black market violations in the average newspaper and trade journal. It is difficult to explain, therefore, why thousands of business concerns, even in those commodities where one may have expected greater violation, appeared to have complied rather fully with the wartime regulations. In some instances it appears that variables other than continuous and extensive contacts with norms favorable to crime, as opposed to unfavorable definitions as Sutherland has suggested, must be introduced to explain the violation. Differential association discounts not only personality factors but also questions of various pressures from suppliers and even sometimes from consumers leading to violation. The question of restriction on profits must also be considered. Inefficiency of government, "red tape," and other factors are also not taken into account in such an analysis.

The theory of differential association, moreover, does not allow sufficiently either for the independent invention of a complex black market technique or for the need for acquiring any technique for those black market violations which were extraordinarily simple. The validity of this particular statement should, of course, be ascertained by further detailed study of a number of black market case histories. Certainly many black market violations, involving similar techniques, appeared in isolated areas. In many violations only a single person seems to have been involved. There was, for example, ample evidence to indicate that rather complex evasive violations of rent regulations appeared in relatively isolated areas. Apparently they were independently devised, since ordinarily association between landlords is limited. . . .

ECONOMIC FACTORS
IN THE BLACK MARKET

Undoubtedly certain economic factors contributed to some violations, but they appear to have been emphasized far more than the evidence warrants. In a system of controls as extensive as these, not all concerns were able to make a profit even if the general profit picture was favorable. The application of controls in a largely uniform fashion, involving the regulation of various sizes and types of business, undoubtedly made staying in business and obeying the law two irreconcilable objectives in some instances. Particularly difficult were the pressures at various levels of business by the violations of suppliers. Some wholesalers, for example, in overcharging, or utilizing tie-in sales, contributed to the predicament for the retailer, who then had to sell at a loss or violate the law.

The alternatives to violating the law in such a situation were either to reduce profit margins and absorb some cases of overcharge—and many did just that as they do in peacetime under somewhat similar circumstances—or to expose the supplier to the OPA and testify against him, an action seldom taken. If there were repercussions, such as having supplies cut off, several concerns could have banded together not only to prevent this squeeze but to promise retaliation after the war. There was also the drastic possibility which some patriotic men did follow, and that was to give up dealing with this supplier or go out of business entirely.

Statements have been made that large firms generally complied with the regulations, while small ones did not. It has been suggested that large firms were better able to absorb any squeeze, considered their reputations more carefully, were more aware

of their social responsibilities, employed so many persons that violations could not possibly have been kept secret, were more frequently and thoroughly investigated, and had larger staffs to become familiar with and explain all regulations. Small firms, on the other hand, were thought to be more liable to a squeeze, to have little reputation to lose, not to keep adequate records and, therefore, to be able to make frequent cash transactions to hide violations and so were not as frequently investigated by the OPA. This explanation, while perhaps valid in some individual cases, does not appear to be substantiated by the facts, and sometimes these arguments were even reversed. No over-all conclusion can be drawn, for many large concerns did violate, whereas many small ones did not. Although the findings were inconclusive, a survey which investigated this particular problem among Chicago business concerns suggested that the size of the firm alone did not appear to be an important factor in violation.[28]

There is no evidence to indicate, then, that businessmen generally had to choose between making a living and entering the black market. Economic restrictions did interfere with the size of the profits and to this extent increased black market activity, but they did not cause it.[29] In general, the

[28] George Katona, *Price Control and Business,* Bloomington, Ind.: The Principia Press, 1945, pp. 128–129.

[29] In this connection one magazine carried a supposedly true story involving an interview with a textile merchant in the club car of a Miami–New York train. Finding that the businessman was wearing a one-thousand-dollar necktie, the interviewer asked him how he got the money. After he described a sordid tale of black market dealings in textiles of a particularly flagrant nature, in violation of the regulations of the War Production Board and the OPA, the businessman was asked, "Couldn't you have made pretty good money if you hadn't gone in for the angles?" "Of course," he replied, caressing his tie, "but then I'd be wearing only a hundred dollar tie instead of a thousand dollar one."— Potomacus, "The Thousand-Dollar Necktie," *New Republic,* March 25, 1946, pp. 407–409. Ties costing this amount of money were a fad and served as a method of displaying wealth at a time when luxuries were not plentiful.

price ceilings did not produce losses, but merely restricted even greater profits, which were available from illegal rather than legal dealings, offering great temptation particularly when others were dipping into the "gravy." Thus many businessmen regarded failure to make the most money possible from a sale as a "loss" which might be regarded as perfectly "normal" economics were it not for the fact it was a violation of the law.

THE ROLE OF GOVERNMENT
IN THE BLACK MARKET

The government contributed in several ways to the extensiveness of the black market, but like the economic factors, these considerations cannot be thought of as a "cause" of the black market. First, the nature of the price and rationing laws was significant in explaining some violations. In some respects the statute represented a major change forced upon American society and the chief reason for expecting its support came from the fact that we were at war and compliance would help us win it. It was unfortunate that there were some who were not as much interested in contributing to the war effort as in making large profits. Although many laws had been passed in the interests of large groups of our citizens, the emergency Price Control Act was actually the first one to affect practically everyone in this country. The federal trade regulations, the Securities and Exchange Act, the Food and Drug Act, and even the National Labor Relations Act directly affected relatively small groups, although indirectly a great many people benefited, if only theoretically, without having to make any particular personal sacrifice. Furthermore, some of the restrictions put upon each of the groups in America were contrary to certain fundamental ideological thinking right up to the passage of the law.

The government itself made mistakes in the issuance and enforcement of these economic controls, although the most serious blunders occurred in the early period of price and rationing controls. Admittedly the problem of price and rationing control was an extremely complex one, as the black market in meat vividly demonstrated. Obviously it is virtually impossible during a war situation to work out an ideal control situation without regard to the urgencies of time, manpower shortages, facilities, and the opinion of both the public and the persons immediately affected by the control program. Without proper enforcement, however, it was difficult to impose earlier and more far-reaching controls over the entire economic system, including wage and price controls. It was also a mistake not to have done more to encourage an even distribution of supplies nationally to take limited supply pressures from certain areas. There were many rather stupid procedures and an unnecessary amount of reporting work or red tape. The absence of hard-hitting enforcement work in dealing with the early black market contributed to a general disrespect for the OPA during much of its existence. Yet nearly all business had previously been under some form of peacetime regulation and subject to government reports. The extent of violations in many commodity areas would seem to disprove the contention that bad regulations alone accounted for most violations, unless one wishes to take the position that all regulations were technically bad.

In addition, because of insufficient manpower, technical skill, and other factors, enforcement efforts throughout the war were generally inadequate to deal with the size of the problem and the black market. Businessmen saw competitors and others making additional profits from illegal activities without being punished, and others felt the impact of the "squeeze," with the government relatively impotent to deal with it. Many businessmen felt that any enforcement efforts of the government destroyed the effectiveness of informal compliance, and some went so far as to maintain that the individual businessman was at liberty to do as he wished and that it was up to the government's enforcement officers to apprehend him.

The enforcement actions which the government did take were undoubtedly too weak. Not only was the actual criminal sanction insufficiently employed, but civil and administrative actions did not recover anywhere near the amount of profit derived from the black market throughout the war.

The government failed to enlist adequately the voluntary support of business and sections of the public in dealing with the black market, even though many efforts were made in this direction. Many businessmen did not voluntarily accept the fact that practices which were legal before the war had become illegal by a temporary law. The public did not seriously condemn violators, with the exception of the ration currency violations. When the amount of the violation was trivial, the public was particularly tolerant, not realizing the aggregate effect of such practices. The sabotage of the government's efforts to control inflation by numerous vocal and irresponsible lobbyists and politicians, representing special interests rather than the consumer, helped to confuse rather than clarify the situation. A government official described this situation in the summer of 1943:

The public is, to a large extent, doubtful of the need for OPA regulations, ignorant of their provisions, and skeptical of their fairness. This is due to a number of factors. In large measure it can be attributed to unwarranted and unfair attacks by business interests, by congressmen and congressional committees, by newspapers, and by various pressure groups. Much of this stems from purely political motives.[30]

There appears, however, to be little substance to the charge that OPA personnel "fixed" many cases because of political considerations. Some black market cases were "fixed" through friends and through political influence, and bribes were taken by some attorneys and investigators, but for the most part the "fix" does not appear to have been involved in most enforcement actions. In terms of the total number of cases or the large number of personnel, cases involving bribery appear to have been but a small percentage[31] and could not have materially affected attitudes toward the government.

[30] Report on Enforcement to Chester A. Bowles, Senior Deputy Administrator, by Thomas I. Emerson, Associate General Counsel for the Office of Price Administration, August 9, 1943, p. 2.

[31] A small staff of investigators was assigned to the OPA Administrator whose work involved the detection of cases involving bribery and other corruption among OPA personnel and the very knowledge of this fact was partially effective in keeping such cases at a minimum. Another factor was the high caliber and integrity of most top-level wartime government appointments. Probably more important still was the fact that most employees thought of themselves as doing "war work."

THE CRIMINAL VIOLATION OF FINANCIAL TRUST*

Donald R. Cressey

After distinguishing trust violation as a particular type of occupational crime, Cressey sought a theory to explain the type. Several hypotheses were formulated and revised in the search for

* Reprinted from American Sociological Review, 15 (December 1950), pp. 738–743, by permission of the author and the publisher.

> *negative cases. The final revision explained trust violation in terms of a sequence of three events in the violator's career: trusted persons become violators when they conceive of themselves as having a financial problem which is nonsharable, have the knowledge or awareness that this problem can be secretly resolved by violation of the position of trust, and are able to apply to their own conduct in that situation verbalizations which enable them to adjust their conceptions of themselves as trusted persons with their conceptions of themselves as users of the entrusted funds or property.*

The notion that a scientist must seek to formulate generalizations which include all of the cases of the phenomena with which he is concerned has been brought to the attention of sociologists many times.[1] The perfect form of scientific knowledge is assumed to be universal generalizations which permit the discernment of exceptions, thus making possible the perfecting or refinement of generalizations. However, this notion, which is essentially an assumption regarding the proper design for scientific research, has been applied only rarely in criminology, and never in an attempt to formulate a sociological theory of trust violation. In fact, while the criminal violation of financial trust poses serious problems for theoretical criminology, text-book writers and other sociologists who have offered theories of criminal causation have for the most part ignored it.[2] As a result, almost

all publications on trust violation have been issued by persons or agencies primarily interested in the techniques used or in prevention of the crime, and the vast majority of the explanations given in the literature merely repeat and emphasize popular views. Few of the explanations have been convincing since little attempt at an integration with an explicit theory has been made.

On the contrary, most of the current explanations are of a multiple factor type, usually stated in terms of the way the trust violator spends the funds which he has dishonestly obtained. Thus, "gambling," "drink," and "extravagant living" are listed as causes of embezzlement, even if behavior of this kind is not present in even a majority of the cases.[3] Such conceptions are in general more in the nature of attempts to place blame or to indicate immorality than they are explanations of the behavior. For example, if it is said that a trust violator who has been considered a "pillar of the community" and a trusted and loyal employee ac-

[1] G. H. Mead, "Scientific Method and the Individual Thinker," in John Dewey, *Creative Intelligence,* New York: H. Holt, 1917; A. D. Ritchie, *Scientific Method: An Inquiry into the Character and Validity of Natural Laws,* New York: Harcourt, Brace and Company, 1923, pp. 53–83; F. Znaniecki, "Social Research in Criminology," *Sociology and Social Research,* 12 (April 1928), 307–322; F. Znaniecki, *The Method of Sociology,* New York: Farrar and Rinehart, 1934, pp. 232–233; Kurt Lewin, *A Dynamic Theory of Personality,* New York: McGraw-Hill, 1935, pp. 18–24; A. R. Lindesmith, *Opiate Addiction,* Bloomington, Indiana: Principia, pp. 12–14; R. H. Turner, "Statistical Logic in Social Research," *Sociology and Social Research,* 32 (Jan.–Feb., 1948), 697–704.

[2] Only three sociologists have published detailed account of research on the subject: E. Redden, *Embezzlement, A Study of One Kind of Criminal*

Behavior, With Prediction Tables Based on Fidelity Insurance Records, Ph.D. Dissertation, University of Chicago, 1939; Svend Riemer, "Embezzlement: Pathological Basis," *Journal of Criminal Law and Criminology,* 32 (Nov.–Dec., 1941), 411–423; S. Lottier, "Tension Theory of Criminal Behavior," *American Sociological Review,* 7 (Dec., 1942), 840–848.

[3] See, for example, The United States Fidelity and Guaranty Company, *1001 Embezzlers,* Baltimore: Author, 1937, and *1001 Embezzlers Post War,* Baltimore: Author, 1950; J. Edgar Hoover, "National Bank Offenses," *Journal of Criminal Law and Criminology,* 24 (Sept.–Oct., 1933), 655–663; V. Peterson, "Why Honest People Steal," *Ibid.,* 38 (July–August, 1947), 94–103.

tually has been gambling with his own and his company's money, an indication of immorality has been revealed, but his behavior has not been explained. Equally in contrast to the assumption regarding proper scientific methodology are those conceptions which assert that trust violation is caused by an assumed hidden variable, such as "moral weakness" or "tensions,"[4] or by weakness in the systems of checks upon the trusted person.[5] The latter "explanation" merely states, in a sense, that trust violation is caused by the existence of institutions whose functioning depends upon varying degrees of trust.[6]

The central problem of this study is that of providing an explanation in keeping with the assumption of proper scientific method and generalization by determining whether a definable sequence of events is always present when trust violation is present, and never present when trust violation is absent. A major related problem is that of accounting for the presence in individual cases of the events which make up the sequence which differentiates violators from nonviolators. These two problems are closely related since the events in the person-situation complex at the time trust violation occurs cannot be completely separated from the prior life experiences of the trust violator. However, only the first problem, that concerned with what Lewin calls "systematic" causation, in contrast to "historical" or "genetic" causation,[7] will be discussed here.

Hypotheses in regard to the first problem, the problem of systematic causation, were formulated progressively. When an hypothesis was formulated, a search for negative cases was conducted, and when such cases were found the hypothesis was reformulated in light of them. The behavior to be explained in this manner was at first defined as embezzlement, and a legal definition of that crime was used.[8] Upon contact with cases, however, it was almost immediately discovered that the term is not used in a consistent manner in the jurisdiction where the research was conducted and that many persons, whose behavior was adequately described by the legal definition actually had been sentenced to the penitentiary on some other charge. Consequently, the legal definition was abandoned and in its place two criteria for inclusion of any particular case in the study were established: (a) The person must have accepted a position of trust in good faith. This is similar to the implication of the legal definition that the "felonious intent" in embezzlement must have been formulated *after* the time of taking possession. All legal definitions are in agreement in this respect. (b) The person must have violated the trust. These criteria permit the inclusion of almost all persons convicted for embezzle-

[4] Cf. H. Koppel, "Other People's Money," Colliers, 67 (April 16, 1921), 11–12; J. Edgar Hoover, op. cit., S. Lottier, op. cit.

[5] Cf. George E. Bennet, Fraud: Its Control Through Accounts, New York: Century, 1930, p. 22; L. A. Pratt, Bank Frauds, Their Detection and Prevention, New York: Ronald, 1947, pp. 7–10.

[6] Hall has pointed out that the economic system in our modern society presupposes business transactions based on a considerable amount of trust. Jerome Hall, Theft, Law and Society, Boston: Little, Brown and Company, 1935.

[7] Kurt Lewin, "Some Social and Psychological Differences between the United States and Germany," Character and Personality, 4 (June 1936), 265–293. For a discussion of these two types of explanation in criminology see E. H. Sutherland,

Principles of Criminology, New York: Lippincott, 1947, p. 5, and J. F. Brown and D. W. Orr, "Field Theoretical Approach to Criminology," Journal of Criminal Psychopathology, 3 (Oct. 1941), 236–252.

[8] "The fraudulent appropriation to his own use or benefit of property or money entrusted to him by another, on the part of a clerk, agent, trustee, public officer or other person acting in a fiduciary capacity." Black's Law Dictionary, St. Paul: West Publishing Co., 1933, p. 633. Almost all studies pertinent to the current research have been studies of embezzlement. But since this term has been used to denote the behavior of all fidelity bond defaulters, the criminal behavior of all persons employed in banks, and the behavior of swindlers as well as embezzlers, it is obvious that the factual conclusions of the studies are not immediately comparable in all respects. The varied usage of the term is due to oversight on the part of some investigators, but it is also due in part to the existence of a variety of legal definitions among the states and foreign countries.

ment and in addition a proportion of those convicted for larceny by bailee, forgery, and confidence game.

The main source of direct information in regard to the behavior, now called "the criminal violation of financial trust," was interview material obtained in informal contacts over a period of five months with all prisoners whose behavior met the criteria and who were confined at the Illinois State Penitentiaries at Joliet.[9] In some cases we were able to write verbatim notes during the interviews without disturbing the subject, but in other cases it seemed appropriate to make only outline notes, and in some cases no notes could be taken at all. In the last two instances the content of the interview was written down in the subject's own words as soon as he left the room.

The length and frequency of interviews with individual subjects depended to a large extent upon the subject himself. Those subjects who seemed reluctant to talk were seen more frequently than those with whom a friendly and confidential relationship was established early in the process, but those who could not present the details of their cases and backgrounds, even if they so desired, were not interviewed as frequently as those who were able to do so. That is, "good" subjects were interviewed more often

and more extensively than were "poor" subjects—those whose intelligence, educational background, and vocabulary restricted the communication of their experiences. Those who described their behavior fluently became crucial cases, their testimony causing the abandonment of the hypotheses which had guided the research up to the time they were encountered. The new hypotheses were then checked against the less fluent cases.

The initial hypothesis, which was abandoned almost immediately, was that positions of financial trust are violated when the incumbent has learned in connection with the business or profession in which he is employed that some forms of trust violations are merely "technical violations" and are not really "illegal" or "wrong," and, on the negative side, that they are not violated if this kind of definition of the behavior has not been learned. This hypothesis was suggested by Sutherland in his writings on white collar crime.[10] In the interviews, however, many trust violators expressed the idea that they knew the behavior to be illegal and wrong at all times and that they merely "kidded themselves" into thinking that it was not illegal. Others reported that they knew of no one in their business or profession who was carrying on practices similar to theirs and some of them defined their offenses as theft rather than as trust violation.

In view of these negative cases, a second hypothesis, which included some of the "multiple factor" ideas of gambling and family emergencies, as well as the potential trust violators' attitudes toward them, was formulated. This hypothesis was in part derived from Riemer's statement that the "opportunities" inherent in trust positions form "temptations" if the incumbents develop anti-social attitudes which make possible an abandonment of the folkways of business behavior.[11] The formulation was

[9] Determination of whether or not a particular prisoner's behavior met the criteria was made by examination of documents in his personal file and by preliminary or "screening" interviews. The document most heavily relied upon for this purpose was the "State's Attorney's Report" (the official statement of facts in each case), but other documents, such as reports of the Chicago Crime Commission, letters from former employers and from friends and relatives, and the prisoner's statement upon admission to the institution also were consulted. In the screening interviews the subjects were never asked the question, "Did you accept your position of trust in good faith?" but instead the interviewer waited for the subject to give the information spontaneously. Ordinarily, evidence of acceptance in good faith came out in the first interview in form of statements such as the following: "I had no idea I was going to do this until the day it happened." Evidence of acceptance in bad faith was presented, for example, as follows: "My case isn't like embezzlement because I knew when I took their money that I was going to use it for myself."

[10] E. H. Sutherland, *White Collar Crime*, New York: Dryden, 1949.
[11] Svend Riemer, *op. cit.*

that positions of trust are violated when the incumbent structures a real or supposed need for extra funds or extended use of property as an "emergency" which cannot be met by legal means, and that if such an emergency does not take place trust violation will not occur. This hypothesis proved fruitful, but like the first one it had to be revised when persons were found who claimed that while an emergency had been present at the time they violated the trust, other, perhaps even more extreme, emergencies had been present in earlier periods when they did not violate it. Others reported that there had been no financial emergency in their cases, and a few "explained" their behavior in terms of antagonistic attitudes toward the employer or feelings of being abused, underpaid, or discriminated against in some other way.

The next revision shifted the emphasis from emergency to psychological isolation, stating that persons become trust violators when they conceive of themselves as having incurred financial obligations which are considered as non-socially-sanctionable and which, consequently, must be satisfied by a private or secret means. Negatively, if such nonshareable obligations are not present, trust violation will not occur. This hypothesis had the advantage of calling attention to the fact that not all emergencies, even if they are created by prior "immoral" behavior on the part of the trusted person, are important to trust violation. It had been suggested by LaPiere and Farnsworth who cite Sutherland as having shown that in cases of white collar crime the person is frequently confronted "with the alternative of committing a crime or losing something he values above his integrity,"[12] but it was brought into the present study by a suggestion from a prisoner who stated that he believed that no embezzlement would ever occur if the trusted person always told his wife and family about his financial problems, no matter what the consequences. However,

12 R. T. LaPiere and P. R. Farnsworth, *Social Psychology*, New York: McGraw-Hill, 1949, p. 344.

when the cases were re-examined in light of this hypothesis it was found that in a few of them there was nothing which could be considered as financial *obligation*, that is, as a debt which had been incurred in the past and for which the person at present felt responsible. Also, in some cases there had been nonsanctionable obligations at a prior time, and these obligations had not been alleviated by means of trust violation. It became increasingly apparent at this point that trust violation could not be attributed to a single event, but that its explanation could be made only in terms of a sequence of events, a process.

Again the hypothesis was reformulated, emphasizing this time not financial *obligations* which were considered as non-socially-sanctionable and hence as nonshareable, but nonshareable *problems* of that nature. This hypothesis also pointed up the idea that not only was a nonshareable problem necessary, but that the person had to possess (a) knowledge or awareness of the fact that the problem could to some extent be solved by means of trust violation and (b) the technical skill necessary for such violation. Negative cases appeared, however, in instances where men reported that what they considered a nonshareable problem had been present for some period of time and that they had known for some time before the violation took place that the problem could be solved by violating their position of trust by using a particular skill. Some stated that they did not violate the trust at the earlier period because the situation was not in sharp enough focus to "break down their ideas of right and wrong."

Such statements suggested the final revision, which took the following form: Trusted persons become trust violators when they conceive of themselves as having a financial problem which is nonshareable, have the knowledge or awareness that this problem can be secretly resolved by violation of the position of financial trust, and are able to apply to their own conduct in that situation verbalizations which enable them to adjust their conceptions of themselves as trusted persons with their conceptions of themselves as users of the entrusted funds or property.

This hypothesis proved to be far superior to the others, and no evidence necessitating its rejection has been found as yet. In all of the cases interviewed the sequence has been found to be present, and when cases were examined with a view to answering the question: "Why did these men not violate their trust at an earlier period?" it was seen that in earlier periods one or more of the events in the sequence had not been present. A search of cases reported in the literature also showed no negative cases, though it should be pointed out that in many of the reports crucial information which would either contradict or affirm the hypothesis is not given. A similar search of about 200 unpublished cases collected by E. H. Sutherland in the 1930s, before he had formulated the differential association theory, likewise showed no negative cases.

The events present in the process cannot be considered in great detail here. However, brief comments about the sequence are in order.

(1) Criteria of an objective nature in regard to the degree of "shareability" which specific types of problems have in our culture were not set up, but instead the subject's definition of the situation was used as a datum.[13] Consequently, a list which would exhaust all of the possible problems which could be considered as nonshareable and which might play a part in the etiology of trust violation is not conceivable. For purposes of illustration, however, we may cite one type of problem which is frequently so defined.

This type of problem is that which the trusted person considers to have resulted from the violation of the obligations "ascribed" to his position of trust, that is,

those obligations of a nonfinancial nature which are expected of persons in consequence of their incumbency in positions of financial trust. Just as persons in trusted positions have obligations not to violate the trust by taking funds, most of them also have obligations, for example, to maintain an enviable position in the community and to refrain from certain types of gambling and from what may be loosely described as riotous living.[14] When persons incur financial responsibilities as a result of violation of these ascribed obligations they often consider that they must be kept secret, and meeting them becomes a nonshareable problem.

The concept of the nonshareable problem and consideration of the type of nonshareable problem just discussed help to make understandable the reported high incidence of "wine, women and wagering" in the behavior of embezzlers and other trust violators, but these modes of behavior are not used as explanatory principles. In fact, it appears that the use of them as explanations of trust violation merely indicates lack of understanding of the problem.[15]

(2) A nonshareable problem becomes a stimulus to violation of a position of trust only when the position is perceived as offering a private solution to this specific problem. In addition to having a financial problem which he feels he cannot share with

---

[13] Evidence of the presence of nonshareable problems was found in the language used by trust violators. None of them, of course, used the words "nonshareable problem," but many of them stated that they were "ashamed" to tell anyone of a certain situation or that they had "too much false pride" to get help from others.

[14] E. C. Hughes has pointed out that in addition to the specifically determining traits, a complex of "auxiliary traits" is expected of incumbents of certain statuses. "Dilemmas and Contradictions of Status," *American Journal of Sociology*, 50 (March 1945), 353–359. In law, this type of obligation is called an "obediential obligation" since it is a consequence of a situation or a relationship, not of a contract.—*Black's Law Dictionary*, p. 1274.

[15] We do not mean to imply that statistical studies of personal and social traits as selective factors in trust violation have no place. A study, for example, showing a precise relationship between the presence of certain personal and social traits and the structuring of a financial problem as nonshareable would be extremely valuable. What we wish to imply is that such studies of selective factors, even if properly carried out, do not solve the problem of etiology. Cf. A. R. Lindesmith, *op. cit.*, pp. 157–158.

persons who, from a more objective point of view, could help him, the trusted person must have a certain amount of knowledge or information about trust violation in general, and he must be able to apply that general information to his own specific situation. The presence of this event is often indicated by trust violators in their use of the language "it occurred to me" or "it dawned on me" that the entrusted funds could be used for such and such purpose. This "dawning" or "insight" or "perception" that the nonshareable problem can and may be solved by trust violation involves both knowledge of this fact and a "rationalization" of the behavior.

(3) The verbalizations ("rationalizations") used by trust violators are reflections of contact with cultural ideologies which adjust for the person contradictory ideas in regard to criminality on the one hand and in regard to integrity, honesty and morality on the other. Upon the appearance of a nonshareable problem the trusted person applies to his own situation a verbalization which the groups in which he has had membership have applied to others, or which he himself has applied to the behavior of others. This is his motivation.[16]

[16] Cf. C. Wright Mills, "Situated Actions and Vocabularies of Motive," *American Sociological Review*, 5 (Dec. 1940), 904–913.

The hypothesized reactions of others to "borrowing" (criminal behavior) in order to solve a nonshareable problem, for example, are much different from the hypothesized reactions to "stealing" or "embezzling," and the trusted person behaves accordingly. It is because of an ability to hypothesize reactions which will not consistently and severely condemn his criminal behavior that the trusted person takes the role of what we have called the "trust violator." *He* often does not think of himself as playing that role, but instead thinks of himself as playing another role, such as that of a special kind of borrower or businessman.

The final hypothesis in its complete form made it possible to account for some of the features of trust violation and for some individual cases of that behavior which could not be accounted for by other hypotheses. However, the fact that it was revised several times probably means that future revision will be necessary if negative cases are found. The location by another investigator of persons who have violated positions of trust which were accepted in good faith, but in whose behavior the sequence was not present, will call for either a new revision of the hypothesis or a redefinition of the behavior included in the scope of the present hypothesis.

OCCUPATIONAL STRUCTURE AND CRIMINAL BEHAVIOR: PRESCRIPTION VIOLATION BY RETAIL PHARMACISTS*

Richard Quinney

In a study of prescription violation as a type of occupational crime, Quinney found that prescription violation by retail pharmacists is related to the structure of the occupation. Because of divergent occupational roles in the occupation—professional and

* Reprinted from *Social Problems*, 11 (Fall 1963), pp. 179–185, by permission of the author and the publisher.

*business—pharmacists must adapt to an occupational role
organization. The types of adaptations vary in the extent to which
they generate tendencies toward prescription violations.*

An increasing number of sociologists have become interested in the study of occupations, noticeably neglecting at the same time the criminal behavior which occurs within occupations.[1] On the other hand, sociologists concerned with the study of white collar crime have not made any systematic attempt to consider the social structure of occupations in their explanations of white collar crime.[2] The purpose of this study is to demonstrate that an analysis of the occupation should be considered in the attempt to explain violations of laws and regulations which control occupational activities and that such an approach makes it possible to learn more about both the structure of the occupation and the criminal behavior which occurs within the occupation. More specifically, the principal problem of the study is to offer an explanation for a type of criminal behavior which occurs in retail pharmacy in terms of an analysis of the occupation.

RESEARCH PROCEDURE

For a study of occupational violation among pharmacists employed in retail establishments—retail pharmacists—it was first necessary to limit the violation to a type which might form a homogeneous unit of behavior and be subject to a common explanation.[3] While violations of the many state and federal statutes and administrative regulations pertaining to retail pharmacy are all regarded legally as misdemeanors and are subject to particular punishments, the behaviors involved are by no means homogeneous. In the attempt to delineate a specific type of behavior which could be explained by a single theory, the various laws and regulations were subjected to a content analysis in terms of basic occupational activity.[4] The laws and regulations (and their accompanying violations) can be classified into three types: regulation of licensure, regulation of the drugstore, and regulation of prescriptions. Although any one type appeared to represent homogeneous behaviors, the most important type of violation both in terms of public welfare and frequency of occurrence is the violation of laws and regulations that control the

[1] Approaches to the sociological study of occupations are presented in Sigmund Nosow and William H. Form, editors, *Man, Work, and Society: A Reader in the Sociology of Occupations*, New York: Basic Books, 1962.

[2] There are several significant studies of white collar crime: Marshall B. Clinard, *The Black Market*, New York: Rinehart, 1952; Donald R. Cressey, *Other People's Money*, Glencoe, Ill.: The Free Press, 1953; Frank E. Hartung, "White Collar Offenses in the Wholesale Meat Industry in Detroit," *American Journal of Sociology*, 56 (July, 1950), pp. 25–34; and Edwin H. Sutherland, *White Collar Crime*, New York: Dryden Press, 1949.

[3] The importance of delineating homogeneous units of criminal behavior for the purpose of explanation is discussed, among other places, in Marshall B. Clinard, *Sociology of Deviant Behavior*, New York: Holt, Rinehart, and Winston, 1963, pp. 204–216; Donald R. Cressey, "Criminological Research and the Definition of Crimes," *American Journal of Sociology*, 56 (May, 1951), pp. 546–551; and A. R. Lindesmith and H. Warren Dunham, "Some Principles of Criminal Typology," *Social Forces*, 19 (March, 1941), pp. 307–314. For application of this approach see Marshall B. Clinard and Andrew L. Wade, "Toward the Delineation of Vandalism as a Subtype of Juvenile Delinquency," *Journal of Criminal Law, Criminology, and Police Science*, 48 (January–February, 1958), pp. 493–499; and Donald R. Cressey, *Other People's Money*, Glencoe, Ill.: The Free Press, 1953. The suggestion that homogeneous units be delimited within white collar crime has been made in Vilhelm Aubert, "White Collar Crime and Social Structure," *American Journal of Sociology*, 58 (November, 1952), pp. 263–271; and Gilbert Geis, "Toward a Delineation of White-Collar Offenses," *Sociological Inquiry*, 32 (Spring, 1962), pp. 160–171.

[4] The laws and regulations pertaining to pharmacy in New York are compiled in the University of the State of New York, *Pharmacy—Laws, Rules and Information*, Albany, New York, 1959.

compounding and dispensing of prescriptions. Prescription violation was therefore selected as the type of behavior for which an explanation would be sought and thus became the dependent variable of the study.

One of the primary aims of the research design was to provide a comparison of prescription violators and nonviolators. These two groups of retail pharmacists were drawn from the population of retail pharmacists within the city limits of Albany, New York. Through the cooperation of the New York State Board of Pharmacy, the names and addresses of the pharmacists, as well as their violation records over a five year period, were secured. The twenty prescription violators who had been officially detected by state and federal investigators as violating a prescription law or regulation made up the group of prescription violators. The nonviolator group consisted of 60 pharmacists randomly selected from the remaining retail pharmacists who had been investigated but had never been found to violate a prescription law or regulation. The final study group, then, consisted of 80 retail pharmacists, 20 prescription violators and 60 nonviolators.

Data were collected through structured interviews with the retail pharmacists. The interview schedule, designed also for a broader range of problems, obtained information about the pharmacist's background, career in pharmacy, experiences in pharmacy and attitudes about the occupation.[5] The respondents were not informed that their violation record was known to the researcher, and any idea that the study was partly concerned with violation could not have occurred until the last few minutes of the interview, after the major information had been secured. In addition to the formal interviews, throughout the study there were informal discussions with persons related in various ways to retail pharmacy, including members of the state board of pharmacy, instructors in pharmacy, pharmacy students, physicians and customers.

OCCUPATIONAL ROLES IN RETAIL PHARMACY

Most of the sociological studies of occupations have either assumed or demonstrated that occupations are characterized by patterned expectations internalized by the incumbents and reflected in their occupational behavior. On the three occasions that retail pharmacy has received sociological attention, it has been observed that the occupation incorporates two different roles, professional and business. Weinlein noted that the professional aspects of retail pharmacy are vitally influenced by the fact that most of the occupational activities take place in a business establishment, the drugstore.[6] In addition to filling prescriptions, he observed, the pharmacist is involved in many activities of a business nature. Likewise, Thorner described retail pharmacy as an occupation which has the characteristics of both a profession and a business.[7] McCormack defined retail pharmacy as a marginal occupation because it contains the conflicting goals of a profession and a business.[8] These observations were given support in the present research when it was found that 94 percent of the pharmacists replied in the affirmative to the question, "Do you find that the public expects the pharmacist to be *both* a business man and a professional man?"

From what was known about retail pharmacy, then, it appeared that various aspects

---

5 For the larger study see the writer's unpublished Ph.D. dissertation, *Retail Pharmacy as a Marginal Occupation: A Study of Prescription Violation,* University of Wisconsin, 1962.

6 Anthony Weinlein, *Pharmacy as a Profession with Special Reference to the State of Wisconsin,* unpublished M.A. thesis, University of Chicago, 1943.

7 Isador Thorner, "Pharmacy: The Functional Significance of an Institutional Pattern," *Social Forces,* 20 (March 1942), pp. 321–328.

8 Thelma H. McCormack, "The Druggists' Dilemma: Problems of a Marginal Occupation," *American Journal of Sociology,* 61 (January 1956), pp. 308–315.

of the social and cultural structure of the occupation would have implications for the study of prescription violation, particularly the status of retail pharmacy as both a profession and a business.[9] Thus, the research was guided by the general hypothesis that social strains in the form of divergent occupational role expectations are structured in the occupation of retail pharmacy and that prescription violation may result, depending upon the individual mode of adaptation. Such a conception that crime (or deviant behavior in general) is structured finds support in Sutherland's idea of "differential social organization," which proposes that in a heterogeneous type of structure alternative and possibly inconsistent standards of conduct are held by the various segments.[10] A similar idea is found in the sociological tradition of functionalism.[11] Both approaches attempt to account for variations in rates of crime between or within social structures. The strategy taken in the present study was to account for variations in rates of criminal behavior within an occupation.

STRUCTURAL STRAIN AND ADAPTATION

To the retail pharmacist, the existence of two different occupational roles can present a personal dilemma in terms of appropriate occupational behavior. The retail pharmacist is faced with the task of performing his occupational activities with definitions which are not always clear, consistent, and compatible. Structural strain is built into retail pharmacy. The pharmacist must, therefore, make some sort of personal adjustment to the situation.[12]

It was hypothesized that retail pharmacists resolve the dilemma of choosing between different occupational roles—professional and business—by adapting to an *occupational role organization*. Occupational

[9] Discussions of profession and business as two separate occupational institutions are found in Talcott Parsons, "The Professions and Social Structure" and "The Motivation of Economic Activities," *Essays in Sociological Theory*, Glencoe, Ill.: The Free Press, 1949, pp. 185–217; and Theodore Caplow, *The Sociology of Work*, Minneapolis: University of Minnesota Press, 1954, pp. 100–123. Accounts of the historical development of retail pharmacy which document the existence of both professional and business roles may be found in Richard A. Deno, Thomas D. Rowe, and Donald C. Brodie, *The Profession of Pharmacy*, Philadelphia: J. B. Lippincott, 1959; and Edward Kremers and George Urdang, *History of Pharmacy*, Philadelphia: J. B. Lippincott, 1951.

[10] Sutherland discussed "differential social organization" or "differential group organization" in "Development of the Theory," in Albert K. Cohen, Alfred R. Lindesmith, and Karl F. Schuessler (eds.), *The Sutherland Papers*, Bloomington: Indiana University Press, 1956, pp. 13–29; and Edwin H. Sutherland and Donald R. Cressey, *Principles of Criminology*, Philadelphia: J. B. Lippincott, 1960, pp. 79–80, 82–85. This aspect of Sutherland's theory has been pointed out by Donald R. Cressey in "Epidemiology and Individual Conduct: A Case from Criminology," *Pacific Sociological Review*, 3 (Fall 1960), pp. 38–58.

[11] Robert K. Merton, "Social Structure and Anomie," *American Sociological Review*, 3 (October 1938), pp. 672–82; and Talcott Parsons, *The Social System*, Glencoe, Ill.: The Free Press, 1951, pp. 249–325.

[12] The idea of structural strain is found in Parsons, *The Social System*. The concept has been recently employed in Neil J. Smelser, *Theory of Collective Behavior*, New York: The Free Press of Glencoe, 1963. Discussions of adjustment to structural role strain (and role conflict) are found in Leonard S. Cottrell, Jr., "The Adjustment of the Individual to His Age and Sex Roles," *American Sociological Review*, 7 (October 1942), pp. 617–630; J. W. Getzels and E. G. Guba, "Role, Role Conflict, and Effectiveness: An Empirical Study," *American Sociological Review*, 19 (February 1954), pp. 164–175; William J. Goode, "A Theory of Role Strain," *American Sociological Review*, 25 (August 1960), pp. 483–496; Neal Gross, Ward S. Mason, and Alexander W. McFachern, *Explorations in Role Analysis*, New York: John Wiley & Sons, 1958, Chaps. 16–17; Samuel A. Stouffer, "An Analysis of Conflicting Social Norms," *American Sociological Review*, 14 (December 1949), pp. 707–717; Jackson Toby, "Some Variables in Role Conflict," *Social Forces*, 30 (March 1952), pp. 323–327; Walter I. Wardwell, "The Reduction of Strain in a Marginal Social Role," *American Journal of Sociology*, 61 (July 1955), pp. 16–25; and Donald M. Wolfe and J. Diedrick Snoek, "A Study of Tensions and Adjustment under Role Conflict," *Journal of Social Issues*, 18 (July 1962), pp. 102–121.

role organization refers to the relative orientation of the retail pharmacist to both the professional and business roles.[13]

The degree to which pharmacists were oriented to the business and professional roles was then measured. By asking the respondents to indicate how important they regard certain activities and goals in pharmacy, it was possible to determine the relative orientation of pharmacists to the two roles.[14] The results suggest that pharmacists orient themselves in different ways to the available roles. It was thus possible to construct a typology of occupational role organizations based on these differences in orientation. Some pharmacists are oriented more to the professional role than to the business role (Professional Pharmacists—16 percent of the sample), while others are oriented more to the business role (Business Pharmacists—20 percent). Other pharmacists are oriented to both roles (Profes-

sional-Business Pharmacists—45 percent), while a few appear not to be oriented to either of the roles (Indifferent Pharmacists —19 percent).[15] Therefore, since there are two possible occupational roles for the retail pharmacist rather than a single, well-defined role, there appears to be a patterned response in orientation to the two different roles. Retail pharmacists resolve the dilemma of choosing between different occupational roles (or, more generally, adjust to role strain) by adapting to an occupational role organization.[16]

PRESCRIPTION VIOLATION

The foregoing analysis provides a point of departure for an investigation of the possible behavioral consequences of structural strain. Prescription violation may be related to the types of occupational role organizations. More specifically, it was hypothesized that prescription violation occurs with greatest frequency among business pharmacists and least among professional pharmacists, with professional-business pharmacists and indifferent pharmacists being intermediate in the frequency of prescription violation.

The hypothesis was tested by cross-tabulating the prescription violation records and the occupational role organizations of the retail pharmacists. As shown in Table 1, there is a significant association between prescription violation and occupational role organization in the direction predicted. Pre-

---

[13] See Ronald G. Corwin, "The Professional Employee: A Study of Conflict in Nursing Roles," *American Journal of Sociology*, 66 (May 1961), pp. 605–615.

[14] After pertinent materials in the sociology of occupations and retail pharmacy were studied, several items were selected through their construct validity to measure professional and business role orientation. The interview schedule contained the question: "In terms of your pharmacy career, how important is each of the following?" (with the possible response categories of very important, important, of minor importance, of no importance). There followed ten items, randomly placed (selected after the discriminative power of each item had been determined in the interview pretest), which measured the respective role orientations. The professional role items were: (1) reading the professional literature, (2) being a part of the public health team, (3) using and encouraging the use of official drugs, (4) attending professional meetings, and (5) compounding and dispensing prescriptions. The business role items were: (1) maintaining a business establishment, (2) being a successful business man, (3) arranging window and counter displays, (4) being a good salesman, and (5) handling a variety of sundry goods. Each respondent had two role orientation scores (professional and business), and each respondent was given a low or high rating for each role. The pharmacists were then categorized according to the four types of occupational role organizations as based on relative orientation to the professional and business roles.

[15] It should be noted that this distribution is skewed slightly in the direction of business pharmacists. The reason for this is that the number of prescription violators in the study sample over-represents the proportion of violators in the population of retail pharmacists; and, as it will be shown, the group of prescription violators contains a disproportionate number of business pharmacists. Thus, an entirely random sample of retail pharmacists would contain a few more professionally oriented pharmacists.

[16] An occupational role organization may be regarded as the integration of the individual's total occupational role system. See Goode, *op. cit.*, pp. 485–487. Each type of occupational role organization represents a particular method for "ego's manipulation of his role structure" in an attempt to reduce role strain.

Table 1.

RELATIONSHIP BETWEEN PRESCRIPTION VIOLATION AND
OCCUPATIONAL ROLE ORGANIZATION

PRESCRIPTION VIOLATION	OCCUPATIONAL ROLE ORGANIZATIONS							
	PROFESSIONAL		PROFESSIONAL-BUSINESS		INDIFFERENT		BUSINESS	
	No.	Pct.	No.	Pct.	No.	Pct.	No.	Pct.
Violators	0	0	5	14	3	20	12	75
Non-Violators	13	100	31	86	12	80	4	25
	13	100	36	100	15	100	16	100

$$X^2 = 28.6, \qquad df = 3, \qquad P < .001.$$

scription violation occurred with greatest frequency among the business pharmacists —75 percent of these pharmacists were violators—and occurred least among professional pharmacists. None of the professional pharmacists were violators. The professional-business pharmacists and indifferent pharmacists were intermediate in violation: 14 percent of the professional-business pharmacists and 20 percent of the indifferent pharmacists were prescription violators. Therefore, in verification of the hypothesis, it was concluded that prescription violation varies according to the types of occupational role organizations in retail pharmacy.

The research findings suggest that pharmacists vary in the degree to which they are affected by the controls of the occupation. Location within the structure of the occupation determines the effectiveness of the controls on the individual pharmacist. Pharmacists with an occupational role organization that includes an orientation to the professional role are bound by a system of occupational control which includes guides for the compounding and dispensing of prescriptions. Pharmacists who lack the professional orientation and are oriented to the business role are less bound by the occupational controls. They stress the merchandising aspects of pharmacy and are primarily interested in monetary gains. The formal controls (particularly legal controls) are made effective by the operation of informal controls (in terms of role expectations) which come mainly from within the occupation.[17]

[17] This interpretation finds support in Howard S.

The results, thus, indicate that prescription violation is related to the structure of the occupation and is an expression of that structure. Furthermore, from the standpoint of the individual pharmacist, prescription violation is related to orientation to the different roles in the occupation. From a social psychological position, then, prescription violation is a matter of *differential orientation*. That is, for each pharmacist, orientation to a particular role more than to another provides a perspective in which violation may seem appropriate.[18] Prescription violation is thus explained in terms of the existence of structural strain in the occupation, because of the existence of divergent occupational roles, and differential orientation of the pharmacists to the roles in the form of adaptations to occupational role organizations.

Becker and James W. Carper, "The Elements of Identification with an Occupation," *American Sociological Review*, 21 (June 1956), pp. 341–348; Caplow, *op. cit.*, pp. 113–121; Edward Gross, *Work and Society*, New York: Thomas Y. Crowell, 1958, pp. 134–139; Oswald Hall, "The Informal Organization of the Medical Profession," *Canadian Journal of Economic and Political Science*, 12 (February 1946), pp. 30–44; Louis Kriesberg, "Occupational Controls among Steel Distributors," *American Journal of Sociology*, 61 (November 1955), pp. 203–212; and Tamotsu Shibutani, *Society and Personality: An Interactionist Approach to Social Psychology*, Englewood Cliffs, N.J.: Prentice-Hall, 1961, especially pp. 60, 91–94, 276–278.

[18] This is essentially the same as Glaser's concept of "differential identification." Daniel Glaser, "Criminality Theories and Behavioral Images," *American Journal of Sociology*, 61 (March 1956), pp. 433–445.

CONCLUSION

A theory of prescription violation by retail pharmacists was formulated and verified in this study. There are two divergent occupational role expectations in retail pharmacy —professional and business. Pharmacists adjust to this situation of structural strain by orienting themselves in varying degree to the roles, by adopting an occupational role organization. The types of occupational role organizations in turn differ in the extent to which they generate tendencies toward prescription violation. The occupational role organizations which include the professional role orientation restrain the pharmacist from violating, while the occupational role organizations which do not include the professional role orientation do not exercise this restraint on the pharmacist. Therefore, prescription violation occurs with greatest frequency among business pharmacists and least among professional pharmacists, with professional-business pharmacists and indifferent pharmacists being intermediate in frequency of prescription violation. It was thus concluded that prescription violation is related to the structure of the occupation and the differential orientation of retail pharmacists.

In an attempt to explain a homogeneous unit of behavior, this study was limited to only prescription violation by retail pharmacists. It is possible, however, that the theory as developed has implications both for other types of violation in retail pharmacy and for violations which occur in other occupations.

Occupational role strain is a common phenomenon in modern society, due in part to the frequency and rapidity with which changes in occupational role definitions occur and new occupational roles appear.[19] Particularly, it seems evident that the occupational roles of business and profession are by no means unique to retail pharmacy. Numerous observations show that some businesses are in the process of becoming professions, some professions are taking on some of the characteristics of business, and other occupations (similar to retail pharmacy) have already firmly incorporated the business and professional roles. For example, such occupations as dentistry, optometry, chiropody, osteopathy, and even independent general medicine are similar to retail pharmacy in that they possess the characteristics of both a profession and a business. Such occupational careers as real estate agent, accountant, and electrician, while traditionally business oriented, are now taking on some professional characteristics. Similarly, some of our traditionally professional careers—such as that of the psychologist— are taking on business characteristics as members become private consultants and counselors.

Also, by way of relating occupational role strain to occupational violation, many of these occupations are subject to laws and regulations similar to those of retail pharmacy. The violation of these laws and regulations is similar to prescription violation in that illegal behavior occurs in the course of serving the customer, as in the failure to retain a dental prescription by the dentist, alteration of a prescription for lenses by an optometrist, and the use of a secret method or procedure of treatment in the case of both osteopathy and medicine. It appears likely that the theoretical orientation employed in this study and the research findings of the study are applicable to other occupations and violations.

Finally, the study of prescription violation adds credence to the increasingly popular conception that deviant behavior is a reflection of social structure.[20] A demonstration of this assumption has been accomplished by bringing together a study of the

[19] See Walter I. Wardwell, "A Marginal Professional Role: The Chiropractor," *Social Forces*, 30 (March 1952), pp. 339–348.

[20] A recent textbook in criminology uses this as a major theme: Herbert A. Bloch and Gilbert Geis, *Man, Crime, and Society*, New York: Random House, 1962.

occupation and a study of criminal behavior in the occupation. If white collar crime is illegal behavior in the course of occupational activity, then it is reasonable to assume that the occupation itself must become the object of study as well as the illegal behavior which occurs within the occupation. White collar crime reflects the particular structure of the occupation and is a normal response to one's particular location within the occupation. Criminologists might consider the importance of understanding the occupation in the process of formulating theories of criminal behavior; and, on the other hand, sociologists who study occupations might give some attention to understanding the occupation by an investigation of the criminal behavior in the occupation. Both the structure of the occupation and criminal behavior within the occupation can be better understood if they are considered together.

CHAPTER 5

Political
Crime

The criminal law, as a form of social control, is characterized by politicality; that is, (1) specific rules of conduct are created by a recognized authority, (2) designated officials interpret and enforce the rules, and (3) the code is binding on all persons within a given political unit. Criminal law is thus an aspect of politics, one of the results of the process of formulating and administering public policy. It follows that the content of the criminal law, including the kind of conduct prohibited and the nature of the sanctions attached, depends upon the values of the groups in the social and political system that influence legislation, court decisions, and administrative rulings. The social values which receive the protection of the criminal law are ultimately those considered important by the dominant groups in the society.[1] Furthermore, the political nature of criminal law affects the administration of the law as well as its content; that is, the decision as to who is the criminal is also made in the enforcement and interpretation of the criminal law. Thus, the values and

[1] Thorsten Sellin, *Culture Conflict and Crime*, New York: Science Research Council, 1938, Chap. 2.

ultimately the actions of the groups in positions of power within a society can enter at any point in establishing the criminality of an individual.

From one point of view, then, all criminal behavior results from the political organization of a society: Formal codes are created and administered in order that certain behaviors and persons may be defined as criminal. The political nature of criminal behavior is perhaps best observed in respect to those behaviors which are defined as criminal because they are regarded as apparent threats and dangers to the political state. These offenses can be broadly classified as *political crime*.

Political crime consists of violations which occur in the course of the attempt to protest, express beliefs about, or alter in some way the existing social structure. The violations—be they in violation of laws created for the suppression of such behavior or be they in violation of laws created for other purposes (such as loitering and parading without a permit) but enforced for political reasons—are regarded by political authorities as detrimental to the state as it exists. Included in political crime is a wide range of behaviors: treason, sedition, espionage, sabotage, assassination, war collaboration, violation of military draft regulations, civil rights violations, student protest violations, violations resulting from the advocacy and support of "radical beliefs," and failure to conform to certain laws because of religious beliefs. Also included in political crime are the behaviors of the officeholders themselves, including law enforcement agents, who in the attempt to preserve a particular social order violate a higher (for example, federal) law, as seen, for example, in police brutality, the denial of free speech, and the restriction of free assembly. Similarly, as in the civil rights struggle, state authorities in the attempt to preserve the status quo may willingly violate federal laws on voting rights and public accommodations.

All of the behaviors mentioned above may be grouped into the category of political crime. These behaviors may be studied in relation to political behavior in general. With similar crimes in mind, Vold has observed that, to the extent crime is the by-product of conflicting interpretations of what is proper conduct by different segments of a population, crime is an aspect of political behavior and those who hold the minority view must either change their behavior or find it regarded as criminal by the dominant majority.[2]

Political crime in general, then, is political in two ways: First, the violating behaviors are political in that the violators are attempting to express their opinions and beliefs about the proper structure of the state, with a possible attempt to bring about change. Second, the enforcement of laws is political in that laws are being invoked for political reasons.

CRIMINAL CAREER OF THE OFFENDER

Of the various types of criminals, the political criminal has probably received the least systematic attention by criminologists. A few criminologists have, however, in various classificatory schemes included types that are similar to the political criminal. Horton and Leslie, for example, included within the category of "legalistic criminals" persons who become known as law violators because of unjust law enforcement or because their alleged crime is merely the pretext for action against

[2] George B. Vold, "Some Basic Problems in Criminological Research," *Federal Probation*, 17 (March 1953), p. 40.

them due to the fact that they hold unpopular social and political ideas. For example, political radicals have been convicted of conventional crime on flimsy evidence and labor organizers have been arrested for loitering and obstructing the sidewalk. Horton and Leslie observed that legalistic criminals have little in common with conventional criminals: "Granted some of them may be very poor citizens, they generally lack criminal intent, lack orientation and need no special treatment. If convicted and punished, they are likely to become worse than before."[3]

Vold has also outlined several criminal subtypes that exist because persons pursue certain activities which are not favored by the political majority.[4] Among these criminals are (1) political offenders whose views are regarded as subversive by the government, (2) religious or philosophical sectarians whose behaviors are contrary to the law, and (3) nonconformist intellectuals who, on the basis of conviction, persist in outlawed behavior. In a not too different fashion, both Newman and Cavan have discussed "ideological crime" that occurs in a particular value framework.[5] They have observed that these crimes must be included in the definitions and theories of crime.

Merton, in making a distinction between "nonconforming" and "aberrant" behavior, has provided some guides to understanding the career of the political criminal.[6] According to Merton, the nonconformer, in contrast to the aberrant, (1) announces his dissent publicly, (2) challenges the legitimacy of the norms and laws he violates, (3) aims to change the norms he is denying in practice, (4) is acknowledged by conventional members of the society to depart from prevailing norms for disinterested purposes and not for what he personally can get out of it, and (5) lays claim to a higher morality and to ultimate values rather than to the particular norms of the society. Criminologists have concentrated attention on the career of the aberrant to the almost total neglect of the nonconformer.

Political behaviors which may result in violation of the law are many and varied. In other words, political crime as a behavior system actually consists of a number of subtypes. Nevertheless, there are certain characteristics shared in common by the violators. Political offenders usually do not engage in criminal activity as a full-time career. Persons who commit political crimes do not conceive of themselves as criminals and do not identify with crime or criminal behavior. They violate the law only when such behavior seems to be the most appropriate means for achieving certain ends. The ends, to the offender, are not personal but are deemed desirable for the larger society. The action taken by the offender is usually public rather than private. The criminal behavior is regarded by the offender as symbolic of a higher purpose. Political offenders carry on their illegal activities in pursuit of an ideal.

There has been only a limited attempt to describe the personal and social

---

[3] Paul B. Horton and Gerald R. Leslie, *The Sociology of Social Problems*, 3d ed., New York: Appleton-Century-Crofts, Inc., 1965, p. 138.

[4] George B. Vold, *Theoretical Criminology*, New York: Oxford University Press, 1958, pp. 299–300.

[5] Donald J. Newman, "Legal Norms and Criminological Definitions," in Joseph S. Roucek (ed.), *Sociology of Crime*, New York: Philosophical Library, Inc., 1961, pp. 71–75; and Ruth S. Cavan, "Underworld, Conventional and Ideological Crime," *Journal of Criminal Law, Criminology and Police Science*, 55 (June 1964), pp. 235–240.

[6] Robert K. Merton, "Social Problems and Sociological Theory," in Robert K. Merton and Robert A. Nisbit (eds.), *Contemporary Social Problems*, 2d ed., New York: Harcourt, Brace & World, Inc., 1966, pp. 808–811.

characteristics of persons who engage in political behavior which may be defined as criminal.[7] However, it seems sound to conclude that such characteristics as age, sex, ethnicity, and social class do not differentiate political offenders as a whole from the population in general. Political offenders differ more from one another according to the type of political crime than they differ from the noncriminal population. For example, in regard to social class, persons in the IWW (Industrial Workers of the World), some of whom were defined by the United States government as criminal, were of the laboring class, while the members of many other radical political organizations have been from the middle class. Likewise, in respect to ethnicity, politically oriented movements have differed greatly from one another in their ethnic composition, with some movements drawing from the population at large. It appears that the crucial factors in the career of the political offender are not personal and social characteristics per se but the values of the offender and the value systems to which he is actively responding.

Political criminals are usually committed to a larger social order. The social order they have in mind, however, may differ from the existing order. It is because of their commitment to something beyond themselves and conventional society that they are willing to engage in criminal behavior. Persons who occasionally engage in political crime are interested in their society, but at times find it lacking in important ways. They may then sever their commitment to the society in place of a social order which could exist. The social order to which they are committed may be a modification of the one that exists or may possibly be an entirely new order. Nevertheless, the existing society always serves as a reference point for political offenders.

The traitor and the spy provide the classic examples of the political offender who is committed to another social order. The traitor is guilty of treason in giving aid to another government making war against his own government, or adhering to enemies of the state. The spy, on the other hand, is more often a citizen of another country and in the course of espionage obtains secret information, often of a valuable military nature, for a foreign power. He is committed to his own country but is anything but attached to the country from which he secures the information, the country in which he is regarded as a political criminal. The entire career of such an offender may be devoted to spying. For both the traitor and the spy, there is a commitment to a larger social order beyond their own self-interest, with the exception of the professional spy, to whom spying is merely a "dirty business." The conscientious adherence by traitors and spies to the principles of some society has been characterized as follows:

> Although some political offenders are persons without integrity who have yielded to the extensive bribes paid either by foreign powers or by local groups, the vast majority are conscientious adherents to a political philosophy which threatens the existence of the government they are opposing. This was true of the attempts to wrest power from a tyrannical monarch and is equally true of those who aim to overthrow our own government or that of any foreign power today. Political offenders thus represent a paradox for they are criminals who carry on their illegal activities in pursuit

[7] See Edwin M. Lemert, *Social Pathology*, New York: McGraw-Hill Book Company, Inc., 1951, pp. 180–187.

of their ideals. They are not imbued with sordid schemes for extracting vast sums of money from unsuspecting victims, nor are they motivated by basic desires to destroy or kill, although these crimes may be necessary in the pursuit of their ideals. They are generally idealists devoted to a cause (however mistaken it may be) which they place higher than patriotism or personal safety. In most cases of treason the traitors place this cause higher than the existence of their own government. In cases of espionage the spies may be loyal agents of their own country and place its survival above that of the country whose national interests they would destroy—or whose secret papers they would secure. Or they may be hired agents of a foreign power and thus are guilty of treason. All spies are heroes, then, to their native land or the country whose cause they are espousing, while they are arch enemies to those governments whose secrets they secure.[8]

While possibly not as dramatic, the source of commitment is crucial in all forms of political crime.

It is apparent that an understanding of the political criminal requires a conception of man that is not usually used in the study of the criminal.[9] The view that the criminal is produced by a variety of impersonal forces beyond his control is not adequate for the study of the political criminal. The introspective nature of man, man as a reflective being, may be seen in the political criminal. Man alone is capable of considering alternative actions, of breaking from the established social order. Once the individual has an awareness of self, acquired as a member of society, he is able to choose his actions. A purposive, voluntaristic conception of man and his behavior is thus essential to the study of human behavior in general and political crime in particular. The ability of the individual to break with the established order is nowhere better illustrated than in some forms of political behavior which may be defined as criminal. Criminal behavior may at times be the only appropriate means for achieving desired ends. Thus, in the analysis of the political criminal, the deterministic, oversocialized conception of man must be balanced by the facts of man's reason, creativity, autonomy, and potential.

GROUP SUPPORT OF CRIMINAL BEHAVIOR

It is generally the case in a political democracy that most groups in the population can make themselves heard at some crucial point in the decision-making process. Some groups, however, for various reasons, are either excluded from the normal political procedures or are unsuccessful in being represented in the policy decisions. When legitimate political means fail, persons and groups may resort to illegitimate and illegal political procedures. The use of these procedures may result in behavior that is defined as criminal.

Individuals are socialized into political behavior, as in other behavior, on the

[8] Mabel A. Elliott, *Crime in Modern Society*, New York: Harper & Row, Publishers, 1951, p. 180.

[9] See Richard Quinney, "A Conception of Man and Society for Criminology," *Sociological Quarterly*, 6 (Spring 1965), pp. 119–127.

basis of group experience.[10] In the course of political socialization and concrete experience, individuals and groups develop a conception regarding the relative legitimacy of existing political institutions. A political system is regarded as legitimate when the authority of those in control is respected and the available procedures in the political process are believed to be appropriate. Groups generally regard a political system as legitimate or illegitimate according to the way in which the values of the system correspond to their own values. The acceptance of particular societal values, such as achievement and religion, tends to maximize the legitimacy of the existing system.[11] Groups that do not share these values are more likely to question the legitimacy of the system at certain times and are likely to engage in political behaviors ("extremist politics") which may be defined as criminal. The extremism may be of a variety either to the "right" or to the "left" of what is defined as politically traditional in a society.

The pursuit of illegal political behavior is not regarded as a serious matter for some persons. After all, selective obedience to the law is a common phenomenon in other social situations. Laws are obeyed according to a person's beliefs. The evasion of a criminal law most likely represents the following of an alternative norm. The political criminal may actually be following an "ideal" or "utopian" norm, a norm held by most people but rarely realized in actual behavior.[12] The conscientious objector, for example, refuses to have qualification placed on the moral injunction against killing another human being, feeling that the situation is no different in war from what it is in peace. The person who is disloyal to his country is nevertheless being true to higher loyalties. The traitor is not disloyal in his own eyes but is loyal to something he regards as more worthy of allegiance.[13] Such criminals are conscientiously following a set of norms and values which differs from that of the political majority.

The fact that political crime has group support is illustrated in the case of conscientious objectors during World War II. The overwhelming majority of persons convicted during the period were members of the "historic peace churches," including Jehovah's Witnesses, the Society of Friends, the Mennonites, and the Church of the Brethren, all of which are committed to the opposition of war by their fundamental doctrines.[14] The philosophical objectors, those not basing their objections on religious grounds, also found group support for their behavior. They were united, often with religious objectors, through such organizations as the Pacifist Research Bureau, the War Resisters League, and the National Council Against Conscription.

The group nature of political crime varies, of course, from one kind of political crime to another. Some political criminals receive less group support than others. Also, the groups to which political offenders may belong differ greatly in their ideologies. In addition, the social organization of groups supporting political crime

[10] See Herbert H. Hyman, *Political Socialization*, New York: The Free Press of Glencoe, 1959; and Robert E. Lane, *Political Life: Why People Get Involved in Politics*, New York: The Free Press of Glencoe, 1959.

[11] Seymour Martin Lipset, "The Value Patterns of Democracy: A Case Study in Comparative Analysis," *American Sociological Review*, 28 (August 1963), pp. 515–531.

[12] Robert M. Williams, Jr., *American Society*, New York: Alfred A. Knopf, Inc., 1960, pp. 379–380.

[13] Morton Grodzins, *The Loyal and Disloyal: Social Boundaries of Patriotism and Treason*, Chicago: University of Chicago Press, 1956.

[14] Mulford Q. Sibley and Ada Wardlaw, *Conscientious Objectors in Prison, 1940–1945*, Ithaca, N.Y.: Pacifist Research Bureau, 1945, Chap. 1.

varies with the size of the group, cohesiveness of the group, formality of organization, duration of the group, geographical dispersion of the members, and patterns of leadership. Finally, groups differ in the techniques and tactics used by members in the course of committing offenses. Techniques and tactics include such diverse forms as oratory, face-to-face persuasion, writing and propaganda, nonviolent coercion, passive resistance, demonstrations, marches, strikes, suicide, street fighting, and guerrilla warfare.

Violence as a political tactic has been supported and encouraged by a number of extremist groups. Perhaps the obvious example in recent American history is found in the rise of the Ku Klux Klan. As early as 1871, during the Reconstruction period, a congressional investigation of the Klan uncovered hangings, shootings, whippings, and mutilations in the thousands. With the increase in Klan membership in the 1960s, stimulated by progress in the civil rights of Negroes, the Klan again resorted to force and violence. One observer has listed a number of the publicized cases of violence which have followed upon the growth of the Klan:

> . . . eighteen bomb blasts in Negro churches and homes in Mc-Comb, Mississippi, alone during 1964 (Klansmen convicted in at least one case); the bombing of the Birmingham church in which four little Negro girls were killed (Klansmen arrested, freed); the 1964 murder of Negro educator Lemuel Penn (four Georgia Klan members arrested, two tried and acquitted by an all-white jury); the 1965 murder of Mrs. Viola Gregg Liuzzo (three Klan members convicted of violating her civil rights); the murder of three civil rights workers in Philadelphia, Mississippi (six Klansmen among those arrested); weeks of violent racial incidents in St. Augustine, Florida, in 1964, during desegregation efforts by Dr. Martin Luther King (the Klan staging open parades and street harangues on the scene).[15]

CORRESPONDENCE BETWEEN CRIMINAL BEHAVIOR AND LEGITIMATE BEHAVIOR PATTERNS

The behavior associated with political crime in American society is initially consistent with the democratic principle of the right of expression and dissent. The right of petition and association is guaranteed in the First Amendment of the United States Constitution, which states that Congress shall make no law abridging "the right of the people peaceably to assemble, and to petition the Government for a redress of grievances." Yet, especially through state constitutions, the rights of the citizen are qualified.[16] While religious freedom is also a constitutional guarantee, religious freedom cannot be regarded as an absolute. In a complex society there are many competing interests and values which in operation often place limits on religious freedom.

[15] Arnold Forster, "Violence on the Fanatical Left and Right," The Annals, 364 (March 1966), p. 146.
[16] David Fellman, The Constitutional Right of Association, Chicago: University of Chicago Press, 1963.

The most familiar illustrations of the limits of religious freedom are found in situations where the peace, safety, and good order of the community impose them. It is clear that however large
the area of religious freedom may be, and however reluctant the
courts may be to set limits to that freedom, there are countervail-
ing interests which are regarded as so vital to society that they serve
as justification for some limitations. These interests include the
protection of public morals and public health, the care of children,
national defense, general welfare, and public order.[17]

Thus, it may be seen that in practice there are limits to the freedom of expression. Although the behaviors included in political crime may correspond in
principle to the democratic values of American society, the actual commission of
the acts is restricted to what is regarded as politically legitimate.

Intrinsic to political democracy is a basic paradox between two opposing ideals,
extremes which are in some way supposed to be balanced.[18] On the one hand,
political democracies claim the power to govern but, on the other hand, grant the
freedom of thought that may result in dissent. An orderly representative government provides the opportunities for political change. The opposing ideals are able
to exist because of the unspoken agreement in political democracies that "the
majority agrees to tolerate the criticism and dissent of the minority (or minorities)
while the minority agrees to seek power only through persuasion and political
activity, not through violence."[19] Thus, in the abstract, the majority is not to perse-
cute the minority, and the minority is not to express dissent through illegitimate
and illegal activity.

The boundaries and definitions of political freedom, however, are by no means
constant within any political democracy. The latitude of dissent that may still be
regarded as legitimate varies from one time to another. During some periods a
considerable amount and degree of dissent may be tolerated, while in other periods
dissent may be suppressed, particularly by means of the criminal law.

Political freedom is especially restricted during periods of international tension
and conflict which result in real or perceived national emergencies. Freedom of
speech, for instance, is abridged in wartime, as indicated in the United States by
the Sedition Act of 1798, which provided for the punishment of anyone who
uttered or published statements against the government, and by the strengthening
of the Espionage Act in 1918.[20] New controls relating to economic as well as to
security matters are created and enforced during the emergencies of war.[21] The
concern over native communism occurs during postwar instability and unrest.[22]
The federal statutes are filled with other antisubversive provisions that have been

[17] David Fellman, The Limits of Freedom, New Brunswick, N.J.: Rutgers University Press, 1959,
p. 25.
[18] The following discussion is adapted from Richard Quinney, "Crime in Political Perspective,"
American Behavioral Scientist, 8 (December 1964), pp. 19–22.
[19] Horton and Leslie, pp. 632–633.
[20] Herbert L. Packer, "Offenses against the State," The Annals, 339 (January 1962), pp. 77–89.
[21] Edgar C. McVoy, "Wartime Controls in a Democratic Society," American Sociological Review, 11 (February 1946), pp. 85–89; and Howard Woolston, "Free Speech in War Time,"
American Sociological Review, 7 (April 1942), pp. 185–193.
[22] Robert K. Murray, Red Scare: A Study in National Hysteria, 1919–1920, Minneapolis: University of Minnesota Press, 1955.

enacted during national emergencies. To name only a few, the Voorhis Act of 1940 restricted the registration of persons and organizations who acted as agents of foreign powers; the Smith Act of 1940 forbade the advocacy of the overthrow of the government; the Internal Security Act of 1950 (McCarran Act) required the registration of Communist and Communist-front organizations as well as strengthened other legislation on subversion; the Immigration and Nationality Act of 1952 (McCarran-Walter Act) provided for the deportation of resident aliens because of "disloyal" beliefs and associates; and the Communist Control Act of 1954 required the registration of Communist party members with the Attorney General. In addition to such legislation, loyalty and security programs have been initiated and black-list procedures have been established.[23]

While political freedom is a delicate and dubious matter in all political democracies, it is a particular problem in the United States. It seems apparent that Americans, as compared to other peoples in representative governments, are especially intolerant of social and political differences.[24] This intolerance is expressed in the denial of various civil rights to certain social and political minority groups, religious groups, racial and ethnic groups, and political dissenters of various persuasions. Numerous criminal laws and rulings have been formulated to handle these differences. Certain behaviors by political minorities committed out of conscience have been made illegal. In addition to the numerous acts that have been defined as subversive (by the groups in power), attempts to express dissatisfaction with nuclear testing, civil defense, military build-ups, and racial discrimination have been subject to criminal action. A host of previously existing laws have been used in the suppression of dissent and protest. Demonstrators for racial civil rights and other causes have been arrested on such charges as disorderly conduct, breach of peace, parading without a permit, trespassing, loitering, and violation of fire ordinances. Under other laws, persons have been arrested for refusing to pay income taxes used for military purposes, for not complying with local civil defense ordinances, for picketing military bases, for refusing to register for the draft, and for violating state laws that require the segregation of races.[25] All of these criminal behaviors share the common element that the offenders are pursuing values out of conscience and conviction, the values being different from those of the groups that are formulating and administering the criminal law. The result, nevertheless, is that some persons are being defined as criminals.

SOCIETAL REACTION

By definition the political offender is regarded as a threat and danger to the existing society. Those who are so regarded are not dealt with lightly. Reaction to the behavior of the political offender is also severe because the offender's loyalty to the state is in question, loyalty being regarded as a requirement for the members of a society. In addition, political crime is treated harshly because of the composition of the groups that react officially. Conservative segments of society usually domi-

[23] Ralph S. Brown, *Loyalty and Security*, New Haven, Conn.: Yale University Press, 1958.
[24] Herbert H. Hyman, "England and America: Climates of Tolerance and Intolerance," in Daniel Bell (ed.), *The Radical Right*, New York: Doubleday & Company, Inc., 1963, pp. 227–257.
[25] See the annual reports of the American Civil Liberties Union, New York.

nate the power structure of the state. Official action in regard to political crime usually represents the attempt to preserve the status quo. The political offender is punished with the hope that similar political behavior will not occur or will at least remain at a minimum.

Public reaction to activity regarded as threatening to political authority has taken many diverse forms. In the United States a stereotyped conception of the political radical has predominated as a very general form of reaction:

> The stereotyped ideas about radicals which lurk in the consciousness of the masses of people are easily provoked in experimental free-association reactions to the term, embracing such associations as "red," "alien," "dirty," "soapbox agitation," "Godless," "free lover," "bewhiskered," "bombs," and "sabotage." Stereotypes such as these, circulated in newspapers, fiction, and artistic representations, have been highly colored by the beliefs which grew up around anarchism in the nineteenth century and the IWW in the twentieth. Reports of assassinations by Russian revolutionaries and by anarchists in European countries, the assassination of President Garfield by an anarchist, along with the Haymarket riots in Chicago and IWW violence at Homestead, Pennsylvania, and elsewhere, did much to shape the American fixed notions of the radical. Not only has this older anarchistic stereotype remained alive, but it tends to be applied indiscriminately to socialists, Communists, pacifists, and other radicals, as well as to progressive or moderate reformers.[26]

The official reactions to political crime have been particularly severe. For example, during World War II the average sentence for conscientious objectors was more stringent than for many other convicted criminals. Nearly 90 percent of the convicted conscientious objectors were sentenced to prison, with over 30 percent receiving a four- to five-year term. For the entire period only a little over 4 percent of the cases were granted probation.[27]

Jailing and deportation have been used in the United States as means of controlling radicalism. The most dramatic use occurred in November 1919 and January 1920 when federal agents, under the direction of Attorney General A. Mitchell Palmer, staged a series of nationwide dragnet raids and detained for deportation several thousand alien members of the Union of Russian Workers, the Communist Labor party, and the Communist party. In this instance no criminal proceedings were involved. Attorney General Palmer did not try to prosecute actual crimes of radicals against the United States because this would have required an indictment and a trial by jury. Rather, he relied on an administrative process for the apprehension and deportation of radical aliens and thereby circumvented normal legal procedures.[28]

More direct and immediate reactions have taken place, as in the intentional killings by police in such disturbances as the Haymarket riot of 1886 and the

26 Lemert, p. 200.
27 Lemert, pp. 203–204.
28 Murray, Chap. 13. Also see William Preston, Jr., *Aliens and Dissenters: Federal Suppression of Radicals, 1903–1933*, Cambridge, Mass.: Harvard University Press, 1963, Chaps. 7 and 8.

Pullman strike of 1894. Police intimidation and brutality have been evident in more recent times in the handling of "race riots." Some of the violence that has occurred in such disorders has been prompted by the police.[29]

The apartheid policy in South Africa is an extreme example of political control being entirely in the hands of one group to the complete subjugation of another. The policy of the control of nonwhites by whites in South Africa has been implemented through laws which require Africans to carry a pass book at all times. Under the system, totalitarian control is maintained by the government, depriving Africans the right of movement, the right of choice of work, freedom of speech, freedom of association and assembly, in short, the denial of all human rights.[30]

Judicial proceedings, as a reaction to political crime, have served to authenticate and limit political action. The services of the courts have been used by most governments in behalf of political goals. Kirchheimer, in an analysis of the court's role in the control of opposing political viewpoints and actions, has noted that three types of political trials have been used to accomplish the goals of the political authority:

> A. The trial involving a common crime committed for political purposes and conducted with a view to the political benefits which might ultimately accrue from successful prosecution.
> B. The classic political trial: a regime's attempt to incriminate its foe's public behavior with a view to evicting him from the political scene.
> C. The derivative political trial, where the weapons of defamation, perjury, and contempt are manipulated in an effort to bring disrepute upon a political foe.[31]

Through political procedures such as these, political foes are eliminated from political competition. As long as politically organized societies regard certain persons and behaviors as threats to their existence, there will be political crime; that is to say, there will be persons and behaviors that will be defined as criminal.

SELECTED BIBLIOGRAPHY

1. Bell, Daniel (ed.), *The Radical Right*, New York: Doubleday & Company, Inc., 1963.
2. Brink, William, and Louis Harris, *The Negro Revolution in America*, New York: Simon and Schuster, Inc., 1964.
3. Brown, Ralph S., *Loyalty and Security*, New Haven, Conn.: Yale University Press, 1958.
4. Broyles, J. Allen, *The John Birch Society: Anatomy of a Protest*, Boston: The Beacon Press, 1964.

[29] Allen D. Grimshaw, "Government and Social Violence: The Complexity of Guilt," *Minnesota Review*, 3 (Winter 1963), pp. 236–245; Grimshaw, "Actions of Police and the Military in American Race Riots," *Phylon*, 24 (Fall 1963), pp. 271–289.
[30] Leo Kuper, *An African Bourgeoisie: Race, Class, and Politics in South Africa*, New Haven, Conn.: Yale University Press, 1965.
[31] Otto Kirchheimer, *Political Justice: The Use of Legal Procedure for Political Ends*, Princeton, N.J.: Princeton University Press, 1961, p. 46.

5. Cavan, Ruth S., "Underworld, Conventional and Ideological Crime," *Journal of Criminal Law, Criminology and Police Science*, 55 (June 1964), pp. 235–240.
6. Chalmers, David M., *Hooded Americanism*, New York: Doubleday & Company, Inc., 1965.
7. Chapin, Bradley, *The American Law of Treason*, Seattle: University of Washington Press, 1964.
8. Dunham, Barrows, *Heroes and Heretics*, New York: Alfred A. Knopf, Inc., 1964.
9. Elliott, Mabel A., *Crime in Modern Society*, New York: Harper & Row, Publishers, 1951, pp. 179–197.
10. Fellman, David, *The Constitutional Right of Association*, Chicago: University of Chicago Press, 1963.
11. ———, *The Defendant's Rights*, New York: Holt, Rinehart and Winston, Inc., 1958.
12. ———, *The Limits of Freedom*, New Brunswick, N.J., Rutgers University Press, 1959.
13. Forster, Arnold, "Violence on the Fanatical Left and Right," *The Annals*, 364 (March 1966), pp. 141–148.
14. Gellhorn, Walter, *Individual Freedom and Governmental Restraints*, Baton Rouge, La.: Louisiana State University Press, 1956.
15. Greenberg, Jack, *Race Relations and American Law*, New York: Columbia University Press, 1959.
16. Grimshaw, Allen D., "Actions of Police and the Military in American Race Riots," *Phylon*, 24 (Fall 1963), pp. 271–289.
17. ———, "Lawlessness and Violence in America and Their Special Manifestations in Changing Negro-White Relationships," *Journal of Negro History*, 44 (January 1959), pp. 52–72.
18. Grodzins, Morton, *The Loyal and the Disloyal*, Chicago: University of Chicago Press, 1956.
19. Higham, John, *Strangers in the Land: Patterns of American Nativism, 1860–1925*, New Brunswick, N.J.: Rutgers University Press, 1955.
20. Hobsbawm, E. J., *Primitive Rebels: Studies in Archaic Forms of Social Movement in the 19th and 20th Centuries*, New York: Frederick A. Praeger, Inc., 1963.
21. Horton, Paul B., and Gerald R. Leslie, *The Sociology of Social Problems*, 3d ed., New York: Appleton-Century-Crofts, Inc., 1965, Chap. 19.
22. Kaplow, Jeffrey (ed.), *New Perspectives on the French Revolution: Readings in Historical Sociology*, New York: John Wiley & Sons, Inc., 1965.
23. Kirchheimer, Otto, *Political Justice: The Use of Legal Procedure for Political Ends*, Princeton, N.J.: Princeton University Press, 1961.
24. Kuper, Leo, *An African Bourgeoisie: Race, Class, and Politics in South Africa*, New Haven, Conn.: Yale University Press, 1965.
25. ———, *Passive Resistance in South Africa*, New Haven, Conn.: Yale University Press, 1957.
26. Lemert, Edwin M., *Social Pathology*, New York: McGraw-Hill Book Company, Inc., 1951, Chap. 7.
27. Lomax, Louis, *The Negro Revolt*, New York: Harper & Row, Publishers, 1962.

28. McVoy, Edgar C., "Wartime Controls in a Democratic Society," *American Sociological Review*, 11 (February 1946), pp. 85–89.
29. Manwaring, David, *Render Unto Ceasar: The Flag-Salute Controversy*, Chicago: University of Chicago Press, 1962.
30. Merton, Robert K., "Social Problems and Sociological Theory," in Robert K. Merton and Robert A. Nisbit (eds), *Contemporary Social Problems*, 2d ed., New York: Harcourt, Brace & World, Inc., 1966, pp. 775–823.
31. Murray, Robert K., *Red Scare: A Study in National Hysteria, 1919–1920*, Minneapolis: University of Minnesota Press, 1965.
32. Newman, Donald J., "Legal Norms and Criminological Definitions," in Joseph S. Roucek (ed.), *Sociology of Crime*, New York: Philosophical Library, 1961, pp. 55–89.
33. Packer, Herbert L., "Offenses against the State," *The Annals*, 339 (January 1962), pp. 77–89.
34. Preston, William, Jr., *Aliens and Dissenters: Federal Suppression of Radicals, 1903–1933*, Cambridge, Mass.: Harvard University Press, 1963.
35. Quinney, Richard, "A Conception of Man and Society for Criminology," *Sociological Quarterly*, 6 (Spring 1965), pp. 119–127.
36. ———, "Crime in Political Perspective," *American Behavioral Scientist*, 8 (December 1964), pp. 19–22.
37. Randel, William Pierce, *The Ku Klux Klan: A Century of Infamy*, Philadelphia: Chilton Company–Book Division, 1965.
38. Roche, John P., *The Quest for the Dream*, New York: Crowell-Collier and Macmillan, Inc., 1963.
39. Rudé, George, *The Crowd in History, 1730–1848*, New York: John Wiley & Sons, Inc., 1964.
40. Rusche, George, and Otto Kirchheimer, *Punishment and Social Structure*, New York: Columbia University Press, 1939.
41. Sellin, Thorsten, *Culture Conflict and Crime*, New York: Social Science Research Council, 1938.
42. Sibley, Mulford Q. (ed), *The Quiet Battle*, New York: Doubleday & Company, Inc., 1963.
43. ——— and Philip E. Jacob, *Conscription of Conscience*, Ithaca, N.Y.: Cornell University Press, 1952.
44. Vahan, Richard, *The Truth about the John Birch Society*, New York: Mcfadden Books, 1962.
45. Van den Berghe, Pierre L., *South Africa: A Study in Conflict*, Middletown, Conn.: Wesleyan University Press, 1965.
46. Vander Zanden, James W., *Race Relations in Transition: The Segregation Crisis in the South*, New York: Random House, Inc., 1965.
47. Vold, George B., "Some Basic Problems in Criminological Research," *Federal Probation*, 17 (March 1953), pp. 37–42.
48. ———, *Theoretical Criminology*, New York: Oxford University Press, 1958, Chap. 11.
49. Wolfgang, Marvin, "Political Crimes and Punishment in Renaissance Florence," *Journal of Criminal Law, Criminology and Police Science*, 44 (January–February 1954), pp. 555–581.
50. Woolston, Howard, "Free Speech in War Time," *American Sociological Review*, 7 (April 1942), pp. 185–193.

THE RED HUNT*

John P. Roche

> *Presented here is a chapter from a larger study of the quest for civil liberty in the United States. In this selection Roche documents the suppression during World War I of Socialism, the Industrial Workers of the World, and related radical movements. The Red Scare of the period resulted in criminal charges regarding subversion, sedition, and obstruction of the war effort. The frenzy culminated in the mass arrest of alleged alien subversives in the Palmer Raids of 1919 and 1920.*

"Such is the unity of all history," wrote the great British historian Frederic W. Maitland, "that anyone who endeavors to tell a piece of it must feel that his first sentence tears a seamless web."[1] In examining the impact of the First World War on civil liberty, it has been necessary to tear the web more drastically than usual. But the fact that writing is inexorably unilinear should not be allowed to conceal the multidimensional character of reality. Events did not occur in compartments, nor did they arrive on the scene by categories. To employ an analogy, the United States in the war period was suffering from several acute diseases of the body politic—concurrently. From a simplistic viewpoint, the country was just "sick," but a political diagnostician can try to single out the particular ailments. In short, the Great War precipitated a massive political, social, and economic malaise, and our task here is to sort out and examine the various components of this agonizing seizure. It should always be kept in mind, however, that each series of events has to be fitted into the perspective of the whole atmosphere of repression. And that events in one category were often meshed with those in the others: Bolsheviks were de-

nounced as German agents; scurrilous attacks were made on Jews as Russians, hence Bolsheviks; and the Prohibition movement thrived on the slogan that beer was a German device to undermine the efficiency of the American worker.[2]

It is hardly possible here to recapitulate the history of American radicalism except to point out that during the first decade of this century the Socialist movement was, by both earlier and later standards, well-organized and flourishing. Formed in 1901, the American Socialist Party was an amalgam of urban Marxists, radical trade unionists, municipal reformers, and agrarian underdogs. While it had in its ranks the usual complement of priestly sectarians who spent their time glossing Marxist texts and hammering out theoretical pronouncements, the great strength that the party accumulated in this era was hardly the outgrowth of its abstract profundity. When in 1912 its candidate for President, Eugene Victor Debs, polled almost a million votes, and the National Secretary could report that 1039 Socialists had been elected to various offices in the nation,[3] there were those both within the

[1] Frederick Pollock and Frederic W. Maitland, *The History of English Law* (Cambridge, Cambridge University Press, 2d ed., 1952), Vol. I, p. 1.

[2] Andrew Sinclair, *Prohibition* (Boston, Little, Brown, 1962), p. 119.

[3] Cited by Daniel Bell, "Marxian Socialism in the United States," in Donald D. Egbert and Stow Persons, *Socialism and American Life* (Princeton, Princeton University Press, 1952), Vol. I, p. 283.

party and without who saw the United States on the verge of a Socialist revolution. But the opposite was in fact the case. The Socialist Party, far from being a nucleus of revolutionaries, had in many areas become accepted as a traditional political organization, one which represented the left wing of the reform movement but which stood firmly in the reformist tradition.

The German Socialists of Milwaukee, for example, brought clean, honest municipal government to their city. In Victor Berger they had a political boss (a *bonze* in the colloquial German of his constituents) who would at a later date have felt thoroughly at home in such a reform political machine as La Guardia's in New York City. To Lenin is attributed the sardonic observation that before German revolutionaries would seize a railroad line, they would buy tickets. Berger and his organization would have confirmed Lenin's bias: they were meticulously legalistic.[4] In hundreds of other cities throughout the country (the South excepted), the Socialist Party provided the launching pad for reform movements which found themselves blocked by the corrupt, undemocratic character of the traditional parties. The supporters of this "gas and water" Socialism were generally uninterested in the labored formulae of the national Socialist platform. They merely wanted to clean up Haverhill, Reading, Schenectady, or South Siwash.

Thus, while the Socialist Party at the outbreak of the war presented a dynamic exterior (it had thirteen daily newspapers and almost three hundred weeklies, with significant foreign language representation), it was actually schizophrenic. The great mass of those who supported its candidates were not in any ideological sense "socialist," and yet the national destinies of the party were in the hands of dedicated ideological activists, men who unlike the leaders of the

German Social Democratic Party or the British Labour Party were unwilling to trim their sails to the nationalistic will of the "masses." A number of analyses of American Socialism have been written in the attempt to explain the collapse of this once-thriving movement, but not one has sufficiently emphasized this basic consideration. The party was a war casualty because its leaders *refused* to betray the ideals of proletarian internationalism. Under the impact of wartime chauvinism, the electoral rank and file simply vanished or went into hiding; the Bolshevik Revolution and subsequent splits in the party merely shattered the militant remnant.

Had the American Socialist leadership imitated their European comrades and become "social patriots," the party might well have survived, adjusted itself to wartime exigencies, and retained its reform constituency. But from the moment the Emergency Conference in St. Louis, meeting the day after war was declared, adopted a firm antiwar position, Socialism became, in the public eye, a front for the Hun. The statement, presented by Morris Hillquit, the great Socialist leader from New York, still has a ring of grandeur about it:

The Socialist Party of the United States in the present grave crisis reaffirms its allegiance to the principle of internationalism and working class solidarity the world over, and proclaims its unalterable opposition to the war just declared by the government of the United States. . . . We brand the declaration of war by our government as a crime against the people of the United States and against the nations of the world.[5]

This position was endorsed by 80 percent of the delegates and, in a referendum, by an overwhelming vote of the membership. But this is deceptive in terms of real support. Party membership reached a high point of about 125,000 in 1912 and had by this time probably dropped to the neighborhood of 75,000. The members may have stood firm, but the nonmembers who had been voting

---

[4] See David A. Shannon, *The Socialist Party of America* (New York, Harcourt, Brace, 1955), on "gas and water" Socialism in pp. 13–17; on Victor Berger, pp. 21–25.

[5] Cited by Ray Ginger, *The Bending Cross* (New Brunswick, Rutgers University Press, 1949), p. 341.

Socialist and providing the party with its broad constituency, which could possibly have developed into a permanent electoral base, took to the hills. Under withering attack from all sides (traditional politicians disturbed by Socialist growth took maximum advantage of the situation), suffering constant desertions (most of the Socialist leaders in the AFL, for example, repudiated the party), these courageous internationalists marched into their private Armageddon. From this point forward, the Socialist Party was to be an instrument of radical protest, not a political movement.

The American Federation of Labor, with Samuel Gompers in the vanguard, went vigorously to war, but there was a segment of the labor movement which took a vociferous and revolutionary antiwar position: the Industrial Workers of the World. The IWW has by now become so clothed in myth that it is difficult to reach a realistic appraisal of either its strength or its objectives. Ostensibly standing for "One Big Union" and the militant class struggle, the "Wobblies" were also curiously akin to European syndicalist movements which subsequently merited the designation of "fascist." There was the same romanticization of violence, the same antirationalism which expressed itself in contempt and hatred of politics. In short, there was a total rejection of "bourgeois values" which often in practice amounted to an endorsement of revolutionary gangsterism. When Big Bill Haywood sent Harry Orchard out to murder the Governor of Idaho or to dynamite a mine shaft full of "scabs," he was less concerned with building a new world than destroying the old. Thus to rob a grocery store was hardly a sin; it was merely expropriating the goods of a "class enemy." There was a classic Wobbly handbill which conveys the essence. "Don't drive copper tacks in fruit trees—it kills them!" it informed agricultural workers. It was distributed with a bag of copper tacks![6]

In terms of members, the IWW was never large. The United States government alleged in 1917 that there were 200,000 in the organization, but this was part of the case for suppression and was fantastically exaggerated.[7] In the same year, the IWW leader Vincent St. John claimed 60,000 dues-paying unionists. If we add to this a substantial body of non-dues-paying sympathizers, a figure in the neighborhood of 100,-000 seems reasonable. It is difficult to get meaningful statistics in part because the IWW took an existential approach toward administration. Keeping records and the like was a bourgeois fixation which they left to the "stool pigeons" of the "American Fakiration of Labor." No true revolutionary would ever waste his subversive potentialities on bookkeeping. Moreover, there was tremendous turnover both of members and locals. In a typical case, an IWW organizer would pop up in a lumber camp where grievances were rife, sign up the loggers, stage a strike. When, as was usually the case, the lumber operators invoked lynch law to break the strike, the organizer was lucky to escape with his life and the freshly baptized local simply vanished. The workers, for their own protection, hid or destroyed their Red Cards—but often remained strong fellow travelers of the IWW and waited for their next chance. Whole locals disappeared in this and other more colorful fashions. One group in San Diego disbanded in 1911 and gave as their rationale "Mexican Revolution"!

The resemblance of the IWW to later syndicalist-fascist movements was also noticeable in its appeal to what Marx and Engels called the "lumpenproletariat," the dregs of society. Unlike the Socialists, who were as followers of Marx pretty much committed to being the heirs of capitalism, the Wobblies were consumed by a ferocious

[6] See Wallace Stegner, The Preacher and the Slave (Boston, Houghton Mifflin, 1950), for a novel-

ist's account which surpasses many of the "scholarly" analyses in its graphic and sophisticated treatment of the ambiguities of the IWW.
[7] Paul F. Brissenden, The I.W.W. (New York, Russell & Russell, 2d ed., 1957), p. 359.

nihilism; they were capitalism's assassins. Like Mussolini's *squadristi* and the early cadres of the National Socialist Party, they built their constituency on the revenge of the alienated, those who could find no hope of a future in bourgeois society.[8] (Any who would deny this charge on the basis of the IWW *Program* should spend a few minutes reading the platforms of the Italian Fascists or the Nazis *before* the latter seized power.)[9] The Socialists, even the so-called revolutionaries of the left wing, were always sustained by a vision of the future; they envisaged bourgeois society as an intermediate station on a historically routed journey. In short, their commitment was to a future *in* history, while the IWW saw history as a plot against the disinherited and defied both past and future in the name of their appalling image of the present.

And from their position at the bottom of the heap, there was a good deal of rough justice in the IWW evaluation. It is all very well to suggest that the Wobblies were not sterling characters, and it is equally important to note that history can grant no absolution—no amount of Allied stupidity at Versailles could *justify* the barbarism of Nazi Germany. But at the same time, the dispassionate observer is torn with shame when he reads the bloody chronicle of the suppression of the IWW. The power and the constituency of the IWW were created by conditions of blind, savage exploitation of the helpless, by that perversion of American ideals which passed as the free enterprise system in the first decades of this century. To repeat, this situation of near-

peonage could not provide moral validation for the excesses of the IWW, but it does help to explain the basis of Wobbly power. While in any historical period one can find brave men who in the name of one nihilistic credo or another engage in daemonic resistance to the status quo (the European Secret Army in Algeria is a recent example of this phenomenon), the question which must be asked is not *why* are these men so committed (a problem for psychiatrists) but *what* rottenness in society threw leaders of this sort to the top?

In the case of the IWW, the answer is not hard to find. The organization was nourished by a ruthless system of economic and political exploitation which had made impossible the development of any decent code of human relations. Let us take one instance of the IWW in action, a case discussed in the following terms by an official publication of the United States Department of Labor: the "Wheatland Riot" of 1913.

Following a practice not unusual among large-scale growers, E. B. Durst, hop rancher, had advertised in newspapers throughout California and Nevada for some 2,700 workers. He subsequently admitted that he could provide employment for only about 1,500, and that living arrangements were inadequate even for that number. Workers of many racial stocks from many areas poured into the community. . . . A great number had no bedding and slept on piles of straw thrown on floors . . . many slept in fields. There were no facilities for sanitation or garbage disposal and only 9 outdoor toilets for 2,800 people; dysentery became prevalent. . . . The water wells were insufficient for the camp . . . workers were forced to buy what supplies they could afford from a concession store on the ranch.[10]

Above and beyond these physical conditions, the pay was appalling and was kept that way by Durst's homemade version of the "reserve army of the unemployed," the surplus labor he had recruited. The workers simply would not take this, and a spontane-

---

[8] For a discussion of the constructive Socialist position versus the nihilist Nazi one, see Peter Drucker, *The End of Economic Man* (New York, John Day, 1939); and Hermann Rauschning, *The Revolution of Nihilism* (New York, Longmans, Green, 1939).

[9] For the Nazi program in the early 1930s see Carl Mayer, "On the Intellectual Origin of National Socialism," *Social Research*, Vol. 9 (1942), pp. 225–47. For a brilliant exposé of Italian fascist development in the early stages, see A. Rossi (pseud. of Angelo Tasca), *The Rise of Italian Fascism* (London, Methuen, 1938).

[10] Stuart Jamieson (Bureau of Labor Statistics, Bulletin No. 836), *Labor Unionism in American Agriculture* (Washington, D.C., 1945), pp. 61–62.

ous demonstration occurred. At this point, the IWW—in the persons of Blackie Ford and Herman Suhr—moved in to organize a "camp local," and Durst struck back. The strikers, after a fruitless attempt to negotiate with Durst, called a second meeting.

The meeting, which the county sheriff later testified was entirely peaceable, was invaded by a band of armed deputies who came to arrest Ford. One of the deputies on the fringe of the crowd fired a shot to "quiet the mob." This precipitated a riot, in the course of which the district attorney, a deputy sheriff, and two workers were killed and many more were injured.

Hysteria apparently gripped the authorities after the outbreak. Mass arrests of "wobblies" or sympathizers were carried out. Many of the arrested men were severely beaten or tortured, and many others were held incommunicado for weeks. Ford and Suhr, the two leading I.W.W. organizers in the camp, were convicted of murder and sentenced to life imprisonment.[11]

Throughout the country, IWW organizers inevitably turned up in the areas of worst labor-management relations; if the AFL had been beaten, or had been unwilling or unable to provide organization, desperate union militants would turn to the Wobblies for one last chance. Sometimes it worked—as in the Spokane area lumber mills or the famous Lawrence, Mass., textile strike of 1912—but more often IWW intervention simply provided an excuse for decisive brutality by police and Pinkertons.[12]

Before we turn to the details of wartime suppression of Socialism, the IWW, and related radical movements, tribute should be paid to the IWW for a great contribution to the civil liberties tradition, the "free speech fight." By now it should be clear that I am not sympathetic toward either the character or the methods of the IWW—too many social historians seem to have assumed that because the Wobblies were rough they were diamonds—but, however motivated, their struggles for freedom of

speech merit the respect of those who have profited from their reckless courage. Characteristically, the free speech fight had that spontaneous, ad hoc quality which was the bench mark of the IWW. Like the anarchists of Barcelona, who allegedly awake in the morning with supernal knowledge that this is the day to strike, there was minimal organization. An IWW delegate in, say, San Diego would be arrested for making a street-corner speech, then the word would drift up the Southern Pacific line, and at every stop local Wobblies with time on their hands would start for San Diego. Vincent St. John noted that the national headquarters had little to do with what followed. It merely notified the locals of the free speech fight and suggested that "if they have any members that are footloose to send them along."[13]

Soon every freight car coming into San Diego would deposit a few free riders with Red Cards, and the latter would head for the street corners to make their IWW pitch and join their "Fellow Worker" in the calaboose. Shortly, groups of Wobblies would short-cut this procedure by simply going to the jail and demanding admission! In this fashion, hundreds of militants would clog the machinery of justice, turn the jail into a shambles, sing rebel songs—"Dump the Bosses off Your Back," "Solidarity Forever," "Paint 'er Red," "Hallelujah! I'm a Bum!"—day and night, and live off the bourgeois taxpayers until their demands were met. They were beaten, shipped out of town, soaked with hoses, starved in their cells, but to no avail. The nastier the treatment, the more Wobblies "joined the party," coming to San Diego or Spokane from as far away as Chicago. Sometimes the local authorities held out a week, sometimes as long as six months. Their sentiments were tersely put by the San Diego Tribune: "Hanging is none too good for [the Wobblies], they would be much better dead, for they are absolutely useless in the human economy; they are the waste material of

11 Ibid., p. 62.
12 See Ralph Chaplin, Wobbly (Chicago, University of Chicago Press, 1948), passim, esp. pp. 135 ff.
13 Brissenden, op. cit., p. 263.

creation and should be drained off into the sewer of oblivion, there to rot in cold obstruction like any other excrement."[14] But generally the IWW came out ahead, and the twenty or more free speech battles that they mounted between 1909 and 1913 were a noble contribution to the libertarian tradition. Whatever may have been the content of their philosophy, in these encounters they were struggling for a key proposition of the American Dream: the right of unpopular people to express dissenting views.

As can easily be imagined, both the Socialists and the IWW had built up a residue of bitterness against them in the years before 1917. When the United States entered the war, the time had come for settling some long-standing scores, and the opportunity was seized to maximum advantage. The Socialist Party opposed American intervention in measured but hardly "disloyal" terms; the IWW excoriated the war and all things connected with it in its usual slam-bang fashion. (The Socialists, for example, challenged the constitutionality of the draft; the IWW urged all and sundry to refuse military service.) This left them easy targets for the chauvinistic counterattack: they were betraying the United States in its hour of crisis, agents of the Hun. As the *Sacramento Bee* put it, "There must be no leniency to the damnable IWW. They are traitors to the Government. There is evidence that they are in the pay of Germany. . . . The safety of the nation itself demands their extermination."[15] Senator Henry Ashurst announced that IWW stood for "Imperial Wilhelm's Warriors."

The key word here, the word which provides the *leitmotiv* of the great Red Hunt, is *extermination*. The events which occurred between April of 1917 and the time when savage wartime fears expired in the banalities of the Harding Administration can only

be understood as a campaign of extermination. No holds were barred, no logic was too absurd, no constitutional or moral values were permitted to intrude when the United States and the state governments set out to extirpate "treason" and "sedition" and joyously loosed an angered populace upon its "radical" neighbors.

The period can be divided, for the sake of convenience, into two stages: wartime suppression, and the postwar follow-up led by Attorney General A. Mitchell Palmer. The major difference between the two is not one of technique, but rather the additional lurid dimension provided to the postwar repression by the Bolshevik Revolution and the emergence of international Communism. Thorough treatment of either is obviously impossible here; what is significant in the scope of this work is the collapse of American ideals which accompanied the extermination of radicalism—and the dogged, feeble, but indomitably courageous efforts of individuals and organizations like the National Civil Liberties Bureau to stem the tide of legal lawlessness. . . .

Keeping in mind the background of surging crowds of super-patriots endlessly in search of pro-Germans, "slackers," or even the merely unenthusiastic, let us turn to the legal proceedings which were instituted during the war against the Socialist Party, its newspapers and leaders, and against the IWW. Of the three top leaders of the Socialist Party—Eugene Victor Debs, Victor Berger, and Morris Hillquit—only Hillquit emerged unscathed, possibly because for a good part of the time he was in a sanitarium for the tuberculosis which sapped his life, possibly because he had run for Mayor of New York in 1917, receiving one-third of the vote, and his arrest would therefore have looked too much like sheer political reprisal.

Debs, a complex man of deep internal torments, had taken an ambiguous position, at least publicly, on the war. He refused to attend the party convention in St. Louis which endorsed the antiwar position, but

---

14 *Ibid.*, p. 266.
15 Cited by Horace C. Peterson and Gilbert C. Fite, *Opponents of War, 1917–1918* (Madison, Wis.: University of Wisconsin Press, 1957), p. 236.

gradually, as the second echelon of the Socialist leadership fell before the sedition
laws, Debs became less circumspect in public statement, particularly in regard to the
gross violations of civil rights involved in
the prosecutions. In the summer of 1918,
Debs apparently crossed his psychological
Rubicon and, at age 62, set out to join his
comrades behind federal bars. There is evidence that the Washington authorities did
not relish a courtroom encounter with this
great tribune, but the matter was taken out
of their hands in June, 1918, when a local
United States Attorney in Cleveland, Ohio,
presumably building his own reputation as a
sedition hunter, brought an indictment
against Debs for obstructing the recruitment
of military personnel, inciting insubordination and disloyalty in the armed forces, and
of uttering words which would encourage
resistance to the authority of the United
States.

It would be pointless to recapitulate
the substance of Debs's speech to the Ohio
Socialists, which was the basis of the indictment, or of his speech to the hand-
picked jury (made up of citizens whose average age was 70 and average income at
least $50,000) which convicted him of sedi-
tion. Suffice it to say that Debs took his
stand on the First Amendment—"I look
upon the Espionage Law as a despotic enactment in flagrant conflict with democratic
principles and with the spirit of free institutions," he told the court before being sentenced to ten years in Atlanta[16]—and that
no evidence of any sort was introduced by
the United States to verify the specific
charges of the indictment. The essence of
the government's case was that if a soldier
had heard Debs, it was reasonable to believe he might have been influenced toward
insubordination. A year later, the Supreme
Court unanimously sustained the conviction; Justice Holmes (who was privately not
impressed with the menace of Socialism)
suggested in the Opinion that the evidence

against Debs was sufficiently strong to convince reasonable men that he did in fact intend to obstruct recruiting.[17] The old fighter
went off to jail, and Woodrow Wilson
sternly rejected pleas for executive clem-
ency. As late as January, 1921, the President
rejected a recommendation from A. Mitchell Palmer (of all people) that the sentence
be commuted. "This man was a traitor to
his country," Wilson told his private secretary, "and he will never be pardoned during
my administration."[18]

Victor Berger's adventures were somewhat more colorful. The Milwaukee Socialist boss was one of the least lovable
figures in the movement—an authoritarian,
he had also built up a reputation as an anti-
Semite by his unrestrained attacks on the
New York Jewish wing of the party, and
was an unabashed white supremacist (he
once warned, in supporting Chinese exclusion, that "this country is absolutely sure to
become a black-and-yellow country within a
few generations" unless strong action was
taken[19]). There is also good reason to believe that Berger, like his constituents, was
strongly pro-German in his antiwar sympathies, and his personal organ, the Milwaukee
Leader, was barred from the mails in September, 1917, for its outspoken opposition
to war measures. In February, 1918, Berger
was successively nominated by the United
States Attorney for incarceration in federal
prison for sedition and by the Wisconsin
Socialists for the United States Senate.
Even though under indictment, he polled
over 100,000 votes in the special April election, and as a consolation prize was elected
in November to the United States House of
Representatives. With one dissenting vote,
the House refused to seat him and called
for a special election to fill the vacancy.
Berger won this election too, and was again

16 Cited by Peterson and Fite, op. cit., p. 254.

17 Debs v. United States, 249 U.S. 211, 216
(1919).
18 Cited by Ginger, op. cit., p. 405.
19 Cited by Ira Kipnis, The American Socialist
Movement, 1877–1912 (New York, Columbia
University Press, 1952), pp. 287 ff.

refused his seat. He was finally defeated at the polls in November, 1920, though in 1922 he won the place again and this time was at last seated.

Meanwhile, back at the federal courthouse, after a trial which even by the standards of that time was judged extraordinary, Judge Kenesaw M. Landis sentenced Berger and four associates to twenty years' imprisonment. Landis we will meet again when he presides over the trial of the IWW. A judicial mountebank, he specialized in sensationalism (he once fined Standard Oil $10,000,000 in an antitrust case) and made a career out of combining the functions of judge and prosecutor. In disposing of Berger and other "Reds," he was in his element and never permitted the total lack of concrete evidence of criminal conspiracy against the Socialists to slow down the trial. Unfortunately, in this case (as in the Standard Oil decision mentioned above), his addiction for "people's justice" took Landis too far out of the bounds of procedural regularity. In 1921 the Supreme Court held that Landis by his bitter attacks on German-Americans before the trial began had revealed "prejudice" and should have granted the Socialist request for a change of venue to another court. By this time the judge had moved to a more appropriate setting for his talents—as "Czar of Baseball."

These were the trials granted to the *leaders* of the Socialist Party. The rank and file leadership received a brand of justice even more summary. "Our judges," wrote Zechariah Chafee, Jr., "condemned at least eleven persons to prison [under the Espionage Acts] for ten years, six for fifteen years, and twenty-four for twenty years," and he noted that this figure covered only reported cases (in an unreported decision in Sacramento, twenty-six were sentenced to ten years' imprisonment) and excludes the mass trial of the IWW leadership in Chicago.[20]

Moreover, this discussion of trials does not take into consideration the tremendous administrative harassment that radicals were subjected to in their efforts, for example, to keep their newspapers going. No one has ever done a careful study of the impact of censorship and the denial of mailing privileges on the radical press, but the attrition was fierce, and the death rate of publications, particularly among the foreign language weeklies, was very high. The New York *Call*, the Socialist Party's leading daily paper, lost its mailing privileges in November, 1917. It managed to stagger on with a makeshift distribution system until the privilege was restored in June, 1921, but few of the other journals under attack had either the resources, the dedication, or the geographically compact readership of the *Call*. The denial of mailing privileges by the Postmaster General, a decision made without trial of the charges or even a hearing by an official vested with great discretionary authority, was a deathblow to most radical papers. Postmaster General Burleson, for example, denied privileges to the *Call* because it was inciting the people to "arson, murder or assassination"—even though its editors were never indicted for this offense, or any other—and the Supreme Court sustained his decision as a legitimate and unreviewable exercise of discretion.[21]

If the authorities were unrestrained in their campaign against the Socialists, they went literally berserk in the wartime assault on the IWW. In the fall of 1917, United States officers raided the various headquarters of the IWW, and 166 alleged leaders of the organization were indicted for conspiring to obstruct the war effort. Subsequently 113 were brought to trial before Judge Landis in Chicago, and later two other mass trials were launched in Sacramento and Kansas City. Although the fiction was maintained that only individuals were on trial, Landis soon made it clear that it was the IWW in its collective capacity that was in the dock. Huge masses of irrele-

20 Zechariah Chafee, *Free Speech in America* (Cambridge, Harvard University Press, 1946), p. 79.

21 *Ibid.*, p. 305.

vant material, some of it going back a decade, were introduced into evidence even
though no connection existed between this
data and any individual on trial, and it bore
no relation to the war effort. The real
offense that called for legal retribution was
membership in the IWW, and the outcome
was a foregone conclusion. After 55 minutes of deliberation, the jury returned with
verdicts of guilty in ninety-six cases and
Landis took over sentencing. The top leaders uniformly got twenty years, thirty-three
received ten-year terms, and another thirty-
three were sent down for five; the remainder
got one year or less. In addition, the judge
fined the guilty an aggregate figure of $2,-
300,000! For some time to come it appeared
that the main locus of IWW activity would
be Leavenworth Prison.[22]

While these trials were under way, action of an even more direct sort was common throughout the country. Any suspected
of IWW sympathies were dealt with under
local, often lynch law. It became, for example, very risky to organize or participate
in IWW defense activities, to try to raise
funds to aid the defendants. While courageous civil libertarians such as John Dewey,
Carlton Hayes, Thorstein Veblen, and the
leaders of the embryonic American Civil
Liberties Union called for fair play, the
Department of Justice (according to the
ACLU) "arrested the active members of
I.W.W. defense committees at many points
in the country, stopped their meetings, and
seized their funds." The national defense
committee in Chicago discovered that its
appeals for aid were piling up in the post
office, undistributed. Everywhere fund-
raisers were given a standard treatment by
the American Protective League: they were

beaten up and/or arrested for sedition. A
recommendation was made in the United
States Senate that disloyal organizations be
forbidden to solicit funds through the mails.

Even this was child's-play by comparison
with the handling of IWW locals, and alleged members, in the Western states. Now,
cloaked in high patriotic garb, the enemies
of the IWW moved in for the kill; the consequence was a state of vigilante martial
law. Listen to the advice of the Tulsa
World, November 9, 1917:

If the I.W.W. . . . gets busy in your neighborhood, kindly take the occasion to decrease the
supply of hemp. A knowledge of how to tie a
knot that will stick might come in handy in a
few days. It is no time to dally with the
enemies of the country. . . . The first step in
the whipping of Germany is to strangle the
I.W.W.'s. Kill 'em just as you would any
other kind of snake. Don't scotch 'em; kill 'em!
And kill 'em dead! It is no time to waste
money on trials . . .[23]

The Sacramento Bee plugged the firing
squad as the cure for IWW "poison," and
The New York Times, while deploring the
hanging of IWW organizer Frank Little in
Butte, Montana, noted in partial exculpa-
tion that "I.W.W. agitators are in effect,
and perhaps in fact, agents of Germany."[24]

It would be fruitless to devote more
space to the "extermination" of the IWW
—a chronicle of brutality becomes dulling
after a while as one, in psychological self-
defense, takes refuge in disembodiment and
refuses to empathize with the victim of the
lash. However, there is one episode which
can be used to close this saga, one which
starkly delineates the degree to which wartime hysteria against the IWW was employed to destroy a legitimate labor organization: the Bisbee Deportation.

Bisbee, Globe, and Miami were small,
isolated communities in the Arizona desert
wholly dominated by copper mining. Labor
troubles had been endemic in the area, the
IWW had been active, and in the summer
of 1917 things came to a head when the

22 Robert K. Murray, Red Scare (Minneapolis, Uni-
versity of Minnesota Press, 1955), p. 30; also
Philip Taft, "The Federal Trials of the I.W.W.,"
Labor History, Vol. 3 (1962), pp. 57–91, passim.
Since this was written Donald Johnson's The
Challenge to American Freedoms: World War I
and the Rise of the American Civil Liberties
Union (University of Kentucky Press, 1963) has
appeared with some interesting material on the
early work of the A.C.L.U.

23 Cited by Peterson and Fite, op. cit., p. 173.
24 Ibid., pp. 55 and 60.

dominant union, affiliated with the American Federation of Labor, called a strike. The situation was complex. The IWW immediately jumped into the strike and attempted to take the leadership away from the AFL, the latter retaliated by denouncing the IWW organizers as stool pigeons and extremist provocateurs in the pay of the bosses, the federal government attempted to mediate, and antilabor groups began to denounce the whole enterprise as IWW–sponsored treason against the United States. Although there had been no violence, the Globe Loyalty League—"a militant body organized to fight the I.W.W. without compromise or quarter"—on July 6 issued a fire-eating manifesto:

. . . terrorism in this community must and shall cease; that all public assemblies of the I.W.W., as well as other meetings shall be suppressed; that we hold the I.W.W. to be a public enemy of the United States; that we absolutely oppose any mediation. . . .[25]

At this point, one of the mine operators, Walter Douglas of Bisbee, threw a match into the powder magazine: "You cannot compromise with a rattlesnake . . . that goes for the International Union [AFL] and the I.W.W. . . . I believe the government will be able to show that there is German influence behind this movement. . . . It is up to the individual communities to drive these agitators out."[26] (An Arizona judge had already suggested a more direct course: "I would like to go up there [to the picket line] and mow those sons of bitches down with a machine gun."[27]) On July 12, Sheriff Harry Wheeler of Cochise County and the Bisbee Loyalty League picked up the cue from Douglas: at dawn about 1200 men organized into posses, rounded up *all* local labor militants, 1186 in all, loaded them into boxcars and shipped them off to Columbus, New Mexico. Authorities in Columbus refused to accept the shipment, so it was taken back and dumped at a remote, virtually abandoned army post in the desert, and, in the words of President Wilson's Mediation Commission, the deportees were "left to shift for themselves" in a situation where they "were wholly without adequate supply of food and water."[28] After two days, the United States Army went to their rescue, and the refugees were established in a camp near Columbus. The *Bisbee Daily Review* chortled over the purge: "no longer does a blot remain on the escutcheon of Bisbee. 'Wobblyism' has passed into the labyrinth of things discarded."[29]

Although, as the President's Mediation Commission pointed out in its careful and detailed report, the action had been taken by the sheriff after consultation with the leading local mine operators, it had involved illegal censorship of outgoing telegrams and telephone messages, and its instigators had grossly violated the constitutional rights of the deportees, those responsible justified their act by invoking the doctrine of anticipatory retaliation ("we had to defend ourselves from certain attack") and escaped punishment.[30] Needless to add, the deportation, in which there had been no attempt to discriminate between IWW and AFL militants, destroyed the trade-union movement in Bisbee: the Loyalty League set up its own union, the Workingmen's Protective League, and refused to permit bona fide trade unionists even to enter the town.

The events which we have been describing all occurred while the United States was actively participating in the First World War. This is no justification, but it does provide some insight into motives when one realizes that decent people in wartime often become consumed with patriotic fervor and lose their perspective. Sheriff Wheeler of Cochise County, for example, had been known as a fair, prolabor man before the war; among the miners it was said that "if

---

25 Cited by Vernon II. Jensen, *Heritage of Conflict* (Ithaca, Cornell University Press, 1950), p. 396.
26 *Ibid.*, p. 397.
27 *Ibid.*, p. 394 f.
28 President's Mediation Commission, *Report on Bisbee Deportation* (Washington, D.C., 1918), *passim*.
29 Cited by Jensen, *op. cit.*, p. 406.
30 *Ibid.*

you were opposed to Wheeler you got a beating before you got home"[31] (a remark which in itself provides a sharp *aperçu* into frontier democracy). With the Armistice in November, 1918, and the subsequent surrender of the Central Powers, one might assume that the frenzy would have abated, that a return to sanity would have left the American people, like the victim of a hangover, with a feeling of sheepish guilt. Yet, for reasons which have never been adequately probed, the opposite was the case. The antiradical sentiments of the wartime years became, if anything, more intense after the Armistice and reached a somber climax of indignity in the Palmer Raids of 1919 and 1920.

The background of the Great Red Scare was provided by a number of objective historical factors—the Bolshevik Revolution and formation of the Comintern; a wave of vicious bombings or attempts at assassination of public officials attributed to the "Reds"; a tremendous surge of strikes as labor abandoned the restraints of wartime and attempted to have wages catch up with prices; demobilization and accompanying uncertainty (and, as John Dos Passos superbly limned in *1919*, which should be required reading for historians of the period, *boredom* with Victorian America); the constitutional absurdity of the Eighteenth Amendment, the Maginot Line of moribund Puritanism; a depression in which everything dropped but prices (in 1919, 2.3 percent of the work force was unemployed; by 1921, this had leaped to 11.9 percent); a reunited Republican Party savagely mauling President Wilson (who collapsed under the strain) and employing the motif of disillusionment with the war to castigate the whole reform tradition. These are the main threads the historian can trace, but there was a deeper social basis for the madness of the immediate postwar years: a generalized but largely unarticulated recognition that the country and the world had been transformed, and an equally widespread inability

31 *Ibid.*, p. 404.

to comprehend the premises of the new, emerging social order. It was, in the phrase of the time, "a cockeyed world," but only the Dadaists and a few other artists of extraordinary cultural sensitivity faced up to the fact and tried to adjust their standards to the reality.

Most Americans simply got frightened and looked for the villains, the daemonic agents of insecurity who had destroyed the nice, comfortable world of 1914. Some rushed to eliminate strong drink, others saw jazz, or modernistic theology, or Darwinian biology, or the League of Nations as the enemy. But the simplest answer, one which fitted neatly into a long tradition of nativism, was to blame foreign influence, and specifically the impending conquest of America by foreign radicals. This attack, of course, meshed beautifully with the antiradical campaign of the war years, but was potentially far more inclusive. American Jews, for example, who had distinguished themselves in supporting the war effort, could be netted by the equation of Jews and Bolshevism; the American Federation of Labor could be lambasted along with the IWW as a radical, foreign conspiracy against the freedom of the American workingman. (The preamble to the AFL Constitution announced that "a struggle is going on in the nations of the civilized world between the oppressors and the oppressed of all countries, a struggle between capital and labor, which must grow in intensity from year to year and work disastrous results to the toiling millions of all nations. . . ." and Gompers was a British-born Jew.)

Unquestionably some who employed this slippery logic did so quite cynically—it provided them with a splendid demagogic basis for destroying their opposition and, say, instituting the "American Plan" (the "open shop") in their factories. However, the evidence suggests that an overwhelming percentage of those who seized upon this amalgam theory were quite sincere, even desperately sincere, people striking out blindly at the seeming protagonists of a novel and terrifying *Zeitgeist*. Essentially the fundamental ideals of the Democratic Dream were repudiated in the name of preserving the American status quo ante 1914. One set of institutions and folkways was fossilized as the "American Way," and spokesmen for change (as well as innocent symbols of change such as the Southern Negroes, who, migrating North during the war years, were greeted with fierce hostility by their new neighbors . . .) were castigated as traitors. This is a not uncommon historical phenomenon—Oswald Garrison Villard once observed at a Republican Lincoln Day dinner that an American conservative was one who worshipped a dead radical, and each generation attempts to impose its standards on its children, even its pattern of revolt. What made the 1918–1921 period distinctive was that this conflict between generations was both uniquely multidimensional and conducted in the atmosphere of lynch law which had encased wartime patriotism.

Three episodes must suffice to buttress the proposition that the American Dream had degenerated into a wild, flailing effort to restore the *ancien régime*: the Abrams Case, the refusal to seat the Socialists in the New York legislature, and the Palmer Raids. The first illustrates the theory of amalgam in judicial operation; the second, the repudiation of the key technique of the democratic political process, the will of the electorate; and, the third, the employment by the national government of authentic police state procedures against alleged subversives. In addition, it should be recalled that the actions of national, state, and local authorities against Socialists and Wobblies, described above, did not stop at the Armistice: the Kansas City trial of IWW activists did not get under way until December 1, 1919.

In August, 1918, Jacob Abrams and six anarchist-Socialist associates were arrested for sedition. The indictment charged that by distributing some leaflets on the lower East Side of New York, they had threatened to impede the war effort. The throwaways, written in English and Yiddish, were a bitter denunciation of President Wilson's decision to intervene against the Bolsheviks in the Murmansk area and called for a general strike to prevent shipment of munitions to the anti-Soviet forces. The leaflet in English contained a postscript: "P.S. It is absurd to call us pro-German. We hate and despise German militarism more than do your hypocritical tyrants. We have more reasons for denouncing German militarism than has the coward in the White House."[32]

It could, perhaps, have been put more courteously, but one may doubt whether the best political manners would have made much difference. The Abrams circle was brought to trial in October—before a federal judge borrowed from Alabama who patently looked on the defendants as exhibits in a museum of un-American horrors—and despite their assertion that nothing they had said could be construed as favoring a disruption of the war *with Germany*, three were sentenced to twenty years' imprisonment, one to fifteen, and one to three. In delivering sentence, Judge Clayton performed the mystic act of amalgamation:

. . . we are not going to help carry out the plans mapped out by the Imperial German Government, and which are being carried out by Lenine [sic] and Trotsky. I have heard of the reported fate of the poor little daughters of the Czar, but I won't talk about that now. I might get mad.[33]

One may speculate on what sentences Clayton would have given if he had gotten "mad"; twenty years was the maximum. As Chafee pointed out in his masterful analysis of this episode, "If they had actually conspired to tie up every munition plant in the country, and succeeded, the punishment could not have been more."[34]

We may leave the Abrams litigation here. The Supreme Court, only Holmes and Brandeis dissenting, confirmed the convic-

[32] Cited by Chafee, *op. cit.*, p. 110.
[33] *Ibid.*, p. 128.
[34] *Ibid.*

tion in 1919;[35] In 1921, the sentences were commuted on condition that the radicals go to Russia. Note the proposition that has emerged: a radical in New York who supported the Bolsheviks was not only un-American, but pro-German. Only one ingredient was missing on the overt level, though it was implicit in the Abrams case: the pro-Bolshevik radical was also a Jew. The possibilities of this racist slogan were not lost on the nativists—who pushed vigorously the thesis of pro-German Jewish Bolshevism. Nor was it taken lightly by American Jewish defense organizations. In the spring of 1920, the Anti-Defamation League sent to the editors of five hundred leading newspapers a series of articles by Isaac Don Levine, former Chicago *Daily News* correspondent in Russia, highlighting the opposition of Russian Jews to Bolshevism. The letter of transmittal noted that Levine's writings contained "a conclusive answer to the many libelous stories recently appearing in the press of this country which . . . charge Jews with responsibility for Bolshevism in Russia and for social and economic unrest in other countries . . ."[36]

It is interesting to note the key role of New York, both state and city, in the events of the Great Red Scare. The enormous polyglot metropolis, full of aliens, Jews, Catholics, atheists, "wets," Bohemians, Bolsheviks, anarchists, DeLeonists, and God knows what else, symbolized in itself the antithesis of the *ancien régime*. It was in New York that a frightful bomb exploded on Wall Street, killing thirty-eight and injuring hundreds; it was in the New York Post Office that sixteen dynamite bombs, each disguised as "Sample—Novelty" from Gimbels, were discovered bearing the addresses of, *inter alios*, Justice Holmes, Judge Landis, Attorney General Palmer, Postmaster General Burleson, and J. P. Morgan; it was New York's distinction to serve as the

locale for the most massive of the Palmer Raids and for the first of the three-ring circuses that resulted when state legislatures established committees to investigate "Revolutionary Radicalism"—the Lusk Committee of 1919–1920.

New York State achieved additional notoriety in 1920 when the State Assembly expelled five Socialist members on the ground that they had "been elected on a platform that is absolutely inimical to the best interests of the State of New York and of the United States." President Wilson made no comment. Indeed, in one sense the expulsion could have been considered as a response to his Congressional message of December 2, 1919, demanding stronger action against Reds.[37] To his eternal credit, Charles Evans Hughes, former Governor of New York, Justice of the Supreme Court, and Republican candidate for President, immediately and in hard, cold phrases which could not be misunderstood castigated the Assembly's action:

If there was anything against these men as individuals, if they were deemed to be guilty of criminal offenses, they should have been charged accordingly. But I understand that the action is not directed against these five elected members as individuals but that the proceeding is virtually an attempt to indict a political party and to deny it representation in the Legislature. This is not, in my judgment, American government.[38]

And Alfred Emanuel Smith, that tragic hero of the winter war for American ideals, whose nobility and courage in the hard campaigns of the twenties has been obscured by his later bitterness at Roosevelt, echoed Hughes's condemnation. "It is inconceivable," said the Governor, "that a minority party, duly constituted and legally organized, should be deprived of its right to expression so long as it has honestly, by lawful methods of education and propaganda, suc-

---

[35] *Abrams v. United States*, 250 U.S. 616 (1919).

[36] From Files of the Anti-Defamation League, Letter from Leon L. Lewis, Executive Secretary of the Anti-Defamation League, April 17, 1920.

[37] Congressional Record, *Proceedings and Debates of the Second Session of the Sixty-Sixth Congress* (Washington, D.C., 1920), Vol. 59, Part I, p. 30.

[38] Cited by Chafee, *op. cit.*, p. 273.

ceeded in securing representation, unless the chosen representatives are unfit as individuals."[39] Smith had enough experience with the rurally dominated legislature to know that the bucolic solons were not just attacking "Reds"; their real target was *The City*, the new Babylon.

The Assembly was unmoved. It conducted a farcical investigation, refused to permit Hughes to testify, denounced the iniquities of Socialism, and then in effect disfranchised 60,000 New York City voters by confirming the expulsion. For good measure, it passed a series of repressive acts against "revolutionary radicals," one of which would have barred the Socialist Party from the ballot entirely, and adjourned in an atmosphere of patriotic euphoria—it had been "a victory for undivided Americanism" the Speaker announced.[40] Governor Smith caustically vetoed all the antiradical statutes, asserting in essence that "Americanism" should be defined as a dedication to certain ideals and that the measures passed by the legislature were consequently a greater threat to the cause of American freedom than the alleged subversion of the "revolutionary radicals." Nonetheless, the deed was done. In the name of protecting the state from unproved subversion, the majority of the State Assembly had expelled duly elected opponents from the chamber. The next logical step was to drive them from the political community entirely— which brings us to the Palmer Raids, the "Red Ark," and the deportations of 1920.

In an ironic passage of *The People, Yes*, Carl Sandburg wrote of the Irish cop in Denver who was heard withering a Pawnee Indian Wobbly with the observation, "If you don't like it here, go back where you come from!"[41] It was not, however, until the Bolshevik Revolution (with perhaps a brief exception during the frenzied anti-

French politics of 1789–1800)[42] that the notion got abroad that radicals, whatever their degree of disaffection with the United States, bore allegiance to a foreign power. . . . the United States had before the turn of the century taken a very free and easy legal approach to aliens. There were few restraints or disabilities arising from alienage, and in some states those who had taken out first papers were given the right to vote.[43] In the early years of this century, the laws governing aliens were tightened up and expanded in coverage at the same time, and as another facet of the systemization of immigration procedures. Most of the restrictions were designed to prevent the United States, in the phrase of the time, from becoming a "dumping ground" for convicts, paupers, and diseased foreigners. But after the assassination of President McKinley, provisions were enacted to bar anarchists or "criminal syndicalists" from entry, and to facilitate their deportation if apprehended on American soil.[44]

During the war, this statute was further expanded to authorize the deportation of a wide range of radicals, but the crucial point was the method of procedure against an allegedly deportable alien: he had absolutely no constitutional protection. There was (and still is) no trial at law of the charges, no jury, no appellate recourse against an administrative determination of guilt: "the decision of the Secretary of Labor shall be final."[45] In other words, the Secretary of Labor (who has been superseded in this function by the Attorney General since 1940), and in fact his subordinates, who handled the day-to-day work of the Immigration Bureau, were given the authority to exile human beings from the United States on the basis of decisions made

[39] Mark Sullivan, *Our Times* (New York, Scribner, 1936), Vol. 6, p. 172.
[40] Cited by Chafee, *op. cit.*, p. 280.
[41] Carl Sandburg, *The People, Yes* (New York, Harcourt, Brace, 1936), p. 58.
[42] See James M. Smith, *Freedom's Fetters: The Alien and Sedition Laws and American Civil Liberties* (Ithaca, 1956), *passim*.
[43] See Leon E. Aylesworth, "The Passing of Alien Suffrage," *American Political Science Review*, Vol. 25 (1931), pp. 114 ff.
[44] Chafee, *op. cit.*, pp. 197 f.
[45] *Ibid.*, p. 179.

by themselves, decisions which were subject to no significant external check. Perhaps on occasion a determined federal judge (Judge George Anderson of Massachusetts was a notable example)[46] could intrude on this plenary exercise of power by determined procedural attrition, by holding, for instance, that the immigration officers had not lived up to *their own rules* in denying an alien a "fair hearing." But in general the government was unhindered by the Constitution or the courts in its purgative endeavors. What Assistant Secretary of Labor Louis Post, who saw the operations from the inside, called the *Deportations Delirium of Nineteen-Twenty* was conducted in utter disregard of traditional concepts of justice.

As a footnote to the handling of "subversive" aliens, it should be mentioned that undesirable naturalized citizens could also be disposed of in this handy fashion if they were first denaturalized. The classic instance of this procedure concerned Emma Goldman, the matriarch of American anarchists, who was deprived of her citizenship and deported to Russia in 1919. The ground for denaturalization was that she had received her American nationality on marriage to a man later denaturalized for fraud, and it seems clear that Jacob Kersner, her former husband, was deprived of his citizenship just to make it possible for the government to "get" Red Emma. Emma was shipped off in December, 1919, on the "Red Ark"—the army transport *Buford*—as part of a cargo of 249 subversives bound for Soviet soil. *The New York Times* gleefully bid good riddance to this "pernicious soldier of disorder."[47]

The story of the Palmer Raids and deportations can be briefly told. In the summer and fall of 1919, against a background of labor unrest and bomb threats, the clamor increased for decisive government action against radical aliens (Senator Kenneth McKellar had earlier suggested that the United States establish a penal colony on Guam for native-born subversives). The Senate on October 19 unanimously passed a resolution demanding that the Attorney General get about the business at once, and Palmer—whose Washington home had recently been blasted by a bomb—took the hint, got himself a sizable appropriation, set up an antiradical unit in the Department of Justice, and the wheels of injustice began to turn. On November 7, 1919, the offices of the Union of Russian Workers, an anarchist-Communist group, were raided and 250 members of the organization arrested. Local authorities, notably in New York, took a hand in the game and conducted their own raids and arrests: over 500 alleged alien subversives were held in New York City alone.

The Congress and the newspapers expressed their gratitude to the Attorney General for saving the country from a "gigantic plot." Palmer overnight became a national hero, and it has been suggested that he reached the conclusion at this point that antiradical notoriety could be his ticket to the White House. With this Presidential bee buzzing in his bonnet, Palmer then set out to organize a *real* dragnet. On December 27, 1919, the Acting Secretary of Labor signed more than three thousand arrest warrants and turned them over to Palmer, and on January 2, 1920, almost five thousand suspected alien members of the Communist Labor Party and the Communist Party (the two factions which had emerged when the pro-Bolsheviks split from the Socialist Party in 1919) were arrested. The raids occurred simultaneously in thirty-three cities—those seized were held in deplorable, makeshift prisons, denied the right to communicate with their families, and often treated brutally. Many understood little English. In Lynn, Massachusetts, thirty-nine Yiddish-speaking bakers were arrested as they gathered in revolutionary strength

[46] See his opinion in *Colyer* v. *Skeffington*, 265 Fed. 17 (D. Mass. 1920).
[47] Richard Drinnon, *Rebel in Paradise: A Biography of Emma Goldman* (Chicago, University of Chicago Press, 1961), p. 223.

on the night of January 2—no one present was able to communicate to the police that they were engaged in organizing a bakery.

Palmer reached his zenith in early 1920, and then, at first imperceptibly, the Red Scare began to lose its potency and degenerated into anticlimax. Most Americans were tired of the whole business of living in crisis and only asked for a chance to change the subject. Senator Warren G. Harding undertook to lift the burden, and with a sigh of nostalgic relief the electorate voted for "normalcy." Most of those arrested by Palmer were eventually released (less than a thousand were actually deported), and as the Republicans took over the government it became apparent that the frame of political reference had been fundamentally altered. For radicals the season of active terror was over. But this was not a consequence of the new administration's dedication to the ideals of liberty. Rather, it was a function of the dominant Republican view that all ideas were un-American. Wilson kept Debs in jail because, in his perverse way, the President respected the force of ideas. Harding freed the old Socialist because he viewed him as a harmless nut. The American Dream, with all other dreams, had become irrelevant.

CONSCIENTIOUS OBJECTORS AS LAW VIOLATORS*

Mulford Q. Sibley and Philip E. Jacob

More than 6000 persons in the United States were prosecuted for conscientious objection during World War II. Discussed in this selection are the various forms of violation of the Selective Training and Service Act of 1940 which pertained to the conscientious objector. The selection also covers the trial and sentencing of conscientious objectors.

Many of those who supported the conscientious-objector section of the Selective Training and Service Act of 1940 hoped that the seemingly liberal provisions for conscience would minimize the necessity for prosecution of objectors. This, however, was not to be. Both because of the provisions of the act itself and because of the nature of its administration and interpretation, relatively large numbers of individuals claiming to be objectors began to be prosecuted after the law had been in effect only two years. Actually, about nine times as many objectors were sent to prison during the Second World War as were incarcerated during the First World War; even in proportion to the total numbers conscripted, there were between two and three times as many. The prosecution, trials, and sentencing of conscientious objectors provide an important chapter in the whole study of the subject. How objectors clashed with the law and why they did so casts a significant light not only on the objectors but also on the agencies of the law which were called upon to deal with them.

* Reprinted from Mulford Q. Sibley and Philip E. Jacob, *Conscription of Conscience*, Chapter 15. Copyright 1952 by Cornell University. Used by permission of Cornell University Press and the authors.

THE LEGAL OFFENSES

According to the Department of Justice, there were 5516 prosecutions of persons claiming to be conscientious objectors down to a month before the conclusion of hostilities with Japan. Table 1 indicates the of-

than one person out of every three prosecuted under the Act was, therefore, a conscientious objector. It is possible that the percentage was even higher, as many of those not classified by the Department of Justice as "objectors" could probably have been placed in that category without strain-

Table 1.

PROSECUTIONS OF CONSCIENTIOUS OBJECTORS*

	OCT. 16, 1940 TO JUNE 30, 1942	JULY 1, 1942 TO JUNE 30, 1943	JULY 1, 1943 TO JUNE 30, 1944	JULY 1, 1944 TO JUNE 30, 1945	TOTAL
Failure to register	112	133	13	8	266
Failure to return questionnaire	26	14	9	1	49
Failure to report for preliminary physical examination	18	32	19	1	70
Failure to report for induction	128	916	1,551	735	3,331
Failure to report to C.O. camp	99	519	618	303	1,539
Failure to comply with C.O. assignment—walkouts, refusals to work, etc.	1	49	79	104	233
Counseling and aiding evasion	2	22	3	1	28
Total	386	1,685	2,292	1,153	5,516

* Adapted from figures of the Department of Justice. See *The Reporter*, Nov. 1, 1945, p. 3.

fenses charged and the total number of prosecutions for the years 1940 to June 30, 1945. Individuals claiming objection continued to be prosecuted until well into 1947, when the Selective Training and Service Act expired (on March 31). All together, more than 6000 objectors, including the Jehovah's Witnesses, were prosecuted down to the expiration of the Act.[1] This represents 37.5 per cent of the total of approximately 16,000 persons prosecuted for violations of the Selective Training and Service Act.[2] More

ing the term too much, for the line between conscientious objector and "draft evader" was often a fine one. Sometimes the so-called evader had genuine objections but was not articulate about them.

THE EXPLANATION FOR LAW VIOLATIONS

The Nonregistrants. There is, of course, but little difficulty in explaining the nonregistrants. For the great bulk of them, their refusal to register under the law was deliberate and not the result of misinformation or of any obviously low intelligence (as might have been true of some nonregistrants who were not conscientious objectors). It is true

[1] *A Program for National Security: Report of the President's Advisory Commission on Universal Training* (Washington, 1947), 256–257. Total prosecutions down to Nov. 1, 1945, were 5652. *The Reporter*, Nov. 1, 1945.
[2] *A Program for National Security*, pp. 256–257.

that it is a bit surprising to find that the largest religious group of nonregistrants was composed of the Negro Moslems. But the Moslems themselves (more than 100 out of the 300 nonregistrants) seemed to have had no doubt about their duty not to comply with the law. They could fight only in a holy war called in the name of Islam, and even the act of registration would constitute a violation of Allah's will.

As for the remaining nonregistrants, they had dramatized their case for nonregistration from the very beginning of the Selective Training and Service Act. As early as October 16, 1940, the first registration day, 8 students at Union Theological Seminary had publicly announced their refusal to register and were later sentenced to prison. The 8 were followed by others, the greatest incidence of conscientious nonregistration occurring in the year July 1, 1942, to July 1, 1943, when 133 objectors (including Negro Moslems) announced their intention of refusing to comply even with the first requirements of the Act. On the other hand, the number of conscientious nonregistrants during the last year of hostilities was only 8.[3]

Nonregistrants usually made some public announcement of their action, often by means of a letter to the federal district attorney or to the local Selective Service Board. This, it was felt, would differentiate them from mere "draft evaders." Conscientious nonregistration was primarily an open protest not only against war but also against the principle of conscription.

The number of prosecutions for nonregistration would have been larger had the Department of Justice chosen to prosecute those men above forty-five who refused to register—about twenty of this group took the nonregistrant position, including A. J. Muste, Evan Thomas, Richard Gregg (author of the pacifist classic, The Power of Non-Violence), Julius Eichel, Walter Longstreth (well-known Philadelphia attorney), and others.[4] But the Department

took the position that since persons in this age group were above the age of service it would regard their letters informing the Department of their attitude as adequate for registration purposes. One exception alone was made: Julius Eichel was prosecuted, for some curious reason.

It should be emphasized that nonregistrants in this older group did not request favored treatment. Indeed, several of them expected to go to jail along with their younger fellow pacifists. And many argued that it was unfair to send younger nonregistrants to jail for a deliberate breach in the law while allowing the older men, who had committed precisely the same offense, to go free. The Department of Justice, nevertheless, had spoken.

The Denial of IV-D. The denial of classification IV-D to Jehovah's Witnesses was the explanation for the great bulk of failures to report to the Army or to Civilian Public Service. As has been shown before, many local boards refused to consider Jehovah's Witnesses for either IV-D (ministerial exemption) or IV-E (conscientious objector to both combatant and noncombatant military service) classification. In such cases the devout Witness could only refuse to report to the Army and thus subject himself to civil prosecution. On the other hand, most Witnesses were equally opposed to Civilian Public Service; when local boards were willing to give IV-E classifications to them, they declined to report to Civilian Public Service camps. All together, about 75 per cent of all conscientious objectors prosecuted during the war were Jehovah's Witnesses, and in the overwhelming majority of these cases the technical offense charged was failure to report to the Army or to Civilian Public Service, as ordered.

The Denial of IV-E. Next to the denial of IV-D, the refusal of the Selective Service System to classify the objector, as requested,

3 See The Reporter, Nov. 1, 1945.
4 See R. Alfred Hassler, Conscripts of Conscience, the Story of Sixteen Objectors to Conscription (New York, 1942).

in IV-E constituted the most important explanation for clashes with the law. An objector would be denied IV-E by his local board; he would go through the hierarchy of appeals and the decision of the local board would be sustained. That exhausted his administrative remedies. He had now to decide whether to surrender his conscientious objection to service in the Army or subject himself to prosecution. The Department of Justice, on the other hand, was obliged to prosecute those who failed to obey the orders of the Selective Service System. Occasionally, confronted by prosecution, the objector would agree belatedly to obey the orders of the local board, in which event the Justice Department would drop its proceedings. Such examples, however, were rare. It was usual, as in the case of nonregistrants, for the defaulter to give notice to the local board and to the federal district attorney of his intention to ignore the summons to report to the Army. Again, as in the case of nonregistrants, the objector was trying to differentiate himself from those who evaded Army service for "unconscientious" reasons; again, the dividing line between a "conscientious" and an "unconscientious" objector was at certain points rather hard to discern.

Objection to Alternative Civilian Service. Some objectors received the classifications they requested but refused at various points to comply with other requirements of the law. Thus they might receive a tentative classification of IV-E and refuse to report for physical examinations. That, of course, violated the law, as they were well aware. Their explanation was that they wished to take this means to protest conscription or, in some cases, the type of alternative civilian service set up under the Act. Similarly, others might obey the law up to the point where they were required to report to Civilian Public Service and at that point announce their disobedience. Sometimes the point of "absolutism" would be at the stage of returning the questionnaire. But what-

ever the point and however the precise explanation was stated, prosecution would follow.

Walkouts and Refusals to Work. As restrictions in Civilian Public Service increased during the course of the war and dissatisfaction with the structure and administration of alternative service became more widespread, many of those who had received IV-E classifications and had actually worked in the system became restive and sought to give expression to their profound dissatisfaction by act as well as word. Some of them carried on "slowdowns" in Civilian Public Service or refused to perform their assigned tasks. Sometimes slowdowns and refusals to work led to prosecution. In other cases, objectors walked out of Civilian Public Service camps to evidence their opposition or disgust. After 1942, slowdowns, refusals to work, and walkouts constituted a gradually increasing proportion of all those objectors prosecuted. Thus in 1942–1943, 2.9 per cent of all the objectors prosecuted were in the category "walk-outs," refusals to work, and slowdowns; in 1943–1944, 3.4 per cent; and in 1944–1945, 9 per cent.

With the end of the war, or at least of the large-scale fighting, dissatisfaction in C.P.S. camps mounted, and it became more and more difficult for Selective Service to justify its continued detention of men. The protest against unpaid labor grew until it became a reverberating and defiant roar. Larger and larger numbers of the obstreperous were transferred to Selective Service's camp at Minersville, California, which became something of a punitive detention barracks.

Slowdowns, refusals to work, and walkouts, particularly in government camps, were accentuated. Would the Department of Justice prosecute vigorously in cases of this kind or would it be lenient? The question took on an added importance in view of the well-known feeling in Selective Service that the Department had been too lenient throughout the war in prosecuting c.o.'s.

The problem was best illustrated, perhaps, in the long drawn-out case of the Glendora government C.P.S. camp strikers. On May 17, 1946, six assignees at Glendora were arrested. Two of them were charged with refusal to transfer to another camp when ordered to do so by Selective Service, and four were accused of refusal to carry out assigned duties. Placed in the county jail originally, they were released on bail and their trial was expected to take place in June, 1946—nearly one year after the conclusion of hostilities.[5] A picket line of 30 other strikers, together with wives and children of the men and ministers of the gospel, kept incessant vigil at the jail before they were released pending trial.

But when the June date for trial arrived, the hearing was postponed. By this time a total of 47 men at the Glendora camp had been arrested and were awaiting trial. Since almost all the other men in the camp were also striking, the government was confronted with what was virtually a mass refusal to work. The American Civil Liberties Union had taken up the cause of the strikers, both those who had been arrested and those who had not yet been formally charged with an offense.

Another month passed by and the protests at Glendora had increased. The general work strike had now lasted one hundred days. The few assignees still working at the camp had been transferred to a side camp. Although the strikers continued to refuse to perform their assigned duties and constantly iterated their protests at lack of pay, boondoggling nature of the work, discrimination in discharges, and other grievances, they were busily engaged in packaging food for European relief. Meanwhile, the trial date for the men who had refused to transfer had been pushed forward to September 17,

1946. A motion for dismissal of the remaining cases was to be heard August 5.

But the September 17 trial date, too, was postponed, while the demand for dismissal of the cases increased in volume. All over the country, groups of objectors and nonobjectors alike were asking that the prosecutions stop. A new trial date was now fixed for October 7, and the defendants had increased to 62. A number of the strikers were attending polio patients at a Los Angeles hospital while their cases were pending in the courts. The Department of Justice and the Selective Service System had in the meantime tried to induce the men to return to work, promising them early discharge if they would do so. The overwhelming majority of the men refused to consider this offer. A Glendora Strikers' Defense Committee was organized and preparations were made for a long legal battle. By September 1, the Glendora legal struggle had won even more attention and sympathy throughout the nation.

It was obvious that by now the Department of Justice was in a quandary. If it pushed the prosecution of the men and insisted on stiff penalties, it would incur the hostility of civil-liberties organizations and many churches. If, on the other hand, it failed to push the case with vigor, it might appear to be encouraging wholesale disregard of the Selective Service Act, which, after all, was still on the statute books. The Department chose to temporize. It had the trial postponed again—this time to March 11, 1947. The number of those under indictment had now been slightly reduced, to 58.

In the meantime, the date for expiration of the Selective Service Act, March 31, was approaching. The Department of Justice now recommended that charges against 36 of the 58 men be dropped. Charges remained against only the 22 supposed "ringleaders." The 36 men who were released protested vigorously, arguing that either all or none of the cases should be dismissed. The Department of Justice, however, re-

5 *The Reporter*, May 31, 1946. Also see *The Reporter* of June 21, 1946; August 2, 1946; September 1, 1946; February 1947; and April 1947.

fused to countenance such a move, but insisted on bringing only the 22 to trial—this time on the postponed date of March 24 (one week before the expiration of the Selective Training and Service Act).

On March 24, then, came the anticlimax. The 2 men who were considered ringleaders by the Department of Justice (Behre and Atherton) were sentenced to two years and were immediately placed on probation. Their parents were to be their probation custodians! A few days later, just before the Act expired, the remaining 20 men were sentenced to ten months for "failure to work according to regulation" and to one month each for "failure to report for roll call on a specific day." All the sentences were suspended and two years' probation was decreed.

The Glendora case had dragged out for nearly a year, and the mighty machinery of prosecution, which had originally planned a mass trial and conviction, ended rather lamely by placing the leaders of the strike in the hands of their parents. The protests of the Strikers' Committee had undoubtedly proven effective when considered in connection with the fact that the general postwar reaction against the war was now in full swing and that the Department of Justice itself had no real enthusiasm for its task.

Counseling and Aiding Evasion. One of the most interesting phenomena with respect to prosecutions was that there were only twenty-eight cases of "counseling and aiding evasion" down to the end of hostilities. This may indicate any number of things, but it surely demonstrates again that there was relatively little "political" opposition to the war. It may also show that the Department of Justice was somewhat careful about charging persons with this offense. Certainly there was no tendency, such as that noticeable in the First World War, to bring charges against every person who might give out public utterances against the war. But on the other hand there were in World War II very few public utterances to

prosecute. There was no prosecution during the Second World War comparable to the Debs case during the first conflict.

THE TRIALS OF OBJECTORS

The offenses of conscientious objectors, being violations of national law, were tried in the several federal district courts. The objector, after arrest (and it was usually not difficult to find him, since he made it a point to inform the district attorney of his whereabouts), would often be lodged in jail for a time and then be released on bail. Bail ranged in amount from $250 to (in one case) $25,000. Most common bail bonds were $1000 to $2000. And some objectors were released on their own recognizance, without bail.

On the day appointed for trial the accused objector would appear with his attorney in the district court. Often a considerable number of friends would accompany him, and in many instances special representatives of defense organizations for conscientious objectors were present. Ministers and sometimes representatives of such organizations as the American Friends Service Committee would give moral support to the objector in court. Girl friends and wives not infrequently were present. And the tenseness of the hearing was in a few cases accentuated by the quiet weeping of sympathizers, as, for example, when the original eight Union Theological nonregistrants were sentenced.

Once in court, the objector could plead "guilty," "not guilty," or "*nolo contendere.*" If he pleaded guilty, he would be sentenced by the judge immediately, although the judge often allowed time for a statement by the objector, his attorney, and the United States district attorney. If the plea were "not guilty" (and in most cases it was not), there would be a trial, either by the judge or by a jury. Most trials of objectors were not jury trials. Many objectors preferred the plea of "*nolo contendere,*" which meant that the charge, while not being contested, was not being admitted with any sense of "guilt." In such an event, the district judge would usually afford ample opportunity for comment by all the parties involved.

It is obvious in going through court records that many judges were puzzled by the problem of conscientious objectors. On the one hand, the judges were under an obligation to apply the law of the land to the particular instance; on the other, the offender, in demeanor and attitude, quite frequently reminded one of George Fox, William Penn, or another of the seventeenth-century Quakers. In at least one instance the judge himself was a member of the Society of Friends; this particular magistrate, Judge George Welsh of Philadelphia, frequently gave expression to the problem which he, a Friend, confronted in sentencing young Friends who claimed to be acting in response to the voice of conscience.

The case of Frederick H. Richards will serve to illustrate one type of objector and the attitude of one kind of judge. Richards was a nonregistrant who had voluntarily returned from Mexico (where he had been working on an American Friends Service Committee reconstruction project) in 1941 to announce his refusal to register. His case came up before the district court on November 26, 1941. He was allowed to make a statement giving his reasons for refusing to register. He said:

I stand before you today, your Honor, for two reasons. The first is conscription. The second is war. . . .

If our draft law contained a clause exempting men who, like myself, cannot conscientiously accept any compulsory service demanded by the State, I would be glad to volunteer for dangerous constructive service for my fellow men. . . . But to perform such service as a slave, under compulsion, and as a conscript, is contrary to both Quaker and American principles. Conscription is the denial of the personal responsibility of a man to live up to the right as he sees it. . . .

As a Quaker, I cannot but oppose this war. I do not believe that the butchery of another

twenty or thirty million people will further the Christian religion. . . .[6]

After the Richards statement, there was a cross-examination by the district attorney:

Q. Just one question, Mr. Richards. Would you take up arms to defend this country in the event of actual military invasion?
A. No sir.
The Court: Doesn't a religion that teaches love of your country require obedience to constituted authority? Don't you embrace obedience to constituted authority as one of the requisites of love of country?
A. I do until it conflicts with my conscience.
The Court: Then you put your conscience above love of country, wouldn't that follow logically?
A. Yes, it would.

The Richards hearing concluded with the following interchange:

Counsel for Richards. Fred's deliberate and voluntary return to the United States from Mexico, when he did not have to do so, for the specific purpose of making a maximum protest against what he considers the greatest of all evils, war and conscription, called to mind the story of the journey and protest of another man in history.

In the year A.D. 404, the custom was to hold gladiatorial fights for public amusement in Rome—A Christian monk, Telemachus, reached the conviction that it was his duty to make an open protest. Leaving Syria, he made the journey all the way to Rome for the specific purpose of protesting against the gladiatorial fights. In the midst of such a fight he ran into the arena, calling upon the Emperor to stop the cruel performance. When his purpose was realized, he was stoned to death before the watching multitude. Losing his life, Telemachus apparently failed to accomplish his purpose. In reality, however, his vicarious sacrifice succeeded, for that gladiatorial fight was the last one ever held in Rome. . . .

District Attorney. If your Honor pleases, there cannot possibly be any comparison between the gladiatorial story and the case before the court today. No one is trying to force that man from becoming a gladiator.

However, what I do not like most about this defendant is that which he apparently brags

[6] *Federal Convicts Numbers 1128 and 1129; College to Prison* (Philadelphia, 1942).

about, and has repeated several times on the stand, that he was not in the country and he deliberately came back here to become a law violator. He was in Mexico where he says he had sufficient money to stay, and could have stayed there, but he took upon himself and thought that it was his duty to add to the trouble we already have here and become a conscientious objector, and give statements to the press, and so forth, as to what his feelings were. . . .

The Court. It is . . . an unpleasant and difficult task for me to perform, Mr. Richards, but you have admitted violating the law of the land, and as I said, if you had chosen to register and have yourself classified as a conscientious objector, there would be no question or no necessity for you to bear arms, as apparently your ancestors for many generations did. . . .

The sentence of the Court is that you . . . undergo imprisonment . . . for a period of one year and one day.

Other district judges showed similar attitudes toward conscientious objectors who came before them. Some were apparently genuinely disturbed by the prospect of sentencing objectors to the penitentiary. They tried to draw out every possible reason for a light sentence. Thus one Los Angeles judge expended his own funds to find out what effect probation for four C.P.S. walkouts would have on other conscientious objectors in Civilian Public Service camps. He reached the conclusion that for him to put the four boys on probation would tend to encourage others to walk out.[7]

On the other hand, some judges seemed to take delight in lecturing objectors on their lack of patriotism. Federal Judge Michael L. Igoe, of Chicago, ordered one conscientious objector under indictment, Robert Chino, from his courtroom while he pronounced sentence on another objector. In the process of ejecting Chino from the courtroom, Judge Igoe attacked the War Resisters League as "that bunch out on the south side that thinks it is greater than the

laws of the United States." Then the Judge turned to Lauren Wispe, graduate student in philosophy at Northwestern University, whose case was at bar. Wispe had refused to register, allegedly at the instigation of Chino, who was of Japanese descent. Judge Igoe shouted at Wispe: "You are a slacker of the worst type, letting yourself be influenced by an alien. When even your own mother wants you to join the army." Wispe's attorney at this point tried to protest that his client was not a "slacker." But the judge would brook no interruption, and continued: "All I can see is that he is unwilling to obey the laws of the United States."

Sentence of three years was imposed on Wispe and a deputy sheriff led him away. Then Judge Igoe remarked: "I hope those smart young people on the south side of Chicago will take that as a lesson." He called for Wispe's friends to come before him before he adjourned court. One of these friends was Georgia Lloyd, of the well-known publishing family. She had provided bail for a number of objectors. Judge Igoe now lectured the little group before him. "Get out of here," he shouted as a final word of warning, "and don't ever let me see you in my court again."[8]

On another occasion a district judge was called upon to hear arguments on a writ of habeas corpus involving a conscientious objector allegedly sent into the Army through wrong classification by a local board. After hearing the pleas of counsel, the judge ordered the objector removed to an adjoining courtroom used for naturalization purposes. Mounting the bench, he heard the oath of allegiance of several hundred new citizens and delivered himself of the following:

There is a person in the rear of the room whom I want to hear what I am going to say. You new citizens have taken an oath which obligates you to defend this country with your lives. There is a man in the rear who is willing to let you do this for him though he was born in this country and you were not. If you violate your oath to defend the country, the govern-

---

[7] *U.S.* v. *Philip Curtis Dolve, Gerald P. Darrow, Charles Vincent Worley, Lloyd Scaff*, Reporter's Transcript of Proceedings, before Hon. Ralph E. Jenney, Los Angeles, Calif., June 23, 1943, p. 14.

[8] See the *Conscientious Objector*, June, 1942.

ment may cancel your citizenship, but it may not revoke the citizenship of a person born here who refuses to carry out his obligations in that regard.[9]

In all fairness to the judges, it should be pointed out that certain cases of conscientious objectors were ample cause for wonder. In some courts, the presiding judge was confronted by defendants whose language and climate of thought were so much at variance with usual modes of reacting that it was not surprising that the judge often found himself angry and at a loss. When Jehovah's Witnesses spoke of Armageddon, members of Mankind United debated the World Conspiracy, and other objectors talked about the mysterious operations of Divine Providence, it is not surprising that rather prosaic judges should become impatient. John Andrew Schubin, a Molokan, had been given a IV-E by his local board but had refused to report to C.P.S. Brought before a federal district judge in Los Angeles, he was asked by the magistrate why he could not chop wood under civilian control. He replied: "Well, it is the foreign cause of the war activity." The judge persisted and the answer now was, "Well, the Holy Ghost forbids me to accept anything." At another point he was asked whether he had not accepted the protection of the government all his life. To this he answered: "No, God is the only protector, Jesus Christ and the Holy Ghost. . . . That is all I need." Finally the judge exploded: "Well, all right. The Holy Ghost won't forbid you to accept a sentence in jail. It is the judgment of the court for the offense for which you stand convicted that you shall be sentenced to an institution of the county jail type for a period of six months. . . . All, right, you fight it out with the Holy Ghost. I say that with all due reverence, gentlemen."[10]

This sampling of hearings and trials should not be taken to mean that every conscientious objector received individual treatment and an individual ceremony, nor does it imply that the judge in many, if not most, cases honored him with either a denunciation or with appreciative words. Indeed, as the war became more and more bitter and all-embracing and the number of Selective Service cases mounted, many judges found it convenient to allow the numerous hearings involving conscientious objectors, particularly Jehovah's Witnesses, to accumulate. When the number became sufficiently large, the judge would hold mass hearings and settle the cases in batches of thirty and forty at a time. This practice was more common in some judicial districts than in others, but was sufficiently common in any event to deserve emphatic notice.

Mass hearings were made practicable partly by reason of legal rulings which denied to the objector the right to raise the question of misclassification (by local or appellate board) in the trial court. The courts ruled right down to the end of hostilities that the question of classification could not be raised in the courts at the point where the objector refused to obey a local-board order. The objector must first obey the order and complete the administrative process (by reporting to the Army or Civilian Public Service, as the case might be) and then petition for a writ of habeas corpus. At that point the problem of classification could be raised, but not before. Since many objectors, and practically all Jehovah's Witnesses, could not in conscience "complete the administrative process," they were limited to a hearing on the simple question of disobedience of a local board. In the hearing or trial for failure to obey a local-board order, the sole question at issue was whether the objector did in fact disobey the order. Since the objector would usually not deny that disobedience—and would sometimes, indeed, proclaim it in stentorian tones—the disposal of his case was relatively simple; many cases, especially of Jehovah's

[9] Judge Matthew T. Abruzzo, in Brooklyn, N.Y., in the case of Randolph Phillips. *New York Times*, March 19, 1943. See also the *Conscientious Objector*, April 1943.
[10] *U.S. v. John Andrew Schubin*, Reporter's Transcript, Jan. 25, 1943. The presiding judge was Leon Yankwich.

Witnesses (which were usually very similar to one another), could be passed upon at a single judicial sitting. Thus the dockets of the courts, filled to overflowing with the extra burden of Selective Service cases during the latter half of the war, could be cleared in some instances with relative rapidity. Whether this was a wise expedient is, of course, another matter.

SENTENCES AND PROBATION

What sentences conscientious objectors received depended largely upon the discretion of the individual judge, subject to the statutory (Selective Training and Service Act) maximum of 5 years and a $10,000 fine. In the latter years of the war, judges within a given geographical area (for example, Philadelphia) would sometimes reach an agreement for standard and uniform sentences for given categories. But by and large, and taking the period of the war as a whole, sentences varied widely in a geographical sense. Thus the average sentence of all Selective Service violators in Vermont up to the middle of 1943 was 1.1 months, while in South Dakota it was 55.7 months.[11] And it should be remembered that a large proportion of Selective Service violators were classified at that time as conscientious objectors.

Down to the middle of 1943, the average sentence of all Selective Service violators was 30.6 months. For violators of the narcotics law, the average was 20.8 months; of the liquor laws, 10.6; of the postal laws, 27.3; of the white-slave laws, 28.3.[12] The philosophical observer of men and affairs, reflecting on these figures, could draw interesting conclusions as to the relative heinousness of the several violations of national law.

Looking at the matter from a different perspective, the average sentence of Jehovah's Witnesses for the year ending June 30, 1944, was 42 months; for other conscientious objectors, it was 34; for those vio-

lators of the Selective Training and Service Act who did not claim conscientious objection, it was only 28. By 1945 the averages had been altered only slightly, being, respectively, 45, 37, and 28 months.[13] Rather consistently throughout the course of the war, Jehovah's Witnesses were more harshly treated in terms of sentences than other conscientious objectors, while conscientious objectors as a class received higher sentences than those violators of the Selective Service act who did not claim to be conscientious objectors. In order of increasing severity of sentences we thus have violators of liquor laws, violators of narcotics laws, defiers of the postal laws, white slavers, Selective Service Act violators who did not claim to be conscientious objectors, conscientious objectors, and Jehovah's Witnesses.

But averages do not reveal the whole story, for they do not indicate anything about highest and lowest sentences, relative proportion of high to low sentences, and the differences, if any, in lengths of sentences imposed as between years. The figures in Table 2 more nearly reveal the complete story. An examination of the tabulated figures discloses that 64 per cent of all objectors sentenced between 1940 and 1942 received sentences of a year and a day or above; between July 1, 1942, and July 1, 1944, the percentage rose sharply to 90; after the cessation of European hostilities—between July 1, 1944, and July 1, 1945—the proportion dropped to 85. After the surrender of Japan, six-month sentences were increasingly common. After Pearl Harbor, then, there was a sharp increase in length of sentences imposed, and after August, 1945, there tended to be a sharp decrease, even though objectors continued to be sent to prison for more than a year after the surrender of Japan. It may be inferred that courts seemed to feel that so long as a "shooting" war was in progress sentences should be relatively stiff, but that when hostilities ceased district attorneys and

---

[11] *Federal Prisons* (published annually) (El Reno, Okla., 1943), pp. 59–60.
[12] *Ibid.*, p. 58.

[13] Based upon figures of the N.S.B.R.O. and the Department of Justice.

Table 2.

SENTENCES OF CONSCIENTIOUS OBJECTORS*

	OCT. 16, 1940 TO JUNE 30, 1942	JULY 1, 1942 TO JUNE 30, 1943	JULY 1, 1943 TO JUNE 30, 1944	JULY 1, 1944 TO JUNE 30, 1945	TOTAL
Fine only	2			2	4
Probation	30	56	77	55	218
1 month or less	5	5	7	3	20
1 month through 6 months	18	18	12	6	54
6 months through 1 year, 1 day	83	87	130	106	406
1 year, 1 day–2 years	112	246	391	268	1,017
2 through 3 years	68	675	713	265	1,721
3 through 4 years	39	191	224	127	581
4 through 5 years	29	405	738	321	1,493
Over 5 years, 2 or more counts		2			2
Total	386	1,685	2,292	1,153	5,516

* Department of Justice figures. See *The Reporter*, Nov. 1, 1945, p. 3.

judges agreed that penalties might well be lightened.

One problem that always arises in connection with the types of offenses committed by conscientious objectors is the question of resentencing for what may be considered to be the same offense but which is technically a separate one. The case of James Ball is typical. Ball refused to register for the draft and was sentenced to a year and a day. He served his sentence, the government registered for him while he was in jail, and his case was reopened by his local board. He was classified a conscientious objector, refused on conscientious grounds to report to Civilian Public Service, and was sentenced for his refusal to five years.[14] Arnold Satterthwait found himself in a similar position: his original sentence had been a year and a day for nonregistration; his registration was completed by the warden of the prison (in accordance with Selective Service regulations); when, after his release from prison, his case had been reopened by

his local board, he refused to report for his medical examination. He was given a second prison term of three years, the judge arguing that as a second offender the more severe sentence should be imposed not as punishment but to deter others.[15]

Similar cases of what was called "cat-and-mouse" treatment occurred all together about one hundred times during the course of the war. It was felt by many objectors and defenders of civil liberties that second sentences of this kind for what was essentially the same offense were unfair, and some argued that they violated the spirit, even though not the letter, of the Fifth Amendment's double-jeopardy clause.

Some objectors who were sentenced did not, of course, actually go to prison; they were placed on probation. About 225 objectors were thus enabled to avoid the problem of prison, even though they had committed breaches of the law. Probation as a technique for handling conscientious objectors was most widespread in the Los Angeles area, where federal judges early decided that

14 Critical comments on the case will be found in Constance Rumbaugh to A. J. Muste, Aug. 6, 1943, and Mrs. Matilda Ball to Evan Thomas, Aug. 22, 1943.

15 *U.S.* v. *Arnold Chase Satterthwait*, Reporter's Transcript, Sept. 8, 1943 (Eastern District of Pennsylvania).

it was generally more intelligent than an outright prison sentence. In the early part of 1943, Federal Judge Ralph E. Jenney of Los Angeles made public an announcement that he would send no more objectors to jail but would place all of them on probation.[16] And by 1945 an Oregon federal judge was stating the same general policy.[17] While eastern judges generally lagged behind those in Los Angeles, by the end of 1943 even a New York City judge had placed his first objector on probation.[18] Despite all this, however, and the genuine sympathy of many judges, fewer than 4 per cent of all the conscientious objectors coming before the courts were placed on probation. The remaining 96 per cent went to prison or were fined, or both.

There are several explanations for the relatively small number placed on probation. In the first place, the Selective Service System in many jurisdictions did all it could to discourage probation, apparently feeling that it was in duty bound to see that violators of the Selective Service law served their time in jail. Also, it was objected that allowing men to go on probation subjected them to different standards from other objectors; men on probation were often paid, for example, and their movements were restricted only by the court and not by Selective Service.

A second reason for the small number of probationers was the pressure exerted by various groups, like the American Legion, who believed that it was particularly heinous to place violators of the Selective Training and Service Act on probation, whatever might be desirable with respect to other types of offenders.

Finally, many objectors could not conscientiously subscribe to the conditions usually required. Each recipient of probation had to promise to "obey all laws, live morally and ethically right." To many objectors, the promise to obey all laws was one which they could not make; after their period of probation had expired, or even during it, they might feel called upon by conscience to violate the law again.

Those who were placed on probation were assigned to a wide variety of work. Some were sent to Civilian Public Service camps, where, of course, they continued (as elsewhere on probation) to be under the general jurisdiction of the court. Others were sent to hospitals, both general and mental, where they might be given nominal wages. One judge in placing a nonregistrant on probation laid it down as a condition of his probation that he not mingle with the "bohemian colony" which had presumably influenced him to violate the law.[19] One probationer was assigned for three years to a seminary, and there was at least one instance of a nonregistrant being sent on probation back to his own farm.[20] Others were directed to work in the Forestry Service of the Department of Agriculture, in the conscientious-objector advisory work of the American Friends Service Committee, and in the National Foundation for Infantile Paralysis.

The case of one probationer will serve to illustrate the pressures and conditions which might affect the working out of the system. Richard Petherbridge had been denied a IV-E by his local board. When it came time to sentence him, he was sent on probation to the C.P.S. camp at Glendora, California. Then the conditions of his probation were changed, on his request, to permit him to work for the California Institute of Technology, which was providing research assistance for the National Foundation for Infantile Paralysis. Petherbridge's task was to care for animals used for experimental purposes. He was at first given $50.00 a month;

16 *New York Sun*, April 14, 1943.
17 Judge Claude McColloch. See the *Conscientious Objector*, April 1945.
18 Federal Judge John C. Knox. See the *Conscientious Objector*, Jan. 1944.

19 Case of David R. Nyvall, III. See the *Chicago Herald-American*, March 9, 1942. The *Herald-American* carried on a public agitation against several nonregistrants, including Nyvall.
20 *Memorandum on Probation for C.O. Violators of the Selective Service Act*, Fellowship of Reconciliation, March 8, 1944.

later this was raised to $75.00. When his services were ended here, the court allowed him to do research for another professor who was interested in a guayule project having for its objective the resettling of Japanese-Americans in northwest Arizona. A little later, however, certain members of the Biology Division of California Institute of Technology apparently objected to any conscientious objector working on any project having anything to do with Japanese-Americans. The result was that later he left this position for yet another.[21] He felt, however, that the real cause for his dismissal was his activity, along with that of several other conscientious objectors, in the interests of racial equality. He and several of his Negro and Japanese-American friends had attempted to attend a dance in the Pasadena Civil Auditorium. They were denied admittance; later on, the manager of the Auditorium, learning that Petherbridge was an objector, called the city manager, a prominent member of the American Legion. That official, in turn, called the secretary to

the head of the California Institute of Technology, who then sent out memos to the members of the department for which Petherbridge was working. The memos stated that he was a conscientious objector, a fact of which many of his colleagues were apparently ignorant. The result was that he was transferred.

On the whole, it was extremely unfortunate that probation was not used much more widely, as it seems fairly evident that it was a principle eminently suitable for application to the cases of conscientious objectors. One curious fact does, however, stand out when considering the problem of probation in relation to the whole question of conscientious objection: many objectors on probation were paid, whereas objectors in regular C.P.S. camps were not. Here were men who had violated the law being assigned to service (in many cases) with salary, however small, while those sent to regular C.P.S. camps and who had violated no law were denied any wages. It illustrates again the curious quirks and paradoxes which characterized American treatment of the conscientious objector during World War II.

[21] Memorandum of conversation with Petherbridge and records of Los Angeles Committee for Conscientious Objectors.

POLITICAL CRIME
AND THE NEGRO REVOLUTION*

Joseph C. Mouledous

As discussed by Mouledous in the following selection, political crime has two dimensions: (1) actions directed against the state, and (2) conduct derived from unlawful state power. Southern political power is judged to be illustrative of unlawful state power. A brief historical survey of legitimate attacks upon Southern power and of the methods used by Southern power in responding illuminates the illegal political techniques by which this unlawful power is maintained.

* This selection, written especially for this book, is published here for the first time.

The tactic of nonviolent civil disobedience used in the Negro "revolution" and the nature of the Southern white response have brought into focus the issue of political crime. Two questions arise from this issue: (1) Under what conditions is civil disobedience to be considered criminal? (2) Cannot the legislators and executors of politically divisive ordinances and statutes be judged to be acting criminally? This paper argues for the reintroduction of the two basic dimensions of political crime. It holds that political crime can consist of behavior by agents of government as well as behavior directed against government, and our major emphasis will be on the politically criminal behavior of representatives of Southern political power; a second and far less fully developed concern will be with the question of civil disobedience.

The distinction between crimes against government and crimes by government is not new to criminological literature, and these two facets have been differentially emphasized by various writers. For example, Beccaria emphasized crimes by government while Lombroso's concern was with crimes against government. In the United States Franklin H. Giddings clearly stated that these were the two significant dimensions of political crime. Writing in 1898 an introduction to Louis Proal's study of political crime, Giddings stated:

The term "political crime" has two meanings. Perhaps the more familiar one is that of crimes against governments, such as treason, insurrection, and rebellion. . . . The other meaning is that of crimes perpetrated by governments for alleged reasons of state, and by politicians for alleged reasons of expedience or for political advantage.[1]

The dual aspect of political crime articulated by Giddings has not been the subject of serious discussion in American criminological literature. Rather, the major emphasis has continued to be on crimes against government: both Packer's article entitled

"Offenses against the State,"[2] and Elliott's classification of "political offenders"[3] are indicative of this limited perspective.

Although American criminologists have largely dropped "crime by government" out of their picture of political crime, there are indications that they are unhappy with the results and are seeking satisfactory alternatives. For example, Marshall Clinard raises the criterion of "socially injurious"—not politically injurious—behavior in his study *The Black Market*. And furthermore, Clinard attempts to broaden and make more meaningful the concept crime by defining crime as "any act punishable by the state, regardless of whether the penalty is a criminal one or is *administrative* or *civil in nature*."[4] While this viewpoint recognizes the state's increasing role in reshaping law and in defining the limits of freedom, it fails to perceive that this development may also threaten the political rights of the individual.[5]

To argue, as most criminologists do, that crime is any act punishable by the state is to imply strongly that government and law are one; that is, that all which government punishes is necessarily unlawful. This notion seriously limits the legitimate behavior of political actors, discourages the use of the concept political crime as crime perpetrated by government or its agents, and encourages one to subsume such acts under the concepts white collar crime, occupational crime, or socially injurious behavior.

The fact of the matter is that Americans, by and large, are comfortable with limiting political crime to crime against government. Not only are Americans reluctant to face the possibility that government can act

[1] Louis Proal, *Political Crime*, with an introduction by Franklin H. Giddings, New York: D. Appleton & Company, Inc., 1898, pp. v–vi.

[2] Herbert L. Packer, "Offenders against the State," *The Annals*, 339 (January 1962), 77–89.

[3] Mabel A. Elliott, *Crime in Modern Society*, New York: Harper & Row, Publishers, 152, pp. 179–197.

[4] Marshall Clinard, *Sociology of Deviant Behavior*, New York: Holt, Rinehart anl Winston, Inc., 1963, p. 160.

[5] See the excellent paper by Charles A. Reich, entitled "The New Property," *Yale Law Journal*, 73 (April 1964), pp. 733–787.

criminally; they avoid the possibility that deliberate political acts against government may be "noncriminal." This is clearly expressed in the punitive sanctions imposed on political criminals. Up to the present civil rights confrontation, American political criminals have seldom received special treatment as political criminals. Rather, they have been defined as "common criminals" and required to serve their sentences along with "common criminals": a condition that is not without unusual difficulties and even dangers to political criminals.

The basis of American attitudes toward political crime and political criminals is deeply rooted. As both Andrew Hacker[6] and Daniel J. Boorstin[7] have indicated, the uniqueness of the American experience is that it has never had a politics. The legitimacy of the political reality that is America has seldom been questioned, partly because of the assumption of human equality and individual dignity which underlie our political order, but also because of the optimism inherent in the Puritanism-turned-pragmatism that has been a predominant orientation of Americans to their environment. It is an optimism colored by a psychology which judges all who, either willingly or because of personal inadequacies, refuse to seek successful participation in the American enterprise and yet who insist on calling into question its legitimacy, to be beyond redemption—to be treated as outcasts rather than as serious questioners and contributors to the American political community. At the same time, this American attitude permits those who participate successfully to judge and question, to select and innovate; in effect, to be politically creative. Such actors as these have often sought to apply the basic presuppositions of liberal democracy: human equality and the political dignity of the individual as distinct and separate from the state. This has produced a theme in our society which stresses the view that government and law are two related yet different orders; government exists as one source of law, but law exists as the superior reality. Government is subsumed under this law, and it is understood that the individual, as a political actor, has not only a right but an obligation to question government in the light of the law.

Within the framework of this paper these presuppositions which are at the root of our American political tradition are used as standards for judging political behavior. It is held that behavior can be judged to be politically legitimate or politically criminal by whether it is oriented toward making law an instrument serving one segment of society through the exclusion of others from the political community, or whether it is directed toward the creative reinterpretation and extension of law consistent with the presuppositions of political dignity and human equality.

A fact of Southern history is the fact of political crime, for the South has denied the Negro entrance into the political community. The Negro has held an integral, if subservient, role in Southern society, but he has been cast out of the political community and thereby denied existence under law. Without a legal identity, the Negro as an individual has no existence. His existence is a group existence. As a group the Negro occupies a status within the Southern social order, but as an individual, being denied legal identity, the Negro is truly the invisible man.

Since Southern political power is based on the exclusion of the Negro from the political community and inclusion of the Negro in Southern society, it became essential for the South to create a no-man identity for the Negro, to make him without individuality, to keep him "Tom" and "boy." And conversely, the Negro revolt has been a revolt against this state of oblivion, and movement toward carving out an identity, a sense of manhood, an existence as an

6 Andrew Hacker, "Liberal Democracy and Social Control," The Political Imagination, Edgar Litt (ed.), Chicago: Scott, Foresman and Company, 1966, pp. 267–277.
7 Daniel J. Boorstin, The Genius of American Politics, Chicago: University of Chicago Press, 1953.

individual among other individuals within the American political community.

It has been asked, "Where do we date the beginning of the Negro revolt?"[8] With the 1870 "sit-ins" and "ride-ins" occurring in Louisville, Kentucky?[9] With 1909 and the founding of the National Association for the Advancement of Colored People (NAACP)? With the Atlanta Civil and Political League of 1936, founded to stimulate Negroes to register to vote? With 1941 and the threatened march on Washington, D.C., led by A. Philip Randolph, which moved President Roosevelt to create the wartime Fair Employment Practices Commission? With the 1942 Southern Conference on Race Relations at Durham, North Carolina, attended by leading Southern Negroes from educational institutions, trade unions, churches, business and professional associations? With the corresponding conference held by white Southerners, April 8, 1943, at Atlanta, Georgia, under the intellectual leadership of Howard W. Odum, Professor of Sociology at the University of North Carolina and involving leading white Southerners from all walks of life? With the Supreme Court's great white primary ruling of 1944? With President Truman's Executive Order of 1946 and the Supreme Court opinion in *Brown v. Board of Education* which cast out of legal philosophy the apartheid conclusions of *Plessy v. Ferguson* and held that any separation of the races must denote the inferiority of the Negro race? With Rosa Parks and the Montgomery, Alabama, bus boycott of 1955–1956?

There have been many beginnings, but none are more appropriate for an understanding of the present Negro revolt than

[8] "Direct Action in the South: A Southern Regional Council Report," *New South*, Vol. 18 (October–November 1963). Our discussion of direct action in the South, 1960–1963, is based upon and closely parallels the account in this report.

[9] Alan F. Westin, "Ride-in's and Sit-in's of the 1870's," *Freedom Now! The Civil Rights Struggle in America*, Alan F. Westin (ed.), New York: Basic Books, Inc., 1964, Chap. 10, pp. 68–74.

the attempt made by the Congress of Industrial Organizations (CIO) during the 1930s and 1940s to unionize the South, largely on an interracial basis. As Daniel Bell[10] has noted, labor's situation and the Negro's situation have had many points in common: the "yellow-dog" contracts were a form of segregation; labor was aided in its struggle by the federal government and by favorable court decisions; still labor was ultimately forced to help itself by direct action. Furthermore, in the South the CIO threatened to accomplish many of the ends that are being accomplished today by the civil rights movement, and in so doing, the unions elicited responses similar to those being shown toward the Negro today. Therefore, the struggle to unionize the South provides us with a preview of the present Southern conflict.

The very existence of the CIO in the South was a direct threat to white supremacy. Many union halls were integrated and white Southerners who joined the unions could experience their first contacts, on the basis of equality, with Negroes. Through their educational programs unions attempted to educate their white memberships, to create in them an awareness of mutual political and economic interests with Negro labor. The Political Action Committee of the CIO attempted to initiate political activity that would involve a broad spectrum of Southern communities.

We may take as a single example union activity directed toward encouraging and aiding Negroes to register and to vote. In June 1944 the white primaries were destroyed by a ruling of the Supreme Court which held that Negroes could not be barred from party primaries. Stimulated by this decision, unions began to encourage their Negro members to register and vote, and unions used their funds and resources to agitate the Negro community to so act. In September 1944 editors of *The Southern*

[10] In a discussion of Arthur Waskow's "Creative Disorder in the Racial Struggle," *The Correspondent*, No. 33 (Winter 1965), p. 103.

Patriot congratulated "the Orleans Parish [Louisiana] Political Action Committee [CIO] for its efforts in adding 1021 new voters to the registration lists."[11] Under union leadership returning Negro GIs in 1946 marched one-hundred strong to the Birmingham Courthouse in a futile attempt to register to vote.[12] Such attempts, for many reasons, were only sporadic, but they did occur, continuing into 1948, when the Progressive party, supported by the left wing-dominated CIO unions, in an attempt to place Henry Wallace on Southern ballots, made their last drive to register Southern Negroes to vote. For example, in September 1948 in St. Bernard Parish, Louisiana, eleven Negroes, accompanied by representatives of the Louisiana Progressive party and the Southern Fur Trappers Union, went to the courthouse to register to vote; they were cursed and turned away by armed deputies.[13]

Labor's attempt to organize the South, under the leadership of left-wing CIO unions, had political as well as social and economic overtones. This fact was clearly understood by most Southern politicians. They knew from the beginning that the CIO's organizational drive, its attempt to initiate a right-to-vote movement, and its struggle to have prolabor legislation passed, could revolutionize the South. As early as January 26, 1938, Senator Richard Russell of Georgia articulated what the Southern power structure most feared—and still fears:

Every Senator on the floor of this body knows that if a measure of this kind were passed, there would be Negro governors and there would be Negro senators. There are many states where two or three or four or five members of the House of Representatives would be Negroes, and no white man would have a chance to be elected. This means that there would be county after county where every officer and every official would be of the Negro race.[14]

[11] *Southern Patriot*, 2 (September 1944), p. 2.
[12] *Southern Patriot*, 4 (March 1946), p. 5.
[13] *Southern Patriot*, 6 (October 1948), p. 4.
[14] As quoted by Pettis Perry, *Negro Representation—A Step towards Negro Freedom*, New York: New Century Publishers, 1952, pp. 22–23.

This fear, expressed on the floor of the United States Senate, was translated into action in the communities of the South. The police undertook to protect the Southern status quo by direct action against union organizers and members.[15] In the Lumberton, North Carolina, textile strike of 1937, sixty-five union men and Myles Horton, Director of Highlander Folk School and a volunteer organizer, were arrested. In spite of the fact that Horton insisted that the strike be conducted according to principles of nonviolence, the police made it known that "Horton will be arrested regardless of whether he is on the scene should any violence occur on the picket line, or elsewhere, concerning the strike."[16] In Jackson, Mississippi, two representatives of the International Woodworkers of America, and the wife of one of them, were arrested and held for thirty-six hours, without charges being filed against them.[17] In Vicksburg, Mississippi, the vice-president of the International Woodworkers was held for investigation. During the interrogation the police captain informed him that he was "inciting trouble for the police department, and he guessed he [the police] would have to shoot up a bunch of these burr-headed Negroes." The police captain said further that "regardless of what federal laws might be passed, if Negroes get out of place they would probably be lynched and the police department would not interfere."[18] In Port Gibson, Mississippi, the sheriff showed up at the picket line waving his gun and threatening

[15] This brief enumeration of instances of police action is not at all exhaustive; it is given only as representative of the type of police behavior which was common with regard to union activists.
[16] Lucy Randolph Mason, *To Win These Rights: A Personal Story of the CIO in the South*, New York: Harper & Row, Publishers, 1952, pp. 44–46. The quotation is from the *Charlotte Observer* of July 8, 1937.
[17] Mason, pp. 72–73.
[18] Mason, p. 76; Miss Mason quotes from a letter from William Botkins, vice-president of the International Woodworkers, CIO, to George Brown, director of organization for the union, April 1944.

to shoot the women strikers full of lead unless they went back to work.[19]

Not only did the executors of law strike out to protect white Southern political power, but the legislators also contributed their part. In Milledgeville, Georgia, an ordinance was passed which required that union organizers be local residents for one year and pay a $5000 license fee. Although this ordinance was ruled unconstitutional in 1941,[20] the legislators of Cuthbert, Georgia, passed a similar ordinance in 1947. Cuthbert's ordinance required that anyone soliciting members for unions should first secure a city license and pay a fee of $1500 per year for organizing labor.[21] In Arkansas an antiviolence-in-strikes law was passed which permitted the arrest of union officials, members, or pickets on the charge of threatening— not committing—violence against nonunion men while depriving them of their right to work. And in the Arkansas strike against the Southern Cotton Oil Mill a strikebreaker fatally stabbed a Negro striker; yet the Little Rock grand jury failed to indict the strikebreaker. Instead, it indicted five union men, four of whom did not even witness the stabbing, under the antiviolence law.[22]

Southern legislators did not limit the scope of their statutes in support of Southern norms to the activities of union men. Even personnel agents, recruiting Southern labor for Northern industry, were recipients of punitive sanctions. The fact that Northern industry was the backbone of the "war effort" had little import; the South, in an attempt to preserve within its region cheap Negro labor, either passed or dug out of the books dating back to 1870, laws requiring payment of prohibitive license fees for the privilege of soliciting labor for employment outside the state. By 1943 ten Southern states had such emigrant agency laws, and applied them.[23] A New Jersey scrap metal company sent an agent to Georgia in 1943 to recruit and transport workers to New Jersey. The agent successfully secured a number of men, but at Cordele, Georgia, the chief of police boarded the train and took the agent and the prospective jobholders to jail. The company agent was found guilty of enticing, without a license, laborers to be employed beyond the state. He was given a six-month suspended sentence, placed on eighteen months' probation, and given twenty-four hours to leave Georgia; his company was fined $1000.[24]

The unions sought to protect their officials and members by securing aid from the federal government and from the courts. In one surprising instance the city marshal of Walnut Ridge, Arkansas, pleaded *nolo contendere* in federal court on the charge of assaulting and abusing a labor organizer. This case was one of the rare instances in which federal civil rights statutes were used.[25] Aid generally came in the form of behind-the-scenes pressure from the federal government. For example, in Memphis, Tennessee, union organizers were assaulted by a mob. Boss Crump was unavailable to union representatives who sought his assistance. And so a direct appeal was made to President Roosevelt, through Mrs. Roosevelt, resulting in the arrival of a special representative of the Attorney General to investigate charges against the city administration concerning the denial of civil rights to union men.[26] Following this in-

---

[19] Mason, p. 78.
[20] *Southern Patriot*, 2 (September 1944), p. 2.
[21] Mason, pp. 81–83.
[22] *Southern Patriot*, 4 (February 1946), p. 4.

[23] These laws were strongly condemned as unconstitutional in articles in *Cornell Law Quarterly*, March 1943 and June 1943.
[24] *Southern Patriot*, 1 (February–March 1943), p. 6.
[25] This alleged assault took place at Walnut Ridge, Arkansas, in 1942; see *Southern Patriot*, 1 (November 1943), p. 3. See also, for a discussion of federal criminal sanctions against unlawful police power, "Federal Civil Sanctions" in *Justice; 1961 Comission on Civil Rights Report*, Washington, D.C.: Government Printing Office, 1961, Chap. 5, pp. 69–78.
[26] Mason, pp. 111–113.

vestigation CIO members were not molested, plants were successfully organized, membership grew, and politicians who had previously opposed the unions with vigor showed a remarkable change of heart. In some cases when the FBI investigated charges of unlawful use of police power the behavior ceased.

The legal phase of the Negro revolt was carried on by the lawyers of the National Association for the Advancement of Colored People (NAACP) and other civil rights groups. Because of their activities, the Supreme Court at each of its sessions from 1938 to 1948 decided at least one case involving the rights of minorities.[27] And beginning in 1948 the Supreme Court began to hand down decisions in the area of education.

The results of these legal struggles cannot be overestimated. The *Smith v. Allwright* case of 1944 gave the Negro the right to vote in primary elections, and thus announced him as a potential political power. The 1945 *Screws v. United States* case, in which a Georgia sheriff was, at first, found guilty of blackjacking a Negro prisoner to death, and later acquitted and elected to a state office, made clear the existence of unlawful police conduct in the maintenance of white power in the South. The 1954 *Brown v. Board of Education* decision led to an aftermath which included the Little Rock, Arkansas, and Clinton, Tennessee, riots and the use of federal troops, all of which further crystallized national opinion in favor of the Negro movement and against white supremacy.

Supporters of white supremacy were not lax in responding to these challenges. Negroes who attempted to vote in the primaries were beaten; in Calhoun Falls, South Carolina, August, 1948, Reverend A. Ware, a Negro minister, was stabbed and beaten after he voted in the primary; in Montgomery County, Georgia, D. C. Carter,

president of the local branch of the NAACP, was beaten after he voted in the state primary elections. Negroes who attempted to register to vote could seldom find the registrar and were frequently beaten. The NAACP came under increasing attack. Four Southern states passed laws making the NAACP an illegal organization and a fifth state imposed a fine of $1,000,000 on it. In Birmingham, wearers of NAACP buttons had them ripped off by police officers, and police brutality grew to such proportions that in April 1948 the NAACP called an emergency meeting to protest police violence after five Negroes were shot and killed by police officers within a one-month period.[28] The increase of private violence was announced with the resurgence of the Ku Klux Klan (KKK). Three Negro homes were bombed in Birmingham in March 1949 and on June 12, 1949, 126 hooded Klansmen paraded in Tuscaloosa, Alabama.[29] On Christmas, 1951, a bomb was set off in the home of Harry T. Moore, state coordinator of the NAACP in Florida; he died on the way to the hospital and his wife died of her injuries on January 3, 1952. In Virginia the state bar brought charges of unprofessional conduct against NAACP attorney Samuel W. Tucker; these charges grew out of his participation in three NAACP cases in 1949.[30] The basic pattern was set: Negroes pursued their constitutional rights in a legal manner, only to be met by a variety of "criminal" responses on the part of the upholders of white supremacy.

The Montgomery bus boycott of 1955–1956[31] involved virtually the entire Negro community. The initial response to it was generally limited to police action. Taxicabs and private Negro vehicles were frequently stopped, and motor vehicle violations increased phenomenally. Arrests for hitch-

[27] Herbert Hill and Jack Greenberg, *Citizen's Guide to Desegregation*, Boston: The Beacon Press, 1955, p. 61.

[28] *Southern Patriot*, 6 (April 1948), p. 1.
[29] *Southern Patriot*, 7 (June 1949), p. 1.
[30] *Southern Patriot*, 18 (February 1960), p. 3.
[31] L. D. Reddick, "The Bus Boycott in Montgomery," *Voices of Dissent*, New York: Grove Press, Inc., 1958, pp. 169–179.

hiking, loud talking, walking on lawns, and congregating in white neighborhoods were all part of the attempt to break the boycott. Finally, Martin Luther King and other leaders were arrested, and a crude bomb was thrown against King's home. Four months after the arrest of Rosa Parks, which had started the boycott, the Supreme Court upheld the ruling of a lower court against segregated seating on municipal buses, and this limited victory was complete.

The period between the end of the Montgomery bus boycott and the beginning of the sit-ins in 1960 was essentially limited to court litigation, as exemplified by the *Gomillion v. Lightfoot* case, arising out of the city of Tuskegee, Alabama, redistricting its city boundaries to exclude Negroes, thus making them ineligible to register and vote in municipal elections. In arguing this case before the United States Supreme Court, the legal representatives of Tuskegee and Alabama were asked the following question by Justice Whittaker: "*Could this lawful power you speak of be used to accomplish an unlawful purpose?*"[32] The unanimous decision in favor of the Negro petitioners was affirmation that state power, used as an instrument for circumventing a federally protected right, was unlawful use of such power.[33] In an equally important case in Fayette and Haywood, two counties in Tennessee, landlords were restrained from evicting 48 tenant farmers. In supporting the tenant farmers a United States Court of Appeal concluded:

If sharecropper-tenants in possession of real estate under contract are threatened, intimidated or coerced by their landlords for purposes of interfering with their rights of franchise, certainly the fact that the coercion relates to land or contracts would furnish no excuse or defense.[34]

Thus the courts judged that economic power could be used unlawfully. In a similar manner legislation passed for the purposes of purging voter registration rolls, and of interposing the state constitution between the federal Constitution and the citizen, and thereby avoiding integration of the schools, and all similar legislation, was struck down as unconstitutional. The major thrust against white supremacy during this period was in the hands of the federal courts, backed up by federal power as in Little Rock, Arkansas, and Clinton, Tennessee.

The next development in the Negro revolt was the entrance of middle class Negro students as nonviolent, direct action "sit-iners," protesting against segregation.[35] Originating as a spontaneous protest on February 1, 1960, in Greensboro, North Carolina, this form of protest spread rapidly across the South, and the activists, with some help from the Southern Christian Leadership Conference (SCLC), organized themselves into the Student Nonviolent Coordinating Committee (SNCC), which was to prove to be the most militant of the civil rights groups, instrumental in transforming the Negro revolt as a protest against segregation into a Negro revolution seeking to destroy white political power and to secure political power for Southern Negroes.[36]

The sit-iners elicited vigorous response. As the Southern Regional Council Report noted, "Following the outbreak of the 1960 sit-ins every [Southern] legislature passed laws to regulate—and restrict—sit-in activities."[37] These civil rights activists found themselves being arrested and convicted on such charges as criminal trespassing, blocking fire exits, vagrancy, criminal anarchy (which carried a possible ten-year sentence), criminal mischief, breach of peace, delinquency, and drawing a poster which "libeled the state."[38] Furthermore, sanctions were

[32] Bernard Taper, *Gomillion Versus Lightfoot*, New York: McGraw-Hill Book Company, Inc., 1962, p. 103.

[33] Taper, p. 113.

[34] Wallace Mendelson, *Discrimination*, Englewood Cliffs, N.J.: Prentice-Hall, Inc., 1962, pp. 22–23.

[35] "Direct Action in the South," pp. 3–6.

[36] Bayard Rustin, "From Protest to Politics," *Commentary*, 39 (February 1965), pp. 25–31.

[37] "Direct Action in the South," p. 25.

[38] See *Southern Patriot*, Vol. 17 (April 1959). Vol. 18 (October 1960), Vol. 18 (November

applied against at least 141 students and 58 faculty members by dismissing them.[39] In spite of such harassment, the sit-ins were relatively successful: Supreme Court rulings overturned the convictions of peaceful, non-violent protesters and thereby acknowledged the legitimacy of this form of civil disobedience, as well as the illegitimacy of so-called "lawful" power which functions for the purpose of attaining unlawful ends.

Following the spontaneous student protests against segregation, the Congress of Racial Equality (CORE), an essentially Northern-based and highly interracial civil rights organization, invaded the South in a series of "freedom rides." It has been questioned whether this tactic was successful, for as a result CORE was overburdened with excessive legal costs and some pro-civil rights elements were estranged.[40] The reaction included the burning of a Greyhound bus and the beating of its passengers. Violence in Birmingham and later in Montgomery led the federal district court in Alabama to this judgment:

The failure of the defendant law enforcement officers to enforce the law in this case clearly amounts to *unlawful state action* in violation of the Equal Protection Clause of the Fourteenth Amendment.[41]

Out of these "rides" came the unmistakable fact that the refusal of police to protect peaceful demonstrators from violence constituted unlawful police action.[42]

Albany, Georgia, was the site of the next big battle of the civil rights movement.[43]

Like Montgomery, it involved a large segment of the community. Beginning as a relatively mild form of protest organized by the NAACP, it was quickly escalated into a more aggressive stage by SNCC activists, who made a direct assault on all forms of segregation. When it became obvious to the Negro leadership that the community supported the SNCC people, the Albany movement, encompassing all civil rights organizations, was born, and Dr. Martin Luther King entered the picture. Protests were made against segregation in train and bus stations, libraries, parks, hospitals, and against police brutality and followed the general pattern of singing and praying marches into the business district, arrests, and then protest marches against these arrests. Violence was not entirely avoided. Some of the marches went through Negro nightspot sections; drinkers entering the marches were not so inclined to nonviolence and on at least one occasion threw objects, rocks and bricks, at the police.

In neighboring Baker County the sheriff was sued by Warren Johnson in the federal district court in Albany, Georgia, on the charge that he had arrested Johnson without a warrant, had handcuffed him, and then in jail had shot him in the neck three times. Following the sheriff's acquittal, civil rights activists picketed the supermarket owned by one of the jurors. The federal government took immediate action against eight members of the Albany movement, charging two with obstructing justice and six with perjury. These indictments and the convictions which followed the verdict of an all-white federal jury, led Martin Luther King to say: "It is tragic that the only instance in which the federal government has moved with vigor has been against Negro leaders who have been working to end the evils of segregation."[44]

On the day of the indictment, street demonstrations held in Americus, a few

1960), Vol. 19 (January 1961), Vol. 19 (February 1961), Vol. 19 (March 1961), and Vol. 19 (April 1961).

39 "Direct Action in the South," p. 4.

40 William Goldsmith, "The Cost of Freedom Rides," *Dissent*, 8 (Autumn 1961), pp. 499–502. See also "Direct Action in the South," pp. 7–9.

41 As quoted in Mendelson, p. 159 (italics added).

42 Howard Zinn has an excellent chapter on the freedom rides in his book, *SNCC: The New Abolitionists*, Boston: Beacon Press, 1964.

43 "Direct Action in the South," pp. 12–16. See also *Upside-Down Justice: The Albany Cases*, Albany, Ga.: National Committee for the Albany Defendants, n.d.; a pamphlet, p. 8. Our material

on the Albany situation including the Americus, Georgia, arrests are taken form these two sources.

44 *Upside-Down Justice . . .*, p. 8.

miles from Albany, resulted in the arrest of three SNCC field workers and a CORE worker; they were charged with unlawful assembly, obstructing lawful arrest, inciting to riot, assault with intent to murder, and attempt to incite insurrection. The latter charge carried the death penalty. The next day, in the demonstrations held to protest these arrests, marchers were clubbed and were burned with cattle prods.

Albany pointed out that mass demonstrations involving the entire community walked on the edge of mob violence. It also demonstrated the vulnerability of civil rights activists to federal sanctions.

In the spring and summer of 1963[45] conflict between Negro demonstrators and the police occurred in a number of Southern communities, such as Birmingham, Alabama; Danville, Virginia; and Cambridge, Maryland. These confrontations were notable in that they made public the willingness of sizable segments of the Negro population in these communities to violate publicly existing laws in the hope of changing these laws. Even children participated; "one estimate had all but 887 of the 7386 pupils of Birmingham's seven Negro high schools absent during one day at the height of the demonstrations."[46]

While the intent of these demonstrations was clearly nonviolent, they seldom avoided violence. In Birmingham, Martin Luther King's headquarters was bombed, and an outraged Negro mob stoned the police, set fire to a vehicle, and stabbed one policeman. In Danville, Virginia, the police broke down the door of a church where demonstrators were gathered and arrested Negro leaders under an ancient law that made it a felony "to incite the colored population to acts of war and violence."[47]

The summer of 1963 ended with the massive march on Washington, D.C., in which some 200,000 persons participated. Although most of the marchers were Negro, the march represented a broadening of the civil rights movement in that Catholic, Protestant, and Jewish white representatives participated. It is ironic that this broadening of the movement, so much a goal of Negro leadership, was greatly extended and transformed into a firm commitment to act on the part of respectable middle-class whites and especially the Protestant clergy and later the Catholics, by the bombing in September of a Negro church in Birmingham which killed four little girls and injured two more. Following this crime, representatives of white middle class America became actively involved in civil rights protests. The wade-ins and demonstrations at St. Augustine, Florida, March 1964 saw white involvement to the extent that Mrs. Malcolm Peabody, mother of a former governor of Massachusetts, came to St. Augustine to join the demonstrators.

The next development in the civil rights movement began as a controversy within SNCC.[48] As early as the summer of 1961, SNCC workers engaged in a searching dialogue over tactics. Some wished to continue direct action campaigns: sit-ins, pray-ins, stand-ins, demonstrations, boycotts, and so on. Others, with the encouragement of such advisers as Myles Horton of Highlander Folk School, argued for an extensive voter education and registration drive. As Howard Zinn writes: "The result was a compromise. Two arms of SNCC were created."[49] Direct action projects were continued, and a voter registration drive was begun.

Following this decision, SNCC workers began voter registration activities in the very bastion of white supremacy, the Black Belt. In 1959 there were 158 counties in eight states with predominantly Negro populations, and in 51 of these counties less than 3 percent of the nonwhite voting age population were registered to vote.[50] Although SNCC workers became active in all

45 "Direct Action in the South," pp. 17–22.
46 "Direct Action in the South," p. 18.
47 "Direct Action in the South," p. 19.
48 Zinn, pp. 57–61.
49 Zinn, p. 59.
50 Quoted by Mendelson, pp. 170–171, from the 1961 Report of the United States Commission on Civil Rights.

of these states, they concentrated on Mississippi, a state outstanding in that it had the largest nonwhite population, and by far the smallest percentage—less than 1 percent for the state as a whole—of nonwhites of voting age registered. By fall of 1963, SNCC workers had expanded their activities to all five congressional districts in Mississippi and had joined with CORE, SCLC, and NAACP to form the Council of Federated Organizations (COFO), which conducted a "Freedom Vote" campaign in which 80,000 votes were cast for Aaron Henry for governor.[51] One result of this political thrust was the formation of the Mississippi Freedom Democratic party, which presented a slate of delegates to the Democratic Party convention, challenging, with some success, the seating of the regular Democratic party delegates.

Voter registration drives, "freedom schools" to educate the Negro population politically, and community centers to provide a number of services for the impoverished and largely illiterate Negro population, proved to have broad appeal, especially among college students. A Mississippi Summer Project was devised, and, aided by the Committee on Race and Religion of the National Council of Churches, almost one thousand students volunteered to participate in the voter registration drives, freedom schools, and community centers.

Mississippi's legislature moved quickly in response to this invasion of "civil rights agitators" by passing a number of bills concerned solely with civil rights workers. The following are given as examples.[52] House Bill 64 authorized cities to restrict the movements of individuals and groups and to set curfew hours. Senate Bill 1545 outlawed the distribution of boycott literature, and provided a maximum penalty of a $500 fine and/or six months in jail. Senate Bill 1517 increased the maximum fine from $100 to $300 and jail terms from thirty to ninety

days for specific traffic violations; such violations were frequently applied against civil rights workers. House Bill 546 prohibited picketing of all public buildings, streets, and sidewalks and other places belonging to the city, county, or state. Senate Bill 1969 made it a misdemeanor to teach in or to conduct an unlicensed school, a measure obviously applicable to the Freedom Schools. House Bill 270 prohibited entry into the state with the intention of violating state laws.

The police, too, were active. Six civil rights workers transferring a trailer of books for the Freedom Schools were arrested on suspicion of carrying materials which advocated the overthrow of the government. The groups of student volunteers for the Mississippi Summer Project began arriving in Mississippi on June 21, 1964, and immediately came in contact with the police: Ruleville, the first carload of volunteers were arrested for questioning; Clarksdale, arriving students were ordered off the streets; Philadelphia, three workers were arrested, released, and then disappeared—until their bodies were unearthed by the FBI; Drew, June 24, 1964, voter registration workers were met by armed whites; Hollandale, June, 24, 1964, civil rights workers were ordered out of town by the mayor, who said they needed a permit to do registration work; Itta Bena, June 25, 1964, two white civil rights workers were picked up by two truckloads of white men and taken out of town; Columbus, June 26, 1964, eight voter registration workers were arrested for distributing leaflets.[53] And so forth; the list is seemingly endless.

---

[51] *Mississippi Freedom Project*, Atlanta: Student Nonviolent Coordinating Committee, n.d.; a pamphlet.
[52] See *Student Voice*, 5 (June 9, 1964), pp. 1–2; and 5 (May 26, 1964), p. 2.

[53] The account of these arrests and harassments is taken from *Student Voice*, Vol. 5 (June 30, 164). The murder of the three civil rights workers is described in detail in *Mississippi Eyewitness*, a special issue of *Ramparts* Magazine edited by Maxwell Geismar, Menlo Park, Calif.: The Layman's Press, 1964. For a full account see also Jack Minnis, *Mississippi; A Chronology of Violence and Intimidation in Mississippi Since 1961*, Atlanta: The Student Nonviolent Coordinating Committee, 1964; this material was first published in the *Congressional Record*, April 4, 1963, and subsequently brought up to date for this article.

And then we come to Selma, Alabama.[54] In a significant respect the two major arms of the civil rights movement, direct action and voter registration, united in one massive thrust against white supremacy in Selma, Alabama. In this community in which less than 2 percent of the nonwhites of voting age were registered to vote, action initially started as a SNCC voter registration project in February 1963. By September and October 1963 the community was mobilized behind the registration drive. On October 7, 1964, approximately 300 Negroes stood in line all day seeking entrance into the voter registration office. At this stage the confrontation in Selma was carried primarily by Negroes; according to Zinn, the only local white to show sympathy to civil rights activists was a Catholic priest, Father Maurice Ouillet.[55] And throughout the remainder of 1963 and 1964, the Selma operation was predominantly a SNCC project, which in spite of repeated demonstrations for voter registration, had failed to crack the white power structure symbolized by Sheriff James Clark.

In January 1965 the Selma confrontation entered a new stage, in that SCLC and Dr. Martin Luther King joined SNCC workers in this struggle. Under their joint leadership massive attempts to register were made once again, but without success. King's arrival heightened the struggle; not only did he bring nationwide publicity to the Selma struggle; he brought respectable, middle class whites, especially the clergy, to Selma to participate in the struggle. Following an unsuccessful attempt to march from Selma to the state capitol, Montgomery, in which Negroes were brutally beaten by Alabama state troopers, Dr. King made a nationwide appeal for aid. The response to his appeal gave tangible proof of the fact that the civil rights movement had significantly broadened its base and gained wide support. Rabbis, ministers, priests, nuns, professors, students, and others, came to Selma im-

mediately. There followed mass marches and demonstrations in Selma; the murder of Reverend James Reeb, a white minister from Boston; and the immediate arrest of alleged KKK members who were charged with the murder. The march from Selma to Montgomery, with massive federal protection, ended in a display of strength which saw more than 25,000 civil rights supporters from all over the country marching in Montgomery. Then followed, that evening, the murder of a white female civil rights worker.

What is clear from our survey is that the South has used all dimensions of its power to maintain the existing white supremacist political structure. It has used private power unlawfully; it has misused lawful power and made it criminal; it has used economic power illegally. Legislatures have passed statutes and ordinances that were obviously unconstitutional; police have violated due process of law; judges have demeaned the bench; administrative sanctions have been applied to schoolteachers, students, and professors; lawyers have been harassed in such a way that civil rights activists could have been denied the right to counsel; individuals and groups such as the KKK have struck out with brutal violence against civil rights workers. Some parts of the South have earned the label "the closed society," and may well deserve being called "a totalitarian order." The Catholic lay magazine, *Ramparts*, in describing details of the Goodman, Schwerner, and Chaney murders, used the following quotations from Adolf Hitler:

Make them live in a valley of fear . . . a valley guarded by our men who will be both their only hope and the source of their fear.[56]

Activists in the civil rights movement either have openly and consciously violated laws they have held to be unlawful or have frequently found themselves in the position of having their behavior defined as a violation of local ordinances and statutes.

Thus civil rights activists have forced us to face the question of political crime, first,

---

[54] Here we follow Howard Zinn, Chap. 8.
[55] Zinn, p. 150.

[56] Zinn, p. 150.

by their choice of action, and, second, by what they have chosen to confront. If we are to seek a valid assessment of their challenge we must acknowledge that the primary objective of law is to encourage certain kinds of behavior while discouraging others.[57] Regardless of the issue at hand, be it civil rights or international affairs, we must ask whether we wish members of the body politic to confront government, in all its forms, and to demand articulation and clarification of issues, and we must know whether we wish to encourage legal forms of protest against government and its agencies when disapproval of and disagreement with the positions and actions of government exist.

What is critical is that the behaviors which we are encouraging or discouraging should not be determined by existing social norms nor by administrative judgment. Sociologists cannot abdicate the responsibility of judgment and accept the state's criteria of crime. A superior referent must be sought.

Civil rights activists, by openly and consciously violating laws they have held to be unlawful, have stimulated sociologists to explore this complicated problem of man, the state, and the rule of law. And in spite of their numerous arrests and their philosophy of civil disobedience, many writers are not disposed to judge these activists as criminals, political or otherwise, but rather to view their behavior favorably. Robert K. Merton,[58] for example, writes in a tone and style which clearly communicate his favorable attitude toward the civil rights movement. Distinguishing between two types of deviant behavior, nonconforming and aberrant, he holds that the nonconformist, in contrast to the aberrant, (1) an-

nounces his dissent publicly, (2) challenges the legitimacy of the norms and laws he violates, (3) aims to change the norms he is denying in practice, (4) is acknowledged by conventional members of society to depart from prevailing norms for disinterested purposes, and not for what he personally can get out of it, and (5) lays claim to a higher morality and to ultimate values, rather than to the particular norms of society. The nonconformist is therefore similar to Max Weber's *saint*, and, of no little importance, he acts, according to Merton, in a social context which acknowledges and respects his other than personal motivations.

Merton's analysis is attractive, but it is doubtful that it can provide us with essential distinguishing criteria. First, in requiring that conventional members of society acknowledge that the nonconformist is behaving "for disinterested purposes," Merton keeps the sociological observer chained to the opinions of these "conventional members of society." Furthermore, simply to state that the nonconformist "lays claim to a higher morality and ultimate values" without specifying a basis for these, makes it extremely doubtful that Merton's classification permits distinguishing between a "radical right-wing" nonconformist and a "civil rights" nonconformist; and, lacking such analytical discrimination, its use is obviously limited.

A more successful attempt to distinguish politically significant forms of behavior is shown in Waskow's article,[59] in which he identifies three types of political action: (1) politics of order, that is, acting within the existing rules of society and making reforms when needed; (2) politics of violence, which is illegal behavior justified in that it is directed either against or toward the destruction of an enemy; and (3) politics of creative disorder, which refuses to do violence, but which seeks to achieve change by a

[57] H. L. A. Hart, "Prolegomenon to the Principles of Punishment," *Philosophy, Politics and Society*, Peter Laslett and W. G. Runciman (eds.), Oxford: Basil Blackwell, & Mott, Ltd., p. 163.

[58] Robert K. Merton, "Social Problems and Sociological Theory," *Contemporary Social Problems*, edited by Robert K. Merton and Robert A. Nisbet, New York: Harcourt, Brace & World, Inc., 1961, Chap. 15, pp. 697–737.

[59] Arthur Waskow, "Creative Disorder in the Racial Struggle," *Correspondent*, No. 32 (Autumn 1964), pp. 61–73.

militant attitude but by nonviolent means. And he has concluded:

The new techniques [of civil disobedience] are also likely to revivify the practice of that kind of democracy in which all citizens participate directly, in which each man has an active share in the shaping of his own destiny and that of his society.[60]

Waskow's three types of political action point the way toward a classification which is consistent with the contents of this paper. It is suggested that behavior can be judged to be (1) apolitical behavior, (2) politically obedient behavior, (3) creative political crime, or (4) destructive political crime. *Apolitical behavior* is behavior which seeks to satisfy the needs and interests of an individual or a group outside the political realm. Such behavior seeks either to deny the need for a political order or to subvert it into essentially nonpolitical forms. *Politically obedient behavior* acknowledges the existing political forms as legitimate and necessary and seeks to work within their framework. It understands that existing forms and instant governmental acts have a constitutional basis, but the politically obedient adheres to and accepts the official interpretation of these constitutional presuppositions. The politically obedient, in effect, removes himself from a creative role in the political order; he plays a passive, conformist, obedient role. *Political crime as creative behavior*, in the United States at least, similarly adheres to the constitutional presuppositions of the political order, but insists on the right and responsibility of the individual to impose an other than official interpretation. Thus, basic to the creative political actor are the premises that all men belong to, and should be encouraged to participate in, the body politic, and that this right is basic to political identity and must be protected by law, a law that applies equally to all. The politically creative actor insists that the state tolerate and refrain from seriously punishing politically deviant actions when these are directed

[60] Waskow, p. 73.

toward the maintenance, through creative interpretation, of the existing political order, rather than toward the destruction of that order. The politically creative actor insists on the right to rebel—in Albert Camus' sense of that word—the right to protest nonviolently, by civil disobedience if necessary, against the actions of the political state. Finally, the *politically criminal* seeks power for himself, his party, or his group by violating the constitutional and ethical presuppositions of the political order and interpreting the law in an exclusive and politically divisive manner. The political criminal seeks to maintain or acquire power by excluding class, race, ethnic, religious, or political groups by denying their participation in the political order.

This survey has examined the politically criminal nature of Southern political power. It has shown that the South, by denying political identity to its Negro population, has violated the basic constitutional presuppositions of political community; that is, the right of all to live under law and to participate in the making and executing of that law. By developing this pattern of "exclusive" politics, the South has created a police state rather than a political community; the Negro has been forced to accept his subservient social status by techniques of extralegal violence supported by police power. And thus the South has moved frighteningly close to a totalitarian political order.[61]

In seeking a political identity, by acting in the public sphere in a nonviolent manner, seeking a meaningful application of existing laws, the creative interpretation and extension of laws, and the making of new laws, the Negro has given legitimacy to, and proven the success of, this form of "crea-

[61] While this writer has strong reservations about characterizing the South as totalitarian, it must be noted that such a characterization has recently been made. See Joseph L. Brent III and Perry H. Howard, "Toward a Sociological History of the American South: Implications of Regional Totalitarianism in a Pluralistic Society," unpublished manuscript; paper read at the Montreal meeting of the American Sociological Association, September 1964.

tive" political activity. This phenomenon may be of great importance for the future, as we move into a "post capitalistic" period,[62] a period characterized by government largesse rather than by "free enterprise," and, correspondingly, a shift from a class society with rights grounded in property to a society generally based on privileges arising from status.[63]

As we advance into this government-

[62] Ralf Dahrendorf, Class and Class Conflict in Industrial Society, Stanford, Calif.: Stanford University Press, 1959.
[63] Reich.

created status society, individuals will be increasingly faced with the struggle to transform the privileges of status into the rights of the individual. This will mean direct confrontation with government; it will sometimes mean action directed against government. But it need not mean political crime in the destructive sense of the word. Rather, the civil rights movement and other contemporary nonviolent protests point the way to a form of political creativity open to man in mass society dominated by government largesse.

COLLABORATORS WITH THE GERMANS IN DENMARK DURING WORLD WAR II*

Karl O. Christiansen

After World War II over 14,000 persons in Denmark were convicted in accordance with a retroactive supplement to the Criminal Code which made "collaboration and other activities injurious to the State" a criminal act. Collaboration of males with the Germans has been studied by Karl O. Christiansen, and several subsequent reports have been published in Danish. Described here is the political, cultural, and socioeconomic situation in Denmark during the war which provided the setting for various types of collaboration. Data from interviews with 2967 collaborators established that three population groups varied in their collaboration and were divergent in respect to a number of social conditions. The hypothesis is advanced that group resistance affects the incidence of collaboration with the occupying power and exerts an influence on who becomes a collaborator.

At the Nuremberg trials, the French Public Prosecutor, Edgar Faure, concluded his indictment for crimes against humanity by calling attention to the Nazi reign of terror in Denmark during the last years of the occupation. The crimes committed were

not random acts of terror perpetrated by chance and by morally worthless subordinates; they were a deliberate link in the Nazi system of suppression, intentionally implemented by the head of the Nazi state and his closest followers. During the Ger-

* This selection, written especially for this book, is published here for the first time.

man occupation of Denmark Danish citizens committed crimes against which the Danish judicial authorities were unable to take any steps because of the criminals' association with the occupying power. The crimes in question were primarily murders and crimes of violence, duress, intimidation, and threats, and a number of crimes endangering the lives of the public, often described as *Schalburgtage*. Collaborators with the Germans were also guilty of crimes against property, though in a far less degree. These crimes included some cases of robbery with violence committed by members of the Hipo Corps and the Schalburg Corps, certain cases of burglary, a few cases of theft, and occasional instances of embezzlement and fraud. There were numerous petty offenses (disturbances of the peace, breaches of the Firearms Act and the ban on wearing uniforms) which were quite harmless and called for light punishment. Also there were a few cases of sexual crimes; but the rumors which circulated about these crimes during the occupation were vastly exaggerated. According to Danish law the criminal nature of these acts is indisputable.

In addition to these offenses, there was general agreement within the resistance movement, among politicians, and in the vast majority of the population that service in the German (or German-sponsored) armed forces and in the forces to which the German occupiers assigned police duties was also punishable. This likewise applied to those guilty of informing, to certain types of propagandist activities, and to certain other forms of collaboration with the occupying power, particularly industrial or economic collaboration.

After the war just over 14,000 persons in Denmark were convicted in accordance with the supplement to the criminal code of June 1, 1945, dealing with "collaboration and other activities injurious to the State" or in accordance with the slightly amended act of June 29, 1946. In the present survey the offenders have been termed "collabora-

tors," a simplified term which describes the behavior of the majority of the convicted persons. According to Section 1 the validity of the act is limited to the period from April 9, 1940, to two years after the act came into force, that is, June 1, 1947. This act is thus a retroactive law. Only a very few of the convicted persons committed their crimes after the liberation in May 1945. According to Section 2 the law is effective only in the case of crimes committed by persons of Danish nationality. The act does not aim at inflicting punishment on foreign, in particular German, war criminals who committed crimes in Denmark during the war.

TYPES OF COLLABORATORS

Several forms of offenses were made punishable by the Criminal Code. According to the prevailing or dominant type of collaboration the persons convicted may be classified into nine groups.

1. Civil guards in Denmark, comprising members of different corps and groups who performed service as civil guards within the frontiers of Denmark, especially naval guards, Schweriner guards (a German corps, which both recruited its members in Denmark and served in the country during the occupation), firemen, several civil guard corps attached to the German airfields in Denmark, the Sommer Corps (a Danish Nazi corps of civil guards, established at the beginning of 1944 and dissolved in February 1945), and some members of the German Organization Todt (Schutz Kommando Manner the SK) who served in Denmark.
2. Civil guardsmen abroad, comprising collaborators who served as watchmen abroad (in Germany, Italy, France, and Norway). Most of them were members of the Organization Todt (OT).
3. Soldiers: members of Free Corps Denmark (a Danish military Nazi corps established in June 1941) and Waffen-SS, members of the German navy and

soldiers serving on airfields as antiaircraft gunners (Flaksoldaten). Most of them served on the Eastern Front.

4. Zeitfreiwillige (part-time volunteers): a corp of members of the German minority in South Jutland, established in January 1943. They received some military training, mostly on Sundays. The corps was to go into action in the event of an Allied invasion of Denmark. This group also included members of the Selbstschutz (Self-Protection), a corps which the Danish inhabitants of South Jutland considered a more serious threat than the Zeitfreiwillige.

5. Members of the Schalburg Corps, formed in February, 1943, by the second commander of Free Corps Denmark and named after the first commander, Von Schalburg, who fell in Russia. It was a Danish Nazi corps which gave its members military training. Toward the end of the occupation it performed police duties in several Danish towns. The corps was dissolved in January 1945, but as early as July 1944, a group broke out from the corps under the name of SS-Ausbildungsbataillon Schalburg. After the dissolution of the Schalburg Corps, the SS-Ausbildungsbataillon was renamed SS-Vagtbataillon Sjaelland, and, in fact, took over the former's functions.

6. Members of the Hipo Corps, a Danish Nazi corps, established in 1944, which acted as a police force (Hipo = Hilfspolizei = Auxiliary Police). The Hipo developed from a division of the Schalburg Corps (Et = Efterretningstjenesten = Intelligence Service). The members of the Hipo Corps collaborated to a certain extent with the Gestapo. Some of the most dangerous gangs which terrorized the Danish population during the occupation were attached to the Hipo Corps.

7. Members of the German Police Corps, most of whom belonged to the Gestapo, but a smaller number of whom were attached to the Sicherheitsdienst (Security Service) or the German (Civil) Police Force. These corps played their most important part from the end of 1943.

8. Propagandists, Nazi leaders, recruiting officers: groups of collaborators whose activities were mainly concentrated in the intellectual fields.

9. Informers, who were not as a rule organized in groups as were the members of the other groups. From a sociological point of view the main characteristic of the informers was that they generally acted as individuals rather than as members of any group. In fact, most of them cannot be classed with any particular group. Nonetheless, they are a type of collaborator.

In 1940 various corps of civil guards and SS-Standarte Nordland were set up. In 1941 the Free Corps Denmark was formed, and the recruitment of SK members for OT and the German Police Corps had begun. The recruitment to the soldier corps culminated in 1941, and in 1942 the recruitment to the civil guard corps was quite considerable. At the beginning of 1943 the Schalburg Corps and the Zeitfreiwillige Corps in South Jutland were formed, and later in the same year the Sommer Corps was created; in the same period the ET parted company with the Schalburg Corps. At the end of 1943 the German Police corps were considerably enlarged. In the spring of 1944 the Selbstschutz Corps was formed. In early 1944 recruitment to the civil guard corps and the Schalburg Corps reached its height. At the end of 1944 the German Police Corps and in particular the ET increased their numbers, Hipo was formed, and during this period and the beginning of 1945 the recruitment of new members to these corps reached its height.

The formation of these corps of collaborators meant a large increase in the number of recruited collaborators up to the beginning of 1944. Even toward the end of 1944 and during the early months of 1945 the number of volunteers was fairly high; approximately 1000 convicted collaborators began their criminal association with the Germans during the last four months of the occupation. The existence of these corps also meant that most of the crimes had a situational character.

THE NATURE
OF THE CRIMINAL
BEHAVIOR

Probably more than any other form of criminality, the criminality of the collaborators was the result of the *general social situation.* The fact that it was impossible to take legal measures against those who collaborated with the Germans during the occupation made it necessary to pass a retroactive law. If this had not been done, the population would most certainly have taken the law into their own hands, and the "Night of the Long Knives," which some people dreamed of, would have become a bloody reality. This was fortunately avoided.

The fact remains, nonetheless, that the majority of the acts which were subsequently punished with severe sentences did not, in the normal sense, constitute criminal offenses at the time. They were either not punishable or only subject to light sentences; they did not warrant charge and conviction; the lawful press of the country was debarred from reporting these crimes, and because none of these cases could be tried the illegal newspapers could not follow the normal practice of the press and refer to an unbroken series of decisions of the courts. Furthermore, psychologically, these acts were not regarded as crimes of the same nature as breaches of the Criminal Code.

From this point of view *the criminal forms of collaboration can be defined as certain violations of what was considered proper behavior in dealings with the Germans by the vast majority of the Danish people during the years of the German occupation, violations which were then criminalized after the liberation, but most of which were in fact not, or at least were not regarded as, punishable at the time they were* committed. For this reason too, it was impossible to prosecute and convict the perpetrators as long as the Germans were occupying the country.

If the fact that society condemns certain acts as being criminal and reacts against the perpetrators of such acts through its judicial authorities has any influence whatsoever on the frequency of crime, on who becomes a criminal, or on the conditions which, so to speak, produce crime, then one cannot expect to find a close consistency between normal criminality and the criminality of collaborators. In one other respect, too, the crimes of collaboration differ from normal criminality. Figuratively speaking, the normal criminals themselves create the framework of their crimes, while for most of the collaborators the framework existed beforehand; the "framework" in their case was the various corps of collaborators which were formed during the occupation.

EXTENT OF COLLABORATION

By national and ideological loyalties the convicted persons may be classified in three population groups: first, the *German minority* in South Jutland; second, the *Danish Nazis;* third, the *non-Nazi population* excluding the first two groups. Collaborators from South Jutland generally described themselves quite simply as "Danish" or "German." It was only in a few cases that the classification had to be made on the basis of information about their extraction, schooling (Danish or German school), language, or national sympathies. They were all members of the German Nazi party (NSDAP). The Danish Nazis were identified on the evidence of substantiated membership of the Danish Nazi party (DNSAP), before they were recruited as collaborators. After the war the archives of the Nazi party fell into the hands of the Danish police; hence

According to information from the Danish Department of Statistics, a total of 13,521 persons (12,877 men and 644 women) out of approximately 4,000,000 persons were convicted in accordance with the supplement to the Criminal Code.[1] This survey does not include the 1114 men who were convicted for economic collaboration only; the remainder, 11,763 men, form the basis from which the material for the present survey was selected. The forms of collaboration for which women were convicted will not be discussed except to add that more than half the women were sentenced for informing.

The male collaborators could be classified according to dominant groups and population groups as shown in Table 1. The Zeitfreiwillige were found only in the German minority group. Soldiers were found with almost equal frequency in all three population groups, though perhaps with a slight preponderance among the Nazis. Civil guards in Denmark accounted for about one fourth in all three population groups, with an apparent predominance in the Danish non-Nazi population group.

[1] *Retsopgøret med landssvigerne.* Det statistiske Department, Copenhagen, 1958. (*The Judicial Purge of Collaborators.* Report published by the Department of Statistics for the Ministry of Justice, Copenhagen, 1958.)

Guards abroad were especially prevalent in the non-Nazi population group and less frequently in the German minority and among the Danish Nazis.

The differences are not particularly striking for the Schalburg Corps, the German Police Corps, and the informers. The fact that the propagandists are most numerous in the Nazi group is to a certain extent self-explanatory. The frequency of collaboration differed considerably in the three population groups. In all, just under 1 percent of the male population over the age of criminal responsibility (15 years) were punished for one of the types of collaboration which were criminalized by the supplements to the Criminal Code. But this figure varies in the three population groups: 25 percent in the German minority group, 10 percent among the Nazis, and 0.4 percent in the non-Nazi population.

It is possible to limit or expand, however, the concept of criminal collaboration. (1) Punishment could be limited to infringement of the Criminal Code in connection with informing and collaborating with the occupying power. In this case the number of convicted persons would

Table 1.

MALE COLLABORATORS ACCORDING TO POPULATION GROUPS
AND TYPE OF COLLABORATION (ESTIMATED FIGURES)*

TYPES OF COLLABORATION	GERMAN MINORITY		DANISH NAZI PARTY		THE REST		TOTAL	
	No.	Pct.	No.	Pct.	No.	Pct.	No.	Pct.
Civil guards in Denmark	594	21.4	838	24.8	1615	28.8	3047	25.9
Civil guards abroad	149	5.4	71	2.1	936	16.7	1156	9.8
Soldiers	727	26.2	1058	31.3	1575	28.1	3360	28.6
Zeitfreiwillige	1212	43.6	0	0	0	0	1212	10.3
Schalburg Corps	0	0	260	7.7	353	6.3	613	5.2
Hipo Corps	6	0.2	301	8.9	303	5.4	610	5.2
German Police Corps	52	1.9	280	8.3	331	5.9	663	5.6
Propagandists	6	0.2	362	10.7	118	2.1	486	4.1
Informers	31	1.1	209	6.2	376	6.7	616	5.2
Total	2777	100.0	3379	100.0	5607	100.0	11763	99.9

* Here as elsewhere the estimations are based on the author's investigation of 5152 male collaborators, see footnote 6.

hardly have exceeded between 1600 and
1700 males. (2) Punishment could include
the subsequently criminal forms of collaboration, for membership in the Nazi parties,
and for civilian work for the Germans. The
number of sentenced persons would hardly
have been less than 150,000; the convictions
in the German minority group and among
the Nazis would have reached 100 percent
but presumably at most 7 to 8 percent in
the non-Nazi population.

The existing differences in the frequency
of collaboration in the three population
groups may be explained by means of the
concept of group resistance.[2] Resistance to
collaboration did not exist in the German
minority; it existed, in a limited degree,
among the Danish Nazis, and was considerably more active and extensive in the non-
Nazi population. This does not mean to
say that group resistance is the only factor
which determines the frequency of crime,
but merely that, in the given circumstances,
it probably is a decisive factor.

It has been asserted that the figure for
the German minority group cannot be compared with the figures for the other two
groups, because the criminal culpability of
the offenses committed by the members of
the Zeitfreiwillige (part-time volunteer
corps) was slight. This would bring down
the crime frequency for the German minority group to 14 percent. The significance of
this argument is, however, entirely dependent on how one interprets the concept of
crime as it is relevant to criminology. These
considerations lose their force if, like Sutherland and Cressey, one defines criminality as
the set of relationships between the following three elements: a value appreciated by
a politically important group; a group whose
members do not appreciate the value and
consequently endanger it; and coercion decently applied by those who appreciate the
value to those who disregard it.[3] On similar

grounds inspired by the theories borrowed
from sociology of law, Christie stresses the
advantages of accepting a definition which
places the main emphasis on the "interplay
between the offender and the legal system."[4] In this case one cannot disregard
the collaboration of the Zeitfreiwillige. In
fact, at the purge, this group received heavy
sentences, most of them exceeding eighteen
months' imprisonment.

If one accedes, however, to these views
and accepts the opinion that membership
in the Zeitfreiwillige Corps could hardly
be described as criminal, exemption from
punishment for this type of collaboration
would mean only a small reduction of the
number of collaborators convicted in the
German minority group, as about 80 percent of the Zeitfreiwillige were punished for
other crimes as well, nearly 40 percent receiving sentences for various forms of service in the armed forces; many also served as
members of the Selbstschutz, which was a
more openly agressive organization; and
about 25 percent took part in the Nazi
leader courses which, in the case of the
Danish Nazis, was generally considered an
aggravating circumstance. The number of
convicted persons in this group would thus
have been about 20 percent of the adult
males in the German minority.

THE DANISH WARTIME SITUATION AND COLLABORATION

The developments which took place during
the occupation were the result of a number
of factors, including the attitude and dispositions of the Danish government and the
German occupiers; the growth of the resistance movement; the attitude of the German minority, the Nazis, and the population as a whole; and, finally, the economic,
occupational, and, in the narrow sense of
the word, the social conditions.[5]

[2] Thorsten Sellin, Culture Conflict and Crime, New York: Social Science Research Council, 1938.
[3] Edwin H. Sutherland and Donald R. Cressey, Principles of Criminology, 6th ed., Philadelphia: J. B. Lippincott Company, 1960, p. 15.
[4] Nils Christie, "Synspunkter pa kriminologien" (Criminology as a Science), Nordisk Tidsskrift for Kriminalvidenskab, 46 (1958), pp. 135 ff.
[5] Regarding sources for the following survey, see Karl O. Christiansen, Landssvigerkriminaliteten

During the first years of the occupation the *policy of the Danish government* was one of adjustment and cooperation. This was manifested in the following ways: (1) Repeated injunctions to the population to preserve calm and order. (2) Official statements confirming the government's faith in a German victory. (3) After the German attack on Soviet Russia, Denmark's status as a nonbelligerent country was maintained but, in the words of an official statement put forward at the time, "the outcome of the war can no longer be regarded as irrelevant." The government banned the Communist party, interned Communist leaders, indirectly sanctioned the formation of the Free Corps Denmark, and signed the Anti-Comintern Pact. (4) Sabotage was energetically combated after 1942, and the population was again and again exhorted to refrain from active resistance. (5) The resistance of the government to the Germans could not be expressed in official declarations or statements.

The break with the Germans on August 23, 1943, brought about a complete change in the government's attitude. (1) The official policy of cooperation and collaboration was rejected. (2) Official exhortations to collaborate with the Germans ceased. (3) The faith in a German victory had faded. (4) The recruitment of Danes to German war service ceased practically entirely. Anti-Communist feeling gradually dwindled; Danish public officials protested strongly against the deportation of Danish Communists. (5) The propaganda against acts of sabotage by the resistance movement was left entirely to the Germans and the Danish Nazis. Police action against the saboteurs was curtailed and ceased entirely when the police were deported or, to avoid deportation, went underground on September 19, 1944. (6) It is open to discussion whether Denmark, after August 29, 1943, was nonbelligerent, at war with Germany,

or in a state "verging on war." This question is still being debated. The majority of the population, however, hardly considered Denmark as being in a *de facto* state of war with Germany; but there was no doubt that their attitude was openly hostile.

Denmark's status as an occupied country differed from that of the other occupied countries. Normal diplomatic relations were maintained and, in principle, all problems were to be solved through negotiation. But the attitude of the *occupying power* was naturally exclusively determined by what served German interests best. The most interference in Danish affairs was in the administration of justice, but the political influence exerted by the Germans, backed by pressure or more or less official threats, was in reality much more serious. The occupation meant a complete readjustment of supplies, trade, and economic policy, but to begin with the Germans attempted to keep up appearances, asserting that "all trade was on a reciprocal basis."

Toward the end of the occupation the situation changed to one marked by violence, terror, and wanton destruction. Some figures will serve to illustrate this. The persecution of the Jews began on the first of October, 1943; between 6000 and 7000 Danish Jews evaded deportation by escaping to Sweden during the following months. In addition to the Jews, about 12,000 other Danes fled to Sweden. The Germans managed to intern 475 Jews in Theresienstadt, a notorious concentration camp in Germany, where 52 of them died. After the Danish police force was dissolved on September 19, 1944, 1984 members were sent to concentration camps in Germany, where 80 of them died. The following list of casualties will give an impression of the effects of German rule:

---

i sociologisk belysning. (Collaboration with the Germans in Denmark during the Occupation: A Sociological Study.) Copenhagen, 1955.

1. Officially executed after being sentenced by a German military tribunal   102
2. a. Shot during "an attempt to escape" August 9–10, 1944   11
   b. Killed in action, under arrest,

during attempt to escape, during interrogation, in German
prisons, etc.   372
   c. Killed during the general strike
     in Copenhagen, 1944   112
   d. Killed during raids, terror,
     "Schalburgtage" etc.   447
   e. Killed as reprisal or assassi-
     nated   117
   f. Various causes   5
3. Died in German concentration
   camps   546
                                                               ————
                                                               1712

The numbers of interned and imprisoned persons can be estimated as follows:

1. Deported to German concentration
   camps   6104
2. Interned in Denmark   6897
3. In German prisons in Denmark   4000
                                                              ————
                                                              17,001

Nevertheless, throughout the occupation
there was a slight resistance among the
Danish Nazis against collaborating with the
Germans. There is no reason to doubt the
patriotic feelings of the Danish Nazi party.
This attitude was not as marked as the
Danish Nazi propagandists represented it to
be, and only occasionally did it influence
the policy of the party, but it did exist.
Reasons of tactics probably explain why it
did not play a more prominent part.

The growth of the resistance movement seems to have been the effect of a
continuous series of causes, the end of 1943
being a particularly important phase of this
development. The firmer organization and
increased activities of the sabotage groups,
the closer contact with Britain, the forma
tion of the Freedom Council, the beginning
of the cooperation between the underground organizations, the politicians, and
the Danish armed force, the growing influ-

ence and circulation of the illegal newspapers, the formation of military groups,
and the liquidation of informers all indicated that the situation had entered upon
a new and vital phase. Table 2 provides
some figures to illustrate this.

The total number of liquidations of informers carried out by the resistance movement amounted to about 380. In 1943 only
a few took place, in 1944 there were somewhat over 100, and in 1945, up to the liberation in May, over 200.

The attitude of the German minority
may be characterized by their national and
political ties with the occupying power. The
minority was pro-German to such a degree
that it could not be otherwise than immune
to Danish influences. Most of the collaborators who belonged to this German minority group regarded collaboration with the
Germans as something which was not only
fully legal but their duty.

For the Danish Nazis the situation was
somewhat different. They felt themselves
closely bound, politically but not nationally, to the occupying power. Their willingness to collaborate with the Germans could
not be doubted. It followed from their ideological sense of solidarity and from tactical
considerations. The Germans made extensive use of this group, and were ready to
pay for its loyalty with money and a certain political support as long as they did
not have to commit themselves decisively.

The attitude of the non-Nazi population underwent considerable changes during the years of the occupation. The resistance against the policy of cooperation with
the Germans was evident in the greater part
of the population from the very beginning
of the occupation. It was far stronger here

Table 2.

	1940	1941	1942	1943	1944	1945
Circulation of illegal newspapers in thousands	1	40	301	2600	10,935	10,131
Number of acts of sabotage by the resistance movement	52	54	188	1319	1195	1988

than among the Nazis and the German minority. The first clear example of this growing reaction was seen in the student demonstrations in 1941; it broke through seriously at the parliamentary elections in March 1943, in the strikes during the summer, and the concerted effort to help the Jews in the autumn of 1943. The climax was reached in the spontaneous general strikes in the summer of 1944 and did not subside until the liberation of the country in May 1945. But the group resistance never became total.

Economic factors played a role. Real wages fell during the first years of the war and reached their lowest level in 1941–1942. In 1943 and 1944 the tendency was toward higher wages, but the wage level was still lower than in the prewar years. The wages of agricultural laborers and farm hands were more satisfactory. The unemployment situation quickly improved; in 1939 it was 11.5, in 1943, 6.3, and in 1944, 4.6. However, 35 percent of the collaborators were unemployed at the time of their recruitment. The recruitment of Danish labor to work in Germany was extensive, particularly in the first three years of the war: over 30,000 in 1941 and 1942. In all, about 110,000 persons worked in Germany during the period 1940–1945. Some of them returned to work in Germany more than once. From 1941 until the liberation, 11,751 persons went to work in Norway.

Recruitment for civilian employment in Germany was partly through the German Employment Offices, and partly through Danish firms or recruiting officers. A number of Danes who were out of work were encouraged by the Danish Public Assistance Offices to seek employment in Germany or to work for the German armed forces in Denmark. A large number of persons were employed on German Wehrmacht installations in Denmark. These figures reached their zenith in May 1944, when 71,000 persons were working on military installations in this country.

During most of the occupation there was a surplus of workers who had returned from employment in Germany and who were unable to find civil employment with the Wehrmacht in Denmark. By March 31, 1943, 77,000 workers had returned from Germany, while the number of workers employed on military installations in Denmark at this time was about 30,000. In December 1944, the number of Wehrmacht workers in Denmark was about 57,000; at the same time, however, there were in this country slightly over 120,000 persons who had returned from Germany. A conservative estimate shows that from the end of 1942 there were constantly between 30,000 and 50,000 returned workers who were unable to find work with the German Wehrmacht in Denmark. Some of this labor reserve was recruited for the activities of the occupying power, activities for which they were subsequently convicted. Fifty-seven percent of the collaborators covered by the present study had previously had civilian employment with the Germans in Germany, Norway, or Denmark.

Crimes of violence and crimes against property more than doubled between 1939 and 1943. There was no rise in sexual criminality during the war. The dissolution of the Danish Police Corps on September 19, 1944, resulted in a rise in the normal criminality, but no statistics are available on this development.

CHARACTERISTICS OF COLLABORATORS

The investigations carried out by the present author[6] cover 5152 male collaborators convicted in accordance with the supple-

[6] *Mandlige landssvigere i Danmark under besaettelsen. En kriminografisk og sociologisk oversigt over 5.107 maend dømt efter straffelovstillaeggene af 1.6.1945 og 29.6.1946.* (Male Collaborators with the Germans in Denmark during the Occupation: A Criminographical and Sociological Survey concerning 5,107 Men, Convicted according to the Supplements of 1.6.1945 and 29.6.1946 to the Civil Penal Law. With a summary in English); *Udgivet af Direktoratet for faengselsvaesenet.* (Published by the Prison Administration) Copenhagen, 1950; and *Landssvigerkriminaliteten i sociologisk belysning.* (Collaboration with the Germans: A Sociological Study.) Copenhagen, 1955.

ments to the Criminal Code of June 1, 1945, and June 29, 1946, but exclude economic collaborators. These 5152 collaborators represent 44 percent of the total number convicted. In all, 2976 were interviewed. The investigation was carried out between 1945 and 1950 at the Registration Office for Collaborators at the Directorate of Prisons. This office was headed by the psychiatric consultant to the prisons, George K. Sturup, M.D., Chief Psychiatrist, and the author. The material comprises a disproportionate number of civil guards, members of the Schalburg Corps and the Gestapo (German Police) in relation to the number of Zeitfreiwillige, Hipos, propagandists, and informers, who are somewhat underrepresented. The higher death rate in some of the corps, differences in the occurrence of hidden criminality, and the above-mentioned skewed distribution of the dominant types may have had the following effects: (1) a smaller frequency of convicted collaborators in the groups comprising the German minority and the Nazis due to variations in the death rate of the three groups; (2) due to the need to reduce the size of the study, a higher frequency of socially deviating persons among the investigated collaborators and among the investigated collaborators recruited at an early stage among the German minority; (3) a higher frequency of socially deviating persons among the investigated collaborators recruited at an early stage, probably in all three population groups. This was a consequence of a higher death rate and a higher incidence of hidden criminality among collaborators recruited early. In analyzing the material, these reductions have been taken into consideration, for the material has been consistently divided into the relevant subgroups.

It is evident from the predominantly negative findings of the two Danish surveys of their psychological and psychiatric background that the criminality of the collaborators was primarily a *sociological* phe-

nomenon,[7] a finding which has been further corroborated by investigations of the social conditions of the collaborators. On this point the three population groups are somewhat divergent. A short survey is given below of the results of the investigation regarding (1) age, (2) education, (3) occupational and economic factors, (4) marital status, (5) previous criminality, and (6) social class.

Age and Education. Like ordinary criminality, the criminality of the collaborators was highest in the youngest age groups and decreased with increasing age, although the fall is not as marked as for ordinary criminality. The collaborators from the German minority included many older persons, among the third group there were relatively many younger persons, while the Nazis formed an intermediate group. It was found that the German minority and the Nazis had a higher education, 56 percent having had supplementary or other higher education; the third group, comprising the rest of the country, 32 percent had a higher education. There was a greater number with only elementary schooling in the membership of the third group and among the Nazis than among the general Danish army recruits investigated in 1946. There was no demonstrable difference for the German minority. These observations seem again to indicate that the collaborators in the German minority did not differ essentially from the Danish population as a whole as far as schooling is concerned. The Nazi collaborators form an intermediate group which in social respects compares unfavorably with the average population. The same applies to

[7] Gunnar Mortensson, "Psykiatrisk undersøgelse af mandlige landssvigere i Denmark" ("Psychiatric Investigation of Male Collaborators in Denmark.") *Nordisk Tidsskrift for Kriminalvidenskab,* 41 (1953), pp. 2 ff.; and Thomas Sigsgard, *Psykologisk undersøgelse af mandlige landssvigere i Danmark under besaettelsen. (Psychological Investigation of Male Collaborators in Denmark during the German Occupation.)* Copenhagen, 1954.

the collaborators in the group comprising the non-Nazi population.

Occupation and Income. The economic and occupational conditions are illustrated by an investigation of the vocational training, the incidence of unemployment at the time of recruitment, and increased income on turning collaborator for the first time. In the third group, among the collaborators over twenty-five living in towns, there were considerably and significantly more unskilled workers than among the Nazis. There was a far greater number of collaborators who were unemployed at the time of their recruitment in the third group than in the two other groups. It is not possible to demonstrate that there was more unemployment among the Nazis than in the German minority. Among collaborators from the

general population the number of unemployed was significantly higher among the guards than among the soldiers.

The statistical analysis of increase in income on turning collaborator showed that those from the non-Nazi population who had been recruited in 1944 or 1945 in Copenhagen more frequently showed an increased income than the corresponding category among the Nazis. Taken together with the results for vocational training and unemployment this seems to mean that the collaborators in the non-Nazi group were financially worse off than the collaborators in the other two population groups.

Marital Status. Age is an important factor in relation to marital status. The large number of unmarried persons (60 percent) in the membership of the third group was

Table 3.

INTERVIEWED COLLABORATORS ACCORDING TO AGE,
MARITAL STATUS, AND POPULATION GROUPS

AGE AND POPULATION GROUP	NUMBER	MARITAL STATUS AND AGE			
		UNMARRIED (percent)	MARRIED (percent)	DIVORCED (percent)	WIDOWERS (percent)
German Minority					
0–20 years	60	100	0	0	0
21–25 years	43	88	12	0	0
26–30 years	40	30	67	3	0
31–40 years	97	8	90	1	1
41+ years	121	1	92	5	2
Total	361	33	64	1	0
Nazis					
0–20 years	160	99	1	0	0
21–25 years	159	78	21	1	0
26–30 years	150	32	63	5	0
31–40 years	197	14	79	6	1
41+ years	193	7	85	7	1
Total	859	44	52	4	0
Non-Nazi					
0–20 years	569	98	2	0	0
21–25 years	490	73	24	3	0
26–30 years	265	32	49	18	1
31–40 years	267	17	64	17	2
41+ years	155	2	81	11	6
Total	1747	60	32	7	1

due to the fact that this group consisted of relatively many young collaborators (Table 3). This group differs from the other two population groups in that it includes slightly more young married persons and relatively fewer older married persons. This group also includes far more separated or divorced persons or widowers than the other groups; higher frequency of divorcees is considerably and significantly above the divorce rate for men. The Danish Nazis had slightly more older unmarried, fewer older married persons, and more divorcees than the German minority.

Previous Criminality. During the occupation there were exaggerated notions about the number of criminals to be found among the collaborators.

Actually about 32 percent of the collaborators forming the subjects of this investigation had been in conflict with the law before joining one of the corps of collaborators. If one disregards petty crimes and considers only the crimes which entail registration in the criminal records, the figure is reduced to 22 percent. Of these 22 percent, about two thirds (16 percent) were previously sentenced to imprisonment, one fourth (5.6 percent) received prison sentences up to five months, and one eighth (2.8 percent) sentences of one year or more. The distribution based on the nature of the crimes committed corresponds fairly closely to the figures in the official statistics: about 90 percent were sentenced for crimes against property, and the remainder for crimes of violence, sexual offenses, and other types of crime.

A survey was made of the occurrence of previous crime in the narrow sense of the word (crimes registered in the criminal records) in the three population groups and within certain of the dominant types. With the usual subdivisions of the material, the statistical analysis reveals that the relative frequency of previous criminals among the collaborators is significantly higher among collaborators from the non-Nazi population

(29 percent) than in the German minority (7 percent) and among the Nazis (14 percent). The difference between the Nazis and the German minority, which in fact is quite evident, cannot be proved significant when the material is divided into such relatively small subgroups. The lowest frequency of previously convicted persons is found among the early collaborators in the German minority (7 percent in the provincial towns and 4 percent in rural districts).

Among the Nazis the frequency of previous criminality varies less. The lowest figure is found among the early recruits from rural districts (8 percent), and the highest among the late recruits in the provincial towns (18 percent). Considering that the Nazis mainly belonged to the middle classes, these figures, which differ significantly from the figures for the total population, appear to be rather high.

The crime frequency among the collaborators in the third group comprising the non-German and non-Nazis is considerably and significantly higher than in the corresponding section of the Danish population who did not collaborate with the Germans.

Previous criminality was also higher than the other two groups of collaborators. The lowest figures represent the early recruits from the provincial towns (22 percent) and the highest the late recruits in the capital and the provincial towns (34 percent and 31 percent, respectively). The age group 21–25 years of age in the capital is particularly remarkable in that the frequency of the previously convicted among the early and late recruits to the ranks of the collaborators was 37 percent and 40 percent, respectively.

Late recruits to the Hipo Corps coming from towns in the non-Nazi group showed a significantly lower rate of previous criminality than other "late" collaborators. This last fact, which concerns the most notorious police corps formed during the occupation, whose members perpetrated some of the most atrocious crimes committed during the last seven months of the war, calls for some explanation. The members of the Hipo

Corps who began their career of crime during the occupation but before the Hipo Corps was formed at the end of 1944, must have started as collaborators in one of the other corps. It seems as if the Hipo Corps was wary of accepting previously convicted persons unless they had formerly served as members of one of the other corps. As the Hipo Corps had its headquarters at the Danish police headquarters, their leaders had easy access to the files of the Central Police Register. In other words, putting it rather paradoxically, in order to be eligible for the Hipo Corps either one had to have been a member of another corps, regardless of previous criminality, or he had to have a clean criminal record.

Social Class. The material was next classified into the following social classes: (1) lower class (unorganized labor and day laborers), (2) lower middle class (organized labor, independent artisans, low-grade officials, agricultural laborers, small holders), (3) upper middle class (higher grades in trade and industry, the majority of university graduates, farmers), and (4) the upper class (top grades in trade and industry, senior civil servants, leading members of the liberal professions, large farmers, and estate owners).

The distribution within the population groups as presented in Table 4 shows that there is a far larger percentage of members of the lower class among the non-Nazi group than in the other two population groups, and more among the Nazis than in the German minority. The distribution differs, however, for the other social classes.

CONCLUSIONS

A comparison of the German minority group with collaborators from the non-Nazi population shows that the latter group include significantly far more "socially deviating persons" than the first group, that is, persons from unfavorable family conditions, with less schooling, less vocational training, unemployed at the time of recruitment, separated or divorced, with a record of previous criminality, and from the lower social class. Much the same findings were made when collaborators from the non-Nazi population were compared with the Nazis. On the other hand, it was possible to demonstrate a large and significant difference between the Nazis and the German minority only in regard to unfavorable family conditions and lower social status.

The question that remained was whether the frequency of social deviation among the collaborators corresponded to the frequency of social deviation in equivalent population groups. There are two points worth mentioning in this connection: (1) Admittedly, it cannot be proved that, on an average, there were more socially deviating collaborators in the German minority and among the Nazis than in the corresponding total popu-

Table 4.

INTERVIEWED COLLABORATORS ACCORDING TO SOCIAL
CLASS AND POPULATION GROUPS

POPULATION GROUPS	NUMBER	SOCIAL CLASS		
		LOWER CLASS *(percent)*	LOWER MIDDLE CLASS *(percent)*	UPPER MIDDLE AND UPPER CLASS *(percent)*
German minority	361	10	77	13
Nazis	859	25	74	1
Non-Nazi	1747	43	56	1
Total	2967	34	63	3

lation groups. The relative figures for the German minority are so small that there is good reason to believe that the frequency is the same. But, on the other hand, it is obvious that the collaborators belonging to the group comprising the non-Nazi population included more socially deviating persons than the population group from which they derived. (2) Furthermore, it has been possible to prove that there were considerably more socially deviating persons among the late than among the early recruits to collaborationist activities in the German minority and among those collaborators from the non-Nazi population.

A possible explanation of this variation in the proportion of "deviating persons" may be *the varying group resistance to collaboration with the occupying power.* It was practically nonexistent in the German minority, it was limited among the Danish Nazis, and it was greatest in the non-Nazi population. It is also a fact that among the latter, group resistance was vastly greater in 1944–1945 than in the first years of the German occupation. It therefore seems obvious to put forward the hypothesis that *group resistance not only affects the incidence of criminality but also exerts an influence on who becomes a criminal:* the greater the group resistance, the higher the relative frequency of social (and/or personality) deviations among those who ignore the demands of the group. Such a hypothesis will be supported by the facts concerning the criminality of the collaborators in Denmark during the occupation adduced in the present survey.

There are two aspects of the problem of recidivism among the collaborators: the first was the subsequent criminality among those collaborators whose history of conviction was about what one might have expected; the second was the higher recidivism rate among the previously convicted collaborators, a rate essentially higher than one might have expected.

The length of the observation period for the majority of the convicted persons (90 percent) from their release until 1955 was at least seven years. For another 8 percent the observation period was 5 to 7 years; in 1955 only 2 percent had been at liberty for less than five years. The material for the follow-up investigation consisted of 2967 interviewed collaborators. Excluded in advance were 21 persons who had no chance of recidivism insofar as they had been either acquitted by a higher court (and therefore cannot be regarded as having been collaborators), had died during their imprisonment, or had been exiled after having served their sentences. Of the remaining 2946 who form the material for this study of recidivism, 46 died after release without recidivating, while 542 were sentenced for more or less serious offenses. Of 542 sentenced, 227 received fines or simple detention for minor offenses, while the remaining 315 were sentenced to imprisonment or to special punishment of a more serious character. In the following survey only these 315 persons are regarded as recidivists, minor criminality being disregarded. The information about their relapse into crime was obtained from the Central Police Register, which can be accepted as reliable for the period under review.

The rates of recidivism are surprisingly low: only 11 percent for the group as a whole. For ordinary prisoners the rate of recidivism in the corresponding age groups would not have been below 40 percent. Not even the group from the non-Nazi population which had the highest rate of recidivism (16 percent) approached the expected rate. The frequency of recidivism for the German minority, under 2 percent, is slightly above the frequency of criminality for this population group, which is generally quite low. The Nazi collaborators were as a whole younger than the collaborators in the German minority group and included more members from urban areas. Here a 4 percent frequency of recidivism is somewhat in excess of the frequency of criminality for previously unconvicted persons.

The investigation also showed (1) that

the frequency of recidivism decreases with rising age, (2) that the frequency of recidivism in all three population groups is higher in urban areas than in the country, and (3) that it is relatively high among civil guards aboard, soldiers, and informers whereas it is low for Zeitfreiwillige, propagandists, and members of the Hipo Corps.

Here, as in so many other respects, a criminal past is of decisive importance. A distribution of the subjects into not previously convicted and previously convicted does not alter the impression obtained of the respective shares of the different population groups in subsequent criminality. The German minority still comes in lowest, with 0.9 percent and 11.5 percent for not previously convicted and previously convicted, respectively, and the group from the non-Nazi population comes highest, with 10.3 percent and 28.1 percent, respectively. The figures for the Nazi group were 2.9 percent and 11.5 percent, respectively.

The differences in the frequency of new criminality among collaborators previously convicted and those not previously convicted of a criminal offense appear surprisingly high. In relation to the two aspects of the problem discussed above it is particularly interesting to compare the recidivism of the not previously convicted with the normal risk of being punished for the population as a whole, and also the recidivism of the previously convicted with the frequency of recidivism for inmates of prisons.[8] For the not previously convicted persons the subsequent criminality of collaborators in all three groups is higher than the expected figures.

[8] Karl O. Christiansen and Arne Nielsen, "Nulevende straffede maend i Danmark." ("The Number of Persons Who Have Been Criminally Punished in Denmark.") Nordisk Tidsskrift for Kriminalvidenskab, 41 (1959), pp. 18 ff.; Karl O. Christiansen, Lise Møller and Arne Nielsen, "Kriminalitetsrisikoen i Denmark før og efter krigen." ("The Risk of Being Punished in Denmark before and after the War"). Nordisk Tidsskrift for Kriminalvidenskab, 48 (1960), pp. 300 ff. and (1961), pp. 73ff.; and Beretning om faengselsvaesenet i Danmark 1961. (Annual Report from the Danish Prison Administration for the Year 1961). Copenhagen, 1964.

The absolute figures for the German minority and the Nazis were small and can hardly be considered decisive. But the difference observed for the group comprising the non-Nazi population is significant, 10.3 percent as against the estimated 1.5 percent.

The results were reversed for the previously convicted. The frequency of recidivism was in all instances lower than expected. Even taking into consideration the relatively small numbers involved in the case of the German minority, the differences are marked: the actual frequency of recidivism is in all three population groups only between one half and one quarter of the expected figure.

It thus seems possible to conclude from this that the purge of collaborators, their imprisonment, and their subsequent release had a favorable effect on the career of the previously convicted, whereas, quite the opposite, the effect of these measures was clearly unfavorable in the case of those not previously convicted. The question, then, is how to explain this extraordinary result.

A number of factors which might possibly have explained the occurrence of a lower frequency of recidivism among the collaborators than among ordinary criminals must be disregarded, as one may presume that their effect on all convicted persons must have been the same, regardless of whether they had previously been convicted or not. There remain, in the opinion of the present author, two hypotheses, of which one in part and the other in its entirety, may account for the differences in the frequency of recidivism among previously and not previously convicted collaborators: (1) The previously convicted had their (ordinary) career of crime, as it were, interrupted not only by their prison sentences but as a rule also through their service in one of the corps of collaborators, where the discipline regarding work was extremely strict. There is no parallel explanation of the higher recidivism of the not previously convicted. (2) It may be asserted that with the previously convicted their status was improved through their sentence in that they were classified in a "higher" category of criminals, which they themselves described as "political criminals." There are hundreds of examples to illustrate how they looked down upon the ordinary criminals as "common thieves, swindlers, sexual criminals, and hooligans."

In the case of those *not previously convicted* their prison sentence, even though it was for something as relatively "respectable" as political crimes, was a considerable fall in status. Despite the nature and motives of their crimes they were nonetheless now classified as "criminals."

personal behavior with customers and colleagues. The philosophy is one of exploiting the exploiters (customers) by whatever means necessary and defining the colleagues of the call girl as being intelligent, self-interested and, in certain important respects, basically honest individuals. The interpersonal techniques addressed during the learning period consist primarily of "pitches," telephone conversations, personal and occasionally sexual hygiene, prohibitions against alcohol and dope while with a "john," how and when to obtain the fee, and specifics concerning the sexual habits of particular customers. Specific sexual techniques are very rarely taught. The current sample included a considerable number of girls who, although capable of articulating this value structure, were not particularly inclined to adopt it.[6]

Girls who become prostitutes tend to develop attitudes and behavior patterns which are part of their social role. They develop an argot, their own professional language, special acts and services, patterns of bartering with customers and an impersonal relationship with them, as well as a large number of rationalizations for their activities.[7] The earnings of most prostitutes, even allowing for deductions in payment to a pimp, or for "protection" from the police, are higher than the earnings of most working women. The prostitute is paid for her loss of esteem through negative societal reaction. In fact, Davis concludes that "since the occupation is lucrative, the interesting question is not why so many women become prostitutes, but why so few of them do."[8]

Many prostitutes are able to leave their occupation for marriage or for employment as waitresses, domestic servants, or salesgirls. A few others are able to achieve and maintain a high standard of living. But for many, some of whom are eventually affected by venereal disease, alcoholism, and drug addiction, the end is a derelict life, punctuated more or less regularly by arrests and jail sentences. From there it is an easy step to petty stealing and shoplifting.

It is difficult to generalize about the self-attitudes of prostitutes. Because the prostitute encounters a duality of social values there is a tendency to justify or rationalize commercial sex behavior by emphasizing certain legitimate values of society, such as financial success or taking care of persons who are financially dependent on them. Self-concept as a prostitute is one role open to a prostitute; she may sustain her role through interaction with others and an emphasis on the accepted values of sex and commercial exploitation of the general society. Undoubtedly, arrests strengthen the self-conception of a prostitute, as do the attitudes of other persons associated with her. Certainly those who are employed in other occupations, such as a secretary or a model, or those whose customers are from the upper socioeconomic groups, are less likely to conceive of themselves in these terms. One study found that the more socially isolated individuals were more likely to define their behavior as acceptable than were those who were less isolated.[9]

[6] Bryan, p. 294. Also see Bryan, "Occupational Ideologies of Call Girls," *Social Problems*, 13 (Spring 1966), pp. 441–450.
[7] Walter C. Reckless, *The Crime Problem*, 3d ed., New York: Appleton-Century-Crofts, Inc., 1961, pp. 276–277.
[8] Kingsley Davis, "Sexual Behavior," in Robert K. Merton and Robert A. Nisbet (eds.), *Contemporary Social Problems*, 2d ed., New York: Harcourt, Brace & World, Inc., 1966, p. 361.
[9] Bryan, "Occupational Ideologies of Call Girls."

One study found that the stated ideology of those who had been call girls for an average length of 27 months included the beliefs that customers are exploitative, that other women are hypocrites about the use of sex to gain advantages, that prostitution provides a valuable social service by producing necessary sexual outlets and psychological comfort to customers and that call girls' relationships are close and honest.[10] However, when the individual opinions of prostitutes were studied the ideologies were generally not supported. The conclusion is that though professional ideology is learned and may serve a function during the apprentice period of prostitution it does not remain of equal importance throughout a call girl's career. For the apprentice the ideology is important in counteracting a negative self-image and reducing moral conflict during the initial period of prostitution.

HOMOSEXUAL BEHAVIOR.   Sex is but one aspect of a person's total life. Generally, it is not independent of a total life pattern and seldom is the dominating one. Thus the term homosexual is somewhat misleading. Labeling a person a homosexual tends to make a single aspect of his life cover his entire life pattern. One is unlikely to speak of a nonhomosexual as a "heterosexual."

There are homosexuals in business and the professions and in lower and upper classes. Some are married, and, like the heterosexual person, have various interests and avocations.

A person must be socialized into the homosexual subculture. This involves the learning of a social role. One must recognize one's self as a homosexual and enter into the stream of homosexual life. One important research study defined a homosexual not by his homosexual experiences but as any adult who "regards himself as a homosexual and is prepared to say so to the interviewer."[11] This self-conception as a homosexual is derived largely from the reaction of others which results in the homosexual's seeking more and more associations within the homosexual subculture. Pressures from society tend to push individuals along a four-stage progression although some individuals do not progress beyond the second stage and others become members of homosexual groups without losing interest in other activities in the community.

> 1. The first stage usually occurs in the late teens or early twenties. As his friends start to go out with girls and eventually marry, the homosexual finds other interests and drifts away from their company. Sometimes he is scarcely aware of his homosexual tendencies or has not come to terms with them, but gradually he becomes conscious of his isolation. Many young homosexuals have described their dismay when they have discovered that the sort of things which interest their friends hold no appeal for them.
>
> 2. Thus the young homosexual finds he is driven away from the company of ordinary men and women at just the time when he most needs their help. As he loses his friends he begins to regard himself as an outcast. He finds to his dismay that will-power and self-control are not the answer to his problem. The more extrovert

---

[10] Norman R. Jackman, Richard O'Toole, and Gilbert Geis, "The Self-Image of the Prostitute," *Sociological Quarterly*, 4 (Spring 1963), pp. 150–161.

[11] Michael Schofield, *Sociological Aspects of Homosexuality: A Comparative Study of Three Types of Homosexuals*, Boston: Little, Brown and Company, 1965, p. 4.

homosexual will soon pass through this second stage and quickly make friends with other homosexuals. But others lead lonely lives, plagued by feelings of guilt and accepting the role of the social isolate.

3. At the third stage the young man meets other homosexuals and begins to go to their meeting places and joins a homosexual group. Some of them soon tire of this opportunity to mix in a group of like-minded individuals, but others accept the chance eagerly. Here a homosexual can feel at ease because he does not have to hide his true inclinations. Indeed, this is such a relief that much of the talk in these groups is about sex. It is here that the two worlds conflict. He must make sure that his friends from the other world do not meet his friends from the homosexual group. He has to explain his absences from the other world, think up convincing stories, and learn to lead two lives. Some homosexuals resolve this dilemma by moving on to the fourth stage.

4. At this last stage the homosexual way of life monopolizes his interests and absorbs all his time. He gives up his efforts to resolve the conflicts between the outside world and the homosexual way of life. He moves exclusively in a homosexual group and adopts a hostile attitude towards all those not in the group. He has, in fact, adopted all the characteristics of an introverted minority group.[12]

Many homosexuals are highly promiscuous; the relationships of such homosexuals with others are short-lived and relatively anonymous, becoming acquainted in public places such as public toilets or other meeting places. The married homosexual may engage in both types of sex relations. In cases of more promiscuous homosexuality "not only are permanent relationships infrequent but even less lengthy affectional-sexual links tend to be overshadowed in homosexual life by the predominant pattern of 'cruising' and relatively impersonal one-night stands."[13] Because of this pattern of temporary sex relationships there are some male homosexual prostitutes and some exploitation particularly by juveniles who make themselves available to homosexuals for a monetary reward.[14]

Promiscuous homosexuals are more likely to be arrested or go to psychiatrists for treatment because their way of life exposes them to arrest or because they have ambivalent feelings about such sporadic activity if they are also heterosexual. A large group of homosexuals, however, consists of those who tend to have more stable homosexual relationships and do not come to the attention of authorities or psychiatric agencies. These are the confirmed homosexuals. In a study of equal groups of 50 homosexuals (1) who had been arrested, (2) who had not been arrested but had been under psychiatric treatment, or (3) who had never been arrested or been under treatment, the latter group was found to be quite different.[15] Members of the latter group more often started homosexual relations with other boys before the age of seventeen; they were more likely to have long-standing relations with men and to have lived with other homosexuals. Over four fifths

12 Schofield, p. 181.
13 Schur, p. 89.
14 Albert J. Reiss, Jr., "The Social Integration of Queers and Peers," *Social Problems*, 9 (Fall 1961), pp. 102–120, and Schofield, pp. 12–13.
15 Schofield, pp. 100–143.

(84 percent) had so arranged their lives that homosexual acts generally took place in the privacy of their homes.

DRUNKENNESS.   Alcohol, a chemical substance, has been produced in most countries for centuries, either, through a process of fermentation or distillation, in the form of distilled spirits such as whiskey or gin, or in the form of fermented beverages such as wine or beer. It is not psychologically habit-forming in the sense that certain narcotics are. As alcohol is consumed, it increasingly acts as a depressant and an anesthetic; it is not a stimulant as is commonly believed. Under the influence of alcohol a person may become aggressive, silent, or even fall into a stupor as a result of the reduction of cortical control rather than as a result of stimulation. With increasing drunkenness there is a dulling of sensory and motor function, a blunted judgment of oneself and one's activities, and an impairment of functions such as walking. "At 0.30 percent from the presence of a pint of whiskey in the body, sensory perception is so dulled that the drinker has little comprehension of what he sees, hears or feels; he is stuporous."[16]

Alcohol drinkers may be classified as the social or controlled drinker, the heavy drinker, and the alcoholic.[17] A *social or controlled drinker* drinks for sociability, conviviality, and conventionality. If he chooses, he can refrain from using intoxicating beverages. There are two types of social drinkers, the occasional and the regular drinker. The former drinks sporadically and may have only a few drinks a year, whereas the regular social drinker may drink three or more times a week. Not only does the *heavy drinker* make more frequent use of alcohol than the regular social drinker; he may become intoxicated as a result of consuming large quantities of alcohol. The excessive drinker, in common with social drinkers but with greater difficulty, may be able to curtail or to cease drinking completely on his own volition. Depending upon circumstances, he may continue drinking in this manner for the rest of his life, may later reduce the frequency and quantity of his alcohol consumption, or he may become an alcoholic. *Alcoholics* are those whose frequent and repeated drinking of alcoholic beverages is in excess of the dietary and social usages of the community and to such an extent that it interferes with health or with social or economic functioning. The alcoholic is unable to control consistently, or to stop at will, either the start of his drinking or its termination, once it has started. Among alcoholics there is (1) a reliance on alcoholic beverages, (2) repetitiveness or chronicity of the drinking in the sense that the drinking does not take place on rare occasions, (3) and ill effects which derive from the drinking and not from other causes. The drinking affects the drinker's life and not just society. The ill effects may be either definite ill-health, social or interpersonal ill effects, such as disruption of the family or ostracism which would not occur if the drinking were stopped, or economic effects, such as inability to keep a job, work efficiently, or take care of one's property as well as one could without the drinking. While the drinking of alcoholic beverages and heavy drinking are the necessary prerequisites, alcoholism should be regarded as a behavioral phenomenon and not as a biological or psychological entity.

Shifts from the stage of excessive drinking to that of chronic alcoholism, with

[16] Leon A. Greenberg, "Intoxication and Alcoholism: Physiological Factors," *The Annals*, 315 (January 1958), p. 27.
[17] See Marshall B. Clinard, *Sociology of Deviant Behavior*, rev. ed., New York: Holt, Rinehart and Winston, Inc., 1963, pp. 337–346.

its social and often physical deterioration, are often imperceptible. The alcoholic process usually extends over a period of ten to twenty years of drinking; one is never a full-blown alcoholic after a few experiences with the effects of liquor. Alcoholism means more than sporadic intoxication. It implies changes in the nature of inter-personal relations with others, in attitudes toward drinking, in social roles, and in conceptions of the self, including increasing dependence on drinking, attitudes which are at variance with those held by others and which were developed through a marginal social existence, numerous rebuffs, arrests, social isolation, and physical deterioration.

Excessive drinking and alcoholism may be perceived by others as extreme devi-ation, and these persons are often frequently arrested. Excessive drinkers may come to conceive of themselves as problems, and even as alcoholics, but not as criminals even though their drinking may result in frequent arrests. They may come to refer to themselves as "drunks" and "drunken bums" but not as criminals; increasingly the more persistent excessive drinkers come to conceive of themselves as alcoholics or "sick" persons.

DRUG ADDICTION.   A federal act, passed in 1914 and subsequently amended makes the sale and use of opiates, cocaine, and marihuana as well as several other drugs illegal without a doctor's prescription. Actually, it made drug users legally "crimi-nals." Although habit-forming narcotic drugs include many types, addiction is generally from morphine and heroin, which are derived from opium, and cocaine and marihuana. The physiological and psychological dependence on drugs makes the drug addict a problem both for himself and often for society.[18] As tolerance for the drug is developed and more and more of it must be taken to relieve the physiological and psychological symptoms of withdrawal distress, the habit becomes well established and costly to maintain.

While addiction to cocaine is physiological, addiction to marihuana is not physiological but more psychological in nature. This means that a marihuana habit may be broken in much the same way as cigarette smoking. Addiction to opiates has been explained as a combination of physical factors and the association of the drug with the distress which accompanies sudden cessation of its use.[19] Addiction to opiates is therefore impossible without recognizing the withdrawal distress. In becoming an opiate addict the individual changes his conception of himself and of the behavior he must play as a "drug addict." The more he associates with other drug addicts and finds he cannot free himself from dependence on drugs, the more he comes to play the social role of an addict. Drug addiction is learned just as other behavior is learned, primarily from association with others who are addicts.

Persons who use drugs seldom think of themselves as real criminals because they tend to regard themselves as being in a unique situation whenever they are "hooked" by a drug and are therefore under necessity to have to violate the law by using the drugs or committing offenses to "support" their habit. Some indication of the fact that drug addiction need not be associated with self-regarding criminal attitudes is the fact that in virtually all Western nations there is, for example, a high incidence of drug addiction among doctors, and to a lesser extent among nurses.[20] This is because of the relative availability of the drug and the knowledge

---

[18] John A. O'Donnell and John C. Ball, *Narcotic Addiction*, Englewood Cliffs, N.J.: Prentice-Hall, 1965, and Clinard, Chap. 11.

[19] Alfred R. Lindesmith, *Opiate Addiction*, Bloomington: Indiana University Press, 1947.

[20] Alfred R. Lindesmith and John Gagnon, "Anomie and Drug Addiction," in Marshall B.

of its effect. Performers in the entertainment world, such as jazz musicians, also have a high rate.[21] Juveniles who use drugs live primarily in slum areas where there is often a ready supply. Addicts may engage in petty thefts or prostitution in order to support their habit. Even when criminal activities become associated with securing funds to maintain the drug habit, crime does not become an end in itself. Those addicts, juvenile or adult, who engage in other crime do so chiefly to obtain funds with which to purchase illicit drugs. There is little evidence to indicate that crimes of violence are associated with addiction.

GAMBLING. Except for those engaged in organized or professional gambling, persons who gamble, even where the law prohibits it, almost never think of themselves as criminals. Gambling appeals because of the chance factor for success regardless of the type of skill involved. It also offers relief from routine and boredom; whether one wins or not there is excitement over the possible results. Participation in gambling is on a large scale even though some participants may be publicly against it.

Gambling differs in its appeal by social class, sex, and other factors.[22] A study of lower class gambling found that it appears to offer more than a means of recreation or monetary gain; it also serves the function of status rewards of success and recognition by others.[23] Chiefly, it represents a way of beating the outside system, for "in picking the winner and becoming the center of attention, the winner leaves the realm of the nobody for the realm of the somebody."[24]

A study of Swedes who gambled regularly on "football" (soccer) matches has failed to show that gambling results in changes in the ordinary career of an individual.[25] Similarly in Sweden gambling is greater among the lower class. In fact, the more advantageous the social position, the less likely for persons to gamble.[26] Gambling appears to afford an unrealistic "hope" for social betterment in seeking to fulfill their mobility aspirations. Compared with nongamblers, it does not affect their involvements with friends, dependence on families, and acceptance of family responsibilities. Gambling also does not lead to unemployment, occupational apathy, and lack of initiative for work involvement. Moreover, gambling does not tend to lead to financial ruin for gamblers and their families; although soccer pools are popular, participation in them is moderate, the betting stakes being proportionate to individual incomes.

TRAFFIC OFFENSES. Traffic offenses may be divided, in order of seriousness, into "moving violations" where a collision is involved, moving violations where no collision is involved, and parking or similar violations. Moving violations are considered the more serious because they involve potential injury to someone through

---

Clinard (ed.), *Anomie and Deviant Behavior: A Discussion and Critique*, New York: The Free Press of Glencoe, 1964, p. 170, and Charles Winick, "Physician Narcotic Addicts," *Social Problems*, 9 (Fall 1961), pp. 174–186.

[21] Charles Winick, "The Use of Drugs by Jazz Musicians," *Social Problems*, 7 (Winter 1959–1960), pp. 240–254.

[22] Herbert A. Bloch, "The Sociology of Gambling," *American Journal of Sociology*, 57 (November 1951), pp. 215–221, and David D. Allen, *The Nature of Gambling*, New York: Coward-McCann, Inc., 1952.

[23] Irving K. Zola, "Gambling in a Lower-Class Setting," *Social Problems*, 10 (Spring 1963), pp. 353–361.

[24] Zola, p. 360.

[25] Nechama Tec, *Gambling in Sweden*, Totowa, N.J.: The Bedminster Press, 1964.

[26] Tec.

speeding, failure to observe a traffic signal, reckless driving, leaving the scene of an accident, or drunken driving. An English study of serious motoring accidents defined them as causing death by dangerous driving (negligent manslaughter), driving recklessly or dangerously, driving a vehicle while under the influence of alcohol or drugs, driving while disqualified, failure to stop after or to report an accident, and driving without third party insurance.[27]

Offenders convicted of serious motoring offenses do not tend to regard themselves as criminals nor are they regarded as such by others. A study classified three fourths of 653 offenders convicted of serious offenses as indifferent to their offenses.[28] A study involving interviews with 43 such offenders found that only 3 used the term criminal in the interview to refer to themselves.[29] The others thought the term inappropriate for their behavior, the term criminal to them involving crimes of violence or dishonesty in which there was intent of harm to someone. They objected to mixing in court with criminal types and sex offenders. Nineteen of those interviewed did believe that some motoring offenses were crimes and their perpetrators criminals, for example, driving under the influence of alcohol and failure to stop or report if there was a question of injury.

There are indications of considerable recidivism in traffic offenses and that a considerable proportion have been convicted of other offenses. Middendorff, for example, in a study of 600 cases in Germany, found that half of those traffic offenders had been found guilty of one or more similar traffic offenses.[30] Twelve percent of 653 offenders convicted for a serious motoring offense had four or more additional motoring convictions.[31] About a third of the drivers who had been convicted of driving after having been disqualified had additional convictions for the same offense and one tenth of those convicted of driving while under the influence of alcohol had been previously convicted.

GROUP SUPPORT OF CRIMINAL BEHAVIOR

Some public order offenses, such as prostitution, homosexual behavior, and drug addiction, grow out of and are heavily supported by rather clearly defined deviant subcultures. Others, such as drunkenness, gambling, and traffic offenses, have group support in the deviant behavior of certain social classes and ethnic groups and also in the general norms of society which support the drinking of alcoholic beverages, favorable attitudes to games of chance, and opposition to many laws regulating motor vehicles.

PROSTITUTION. Prostitutes can generally be classified according to their methods of operation. There are individual common prostitutes, organized houses of prostitution, call-girl and similar arrangements, and the "high-class," independent prostitute. One type is the girl who works in an organized house or brothel. New girls are "broken in" to the rules and regulations of the house and each new prostitute

[27] T. C. Willett, Criminal on the Road; A Study of Serious Motoring Offenses and Those Who Commit Them, London: Tavistock Publications, 1964, pp. 130–131.
[28] Willett, p. 279.
[29] Willett, pp. 277–279.
[30] Wolf Middendorff, "A Criminology of Traffic Offenses," Federal Probation, 27 (September 1963), p. 39.
[31] Willett, pp. 214–225.

soon learns various sex techniques. She learns how to handle a large number of customers without running the risk of losing them as patrons, how to deal with certain types of men, and how to protect herself against venereal disease. Another type of organized prostitution is the so-called call-girl, who has contributed greatly to the elimination of street soliciting and red-light houses. The call-girl often depends upon some organization for recruiting her patrons, although she may operate independently and have her own list of patrons who call upon her directly. More frequently, patrons are secured through the intermediary services of a bell-hop, a hotel desk clerk, a taxi driver, or other agent who, for a fee, will give the patron the telephone number used by the girl or arrange for a hotel or motel room. Prostitution is usually associated with panderers or pimps who solicit for the girls and often live off their earnings.

Some prostitution is not strictly organized as such, but is knowingly permitted and may be even encouraged through legitimate, but often shady, businesses, especially those in such commercial recreation as burlesque shows, night clubs, or amusement parks. Taxi dance halls particularly afford opportunities for the dancers to make engagements with their patrons, either in a room hired for the occasion or in the dancer's own room or apartment.[32] Through a variety of techniques performers in cabarets or burlesque shows recruit patrons for later dates.

Prostitutes have often been indoctrinated into the profession by those who have been closely associated with prostitution. Usually from a lower class background of more freedom in sexual norms, they seldom develop a high degree of organization within their profession. Its very nature is competitive, each prostitute attempting to build up and keep her own clientele; hence such personal group solidarity that exists is mainly for protection from the police or from others who threaten their profession. Prostitutes have a limited argot or special language of their own, which is a mark of a degree of association and group cohesiveness.[33]

HOMOSEXUAL BEHAVIOR. Homosexual behavior appears to be a product of the adoption of certain homosexual subcultural norms and a conception of self. Homosexual experience itself does not make one a homosexual; one research study concluded that "homosexual behavior when young is neither a sign that a boy will grow up to be a homosexual, nor is the absence of such behavior a guarantee that a boy will make a successful heterosexual adjustment."[34] A study of three groups of homosexuals—those who had been imprisoned, those only under psychiatric treatment, and those who had not been imprisoned or treated—showed that nearly all those in the three groups had been introduced into homosexual activities by other boys before the age of sixteen.[35] Only a small proportion in each group had a homosexual initiation by an adult. The channeling of sexual expression into homosexual patterns must come through some cultural or subcultural definitions, just as do heterosexual relations. The very first homosexual experience among 127 homosexuals studied in Great Britain was usually with a schoolboy of the same age and generally constituted sex play, often in a school situation.[36] These ex-

---

[32] Paul Cressey, *Taxi-Dance Hall*, Chicago: University of Chicago Press, 1932.
[33] David Mauer, "Prostitutes and Criminal Argots," *American Journal of Sociology*, 44 (January 1939), pp. 546–550.
[34] Schofield, p. 135.
[35] Schofield, p. 82.
[36] Gordon Westwood, *A Minority: A Report on the Life of the Male Homosexual in Great Britain*, London: Longmans, Green & Co., Ltd., 1960, pp. 24–39.

periences, however, did not necessarily lead to homosexuality as a pattern of sex behavior. The first "significant homosexual experience" can be defined as one carried out with an adult or repeated acts carried out with the same boy over a year or so. Over two thirds of such experiences were with another boy. Only 18 percent were first introduced to homosexuality as boys by adults; another 11 percent had no experience of any sort until they were adults, and in all such cases their partner was an adult. Another study, however, showed that homosexuals are likely to have had sexual experiences with adult males even before puberty; in one study a third had been approached by men and 27 percent had had physical contact with men.[37]

The subcultural "world" of the homosexual has its own special language where a special vocabulary, with words such as "gay," "straight," and "queen," is "similar in some respects to that of the underworld; in others to that of the theater."[38] There are also subculturally defined ways in which homosexual relations are established. Many communities have special meeting places where homosexuals gather, usually at certain street corners, parks, taverns, clubs, or lavatories.[39] Recognition by other homosexuals appears to involve particularly gestures, walk, clothes, and a special vocabulary.[40] Consequently a homosexual group as a subcommunity comes to have its "own status symbols and mythology, and may provide the same kind of social and psychological support that a family group provides for other people. All this means that before long the homosexual becomes alienated from the conventional culture."[41]

DRUNKENNESS. The excessive use of alcohol appears to be learned from others, group associations and cultural factors playing an important role. Differences exist not only in the drinking customs of societies but in those of subgroups within a society. The drinking mores of the individual are correlated with those of his associates. People learn to drink excessively because of the type of drinking behavior of their companions, social class, occupation, or ethnic status. Group associations determine the kind of beverage and the amount used, the circumstances under which drinking takes place, the time of drinking, and the individual's, as well as others', attitudes toward excessive drinking.

A study of 187 chronic police case inebriates, most of them with lower class backgrounds, showed that their drinking occurred in small intimate groups, less than 8 percent being usually solitary drinkers.[42] "The major function of these drinking groups . . . is in providing the context, social and psychological, for drinking behavior. In reality we have subcommunities of inebriates organized around one cardinal principle: drinking. The fantasies concerning the rewards of the drinking experiences are enforced in the interaction of the members, who mutually support each other in obtaining alcohol and mutually share it."[43]

[37] Paul H. Gebhard, John H. Gagnon, Wardell B. Pomeroy, and Cornelia V. Christenson, Sex Offenders: An Analysis of Types, New York: Harper & Row, Publishers, 1965, p. 329.
[38] Donald W. Cory, The Homosexual in America, New York: Greenberg: Publisher, Inc., 1951, p. 90. Also see D. J. Mercer, They Walk in the Shadow, New York: Comet Press, 1959.
[39] For discussion, see Gordon Westwood, Society and the Homosexual, New York: E. P. Dutton & Co., Inc., 1953, Chaps. 19–21, and Cory, p. 90. Also see Westwood, A Minority, pp. 68–77.
[40] Westwood, A Minority, pp. 83–86. Also see Gebhard, et al., p. 348.
[41] Schofield, p. 183.
[42] David L. Pittman and C. Wayne Gordon, Revolving Door, New York: The Free Press of Glencoe, 1958. Also see Earl Rubington, "Relapse and the Chronic Drunkenness Offender," Connecticut Review on Alcoholism, 12 (November 1960), pp. 9–12.
[43] Rubington, p. 71.

The role of group factors in perpetuating chronic drunkenness is seen, for example, particularly in "Skid Rows," where there are group definitions of behavior in drinking practices. Members of Skid Rows protect each other from the police and offer each other the mutual social support which is particularly important for those who have descended to Skid Rows from higher positions of social status.[44] Skid Row drinking is done in association with small groups who mutually support each other in their drinking habits and offer necessary companionship.

DRUG ADDICTION.   Drug addiction involves an elaborate subculture supported by group norms which one writer calls a "survival system."[45] This involves the justification or ideology for drug usage and the "reproductive" system: that addicted persons must continually recruit new members in order to sell them drugs to support their habit. There is also defensive communication with its own argot for drugs, supplies, and drug users, which must be learned by the initiates, and the "neighborhood warning systems" by which addicts are protected by others. The support of the habit requires a complex distribution network of the illegal drugs. This has been termed the "circulatory" system of the drug subculture, namely, the system by which addicts learn to secure illegal drugs.[46]

Most persons are knowingly initiated into drug usage, usually by friends or marital partners. Rarely does the use of drugs during illness lead to addiction. Most start taking drugs out of curiosity as to its effects or because of association with persons already addicted. Some adolescents and others take drugs for the "kick," as something tabooed by "squares" and to heighten and intensify the present moment of experience and differentiate it from the routine of daily life.[47]

TRAFFIC OFFENSES.   There is evidence that traffic violators, like gamblers, are for the most part normal persons who have acquired from others automobile driving attitudes and behavior that make them violate traffic laws. Vold has written, "How does it happen that such a large proportion of the total population undertakes to drive on streets and highways in violation of traffic laws? Most traffic offenses appear to be the behavior of normal people who have acquired attitudes and learned behavior in driving an automobile that are often dangerous and that are frequently contrary to traffic regulations and in violation of traffic law. Yet to any suggestion that they may have been in error, or that they may be undesirable drivers, they react with few exceptions in the manner of outraged innocence expressed by the popular exclamation: 'Who, me?' But . . . explanation in terms of the normal learning process of normal people seems a much more realistic approach to this problem than any attempt to discover evidence of individual deviance."[48]

An English study of a sample of persons convicted of serious motoring offenses

[44] Earl Rubington, "The Chronic Drunkenness Offender," *The Annals*, 315 (January 1958), pp. 65–72; W. Jack Peterson and Milton A. Maxwell, "The Skid Road 'Wino,'" *Social Problems*, 5 (Spring 1958), pp. 308–316; Joan K. Jackson and Ralph Connor, "The Skid Road Alcoholic," *Quarterly Journal of Studies on Alcohol*, 14 (September 1953), p. 475; and Donald Bogue, *Skid Row*, Chicago: University of Chicago Press, 1963.
[45] Seymour Fiddle, "The Addict Culture and Movement into and out of Hospitals," as reprinted in Senate Committee on the Judiciary, Subcommittee to Investigate Juvenile Delinquency, *Hearings*, Pt. 13, New York City, September 20–21, 1962, Washington, D.C.: Government Printing Office, 1963, p. 3156.
[46] Fiddle, p. 3156.
[47] Harold Finestone, "Cats, Kicks, and Color," *Social Problems*, 5 (July 1957), pp. 3–14.
[48] George B. Vold, *Theoretical Criminology*, New York: Oxford University Press, 1958, p. 201.

revealed a preponderance of them to be members of the working class. In six classes of offenders, working class persons were predominant in all but drunken driving, where they still constituted 46 percent of the offenders.[49]

CORRESPONDENCE BETWEEN CRIMINAL BEHAVIOR AND LEGITIMATE BEHAVIOR PATTERNS

It is difficult to differentiate the goals and general life orientation of homosexuals from heterosexuals except in the means of sex gratification, of gamblers from non-gamblers, or those who commit traffic offenses from those who do not. Likewise, except for those who are highly involved in their way of life, prostitutes, users of drugs, and excessive drinkers are probably not much different in their attitudes toward the general goals of society from those who are not so engaged. Where the behavior becomes more fully an important part of the individual's life organization and there is a degree of isolation from conventional society, however, such offenders may become more committed to the goals of a deviant subgroup, such as the subculture of drug addicts or homosexuals, and less to the larger society.

Much of the behavior of public order offenders is consistent with legitimate behavior patterns. The prostitutes' behavior is simply one way of satisfying legitimate male heterosexual needs and is a commercial occupation following the same goal of many other occupations. The homosexual, while deriving satisfaction in a different way, is engaging in sex behavior which is widely practiced. A drunken person is engaging in the drinking of alcoholic beverages which is approved and widely practiced behavior for adults. The use of drugs, while disapproved, has its physiological counterparts in the use of alcohol and cigarettes and the taking of minor nonaddictive drugs, such as aspirin and stimulants. Commercial gambling has many counterparts in a society. In various forms gambling is widely engaged in by the population, in such games of chance for small stakes as poker, blackjack, bridge, and bingo, although this gambling rarely brings arrests by the police. It is difficult to distinguish between situations in which the chance element is called gambling and those, like stock-market operations, commodity speculation, or, indeed, many other financial transactions, where there is a chance element but one not officially classified as a form of gambling.

In many of these public order offenses, as in the United States, there are economic and cultural considerations common to the general society, as Vold has indicated.[50] In such offenses as drunkenness, narcotic addiction and prostitution commercial gain plays a prominent part. Prostitution is an economic commodity, the sale of sex. A large economic interest enters the production and sale of alcoholic beverages, and there are large financial gains resulting from the illegitimate sale of narcotics. Gambling is a large-scale economic enterprise catering primarily to the small bettor.

The illegal behavior represents an occupation for many of the offenders in this group. Prostitution is a "job" as much as any other. Many gamblers live well from their occupations. There are even opportunities to develop a degree of professional

[49] Willett, pp. 194–199. A study in the United States found that traffic law violators follow closely the distribution of the total male labor forces but that traffic law violators have a higher social status than violators of criminal laws.—H. Lawrence Ross, "Traffic Law Violation: A Folk Crime," Social Problems, 8 (Winter 1960–1961), pp. 231–241.
[50] Vold, pp. 151–154.

skill with resulting status among one's associates. "The great majority of the participants in these criminal activities are not thought to be either clever or particularly skilled, but nevertheless the normal 'success goals' of the American cultural tradition urge the individual on to attempt to become a 'big shot' in the 'racket.' This is especially true in the case of gambling, prostitution, and the promotion of a more profitable use of drugs."[51] Prostitution is linked, for example, with many values of normal society. The general culture emphasizes the importance of sexual values and the unmarried, or even the married, man might find the satisfaction of these sexual stimulations unsatisfactory. Prostitution thus becomes closely allied to normal economic forces. "Our laissez-faire economy and its integration through a price system allows the relatively free operation of supply and demand whether it be commerce in grain futures or sex service."[52] The culture also generally makes it possible for women to exploit sex commercially in other ways besides prostitution, such as the "femininity" displayed to a male customer by a salesgirl, secretary, or waitress. The sex act may also play a part in premarital courtship and even in some marriages that is analogous to commercial exploitation in prostitution.

One study of 653 serious offenses showed that "the majority of these serious motoring offenders were normal people who succumbed to temptation when circumstances were favorable and it was expedient to take a chance."[53] Males are given to this behavior more than females, with the estimated ratio being 3 to 1. The ratio decreases for hit and run driving, which has been termed a more typically "feminine" offense.[54] In the great majority of cases, the offenses were largely of the offenders' own making and seemed to be due to an absence of constraints upon behavior. Offenders of traffic laws could be grouped into three categories, according to their attitudes toward their offenses.

> (a) The ruthless, shameless, or violent offender, who has little apparent concern for the needs or the safety of others, and seems to be quite indifferent to social or legal sanctions. About 11 percent of the 653 were of this type.
>
> (b) The driver who is neither ruthless nor violent, but who seems prepared to break the motoring law whenever it is expedient and sees nothing wrong in doing so "if one can get away with it." About 75 percent of the 653 were in this group.
>
> (c) The definitely law-conscious driver, who appears to be upset and conscience-stricken about breaking the law, especially when he has caused damage. About 14 percent were in this category.[55]

SOCIETAL REACTION

Public order offenses are numerous. They constitute behavior which is considered by law to be contrary to the system of morals or the standards of proper conduct

[51] Vold, p. 153.
[52] Edwin H. Lemert, *Social Pathology: A Systematic Approach to the Theory of Sociopathic Behavior*, New York: McGraw-Hill Book Company, Inc., 1951, p. 246.
[53] Willett, pp. 231–232.
[54] Willett, p. 301.
[55] Willett, pp. 231–232.

for an individual. Yet the condemnation for the most part is not strong, and one writer consequently has referred to certain offenders of this type as the "petty offender," one who is defined as a criminal because he breaks criminal laws which are chiefly misdemeanors and mainly city ordinances. The petty offender "is arrested on such charges as being drunk in public view, committing a public nuisance, disturbing the peace, loitering, trespassing, vagrancy, family disturbance, and so on."[56] There are indications that the attitude of the general public toward some of these offenses, such as drunkenness, use of drugs, and homosexuality, may eventually lead to their not being regarded as crimes. On the other hand, there is likelihood that motor vehicle offenses may eventually be regarded more seriously. The behavior involved in these offenses reflects, in part, the changing definitions of what is and what is not proper in behavior. As Vold has pointed out, blasphemy and heresy were once commonly prosecuted offenses. "Both of these have disappeared from the categories of crimes calling for police control in the world of today, though both types of behavior persist in the community. But ideas and events in the world at large have changed and we no longer seek to make men religious by law and police action. Could it be that we may be in the process of a similar transformation in the matter of control of personal habits and morality represented by these categories of petty crime, as they appear in the American world of today?"[57] In other parts of the world many of these public order offenses are not considered to be crimes.

Some public order crimes represent efforts to control certain moral and personal behavior through laws, often without attempts to mold public opinion to support the legislative and police activity. Undoubtedly, only a small proportion of these offenses actually committed are ever apprehended. Indeed, there is a dilemma between criminal action as opposed to no action at all against such behavior as prostitution, drunkenness, the use of drugs, gambling, and homosexual behavior.

> After many years of penalizing these areas of behavior as crime, we still have the problem behavior with us, and we have as well a large number of officially designated criminals convicted under such procedure. Furthermore, there is widespread recognition of the fact that the behavior is much more prevalent than that reached by criminal prosecution and conviction. Penalizing behavior in these areas as crime does not seem to have been particularly successful in controlling or eliminating the problem behavior. It is entirely possible that we have a larger proportion of our population involved in these behaviors than is the case in some of the countries that do not include them under the criminal law. Behavior in these several areas is criminal because we so define it, but if we should not penalize it as criminal, would the behavior become rampant and without control? That is the dilemma confronting present-day thinking and practices in the United States.[58]

PROSTITUTION.   Attitudes toward prostitution have varied historically, and today they differ widely by country. The attitude toward, and the social status of, the

[56] Irwin Deutscher, "The Petty Offender: A Sociological Alien," *Journal of Criminal Law, Criminology and Police Science*, 44 (January–February 1954), p. 592.
[57] Vold, p. 148.
[58] Vold, p. 156. He does not refer to homosexual behavior in this statement.

prostitute, as Davis has suggested, vary according to three conditions: (1) if the prostitute practices a certain discrimination in her customers, (2) if the earnings are used for some socially desirable goal, and (3) if the prostitute combines with her sexual role others which are more acceptable.[59] In France prostitution is illegal but condoned, as it is in many other parts of the world, particularly in Latin America. Prostitution, particularly soliciting, is strongly disapproved under Anglo-American law, but some persons would tolerate it as necessary, with certain urban areas set aside for prostitutes who could, in this way, they naively believe, be regularly inspected for venereal diseases. Prostitution is opposed on many grounds: (1) degradation of the women who engage in it; (2) effects on general law enforcement through police protection; (3) effect on marital relations where recourse is had to prostitutes; and (4) the patronage of prostitutes by young persons, soldiers in particular, and its effect on national values.

Prostitution, or the act of solicitation, is generally regarded as a misdemeanor and punished with a fine or a jail sentence of under one year. While punishments are usually not severe, repeated apprehensions may be treated as felonies with a longer sentence. England revised its statutes in 1960 to provide a graduated system of fines for prostitutes who loiter or who solicit for prostitution in a public place: £10 for the first offense, £25 for the second, and for the third £25 or three months' imprisonment, or both. The Wolfenden Report in which this legislation was proposed stated rather clearly the reasons for the English public attitude toward prostitution, much of which would be applicable in the United States.

> If it were the law's intention to punish prostitution *per se*, on the ground that it is immoral conduct, then it would be right that it should provide for the punishment of the man as well as the woman. But that is not the function of the law. It should confine itself to those activities which offend against public order and decency or expose the ordinary citizen to what is offensive or injurious; and the simple fact is that prostitutes do parade themselves more habitually and openly than their prospective customers, and do by their continual presence affront the sense of decency of the ordinary citizen. In doing so they create a nuisance which, in our view, the law is entitled to recognize and deal with.[60]

HOMOSEXUAL BEHAVIOR. Attitudes toward homoeosexual behavior have differed from one period in history to another. This behavior was prevalent in Greek and Roman times and in some societies homosexual practices were related to certain religious rites. Ford and Beach studied 76 folk societies and found that among 49 of them, or 64 percent, "homosexual activities of one sort or another are considered normal and socially acceptable for certain members of the community."[61] Some of the negative attitudes in parts of Western society that homosexuality is deviant behavior can be explained by certain aspects of the Christian

---

[59] Davis, p. 532.
[60] The Wolfenden Report, *Report of the Committee on Homosexual Offenses and Prostitution*, New York: Stein and Day, 1963, pp. 143–144.
[61] Clellan S. Ford and Frank A. Beach, *Patterns of Sexual Behavior*, New York: Harper & Row, Publishers, 1951, p. 130. Also see Ruth Benedict, *Patterns of Culture*, Boston: Houghton Mifflin Company, 1934.

tradition.[62] In fact, until 1553 homosexual practices in England were exclusively ecclesiastical offenses; the early Christians preached that homosexual behavior was a sin and in the Medieval ages the ecclesiastical courts imposed severe penalties. Certainly much of contemporary public opposition to homosexual acts is that they are "unnatural" in the sense that they do not lead to procreation.

The reactions of people in the United States today to homosexuality are conditioned by subcultural and situational factors. The processes by which persons come to be defined as homosexuals are contingent upon the varying interpretation of others and the treatment as a result of this definition. Interpretation of homosexuality may result in several different societal reactions by nonhomosexuals.[63] These may be explicit disapproval and immediate withdrawal of relationships, explicit disapproval and subsequent withdrawal, no disapproval and relationship sustained or a policy of "live and let live" response to homosexuals.

Homosexuality per se is not a crime: it is a social psychological state of mind in which one is favorably disposed toward sex relations with a person of one's own sex. Criminal penalties provided for homosexual acts in the United States, such as sodomy, are often quite severe. Some states provide penalties as high as ten or more years imprisonment. There are great variations in penalties, ranging from three years to a maximum of thirty years. In other cases, homosexual offenders may be detained for an indefinite period under sexual psychopath laws for "treatment," which is seldom adequate. In actuality, however, a relatively small proportion of persons are arrested for these acts and the courts and juries tend to be lenient toward the offenders. Considerable reliance is placed on the shame or stigma that will result from the apprehension. Apprehension is difficult because there is generally no complaining witness and because such acts occur largely in private.

While most other Western societies seek to protect younger adults from homosexual acts and to protect public decency, France, Spain, Italy, Denmark, and Finland, for example, do not consider homosexual acts, committed in private by adults, to be a criminal matter; West Germany is almost the only exception in Europe. As in England, there have been efforts in the United States to remove homosexual acts above a certain age limit from the list of crimes on the grounds that it is purely a personal act. In England, as a result of the Wolfenden Report, the law has been recently changed so that homosexual acts between persons twenty-one years of age and over and carried out privately are no longer crimes.

DRUNKENNESS. If excessive drinking is continued over a long enough period of time the individual may increasingly become involved in difficulties which arise from the drunkenness itself. He may lose his wife and his job and be ostracized by neighbors and friends. The Protestant ethic may play an important role in the attitudes of others because drunkenness is regarded as a lack of moral strength, of devotion to the goals of personal discipline, of will power, and of dedication to work. Societal reaction is experienced through family members, employers, neighbors, church associates, and the police representing the larger community.

The excessive drinker who becomes the alcoholic is often the chronic drunkenness offender before the courts. He may, with increasing frequency, be arrested and

[62] David S. Bailey, Homosexuality and the Western Christian Tradition, New York: David McKay Company, Inc., 1955.
[63] See John I. Kitsuse, "Societal Reaction to Deviant Behavior: Problems of Theory and Method," in Howard S. Becker, The Other Side: Perspectives on Deviance, New York: The Free Press of Glencoe, 1964, pp. 87–102.

jailed. Drinking may become a way of getting away from the societal reaction to problems caused by the drinking. His drinking problems can be faced only by more excessive drinking, which in turn leads to more arrests for public order disturbances. Final rejection is taking up his life on Skid Row.

There are indications that the drunkenness of chronic alcoholics, some of whom may have been arrested over a hundred times, may in the future not be treated as a crime. The District of Columbia's highest court ruled during 1966 that a chronic alcoholic cannot be convicted of the crime of public drunkenness. In an 8 to 0 decision, the United States Court of Appeals for the District of Columbia said that proof of chronic alcoholism is a defense to a drunkenness charge because the defendant "has lost the power of self-control in the use of intoxicating beverages." Since such a defendant lacks the necessary criminal intent to be guilty of a crime, he cannot be punished under the criminal law, the court ruled. At issue in the case was the ninety-day suspended sentence of a man of 59 who was convicted of public drunkenness in 1964 for the seventieth time since 1936. The Court of Appeals ruled that the trial judge committed an error when he refused to hear expert medical and psychiatric evidence that the man was an alcoholic who had lost his control over the consumption of alcoholic beverages.

DRUG ADDICTION.   Prior to the passage of the Harrison Act in 1914 outlawing the use of certain drugs without a physician's prescription, there was considerable public tolerance for the use of drugs, which was regarded as a personal problem. By this law and others passed by the states, drug users became "criminals" and drugs something mysterious and evil. Public attitudes approved making the unauthorized possession, sale, or transfer of drugs, particularly to juveniles, subject to severe punishment. State penalties have become more severe in recent years, and the possession of narcotics, for example, has been made a felony instead of a misdemeanor.[64]

The public attitude toward drug addicts represents largely a stereotype toward what has been termed the "dope fiend" myth. The fact that many drug addicts become unproductive is disapproved, as is drunkenness, by the work-oriented Protestant ethic of American society. Greater understanding of the problem is emerging, however, particularly about the role that repressive legislation plays: by making drugs difficult to secure and at a high price, it has encouraged the development of a drug subculture and consequent influences toward addiction. Efforts are being made to consider drug addiction as a disease and not as a criminal or police problem. In order to deal more effectively with the drug problem by prevention, that is, curing addicts of their habits, to eliminate the exploitation of drug addicts for mercenary gain, and to reduce the number of crimes committed by addicts as a consequence of their habits, Lindesmith has made several proposals:

> (1) Antinarcotic laws should be so written that addicts do not have to violate them solely because they are addicts.
> (2) Drug users are admittedly handicapped by their habits but they should nevertheless be encouraged to engage in productive labor even when they are using drugs.

[64] Alfred R. Lindesmith, *The Addict and the Law*, Bloomington: Indiana University Press, 1965, p. 80.

(3) Cures should not be imposed upon narcotics victims by force but should be voluntary.

(4) Police officers should be prevented from exploiting drug addicts as stool pigeons solely because they are addicts.

(5) Heroin and morphine addicts should be handled according to the same principles and moral precepts applied to barbiturate and alcohol addicts because these three forms of addiction are basically similar.[65]

In the United Kingdom drug addiction is considered a medical rather than a legal problem, and authorized physicians may prescribe drugs at low cost. The addict is therefore not regarded by the British public as a criminal. He does not have to steal or sell drugs to secure some sources of supply for himself and a woman does not have to turn to prostitution. Addicts are consequently relatively non-criminal in the United Kingdom.[66]

GAMBLING. Gambling is usually defined as wagering money or other objects upon an outcome which largely depends upon chance. It is illegal in nearly all parts of the United States, although it is not necessarily so in other countries. Great variations exist in the type of games restricted or prohibited. In England the law is much more generous. "Unlawful gaming" consists of gambling in which the chances of the players are not equal or a toll is levied on the stakes or a charge is made for the right to take part in the gaming. Gaming on the public street is also an offense.

Attitudes of people toward private and public gambling vary widely in the United States. Gambling for small stakes and among friends is generally regarded as sometimes not in good taste but not a serious infraction of the moral or legal codes. On the other hand, reaction of some sections of the public is likely to be more severe if the gambling is commercialized or carried out in association with organized crime, as in the case of organized betting on sports contests and the numbers racket.

Opposition to gambling seems to be based on the position that gambling does not perform a socially productive economic function. It is securing economic rewards without work. The fact that persons may lose money through gambling has caused some to oppose it. In commercialized gambling it is generally necessary to arrange a "fix" with law enforcement officials and this arouses negative reactions because of the effect on law enforcement generally.

Evidence exists that commercialized gambling need not necessarily be linked with organized crime as has so often happened in the United States. In fact, some have suggested that greater opportunities for legalized gambling through providing controlled opportunities to bet on football games, horse races, and lotteries might diminish the influence of organized criminal groups in this area.[67]

65 Lindesmith, The Addict and the Law, p. 270. Also see Drug Addiction: Crime or Disease. Interim and Final Reports of the Joint Committee of the American Bar Association and the American Medical Association on Narcotic Drugs, Bloomington: Indiana University Press, 1960.
66 Edwin M. Schur, Narcotic Addiction in Britain and America: The Impact of Public Policy, Bloomington: Indiana University Press, 1962. Because of an increase in drug addiction, proposals were made in 1967 to create a degree of centralization in issuing prescriptions to drug users through hospital psychiatrists. Previously, any general physician could prescribe drugs.
67 Tec.

TRAFFIC OFFENSES.   On the whole, the punishments for moving traffic offenses, considering the potential danger, are relatively light. Most traffic offenses carry little moral stigma, even after a fine or a jail sentence has been imposed. Most are not regarded as antisocial, primarily because these offenses involve, potentially, practically everyone. Traffic laws are of fairly recent origin and appear as yet to have little support from the mores. Because the societal reaction is seldom strong, they have been referred to as a "folk crime."[68]

In a study of 43 convicted serious traffic offenders the social repercussions were negligible in all but four cases, and even they were not seriously affected.[69] There was little inclination on the part of the police to apply the term criminal or any social stigma, distinguishing clearly between what they regarded as motoring offenses and real crime. Treatment of serious motoring offenders by the courts tended to be much more lenient in terms of fines and probation than the treatment of those charged for other serious offenses. There is some indication that these attitudes may be reversed because of the increasing toll in injuries and deaths from motor vehicle accidents.

VAGRANCY.   Vagrancy, a public order crime, has not been discussed in any detail but in this chapter it is treated as an example of how certain behaviors become defined as a public order crime by certain power groups in a society. A vagrant by law is an individual with no money or apparent means of support. Such vagrancy statutes are our heritage from English and other European laws which were enacted as early as the fourteenth century but became common by the sixteenth century. These vagrancy statutes derive primarily from the early English poor laws which came into existence after the feudal system declined and turned loose large numbers of peasants on society. The basic aims of such laws were to force persons into employment or into public works at low wages or to force them into private employment at prevailing rates. The Calvinistic view, as expressed by the Protestant ethic, held that the middle class, the poor, and the unemployed should work to produce worldly goods as God's will.[70]

Today vagrancy statutes are also widely used by police to detain suspects, some of them actual criminals and others simply lower class persons who were caught in a police "dragnet." One writer, in commenting on today's vagrancy laws, has stated: "The time is surely at hand to modernize the vagrancy concept or, better yet, to abandon it altogether for statutes which will harmonize with notions of a decent, fair, and just administration of criminal justice, and which will at the same time make it possible for police departments to discharge their responsibilities in a reasonable manner."[71]

SELECTED BIBLIOGRAPHY

1. Allen, David D., *The Nature of Gambling*, New York: Coward-McCann, Inc., 1952.

[68] Ross, pp. 231–241.
[69] Willett, p. 302.
[70] George Rusche and Otto Kirchheimer, *Punishment and Social Structure*, New York: Columbia University Press, 1939, pp. 32–41. Also see William J. Chambliss, "A Sociological Analysis of the Law of Vagrancy," *Social Problems*, 12 (Summer 1964), pp. 67–77.
[71] Arthur H. Sherry, "Vagrants, Rogues, and Vagabonds—Old Concepts in Need of Revision," *California Law Review*, 48 (October 1960), pp. 557–73.

2. Bailey, David S., *Homosexuality and the Western Christian Tradition*, New York: David McKay Company, Inc., 1955.
3. Barker, Gordon H. and W. Thomas Adams, "Glue Sniffers," *Sociology and Social Research*, 47 (April 1963), pp. 298–310.
4. Becker, Howard S., "Becoming a Marihuana User," *American Journal of Sociology*, 59 (November 1953), pp. 235–242.
5. Bloch, Herbert A., "The Sociology of Gambling," *American Journal of Sociology*, 57 (November 1951), pp. 215–221.
6. Bogue, Donald, *Skid Row*, Chicago: University of Chicago Press, 1963.
7. Bryan, James H., "Apprenticeships in Prostitution," *Social Problems*, 12 (Winter 1965), pp. 287–296.
8. ———, "Occupational Ideologies of Call Girls," *Social Problems*, 13 (Spring 1966), pp. 441–450.
9. William J. Chambliss, "A Sociological Analysis of the Law of Vagrancy," *Social Problems*, 12 (Summer 1964), pp. 67–77.
10. Chein, Isidor, Donald L. Gerard, Robert S. Lee, and Eva Rosenfield with the collaboration of Daniel M. Wilner, *The Road to H*, New York: Basic Books, Inc., 1964.
11. Chein, Isidor, and Eva Rosenfield, "Juvenile Narcotics Use," *Law and Contemporary Problems*, 22 (Winter 1957), pp. 52–69.
12. Cory, Donald W., *The Homosexual in America*, New York: Greenberg: Publisher, Inc., 1951.
13. Cressey, Paul, *Taxi-Dance Hall*, Chicago: University of Chicago Press, 1932.
14. Davis, Kingsley, "Sexual Behavior," in Robert K. Merton and Robert A. Nisbet (eds.), *Contemporary Social Problems*, 2nd ed. New York: Harcourt, Brace & World, Inc., 1966, Chap. 7.
15. Deutscher, Irwin, "The Petty Offender: A Sociological Alien," *Journal of Criminal Law, Criminology and Police Science*, 44 (January–February, 1954), pp. 592–595.
16. ———, "The White Petty Offender in the Small City," *Social Problems*, 1 (October 1953), pp. 70–73.
17. *Drug Addiction: Crime or Disease*. Interim and Final Reports of the Joint Committee of the American Bar Association and the American Medical Association on Narcotic Drugs, Bloomington: Indiana University Press, 1960.
18. Fiddle, Seymour, "The Addict Culture and Movement into and out of Hospitals," as reprinted in Senate Committee on the Judiciary, Subcommittee to Investigate Juvenile Delinquency, *Hearings*, Pt. 13, New York City, September 20–21, 1962; Washington, D.C.: Government Printing Office, 1963.
19. Finestone, Harold, "Cats, Kicks, and Color," *Social Problems*, 5 (July 1957), pp. 3–14.
20. ———, "Narcotics and Criminality," *Law and Contemporary Problems*, 22 (Winter 1957), pp. 69–85.
21. Ford, Clellan, and Frank A. Beach, *Patterns of Sexual Behavior*, New York: Harper & Row, Publishers, 1951.
22. Gebhard, Paul H., John H. Gagnon, Wardell B. Pomeroy, and Cornelia V. Christenson, *Sex Offenders: An Analysis of Types*, New York: Harper & Row, Publishers, 1965.

23. Jackman, Norman R., Richard O'Toole, and Gilbert Geis, "The Self-Image of the Prostitute," *Sociological Quarterly*, 4 (Spring 1963), pp. 150–161.

24. Jackson, Joan K., and Ralph Connor, "The Skid Road Alcoholic," *Quarterly Journal of Studies on Alcohol*, 14 (September 1953), pp. 468–486.

25. Kitsuse, John I., "Societal Reaction to Deviant Behavior: Problems of Theory and Method," in Howard S. Becker, *The Other Side: Perspectives on Deviance*, New York: The Free Press of Glencoe, 1964, pp. 87–102.

26. Lemert, Edwin M., *Social Pathology*, New York: McGraw-Hill Book Company, Inc., 1951, Chap. 8.

27. Leznoff, Maurice, and William A. Westley, "The Homosexual Community," *Social Problems*, 3 (April 1956), pp. 257–263.

28. Lindesmith, Alfred R., *The Addict and the Law*, Bloomington: Indiana University Press, 1965.

29. ———, *Opiate Addiction*, Bloomington: Principia Press, 1952.

30. ———, and John H. Gagnon, "Anomie and Drug Addiction," in Marshall B. Clinard (ed.), *Anomie and Deviant Behavior: A Discussion and Critique*, New York: The Free Press of Glencoe, 1964.

31. Mauer, David W., "Prostitutes and Criminal Argots," *American Journal of Sociology*, 44 (January 1939), pp. 546–550.

32. Mercer, D. J., *They Walk in the Shadow*, New York: Comet Press, 1959.

33. Middendorff, Wolf, "A Criminology of Traffic Offenses," *Federal Probation*, 27 (September 1963), pp. 36–42.

34. Murtagh, John M., and Sara Harris, *Cast the First Stone*, New York: McGraw-Hill Book Company, Inc., 1957.

35. O'Donnell, John A., "Narcotic Addiction and Crime," *Social Problems*, 13 (Spring 1966), pp. 374–385.

36. Peterson, W. Jack, and Milton A. Maxwell, "The Skid Road 'Wino,'" *Social Problems*, 5 (Spring 1958), pp. 308–316.

37. Pittman, David J. and C. Wayne Gordon, *Revolving Door*, New York: The Free Press of Glencoe, 1958.

38. Reckless, Walter C., *The Crime Problem*, 3d ed., New York: Appleton-Century-Crofts, 1961.

39. Reiss, Albert J., Jr., "Sex Offenses: The Marginal Status of the Adolescent," *Law and Contemporary Problems*, 25 (Spring 1960), pp. 309–334.

40. ———, "The Social Integration of Queers and Peers," *Social Problems*, 9 (Fall 1961), pp. 102–120.

41. Roebuck, Julian B., "The Negro Drug Addict as an Offender Type," *Journal of Criminal Law, Criminology and Police Science*, 53 (1962), pp. 36–43.

42. Rooney, Elizabeth A., and Don C. Gibbons, "Reactions to 'Crimes without Victims,'" *Social Problems*, 13 (Spring 1966), pp. 400–411.

43. Ross, H. Lawrence, "Traffic Law Violation: A Folk Crime," *Social Problems*, 8 (Winter 1960–1961), pp. 231–241.

44. Rubington, Earl, "The Chronic Drunkenness Offender," *The Annals*, 315 (January 1958), pp. 65–72.

45. Rusche, George, and Otto Kirchheimer, *Punishment and Social Structure*, New York: Columbia University Press, 1939.

46. Schofield, Michael, *Sociological Aspects of Homosexuality: A Comparative Study of Three Types of Homosexuals*, Boston: Little, Brown and Company, 1965.

47. Schur, Edwin M., *Crimes without Victims*, Englewood Cliffs, N.J.: Prentice-Hall, Inc., 1965.

48. ———, *Narcotic Addiction in Britain and America: The Impact of Public Policy*, Bloomington: Indiana University Press, 1962.

49. Sherry, Arthur H., "Vagrants, Rogues, and Vagabonds—Old Concept in Need of Revision," *California Law Review*, 48 (October 1960), pp. 557–573.

50. Sutherland, Edwin H., and Donald R. Cressey, *Principles of Criminology*, 7th ed., Philadelphia: J. B. Lippincott Company, 1966.

51. Tec, Nechama, *Gambling in Sweden*, Totowa, N.J.: The Bedminster Press, 1964.

52. Vincent, Clark, *Unmarried Mothers*, New York: The Free Press of Glencoe, 1961.

53. Vold, George B., *Theoretical Criminology*, New York: Oxford University Press, 1958.

54. Weinberg, S. Kirson, *Incest Behavior*, New York: The Citadel Press, 1955.

55. Westwood, Gordon, *A Minority: A Report on the Life of the Male Homosexual in Great Britain*, London: Longmans, Green & Co., Ltd., 1960.

56. ———, *Society and the Homosexual*, New York: E. P. Dutton & Co., Inc., 1953.

57. Wheeler, Stanton, "Sex Offenses: A Sociological Critique," *Law and Contemporary Problems*, 25 (Spring 1960), pp. 258–292.

58. Willett, T. C., *Criminal on the Road: A Study of Serious Motoring Offenses and Those Who Commit Them*, London: Tavistock Publications, 1964.

59. Winick, Charles, "Physician Narcotic Addicts," *Social Problems*, 9 (Fall 1961), pp. 174–186.

60. ———, "The Use of Drugs by Jazz Musicians," *Social Problems*, 7 (Winter 1959–1960), pp. 240–254.

61. *The Wolfenden Report: Report on the Committee on Homosexual Offenses and Prostitution*, New York: Stein and Day, 1963.

62. Zola, Irving K., "Gambling in a Lower-Class Setting," *Social Problems*, 10 (Spring 1963), pp. 353–361.

THE CHRONIC DRUNKENNESS OFFENDER*

Earl Rubington

> *The social roles which men play are more often the result of networks of social relations than the product of any individual's attributes. The behavior of chronic drunkenness offenders,*

* Reprinted from the *Annals of the American Academy of Political and Social Science*, 315 (January 1958), pp. 65–72, by permission of the author and the publisher.

*ordinarily explained by their properties as individuals, is viewed
here as a consequence of conformity to Skid Row social norms.
Skid Row subculture, its social functions, how people come to it
and behave once there are discussed.*

Chronic drunkenness offenders are usually considered to be closely attached to alcohol and relatively detached from people. Their interest in other people is said to proceed in inverse ratio to their interest in drinking. Current therapeutic and punitive approaches, hoping to reverse this interest ratio, seek to separate the offender from alcohol and thereby increase the chances of sober association.

This paper suggests that offenders are actually connected with other people through excessive use of alcohol, that knowledge of these connections may prove useful in social rehabilitation. The first part of this article traces the connections between offenders; the second describes briefly a new technique of rehabilitation which tries to take these connections into account.

Agencies which deal with chronic drunkenness offenders regard their behavior as a product of certain individual attributes. Offenders, they believe, suffer from a variety of biological, psychological and moral defects. These defects, they argue, compel offenders to rely more and more upon alcohol and less and less on other people for satisfactions. According to agency opinion, these attributes sustain the offender in a pattern of socially irresponsible behavior which recurs with such amazing regularity as to constitute a major social problem.

Agency concern with chronic public drunkenness, the outstanding feature of this behavior pattern, has not been matched with any appreciable success in controlling chronic drunkenness offenders. By locating the mainsprings of behavior in certain offender attributes, agencies see their task as modifying these attributes, employing what is called here "the individualistic approach." In theory, modifying attributes should decrease the frequency of chronic public drunkenness. In fact, modification, even where successful, has had little effect on the chronicity of offense. Arrests for chronic public drunkenness have been almost uniformly constant or increasing for generations, while traditional attribute-focused techniques of punishment and rehabilitation have reclaimed few chronic drunkenness offenders.

Making a whole behavior pattern dependent upon an exclusive number of individual attributes appears to have been a case of misplaced agency emphasis. It seems more likely that these attributes are in themselves dependent in some ways upon the behavior pattern. Agencies of social control argue that these attributes of offenders, whether moral failure, personality disturbance, or social isolation, result in chronic public drunkenness. Yet chronic public drunkenness itself is only one aspect of a broader behavior pattern. In the study, treatment, and punishment of offenders, exclusive concern with these attributes has deflected attention from this larger pattern of behavior—the offender's way of life or subculture.

Some consideration must be given to the social environment of chronic drunkenness offenders in order to supplement the individualistic approach, explain the persistence of public drunkenness, and improve methods of social control. It is the position of this paper that the most important factor common to chronic drunkenness offenders is their participation in a deviant subculture. The system of social relationships prescribed by this subculture may serve to explain aspects of the offender's drinking which are obscured by the individualistic approach. Offenders are all part of a large whole, Skid Row subculture, and unless their relationship to that subculture is understood, no satisfactory explanation of their behavior can result.

All large cities have their Skid Row sections; smaller cities, their equivalent. Here the homeless, the outcasts, the derelicts, the drifters all congregate and make for themselves a way of life substantially at variance with dominant social norms. Here the chronic drunkenness offender—a person who is arrested for public intoxication three or more times each year—also finds a congenial habitat. Skid Row is not, then, a random collection of individuals who all share an individual peculiarity, the craving for alcohol. It is, rather, a collection of people with different personalities who are all bound up in Skid Row subculture in different ways.

If these observations are correct, they carry important implications for current methods of modifying the behavior of chronic drunkenness offenders. One important implication, to be treated later, is that opportunities for departing this way of life depend upon Skid Row status. Before examining this implication, however, it is first necessary to account for Skid Row as a way of life, its existence, the functions it fulfills, how people come to it, and once there how they act.

SKID ROW SUBCULTURE

The behavior of chronic drunkenness offenders is expressive of a common group membership. The obvious facts offenders share in common, excessive social drinking and repeated arrests for intoxication, are in themselves reliable indices of group membership. It is practically impossible to remain on Skid Row and not drink. Drinking there takes place most often in groups and frequently results in intoxication. When intoxicated, it is difficult for some offenders to escape arrest. The coexistence of drinking and frequent arrests binds offenders to the Skid Row way of life. The more the offender is bound to this way of life, the more he exhibits the characteristics of group membership.

Punitive social reactions to drunkenness play an important role in the establishment of this group membership. Arrest, the traditional reaction to intoxication, defines the offender as a person who is something less than human, thus not eligible to receive the benefits of customary social participation. Conversely, the offender is now socially defined as a member of the deviant community, thus eligible to receive the benefits of nonconformist social participation.

Each time the offender is arrested he is exposed to the sentiments of moral indignation symbolized for society by police action. To this he responds with increasing sentiments of solidarity with the category of oppressed peoples, other offenders like himself. The increasing frequency of arrest marks the stages in alienation from society and in identification with the deviant subculture.

The punitive social reaction to public intoxication sets in motion the typical vicious circle which characterizes relations between conformists and deviants. The more the chronic offender is punished for deviant acts by conformists, the more he is rewarded for the same acts by deviants. As a consequence, the major sources of approval and self-esteem can only come from a group of people who are exposed to the sentiments of moral indignation of the society at large. To the degree that he confines social participation to other deviants, he defends himself against these sentiments. The fundamental dilemma for the Skid Row inhabitant is that conformity to Skid Row drinking norms does not completely insulate him from punishment.

Other indices of membership which denote the existence of a subculture are shared ways of acting, thinking, and feeling. Skid Row has a language of its own, an argot made up of Elizabethan thieves' cant, American underworld and tramp slang, and the idiom of contemporary lower-class culture. This argot is the major vehicle for the transmission of the subcultural heritage. Its usage communicates Skid Row values and orients newcomers and old-timers alike to their social environment. Its proper usage marks one as a member in good standing.

Additional indices are techniques of obtaining and consuming alcohol which are learned, shared, and transmitted to members of the group. Perhaps more important as indices are sanctions, both positive and negative. Refusing a drink, drinking more than one's share from a communal bottle, and absconding with funds intended for the purchase of a group bottle all invite negative sanction. Notable among positive sanctions are sharing values—money, drink, and housing being most frequently shared —and assisting members who are "sick"— a generic term on Skid Row for the effects of acute hangover.

The pattern of sharing money and drink is perhaps the most conclusive proof that this is not a way of life based upon the personality traits of alcoholics, although confirmed addicts can participate. Respectable alcoholics are more likely to drink alone; chronic offenders drink, for the most part, in a group. Despite the fact that a supply of alcohol is readily available, many Skid Row habitués do not drink until a group can be assembled. The confirmed addict would find it almost impossible to exert such control. This widespread group drinking has led some authorities to believe that probably not more than 8 per cent of the excessive drinkers on Skid Row are alcoholics.[1]

Its Existence. How are we to account for the existence of the Skid Row way of life in our large cities and its counterpart in the many small towns around the country? Alienation from major value-patterns is one of the prices a complex society must pay for ineffective socialization. Those alienated

from basic cultural traditions fend for themselves in one way or another. A certain proportion of the alienated find it convenient to fend together, and they do so by banding together and expressing their alienation as part of a pattern of organized behavior. Denied status in respectable society, they develop or seek out a social organization in which a role more suitable to their own needs is possible. If that role prescribes social drinking as defined on Skid Row, the alienated are quite willing to comply.

Not all of the people alienated from dominant cultural traditions find their way into Skid Row subculture. Unless they establish some connections with people who can provide group support for the expression of their alienation, they are not likely to identify themselves with Skid Row subculture.

The failure to account for the absence of some alienated individuals on Skid Row casts doubt on the individualistic literature on chronic drunkenness offenders. The bulk of this literature stresses undersocialization, broken homes, low educational attainment, low occupational rank, high residential mobility, mental illness, psychopathic personalities, and physical defects as factors which cause persons to take up the Skid Row way of life.[2] Nevertheless, many other people having similar characteristics fail to select the Skid Row alternative.

If people with similar characteristics do not select the Skid Row alternative, then theories which assign causality to these attributes are insufficient. The literature, stressing individual attributes as the major determinants of behavior, assumes that all people possessing these attributes will ultimately withdraw from society and become completely dependent upon alcohol. In this view, the final stage of withdrawal from society takes place when the social isolate is

[1] Wayne M. Wellman, Milton A. Maxwell, and Paul O'Hollaren, "Private Hospital Alcoholic Patients and the Changing Conception of the 'Typical' Alcoholic," *Quarterly Journal of Studies on Alcohol*, Vol. 18, September 1957, p. 401.

[2] A representative example is Robert Straus, "Alcohol and the Homeless Man," *Quarterly Journal of Studies on Alcohol*, Vol. 7, December 1946, pp. 360–404.

alone on Skid Row with his bottle as a substitute for people.

Since, however, these attributes are necessary but not sufficient conditions of alienation, the explanation for Skid Row recruitment must lie elsewhere. The position taken here is that these attributes are indices of disrupted social relationships. Where the attribute theorists argue that absence of rewarding social relationships necessarily leads to further withdrawal and ultimate dependence on alcohol, the contention here is that the absence of rewarding social relationships creates the search for a primary group. Ultimate dependence on alcohol is a possible consequence of this search, but it is neither the most likely nor the only consequence.

Under certain conditions, the establishment of new primary-group ties may result in abstinence, moderate drinking, or even alcoholism. It may also result in a host of entirely different patterns of behavior. Under certain other conditions, new primary-group ties may be the cause of habituation to alcohol. For the incipient offender, dependence upon an alienated primary group sets in motion the habituation to alcohol. Habituation, for chronic drunkenness offenders, is more likely to be the result of a new system of social relationships rather than the effect of no relationships at all.

The establishment of new primary-group ties following a disruption of previous social ties would seem to be, then, the most satisfactory hypothesis to account for the selection of subcultural alternatives.[3] Given two individuals subjected to similar stress and strain in their social relationships, one avoids the Skid Row alternative because a different system of interpersonal relations binds the prospective deviant to major value-patterns. This suggests that the next primary group into which the person enters consequent to major stress determines the sub-

sequent degree of conformity to dominant social norms. The high rate of informal social participation of juvenile delinquents[4] and incipient alcoholics in their teens[5] lends strong support to this hypothesis.

Skid Row Functions. What are the functions Skid Row fulfills? An achievement-oriented society which accords status to individuals upon the basis of socially recognized effort requires certain negative reference groups in order to maintain achievement striving. These groups are composed of "failures" and "social misfits" who collect in the "blighted areas" of many American cities. Residence in these areas is typically explained as the result of inability to comply with the ethics of individual responsibility. Residence there symbolizes rejection of the dominant emphasis upon upward social mobility. Upward social mobility requires downward social mobility as a condition for the further status striving of some, the validation of present status for others. Skid Row, an area in which recruits have descended from earlier statuses, provides strong support for out-group achievement norms.

For the derelict in-group, the functions are somewhat similar. Association with people who have undergone similar experiences compensates for the effects of alienation. The fall from status is broken by the knowledge that one is no longer alone. Social support, which the respectable world withdraws, can be had from one's associates on Skid Row with less effort.

Recruitment Patterns. Who gets there and how? Only a process of selective drift could account for the replenishment of Skid Row populations since Skid Row is not self-perpetuating like most societies. Periodic mi-

---

[3] For a lucid account of the genesis of subcultures cf. Albert K. Cohen, *Delinquent Boys: The Culture of the Gang* (Glencoe, Ill.: Free Press, 1955). Those who have read Cohen will recognize the author's indebtedness to him.

[4] Bartlett S. Atwood and E. H. Shideler, "Social Participation and Juvenile Delinquency," *Sociology and Social Research*, Vol. 18, May–June 1934, pp. 436–44.

[5] Charles William Wahl, "Some Antecedent Factors in the Family Histories of 109 Alcoholics," *Quarterly Journal of Studies on Alcohol*, Vol. 17, December 1956, p. 653.

gration of the alienated guarantees stability and continuity of Skid Row subculture beyond the life cycle of any of its current members. Uprooted and alienated from the American value-system and from the social structure which supports and distributes those values, some unattached individuals find their way into the subculture once they have "hit the skids."

Despite popular stereotypes, the several social strata which make up American society do not contribute equal shares of Skid Row recruits. These strata differ in the access they offer the alienated for orientation and induction into Skid Row subculture. Because of these differences, the majority of the homeless on Skid Row appear to have emerged from the lower and lower-middle classes. These strata appear to be more vulnerable to physical and mental illness, economic insecurity, broken homes, and cultural inconsistencies. These are some of the social conditions which precipitate alienation. Under appropriate conditions, a certain number of the alienated become oriented towards and later inducted into Skid Row life.

The social strata from which recruits have been alienated shape the different modes of orientation for and induction in Skid Row subculture. These differences bear heavily upon the different ways men participate in the culture once they have become introduced to it.

Skid Row Social Groups. On Skid Row men are connected to each other by the ways in which they use alcohol. These connections, which depend upon the strata from which they were alienated and their induction into Skid Row subculture, make for a system of statuses and roles. Thus, for example, those who prefer whisky look down upon those who drink only wine or non-beverage alcohol. One study[6] reports that this group of men are known as "lushes,"

that they are the "elite," and that their rejection of wine drinkers forces "winos" to group together. This elite group seems to be more organized, more protective of its members, and less likely to get arrested for intoxication than other Skid Row social groups.

In a sense, the elite group is marginal to Skid Row society, thus more likely to leave it. It is commonly held that men at this level of Skid Row society are better risks for therapy because they have known "a better way of life" and have something to which they can "return."[7] Men at increasingly lower levels have known little which differs significantly from what they currently experience, hence have nowhere to "return." In this view, position in the Skid Row status system determines the chances of social reintegration. The elite, aware of the discrepancy between their past and present status, find fewer satisfactions in Skid Row subculture than their less-esteemed associates.

THE INDIVIDUALISTIC APPROACH

Consideration of the social environment in which the chronic drunkenness offender exists plays no prominent part in the individualistic approach to modifying offender behavior. The individualistic approach, whether in punishment or in rehabilitation, focuses upon specific urges to deviance—for example, the craving for alcohol—or personality dynamics—for example, psychopathic personality. Ignoring the fact that personality itself is largely a product of systems of social interaction, the individualistic approach seeks to eliminate urges or alter personality structure.

Jail, outpatient clinic, and inpatient service rip the offender from his customary network of social relations in order to modify behavior. When they have finished

[6] Joan K. Jackson and Ralph Connor, "The Skid Road Alcoholic," *Quarterly Journal of Studies on Alcohol,* Vol. 14, September 1953, pp. 468–86.

[7] Ralph M. Henderson, "The Skid Road Alcoholic," *Proceedings of First Annual Alberta Conference on Alcohol Studies,* August 30–September 2, 1954, p. 92.

incarcerating, exhorting, or treating him as an isolated individual, they thrust him out again into the world. Their practices only confirm the offender's isolation from respectable society while cementing his existing ties with deviant social organization. Any success in altering drinking behavior is vitiated when the offender returns to a social environment which insists upon that very pattern. Manipulating the individual without regard for his customary social environment has cost many communities enormous sums of money and yielded few significant changes in behavior.

A NEW APPROACH: THE HALF-WAY HOUSE

In recent years, a new approach to the problem of chronic public drunkenness has appeared. This approach, which usually takes the name of "half-way house," blends individualistic techniques of social control with the offender's social environment. The outstanding characteristics of the half-way house are the following.

Offenders, once they have voluntarily affiliated with the half-way house, are expected to comply with its few and simple rules. They are expected to get jobs, pay for their room and board, assist in upkeep and maintenance of the house, stay sober while members, and participate actively in the therapeutic program. Half-way houses vary in the length of time a man is permitted to stay, yet most staff personnel agree that maximum benefit comes with a maximum stay, usually three months. Unlike jail, clinic, and hospital staffs, half-way house personnel are usually recovered alcoholics themselves, very often members of Alcoholics Anonymous, and, occasionally, former participants in Skid Row living. The staff, because of their past experiences, are in many ways well-equipped to conduct formal and informal counseling sessions designed to get the individual to recognize the problem he has with alcohol and to help him modify his way of life.

Conformity to half-way house norms is no different in principle from conformity with Skid Row norms. In both instances, group pressures operate; in the first instance, to create abstinence, in the second, inebriety. Group pressures may cause sobriety in a jail or in a hospital; these pressures are short-lived for two reasons. One, the offender is confined against his will, and, two, the pressures emanate from people who are not members of his group. A half-way house is a voluntary association, a man coming into it and leaving it of his own accord. The pressure to remain sober and to live a more stable life emanates from staff and members alike, all of whom have shared similar experiences. In effect, the half-way house seeks to capitalize on the effects of the previous network of social relations developed among chronic drunkenness offenders. This is in sharp contrast with jails, clinics, and hospitals which either deny the existence of such a network or reject it as a possible therapeutic tool.

The half-way house serves as a middle ground between both therapeutic and punitive agencies and organized, respectable society. The offender ordinarily has nowhere to go when he leaves these agencies. Whether he wants to or not, he is drawn back into the Skid Row setting. Compliance with its norms means that he will be back in jail in a short time. A half-way house seeks to fill the gap, to provide a protective environment where the offender can live and work with men like himself, where he can derive his usual satisfactions from group membership without recourse to alcohol.

Program. All half-way houses take drinking to be the major difficulty and provide some kind of therapy for alcoholism. Whether alcoholism is the central problem or not, while men live in a half-way house, they comply with its norms of abstinence and achieve satisfactions in a group comparable to their past drinking group. The same men on Skid Row drank in order to achieve similar satisfactions. These same men, no different in personality when they lived on Skid Row, now actively pursue a more conventional set of goals. Manipulating the system of social relationships rather than the individual alone results in a different pattern of behavior.

Experience with these half-way houses has indicated that substantial changes can occur in men whom their society had long ago given up as lost. While they live in the half-way house, chronic drunkenness offenders become sober and productive members of the community who earn their keep at regular employment and who meet the obligations of half-way house life. While members, they no longer are a drain on community resources. The half-way house appears to be, then, for a certain proportion of chronic drunkenness offenders, a more efficient response to the stubborn problem of chronic public drunkenness than continual jailing.

At the present time, there are more than twenty programs for chronic drunkenness offenders based on the theory of the half-way house. While there may be considerable variation in aims and philosophy, the common factor is the idea that the chronic drunkenness offender must continue his membership in a group of people like himself and that this group can be manipulated to change the offender's pattern of behavior, once the properties of this group membership are better understood.

Research on patterns of half-way house life may provide systematic data on the properties of this group membership. The Compass Club in New Haven, a half-way house run by the Connecticut Commission on Alcoholism, is one program for chronic drunkenness offenders which conducts research on its own operations. Since its inception in February of 1956 a sociologist, the present writer, has been gathering data on social life in the half-way house. This research has uncovered distinctive Club membership careers, long-term members differing in some important ways from short-term members. These differences bear upon the person's career while in the half-way house and in the difficult transition period when he seeks to "make it" on his own, after leaving the Club.

Skid Row presents differential opportunities for leaving; the larger society offers differential opportunities for returning to a more respectable way of life. These opportunities, for leaving and returning, appear to be related to previous status in respectable society and status on Skid Row. These statuses regulate experience while on Skid Row, either limiting or expanding social participation in the subculture. Long-term members of the half-way house appear to be men who were limited in the extent to which they shared in Skid Row culture patterns, and, to that extent, had more opportunities of being accepted back into respectable society.

When these different levels of participation in Skid Row subculture are more carefully worked out, it should be possible to determine potentials for rehabilitation among the population of chronic drunkenness offenders, screen applicants in accordance with these potentials, and adapt therapeutic programs to the different levels of participation. From the outside, all chronic drunkenness offenders look alike. Observed in a half-way house, it becomes clear that there are significant differences among them. Effective social therapy with chronic drunkenness offenders requires knowledge of the way they have participated in Skid Row life and selection of a future social role which may provide similar benefits to the individual without the usual costs to the community.

APPRENTICESHIPS IN PROSTITUTION*

James H. Bryan

On the basis of interviews with call girls in the Los Angeles area, information was obtained about entrance into prostitution. As an occupation, prostitution requires little formal knowledge or practice for its successful pursuit, the result being little occupational socialization and great occupational instability. While there is a definite apprenticeship period for the call girl, it is the secrecy rather than the complexity of the occupation that makes apprenticeship necessary. The primary purpose of the apprenticeship period is the development of an adequate clientele.

While theoretical conceptions of deviant behavior range from role strain to psychoanalytic theory, orientations to the study of the prostitute have shown considerable homogeneity. Twentieth century theorizing concerning this occupational group has employed, almost exclusively, a Freudian psychiatric model. The prostitute has thus been variously described as masochistic, of infantile mentality, unable to form mature interpersonal relationships, regressed, emotionally dangerous to males and as normal as the average woman.[1] The call girl, the specific focus of this paper, has been accused of being anxious, possessing a confused self-image, being excessively dependent, demonstrating gender-role confusion, being aggressive, lacking internal controls and being masochistic.[2]

The exclusive use of psychoanalytic models in attempting to predict behavior, and the consequent neglect of situational and cognitive processes, has been steadily lessening in the field of psychology. Their inadequacy as models for understanding deviancy has been specifically explicated by Becker, and implied by London.[3] The new look in the conceptualization and study of deviant behavior has focused on the interpersonal processes which help define the deviant role, the surroundings in which the role is learned, and limits upon the enactment of the role. As Hooker has indicated regarding the study of homosexuals, one must consider not only the personality structure of the participants, but also the structure of their community and the pathways

[1] H. Benjamin "Prostitution Reassessed," *International Journal of Sexology*, 26 (1951), pp. 154–160; H. Benjamin & A. Ellis, "An Objective Examination of Prostitution," *International Journal of Sexology*, 29 (1955), pp. 100–105; E. Glover, "The Abnormality of Prostitution," in A. M. Krich, editor, *Women*, New York: Dell Publishing Company, Inc., 1953; M. H. Hollander, "Prostitution, the Body, and Human Relatedness," *International Journal of Psychoanalysis*, 42 (1961), pp. 404–413; M. Karpf, "Effects of Prostitution on Marital Sex Adjustment," *International Journal of Sexology*, 29 (1953), pp. 149–154; J. F. Oliven, *Sexual Hygiene and Pathology*, Philadelphia: J. B. Lippencott Co., 1955; W. J. Robinson, *The Oldest Profession in the World*, New York: Eugenics Publishing Co., 1929.

[2] H. Greenwald, *The Call Girl*, New York: Ballantine Books, 1960.

[3] H. S. Becker, *Outsiders: Studies in the Sociology of Deviance*, New York: Free Press of Glencoe, 1963. Also see *The Other Side*, H. S. Becker, editor, New York: Free Press of Glencoe, 1964. P. London, *The Modes and Morals of Psychotherapy*, New York: Holt, Rinehart and Winston, Inc., 1954. For recent trends in personality theory, see N. Sanford, "Personality: Its Place in Psychology," and D. R. Miller, "The Study of Social Relationships: Situation, Identity, and Social Interaction." Both papers are presented in S. Koch, editor, *Psychology: A Study of a Science*, Vol. 5, New York: McGraw-Hill Book Co., Inc., 1963.

* Reprinted from *Social Problems*, 12 (Winter 1965), pp. 287–297, by permission of the author and the publisher.

and routes into the learning and enactment of the behavior.[4] Such "training periods" have been alluded to by Maurer in his study of the con man, and by Sutherland in his report on professional thieves. More recently, Lindesmith and Becker have conceptualized the development of drug use as a series of learning sequences necessary for the development of steady use.[5]

This paper provides some detailed, albeit preliminary, information concerning induction and training in a particular type of deviant career: prostitution, at the call girl level. It describes the order of events, and their surrounding structure, which future call girls experience in entering their occupation.

The respondents in this study were 33 prostitutes, all currently or previously working in the Los Angeles area. They ranged in age from 18 to 32, most being in their mid-twenties. None of the interviewees were obtained through official law enforcement agencies, but seven were found within the context of a neuropsychiatric hospital. The remaining respondents were gathered primarily through individual referrals from previous participants in the study. There were no obvious differences between the "psychiatric sample" and the other interviewees on the data to be reported.

All subjects in the sample were call girls. that is, they typically obtained their clients by individual referrals, primarily by telephone, and enacted the sexual contract in their own or their clients' place of residence or employment. They did not initiate contact with their customers in bars, streets, or houses of prostitution, although they might meet their customers at any number of

locations by pre-arrangement. The minimum fee charged per sexual encounter was $20.00. As an adjunct to the call girl interviews, three pimps and two "call boys" were interviewed as well.[6]

Approximately two thirds of the sample were what are sometimes known as "outlaw broads"; that is, they were not under the supervision of a pimp when interviewed. There is evidence that the majority of pimps who were aware of the study prohibited the girls under their direction from participating in it. It should be noted that many members of the sample belonged to one or another clique; their individually expresssed opinions may not be independent.

The interviews strongly suggest that there are marked idiosyncrasies from one geographical area to another in such practices as fee-splitting, involvement with peripheral occupations (e.g., cabbies), and so forth. For example, there appears to be little direct involvement of peripheral occupations with call girl activities in the Los Angeles area, while it has been estimated that up to 10% of the population of Las Vegas is directly involved in activities of prostitutes.[7] What may be typical for a call girl in the Los Angeles area is not necessarily typical for a girl in New York, Chicago, Las Vegas, or Miami.

Since the professional literature (e.g., Greenwald; Pomeroy) concerning this occupation and its participants is so limited in quantity, and is not concerned with training per se, the present data may have some utility for the social sciences.[8]

All but two interviews were tape re-

[4] Evelyn Hooker, "The Homosexual Community." *Proceedings of the XIV International Congress of Applied Psychology,* 1961, pp. 40–59. See also A. Reiss. "The Social Integration of Queens and Peers." *Social Problems,* 9 (1961), pp. 102–120.
[5] D. W. Maurer, *The Big Con,* New York: Signet Books, 1940. H. S. Becker, *Outsiders.* E. H. Sutherland, *The Professional Thief,* Chicago: University of Chicago Press, 1937. A. R. Lindesmith, *Opiate Addiction,* Evanston: Principia Press, 1955.

[6] This definition departs somewhat from that offered by Clinard. He defines the call girl as one dependent upon an organization for recruiting patrons and one who typically works in lower-class hotels. The present sample is best described by Clinard's category high-class independent professional prostitute. M. D. Clinard, *Sociology of Deviant Behavior,* New York: Rinehart & Co., Inc., 1957.
[7] E. Reid and O. Demaris, *The Green Felt Jungle,* New York: Pocket Books, Inc., 1963.
[8] H. Greenwald, *op. cit.,* W. Pomeroy, *Some Aspects of Prostitution,* unpublished paper.

corded. All respondents had prior knowledge that the interview would be tape recorded. The interviewing was, for the most part, done at the girls' place of work and/or residence. Occasional interviews were conducted in the investigator's office, and one in a public park. Interviews were semi-structured and employed open-ended questions. One part of the interview concerned the apprenticeship period or "turning out" process.

THE ENTRANCE

I had been thinking about it [becoming a call girl] before a lot. . . . Thinking about wanting to do it, but I had no connections. Had I not had a connection, I probably wouldn't have started working. . . . I thought about starting out. . . . Once I tried it [without a contact]. . . . I met this guy at a bar and I tried to make him pay me, but the thing is, you can't do it that way because they are romantically interested in you, and they don't think that it is on that kind of basis. You can't all of a sudden come up and want money for it, you have to be known beforehand. . . . I think that is what holds a lot of girls back who might work. I think I might have started a year sooner had I had a connection. You seem to make one contact or another . . . if it's another girl or a pimp or just someone who will set you up and get you a client. . . . You can't just, say, get an apartment and get a phone in and everything and say, "Well, I'm gonna start business," because you gotta get clients from somewhere. There has to be a contact.

Immediately prior to entrance into the occupation, all but one girl had personal contact with someone professionally involved in call girl activities (pimps or other call girls). The one exception had contact with a customer of call girls. While various occupational groups (e.g., photographers) seem to be peripherally involved, often unwittingly, with the call girl, there was no report of individuals involved in such occupations being contacts for new recruits. The novice's initial contact is someone at the level at which she will eventually enter the occupation: not a streetwalker, but a call girl; not a pimp who manages girls out of a house of prostitution, but a pimp who manages call girls.

Approximately half of the girls reported that their initial contact for entrance into the profession was another "working girl." The nature of these relationships is quite variable. In some cases, the girls have been long standing friends. Other initial contacts involved sexual relationships between a Lesbian and the novice. Most, however, had known each other less than a year, and did not appear to have a very close relationship, either in the sense of time spent together or of biographical information exchanged. The relationship may begin with the aspiring call girl soliciting the contact. That is, if a professional is known to others as a call girl, she will be sought out and approached by females who are strangers:[9]

I haven't ever gone out and looked for one. All of these have fell right into my hands. . . . They turned themselfs out. . . . They come to me for help.

Whatever their relationship, whenever the professional agrees to aid the beginner, she also, it appears, implicitly assumes responsibility for training her. This is evidenced by the fact that only one such female contact referred the aspirant to another girl for any type of help. Data are not available as to the reason for this unusual referral.

If the original contact was not another call girl but a pimp, a much different relationship is developed and the career follows a somewhat different course. The relationship between pimp and girl is typically one of lovers, not friends:

. . . because I love him very much. Obviously, I'm doing this mostly for him. . . . I'd do anything for him. I'm not just saying I will, I am. . . . [After discussing his affair with another woman] I just decided that I knew what he was when I decided to do this for him and I decided I had two choices—either accept it

[9] A point also made in the autobiographical account of a retired call girl. Virginia McManus, *Not for Love*, New York: Dell Publishing Co., Inc., 1960, p. 160.

or not, and I accepted it, and I have no excuse.

Occasionally, however, a strictly business relationship will be formed:

Right now I am buying properties, and as soon as I can afford it, I am buying stocks. . . . It is strictly a business deal. This man and I are friends, our relationship ends there. He handles all the money, he is making all the investments and I trust him. We have a legal document drawn up which states that half the investments are mine, half of them his, so I am protected.

Whether the relationship is love or business, the pimp solicits the new girl.[10] It is usually agreed that the male will have an important managerial role in the course of girl's career, and that both will enjoy the gains from the girl's activities for an indefinite period:

Actually a pimp has to have complete control or else its like trouble with him. Because if a pimp doesn't, if she is not madly in love with him or something in some way, a pimp won't keep a girl.

Once the girl agrees to function as a call girl, the male, like his female counterpart, undertakes the training of the girl, or refers the girl to another call girl for training. Either course seems equally probable. Referrals, when employed, are typically to friends and, in some cases, wives or ex-wives.

Although the data are limited, it appears that the pimp retains his dominance over the trainee even when the latter is being trained by a call girl. The girl trainer remains deferential to the pimp's wishes regarding the novice.

APPRENTICESHIP

Once a contact is acquired and the decision to become a call girl made, the recruit

10 Two of the pimps denied that this was very often so and maintained that the girls will solicit them. The degree to which they are solicited seems to depend upon the nature and extent of their reputations. It is difficult to judge the accuracy of these reports as there appears to be a strong taboo against admitting to such a solicitation.

moves to the next stage in the career sequence: the apprenticeship period. The structure of the apprenticeship will be described, followed by a description of the content most frequently communicated during this period.

The apprenticeship is typically served under the direction of another call girl, but may occasionally be supervised by a pimp. Twenty-four girls in the sample initially worked under the supervision of other girls. The classroom is, like the future place of work, an apartment. The apprentice typically serves in the trainer's apartment, either temporarily residing with the trainer or commuting there almost daily. The novice rarely serves her apprenticeship in such places as a house of prostitution, motel, or on the street. It is also infrequent that the girl is transported out of her own city to serve an apprenticeship. Although the data are not extensive, the number of girls being trained simultaneously by a particular trainer has rarely been reported to be greater than three. Girls sometimes report spending up to eight months in training, but the average stay seems to be two or three months. The trainer controls all referrals and appointments, novices seemingly not having much control over the type of sexual contract made or the circumstances surrounding the enactment of the contract.

The structure of training under the direction of a pimp seems similar, though information is more limited. The girls are trained in an apartment in the city they intend to work and for a short period of time. There is some evidence that the pimp and the novice often do not share the same apartment as might the novice and the girl trainer. There appear to be two reasons for the separation of pimp and girl. First, it is not uncommonly thought that cues which suggest the presence of other men displease the girl's customers:

Well, I would never let them know that I had a lover, which is something that you never ever let a john know, because this makes them very reticent to give you money, because they think you are going to go and spend it with your lover, which is what usually happens.

(Interestingly, the work of Winick suggests that such prejudices may not actually be held by many customers.)[11] Secondly, the legal repercussions are much greater, of course, for the pimp who lives with his girl than for two girls rooming together. As one pimp of 19 years experience puts it:

It is because of the law. There is a law that is called the illegal cohabitation that they rarely use unless the man becomes big in stature. If he is a big man in the hustling world, the law then employs any means at their command. . . .

Because of the convenience in separation of housing, it is quite likely that the pimp is less directly involved with the day-to-day training of the girls than the call girl trainer.

The content of the training period seems to consist of two broad, interrelated dimensions, one philosophical, the other interpersonal. The former refers to the imparting of a value structure, the latter to "do's" and "don'ts" of relating to customers and, secondarily, to other "working girls" and pimps. The latter teaching is perhaps best described by the concept of a short range perspective. That is, most of the "do's" and "don't's" pertain to ideas and actions that the call girl uses in problematic situations.[12] Not all girls absorb these teachings, and those who do incorporate them in varying degrees.

Insofar as a value structure is transmitted it is that of maximizing gains while minimizing effort, even if this requires transgressions of either a legal or moral nature. Frequently, it is postulated that people, particularly men, are corrupt or easily corruptible, that all social relationships are but a reflection of a "con," and that prostitution is simply a

more honest or at least no more dishonest act than the everyday behavior of "squares." Furthermore, not only are "johns" basically exploitative, but they are easily exploited; hence they are, in some respects, stupid. As explained by a pimp:

. . . [in the hustling world] the trick or the john is known as a fool . . . this is not the truth. . . . He [the younger pimp] would teach his woman that a trick was a fool.

Since the male is corrupt, or honest only because he lacks the opportunity to be corrupt, then it is only appropriate that he be exploited as he exploits.

Girls first start making their "scores"—say one guy keeps them for a while or maybe she gets, you know, three or four grand out of him, say a car or a coat. These are your scores. . . .

The general assumption that man is corrupt is empirically confirmed when the married male betrays his wife, when the moralist, secular or religious, betrays his publicly stated values, or when the "john" "stiffs" (cheats) the girl. An example of the latter is described by a girl as she reflects upon her disillusionment during her training period.

It is pretty rough when you are starting out. You get stiffed a lot of times. . . . Oh sure. They'll take advantage of you anytime they can. And I'm a trusting soul, I really am. I'll believe anybody till they prove different. I've made a lot of mistakes that way. You get to the point, well, Christ, what the heck can I believe in people, they tell me one thing and here's what they do to me.

Values such as fairness with other working girls, or fidelity to a pimp, may occasionally be taught. To quote a pimp:

So when you ask me if I teach a kind of basic philosophy, I would say that you could say that. Because you try to teach them in an amoral way that there is a right and wrong way as pertains to this game . . . and then you teach them that when working with other girls to try to treat the other girl fairly because a woman's worst enemy in the street [used in both a literal and figurative sense] is the other woman and only by treating the other women decently can she expect to get along. . . . Therefore the basic philosophy I guess would

[11] C. Winick, "Prostitutes' Clients' Perception of the Prostitute and Themselves," *International Journal of Social Psychiatry*, 8 (1961–62), pp. 289–297.
[12] H. S. Becker, Blanche Geer, E. C. Hughes, and A. L. Strauss, *Boys in White*, Chicago: University of Chicago Press, 1961.

consist of a form of honesty, a form of sincerity and complete fidelity to her man [pimp].

It should be noted, however, that behavior based on enlightened self-interest with concomitant exploitation is not limited to customer relationships. Interviewees frequently mentioned a pervasive feeling of distrust between trainer and trainee, and such incidents as thefts or betrayal of confidences are occasionally reported and chronically guarded against.

Even though there may be considerable pressure upon the girl to accept this value structure, many of them (perhaps the majority of the sample) reject it.

People have told me that I wasn't turned out, but turned loose instead. . . . Someone who is turned out is turned out to believe in a certain code of behavior, and this involves having a pimp, for one thing. It also involves never experiencing anything but hatred or revulsion for "tricks" for another thing. It involves always getting the money in front [before the sexual act] and a million little things that are very strictly adhered to by those in the "in group," which I am not. . . . Never being nice or pleasant to a trick unless you are doing it for the money, getting more money. [How did you learn that?] It was explained to me over a period of about six months. I learned that you were doing it to make money for yourself so that you could have nice things and security. . . . [Who would teach you this?] [The trainer] would teach me this.[13]

It seems reasonable to assume that the value structure serves, in general, to create in-group solidarity and to alienate the girl from "square" society, and that this structure serves the political advantage of the trainer and the economic gains of the trainee more than it allays the personal anxieties of either. In fact, failure to adopt these values at the outset does not appear to be correlated with much personal dis-

tress.[14] As one girl describes her education experiences:

Some moral code. We're taught, as a culture . . . it's there and after awhile you live, breathe, and eat it. Now, what makes you go completely against everything that's inside you, everything that you have been taught, and the whole society, to do things like this?

Good empirical evidence, however, concerning the functions and effectiveness of this value structure with regard to subjective comfort is lacking.

A series of deductions derived from the premises indicated above serve to provide, in part, the "rules" of interpersonal contact with the customer. Each customer is to be seen as a "mark," and "pitches" are to be made.

[Did you have a standard pitch?] It's sort of amusing. I used to listen to my girl friend [trainer]. She was the greatest at this telephone type of situation. She would call up and cry and say that people had come to her door. . . . She'd cry and she'd complain and she'd say "I have a bad check at the liquor store, and they sent the police over," and really . . . a girl has a story she tells the man. . . . Anything, you know, so he'll help her out. Either it's the rent or she needs a car, or doctor's bills, or any number of things.

Any unnecessary interaction with the customer is typically frowned upon, and the trainee will receive exhortations to be quick about her business. One girl in her fourth week of work explains:

[What are some of the other don't's that you have learned about?] Don't take so much time. . . . The idea is to get rid of them as quickly as possible.

Other content taught concerns specific information about specific customers.

. . . she would go around the bar and say, now look at that man over there, he's this way and that way, and this is what he would like and these are what his problems are. . . .

---

[13] The statements made by prostitutes to previous investigators and mental helpers may have been parroting this particular value structure and perhaps have misled previous investigators into making the assumption that "all whores hate men." While space prohibits a complete presentation of the data, neither our questionnaire nor interview data suggest that this is a predominant attitude among call girls.

[14] There is, from the present study, little support for the hypothesis of Reckless concerning the association of experience trauma and guilt with abruptness of entry into the occupation. W. C. Reckless, *The Crime Problem*, New York: Appleton-Century-Crofts, Inc., 1950.

. . . she would teach me what the men wanted and how much to get, what to say when I got there . . . just a line to hand them.

Training may also include proprieties concerning consuming alcohol and drugs, when and how to obtain the fee, how to converse with the customers and, occasionally, physical and sexual hygiene. As a girl trainer explains:

First of all, impress cleanliness. Because, on the whole, the majority of girls, I would say, I don't believe there are any cleaner women walking the streets, because they've got to be aware of any type of body odor. . . . You teach them to French [fellatio] and how to talk to men.

[Do they (pimps) teach you during the turning out period how to make a telephone call?] Oh, usually, yes. They don't teach you, they just tell you how to do it and you do it with your good common sense, but if you have trouble, they tell you more about it.

Interestingly, the specific act of tele phoning a client is often distressing to the novice and is of importance in her training. Unfortunately for the girl, it is an act she must perform with regularity as she does considerable soliciting. One suspects that such behavior is embarrassing for her because it is an unaccustomed role for her to play— she has so recently come from a culture where young women do not telephone men for dates. Inappropriate sex-role behavior seems to produce greater personal distress than does appropriate sex-role behavior even when it is morally reprehensible.

Well, it is rather difficult to get on the telephone, when you've never worked before, and talk to a man about a subject like that, and it is very new to you.

What is omitted from the training should be noted as well. There seems to be little instruction concerning sexual techniques as such, even though the previous sexual experience of the trainee may have been quite limited. What instruction there is typically revolves around the practice of fellatio. There seems to be some encouragement not to experience sexual orgasms with the client, though this may be quite variable with the trainer.

. . . and sometimes, I don't know if it's a set rule or maybe it's an unspoken rule, you don't enjoy your dates.

Yes, he did [teach attitudes]. He taught me to be cold. . . .

It should be stressed that, if the girls originally accepted such instructions and values, many of them, at least at the time of interviewing, verbalized a rejection of these values and reported behavior which departed considerably from the interpersonal rules stipulated as "correct" by their trainers. Some experience orgasms with the customer, some show considerable affect toward "johns," others remain drunk or "high" throughout the contact.[15] While there seems to be general agreement as to what the rules of interpersonal conduct are, there appears to be considerable variation in the adoption of such rules.

A variety of methods are employed to communicate the content described above. The trainer may arrange to eavesdrop on the interactions of girl and client and then discuss the interaction with her. One trainer, for example, listened through a closed door to the interaction of a new girl with a customer, then immediately after he left, discussed, in a rather heated way, methods by which his exit may have been facilitated. A pimp relates:

The best way to do this [teaching conversation] is, in the beginning, when the phone rings, for instance . . . is to listen to what she says and then check and see how big a trick he is and then correct her from there.

. . . with everyone of them [trainees] I would make it a point to see two guys to see how they [the girls] operate.

In one case a girl reported that her pimp left a written list of rules pertaining to relating to "johns." Direct teaching, however, seems to be uncommon. The bulk of whatever learning takes place seems to take place through observation.

It's hard to tell you, because we learn through observations.

15 In the unpublished paper referred to above, Pomeroy has indicated that, of 31 call girls interviewed, only 23% reported never experiencing orgasms with customers.

But I watched her and listened to what her bit was on the telephone.

To summarize, the structure of the apprenticeship period seems quite standard. The novice receives her training either from a pimp or from another more experienced call girl, more often the latter. She serves her initial two to eight months of work under the trainer's supervision and often serves this period in the trainer's apartment. The trainer assumes responsibility for arranging contacts and negotiating the type and place of the sexual encounter.

The content of the training pertains both to a general philosophical stance and to some specifics (usually not sexual) of interpersonal behavior with customers and colleagues. The philosophy is one of exploiting the exploiters (customers) by whatever means necessary and defining the colleagues of the call girl as being intelligent, self-interested and, in certain important respects, basically honest individuals. The interpersonal techniques addressed during the learning period consist primarily of "pitches," telephone conversations, personal and occasionally sexual hygiene, prohibitions against alcohol and dope while with a "john," how and when to obtain the fee, and specifics concerning the sexual habits of particular customers. Specific sexual techniques are very rarely taught. The current sample included a considerable number of girls who, although capable of articulating this value structure, were not particularly inclined to adopt it.

CONTACTS AND CONTRACTS

While the imparting of ideologies and proprieties to the prospective call girl is emphasized during the apprenticeship period, it appears that the primary function of the apprenticeship, at least for the trainee, is building a clientele. Since this latter function limits the degree of occupational socialization, the process of developing the clientele and the arrangements made between trainer and trainee will be discussed.

Lists ("books") with the names and telephone numbers of customers are available for purchase from other call girls or pimps, but such books are often considered unreliable. While it is also true that an occasional pimp will refer customers to girls, this does not appear to be a frequent practice. The most frequent method of obtaining such names seems to be through contacts developed during the apprenticeship. The trainer refers customers to the apprentice and oversees the latter in terms of her responsibility and adequacy in dealing with the customer. For referring the customer, the trainer receives forty to fifty percent of the total price agreed upon in the contract negotiated by the trainer and the customer.[16] The trainer and trainees further agree, most often explicitly, on the apprentice's "right" to obtain and to use, on further occasions, information necessary for arranging another sexual contract with the "john" without the obligation of further "kick-back" to the trainer. That is, if she can obtain the name and telephone number of the customer, she can negotiate another contract without fee-splitting. During this period, then, the girl is not only introduced to other working colleagues (pimps and girls alike) but also develops a clientele.

There are two obvious advantages for a call girl in assuming the trainer role. First, since there seems to be an abundant demand for new girls, and since certain service requirements demand more than one girl, even the well established call girl chronically confronts the necessity for making referrals. It is then reasonable to assume that the extra profit derived from the fee-splitting activities, together with the added conveniences of having a girl "on call," allows the

[16] The fee-splitting arrangement is quite common at all levels of career activity. For example, cooperative activity between two girls is often required for a particular type of sexual contract. In these cases, the girl who has contracted with the customer will contact a colleague, usually a friend, and will obtain 40%–50% of the latter's earnings. There is suggestive evidence that fee-splitting activities vary according to geographical areas and that Los Angeles is unique for both its fee-splitting patterns and the rigidity of its fee-splitting structure.

trainer to profit considerably from this arrangement. Secondly, contacts with customers are reputedly extremely difficult to maintain if services are not rendered on demand. Thus, the adoption of the trainer role enables the girl to maintain contacts with "fickle" customers under circumstances where she may wish a respite from the sexual encounter without terminating the contacts necessary for re-entry into the call girl role. It is also possible that the financial gains may conceivably be much greater for most trainers than for most call girls, but this is a moot point.

A final aspect of the apprenticeship period that should be noted is the novice's income. It is possible for the novice, under the supervision of a competent and efficient trainer, to earn a great deal of money, or at least to get a favorable glimpse of the great financial possibilities of the occupation and, in effect, be heavily rewarded for her decision to enter it. Even though the novice may be inexperienced in both the sexual and interpersonal techniques of prostitution, her novelty on the market gives her an immediate advantage over her more experienced competitors. It seems quite likely that the new girl, irrespective of her particular physical or mental qualities, has considerable drawing power because she provides new sexual experience to the customer. Early success and financial reward may well provide considerable incentive to continue in the occupation.

A final word is needed regarding the position of the pimp vis-à-vis the call girl during the apprenticeship period. While some pimps assume the responsibility for training the girl personally, as indicated above, as many send the novice to another girl. The most apparent reason for such referral is that it facilitates the development of the "book." Purposes of training appear to be secondary for two reasons: (1) The pimp often lacks direct contact with the customers, so he personally cannot aid directly in the development of the girl's clientele. (2) When the pimp withdraws his girl from the training context, it is rarely

because she has obtained adequate knowledge of the profession. This is not to say that all pimps are totally unconcerned with the type of knowledge being imparted to the girl. Rather, the primary concern of the pimp is the girl's developing a clientele, not learning the techniques of sex or conversation.

The apprenticeship period usually ends abruptly, not smoothly. Its termination may be but a reflection of interpersonal difficulties between trainer and trainee, novice and pimp, or between two novices. Occasionally termination of training is brought about through the novice's discovery and subsequent theft of the trainer's "book." Quite frequently, the termination is due to the novice's developing a sufficient trade or other business opportunities. The point is, however, that no respondent has reported that the final disruption of the apprenticeship was the result of the completion of adequate training. While disruptions of this relationship may be due to personal or impersonal events, termination is not directly due to the development of sufficient skills.

DISCUSSION AND SUMMARY

On the basis of interviews with 33 call girls in the Los Angeles area, information was obtained about entrance into the call girl occupation and the initial training period or apprenticeship therein.

The novice call girl is acclimated to her new job primarily by being thoroughly immersed in the call girl subculture, where she learns the trade through imitation as much as through explicit tutoring. The outstanding concern at this stage is the development of a sizable and lucrative clientele. The specific skills and values which are acquired during this period are rather simple and quickly learned.

In spite of the girls' protests and their extensive folklore, the art of prostitution, at least at this level, seems to be technically a low-level skill. That is, it seems to be an occupation which requires little formal knowledge or practice for its successful pursuit and appears best categorized as an un-skilled job. Evidence for this point comes from two separate sources. First, there seems to be little technical training during this period, and the training seems of little importance to the career progress. Length or type of training does not appear correlated with success (i.e., money earned, lack of subjective distress, minimum fee per "trick," etc.). Secondly, the termination of the apprenticeship period is often brought about for reasons unrelated to training. It seems that the need for an apprenticeship period is created more by the secrecy surrounding the rendering or the utilization of the call girl service than by the complexity of the role. In fact, it is reasonable to assume that the complexity of the job confronting a streetwalker may be considerably greater than that confronting a call girl. The tasks of avoiding the police, sampling among strangers for potential customers, and arrangements for the completion of the sexual contract not only require different skills on the part of the streetwalker, but are performances requiring a higher degree of professional "know-how" than is generally required of the call girl.[17]

[17] Needless to say, however, all of the sample of call girls who were asked for status hierarchies of prostitution felt that the streetwalker had both less status and a less complex job. It may well be that the verbal exchange required of the call girl requires greater knowledge than that required of a streetwalker, but the nonverbal skills required of the streetwalker may be considerably greater than those of the call girl.

As a pimp who manages both call girls and "high class" streetwalkers explains:

The girl that goes out into the street is the sharper of the two, because she is capable of handling herself in the street, getting around the law, picking out the trick that is not absolutely psycho . . . and capable of getting along in the street. . . . The streetwalker, as you term her, is really a prima donna of the prostitutes . . . her field is unlimited, she goes to all of the top places so she meets the top people. . . .

The fact that the enactment of the call girl role requires little training, and the introduction of the girl to clients and colleagues alike is rather rapid, gives little time or incentive for adequate occupational socialization. It is perhaps for this reason rather than, for example, reasons related to personality factors, that occupational instability is great and cultural homogeneity small.

In closing, while it appears that there is a rather well defined apprenticeship period in the career of the call girl, it seems that it is the secrecy rather than the complexity of the occupation which generates such a period. While there is good evidence that initial contacts, primarily with other "working girls," are necessary for entrance into this career, there seems no reason, at this point, to assume that the primary intent of the participants in training is anything but the development of an adequate clientele.

THE HOMOSEXUAL COMMUNITY*

Maurice Leznoff and William A. Westley

As the authors of the following selection note, homosexuality is defined both legally and socially as a criminal and depraved

* Reprinted from *Social Problems*, 3 (April 1956), pp. 257–263, by permission of the authors and the publisher.

*practice, and the homosexual is threatened by powerful legal and
social sanctions such as imprisonment, physical violence, ostracism,
and ridicule. The social organization of a homosexual community
is discussed below. The selection considers the homosexual group
in the community, its function, etiology, and interrelationships.*

The significance of homosexuality in our society has been minimized and obscured by the force of social taboo. Yet there is evidence that homosexuals are distributed throughout all geographical areas and socio-economic strata.[1] Furthermore, the subjection of homosexuals to legal punishments and social condemnation has produced a complex structure of concealed social relations which merit sociological investigation. The psychological isolation of the homosexual from society, his dependence upon other deviants for the satisfaction of sexual needs and self-expression, the crystallization of social roles and behavior patterns within the deviant group, the reciprocal obligations and demands within the homosexual community, and their significance for the larger society in which they occur, are but a few of the areas of theoretical interest to the sociologist.

In this paper we shall confine our discussion to the social organization of one homosexual community and its constituent social groups: their function, etiology, and interrelationships.

[1] Kinsey reports that 37 percent of the total male population have at least some overt homosexual experience to the point of orgasm between adolescence and old age; 30 percent of all males have at least incidental homosexual experience or reactions over at least a three year period between the ages of 16 and 55; 25 percent of the male population have more than incidental homosexual experience or reactions for at least three years between the ages of 16 and 55; 18 percent of the males have at least as much of the homosexual as the heterosexual in their histories for at least three years between the ages of 16 and 55; 4 percent of the white males are exclusively homosexual throughout their lives, after the onset of adolescence. Homosexual practices are reported among all occupational groups with the percentage for professionals approximately 50 percent lower than those of other groups. Further confirmation of the distribution of homosexuals among all social strata was obtained from police files and the testimony of homosexuals.

The report is based upon an intensive study of 60 homosexuals in a large Canadian city. The data consist of four-hour interviews with 40 homosexuals and briefer interviews with 20 others.[2] In addition, the data include information based on the observation of many homosexual parties and gatherings in bars and restaurants, and a series of 30 letters written by one homosexual to another.

FUNCTIONS OF HOMOSEXUAL GROUPS

The primary function of the homosexual group is psychological in that it provides a social context within which the homosexual can find acceptance as a homosexual and collective support for his deviant tendencies. Most homosexuals fear detection and are often insecure and anxious because of this. The following statement illustrates this:

The thought that you are "gay" is always with you and you know it's there even when other people don't. You also think to yourself that certain of your mannerisms and your ways of expression are liable to give you away. That means that there is always a certain amount of strain. I don't say that it's a relief to get away from normal people, but there isn't the liberty that you feel in a gay crowd. When I associate with normal people I prefer very small groups of them. I don't like large groups and I think I try to avoid them when I can. You know, the only time when I really forget I'm gay is when I'm in a gay crowd.

To relieve this anxiety the deviant seeks collective support and social acceptance. Since the homosexual group provides the only social context in which homosexuality is normal, deviant practices moral, and homosexual responses rewarded, the homo-

[2] Access to this homosexual community was obtained through a client at a social welfare agency.

sexual develops a deep emotional involvement with his group, tending toward a
ready acceptance of its norms and dictates,
and subjection to its behavior patterns. The
regularity with which he seeks the company
of his group is a clear expression of this dependency.

A prohibition against sexual relationships
within the group, in a manner suggestive of
the incest taboo, indicates the extent to
which the group culture is oriented to this
function. The quotation which follows is
indicative of this taboo:

As far as I know, people who hang around
with each other don't have affairs. The people
who are friends don't sleep with each other.
I can't tell you why that is, but they just don't.
Unless you are married[3] you have sex with
strangers mostly. I think if you have sex with a
friend it will destroy the friendship. I think
that in the inner mind we all respect high
moral standards, and none of us want to feel
low in the eyes of anybody else. It's always
easier to get along with your gay friends if
there has been no sex. Mind you, you might
have sex with somebody you just met and
then he might become your friend. But you
won't have sex with him any more as soon as
he joins the same gang you hang around with.

Within these groups the narration of
sexual experiences and gossip about the sexual exploits of others is a major form of
recreation. The narration of sexual experiences functions to allocate prestige among
the members because of the high evaluation
placed upon physical attraction and sexual
prowess. Yet it creates hostility and sexual
rivalry. The intense involvement of homosexuals in the results of this sexual competition is illustrated in the following statement which was overheard in a restaurant:

Who wouldn't blow up. That bitch is trying
to get her[4] clutches into Richard. She can't
leave anybody alone. I wouldn't be surprised if
she ended up with a knife in her back. I don't
mean to say I'm threatening her. But she's not

---

[3] A stable social and sexual relationship between two
    homosexuals is frequently referred to as "marriage."
[4] The substitution of the female for the male pro-
    noun is a common practice within homosexual
    groups.

going to get away with that stuff forever . . .
playing kneesies under the table all night long.
I had to get her away from Richard. That
lousy bitch. From now on she better keep
away from me.

An additional function is the provision
of a social situation in which the members
can dramatize their adherence to homosexual values. Thus, the gossip about sex,
the adoption and exaggeration of feminine
behavior, and the affectation of speech,
represent a way of affirming that homosexuality is frankly accepted and has the collective support of the group. The extreme but
not uncommon instance of this is the homosexual institution of the "drag" in which
the members of the group dress and make
themselves up as women. A good description of a drag is contained in the following
letter:

Well, doll, last night was one to remember.
Raymond of B. (city) gave me a letter of introduction to one of the local belles. He
'phoned yesterday and we arranged to go out
in the evening. Met at my room and proceeded
to the Frederick Hotel where I was introduced
to my new acquaintances. It was decided to
hold a party afterwards, Chez Norman, my
new acquaintance. He told me they were supposed to be discontinued but we were going
ahead in my honor. And in drag. One queen
about 45-50 who is a window dresser brought
some materials of fine nylon net, 2 yards wide
and changing color across the width from
yellow to flaming orange. There must have
been about 25 yds. Well, he made his entrance
wearing nothing but his shorts and this stuff
wound around him and proceeded to do an
exotic dance. Included in the costume was a
blond wig from one of the store mannequins
and artificial tropical fruits. It was something
to see. It was very ludicrous to begin with
and much more so when you realize that he is
by no means graceful and has so much hair
on him that I am smooth by comparison.
Throughout the evening he kept on making
variations of the costume—each becoming
briefer until he was down to nothing. Really!

Another one, very slim, put on a pair of falsies,
a turban hat to hide short hair, and a dress
with a wide flair skirt. Other than hair on the
chest which showed, the effect of femininity
was so convincing (even his heels) that I

promptly lost interest. Actually produced a beautiful effect—the kind of woman I would like if I could. Beautiful dancer, and performed all evening. Later borrowed some of the nylon net of the old queen and did a dance with flowing material and wearing *nothing*, but nothing else.

There were only three of us not in drag, including yrs. truly. But when it came time to leave (not alone, I might add) I couldn't resist flinging about my coat a fox fur which happened to be lying around. Really, my dear, it was quite an affair.

These functions reflect the common needs and problems which homosexuals face in hostile society.

ETIOLOGY: THE EVASION OF SOCIAL CONTROLS

In our society, homosexuality is defined both legally and socially as a criminal and depraved practice and the homosexual is threatened by powerful legal and social sanctions such as imprisonment, physical violence,[5] social and occupational ostracism, and ridicule. Therefore, all homosexuals face the problem of evading social controls. They do this in two predominant ways.

Some pass for heterosexuals on the job and in most of their social relationships. They mix regularly with heterosexuals for business, entertainment, and other social activities. They avoid situations and persons publicly recognized as homosexual for they fear that discovery will threaten their career and expose them to sanctions. This is illustrated in the following statement of a lawyer:

I know a few people who don't care. They are really pitiful. They are either people who are in very insignificant positions or they are in good positions but are independent. I know of one who is in the retail business. He doesn't care. A lot of the artists don't care. For that reason I have never cultivated the friendship of artists. I just don't get along with anybody who doesn't care. That's why I really can't give you information about those who don't. It's

5 William A. Westley. "Violence and the Police," *American Journal of Sociology*, 59 (July, 1953).

just that I can't afford to get to know them very well, and I try to avoid them. Sometimes personal friends become this way. Then there is a mutual rejection of the friendship. From my point of view I am just no longer interested when they adopt that kind of attitude. From their point of view it means completely living outside of society and they are no longer interested in people who they consider hypocrites.

Others openly admit and practice homosexuality. They usually work in occupations where the homosexual is tolerated, withdraw from uncompromising heterosexual groups, and confine most of their social life to homosexual circles. This attitude is expressed in the following statement by a hairdresser:

Rosenstein can go to hell as far as I care. She works you to the bone if she can get away with it. She told me I run around the place like a regular pansy. So I told her I am a pansy and if she doesn't like it she can get somebody else to do her dirty work for her. I knew she wouldn't fire me. All the ladies ask for me and I don't have to pretend to nobody.

While the problem of evasion is common to all homosexuals, the mechanisms of evasion present various alternatives. Most homosexuals find themselves compelled to conform outwardly to societal demands. They are conscious of their social position within society and seek such satisfactions as occupational mobility and prestige. They endeavor to retain intimate associations within the heterosexual community, and fear recognition as a status threat. Such homosexuals rely upon secrecy and the concealment of their deviant practices. They will therefore be referred to as "secret" homosexuals. A minority retreats from the demands of society and renounces societal goals. Such individuals will be referred to as "overt" homosexuals.

The mode of adaption is largely dependent upon the extent to which identification as a homosexual is a status threat. While economic status cannot be equated with social status, the individual's position within the work world represents the most significant single factor in the prestige scale.

Therefore, the extent to which homosexuality is tolerated in various occupations determines to a great extent the mode of evasion chosen by the homosexual. Thus, there are many occupations, of which the professions are an obvious example, where homosexuals are not tolerated. In other areas, the particular occupation may have traditionally accepted homosexual linkages in the popular image or be of such low rank as to permit homosexuals to function on the job. The artist, the interior decorator, and the hairdresser exemplify the former type; such positions as counter man or bell-hop, the latter. Thus we find a rough relationship between form of evasion and occupation. The overt homosexual tends to fit into an occupation of low status rank; the secret homosexual into an occupation with a relatively high status rank. The relationship is shown in Table 1.

Table 1.

OCCUPATION OF 40 SECRET
AND OVERT HOMOSEXUALS

OCCUPATION*	SECRET†	OVERT	TOTAL
Professional & Managerial	13	0	13
Clerical & Sales	9	4	13
Craftsmen	2	1	3
Operatives	1	1	2
Service	0	6	6
Artists	0	3	3
Totals	25	15	40

* Except for artists the categories and ranking are those established by the National Opinion Research Center. Artists have been listed as a separate category because they often represent a group which is apart from the status structure of the community.

† The secret homosexuals gave the following reasons for concealment: (a) desire to avoid social ridicule—22 cases; (b) fear of dismissal from the job, or where self-employed, inability to get clients—20 cases; (c) a desire to protect others such as family or friends—18 cases.

DISTINCTIONS BETWEEN THE SECRET AND OVERT GROUPS

The chief distinctions between homosexual groups correspond to the differences in the general modes of evading social controls which homosexuals have developed. Thus, secret and overt homosexuals form distinctive groups.

The distinctions between these groups are maintained by the secret homosexuals who fear identification and refuse to associate with overt homosexuals. This statement by a secret homosexual is illustrative:

If someone who is gay wanted to be spiteful they could say something in the wrong quarter. Nobody who cared about himself would say anything. The trouble is that some don't care. I make it a rule to avoid anybody who is perfectly open about himself. It's easy not to become friendly with those people but it's hard to avoid them entirely. You certainly don't want to snub them because that might make them antagonistic. You just don't call them or see them at social gatherings. But you do meet them at bars and that's where you can be introduced to them. If they remember you and continue to say hello to you on the street, you have to acknowledge them or they might feel that you are trying to snub them.

As a result of this social distance a certain amount of reciprocal hostility has developed between the members of secret and overt groups. This hostility helps maintain the social distance and distinctions between these groups. This is demonstrated in the following statements by an overt and a secret homosexual respectively:

I know some of them because sometimes they stoop down and have an affair with somebody from our gang. They even come to a party over at Robert's once in a while but they never hang around for very long and then you don't see them again. They go over to the Red Room sometimes but we don't have much to say to each other and the same thing happens when we go over to the Burning Flame.[6] We just might say hello. But sometimes they will cruise us and try to take someone home to bed. I think you could say we mix sexually but not socially.

There are some people who I don't like and I wish these people didn't know about me. Then there are the people I don't know too

[6] The burning Flame refers to a bar which tended to draw its clientele from secret homosexuals; the Red Room was the acknowledged gathering place of overt homosexuals.

well: people who are obvious or what I uncharitably call the riff-raff. I have always attempted to avoid them and I avoid them now. It is inevitable that you bump into a lot of people you would rather not know. Homosexuals are very democratic people. To achieve their own ends they overlook a lot they wouldn't overlook in other fields. People are bound to each other like a link of a chain. You try to avoid being a link in this chain by carefully choosing.

This poses serious problems for the homosexual who is socially mobile. He is forced to change his primary group affiliations within the homosexual community.

The following statement by the manager of an appliance shop shows how the homosexual tends to change his orientation from "overt" to "secret" as he becomes upwardly mobile.

My promotions have made me more conscious of the gang I hang around with. You see, for the first time in my life I have a job that I would really like to keep and where I can have a pretty secure future. I realize that if word were to get around that I am gay I would probably lose my job. I don't see why that should be, because I know that I'm the same person gay or not. But still that's the way it works. I don't want to hang around with Robert[7] any more or any of the people who are like Robert. I don't mind seeing them once in a while at somebody's house, but I won't be seen with them on the street any more.

Both types of groups were identified and observed in the course of this research. Each group consisted of fourteen members. The descriptions which follow are based on the study of these groups.

Secret Groups. The secret homosexuals form groups which consist of a loose amalgamation of small cliques. Interaction within the cliques is frequent, with members meeting at each other's homes and in bars and restaurants. The clique's structure is a product of the diverse interests and occupations and of the desire to limit homo-

sexual contacts which characterize secret homosexuals. The clique unites its several members in common specialized interests apart from the larger group.

The following chart shows the clique structure and occupational composition of a secret homosexual group.

Clique A	Clique B
Lawyer	Clerk-bookkeeper
Personnel Manager	Auditing clerk
University student	Assistant Office Manager
Economist	University student
	Secretary
Clique C	Clique D
Stenographer	Accountant
Store Manager	Interior Decorator
Manager of Statistical Dept.	

A secret homosexual group is generally characterized by: (a) informal standards of admission; (b) discretion in the manner in which homosexuality is practiced; (c) an attempt at concealment; (d) partial rather than complete involvement in the homosexual world.

Overt Groups. Overt homosexuals gather in cohesive social groups which become the dominant focus of their lives. These groups are openly homosexual in character. The members make little effort to conceal their deviation, spend almost all their free time with the group, and tend to regard their other activities as peripheral.

These groups generally draw their members from persons of low socioeconomic status who have jobs where concealment is not a prerequisite. Table 2 presents the occupational composition of the overt group identified in this study.

The members of the group met daily either at a bar, a restaurant, or at the house of the acknowledged leader or "queen."[8] They spent their time in endless gossip

---

[7] Robert is the leader of an overt group of which the respondent was a member at the time he was contacted.

[8] Our data with respect to the prevalence of this role are incomplete. However, homosexuals regularly refer to the queens of other cities, suggesting that the practice is widespread.

Table 2.

OCCUPATIONAL COMPOSITION OF AN OVERT HOMOSEXUAL GROUP

OCCUPATION	FREQUENCY
Manager of appliance shop*	1
School teacher	1
Hospital attendant	1
Hairdresser	4
Sales clerk	2
Foundry worker	1
Baker	1
Salesman	1
Waiter	1
Cashier	1
Total	14

* This individual had just been promoted and was beginning to leave the group. Both he and the school teacher retained for a time their affiliation with an overt group while at the same time concealing their homosexuality at work.

about the sexual affairs of the members or other homosexuals known to them. Often they would go to bars and restaurants in the attempt to make a "pick-up," or spend the evening "cruising" individually or in groups of two's and three's.

The queen seems to characterize only "overt" groups. Functionally, the role of the queen is very important in the life of these groups. He provides a place where the group may gather and where its individual members may have their "affairs." He helps finance members in distress, functions as an intermediary in making sexual contacts, partially controls the entrance of new members, and warns the members of hoodlums who would prey upon them. Generally the queen is an older homosexual who has had wide experience in the homosexual world.

The following statement about the queen by a member of the overt group provides insight into the functioning of the queen and tells something of the way in which the individuals relate to him.

A queen really means the leader of the group. You see how that is in a small town where there are not many people who are gay and willing to admit it. She knows who's who and what's what. She will know every gay person

in town and will arrange things just the way Roberta does.[9] The queen is always somebody pretty old and pretty much out of the game as far as getting anything for herself is concerned. But she doesn't have anything else to do, so she spends all her time on this. I don't know of any queen as commercial as Roberta. But that's because Roberta is so goddam crude. I know the queen in Hillsburg and she was a perfect lady if I ever saw one. She knows everything. She used to make quite a bit but it was always in the form of getting invitations for dinner or as a present. You feel grateful to somebody who does something for you and you pay off. It's like a debt.

Overt groups are characterized by: (a) no particular standards of admission; (b) unselfconscious and unrestrained practice of homosexuality; (c) little or no concealment; (d) high degree of social isolation with little involvement in heterosexual activities; (e) little concern with identification as a status threat or the sanctions of heterosexual society.

THE HOMOSEXUAL COMMUNITY

The diverse secret and overt homosexuals are linked together either through bonds of sex or of friendship. Within the primary group, the emphasis upon friendship rather than sex serves to eliminate excessive sexual competition and preserves group unity. However, this creates a sexual interdependency upon those outside the group with important social consequences.

In the first place, it forces the secret homosexual out into the open in an attempt to solicit sexual partners. He thus frequents the known homosexual meeting places within the city such as specific bars, hotel lobbies, street corners, and lavatories. These activities make him an increasingly familiar figure within the homosexual world.

Secondly, this solicitation leads to the interaction of secret and overt homosexuals on a sexual as opposed to a social basis. While these contacts occur in a spirit of

[9] The adoption of feminine names is a widespread practice among all homosexuals interviewed.

anonymity, an approach to the other often requires an exchange of confidences.

Thirdly, this sexual interdependency increases the anxiety of secret homosexuals since it forces them to contact the overt ones whom they fear as a threat to their security.

Thus, it is the casual and promiscuous sexual contacts between the members of different categories of evasion (i.e. the secret and the overt) which weld the city's homosexuals into a community.

CONCLUSION

The homosexual community thus consists of a large number of distinctive groups within which friendship binds the members together in a strong and relatively enduring bond and between which the members are linked by tenuous but repeated sexual contacts. The result is that homosexuals within the city tend to know or know of each other, to recognize a number of common interests and common moral norms, and to interact on the basis of antagonistic cooperation. This community is in turn linked with other homosexual communities in Canada and the United States, chiefly through the geographical mobility of its members.[10]

[10] The queen of the overt group studied maintained an address book containing the names of approximately 3000 homosexuals scattered across North America.

NARCOTICS AND CRIMINALITY*

Harold Finestone

In discussing the nature of the relationship between narcotics use and criminality among male adolescents and young adults, Finestone observes that both criminality and experimentation with narcotics stem from a similar source. Both are prestigeful forms of activity learned by members of the street-corner society of the disadvantaged areas of the city. Once the street-corner boy is addicted, however, criminal activity may be perpetuated in order to maintain the supply of narcotics.

Of the many controversial aspects of narcotics addiction in this country, perhaps the most emotionally freighted one has been the nature of its relationship to criminality.[1] This relationship, which has always appealed

[1] This paper is restricted to a discussion of the relationship between opiate use and criminality. The relationship between cocaine or marijuana use and criminality raises somewhat different and less urgent problems.

to popular imagination, has become the focus of even greater attention in these postwar years, as the use of narcotics has spread in almost epidemic proportions among some sectors of our adolescent and young-adult population, and as these youthful addicts, in increasing numbers, have collided with the police for violations of the narcotic drug laws and for other criminal offenses. This

* Reprinted from *Law and Contemporary Problems*, 22 (Winter 1957), pp. 69–85, published by the Duke University School of Law, Durham, North Carolina. Copyright, 1957 by Duke University, by permission of the author and the publisher.

recruitment of growing numbers of young persons to the use of narcotics has, indeed, invested the relationship with a novel character, and it is with the exploration of this somewhat recent development that this paper is primarily concerned. To this end, an attempt will be made to explain how narcotics use and criminality came to coincide in the experience of many young narcotics users, how the narcotics use is related to their criminality, and, then, how this relationship typically changes during the career of the individual addict.

I

The *Uniform Crime Reports*[2] and the data collected in the course of the Chicago Narcotics Survey, 1951–53,[3] both indicate a trend, in evidence since the early thirties and interrupted only during the war years, towards not only an increasing number of, but also a correspondingly increased involvement of young persons in, narcotic drug law violations. Thus, the *Uniform Crime Reports* recorded 2648 arrests for narcotic drug law violations in 1932, which figure rose to 5014 in 1940, fell to 1123 in 1942, and rose again to 2807 in 1946, 6546 in 1949, and 13,030 (the apogee) in 1950. The trend from 1952 onwards cannot, unfortunately, be inferred from these data, since the basis of reporting arrests for the *Uniform Crime Reports* was revised and the population base restricted in that year; but even with the revised procedure of reporting, the number of arrests annually reported has never fallen below the figure reached in 1940. In 1953, for example, 5681 arrests were reported. The Chicago Narcotics Survey data clearly reflect the same trend. The annual number of arrests averaged 330 for the period 1934–38, rose to 433 in 1939, declined during the war period, but resurged during the postwar period, rising to 424 in 1946 and increasing

annually thereafter until a peak of 1188 was reported in 1951. The most recent years for which comparable data are available, 1954 and 1955, however, show some tendency towards a diminution in the number of arrests.

Closely paralleling this increase in the absolute number of arrests for narcotic drug law violations is the trend, both on the national level and in Chicago, towards a gradually increasing proportionate number of such arrests in the younger age groups. The data from the *Uniform Crime Reports* indicate that in 1932, the proportion of total arrests for narcotic drug law violations in the twenty-four-and-under age group was fifteen per cent; in 1941, this proportion was twenty-nine per cent; and in 1951, it was forty-six per cent. The operation of a similar trend in Chicago is revealed by the fact that the proportion of total arrests falling in the sixteen-to-twenty age group was four per cent in 1934–38, seven per cent in 1941, and twenty-four per cent in both 1950 and 1951. During the same period, the proportion of total arrests in Chicago falling in the thirty-one-and-over age group decreased from an annual average of fifty-five per cent for the period 1934–38 to twenty-five per cent in 1951. Another method of portraying the same trend for Chicago is through the rates of arrest for narcotic drug law violations in each age group. Table 1 permits a comparison. And additional evidence of the trend towards the growing recruitment of new narcotics users among young people is provided by the data on first admissions of Chicago residents to the United States Public Health Service Hospital, Lexington, Kentucky, for two separate periods, 1937–41 and 1947–51. For the period 1937–41, the sixteen-to-twenty age group constituted four out of a total of 282, or 1.4 per cent of the first admissions; in the later period, 1947–51, it constituted 354 out of 1476, or twenty-four per cent of the first admissions. In contrast to this younger age group, the thirty-one-and-over age group comprised seventy-two per cent of the total first ad-

2 FBI. U.S. Dep't of Justice, *Uniform Crime Reports for the United States* (1932–55).
3 Cf. Chicago Police Department, *1934–53 Annual Reports* (n.d.).

Table 1.

RATES OF ARREST FOR NARCOTIC DRUG LAW VIOLATIONS
(CHICAGO) PER 10,000 POPULATION FOR DIFFERENT
AGE GROUPS DURING THE PERIODS 1934–38 AND 1951

AGE GROUPS	1934–38	1951
16–20	.43	13.64
21–30	2.10	10.08
31 and over	1.09	1.48

missions in the period 1937–41, and only twenty-seven per cent of such admissions in the period 1947–51.

These data appear unequivocally to evince the changing character of the narcotics addict population, which, since the early thirties, has more and more, both absolutely and proportionately, come to be comprised of adolescent and young-adult age groups.

But what are the types of offenses, apart from narcotic drug law violations, for which these addicts have been arrested? Is there any substance to the common notion that a high proportion of crimes committed by addicts are crimes of violence? The organization of the Narcotic Bureau of the Chicago Police Department in 1950 made possible the collection of data about the arrests of all known narcotics users which sheds some light in this area. From these data for the year 1951, it has been possible to classify these arrests and to determine the percentage distribution of the more serious types of offenses among addicts vis-á-vis the population at large.[4] These figures are presented in Table 2, and they would seem to indicate that the number of arrests for nonviolent, property crimes was proportionately higher among addicts. In contrast, however, the number of arrests of addicts for violent offenses against the person, such as rape and aggravated assault, was only a fraction of the proportion constituted by such arrests among the population at large.

Another kind of datum that bears di-

[4] Arrests for criminal homicide were not tabulated separately by the Narcotic Bureau, however, because their number was too small to justify a separate category.

Table 2.

THE PERCENTAGE DISTRIBUTION OF ARRESTS FOR THE MOST
SERIOUS TYPES OF OFFENSES IN THE NARCOTIC BUREAU
AND THE CHICAGO POLICE DEPARTMENT, 1951*

	NARCOTIC BUREAU	CHICAGO POLICE DEPARTMENT
Larceny—Theft (except auto theft)	58.8	31.0
Robbery	16.2	7.3
Burglary—Breaking and entering	9.9	9.4
Stolen property: buying, receiving, possessing	5.1	3.2
Forgery and Counterfeiting; Embezzlement and Fraud	4.2	4.9
Sex offenses; Rape	1.6	11.0
Auto theft	1.5	9.1
Weapons: carrying, possessing, etc.	1.4	4.4
Aggravated assault; other assault	1.3	19.7
	100.0	100.0

* Chicago Police Department, *1951 Annual Report*, 13 (n.d.).

rectly on the relationship between narcotics use and criminality is that showing the spatial distribution of narcotics additcs within the urban community. Faris and Dunham, in their study of 772 cases of addicts admitted to four Illinois State Hospitals and eight private institutions from the city of Chicago in the period 1922–34, observed that there appeared to be a general concentration of such cases in and near the center of the city. "It is noted that almost 50 per cent of the cases are in the hobo and rooming-house areas at the center of the city."[5] Since the period of the Faris and Dunham study, the character of the addiction problem has been changing in the direction indicated in the previous discussion, but ecologically, the incidence of addiction has remained heavily concentrated in a few of the disadvantaged areas of the city:

The drug use problem is concentrated with extraordinary sharpness in a very limited segment of the city's population. . . . Almost two thirds of Chicago's drug users may be found in the decile, or tenth, of the population whose community rates [of drug users by community areas] are the very highest. Almost nine of every ten drug users may be found in the upper deciles, representing 20 percent of the city's population.[6]

And other types of data indicate that where the incidence of addiction is highest, there is the heaviest concentration of many other types of social problems:

The highest concentrations of drug users are found in the communities displaying the highest rates of Juvenile Court delinquents, of Boys' Court cases, of tuberculosis, and of infant mortality. These are the communities of lowest income in the city.[7]

Similar findings concerning the ecology of narcotics addiction in New York City

[5] Robert E. L. Faris and H. Warren Dunham, *Mental Disorders in Urban Areas*, 122 (1939).

[6] Illinois Institute for Juvenile Research and the Chicago Area Project, *Report of the Chicago Narcotics Survey*, 44 (unpublished manuscript 1953).

[7] Illinois Institute for Juvenile Research, *Drug Addiction among Young Persons in Chicago*, 6 (1953).

were established in recent studies conducted by the Research Center for Human Relations New York University. This agreement in the findings of these recent studies, together with the observation that the distribution of many deviant social phenomena has tended to exhibit a similarity in spatial pattern in many other ecological studies, affords some basis for the tentative hypothesis, here advanced, that the findings of the Chicago study may also apply to other large cities where there is a problem of narcotics use among young persons.

A comparison of the distribution of cases of narcotics addiction in the Faris and Dunham study with the distribution of cases in the Chicago study almost a generation later reveals a definite relationship between the two. In the earlier study, as has been noted, the cases were concentrated in and near the center of the city, in the hobo and rooming-house districts, which were part of the "zone of transition." The more recent Chicago study established that the cases were concentrated in the disadvantaged areas farther out from the center of the city, but immediately adjoining the "zone of transition." The changing from the earlier to the later pattern of distribution involved no spatial discontinuity—that is, the new areas of concentration were immediately contiguous to the areas where the problem was formerly most highly concentrated—and this suggests that narcotics use may have diffused from onc area to the next.

In the light of these data, let us now address the central problem of the relationship of narcotics use and criminality: How did narcotics use and criminality come to coincide in the life experience of many adolescents and young adults in the disadvantaged areas of large cities, such as Chicago? What is the nature of the relationship between the narcotics use and criminality in this sector of the population? The central theme of the interpretation to be offered is that this conjunction has been, in part, a consequence of influences having their origin in the social life, or "subculture," of these young persons and, in part, a consequence of influences having their origin in the local communities which impinge on the young persons residing there.

In spreading to young persons, as it did, narcotics use made its inroads within a distinctive and uniquely vulnerable social milieu, the world of the adolescent in the most disadvantaged areas of the city. Like their age-mates everywhere, these adolescents spontaneously form peer groups, which exert a significant influence upon their conduct. In other types of communities, however, particularly those of higher socioeconomic status, the control over behavior exerted by the peer group is subject to restraint by the obligations and loyalties binding the individual adolescent members to other conventional groups, such as the family and the school. By way of contrast, such competing obligations and loyalties fail to exert their limiting and moderating influences in the most disadvantaged areas, and the peer group assumes a virtually sovereign control over the behavior of the individual adolescent. Under such conditions, the introduction of a novel practice may lead to its rapid diffusion, and, because it is unchecked by pressures counter to those exerted by the peer group itself, go to extremes that are not possible among adolescents elsewhere. In this milieu, narcotics use could spread more selectively and with somewhat greater difficulty, perhaps, but in a manner analogous to a new fashion in language, dress, or music.

The social world of the adolescent male in the disadvantaged areas has been aptly characterized by the term "street-corner society." This concept, which will be referred to frequently in the subsequent discussion, has been developed as follows:[8]

This term has come into use in recent years to describe the street gangs which abound in certain quarters of the city. The use of the expression "society" in connection with such gangs is meant to suggest that all members of street gangs share a distinctive set of ideas and

attitudes, much as would, say, the members of "cafe society." It is, moreover, a society in the sense that a large enough number of young persons have participated in it over a long enough period of time so that it exists independently of particular persons entering or leaving its ranks.

This society flourishes in those communities where the traditional influences and controls over the conduct of the youth group tend to be weak and uncertain. In such communities all young persons either participate in or are exposed to the activities of this society. In the face of counteracting pressures for conformity to the rules and morals of the wider society, of varying degrees of effectiveness, some youngsters merely dabble in street society, taking on only some of its superficial traits; others participate fully but for relatively short periods; and still others become full-fledged members and ultimately the bearers and agents of its code and its culture.

The central feature of this society and its body of practices, or "culture," is the support it gives to behavior which is generally inconsistent with the norms of conventional society, and often openly hostile to many of its expectations. This orientation on the part of street boys is expressed in a variety of ways, but is most clearly and dramatically manifested in delinquency, and in the search for and exploitation of "kicks."

It is evident from this description that there are significant influences originating in street-corner society itself that would be hospitable to experimentation with narcotics. An orientation to life which gives zestful sanction to many forms of unconventional activity appears to have spread the welcome mat for narcotics use. Much of the behavior reported by these young addicts clearly indicates that they had actively sought out narcotics—and not only heroin, but every other substance of which they had heard which yielded a "kick," such as marijuana, cocaine, benzedrine, and the barbiturates. The activity centering around these narcotics had many of the characteristics of a fad—that is, the restless searching, the uncertainty and excitement and exclusive preoccupation with a novel experience, the pressures to "go along," and the final capitulation on the part of many, despite

8 Illinois Institute for Juvenile Research, op. cit. supra note 8, at 9–10.

the existence of strong initial doubts and inhibitions.

While the spread of narcotics use to young persons was tightly restricted to those local areas which also had high rates of juvenile delinquency and young-adult criminality, there were some communities with rates of juvenile delinquency almost as high where adolescent narcotics use was virtually unknown. In a community of the latter type, it was actually possible to observe a situation where the coming to light of several cases of narcotics use by young people of the locality evoked such strong moral disapproval and community resistance that any potential epidemic was quickly averted in its incipient stages. By way of contrast, in many of the areas to which narcotics use spread, the local residents were just as morally aroused, but their opposition was ineffective. In the first type of local community, the local residents were capable of collective action to insure effective law enforcement and other direct measures to deal with the problem; in the latter type of community, the local residents were not able to turn their strong moral disapproval into effective collective action.

This discussion suggests that narcotics use spread to adolescents in communities deficient in two essential types of social control: first, the controls originating in conventional institutions which define the limits of permissible behavior for adolescents; and secondly, the controls by means of which the community is enabled to resist encroachments by those espousing values to which it is strongly antagonistic. These deficiencies constitute an essential part of the "slum-making process." It was apparently the operation of similar processes that led to the concentration of such deviant occupational types as criminals, racketeers, prostitutes, and drug peddlers in the same disadvantaged areas in which narcotics use was later to spread among young people. The location of such aberrant types in these areas is fraught with significance, because in time they come to symbolize both opportunity and hazard for many street-corner boys.

In view of the weakness of community solidarity in the disadvantaged areas, the location there of such deviant types is not to be construed as an expression of the moral qualities of the local residents, but rather as part of a process of selection whereby these types locate where they can survive and perform their function. Although at first an alien influence in the slum community, these deviant types do, however, in time attract local, and particularly younger, residents to perform their illegal functions. Lohman has commented upon a similar process in his observation of the consequences of the location of gambling and prostitution in the Near North-Side Communities of Chicago in the late thirties:

. . . Occupational opportunities are limited in character. The first and foremost facet for the gaining of a livelihood which competition in the whole life of the city assigns to communities such as the Italian or the Negro on Chicago's Near North Side is of course unskilled labor. The low income standard which such work provides stands in strong contra-distinction to standards of success and personal property which society at large exhibits. On the other hand, the community has, within its environs, pursuits which afford a higher income. These opportunities may not in themselves be morally approved by conventional society but the whole society gives rise to their being and they singularly afford what other limited laboring opportunities deny.

The location of such institutions of vice and disorganization, through the impersonal distribution of function throughout the city has established an order to which the local community subscribes. The shills, stickmen, dealers, doormen, in short, the professional staff of C-Street's bookies and gambling resorts are provided largely by the local community to the west. Prostitution along D-Street, with the first invasion of the Colored community supplied largely by recruited inmates from the south side, is now a matter entirely of local occupation not only for the girls, but for the operators as well. . . .[9]

In the localities frequented by adult criminals, the notoriety, glamor, and symbols of material success that are sometimes

[9] Lohman, *The Participant Observer in Community Studies*, 2 Am. Sociological Rev. 890, 894 (1937).

associated with them enhance their attractiveness as role-models to members of street-corner society, who, as adolescents, may find it easier to identify with them than with conventional role-models. In a similar vein, interviews with young narcotic addicts in 1952 suggested the observation that in at least certain social circles where these youngsters sought status and recognition, adult addicts or "junkies" enjoyed a certain prestige. Many of these young addicts reported that they and others had tried to simulate the mannerisms and philosophy of life of addicts before they themselves had become addicted.

Reverting now to the relationship between narcotics and criminality, the principal observation to be made is that narcotics use spread to adolescent groups who simultaneously evaluated highly adults who were engaged in a wide variety of criminal activity and adults who were addicted; and these valuations were reflected in both criminal activity and experimentation with narcotics. Thus, both the criminality and experimentation with narcotics stemmed, at least in part, from influences to which the youngsters were exposed, as represented by adult models within the local community. Both criminality and narcotics use came to be prestigeful forms of activity. In this sense, it is irrelevant to ask whether the delinquency preceded the addiction or vice versa. Many of those who became addicted and were forced to engage in crime to support the high cost of their addiction would probably have gone on to engage in crime as adolescents regardless of whether or not they had become addicted.

The statement that both delinquency and narcotics use existed side by side as independently valued patterns of behavior is not inconsistent with the observation that for specific individuals, delinquency or narcotics use may have initially represented alternative forms of behavior.[10] Nor is it inconsistent to observe that each activity

became modified within the individual's behavior when conditioned by the other. For example, in some instances, adolescents on the fringes of street-corner society and only marginally involved in criminal activity apparently seized on the possibility of narcotics use as a means of enhancing their status in the group, since it was not always the existing leaders who were the first to experiment with narcotics. Once addicted, however, these adolescents, who previously had been only marginally involved in delinquency, were forced into regular criminal activity in order to raise money to maintain their supply of narcotics.

What kind of image can be formed of the young addict or "junky" and of his milieu that may be of assistance in understanding the relationship between narcotics use and crime? At the time when many of these young addicts were interviewed in 1952, most were still in the early stages of their addiction. They were "snatch-and-grab" junkies, supporting their habits through petty thievery, breaking into cars, shoplifting, and a variety of "scheming," such as "laying a story" on "a sucker" in the hope of gaining sympathy and some cash. Some enterprising ones actually had girls out "hustling" for them through "boosting" (shoplifting) and "turning tricks" (prostitution). Despite the ragged state of their clothing and the harried nature of their existence, they regarded themselves as the members of an elite, the true "down cats" on the best "kick" of them all, "Horse" (heroin). Many of them were still living at home, although they had long since exhausted the last reserves of patience of their families and "fenced" much of their movable property. Few, if any, of them had finished high school, and, on the average, they had little or no employment experience. Their attitudes towards work and the daily routine that steady employment presupposed were entirely negative. Their number-one hazard was the "man" (the police). Once they became "known junkies"—that is, known to the police—they were frequently picked up and sometimes sentenced

---

[10] Cf. Dumpson, Gang and Narcotic Problems of Teen Age Youth, 6 Am. J. Psychotherapy 312 (1952).

—mostly for misdemeanors and, consequently, for short sentences. In their own words, they would begin to "ride the horse to California" (in Chicago, the criminal and narcotic courts, as well as the County Jail and the House of Correction, are located on the street with this name). The police became a symbol of the "revolving door through whose entrance and exit the same persons form a constant procession."[11]

After months and sometimes years of this kind of existence, the morale of the young junky drops very low, or his health deteriorates, or his daily requirement of narcotics gets beyond his ability to support, and he finally considers attempting to cure himself of the habit. Because these addicts were constantly being picked up by the police and held at the police lockup or receiving short sentences, they were frequently forced to "kick the habit cold turkey"—that is, to undergo the abrupt withdrawal of the narcotic. This would remove their physical dependence on it, but they would inevitably relapse shortly upon release. Consequently, when they sought a "cure," they hoped for more than mere withdrawal of the narcotic. At this point, their motivation was never clear, but it led many of them to seek treatment at the United States Public Health Service Hospital at Lexington. The treatment at Lexington, too, was very frequently followed by relapse.

The question arises as to the relationship of the young narcotics addict to the rest of the criminal world. The impression gained from interviewing them was that these addicts were petty thieves and petty "operators" who, status-wise, were at the bottom of the criminal population or underworld. It is difficult to see how they could be otherwise. The typical young junky spent so much of his time in a harried quest for narcotics, dodging the police, and in lockups, that he was hardly in a position to plan major crimes.

It is to be observed that narcotics use

spread to areas and to parts of the city and to groups of adolescents and young adult males who have traditionally been responsible for a high proportion of the larceny and robbery and other serious property crimes committed in the city. Accordingly, it would be expected that a certain proportion of young addicts would also be responsible for these major offenses. This was found to be true, but the interviews suggested two further relevant observations: First, a number of addicts did commit serious offenses against property and persons, but usually such individuals had also committed similar offenses before becoming addicted. Second, the number of offenses coupled with violence appeared to be but a small proportion of the total, an observation which is corroborated by the data from the Narcotic Bureau of the Chicago Police Department for 1951, presented earlier. Addiction, thus, appears to reduce both the inclination to violent crime and the capacity to engage in sophisticated types of crime requiring much planning.

If the present public policy towards addiction remains unchanged, it is a moot question as to what will happen to these young addicts as they grow older. It seems unlikely that they can rise in status among their nonaddicted associates who are engaged in criminal activity, nor are they likely to become engaged in more serious types of crimes. The possibility that most plausibly suggests itself is that as they grow older and wiser in the ways of coping with their addiction, they will increasingly learn to "cool it"—that is, they will leave behind them the days of the "frantic" and the "snatch-and-grab" junky and learn to conceal their addiction. Through trial and error, they will grope for unconventional and illegal ways of making money that will involve a minimum of risk-taking. They will also learn to take the occasional "bust" and short sentence. As public concern over the problem of narcotics use falls off, many will find ways and means of establishing a modus vivendi with the police. And, although the evidence for this is obscure and inconclu-

---

[11] Collins, *Law and the Woman Narcotic*, in Proceedings of the Sixty-Seventh Annual Congress of the American Prison Ass'n 66, 68 (1937).

sive, some few of them may be able to "kick the habit" for relatively long periods of time and achieve some semblance of conventional life. Those few engaged in serious criminality will probably continue to engage in it. For them, penitentiaries rather than the House of Correction or the County Jail will punctuate their sojourn on the streets.

What, finally, are the implications of the spread of narcotics use to street-corner society? One of the most intractable features of that society is its detachment from conventional institutions and controls and its opposition to social expectations having their origin in the conventional world. This detachment represents the greatest obstacle to any attempted intervention to modify the behavior of its members. The spread of narcotics use to this segment of the community has increased its sense of alienation and has intensified the difficulties of effective intervention. These young addicts have come increasingly to live in a world apart, and all their experiences are such as to make them, realistically, increasingly unemployable as time goes on. This alienation of the young junky, this widening spatial and social distance separating him from the conventional sectors of the community and of public opinion, has, unfortunately, by making his behavior so apparently unintelligible, further tended to reinforce the common stereotype of the "drug fiend." Such stereotypes have impeded more humane and realistic measures to cope with the plight of the young addict.

Observers have expressed surprise at the metamorphosis by which the street-corner boy evolves into the young adult who becomes a hard-working conventional family man. This transformation takes place despite the occasional handicap of a juvenile or adult criminal record and the stigma of being an "ex-con." It is a transition that can be explained, at least in many cases, as a change from the adolescent to the adult role. The adult male has occupation and family as incentives for him to achieve a stable life organization. The adolescent, particularly in the disadvantaged areas, often does not have such powerful incentives until he reaches young adulthood. It has been noticed that young addicts, as they near adulthood, sometimes attempt to re-evaluate their modes of behavior, including their addiction, from an adult perspective and even make some gestures to achieve a conventional adult role. Rarely does it get beyond the stage of gesture, however, because of the demands of their addiction. The spread of narcotics use to street-corner society, thus, has had the effect of perpetuating petty criminal careers which otherwise might have been merely an episodic part of the individual's life as an adolescent and as a street-corner boy.

OBSERVATIONS ON GAMBLING IN A LOWER CLASS SETTING*

Irving Kenneth Zola

Although legal action is seldom taken, the person who places a small gambling wager usually violates a criminal statute. Zola has observed the behavior of a group of working-class men who

* Reprinted from Social Problems, 10 (Spring 1963), pp. 353–361, by permission of the author and the publisher.

*regularly engage in off-track betting. Such gambling is seen as a
means of allowing the players to function in the larger society
without suffering the consequences of the realization that they
have little else. Some of the reasons for the persistence of gambling
and its functions are considered.*

Introduction. Studies in gambling have often focused on matters of individual pathology[1] and yet, on a number of psychological dimensions, no significant differences have been found between gamblers and non-gamblers.[2] Part of the explanation for this lack of difference is the fact that so widespread an activity as gambling can be "many things to many people."[3] Another reason is that while recognized as one of our major social problems, gambling also constitutes a major American paradox, fluctuating as it does between tolerance and condemnation, with a very thin line drawn between legal and illegal forms.[4] It seems obvious that to exist in this state of limbo, gambling must serve important social and psychological functions. This report is an attempt to delineate some functions of one form of gambling as it occurs in a small lower-class residential community.

THE SETTING

East Side was a small working-class area within a large New England city. Successive waves of immigrants once flooded the streets, but in recent years the population had become more stable, predominantly Italian with smaller segments of Eastern European Jews and Poles. As part of an anthropological field team, the observer spent several months in East Side, becoming a habitué of meeting places, bars, and taverns and participating actively with several sub-groups. His identity and role were, however, unknown to the community. Most of the observations on gambling were made at Hoff's Place, one of many taverns along the main street of East Side. It was a bar and grill frequented mostly by Italians and Poles who were either present or former residents of the immediate neighborhood. At Hoff's one type of gambling predominated: off-track betting where wagers are made with a "bookie" or "bookmaker." Though the men spent much of the day here, virtually all over thirty were married and relatively few were unemployed. Some were on vacation or on their day off. Some worked nearby, drove delivery trucks or taxis and dropped in and out while ostensibly working. Others worked on split shifts and visited between them. Still others had jobs which ended early in the day or started very late.

One of the first observations made of Hoff's was the dissociation of the bar from other spheres of the men's social life. Violent reactions often greeted any invasion or intrusion.

One wife became concerned when her husband did not return for supper and so she called and asked the bartender about his whereabouts. Although he knew, he gruffly denied any knowledge. Whereupon she burst into tears, pleading with him, "Please don't tell him I called, 'cause he would beat the shit out of me if he knew."

"One day my mother sent me after my father. It was gettin' late. When he came home was

[1] Edmund Bergler, *The Psychology of Gambling,* New York: Hill and Wang, 1957; and "The Gambler—A Misunderstood Neurotic," *Journal of Criminal Psychopathology,* 4 (1943), pp. 379–393.
[2] James Hunter and Arthur Bruner, "Emotional Outlets of Gamblers," *Journal of Abnormal and Social Psychology,* 23 (1928), pp. 38–39; and Robert P. Morris, "An Exploratory Study of Some Personality Characteristics of Gamblers," *Journal of Clinical Psychology,* 13 (1957), pp. 191–193.
[3] Edward C. Devereux, Jr., "Gambling and the Social Structure—A Sociological Study of Lotteries and Horse Racing in Contemporary America," unpublished doctoral dissertation, Harvard University, 1949.
[4] Herbert A. Bloch, "The Sociology of Gambling," *American Journal of Sociology,* 57 (1951), pp. 215–222; and "The Gambling Business: An American Paradox," *Crime and Delinquency,* 8 (1962), pp. 355–364.

he mad! He kicked her all the way down Lawrence Street and back and said to her, 'Don't you never send anyone after me here. No buts, anything can wait till I get here.' And she never did it again."

A further distinction was made between gambling and other spheres of economic activity. A man was not expected to share his profits with his family and was thought a "damn fool" if he even told them of his winnings. The fact that most gambling activities take place in a context institutionally defined as "recreation" helps to emphasize this dissociation from ordinary utilitarian activities.[5]

A GROUP IN PROCESS

The men at Hoff's, however, did not constitute a group in the formal sense. Regardless of when in the day one entered, the men in the bar seemed only to be whiling away their time drinking, barely taking notice of one another. On any day the pattern would be quite similar.

In the first booth, Hal reads the Morning Telegraph while Sammy naps in a corner. Behind them Smiley studies the Star Racing Section and Silvio looks at Phil's Armstrong. Phil, the bookie, sits at the bar going over his slips. Beside him Nick stares blankly at the wall and not two stools away Johnnie and Joe sip beer without speaking. Further down the bar sits an unidentified man and next to him stands Al, the bartender, gazing aimlessly out the window as he washes glasses.

Ten minutes before the start of each race, however, this changed. Men who were outside came in and those previously silent began to talk.

"Do you think he's got a chance?"
"I don't like the jockey."
"He likes muddy tracks."
"He's long overdue."
"They've been keeping him for this one."

Some of the remarks were addressed to one's neighbor, some to no one in particular. The bookie began to take bets. Gradually, the

"Get your bets in while you can," kids Phil. Silvio turns and hands him five dollars while conversation became more agitated.

Devereux, op. cit.

Smiley shakes his head, "He'll never win." Sal laughs, "Here Phil, a bean on the nose, number seven, a 'sure thing.'" "I'm the one who's got that," roars Al, reaching into his pocket and taking out a twenty-dollar bill. "Twenty thousand on number one. C'mon Irv, stick with me." "Uh, uh," I answer. "You're bad news, I like Principio." Meanwhile Phil proceeds gingerly down the bar as others turn and bet, rise from their booths or motion him toward them.

Some last minute bets or changes were made and then the race began. If the race was broadcast, a group formed near the radio. The cheering was restrained and muffled.

"See, look what's happening."
"Why is the jockey holding him back?"
"Just watch him finish with a spurt."

Regardless of whether the race was broadcast, the announcement of the winner always led to the same discussion. All attention focused on the winners.

"How did you figure it?"
"How come you picked her?"
"How did you know?"

And their answers. . . .

"I've noticed that jockey. . . ."
"Did you see the weight shift? Well. . . ."
"I figure they've been saving him. . . ."
"His last time out, he. . . ."

If no one picked the winning horse, the discussion was still the same, but more philosophical and not as prolonged. Within five minutes, however, it was quiet again.

Al is back washing glasses. Silvio and Smiley return, each to a separate booth. Hal goes outside and Sammy goes back to sleep. Joe and Johnnie leave but Paul and Charlie replace them at the bar sipping beer without speaking. Nick studies the chart for the next race. Sal stands at the door looking at the sky and Phil, slips of paper in his hand, walks slowly toward the phone.

Once more they appeared to be strangers . . . until the next race.

Yet gambling is more than a mode of communication. It creates a bond between the men—a bond which defines insiders and outsiders. This function of gambling first became apparent when a newcomer arrived at Hoff's.

Joe did not live in East Side, though he was distantly related to one of the bookies. He worked on a nearby construction gang and gradually began to patronize Hoff's. At every opportunity, he would come in, order a drink, and sit at the bar or in one of the empty booths. Although he was through work at 4:00 P.M., he often remained until 5:00 or 6:00. When he offered to buy someone a drink, he was gently, but firmly, refused. All he gained was an occasional nod; until, in an off-hand manner, he asked questions about the races, horses, odds, and ways to bet. At first he bet the choices of others and then finally his own. Only when he started betting did others begin to interact with him, respond more than monosyllabically, and "allow" him to join them as they sat at the bar or in the booths.

For the younger residents of East Side, gambling seemed a way of preparing them for later adulthood. A number of teenagers always hung around Hoff's; and, although they were not allowed in the bar to drink, they were welcome to place bets. It was during such times that they first initiated conversation with the younger men (19–21) —a preliminary step in "anticipatory socialization."

Thus, even though someone might appear at the same time every day, or the same day every week, this was insufficient to designate one a "member," a "regular," or an "insider." At Hoff's, this was accomplished only by off-track betting—an activity which served as the entrance fee, defining membership and initiating newcomers.

THE PRESERVATION OF GROUP ATTACHMENT

Three observations made by Devereux in his analysis of gambling and the social structure are relevant here: (1) Although the making of a wager polarizes the field and artificially creates the gambler's bond of interest in the event, it does not follow that winning money is the dominant motivational force; (2) many gamblers go to great lengths to deny their emotional involvement in specific events; (3) the importance and relevance of competition to gambling varies with the

social context in which it occurs.[6] Each of these observations was found to hold true for Hoff's, but here in East Side, they have yet a secondary function. In de-emphasizing emotionality, monetary gain, and competition, not only were several basic sources of hostility often emanating from gambling eliminated but, at the same time, attachment to the "group at Hoff's" was thereby reaffirmed.

While the excitement accompanying any sporting event was present, it was restrained. The extremes of overexcitement and depression were both negatively sanctioned. On more than one occasion, a person who went "over the line" when he won was called "nuts" or told to stop "acting like a jerk"; or if one persisted in bemoaning his "hard luck," he too was reprimanded. Even overconcern during a race or contest was regarded with skepticism.

Donnie was disturbed about the ball game— he had bet $10 on the outcome. He would get up, pace back and forth, sit down again. Each time he asked questions about the ability of the players or the manager. "Do you think he knows what he's doing?" As he returned to his seat once more, Mario shook his head indicating Donnie. He commented on his nervousness, adding, "After all, it's only money."

While these men cared when they lost, such depression was remarkably short-lived, perhaps until post-time of the next race. Little systematic effort was made to retain one's winnings. These men never stopped while ahead, nor reduced or even maintained the size of their bets after having won. If a person was ahead at the end of the day, it was more likely because there were no more races than through any conscious effort to accumulate profits. At Hoff's, there was no prototype of the conservative gambler who quit while ahead. People who did were disliked, and not only by the bookies. Instead of admiring them, the regulars shook their heads and called them "cheap bastards." One would have to increase the bet continually in order to gain any substantial

6 Devereux, op. cit.

amount of money, and yet there is still the problem of a stopping or cutting-off point. The following legend is illustrative of this:

Bob was relating the experiences of an old East Sider. "I know a guy who won a $100,-000. First here and then he wanted to gamble so badly he flew to New York and then back here and kept losing till he had nothing." "Yeah," added Spike. "It could happen. You lost twenty G's and figure you've still got eighty, so you take another shot, and finally you've got nothing."

Thus, if no limit, no matter how theoretical, exists then monetary gain *per se* becomes an indefinite goal and one impossible of attainment. Finally, individual competition was almost nonexistent. Within the group itself, members were not explicitly compared with one another as being better or worse players. In part to salve the wounds of defeat, and to share the fruits of victory, there was the common practice of mutual treats where the winner paid for the drinks of his closer acquaintances.

Particularly striking was the shift of competition from within the group to "the system." There was continual talk of "beating the system," "cracking the system," "not letting the system beat you." While this ostensibly referred to the scheme or principle governing the results of races, the actual hostility was more often expressed against the agent of that system—the bookie. The group complained that "he can't be hit" or dubbed him "the undertaker," and alluded to how they would "like to bury him . . . in an avalanche of losses."

Joe told of one bookie. "Why, you know why that son-of-a-bitch makes more money than anyone else? It's because all the bettors hate his guts, so they make all bets with him, even 'hot tips' just in the hope they'll break him."

"Remember the time that 'Happy' bet 20-20-0 on a long shot and won? Do you remember Sam's face? I thought he would bust a gut."

"Well, I took care of that bookie. I bet $5 on the fifth race and kept betting it all on each race. By the eighth, he had to close up shop."

In this situation, the bookie served a dual function. As the personification of the system they were trying to beat, he facilitated the shifting of competition from within the group to outside the group; and by serving as the target for their hostility, he also became an integrating force of the group— their scapegoat.

Thus the de-emphasis on thrill, money, and competition not only prevented the individual member from becoming too involved with his own personal success and failure; it also made him more dependent on the group and reinforced his attachment to it and the rewards which it alone can bestow—prestige and group recognition. To understand these rewards, it is necessary to examine their dispensation.

SYSTEMS OF BETTING AND THE PRESTIGE HIERARCHY

As depicted in the opening illustration, at Hoff's all available attention and admiration was focused on those men who had chosen winners. Everyone clustered about them, prodded them to reveal the basis of their choice, praised them on their good judgment, and regarded their subsequent opinions highly. Rewarding someone in this manner assumes that he has *done* something to merit such an action. Not all types of gambling warrant such behavior. In the "numbers" or "policy game" where full rein is given to hunches, omens, dreams, and where a person may have his own special number and play it day after day, year after year, no one is congratulated on his ability if he wins, nor asked to explain the rational basis for his choice; he is rather congratulated on his good fortune or luck. In short, methods of selection and the social rewards for winning reflect a conception of the numbers as a game of chance, whose outcome is beyond human control and comprehension, explainable only in terms of luck, fortune or fate.[7]

[7] Gustav G. Carlson, "Number Gambling—A Study of a Culture Complex," unpublished doctoral dissertation, University of Michigan, 1939; and Devereux, *op. cit.*

The methods and social rewards of off-track betting reflect a different assumption, i.e., the existence of an unknown order, a principle which can be figured out and mastered by a skilled observer.[8] While segments of the larger society deny this in their educational and legal attempts to eliminate gambling, there is hardly a single major newspaper which does not publish the opinions of at least one professional racing expert. As a rule, the latter not only names his choices but gives his reasoning. This was similar to the behavior of the bettors at Hoff's, who consulted with the winners or joined in a general discussion to explain the results, to figure out why it happened or what factors had not been sufficiently considered.

Not all criteria for making decisions were equally regarded. Basically, there were two positively valued modes, one subtype of these, and one devalued mode. Generally, an individual was characterized by his reliance on a particular mode, though it was possible that he might use more than one method on any given day. The four systems were differentiated not only by their basis of selection but also by the degree, amount, and quality of attention and recognition the group bestowed on the successful user of such methods.

Handicapping, the method which elicited the highest respect, was based on some pragmatic system of integration of available information such as past performances of horses and jockeys, weight shifts, post position, track conditions, etc. Using any available factual data, there was an attempt to figure out one's choice. Calling an individual a "handicapper" was the highest compliment that could be paid. When someone wanted information about a particular horse or race, the "handicappers" were the ones to whom questions were directed. Moreover, their opinions were solicited even though their total losses might actually outweigh their gains.

[8] Devereux, op. cit.

At one time, I hit upon a system of betting a number of horses in combination. For three straight days, I won the daily double and in the next five days, at least one of my choices won while the other finished second or third. Each of these bets, however, was only for fifty cents and thus the net profit on each day was between five and ten dollars and after the first three days I lost. For this eight-day period I was operating at a loss, and yet for the next few weeks I was consulted by other bettors and kidded by the bookies as being "too good." One even joked about barring me.

Thus, it seems apparent that the "handicapper" gains and retains prestige not because of monetary profits or a preponderance of winners, but because he has demonstrated some technique or skill enabling him to select winners or at least come close.

The "hot tip" was the second positively valued mode. It was based on the use of "inside information," facts about the horses not published or known to the general public. Though the knowledge was supposedly secret, "hot tipsters" usually revealed its possession. For only in so doing could they be acknowledged by the group. While the method of selection is a rational one, the distinguishing feature is access to information and not the exercise of any particular skill. This fact was recognized by the men at Hoff's and though they would ask tipsters, "Got anything hot?", "Any inside dope?", their seeking of advice would not usually go beyond this. Nor were the personal choices of such men given undue weight or consideration unless they had also achieved some recognition as handicappers.

The "hedge" is more complex and seems to be a subtype of the above two methods. One or more of the following statements usually introduced the "hedge."

"You saw me give that to Spike and Angelo and the others and I told them it would win and then I go and bet on another. Whatta dope!"

"I couldn't decide which one of these would win so I didn't bet any."

"I had him [the winning horse] but I had to do an errand before I got here so I arrived too late to bet."

"Remember how I figured it out at home and picked number three to win but then I came here and saw the Armstrong so I bet the six. If only I hadn't seen 'the Arm.'"

The groundwork was usually laid before the race and the sequence was often as follows:

Before: "I like Ocean Rock but Principio is long overdue and that blasted Pilot's Express is always a threat with Hobbes aboard."

After: The fact that he bet Ocean Rock is ignored. "See, what did I tell you, that son-of-a-bitch Hobbes brought him in. I told you that would happen."

These remarks not only covered the bettor if his choice did not win, but also communicated to the group, "See, I also picked the winner, even though I didn't play it." For the most part, it succeeded. The group listened to the "hedgers," included them in the discussion of the results, and so allowed them to share to some extent the rewards of picking a winner. Considering their verbalization, it also seems likely that acceptance hinged on the presumption that the basis of their "unbet" choice was really handicapping or a "hot tip."

At the bottom of this prestige ladder was the hunch or random choice bet—lowest because it embodied a denial of the rationality which underlies the concept of "system" and hence "figuring out" of race results. Although "hunch betting" was chided as a "woman's bet," it was difficult to ignore if it produced a winner. Congratulations might be offered, but the reasoning behind the choice was never seriously solicited nor was future advice sought. The underlying attitude toward this technique was best shown when it produced a loser.

Jack bet on a dog called Cerullo because it was the name of a local hockey player. When it finished second, he was furious. "Damn it, that's what happens when you only have a bean [a dollar]—if I'd had more, I'd have bet him for second too." He barely uttered this when his friends began to tease him. "Say Mickey Mantle is running in the third and Williams in the ninth." They harped on the "why" of his bet. Jack fought back, shouting, "You wouldn't act that way if the shoe was on the other foot." But this only encouraged

them. They continued berating him till he began to sulk and finally walked out.

Only in "hunch" betting and only when it lost did such hostility occur in the group.

THE FUNCTIONAL ASPECTS AND SATISFACTIONS OF BETTING

A rationale-cognitive dimension seems to pervade these methods of selection. Since the races were considered capable of human understanding, this emphasis on rationality reflected and manifested the idea of understanding. By using these methods, the players were "beating the system." The "system," which they frequently mentioned, referred to more than a principle underlying the races but rather to life or fate. Miller claims that many lower-class individuals feel that their lives are subject to a set of forces over which they have relatively little control and that furthermore this world view is associated with a conception of the ultimate futility of direct effort towards a goal.[9] Gambling can help deny this futility, as illustrated by the response of one "regular."

Joe continually talked about "hitting it big." Today was no exception as he spoke of just missing a $1000 double. I looked at him quizzically, "You know you always talk about your ship coming in. Do you ever think it will?" Startled, he raised his head and without looking at me, muttered, "No . . . but what else have I got besides this?" [betting on the races].

By "beating the system," outsmarting it by rational means, these men demonstrated they *can* exercise control and that for a brief moment they *can* control their fate. Off-track betting is thus a kind of escape. It denies the vagaries of life and gives these men a chance to regulate it. At Hoff's, there was an emphasis on rewards rather than punishments, on how much can be gained rather than lost. One was rewarded by increased attention and recognition when he won but never punished or ignored when he lost except when the very structure of the

9 Walter B. Miller, "Lower Class Cultures as a Generating Milieu of Gang Delinquency," *Journal of Social Issues,* 14 (1958), pp. 5–19.

group was threatened. "Hunch" betting was just such a threat because it not only denied the concept of an underlying order but also was a way of admitting defeat, of granting that everything was beyond one's control.

Recognition was the supreme reward of the winner. By competing against the system rather than against themselves, however, recognition was no longer a scarce commodity, for theoretically there was no limit to the number of winners. Thus, wherever possible success and recognition were shared, whether by extending the definition of winners in the acceptance of "hedgers" or sharing the fruits of victory by "mutual treats." One regular revealed the meaning of being a winner when amid the talk and praise of his selection, he yelled, "What do you think I am, a nobody?" It was a statement so appealing that it was taken up as a byword and used over and over again by the group. In some ways, it was an insightful joke, for in picking the winner and becoming the center of attention, the winner leaves the realm of the nobody for the realm of the somebody.

CONCLUSION

Although betting doubtless serves many idiosyncratic needs, much of its structure, function, and persistence can only be understood by an examination of the social context in which it occurs. Gambling offers these men more than a means of recreation, just as Hoff's offers them more than a place to drink. Though such betting may produce neither recreation nor monetary gain, this does not necessarily mean that it is a sterile, nonproductive, or even dysfunctional activity. As many observers have pointed out, these men are aware of the major goals and values of middle-class society but are either unwilling[10] or incapable of achieving them by the use of the ordinary methods.[11] How-

[10] Ibid.
[11] Albert K. Cohen, Delinquent Boys. Glencoe, Illinois: Free Press, 1955; and Robert K. Merton, Social Theory and Social Structure, Rev. and Enl. Ed., Glencoe, Illinois: Free Press, 1957, Chaps. IV and V.

ever, as recent empirical[12] and theoretical[13] literature has demonstrated, deviance may be more than a symptom of dysfunctional structures. For these men, gambling may be a way of harnessing or channeling their otherwise destructive frustrations. Instead of lashing out at society, they lash out at "the system." In this sense, gambling may be an activity which helps reinforce and preserve some of the major values of the larger social system. At Hoff's, they can "achieve" and can gain recognition for their accomplishments—by exercising skill or knowledge in the selection of horses.

Moreover, these goals of achievement and recognition can be aspired to with few of the conventional risks. In the society at large, one's success or failure alters and affects one's whole way of life while here it is completely incidental to it—a reflection of the isolation of gambling from other spheres of life. Here there is an emphasis on rewards rather than punishments, on gains rather than losses, on being a "somebody" and not a "nobody." For these men, gambling, or at least off-track betting, is not simply the flight, the withdrawal, or the escape as so often claimed. By making success and recognition possible, it allows the players to function in the larger society without suffering the consequences of the realization that they indeed have little else.

This paper is necessarily limited by the way the observations were made and thus depicts only one small but significant slice of the social context of gambling—the relation of bettors to one another. Unfortunately little was known of the lives of these men outside this particular setting, so no explanation is possible of how or why the groups at such places as Hoff's originated

[12] Robert A. Dentler and Kai T. Erikson, "The Functions of Deviance in Groups," Social Problems, 7 (1959), pp. 98–107.
[13] Lewis A. Coser, "Some Functions of Deviant Behavior and Normative Flexibility," American Journal of Sociology, 68 (1962), pp. 172–181; and Kai T. Erikson, "Notes on the Sociology of Deviance," Social Problems, 9 (1962), pp. 307–314.

nor of the origins of gambling in general. As with so many other phenomena, the sources or causes have long faded into the background and may even be unimportant. This report is but a single case study—an attempt to delineate some of the possible reasons for the persistence of gambling and some of the functions it may presently serve. Whether similar observations hold for different settings[14] and for different types of gambling will have to be settled by further empirical and more systematic investigations.

[14] Robert D. Herman, "Gambling Institutions: The Race Track," unpublished manuscript presented at the 1963 Meeting of the Pacific Sociological Association.

TRAFFIC LAW VIOLATION: A FOLK CRIME*

H. Laurence Ross

Traffic violations are the most common form of reported crime in the United States. The offenses differ from many other forms of crime in that the social status of the offender is high (similar to that of the population at large), the number of offenses is great, and the laws are of recent origin and appear to be unsupported by the mores. Societal reaction to traffic violation is related to the special characteristics of this "folk crime."

Violations of the traffic laws are the most common form of reported crime in the United States, and the accidents associated with these violations are perhaps the most costly of our social problems. In 1958, 37,000 people died in auto accidents in this country. In that same year, 3,850 cases of murder and non-negligent manslaughter were reported to the F.B.I.—a ratio of ten traffic fatalities to every murder. A most conservative estimate of injuries received in traffic accidents is 1,350,000, as compared with 72,460 cases of aggravated assault reported for the same year. Property damage to the amount of almost two billion dollars was accumulated in traffic accidents, compared with $266 million stolen by thieves, and more than half the latter was recovered, while the damage from accidents represents a total loss. The combined costs of wage losses, medical expenses, and insurance overhead because of traffic accidents in 1958 are estimated to be $3.7 billion, in addition to the costs of property damage.

This paper will offer support for the hypothesis that accidents are generally the result of law violations. It will suggest resemblances and differences between traffic law violators and other types of law violators, with particular attention being paid to the "white-collar criminal." It will further point to significant trends in law and procedure concerning traffic law violators.

LAW VIOLATIONS AND TRAFFIC ACCIDENTS

It should be recognized that the highway is a social situation, in which people are interacting. However, the highway is a very spe-

* Reprinted from *Social Problems*, 8 (Winter 1960–61), pp. 231–241, by permission of the author and the publisher.

cial kind of social situation. Drivers are typically anonymous, and interaction between them is brief and non-recurring. Communications are limited in content and are mediated through mechanical aids, such as lights and horns. Despite these conditions unfavorable to social order, the highway is a place of impressive orderliness in which accidents are rare events. Social control on the highway is maintained in large part through the traffic law.

The manifest function of the traffic law is to minimize conflict between vehicles traveling on the highway. It does so through several means. Some of the laws, which can be called rules of position, allocate the use of parts of the highway according to the direction and speed of the vehicles. Examples are lane laws, passing regulations, and the like. A second group of laws, which can be called rules of priority, determines an order of precedence at intersections. Examples are rules pertaining to stop signs, traffic signals, and similar devices. A third group of laws, which can be called rules of responsibility, requires drivers to possess a minimum level of competence in manipulating the automobile and understanding other laws regulating driving, as a condition of using the public roads. Examples are laws concerning possession of a driver's license and driving under the influence of intoxicating beverages.

It is, of course, true that a violation of one of these laws is not sufficient for an accident to occur. Moreover, the probability of an accident resulting from a given law violation is extremely low. On the other hand, there is evidence that a law violation may be necessary for most traffic accidents. According to the National Safety Council, violations of a traffic law were reported in 88 out of every 100 accidents in 1958. Since police tend not to report suspected violations where they believe a conviction is unlikely, this figure probably underestimates the true proportion of accidents involving law violations. Furthermore, a correlation between law violations and participation in accidents has been demonstrated in the literature, lending further support to the posited relationship.

In sum, it is suggested that traffic law functions to maintain order on the highway, and that violations of this law result in accidents. The responsibility that law must assume for order is particularly great in the realm of traffic, where other forms of social control are limited in their effectiveness.

TRAFFIC LAW VIOLATION AND WHITE COLLAR CRIME

Since most traffic law violations in most states are legally classified as misdemeanors, traffic law violation can be considered crime in both the legalistic school of criminological discussion and in the socio-legal tradition of Sutherland. That is to say, traffic law violation is socially harmful behavior that is legally punishable, and the legal proscription of this behavior is generally embodied in the criminal law. For instance, in the Uniform Vehicle Code, the standard for state motor vehicle laws, the following provisions are found:

It is a misdemeanor for any person to violate any of the provisions of this act unless such violation is by this act or other law of this State declared to be a felony. . . . Every person convicted of a misdemeanor for a violation of any of the provisions of Chapters 10, 11, 12, 13 or 14 for which another penalty is not provided shall for a first conviction thereof be punished by a fine of not more than $100 or by imprisonment for not more than 10 days . . .[1]

Heavier penalties are imposed by the Code for second and subsequent convictions, and for such violations as reckless driving, driving under the influence of liquor, and negligent homicide.

Lack of Social Stigmatization. While traffic law violation fits the above definition of crime, it appears that in most cases it is not

[1] National Committee on Uniform Traffic Laws and Ordinances, *Uniform Vehicle Code*, Washington: 1956.

considered in public opinion to be "real" criminality, and it has generally not been treated as a subject for criminological study. In these aspects, traffic law violation resembles the activities that Sutherland termed "white-collar crime." Sutherland designated by this term those law violations engaged in by high status people while pursuing a white-collar occupation. Traffic law violations and white-collar crime have in common the fact that they are illegal acts which are not stigmatized by the public as criminal. The remainder of this section will probe other parallels between these two groups of illegal acts.

Social Status of the Traffic Law Violator.
Sutherland's "white-collar criminals" come from the ranks of business and professional men. An idea of the social status of traffic law violators, as compared with white-collar criminals, can be obtained from the following tables. Because of the obvious limitations of these tables in terms of the populations studied and the criteria of social status utilized, they should be interpreted as suggestive rather than as demonstrative.

Table 1 is based on the police files in Evanston, Illinois, for the past ten years. Seventeen common traffic violations and

Table 1.

PROPORTION IN WHITE-COLLAR OCCUPATIONS AMONG VIOLATORS
OF SELECTED LAWS IN EVANSTON, ILLINOIS, 1949–1959

VIOLATION	TYPE	PROPORTION WHITE-COLLAR*
Improper left turn	Traffic—position	.87
Improper right turn	Traffic—position	.73
Disregarding red light	Traffic—priority	.73
Disregarding stop sign	Traffic—priority	.73
Disregarding flashing red	Traffic—priority	.70
Passing in intersection	Traffic—position	.70
Wrong way on one-way street	Traffic—position	.70
Failing to yield right-of-way to automobile	Traffic—priority	.63
Reckless driving	Traffic—responsibility	.53†
Following too closely	Traffic—position	.50
Speeding	Traffic—position	.50
Failure to signal	Traffic—position	.43
Driving on the left	Traffic—position	.43
Leaving scene of accident	Traffic—responsibility	.40
Failure to yield right-of-way to pedestrian	Traffic—priority	.37†
Drunken driving	Traffic—responsibility	.37
Obtaining money under false pretenses	Non-traffic	.36
Disorderly conduct	Non-traffic	.23
Narcotics	Non-traffic	.22‡
Driving after license is suspended	Traffic—responsibility	.20
Petty larceny	Non-traffic	.20
Non-support	Non-traffic	.17
Assault	Non-traffic	.13
Burglary	Non-traffic	.10
Intoxication	Non-traffic	.07
Gambling and prostitution	Non-traffic	.06§

* N = unless otherwise specified.
† N = 15
‡ N = 24
§ N = 18

nine common non-traffic violations were chosen for study, and the files were systematically searched for thirty cases of each offense. The occupation of the offender was noted in each case. Persons with the occupation of "housewife" and "student" were excluded from the sample because of the difficulty of classifying these occupations in terms of social status.

The proportion of violators with white-collar[2] occupations was computed for each offense category. Since the white-collar proportion of the male labor force in this community is .67, it can be seen from Table 1 that traffic law violators have a higher social status than violators of other criminal laws,

[2] Professional, and semi-professional, proprietors, managers and officials, and clerical and sales occupations.

and that the status distribution of traffic law violators is close to the distribution of the total male labor force in most cases. This is particularly true for violators of position and priority rules.

The results of Table 1 are limited by the fact that the table is based on a sample of a small and special universe. Table 2, based on national figures reported by the F.B.I., suggests that the findings of Table 1 are more generally applicable. The *Uniform Crime Reports* for 1958 tabulate driving while intoxicated—a traffic law violation—with twenty-three other categories of crime in a racial analysis. Table 2, derived from this analysis, presents the proportions of each criminal category listed as white. Accepting race, rather than occupation, as the

Table 2.

PROPORTION OF WHITE RACE AMONG VIOLATORS OF LAWS
REPORTED IN THE UNIFORM CRIME REPORTS FOR 1958*

VIOLATION	TYPE	PROPORTION WHITE RACE
Forgery and counterfeiting	Non-traffic	.85
Driving while intoxicated	Traffic—responsibility	.83
Embezzlement and fraud	Non-traffic	.80
Auto theft	Non-traffic	.78
Manslaughter by negligence	Non-traffic	.78
Drunkenness	Non-traffic	.74
Vagrancy	Non-traffic	.73
Other sex offenses (except forcible rape)	Non-traffic	.70
Burglary—breaking and entering	Non-traffic	.68
Larceny	Non-traffic	.68
Stolen property, buying, receiving, etc.	Non-traffic	.67
Suspicion	Non-traffic	.65
Liquor laws	Non-traffic	.65
Offenses against family and children	Non-traffic	.64
Disorderly conduct	Non-traffic	.57
Other (non-aggravated) assaults	Non-traffic	.55
Prostitution and commercialized vice	Non-traffic	.53
Forcible rape	Non-traffic	.49
Weapons, carrying, possession, etc.	Non-traffic	.47
Robbery	Non-traffic	.45
Narcotic drug laws	Non-traffic	.39
Murder and non-negligent manslaughter	Non-traffic	.36
Aggravated assault	Non-traffic	.35
Gambling	Non-traffic	.22

* Source: Federal Bureau of Investigation, *Uniform Crime Reports.* 1958 (Washington: Government Printing Office, 1959), Table 21, p. 97.

index of status, it is seen that the traffic law violation is committed by high status people more than all the other tabulated offenses but one. Given the information that the proportion of whites in the United States runs about nine in ten, it is further seen that the status distribution of the traffic law violators is close to that of the population as a whole, supporting on a more general level the observations made in Table 1.

While traffic law violators come from generally higher social strata than the more familiar type of criminal, the above materials indicate that they are not an exclusively white-collar group. Furthermore, except for members of such blue-collar occupational groups as bus- and truck-drivers and chauffeurs, their violations are not committed in the course of their occupations. Thus, it cannot be said that traffic law violators are white-collar criminals in Sutherland's sense. However, their superiority in status to the stereotyped criminal may be partially responsible for the differential social and legal treatment that traffic law violators share with white-collar criminals.

Prevalence of Traffic Law Violation. One of Sutherland's reasons for concern with white-collar criminality was the lack of recognition, among the public and among criminologists, of the numbers of violations being committed. In this respect, traffic law violation resembles white-collar crime. The volume of traffic offenses is overwhelming when compared with all other reported offenses, and probably also surpasses the volume of white-collar criminal activity which is given administrative treatment and thus is not included in statistics of reported crime. The American Bar Association reports that in 1955, in 889 cities, there were 21 million traffic cases filed (including parking), of which 8.5 million were "moving" violations (excluding parking). These figures can be compared with the 2.2 million nontraffic offenses of all types reported to the F.B.I. from 1586 cities—and more than half of these were the minor charges of drunken-

ness and disorderly conduct. Similarly, Wootton reports that, in Britain, motorists constitute over 48 percent of all those convicted of criminal charges.

Relationship to the Mores. Sutherland traced the lack of stigmatization of white-collar crime to the recency of the legislation involved and a lack of correspondence between the law and the mores. Traffic law violation presents a clear case of these conditions, recognized in the following statement by Barbara Wootton:

In half a century the invention of the internal combustion engine has completely revolutionized the business of our criminal courts. Yet this revolution is generally ignored by the public and by the professional sociologist—to a degree that really queers all criminological discussion. Apparently on the Marxian principle that law is made and operated in the interests of the well-to-do, motoring offenses generally, and infringement of speed limits in particular, are not ordinarily thought to "count" as crimes at all.[3]

The discrepancy between the crime and the mores in the case of traffic law violations is enhanced by the fact that conviction for violations of many traffic ordinances need not involve criminal intent, or *mens rea*, on the part of the violator. This is because these ordinances are in the legal realm of *mala prohibita*, rather than *mala in se*. The distinction is one between acts which "are forbidden . . . by statute, but not otherwise wrong" and those done "willfully and corruptly."

There is no offense *malum in se* without some form of *mens rea*, but the normal *mens rea* requirement is not a necessary ingredient of an offense *malum prohibitum*. The typical case involves a mistake of fact. An act has been done under an innocent and non-negligent mistake of fact of such a nature that what was done would have been not only lawful but entirely proper had the facts been as they were reasonably supposed to be. This is a complete defense to a prosecution for an offense *malum*

[3] Barbara Wootton, *Social Science and Social Pathology*, London: George Allen and Unwin, 1959, pp. 25–26.

in se. It is no defense to a prosecution for an offense *malum prohibitum*.[4]

It should be noted furthermore that in these cases, the criterion for conviction is a preponderance of evidence, rather than the usual criminal criterion of guilt beyond reasonable doubt.

In fact, *mens rea* would appear to be the exception, rather than the rule, in traffic law violations. Interviews with traffic law violators in a recent project at Northwestern University—participants in almost fifty accidents—failed to reveal a single case of such intent, although many people claimed they knew the laws and admitted their violations.

Many law violations appeared to be the result of minor skill failures and perceptual errors. Respondents failed to stop at stop signs when they did not see the signs; misjudging the slickness of a roadway surface became a violation of a reasonable speed law; a poorly performed maneuver of the steering wheel became an "improper" turn, etc. The following citations from juristic discussions of traffic law violators are relevant to this point:

In these courts whose criminal jurisdiction previously covered the drunk, the tramp, the petty thief, the masher, the assaulter, and persons generally of ill repute in the community, there began to arise the victim (*sic*) of an increased tempo of life: the age of speed. . . . They were definitely not the type person who either associated with the normal non-traffic defendant or of whom it could be said that they understood only the "rod."[5]

The attitude is generally held that the traffic violator cannot be regarded as a criminal in the usual sense of the word, even though he has broken the law. The traffic offender differs from the average criminal court defendant, both in character and with regard to state of mind.[6]

Folk Crime. This section has suggested many parallels between traffic law violations and those law violations termed white-collar crime by Sutherland. While both are criminal according to socio-legal criteria, both are ignored or condoned by the criminological profession and by the general public. Yet both types of violation are widespread and socially costly. The leaders of society, without thinking of themselves as criminals, participate extensively in both kinds of law violations, although violation of the traffic laws is not confined to these leaders.

It may be useful to think of both white-collar crime and traffic law violations as subspecies of folk crime.[7] This category is proposed in order to group together violations of laws that are introduced to regulate the novel kinds of behavior that an increasingly advanced technology and an increasing division of labor generate. It should be noted, as Aubert states in connection with white-collar crime, that "the laws . . . are usually not in obvious or apparent harmony with the mores. They are largely an outcome of the increased complexity of modern industrial society, a complexity which requires legal control of activities with long-range and often very indirectly damaging effects."[8]

The characteristics of folk crime are present in Sutherland's description of white-collar crime. However, in proposing the more general category of folk crime, these characteristics are emphasized to the exclusion of Sutherland's focus on the occupational context of the act and the white-collar status of the criminal.

The following propositions are speculatively offered concerning folk crime:

(a) Major increments to the complexity of a society, of which the automobile is a technological example, create a need for regulation where none was previously necessary.

[4] Rollin M. Perkins, *Criminal Law*, Brooklyn: Foundation Press, 1957, pp. 693–695.

[5] George Warren, *Traffic Courts*, Boston: Little Brown, 1942.

[6] Edward C. Fisher, *People's Court*, Evanston: Northwestern University Traffic Institute, 1947, p. 17.

[7] This term was suggested by Erwin O. Smigel, in a private communication.

[8] Vilhelm Aubert, "White Collar Crime and Social Structure," *American Journal of Sociology*, 58 (November 1952), p. 266.

(b) Legislation to regulate the conditions brought about by increasing complexity reclassifies certain prevalent non-criminal behavior as crime.

(c) Especially where the harmful effect of the proscribed behavior is indirect or improbable in most instances, the novel legislation may not be related to previously existing norms.

(d) Criminal behavior in folk crime is rooted, not necessarily in lower-class culture, but in the culture of groups most affected by the social or technological changes that the legislation attempts to control. White-collar crime is the special case of folk crime resulting from legislation regulating business and finance. The automobile, with its impact on all social classes, generates more pervasive forms of folk crime.

(e) In particular instances, large numbers of people, including those of high status, will be involved in law violations related to major social changes.

(f) The lack of congruence between the new laws and established mores, the generally higher social status of the violators, and the possibly large size of the group of violators among the total population, will tend to be associated with preferential treatment of folk criminals in the public image and in the judicial process.

Examples of other law violations with the characteristics of folk crime can be found in the literature. Among them is "chiseling" in unemployment compensation. According to Smigel,[9] chiseling shares with white-collar crime (and traffic law violation) the following characteristics; the participant is not a professional criminal, he is not stigmatized as criminal, he may lack criminal intent, and he is treated differently from "ordinary" criminals. Smigel notes that the chiseler differs from the white-collar criminal in that his action need not be committed in the course of his occupation, and he may be found in any social class.

Another example is participation in the wartime black market.[10] Although Clinard claims this is white-collar crime, he presents statistics showing that 65 percent of the people imprisoned for these violations had less than a high-school education, thus indicating that high social status need not be involved. Furthermore, it is obvious that at least the consumers engaging in black market transactions did not necessarily commit these crimes in the course of their occupations.

In sum, the category of folk crime is proposed as a convenient way of thinking about traffic law violations, white-collar crime, chiseling, black market dealings, and many other illegal actions that have in common a source in social complexity. As opposed to "ordinary criminals," folk criminals are relatively numerous, unstigmatized, and differentially treated in the legal process. While they tend to be from higher social classes than the typical stigmatized criminal, they need not be predominantly white-collar, and the proscribed acts need not be committed in the course of business.

JUDICIAL TREATMENT OF TRAFFIC LAW VIOLATORS

The factors that distinguish traffic law violation from other crimes appear to have resulted in differential treatment for the traffic violator, in a manner analogous to the treatment of other folk crimes. Because of the large numbers of offenses committed, there has been a strain on traditional criminal procedures, resulting in new institutional forms. Because of the status of the offenders and their lack of criminal intent, there has arisen the necessity for new kinds of sanctions. Because of the dependence of traffic law on technology, there have developed new attitudes toward the law.

New Institutional Forms. With traffic prosecutions numbering in the millions, the need

[9] Erwin O. Smigel, "Public Attitudes toward 'Chiseling' with Reference to Unemployment Compensation," *American Sociological Review*, 18 (February, 1953), pp. 59–67.

[10] Marshall B. Clinard, *The Black Market: A Study of White Collar Crime*, New York: Holt, Rinehart and Winston, Inc., 1952.

for judicial processing of these offenses has exceeded the capacity of the traditional court system. Trial by jury for every case would not be possible. One response to this situation has been the development of violations bureaus to handle the less serious charges. The legal basis for the bureaucratic treatment of criminal acts is a signed plea of guilt and a waiver of trial. Standard schedules of fines are used, and payment of these penalties by mail is often permitted. The violations bureau has become a standard and integral part of the institutional machinery for handling violations of traffic laws. Three-quarters of the traffic cases in 1955 cited in the American Bar Association report[11] were processed through violations bureaus. Not all of these were minor infractions. Forty percent of the "moving" violations were handled in violations bureaus. Bureaucratic processing of criminal acts on a large scale in the traffic field represents an extreme of the trend to administrative treatment noted by Sutherland for white-collar crime, and constitutes a recognition of the impracticability of alternative methods of procedure. It would be extremely unlikely that a committee of the American Bar Association would recommend the use of such procedures in cases of petty theft or disorderly conduct as it does in the case of minor traffic infractions, although in a few instances, such as in the Recorder's Court in Detroit, the violations bureau has expanded to cover certain minor non-traffic offenses.

Yet the violations bureau has not solved the problem of processing millions of traffic offenses. In San Francisco, where only four percent of the parking violations and sixteen percent of the more serious "moving" violations are processed in court, the average traffic judge was handling 91 cases a day in 1955.[12] A streamlining of court procedure has accordingly taken place. The jury trial

is exceedingly rare in the processing of traffic violations today. The typical court for the trial of traffic charges meets in a special session for the consideration of traffic cases only. Special training is advised for the presiding judge. Cases are of necessity heard quickly. As noted above, in many instances the criterion of guilt beyond a reasonable doubt is replaced by the criterion of a preponderance of evidence for guilt.

The work of courts and violations bureaus in the attempted control of traffic infractions is aided by the technique of police "warnings" without arrests.[13] In certain notorious situations the stopping of a motorist by a policeman has become a situation of informal trial, with a "fine" in the form of a bribe collected by the policeman. The ethics of the situation aside, large scale bribery of police functions to relieve the strains on the legitimate processing system caused by volume of cases.

New Kinds of Sanctions. Punishment of law violators in terms of fines and jail sentences is in large part dependent on the assumption of criminal intent and moral guilt to be expiated by imposed sacrifice. The traffic law violator who lacks criminal guilt often reacts to punishment for traffic law infraction as either "a cost of doing business" or an unjust penalty for something that could not possibly have been avoided. Furthermore, the concept of uniform fines for similar acts results in subjectively unequal penalties for law violators of different economic status. Associated with these facts, the prevailing trend in the field of traffic law enforcement is an attempt to educate the violator, with little intent to punish except in the most serious cases. Traffic judges try to include a lecture as a part of every conviction procedure. An increasingly popular "sentence" is to attend a traffic safety school, usually conducted by local police. Examples of more idiosyncratic at-

[11] American Bar Association, Standing Committee on Traffic Court Program, "The Traffic Problem, Traffic Laws, and Traffic Courts," Chicago: 1957.
[12] Orla St. Clair, "The Traffic Problem: The Lawyer's Responsibilities," *American Bar Association Journal,* 44 (July 1958), pp. 633–641.
[13] Joseph Goldstein, "Police Discretion Not to Invoke the Criminal Process: Low Visibility Decisions in the Administration of Justice," *Yale Law Journal,* 69 (March 1960), pp. 543–594.

tempts at education are the requirement to visit the accident ward of a hospital, suspension of a fine if a car is junked, and an enforced ten-second stop at a frequently violated stop sign. The trend to education is experimental in the sense that its success in controlling behavior depends on the existence of an undemonstrated relationship between law violation and knowledge, and on the assumption that the proper knowledge can be imparted by these techniques.

A second trend in new kinds of sanctions is the use of a functional equivalent to incarceration in the form of license suspension and revocation. Assuming that the loss of a driver's license will keep the driver off the road, the offending behavior is eliminated while the individual keeps his freedom. The legal basis for this action is the assumption that driving is a privilege granted by the state, rather than an individual right. While this assumption has often been supported in the courts, there is reason to doubt its sociological realism, for with metropolitan decentralization many people living in suburban areas have become completely dependent on private automobile transportation. The judge or state motor vehicle bureau suspending the license of a driver runs the risk of forcing the driver into the more serious violation of licensing laws because of his dependence on his automobile for his livelihood. When, for instance, Connecticut started suspending licenses for speeding and total suspensions rose from 17,651 in 1955 to 33,075 in 1956, revocations of licenses resulting from driving while previously suspended went from zero to 1518.[14]

New Attitudes toward the Law. While the institutional forms and kinds of sanctions noted above are important, perhaps the most interesting development in the field of traffic law enforcement is the appearance of new attitudes toward the laws. The novelty of the traffic situation has resulted in over-

shadowing of the charismatic and traditional bases of legitimacy for the law by rational-legal ones. It is common for laws in the traffic field to be labeled by prestigious authorities as defective and inappropriate. The main reason for this is that the technology of the automobile and the trafficways is constantly changing. Speed laws, auto inspection laws, and financial responsibility laws of twenty years ago are already outmoded under today's conditions. Another reason may be legislative recognition of widespread violations. The American Bar Association recommends that: "Traffic laws with inherent defects should be revised and those which are unenforceable or unnecessary should be repealed."[15] The criterion of a proper speed limit is not what was stated in the original set of traffic control enactments, but rather a quasi-scientific criterion of "safety" and "convenience." Traffic enforcement officials often express the opinion that the best law is the most efficient one, regardless of when it was put into existence or the stature of the legislator who proposed it. For example, the Automobile Club of Hartford proposes the following:

Since many studies have proved that basically, regardless of posted signs, most motorists drive at a speed they consider reasonable and prudent according to constantly changing conditions, it follows that whatever this speed may be, it should become the speed limit, and be so posted and enforced.[16]

In line with the rational-legal bases of traffic law, and the decreased emphasis on punishment noted above, there have also been instances of legislative bodies refusing the misdemeanor classification to ordinary traffic offenses. In New York, traffic violations are termed "traffic infractions." According to Article 1, Section 29 of the New York Vehicle and Traffic Law, "A traffic infraction is not a crime, and the penalty and punishment therefore shall not be deemed for any purpose a penal or criminal

[14] Connecticut Department of Motor Vehicles, *Facts: 1958,* Hartford: 1959, p. 39.

[15] American Bar Association, op. cit., p. 4.
[16] Automobile Club of Hartford, "Speed," mimeographed report, 1960, p. 7.

penalty or punishment." Traffic law violations in Pennsylvania are known as "summary offenses." In New Jersey they are
"disorderly offenses." In neither state are
these considered to be crimes, although the
procedures for prosecution are identical with
criminal procedures. In defining traffic law
violation out of the realm of criminality,
these legislators are working toward the congruence of law and the mores sought by
Sutherland, but in a direction opposite to
the one he implied in his writings to be
desirable. Instead of working to get the
criminal nature of the laws sanctioned in
public opinion, they are modifying the laws
to fit the present condition of opinion,
which denies the criminality of traffic law
violations. Assuming the desirability of congruence between law and mores, and assuming that the contribution of the criminal
stigma to control of behavior is minor—
both implied by Sutherland—this seems as
reasonable an action as Sutherland's alternative.

SUMMARY

Traffic law violations are a costly and widespread form of criminal activity. Like white-
collar crime, they represent activity that is
both harmful to society and legally proscribed, yet condoned in public opinion and
ignored by students of criminality.

Violation of the traffic law resembles
white-collar crime in that the social status of
the offenders is high, the number of offenses
is great, and the laws involved are of recent
origin and appear unsupported by the mores.

However, differences between these categories exist in that traffic law violators do
not appear to possess significantly higher
social status than the population at large,
and opportunities for the offenses are not
dependent on occupational duties. It is suggested that the resemblances between white-
collar crime and traffic law violation may
arise from their relation to social complexity,
and that they may both be considered folk
crime.

Several trends in the judicial treatment
of traffic law violators appear related to the
special characteristics of folk crime. Among
these trends are new institutional forms,
such as violations bureaus; new kinds of
sanctions, such as attendance at traffic safety
school; and new attitudes toward the law,
replacing charismatic and traditional bases
of legitimacy with rational-legal ones.

Consideration of traffic law violation,
like consideration of white-collar crime,
should remind criminologists that their
theory neglects the most frequent and costly
kinds of anti-social behavior. Furthermore,
the elements of the social control system in
modern society—the police and the courts—
are far more involved in the regulation of
traffic than in the pursuit of bandits, yet
the study of social control emphasizes the
latter to the virtual exclusion of the former.
If death, injury, and damage to property are
the criteria of importance, traffic law violations in particular, and folk crime in general,
can legitimately claim a high priority among
our major social problems, and recognition
in our social problems theory.

CHAPTER 7

Conventional
Crime

Three types of criminal behavior systems can be broadly categorized as career crimes: conventional crime, organized crime, and professional crime. Career crimes differ markedly from the noncareer cimes that have been discussed thus far. While the types of career crime differ from one another, career crimes have some characteristics in common.[1]

First, persons engaged in career crime usually pursue crimes of gain, mostly property crimes. Career criminals either supplement an income through property crime or, as with organized criminals and professional criminals, make a living from criminal activity. In comparison to persons in legitimate occupations, career criminals make part or all of their living by pursuing activities which have been defined as illegal. One of the occupational hazards for the career criminal, however, is the risk of being arrested and convicted. But since only about a quarter of all property offenses (and only those that are known by the police) are cleared by arrest, the risks are not exceptionally high. For many career criminals, the often-quoted adage

[1] Walter C. Reckless, *The Crime Problem*, 3d ed., New York: Appleton-Century-Crofts, Inc., 1961, pp. 159–161.

that "crime does not pay" is a fiction, a myth maintained by and for law-abiding members of society.

Second, criminal activity is a part of the way of life of the career offender. A career in crime involves a life organization of roles built around criminal activities, which includes identification with crime, a conception of the self as a criminal, and extensive association with other criminals.[2] In career crime there is a progression in crime which includes the acquisition of more complex techniques, more frequent offenses, and, ultimately, dependence on crime as a partial or sole means of livelihood.

Third, persons in career crime tend either to develop a pattern of property violations or in some cases to specialize in a particular kind of offense. A professional criminal, for example, will specialize in one of a number of violations, such as picking pockets, sneak thieving, passing illegal checks, or shoplifting. Career criminals also develop over a period of time special skills and techniques for committing offenses.

Fourth, career criminals are engaged in systematic behavior which requires both personal and social organization. In contrast to noncareer crime, the violations of career criminals are not the result of personal conflicts and immediate circumstances. Career criminals commit their offenses only through awareness of the situation and after planning the offense. Career criminals depend upon the assistance of other criminals and may be involved in an organization of criminals. Because of the involvement of career criminals in crime, there is the prospect of a lifetime career in crime with increased isolation from the legitimate work patterns of society.

Conventional crime as a behavior system is at the bottom of the scale of career crime. The degree of development of conventional criminals and their sophistication in crime is much less than that found among organized and professional criminals. Compared to the other career criminals, conventional property criminals are less skillful in committing offenses and are not as well organized to avoid arrest and conviction. Conventional offenders often begin their illegal activities as juveniles. Many terminate their careers before they reach the age of thirty.

CRIMINAL CAREER OF THE OFFENDER

Conventional criminals begin their careers early in life as juvenile delinquents. Their early life histories are likely to show a pattern of truancy, destruction of property, street fighting, and delinquent gang membership. By the time they are young adults, they have an extensive history of contact with the law, and possibly have had some experience in an institution.

Conventional criminals usually begin their careers in association with juveniles of similar social origins. As juveniles they become involved in a culture which is either neutral or opposed to the law of legitimate society. Their acts are not isolated and personal, but rather are often part of the way of life and norms of a local slum community.[3] At an early age they learn to commit illegal acts and find group support for their behavior. From early experience in such a setting they readily progress

[2] Marshall B. Clinard, *Sociology of Deviant Behavior*, rev. ed., New York: Holt, Rinehart and Winston, Inc., 1963, p. 210.
[3] Marshall B. Clinard, *Slum and Community Development: Experiments in Self-Help*, New York: The Free Press of Glencoe, 1966.

to adult criminal behavior in which thefts are more frequent, substantial, and sophisticated.[4]

The progression from early juvenile gang delinquency to adult conventional crime is shown in a study of Negro armed robbers. Their arrest histories were as follows:

> An early patterning of stealing from their parents, from school, and on the street; truancy, and suspension or expulsion from school; street fighting, association with older delinquents, and juvenile delinquent gang memberships, all were usually evident in their social backgrounds. When compared with the men in the other criminal categories, it was found that there was more destruction of property in their delinquent activities, and there were more frequent fights with schoolmates, male teachers, and delinquent companions. There was a higher incidence of "mugging" and purse snatching. They had more often been the leaders of delinquent gangs, and, they claimed they were leaders because of their superior size and physical strength.[5]

A similar background in gang delinquency has been noted for the conventional career criminal in what Gibbons has called the "semiprofessional property criminal." He observed that these offenders represent the usual outcome of patterns of gang delinquency and, in turn, that "many juvenile gang offenders continue in criminality as semiprofessionals."[6]

As juvenile offenders progress into conventional career crime, they become more committed to crime as a way of life and develop a criminal self-conception. Because of repeated offenses, and because of subsequent arrests and convictions, conventional offenders eventually identify with crime. For occasional property offenders who pursue criminal activity only sporadically, there is vacillation in self-conception. But for conventional criminals who regularly commit offenses and who are continually isolated from law-abiding segments of society, a criminal self-conception is virtually inescapable. In addition, because property offenders are dealt with rather severely before the law, through arrest and sentencing, such offenders readily come to regard themselves as criminals. The criminal record is a constant reminder that the person has been stigmatized by the society. The record may provide a vicious circle whereby the offender, once stigmatized, often cannot enter into law-abiding society and must continue in a life of crime.

Most of the offenses included in conventional crime, whether juvenile or adult, are related to property and other material possessions in one way or another. Within the boundary of property offenses, conventional property criminals are likely to have a diversified offense record. These offenders commit a series of offenses which may include theft, larceny, robbery, and burglary. The amount of money involved in each offense is relatively small. As a result the offenses provide a part of the offenders' livelihood and they must be repeated regularly. Thus, because

[4] Cf. Harold S. Frum, "Adult Criminal Offense Trends Following Juvenile Delinquency," *Journal of Criminal Law, Criminology and Police Science*, 49 (May–June 1958), pp. 29–49.
[5] Julian B. Roebuck and Mervyn L. Cadwallader, "The Negro Armed Robber as a Criminal Type: The Construction and Application of a Typology," *Pacific Sociological Review*, 4 (Spring 1961), p. 24.
[6] Don C. Gibbons, *Changing the Lawbreaker*, Englewood Cliffs, N.J.: Prentice-Hall, Inc., 1965, p. 105.

of the relative lack of skill and organization, conventional criminals, in comparison to organized and professional criminals, are likely to be eventually arrested. Consequently, conventional offenders constitute a large portion of the prison population. Perhaps as many as half of all prison inmates are conventional offenders.[7] With similar offenders in mind, the following remarks were made by Gibbons in reference to the career of the semiprofessional criminals:

> Because of the low degree of skill involved in the criminality of the semiprofessionals, the risks of apprehension, conviction, and incarceration are high. Many semiprofessionals spend a considerable part of their early adult years in penal institutions where they are likely to be identified as "right guys" or antiadministration inmates. It does not appear that conventional treatment efforts are successful in deflecting many of these persons away from continuation in crime. On the other hand, many of them ultimately do withdraw from crime careers upon reaching the early middle-age period.[8]

While many juvenile gang delinquents continue to engage in illegal activities as adults, particularly as adult conventional career criminals, it is unclear why a large number of them discontinue criminal behavior in their mid-twenties or early thirties. Reckless has pointed out that "it is much easier to determine why offenders continue in criminal careers than it is to understand what makes them quit."[9] It has been suggested that, except for certain types of crime, as a person grows older, he tends to lose touch with deviant and criminal associates because of marriage and family responsibilities.[10] Such a change in life style is more important in breaking a criminal pattern than are the present attempts at rehabilitation in correctional institutions.

When crime is pursued as a way of life, as it is with conventional career criminals, other ways of living are not readily observed, understood, nor desired by the offenders. Furthermore, the excitement and notoriety of a criminal career may seem more rewarding to the criminal than the prospects of hard work, responsibility, mediocrity, and monotony provided by a respectable, law-abiding career. A group consciousness among criminals makes movement to a law-abiding life less comprehensible and desirable. Why some career criminals break this group barrier is the problem to be explained. With early middle age, for many conventional offenders, however, a law-abiding career may hold greater possibility than a criminal career which has not been particularly successful.

GROUP SUPPORT OF CRIMINAL BEHAVIOR

Like other types of career criminals, conventional career criminals associate extensively with other criminals and depend to a great extent upon their assistance and

[7] A similar estimation is made in Russell R. Dynes, Alfred C. Clarke, Simon Dinitz, and Iwao Ishino, *Social Problems: Dissensus and Deviation in an Industrial Society*, New York: Oxford University Press, 1964, p. 543.
[8] Gibbons, p. 105.
[9] Reckless, p. 164.
[10] Clinard, *Sociology of Deviant Behavior*, p. 209.

support. Such support for illegal behavior begins for many offenders at an early age. Thrasher noted some time ago in his classic study of gangs that children and adolescents in play groups, in the course of fun and adventure, engage in a variety of activities which are both legal and illegal in nature.[11] The extent to which these groups engage in illegal behavior depends upon such factors as the organization of the neighborhood, family characteristics, community values, and community reaction to gang activity. In some residental areas delinquency may be the principal means of adjusting to the problems of growing up. One delinquent described his illegal activity in relation to his social experiences as follows:

> My neighborhood was filled with rackets of all kinds, from stealing pennies from news stands to stick-ups. The little fellows begin by stealing little things and bumming from school. They drive around in swell cars and strut their stuff and have a swell broad on the string. No kid wants to be in a piker's racket very long and steal coal and junk, because he sees bigger money in the stick-up game, and if you make a hit with the right mob, you're all set.[12]

Play groups, given the appropriate conditions, such as insulation from conventional controls, contact with law-violating values, and conflict with other groups, may over a period of time develop into delinquent gangs. The activities which become most important to the gang may be in violation of the law. The illegal activities of the gangs are at first relatively minor. The members engage in a variety of conventional property offenses, such as stealing from stores, empty houses, drunks, and other sources of property. Gradually the offenses become more like those engaged in by adults, such as burglary, armed robbery, and grand larceny. As gangs increase in organization and tradition, they may come in conflict with other gangs in the vicinity. Personal offenses and violence of various forms may then become common.

The group nature of conventional offense behavior has been illustrated in the case studies compiled by Shaw. One study described five brothers whose criminal careers began at around the age of five, when they started begging, and progressed to truancy and petty stealing, then to stealing more valuable objects.[13] They were arrested by the police many times, appeared frequently in court, and served periods of confinement in correctional and penal institutions, besides being placed on probation and parole several times. They began their delinquency in the company of a gang of boys. The more experienced and older delinquents encouraged the younger and less experienced to engage in more serious thefts. In a study of one delinquent in particular, Shaw described the group nature of delinquency as follows:

> The next step in the development of Sidney's delinquent trend, perhaps the most important, was his participation in the shop-

[11] Frederick M. Thrasher, The Gang, Chicago: University of Chicago Press, 1927.
[12] Clifford R. Shaw and Henry D. McKay, "Social Factors in Juvenile Delinquency," National Commission on Law Observance and Enforcement, Report No. 13, The Causes of Crime, Vol. II, Washington, D.C.: Government Printing Office, 1931, p. 132. Also see William F. Whyte, Street Corner Society, Chicago: University of Chicago Press, 1943.
[13] Clifford R. Shaw, Henry D. McKay, and James F. McDonald, Brothers in Crime, Chicago: University of Chicago Press, 1938.

lifting activities of his play group. This type of delinquency was obviously an accepted tradition of the group, as indicated by the fact that three of its members had been involved in a number of instances of shoplifting prior to Sidney's initial contact with the group. It may be assumed that Sidney not only acquired the shop-lifting techniques and moral code prevailing in this delinquent group, but that through his numerous experiences in shoplifting his delinquent attitudes and interests were more clearly defined and he became more closely identified with the criminal world.[14]

Patterns of social interaction develop in each juvenile gang. The members adapt to a number of social roles and achieve social status through participation in gang activity. Group solidarity and tradition develop in the course of the common experience of the members. The gang may become of such importance to the members that they participate very little in the larger society. Gang boys become dependent upon each other for a large share of their interpersonal gratifications. Nevertheless, as Short and Strodtbeck have recently found, the gang is less than satisfactory as a source of complete personal gratification. While important friendships and loyalties develop within the gang, "the unstable gang context, serving as an arena in which status threats are played out, tends to undermine these friendships and loyalties and makes them shorter lived and less binding."[15]

Some of the juvenile gangs which are involved in conventional offenses in large cities have an existence of many years. Others are more transitory and have relatively little organization.[16] The social roles, traditions, values, and location of the gang may remain relatively intact as members grow out of delinquency into adult crime and as new members become active. Gangs are not dependent upon their present membership for existence. Juvenile gangs are able to continue in spite of the necessary fluctuations in personnel.

CORRESPONDENCE BETWEEN CRIMINAL BEHAVIOR AND LEGITIMATE BEHAVIOR PATTERNS

Probably in no other area of criminology today is there the effort to develop theories as in the study of gang delinquency. As a major form of conventional offenses, gang delinquency has been viewed in relation to the legitimate behavior patterns of society. There have been variations on the theme because of the realization that gang delinquency does not represent a single category of behavior and that it is necessary to construct separate theories for the various types of gang delinquency. Several subtypes of gang delinquency have been distinguished. Cohen and Short divided male delinquency into five types: the parent male subculture, the conflict-oriented subculture, the drug-addict subculture, the semiprofessional theft subculture, and the middle-class delinquent subculture.[17] (1) The parent

---

[14] Clifford R. Shaw, The Natural History of a Delinquent Career, Chicago: University of Chicago Press, 1931, pp. 230–231.

[15] James F. Short, Jr., and Fred L. Strodtbeck, Group Process and Gang Delinquency, Chicago: University of Chicago Press, 1965, p. 283.

[16] Short and Strodtbeck, especially chap. 12.

[17] Albert K. Cohen and James F. Short, Jr., "Research in Delinquent Subcultures," Journal of Social Issues, 14 (No. 3, 1958), pp. 20–37.

male subculture is the more common variety, involving a small gang whose behavior is nonutilitarian, malicious, negativistic, versatile and characterized by short-run hedonism and group autonomy. These characteristics form the common core from which the other types develop, hence the idea of "parent." (2) The conflict-oriented gang may be a much larger group with a high degree of organization, a definite territory, and a readiness to engage in physical conflict and "rumbles" with other gangs. (3) The drug-addict subculture centers on the use of narcotic drugs and a distinct way of dress; its members are often referred to as the "cats." (4) The semiprofessional theft subculture has a utilitarian, systematic, and pecuniary character in which strong-arm methods are used and stolen articles are sold. (5) The middle-class delinquent fosters the deliberate courting of danger, and there is a sophisticated, irresponsible "playboy" approach to activities, symbolic of adult roles and centering largely on sex, liquor, and automobiles. A more limited typology of delinquent subcultures has been made by Cloward and Ohlin: the criminal, the conflict, and the retreatist or drug-culture gang.[18]

The various theories that have been advanced for the types of gang delinquency or for gang delinquency in general have been concerned with the legitimacy of the means and goals of gang members. The theories have emphasized (1) hostility toward middle class norms, (2) lower class culture, (3) differential opportunity, (4) the near group, (5) neutralization and drift, and (6) age transition.

HOSTILITY TOWARD MIDDLE CLASS NORMS. Cohen's analysis of gang delinquency as found among working class males has stimulated the modern study of gang delinquency.[19] Cohen's thesis was that working class boys, because they share the problem of adjustment to middle class standards, act in opposition to these standards, thereby creating a delinquent subculture. These middle class values include ambition, self-reliance, the postponement of immediate satisfactions, good manners and courtesy, wholesome recreation, opposition to physical violence, and respect for property. According to this theory, working class boys resent these dominant values because they have not been part of their own world. They also, consequently, resent middle-class people who assign them to low status because they do not exhibit middle-class values. Delinquent gangs are a natural consequence of working class boys coming together because of common hostilities. The subculture which they form is the opposite of middle class values and is characterized by malice toward things that are regarded as virtuous, a versatility in types of delinquent behavior, short-run hedonism involving nonutilitarian types of "fun" rather than long-range goals, and group autonomy or opposition to social control other than control by the group itself.

LOWER CLASS CULTURE. In sharp contrast to the previous formulation is the delinquent gang theory based on the characteristics of the lower class culture.[20] Ac-

[18] Richard A. Cloward and Lloyd E. Ohlin, Delinquency and Opportunity: A Theory of Delinquent Gangs, New York: The Free Press of Glencoe, 1960.
[19] Albert K. Cohen, Delinquent Boys: The Culture of the Gang, New York: The Free Press of Glencoe, 1955. For an attempt to test the application to England of the various theories presented here, see David M. Downes, The Delinquent Solution: A Study in Subcultural Theory, (New York: The Free Press of Glencoe, 1966). For a critical appraisal of these theories, see David J. Bordua, "Delinquent Subcultures: Sociological Interpretations of Gang Delinquency," (The Annals, 338 (November 1961), pp. 119–136.
[20] Walter B. Miller, "Lower Class Culture as a Generating Milieu of Gang Delinquency," Journal of Social Issues, 14 (No. 3, 1958), pp. 5–19.

cording to Miller, gang activity leads to delinquency as a result of the expression of the lower class focal concerns of trouble, toughness, smartness, excitement, fate, and autonomy. Thus, gang delinquency as seen by Miller is a natural product of a hard-core lower class culture and is not a reaction, as suggested by Cohen, of lower class youth to middle class standards. The lower class boy, therefore, wishing to belong and to achieve status, often participates in delinquent groups which express these values. Delinquent acts not only provide status but are means for satisfying those factors which dominate the way of life of the lower class.

DIFFERENTIAL OPPORTUNITY.   The theory developed by Cloward and Ohlin explains gang delinquency of the subcultural type as arising from differentials in access to legitimate and illegitimate goals.[21] Whether a delinquent subculture develops in a particular area of the city depends upon the availability of illegitimate means. The disparity between what lower class youth are led to want and what is actually available to them is the source of a major problem of adjustment. Adolescents who form delinquent subcultures, according to Cloward and Ohlin, are faced with limitations on legitimate avenues of access to legitimate goals. These adolescents experience intense frustrations and explore nonconformist alternatives. Whether this deprivation will result in delinquency depends, however, on the opportunity or availability of illegitimate means to obtain their goals. In integrated slum areas where adult criminal patterns serve as models and opportunity structures are available, the subcultures will be *criminal* and the gangs will engage in theft, extortion, and similar activities to achieve status and an illegal income. In unintegrated areas, characterized by mobility, transiency, and instability, such as in new urban housing developments, where criminal patterns and opportunity structures are unavailable, models for development of delinquent behavior come from other subcultures, with the gang members engaging in various forms of *conflict*. In the *retreatist* subculture, located in the slum, the members use drugs and engage in other sensual experiences because they find both legitimate and other illegitimate means to success closed to them and refuse to accept the moral validity of illegitimate means to status and success exemplified by stealing and vandalism.

THE NEAR GROUP.   In an interpretation of large conflict-oriented gangs, Yablonsky has suggested that such gangs do not have the stability of membership and the high degree of organization often attributed to them.[22] He has suggested that the violent gang is a "near group" in that this type of gang is characterized by diffuse role definitions, limited cohesion, impermanence, minimal consensus on norms, and shifting membership. In a somewhat different interpretation of the violent gang, Pfautz has suggested that Yablonsky's findings can be more productively recast in the theoretical traditions of collective behavior and social movements.[23] As Pfautz indicates, violent gang activity may represent the attempt on the part of adolescents living in lower class urban slums to act together in the face of social unrest. Some delinquency may be the collective response of adolescents to the problems of growing up in contemporary society. The means and goals of the youths engaged in con-

21 Cloward and Ohlin.
22 Lewis Yablonsky, *The Violent Gang*, New York: The Free Press of Glencoe, 1962.
23 Harold W. Pfautz, "Near-Group Theory and Collective Behavior: A Critical Reformulation," *Social Problems*, 9 (Fall 1961), pp. 167–174.

ventional gang delinquency, however, are likely to be in conflict with the values that are regarded as legitimate by the dominant power segments of society.

NEUTRALIZATION AND DRIFT.   Conventional offenders are only partially committed to legitimate society. When there is commitment, it is usually sporadic and temporary. A fluctuation in commitment to legitimate society, outside a delinquent or criminal subculture, is evident in much of juvenile delinquency. Sykes and Matza have suggested that delinquents do not completely reject the dominant values and norms of the larger society but only neutralize the values and norms in the course of violating the law. In addition, such delinquents make use of the "subterranean values" of the dominant society, allowing these values to serve as a code of behavior rather than reserving them for only leisure-time activities.[24] Similarly, in a participant observation study of middle class gangs, Myerhoff and Myerhoff concluded that middle class gang delinquency is in part an extension of values held by most members of society.[25] But it appears that delinquents are not fully committed to any particular value system. Matza has suggested that in being uncommitted the delinquent "drifts" between a delinquent and a nondelinquent way of life.

> Drift stands midway between freedom and control. Its basis is an area of the social structure in which control has been loosened, coupled with the abortiveness of adolescent endeavor to organize an autonomous subculture, and thus an independent source of control, around illegal action. The delinquent *transiently* exists in a limbo between convention and crime, responding in turn to the demands of each, flirting now with one, now the other, but postponing commitment, evading decision. Thus, he drifts between criminal and conventional action.[26]

AGE TRANSITION.   The relation of the delinquent to the larger society has been viewed in other ways by a number of writers. Bloch and Niederhoffer have taken the position that gang delinquency is in part a result of age grading in the larger society.[27] They have argued that the gang arises as an attempt by adolescents to gain the status not granted to them by adults. Gang membership serves to fill the gap between childhood and adulthood. Paul Goodman, in a similar manner, has pointed to the delinquency problems which result when a society does not provide meaningful functions for adolescents.[28] These ideas seem to apply in particular to recent gang delinquency in Great Britain. Fyvel has seen the increase of gang

---

[24] Gresham M. Sykes and David Matza, "Techniques of Neutralization: A Theory of Delinquency," *American Sociological Review*, 22 (December 1957), pp. 664–670; and David Matza and Gresham M. Sykes, "Juvenile Delinquency and Subterranean Values," *American Sociological Review*, 26 (October 1961), pp. 712–719.

[25] Harold L. Myerhoff and Barbara G. Myerhoff, "Field Observations of Middle Class 'Gangs,'" *Social Forces*, 42 (March 1964), pp. 328–336. Also see Ralph W. England, Jr., "A Theory of Middle Class Juvenile Delinquency," *Journal of Criminal Law, Criminology and Police Science*, 50 (March–April 1960), pp. 535–540.

[26] David Matza, *Delinquency and Drift*, New York: John Wiley & Sons, Inc., 1964, p. 28.

[27] Herbert A. Bloch and Arthur Niederhoffer, *The Gang: A Study of Adolescent Behavior*, New York: Philosophical Library, Inc., 1958. This approach finds support in S. N. Eisenstadt, *From Generation to Generation*, New York: The Free Press of Glencoe, 1956.

[28] Paul Goodman, *Growing Up Absurd*, New York: Random House, Inc., 1960.

delinquency in Great Britain, and in other "affluent" societies, as the failure to provide meaningful symbols for adjustment and fulfillment in place of the symbols once provided by a class-dominated society.[29]

The writings of other writers are also relevant to the age transition hypothesis of gang delinquency. In separate works, Erikson and Friedenberg have argued that adolescence is a time for experimentation, a period for establishing an identity prior to the adoption of adult roles.[30] Problems of identity appear to be particularly pressing in contemporary society. Gang delinquency may be one of the attempts to achieve identity and meaningfulness. The question is why does gang delinquency serve this function for some youths while other social arrangements serve this function for other youths. The answer is probably related to the location of the youth in the general structure of the society.

SOCIETAL REACTION

The reaction against persons who engage in conventional offenses is influenced by the value placed on private property in American society. Conventional offenders represent in part the conflict which exists in respect to property rights. In general, the defining of certain behaviors as criminal (through the formulation and administration of criminal law) is the domain of groups in positions of power.[31] Since, in most societies, the groups which are in power value private property, persons who interfere with property rights are regarded as criminals. The conventional property offender may be viewed as a member of a minority that has little power in the political process. As Bloch and Geis have written in respect to the law on property crime, "Legislation will tend to erect the most formidable barriers against vulnerable segments of the society which attempt to usurp the properties of the entrenched elements."[32] An understanding of who defines behavior as criminal is as essential in the study of conventional crime as it is in the study of criminal behavior in general.

In the administration of the law, conventional offenders are handled according to certain preconceived notions about their characteristics and behavior. Conventional offenders are among those offenders who usually do not reach the trial stage of the judicial process because their cases are settled by a plea of guilty. The prosecuting attorney and defending attorney through "bargaining" often alter the charge in order to avoid a trial.[33] Since the penal code does not provide instructions for making decisions on complaint alterations, other guides must be devised by the attorneys. According to Sudnow, attorneys place concrete cases into more general

[29] T. R. Fyvel, Troublemakers: Rebellious Youth in an Affluent Society, New York: Schocken Books, Inc., 1961.

[30] Erik H. Erikson, Childhood and Society, New York: W. W. Norton Publishing Company, 1950; and Edgar Z. Friedenberg, The Vanishing Adolescent, New York: Dell & Company, 1962.

[31] Thorsten Sellin, Culture Conflict and Crime, New York: Social Science Research Council, 1938, Chap. 2; and Richard Quinney, "Crime in Political Perspective, American Behavioral Scientist, 8 (December 1964), pp. 19–22.

[32] Herbert A. Bloch and Gilbert Geis, Man, Crime, and Society, New York: Random House, Inc., 1962, p. 316.

[33] Donald J. Newman, "Pleading Guilty for Considerations: A Study of Bargain Justice," Journal of Criminal Law, Criminology and Police Science, 46 (March–April 1956), pp. 780–790. Also see Donald C. Newman, Conviction: The Determination of Guilt or Innocence without Trial, Boston: Little, Brown & Company, 1966.

categories of behavioral events.[34] For example, rather than referring to the statutory definition of burglary, reference is made to a nonstatutorily defined class of "burglaries," which Sudnow terms *normal burglaries*. On the basis of a characterization of a normal or typical burglary, attorneys are able to agree upon an appropriate reduction from the original charge, such as reducing a "typical" burglary to petty theft. Thus, an abstract behavioral type is used by those who officially react to conventional crime, as well as by those who study crime.

The programs used in the treatment and prevention of conventional crime are generally based on a conservative ideology. The approaches to juvenile delinquency, for example, have usually consisted of custody, rehabilitation, or redirection of individuals and families, overlooking the relation of offenders to more basic social conditions. As Martin and Fitzpatrick have stated: "None of these efforts aims at social change conceived of in broad terms. They take the side of discipline, law and order, and rehabilitation, but not of social reform."[35] In general, little effort is made to change a local community, such as a slum, by enlisting large-scale citizen participation and developing indigenous leadership and self-help to overcome norms, values, and situations which contribute to delinquency and crime.[36]

> By nature of the function they are asked to fulfill, and the methods by which they are expected to fulfill it, most agencies aimed at curbing delinquency tend to be conservative. By public definition, they are caring for youths who have deviated from the expected values or behavior of the established community and they are seeking to train youths to maintain a greater degree of conformity. In doing this, juvenile courts, psychiatric clinics, training schools, and similar agencies act to conserve the accepted values and behavior patterns of the community. They are a force for the preservation of the *status quo*. Traditionally, then, such agencies have either provided custodial care for the delinquent or sought to change the character of the delinquent. They have given very little attention to the nature of the social institutions from which their cases have deviated.[37]

Only recently have a considerable number of programs been instituted which go beyond the conservative ideology that has long dominated the social reaction to crime.

SELECTED BIBLIOGRAPHY

1. Bloch, Herbert A., and Arthur Niederhoffer, *The Gang: A Study in Adolescent Behavior*, New York: Philosophical Library, Inc., 1958.
2. Bohlke, Robert H., "Social Mobility, Stratification, Inconsistency, and Middle Class Delinquency," *Social Problems*, 8 (Spring 1961), pp. 351–363.

[34] David Sudnow, "Normal Crimes: Sociological Features of the Penal Code in a Public Defender Office," *Social Problems*, 12 (Winter 1965), pp. 255–276.
[35] John M. Martin and Joseph P. Fitzpatrick, *Delinquent Behavior: A Redefinition of the Problem*, New York, Random House, Inc., 1964, p. 37.
[36] Marshall B. Clinard, *Slums and Community Development*.
[37] Martin and Fitzpatrick, pp. 10–11.

3. Bordua, David J., "A Critique of Sociological Interpretations of Gang Delinquency," *The Annals*, 338 (November 1961), pp. 119–136.

4. Clinard, Marshall B., *Sociology of Deviant Behavior*, rev. ed., New York: Holt, Rinehart and Winston, Inc., 1963, Chap. 10.

5. Cloward, Richard A., and Lloyd E. Ohlin, *Delinquency and Opportunity: A Theory of Delinquent Gangs*, New York: The Free Press of Glencoe, 1960.

6. Cohen, Albert K., *Delinquent Boys: The Culture of the Gang*, New York: The Free Press of Glencoe, 1955.

7. ———, and James F. Short, Jr., "Research in Delinquent Subcultures," *Journal of Social Issues*, 14 (No. 3, 1958), pp. 20–37.

8. Cressey, Paul F., "The Criminal Tribes of India," *Sociology and Social Research*, 20 (1935), pp. 503–155, and 21 (July–September 1936), pp. 18–25.

9. Dynes, Russell R., Alfred C. Clarke, Simon Dinitz, and Iwao Ishino, *Social Problems: Dissensus and Deviation in an Industrial Society*, New York: Oxford University Press, 1964, Chap. 18.

10. England, Ralph W., Jr., "A Theory of Middle Class Juvenile Delinquency," *Journal of Criminal Law, Criminology and Police Science*, 50 (March–April 1960), pp. 535–540.

11. Ferdinand, Theodore N., *Typologies of Delinquency: A Critical Analysis*, New York: Random House, Inc., 1966.

12. Frum, Harold S., "Adult Criminal Offense Trends Following Juvenile Delinquency," *Journal of Criminal Law, Criminology and Police Science*, 49 (May–June 1958), pp. 29–49.

13. Fyvel, T. R., *Troublemakers: Rebellious Youth in an Affluent Society*, New York: Schocken Books, Inc., 1961.

14. Gibbons, Don C., *Changing the Lawbreaker*, Englewood Cliffs, N.J.: Prentice-Hall, Inc., 1965.

15. Hall, Jerome, *Theft, Law and Society*, 2d ed., Indianapolis: The Bobbs-Merrill Company, Inc., 1960.

16. Kobrin, Solomon, "The Conflict of Values in Delinquency Areas," *American Sociological Review* 16 (October 1951), pp. 653–661.

17. Lentz, William P., "Rural-Urban Differentials and Juvenile Delinquency," *Journal of Criminal Law, Criminology and Police Science*, 47 (September–October 1956), pp. 331–339.

18. McClintock, F. H., and Evelyn Gibson, *Robbery in London: An Enquiry by the Cambridge Institute of Technology*, London: Macmillan & Co., Ltd., 1961.

19. Matza, David, *Delinquency and Drift*, New York: John Wiley & Sons, Inc., 1964.

20. ———, and Gresham M. Sykes, "Juvenile Delinquency and Subterranean Values," *American Sociological Review*, 26 (October 1961), pp. 712–719.

21. Miller, Walter B., "Lower Class Culture as a Generating Milieu of Gang Delinquency," *Journal of Social Issues*, 14 (No. 3, 1958), pp. 5–19.

22. Myerhoff, Harold L., and Barbara G. Myerhoff, "Field Observations of Middle Class 'Gangs,'" *Social Forces*, 42 (March 1964), pp. 328–336.

23. Pfautz, Harold W., "Near-Group Theory and Collective Behavior: A Critical Reformulation," *Social Problems*, 9 (Fall 1961), pp. 167–174.

24. Reckless, Walter C., *The Crime Problem*, 3d ed., New York: Appleton-Century-Crofts, Inc., 1961, Chap. 9.

25. Roebuck, Julian B., and Mervyn L. Cadwallader, "The Negro Armed Robber as a Criminal Type: The Construction and Application of a Typology," *Pacific Sociological Review* 4 (Spring 1961), pp. 21–26.
26. ———, and Ronald Johnson, "The Jack-of-All-Trades Offender," *Crime and Delinquency*, 8 (April 1962), pp. 172–181.
27. Salisbury, Harrison E., *The Shook-Up Generation*, New York: Crest Books, 1958.
28. Scott, Peter, "Gangs and Delinquent Groups in London," *British Journal of Delinquency*, 7 (July 1956), pp. 4–26.
29. Shaw, Clifford R., *The Jack Roller*, Chicago: University of Chicago Press, 1930.
30. ———, *The Natural History of a Delinquent Career*, Chicago: University of Chicago Press, 1931.
31. ———, Henry D. McKay, and James F. McDonald, *Brothers in Crime*, Chicago: University of Chicago Press, 1938.
32. Short, James F., Jr., and Fred L. Strodtbeck, *Group Process and Gang Delinquency*, Chicago: University of Chicago Press, 1965.
33. Spergel, Irving, *Racketville, Slumtown, Haulburg: An Exploratory Study of Delinquent Subcultures*, Chicago: University of Chicago Press, 1964.
34. Sykes, Gresham M., and David Matza, "Techniques of Neutralization: A Theory of Delinquency," *American Sociological Review*, 22 (December 1957), pp. 664–670.
35. Thrasher, Frederick M., *The Gang: A Study of 1,313 Gangs in Chicago*, abr. ed., Chicago: University of Chicago Press, 1963.
36. Vaz, Edmund W., "Juvenile Gang Delinquency in Paris," *Social Problems*, 10 (Summer 1962), pp. 23–31.
37. Yablonsky, Lewis, *The Violent Gang*, New York: The Free Press of Glencoe, 1962.

THE NATURAL HISTORY OF A DELINQUENT CAREER*

Clifford R. Shaw

The work of Clifford R. Shaw stands as a landmark in the study of crime and delinquency. Shaw clearly showed that illegal behavior was learned in a social and cultural setting. The selection below is a portion from Shaw's case study of a delinquent boy. Association with a group of delinquents marked the beginning of Sidney's career in delinquency. Sidney engaged in a variety of conventional property offenses, ranging from pilfering and petty theft to shoplifting. Also mentioned are such social factors as the community situation and the family in relation to the development of the delinquent career.

* Reprinted from Clifford R. Shaw, *The Natural History of a Delinquent Career*, Chicago: University of Chicago Press, 1931, Chap. 12, by permission of the publisher.

In the foregoing discussion materials have been presented to indicate the nature of the successive social situations in which Sidney lived, the attitudes which developed in relation to these situations, and the various delinquencies and crimes in which he was implicated. To be presented now is a brief summary and tentative interpretation of the more important social aspects of his career in delinquency and crime. It is recognized that the case history is not complete; it is particularly lacking with regard to Sidney's experiences during the first five years of his life.

Underlying our tentative interpretation of this case is the assumption that behavior traits have a natural evolution in the life-history of the individual, developing in the process of interaction between the individual and the successive situations in which he lives. The character of this process is determined both by the nature of the organism and by the conditions of the social and cultural situation to which the organism must make an adjustment. The child is born into the world a physical organism endowed with certain physical characteristics, reflexes, mental capacities, and undefined tendencies to act. Furthermore, he is always born into a social world in which certain cultural norms, social activities, and group expectations already exist. Through participation in the activities of this social world, beginning in such intimate groups as the family, the play group, and the neighborhood, the original activities of the child are conditioned and organized and come to assume the character of well-defined attitudes, interests, and behavior trends. From this standpoint the direction which the development of the original tendencies takes is determined to a great extent by the attitudes and social values prevailing in the situations which the child encounters. This point of view is briefly summarized in the following quotation from Thomas:

Now, it appears that behavior traits and their totality as represented by the personality are the outcome of a series of definitions or situa-

tions with the resulting reactions and their fixation in a body of attitudes or psychological sets. Obviously, the institutions of a society, beginning with the family, form the character of its members almost as the daily nutrition forms their bodies, but this is for everybody, and the unique attitudes of the individual and his unique personality are closely connected with certain incidents or critical experiences particular to himself, defining the situation, giving the psychological set, and often determining the whole life direction.[1]

During the last few years increasing emphasis has been placed upon the importance of the period of infancy, childhood, and early youth in the development of personality and behavior traits. It is quite generally assumed that many of the behavior traits of adults may be traced back to habits and attitudes which were fixed during this early formative period.[2] This period is of particular significance in the development of tendencies toward delinquency and crime.[3] Case histories of older offenders show that frequently the delinquent trend originated during the early years of the individual's life. In many of these cases it is possible to describe, in a general way at least, the successive steps or continuous process involved in the gradual formation and fixation of the delinquent-behavior traits. This process is

---

[1] W. I. Thomas, "The Problem of Personality in the Urban Environment," *The Urban Community* (University of Chicago Press, 1926), pp. 38–39. For further elaboration of this point of view see John Dewey, *Human Nature and Conduct* (New York, 1922); George H. Mead, "The Genesis of the Self and Social Control," *International Journal of Ethics*, XXXV (April, 1925), 251–77; Charles H. Cooley, *Human Nature and the Social Order* (rev. ed.; New York, 1922); Ellsworth Faris, "The Nature of Human Nature," *The Urban Community* (University of Chicago Press, 1926), pp. 21–37.

[2] In this connection see W. A. White, "The Golden Period for Mental Hygiene," *Mental Hygiene*, Reprint No. 81, April, 1920; Cyril Burt, *The Young Delinquent* (1925), p. 584; J. B. Watson, *Behaviorism* (1925), p. 216; A. Gesell, "The Nursery School Movement," *School and Society*, Nov. 22, 1924, pp. 1–19; and F. H. Richardson, *Parenthood and the Newer Psychology* (1926).

[3] See William Healy, *The Individual Delinquent* (Little, Brown & Co., 1920), p. 10.

rather clearly illustrated in the case history of Sidney.

We have, in this case, a young male offender of superior intelligence and apparently normal physical condition, whose career in delinquency began at the early age of seven years. The record of his offenses includes a great number of delinquent practices. In fact, it would be quite impossible to make a complete inventory of all the specific instances of delinquency and crime in which he was involved. Those included in the official record probably comprise only a small proportion of the total number in which he was either directly or indirectly implicated. During the course of his career in delinquency, from the time he was seven to seventeen years of age, Sidney was arrested at least sixteen times, was brought to court on petitions alleging truancy or delinquency ten times, and received seven commitments to four different correctional institutions. His delinquencies became increasingly serious as he grew older, beginning as petty stealing in the neighborhood and truancy from school, and progressing to such serious crimes as holdup with a gun and rape. His offenses in the order of their occurrence included pilfering in the neighborhood, breaking into neighborhood stores, shoplifting, jackrolling, stealing accessories from automobiles, larceny of automobiles, holdup with a gun, and rape. The holdup and rape offenses, as suggested earlier, were the natural consequence of a long chain of delinquent experiences. The attitudes, habits, and philosophy of life underlying these latter crimes were undoubtedly built up in the course of the earlier experiences in delinquency.

SOCIAL FACTORS

In order to understand the origin and early development of Sidney's delinquent behavior traits it is important, at the very outset, to draw attention to certain facts pertaining to the more general social situation in which he was living at the time his career in delinquency began. In the first place, he lived in one of the most deteriorated and disorganized sections of the city. In this area the conventional traditions, neighborhood institutions, and public opinion, through which neighborhoods usually effect a control over the behavior child, were largely disintegrated. Consequently, Sidney had very little access to the cultural heritages of conventional society and he was not subject to the constructive and restraining influences which surround the child in the more highly integrated and conventional residential neighborhoods of the city. In the area in which he lived neighborhood control was limited largely to the control that was exerted through such formal agencies as the school, the courts, and the police.

This community situation was not only disorganized and thus ineffective as a unit of control, but it was characterized by a high rate of juvenile delinquency and adult crime, not to mention the widespread political corruption which had long existed in the area. Various forms of stealing and many organized delinquent and criminal gangs were prevalent in the area. These groups exercised a powerful influence and tended to create a community spirit which not only tolerated but actually fostered delinquent and criminal practices.

Another aspect of Sidney's general social background which seems to be important was the very inferior economic status of his family. At various times the family was destitute and wholly dependent upon charity. It is apparent from the study of the case that the home afforded practically no facilities for the satisfaction of Sidney's fundamental wishes and the stimulation of wholesome play interests. It is probable also that Sidney's feelings of inferiority and insecurity, which are apparent throughout his autobiography, were partly due to the economic inadequacy of the family.

Attention should be directed, also, to the disorganized family situation in this case. Because of the father's repeated desertions, the mother was forced to seek employment outside the home. . . . The family never constituted an integrated unit capable of exercising consistent control of Sidney's behavior. In the absence of effective moral restraints in the family and in the community, the development of his group relationships and his choice of companions outside of the home were almost entirely undirected.

Sidney's first social contacts outside the home were with a group of delinquent boys most of whom were considerably older than himself. His association with this group marked the beginning of his career in delinquency. The first stealing episode consisted of pilfering fruit from the front of a local store. This experience occurred when Sidney was seven years old, while he was in the company of a boy (Joseph Kratz) who was five years his senior. Judging from his own story Sidney's participation in this initial delinquency was due largely to the influence of his companion, who was already skilled in various forms of stealing. This type of petty stealing was a common practice in the area and was closely associated with the interests and activities indulged in by neighborhood play groups and gangs. Soon after the first stealing experience Sidney became involved in a burglary episode. This experience occurred while he was in the company of the same older companion. The next step in the development of Sidney's delinquent trend, perhaps the most important, was his participation in the shoplifting activities of his play group. This type of delinquency was obviously an accepted tradition of the group, as indicated by the fact that three of its members had been involved in a number of instances of shoplifting prior to Sidney's initial contact with the group. It may be assumed that Sidney not only acquired the shoplifting techniques and moral code prevailing in this delinquent group, but that through his numerous experiences in shoplifting his delinquent attitudes and interests were more clearly defined and he became more closely identified with the criminal world.

Along with his early stealing experiences

Sidney began to play truant from school. These two types of behavior are closely associated and, as in the present case, frequently occur together. It is clear that school attendance interfered with Sidney's participation in his play-group activities which were far more thrilling, enticing, and stimulating than the formal routine of the school. From Sidney's point of view the school "was a necessary evil that grown-up folks expected little children to endure." It is significant that truancy from school was a rather common practice among his older companions. On the whole, Sidney's truancy seems to have been a response to the play-group situation rather than to any conflict or difficulty within the school. Despite his repeated truancy, his school report shows a record of good scholarship.

We have assumed in the foregoing paragraphs that Sidney's delinquent-behavior trend originated in the course of his participation in the activities of his play group. On the other hand, one may ask whether Sidney was delinquent because of the influence of his play group or whether he selected delinquent companions because of a predisposition toward delinquency. Obviously it is not possible to secure a conclusive answer to this question. It is possible that certain underlying factors, not disclosed in this case history, were operating to determine his early tendency toward delinquency. It may be pointed out, however, that his first contact with the gang occurred earlier in the chronological sequence of events in his life than his initial delinquencies, and that the character of these initial delinquencies was identical with the traditional patterns of the group. If there was a predisposition toward delinquency prior to his first contact with the gang, it was not expressed in such a form as to be apparent to those who had intimate contact with him during his very early years. Both the mother and the brother, for example, are quite emphatic in stating that the first indication of delinquency appeared subsequent to his association with "Joseph Kratz and his gang." Since the members of the gang lived in the immediate vicinity of Sidney's home, it may be assumed that he was thrown into contact with them in the course of his spontaneous and unsupervised play life outside of the home. Furthermore, it is not improbable that his first delinquencies represent an adjustment to the behavior norms, activities, and expectations of his early play group.

Prior to Sidney's contact with the Burns Athletic Club his delinquencies had been limited very largely to pilfering, burglary, and shoplifting. This contact, however, marked the beginning of a very significant extension of his delinquent activities. It was immediately following his association with this group and while in the company of some of its younger members that Sidney's first experience in the larceny of automobiles and holdup with a gun took place. Such crimes, along with bootlegging, racketeering, hijacking, and other forms of violence, were not uncommon among the members of the Club. Sidney's prompt acceptance of the adult criminal patterns of this group is not surprising in view of the fact that his attitudes and interests were already decidedly delinquent in character. Furthermore, he had never developed vocational and leisure-time interests which might serve to stabilize his behavior and to counteract the influence of the delinquent and criminal characters whom he met at the Club. It seems quite clear that the new criminal patterns of robbery with a gun and larceny of automobiles which he acquired in the course of his associations in this Club represent a continuation or further development of his previously established tendency toward delinquency.

In order to understand Sidney's apparent lack of appreciation of the moral significance of his crime it is necessary to bear in mind that his vital social contacts outside of his home were limited largely to delinquent and criminal groups. It may be assumed that his attitudes toward women and sex behavior were defined through his experience with prostitutes and in the course of his conversations with other delinquents. He was never incorporated into a conventional group through which he might assimilate the conventional attitudes and moral values of society. For the most part, his contacts with conventional groups were not only casual and infrequent but essentially formal and external in character.

It is interesting to observe that the usual formal methods of treatment—special supervision, probation, repeated incarceration in correctional institutions, and parole—failed to check the development of Sidney's career in delinquency. While it is not possible to prove that any method of treatment would have been effective in this case, even at the time of the onset of the career in delinquency, the available records in the case fail to reveal any definite attempt to understand the nature of Sidney's delinquency or to formulate a plan of treatment adapted to his particular needs. Throughout the ten-year period in which he was engaged in delinquency the treatment administered was largely formal and external. Each time that he was placed on probation or released on parole he was returned to the same situation in which his delinquent behavior had occurred, without any attempt made to modify the situation or to develop new group contacts. . . .

Another very interesting aspect of this case is the fact that, while Sidney from a very early age presented numerous behavior problems, his brother was in most respects a model person. Whether this divergence of behavior is due to individual differences or to differences in social contacts cannot be determined upon the basis of the material now available. Abe, seven years older than Sidney, is a plodding, methodical young man of average intelligence. . . . The mother exercised much closer supervision of Abe than it was possible for her to exercise in the case of Sidney. At a very early age Abe became closely associated with the synagogue and thus formed permanent contacts with conventional groups. Sidney, on the other hand, never became identified with groups of this type. From personal interviews it is clear that during his early years Sidney was resentful of the fact that his parents compared his conduct unfavorably with that of his brother. In fact, it is possible that his drive toward unsanctioned behavior was in part a reaction against the model behavior of Abe and the manner in which that behavior was defined in the family situation. Cases such as this suggest the need for comparative studies of delinquent and nondelinquent children living within the same community and, in so far as possible, within the same family. Such studies should reveal the factors which determine the widely divergent behavior tendencies that occur among children living in the same general social situation.

THE GANG*

Frederic M. Thrasher

> Thrasher's The Gang *is a classic in the study of gang delinquency. Presented below is a portion of Thrasher's observations of the gang, derived from an investigation of 1313 gangs in Chicago. The gang begins as a spontaneous play group and eventually develops into a gang through conflict with other gangs and with society in general. The gang fulfills needs which are not satisfied by other social means.*

The beginnings of the gang can best be studied in the slums of the city where an inordinately large number of children are crowded into a limited area. On a warm summer evening children fairly swarm over areaways and sidewalks, vacant lots and rubbish dumps, streets and alleys. The buzzing chatter and constant motion remind one of insects which hover in a swarm, yet ceaselessly dart hither and thither within the animated mass. This endless activity has a tremendous fascination, even for the casual visitor to the district, and it would be a marvel indeed if any healthy boy could hold himself aloof from it.

In this ubiquitous crowd of children, spontaneous play-groups are forming everywhere—gangs in embryo. Such a crowded environment is full of opportunities for conflict with some antagonistic person or group within or without the gang's own social milieu. The conflict arises on the one hand with groups of its own class in disputes over the valued prerogatives of gangland—territory, loot, play spaces, patronage in illicit business, privileges to exploit, and so on; it comes about on the other, through opposition on the part of the conventional social order to the gang's unsupervised activities. Thus, the gang is faced with a real struggle for existence with other gangs and with the antagonistic forces in its wider social environment.

Play-groups easily meet these hostile forces, which give their members a "we" feeling and start the process of ganging so

---

* Reprinted from Frederic M. Thrasher, *The Gang: A Study of 1,313 Gangs in Chicago*, abr. ed., Chicago: University of Chicago Press, 1963 (original copyright 1927), Chap. 2, by permission of the publisher.

characteristic of the life of these unorganized areas.

On a brisk day in May we visited the Hull-House region. Streets and open spaces were alive with boys. With very little direction, there were under way energetic games of all sorts.

At one side of the Goodrich school grounds the "Peorias" were matching skill with a "pick-up" team, the nucleus for some future gang, in a game of playground ball. The "Peoria Strangers," the younger satellites of the group, looked on. In an adjoining portion of the yard, the "Tanners" were playing the "Forquers" for a "pool" of $3.75 which had been put up by the opposing teams. A fight was narrowly averted when the umpire made a "bum" decision and the boys massed about him in a threatening way. At the other end of the lot two more teams were playing.

Small groups here and there were engaged in conversation or side play. Not far away a man was playing "rummie" with four or five young boys with no attempt to conceal the money. A fight in the alley caused a stampede in which the whole "field" rushed precipitately to the fence to see what was the matter.

At the corner of Blue Island and Forquer we found a lively game of ball between the "Reveres" and the "loogins" (second team) of the "Red Oaks." The first team was rooting lustily for its protégés. A gang of little boys had a camp fire in the alley about which they played in Indian fashion. Their fantastic motions gave us an insight into the imaginative world of adventure in which gang boys often live.

Crossing Halsted on Forquer, we met the "Orioles" playing a game of handball against the wall of a building. Although they had developed great skill in dodging, they were greatly handicapped by the interference of vehicles and pedestrians. In the Dore schoolyard the "Guardian Angel Alley Gang" was playing a similar group at ball. Crawling through a hole in the fence, we found the "Arabian Nights," the "Taylors," and the "Comets." At the conclusion of their play, they sang their paeans of victory, like college "pep" songs.

On our return journey, we met the "Black Circles" playing on the corners of Polk and Halsted. Our final stop was at the clubroom of the "Red Oaks," a newly formed social and athletic club which had purchased the charter and equipment of an older organization. The members were sitting quietly about the room playing cards and talking.[1]

THE GANG AND THE PLAY-GROUP

There is a definite geographical basis for the play-group and the gang in these areas.

In the more crowded sections of the city, the geographical basis of a gang is both sides of the same street for a distance of two blocks. The members are those boys who have played together while their mothers and fathers, as is the custom in those regions, sat in front of their homes and gossiped during the long summer evenings. They know each other as well as brothers or sisters, and as they grow older continue to play together. An investigation showed that groups playing in the schoolyard after school hours are composed of boys living in the vicinity, many of whom do not attend that school during the day. The school is not the basis of this type of gang.

In the less crowded sections where the parks are available, the play-groups which frequent them usually live within a radius of only a few blocks. The whole group has simply transplanted itself to the park. The same thing is true of groups playing on vacant lots: they all come from nearby streets. One may see a group from one section playing against a group from another area, but never parts of two groups from different sections on the same team. From childhood up, members of these play-groups and gangs have been together; they would be in an unnatural atmosphere, were they to play in any other group.[2]

The majority of gangs develop from the spontaneous play-group. As the boys or older fellows of a block or a neighborhood come together in the course of business or pleasure, a crowd, in the sense of a mere gathering of persons, is formed.

The new poolroom which came to the neighborhood was a great attraction to the boys. The beginning of the gang came when the group developed an enmity toward two Greeks who owned a fruit store on the opposite corner. The boys began to steal fruit on a small scale. Finally they attempted to

[1] Observations by the author.
[2] Unpublished study by an experienced boys' worker in gangland.

carry off a large quantity of oranges and bananas which were displayed on the sidewalks, but the Greeks gave chase. This was the signal for a general attack, and the fruit was used as ammunition. The gang had a good start from this episode.[3]

On this basis of interests and aptitudes, a play-group emerges whose activities vary from "hide-and-go-seek" to crap-shooting.

This was a group of about nine boys, whose ages varied from sixteen to twenty years. There were both Protestants and Catholics, some of whom attended school, while others worked. Their hang-out was in the front room of the home of one of the members, whose mother, known as "Aunt Sarah," allowed the boys the freedom of her house. Two of the number were piano-players. The boys sang, jigged, played cards, or just talked. There was no formal organization, no one was considered as leader, but the word of one or two had more weight than that of others. There was a group-consciousness and most of the wishes of the members were met in the bunch; yet there was no antagonism to outsiders; they never intruded. During the years the bunch lasted no new members were taken in. It disintegrated as members grew up and moved away or married.[4]

Such a play-group may acquire a real organization. Natural leaders emerge, a relative standing is assigned to various members and traditions develop. *It does not become a gang, however, until it begins to excite disapproval and opposition, and thus acquires a more definite group-consciousness.* It discovers a rival or an enemy in the gang in the next block; its baseball or football team is pitted against some other team; parents or neighbors look upon it with suspicion or hostility; "the old man around the corner," the storekeepers, or the "cops" begin to give it "shags" (chase it); or some representative of the community steps in and tries to break it up. This is the real beginning of the gang, for now it starts to draw itself more closely together. It becomes a conflict group.

It would be erroneous, however, to suppose that a gang springs immediately from

an ordinary street crowd like Minerva, full-grown from Jove's forehead. The gang has its beginning in acquaintanceship and intimate relations which have already developed on the basis of some common interest. These preliminary bonds may serve to unite pairs or trios among the boys rather than the group as a whole. The so-called "two-boy gang" is often a center to which other boys are attracted and about which they form like a constellation. Thus, the gang may grow by additions of twos and threes as well as of single individuals. The notorious Gloriannas were originally a two-boy gang.

Our gang was the outgrowth of a play-group formed by nine boys living in the same block, who became acquainted through the usual outdoor games. Then we began to meet in Tommy's attic. For greater privacy, we built a shack on the alley where we could temporarily isolate ourselves and smoke without the interference of our parents. When my parents were away, we used our basement for a rendezvous, but we were careful to enter by a window so as to escape the attention of the housekeeper.

This desire to escape family supervision marked the beginning of our feeling of solidarity. Our first loyalties were to protect each other against our parents. Sometimes the latter were regarded with great dislike by the gang. The mother of one of the boys, who was very unkind to him, viewed us with equal hatred and once threw a pan of dishwater on us when we were whistling for our pal.

First it was the gang against the members of our households, and then it was the gang against the neighbors. One Saturday morning when we were playing "ditch," Mrs. Apple called the police and told them that we were molesting her property. It proved that we had only run across her lawn, and the cop laughed and said that she was too crabby to be living.

Our collective enterprises soon gave us the name "Cornell Crowd," but we preferred to call ourselves the "Cornell Athletic Club" or the "C.A.C." We took in only two new members during our six years' existence, but for them we devised a special initiation, copying some of our stunts from the "Penrod and Sam" stories by Tarkington.

Our solidarity was greatly augmented by our clashes with other gangs, whether in raids or

[3] Records of the Juvenile Protective Association.
[4] Unpublished manuscript by an experienced boys' worker in gangland.

football games. On one occasion when we beat the Harper gang at football, the game ended in a free-for-all fight. We licked them, and after that they were much more friendly, even though we continued to raid each other's hang-outs. We formed an alliance with the Dorchester gang against the "Kenwoods," who called us "sissies" and "rich kids," and when the latter stole the stove out of the Dorchester shanty, we joined forces and invaded Fifty-fifth Street to bring it back.

Danger from other gangs was always sufficient to eliminate internal friction and unite us against the common enemy. On one Hallowe'en, two of our members engaged in a fight, and no argument or pulling could get them apart. Just then another gang came along and hit Tommie with a soot bag, whereupon the combatants immediately forgot their quarrel and helped us chase and beat up the invaders.[5]

THE GANG
AND THE FORMAL GROUP

Curiously enough, the gang sometimes develops within a group which is quite different from it in every way. A number of boys, perhaps entire strangers, are brought together by some interested agency and a club is formed. A conventional form of organization is imposed, and activities are directed and supervised. Friendships within the group begin to develop on the basis of common interests and lead to factions and cliques which oppose each other or incur the hostility of the directors. In either case, the clique may serve as the basis for a gang, and its members may begin to meet without supervision at other than the regular times.

A group of Irish, Jewish, and Italian boys were enrolled in classes for dancing and dramatics at the settlement. As a result of the new friendships and activities which developed, the Italian boys soon formed a gang which, although leaderless, held closely together and carried on many exploits outside the settlement, including civil war with rival gangs. A strong group spirit arose, and the loyalty of the members to each other became marked, manifesting itself especially in times of unemployment. The settlement saw its oppor-

tunity and accepted the new group, directing its activities along the lines of hiking and camping.[6]

It often happens that boys expelled either as individuals or as a group from some formal organization are drawn together to form a gang. They have become outlaws, and it is the old story of Robin Hood against the state.

A group of eight boys, who had been associated with a club as individuals from two to five years, were suspended because they broke an agreement not to play other baseball teams for money. Twelve sympathizers left the club and joined the outlaws who with their hangers-on now number about one hundred. They met first in a candy store and later rented a cottage. They play baseball for as much as $100 a game. They plan a basketball team, equipment for which they will buy from proceeds of a raffle and a dance.

Their problem is to get access to a gymnasium; the playgrounds are full.[7]

About twenty Polish boys, "canned" from the settlement, organized a gang that they called the "Corporation." The common object of the group was to do away with the settlement which was notified to this effect. Their hang-out was at a Greek fruit store. Only half of them worked at a time. They shared their spending money but not their earnings. They all tended to work at the same place, quitting as a group. They stole balls from the settlement, broke gymnasium windows, and put fake notices on the bulletin boards, but did not cause any serious trouble. Their other activities were robbing fruit stands, cheap holdups, gambling, and baseball. Some of them saw service in the war, which seemed to steady them. Many of them are now drivers of taxicabs and North Side busses, but they still hang together on the street corners.[8]

In all cases of this type, the function of the common enemy in knitting the gangs together is clearly indicated.

INSTABILITY AND DISINTEGRATION

The ganging process is a continuous flux and flow, and there is little permanence in

[5] Manuscript prepared by a former member of the gang.

[6] Study by a settlement worker (manuscript).
[7] Interview with a club director.
[8] Interview with a settlement worker.

most of the groups. New nuclei are constantly appearing, and the business of coalescing and recoalescing is going on everywhere in the congested areas. Both conflict and competition threaten the embryonic gangs with disintegration. The attention of the individual is often diverted to some new pal or to some other gang that holds more attractions. When delinquency is detected the police break up the group and at least temporarily interrupt its career. Some new activity of settlement, playground, or club frequently depletes its membership.

There were several factors in the break-up of our gang. Two of the members and later others became interested in a boys' club. Dissension then arose because the fellows in the club would not swear and play dice. Mutual dislike came out of this division of interest. Another factor was the building of a Y.M.C.A. on the lot where the gang had its playground.[9]

More often the families of the boys move to other neighborhoods, and unless connections are tenacious the old gang is soon forgotten in alliance with the new. One boy joined an enemy gang when his family moved into hostile territory, because he "did not feel like walking so far."

When we lived on Nineteenth and Paulina, I joined the "Nineteenth Streeters," a gang of twelve or thirteen Polish boys. We would gather wood together, go swimming, or rob the Jews on Twelfth Street. When we moved to Twenty-first and Paulina I joined the "Wood Streeters." It was like this. I met a kid and got in a scrap with him. He got two more kids and tried to lick me. A couple of days later on the way to school the same kid came up and said, "Got any snuff?" "Sure!" "Shake a hand!" "Sure! You're the kid who hit me." Then we were friends, and I joined the gang. Then we moved to Twenty-third and Wood, then to Hoyne, next to a suburb, and finally back to Twenty-third and Wood. At each of these places I usually went with a different gang.[10]

Sometimes a quarrel splits the gang, and the disgruntled faction secedes.

It is interesting to note that marriage is one of the most potent causes for the disin-

tegration of the older groups. The gang is largely an adolescent phenomenon, and where conditions are favorable to its development it occupies a period in the life of the boy between childhood, when he is usually incorporated in a family structure, and marriage, when he is reincorporated into a family and other orderly relations of work, religion, and pleasure. For this reason, the adult gang, unless conventionalized, is comparatively rare and is the result of special selection. From this point of view also, then, the gang appears to be an interstitial group, a manifestation of the period of readjustment between childhood and maturity.

Most gangs are in a condition of unstable equilibrium. Those which endure over a period of years are relatively rare in comparison with the great number of rudimentary forms. It is important to note, however, that the volume of gang life and the sum total of gangs do not change appreciably with changing personnel. With few exceptions, the old gangs are replaced by new ones.

THE ROOTS OF THE GANG

Gangs represent the spontaneous effort of boys to create a society for themselves where none adequate to their needs exists. What boys get out of such association that they do not get otherwise under the conditions that adult society imposes is the thrill and zest of participation in common interests, more especially in corporate action, in hunting, capture, conflict, flight, and escape. Conflict with other gangs and the world about them furnishes the occasion for many of their exciting group activities.

The failure of the normally directing and controlling customs and institutions to function efficiently in the boy's experience is indicated by disintegration of family life, inefficiency of schools, formalism and externality of religion, corruption and indifference in local politics, low wages and monotony in occupational activities, unemployment, and lack of opportunity for

---

[9] Gang boy's own story.
[10] Gang boy's own story.

wholesome recreation. All these factors enter into the picture of the moral and economic frontier, and, coupled with deterioration in housing, sanitation, and other conditions of life in the slum, give the impression of general disorganization and decay.

The gang functions with reference to these conditions in two ways: It offers a substitute for what society fails to give; and it provides a relief from suppression and distasteful behavior. It fills a gap and affords an escape. Here again we may conceive of it as an interstitial group providing interstitial activities for its members. Thus the gang, itself a natural and spontaneous type of organization arising through conflict, is a symptom of disorganization in the larger social framework.

These conclusions, suggested by the present study, seem amply verified by data from other cities in the United States and in other countries.

THE GANG AND THE FRONTIER

That the conception of the gang as a symptom of an economic, moral, and cultural frontier is not merely fanciful and figurative is indicated by the operation of similar groups on other than urban frontiers. The advance of civilization into a wild country is heralded by marauding bands which result both from relaxed social controls and attempts to escape authority. The period before and following the Civil War has been called the "era of banditry," so numerous and so desperate were the outlaw gangs. And what are pirates but "gangs of the seas," which, with some of their lonely or lawless coasts, represent interstitial reaches that fall beyond the scope of organized authority and civil society?[11]

IS THERE A GANG INSTINCT?

The traditional explanation of the gang

and one supported by the older type of individual psychology has been to dismiss gang behavior as due to an instinct. ". . . The gang instinct . . . is a natural characteristic of our social order, and it would be impossible to uproot it or destroy it. . . ."[12] "The gang instinct . . . is recognized in the formation of the small group clubs. . . ."[13] "Somewhere about the age of ten, the little boy . . . begins to develop the gang-forming instinct."[14] These are typical statements of the "gang-instinct" explanation. Other writers consider ganging as a special form of the "social instinct"—a difference in phrasing only.[15]

What writers on the gang have attributed to instinct is the result of pervasive social habits arising out of the human struggle for existence and social preferment. It is apparent also that use of the phrases "gang instinct" or "social instinct" in the passages quoted is made without much attempt at a thoroughgoing analysis of the complex conditions underlying the formation and behavior of the gang.

The gang, as has already been indicated, is a function of specific conditions, and it does not tend to appear in the absence of these conditions. Under other circumstances the boy becomes a "solitary type," enters into a relation of palship or intimacy with one or more other boys in separate pairs, or is incorporated into play-groups of a different sort or into more conventional or older groups. What relationships he has with others are determined by a complex of conditioning factors which direct his interests and his habits. It is not instinct, but experience—the way he is conditioned—that fixes his social relations.

11 The first known use of the term gang in the English language in the common disparaging sense

was with reference to pirates (1623). See Murray's A New English Dictionary (Oxford).
12 Franklin Chase Hoyt, Quicksands of Youth, p. 170.
13 Annual Report, Chicago Commons, 1919, p. 19.
14 J. Adams Puffer, The Boy and His Gang, p. 72.
15 N. E. Richardson and O. E. Loomis, The Boy Scout Movement Applied by the Church, pp. 206–7.

SOCIAL STRUCTURE AND GROUP PROCESSES IN GANG DELINQUENCY*

James F. Short, Jr.

Reported below are some of the findings from a study of delinquent gangs in Chicago. Short first considers some of the theoretical issues regarding gang delinquency. He then considers the existence of varieties of delinquent subcultures. The relationship between community structure and delinquency is mentioned. Finally the social disability *hypothesis is advanced for further understanding of gang delinquency.*

While this paper draws heavily on the work of others, both theoretical and empirical, I shall be most concerned with data from an ongoing study of delinquent gangs in Chicago with which I have been associated since the fall of 1958.[1] At that time, the YMCA of metropolitan Chicago and the Department of Sociology at the University of Chicago brought together several academicians. Lay and professional leaders of the YMCA met with us also and made important contributions and commitments to the action-research collaboration which emerged. At that meeting the academicians were encouraged to present and argue about alternative theoretical positions and their implications for research design and for possibilities of working with the new Y program. The others doubtless were curious to know what research and theory had to say about problems which they considered most pressing, and whether, after all, academicians might have some contribution to make to action problems. That conference was the springboard for our action-research program of

considerable proportions, with very generous foundation, university, and YMCA support.

The notion of varieties of delinquent subcultures provided the basis for research design of the Chicago research concerning "street corner groups and patterns of delinquency."[2] Theoretical focus was derived from Cohen's *Delinquent Boys*, from Cloward and Ohlin's *Delinquency and Opportunity*, from Walter Miller's thesis of lower class culture as the "Generating Milieu of Gang Delinquency,"[3] and from our own determination, at first only vaguely formulated, to keep a window open on the gangs in order to gather data on group processes, and later to study characteristics of individual gang members as well as the cultural and social structural data implied by the other theories. I will summarize our research procedures and findings rather than

[1] A more complete report of this research will be found in James F. Short, Jr., and Fred L. Strodtbeck, *Group Process and Gang Delinquency*, Chicago: University of Chicago Press, 1965; several other papers are footnoted at later points in this paper.

[2] James F. Short, Jr., "Street Corner Groups and Patterns of Delinquency: A Progress Report," *American Catholic Sociological Review*, 24 (March 1963), pp. 13–32.

[3] Albert K. Cohen, *Delinquent Boys: The Culture of the Gang*, New York: The Free Press of Glencoe, 1955; Richard A. Cloward and Lloyd E. Ohlin, *Delinquency and Opportunity*, New York: The Free Press of Glencoe, 1960; and Walter B. Miller, "Lower Class Culture as a Generating Milieu of Gang Delinquency," *Journal of Social Issues*, 24 (No. 3, 1958), pp. 5–19.

* This selection is adapted from a paper presented at a social psychology symposium, University of Oklahoma, 1964, by permission of the author. The original paper is published in Muzafer Sherif and Carolyn W. Sherif (eds.), *Problems of Youth: Transition to Adulthood in a Changing World*, Chicago: Adline Publishing Company, 1965, by permission of the publisher and the editors.

present detailed data on these myriad matters. The synthesis which I shall attempt must be seen as an approximation, based on data at hand, from our own work and from the work of others, and subject, of course, to revision in the process of successive approximations to reality which is the hallmark of the scientific endeavor.

I will bring to bear findings from a considerable variety of data generation procedures, including field observation by members of the research team as well as by detached workers, ratings on the basis of such observation, interviews with gang boys, workers, and local community adults, paper and pencil instruments, and laboratory assessments of gang boys carried out under carefully controlled conditions. With the exception of field observations, data were gathered on nongang boys from the gang neighborhoods and on middle class youngsters as well as gang boys, for comparative purposes. We have studied Negro and white boys in each of these categories.

FROM SOCIAL STRUCTURE TO GANG DELINQUENCY: AN INTERPRETATION

In the interest of clarity of organization and intent, I will first summarize some notions about the classes of variables and the nature of their relation to one another, which, on the basis of our research, appear to be involved in the "translation" of social structure into gang delinquency (and at least some other forms of "deviant" behavior).

Realities of social structure such as class and ethnic differentiation and the operation of ecological processes place severe limitations on the realization of cultural universals such as the high value placed on material wealth and status achievement in important institutional contexts such as school and the world of work. At the individual level, failure to achieve these goals begins early in life for many lower class and ethnically disadvantaged persons, because of socialization practices which are defective in

terms of the criteria of achievement of the larger society. This process is complicated by the existence of subcultures with distinctive ethnic and lower class characteristics, and by youth subcultures, some of which are delinquent in a variety of ways. These subcultures have both historical and contemporary roots. They serve both to insulate their adherents from experiences which might make possible achievement of many "respectable" goals in terms of "respectable" criteria for their achievement, and to compensate in some measure for failure, or the likelihood of failure, in these areas. Indeed, the latter appears to be one of the chief functions of peer group participation in every strata of society and at every age.

Important *goals* of the larger society are quite successfully communicated, as Merton suggests.[4] So, also, are values concerning legitimate means for their achievement. Evidence from a variety of sources, for example, the Flint Youth Study and our own, suggests that disadvantaged youngsters do not become alienated, that even the gang ethic is not one of "reaction formation" *against* widely shared values in society.[5]

Peer groups in the lower class come often to serve important *status functions* for youngsters who are disadvantaged with respect to success criteria of the larger society as these are institutionalized in the form of schools, churches, places of business, and so on. Peer groups become the most salient status universe of such youngsters. Group norms and values come to stress means of achievement which are not prescribed by conventional norms and values, which in effect provide alternative means of achievement for group members. Delinquency arises sometimes as a by-product and sometimes as a direct product of peer group activity.

The groups and institutions which are the primary carriers of lower class, ethnic,

[4] Robert K. Merton, *Social Theory and Social Structure*, rev. ed., New York: The Free Press of Glencoe, 1957.
[5] See Martin Gold, *Status Forces in Delinquent Boys*, Ann Arbor, Mich.: Institute for Social Research, 1963.

and delinquent subcultures are marked in many cases by instability and by a high incidence of physical objects and social situations which combine to create high risk of involvement in delinquency. One need only mention the public nature of drinking and "party" behavior, shifting sexual and economic liaisons, a high incidence of guns and the acceptance of violence as a means of settling disputes as available elements for such situations.

There is evidence that the gang is less solidary and less satisfactory to its participants as a source of gratification than nostalgic accounts of "that old gang of mine" suggest. There is evidence, too, that the "lack of social assurance" which Whyte attributed to his corner boys is especially aggravated among these seriously delinquent youngsters, and that they are characterized by other social disabilities which contribute to delinquency-producing status threats within and outside the gang.[6]

Though evidence from our own study is incompletely analyzed, such measures as we have been able to obtain of social structural variables (such as race, class, and gang status, some, but not all, measures of "position discontent," and perceptions of opportunity structures), and of individual social disabilities (such as negative self-concept and low intelligence) are found to order the race, by class, by gang status groups in much the same way as their delinquency rates, but they are not highly correlated with individual behavior in the group context. That is, these variables generally are not predictive of behavioral variations of individual gang members. It is insufficient, in accounting for this finding, simply to regard the group as a catalyst, releasing potentials for delinquency not readily apparent from knowledge of characteristics of participating individuals. We have looked for specific group processes

and mechanisms which are involved in delinquency episodes as a means of further specifying the relation between the group and the behavior of its members. Three of these have been suggested in our recent work:

(1) *Reactions to status threats.* When gang boys perceive threats to some valued status, delinquency often follows.[7] This mechanism has been found to operate in response to perceived threats to leadership status, to a boy's status as a male, as a member of a particular gang, as an aspiring adult. It may operate individually or collectively, though the delinquent solution characteristically involves other members of the group. Why status threats should produce delinquency episodes doubtless is a very complex matter, but we have observed several characteristics of gang boys and their social worlds which apparently are related to this mechanism. There is, first of all, the lack among gangs of formal structure which lends itself to group continuity and stability. There is further the lack of institutionalized support in adversity which characterizes more formal organizations such as voluntary associations, schools, churches, businesses, and governments. At a more individual level, leaders are able to control few resources of crucial value to the group and so their own ability to dominate the group by internally directed aggression is severely restricted. Gang members tend to lack social skills which might permit them to meet status threats in more creative, less delinquent ways. At the group level, delinquent actions often are acceptable, if not generally prescribed by, group norms. They constitute a sort of "least common denominator" around which members can rally. Finally, externally directed delinquency, particularly of an aggressive nature, serves to unify these loosely structured groups in common cause. Indeed, the latter appears to operate not

[6] Cf. William Foote Whyte, *Street Corner Society: The Social Structure of an Italian Slum*, Chicago: University of Chicago Press, 1943; Robert A. Gordon "Social Level, Social Disability, and Gang Interaction," unpublished paper; and Chap. 10 in Short and Strodtbeck.

[7] See James F. Short, Jr., and Fred L. Strodtbeck, "The Response of Gang Leaders to Status Threats: An Observation on Group Process and Delinquent Behavior," *American Journal of Sociology*, 68 (March 1963), pp. 571–579.

only in conjunction with status threats, but independently, as a basic mechanism accounting for delinquency involvement by these youngsters.[8] The point will be further developed at a later point in the chapter.

(2) *The gamble of status v. punishment risk.* In the calculus of decision making, status rewards within the group often tip the scales toward "joining the action," and therefore becoming involved in delinquency, when the chief *risk* in such behavior appears to be the probability of punishment at the hands of a society which seems disinterested in one's personal fate.[9] Episodes which seem to reflect simply a hedonistic orientation to life thus may be seen to involve a rational assessment of probabilities with the resultant decision to risk the consequences of joining the action, going along with the boys, and so on. The decision is understandable in view of the low risk of serious consequences associated with most delinquency episodes, and the somewhat higher probability of associated group rewards consequent to joining the action—the affirmation of friendship bonds, status accruals from performance in an episode, personal satisfaction derived from demonstration of toughness, masculinity, and the like.

(3) *The discharge of group role obligations.* As obvious examples, a leader may be *required* to "join the action," or even to precipitate it, given a situation involving group threat; a "war counselor" is required to perform when gang conflict appears imminent or is engaged. Centrality in the group, or striving toward this goal, exposes one to involvement in situations with a high "delinquency potential," by means of the previously discussed mechanisms, including those associated with specific roles in the group. Thus, an apparent paradox in our self-concept data may be resolved. As reported elsewhere, boys who describe them-

selves in "scoutlike" terms (loyal, polite, helpful, religious, obedient) are more involved in conflict behavior than are boys who describe themselves as "cool aggressives" (mean, tough, troublesome, and cool).[10] Our interpretation rests upon the connotation of *responsibility* in personal relations and recognition of their implied obligations, characteristic of the scout terms; this, in contrast with cool aggressive terms, each of which carries overtones of disruption or disregard of obligations to associates, or to convention, and of a type of detachment which is the antithesis of reciprocity in personal relations. The scouts, we believe, facilitate cohesive relations and reduce interpersonal tensions in these loosely structured groups. This, in turn, enhances their centrality in the group and so exposes them to situations in which role expectations, status threats, and potential rewards associated with joining the action make more likely their involvement in episodes of aggression.

BEHAVIOR PATTERNS: SUBCULTURES?

Turning now to behavioral variations among gang boys, we may assess behavior patterns in terms of various proposed delinquent subcultures. From the beginning of the study we had been impressed by the lack of "purity" of the hypothesized types, despite the fact that our selection of gangs, with the full cooperation of the YMCA detached workers, was oriented toward obtaining the best possible representatives of the three most discussed types in the literature, viz., conflict, criminal, and retreatist. Negro conflict gangs were plentiful, but they were involved also in a great deal of stealing, and we were unable to locate a real criminal gang, despite our determined and prolonged effort to do so. We did find occasional cliques or other subunits within larger gangs which engaged in special criminal activities, for example, systematic theft or strong-arm-

[8] Gordon.

[9] See Fred L. Strodtbeck and James F. Short, Jr., "Aleatory Risks v. Short-Run Hedonism in Explanation of Gang Action," *Social Problems,* 12 (Fall 1964).

[10] Short and Strodtbeck, *Group Process,* Chap. 7.

ing. In one group there was a clique of "winos," and several had "singing" cliques. After a full year of investigation we located what appeared to be a genuine retreatist group. It became clear that the subcultural emphases specified in the literature were not as exclusive as their descriptions in the literature suggested. Our factor analysis of detached worker ratings isolated a conflict pattern, and a combination of drug use, homosexuality, common-law marriage, attempted suicide, and pimping which we could label as retreatist, but no criminal factor was found. Neither conflict nor retreatism characterized exclusively any one of the gangs under study. Other activities emerged also as factors and blended into the behavior patterning of these boys, for example, stable corner boy activities, heterosexual behavior, and an "authority protest" factor involving chiefly auto theft, truancy, running away from home, vandalism, and creating public disturbance.[11] The *simplicity* of subcultural patterns described clearly was challenged by these data, if not their hypothesized etiology.

Field observation, coupled with systematic measures of the values of the boys by means of a semantic differential, indicated that gang boys' commitment to delinquent norms was quite tenuous,[12] indeed, virtually nonexistent except in specific types of situations which involved the group, such as threat to the group from another gang, or, in some instances, threats to the status of boys individually. Analysis of behavior patterns and self-concept measures suggested that the gangs contained considerable numbers of stable "corner boys" and even a few "college boys"; there were "scouts" as well as "cool aggressives" within the same gang. This led us to question the homogeneity of gangs as well as the degree of

normative commitment which the gang places on its members.

Yet there was within each of these gangs a shared attitude, and often this was shared as well with members of other groups. For some gangs, in contrast with others, conflict with other gangs was a major focus of group activity and a source of considerable status within the gang. These gangs more often than others engaged in a variety of violent episodes in addition to gang conflict. Those gangs were *invested* in their reputation for fighting. The "boundaries" of their concern for such a "rep" are not clear. We know it includes other fighting gangs, but there is evidence, also, that it includes a much broader public. Members of such gangs often evidenced great pride when the mass media took note of their activities, even though the notices often were derogatory. A prominent member of one such gang compiled a scrapbook filled with newspaper articles featuring his gang. Gang boys at first would be suspicious and ambivalent about having newsmen follow them around in search of a story, but to the best of my knowledge reporters never experienced prolonged difficulty, and willing informants were always at hand.

Conflict gangs created roles expressive of their conflict orientation, thus differing in structure from other gangs. Such positions as "war counselor" and "armorer" were jealously guarded, even though the duties and privileges of office were rarely defined in a formal way. These roles served as a focus of ceremonial deference within the group, and they provided still another basis for individual status and for group identity. The nature of the "guerrilla warfare" typical of these groups, and its function for the participants is dramatically portrayed by a detached worker's report of a minor skirmish between the Knights and the Vice Kings, two groups which had been feuding for some months:[13]

. . . [I] was sitting there talking to the Knights . . . re-emphasizing my stand on

[11] James F. Short, Jr., Ray A. Tennyson, and Kenneth I. Howard, "Behavior Dimensions of Gang Delinquency," *American Sociological Review*, 28 (June 1963), pp. 412–428.

[12] See James F. Short, Jr., Fred L. Strodtbeck, and Desmond S. Cartwright, "A Strategy for Utilizing Research Dilemmas: A Case from the Study of Parenthood in a Street Corner Gang," *Sociological Inquiry*, 32 (Spring 1962), pp. 185–202.

[13] The case and commentary are taken from Short and Strodtbeck, *Group Process*, Chap. 9.

guns, because they told me that they had collected quite a few and were waiting for the Vice Kings to come down and start some trouble . . . I told them flatly that it was better that I got the gun rather than the police, and though they agreed with me, they repeated their stand that they were tired of running from the Vice Kings and that if they gave them trouble, from now on they were fighting back.

. . . while I was sitting there in the car talking to William (the remaining guys having gotten out of the car in pursuit of some girls around the corner), William told me that a couple of Vice Kings were approaching. I looked out the window and noticed two Vice Kings and two girls walking down the street by the car. . . . William then turned around and made the observation that there were about fifteen or twenty Vice Kings across the street in the alley and wandering up the street in ones and twos.

At this point, I heard three shots go off. I don't know who fired these shots, and no one else seemed to know, because the Vice Kings at this point had encountered Commando, Jones, and a couple of other Knights who were coming from around the corner talking to the girls. The Vice Kings yelled across the street to Commando and his boys, and Commando yelled back. They traded insults and challenges, Commando being the leader of the Knights and a guy named Bear being the leader of the Vice Kings. . . . I got out of the car to try to cool Commando down, inasmuch as he was halfway across the street hurling insults across the street and daring them to do something about it, and they were doing the same thing to him. I grabbed Commando and began to pull him back across the street.

By this time the Vice Kings had worked themselves into a rage, and three of them came across the street yelling that they were mighty Vice Kings and [were going] to attack Commando and the Knights. In trying to break this up, I was not too successful. I didn't know the Vice Kings involved, and they were really determined to swing on the Knights, so we had a little scuffle around there. . . . At this point, along the street comes Henry Brown, with a revolver, shooting at the Vice Kings. Everybody ducked and the Vice Kings ran, and Henry Brown ran around the corner. When he ran around the corner I began to throw Knights into my car because I knew that the area was "hot," and I was trying to get them

out of there. Henry Brown came back around the corner and leaped into my car also. I asked him if he had the gun, and he told me that he did not, and since I was in a hurry, I pulled off in the car and took him and the rest of the boys with me.

* * *

In the car Commando and the other boys were extremely elated. There were expressions like: "Baby, did you see the way I swung on that kid"; "Man, did we tell them off"; "I really let that one kid have it"; "Did you see them take off when I leveled my gun on them"; "You were great, Baby. And did you see the way I . . . ," etc. It was just like we used to feel when we got back from a patrol where everything went just right [the worker had been a paratrooper in the Korean conflict]. The tension was relieved, we had performed well and could be proud.

"Here," as we say in Chapter 9 of *Group Process*, "the status function of the conflict subculture is seen in bold relief. No doubt the Vice Kings, too, felt the thrill of the conflict. They had faced great danger and had a perfect alibi for not winning an unequivocal victory, namely, the fact that the opposition had a gun—and so, of course, did the Knights, for the worker intervened to prevent them from following up their advantage. Thus, participants on both sides of such a conflict can share the elation and the status-conferring glow of an encounter such as this. It is, in effect, *not* a 'zero-sum game' in the sense that points won by a party to the conflict are not necessarily lost by his adversary. No one need necessarily be defeated; behavior in conformity with the norms of the subculture takes place and is rewarded, and law and order are restored. In this way society, too, shares in this non-zero-sum game. Lest we be accused of too sanguine a view of gang behavior, we note that boys may be defeated, individually and collectively, and much injury and property damage may and often does result from this 'game.'"

We know from study of numerous incidents that not all members of conflict gangs participated in such skirmishes even though they may have been on the scene.

We do not fully understand why this is the case, in part because much of the analysis to this point has not concerned intergang differences, and the focus of that which has is on hypothesis formation rather than testing, and on illustration rather than demonstration. Our suspicion, however, is that boys who are involved at any one time are those who are most heavily committed to the gang at the moment, usually gang leaders or other boys who aspire to prominence in the gang. Outstanding performance on such occasions is one of the few avenues to achievement of real prominence which is open in gangs such as these, for reasons which we shall note presently.

So much for conflict. What of retreatism? The contrast between our one group of retreatists and all other gangs under observation was striking. I quote from an earlier description of these young men:[14]

. . . The basis of camaraderie among the drug users was their common interest in kicks. Past and present exploits concerned experiences while high, and "crazy" behavior rather than bravery or toughness. Use of pills and other drugs seemed virtually a way of life with these boys, interspersed with other kicks such as sex, alcohol, and "way out" experiences which distinguished them, individually and collectively. After several observations of this group in their area, a member of the research team reported:

"The guys make continual references to dope. They talk about it much as a group of drinkers might talk about liquor. It comes up freely, easily in the conversation, a couple of remarks are made about it, who's taken it recently, how it affected this or that person, etc., and then it is dropped only to come up again before long. Today the guys made comments about dope and baseball. (You get the feeling that whatever the activity of the moment, the guys will talk about it in relation to dope—how taking dope affects their participation in the activity.) A commonly expressed notion was that so and so played baseball better when he was 'high' than at any other time. Whether they believed this was hard to tell. It sounded much like oft heard remarks that 'I play poker better when I'm half drunk or high.' (i.e. remarks made in the com-

munity at large). . . . The guys like to talk about their 'highs,' how much they have taken, how high they were, what they did while high, etc. . . . Perhaps one attitude is implicitly expressed, though, in these remarks; the attitude of acceptance."

Five months later this same observer reported on a hanging session in which the group related "tales about some of the crazy and humorous things" in which various of the drug users had been involved.

The relating of these tales was greeted by laughter from all. Often the worker or observer would mention an incident and Butch would fill us in or correct us on details. Some of the incidents mentioned:

1. The time Willie was so high he walked off a roof and fell a story or two and broke his nose. . . . Butch said it was over a week before he went to the doctor. . . . Harry said he walked around the hospital in a crazy looking green coat whenever the guys went to visit him.
2. The time Snooks, Baby, and Jerry climbed on a roof to wake Elizabeth. One of the guys reached through the window and grabbed what he thought was Elizabeth's leg and shook it to wake her up. It turned out to be her old man's leg and it woke him up.
3. The more recent incident in which Sonny leaped over the counter to rob a Chinaman who proceeded to beat him badly. When the police came, Sonny asked that they arrest this man for having beaten him so. He was doped out of his mind and didn't know what was happening.
4. Walter got into an argument with a woman over whose car it was they were standing by. He insisted they call the police, and waited confidently until the police showed and took him away.
5. Sonny tried to break into a building and was ripping off a door when the police found him.
6. Some of the guys slept out in a car and woke the next morning to find the car was being pulled away. They asked the tower to stop just long enough so they could get out.
7. One of the guys broke into a car and just about tore the door off doing so—this was a car with all the windows broken out—he was too high to notice.
8. One of the boys tried to start a car but just could not manage it. The car had no motor.

[14] Short and Strodtbeck, Group Process, Chap. 9.

All laughed at these true tales. Butch even

noted that he had been with the guy who broke into the car with no windows.

[The observer then remarked] "These tales may be in the process of becoming legendary within the group. They are so characteristic of this group and describe it so well."

Though several of these boys had "grown up" together, they were not bound to each other by feelings of loyalty. Virtually their only common bond appeared to be use of drugs and the type of experiences which are recounted above. They did not really *share* drugs. Every boy was expected to "cop" (purchase drugs) on his own. In a peculiar way this was functional to the group, for although all of the boys who were financially and otherwise able to do so would get high, seldom were more than a few heavily under the influence of drugs at any one time. They liked to get high together, but boys who were not high appeared to enjoy the antics of others who were. They were really quite individualistic in their pursuit of kicks. Often the worker would find a boy off by himself, or with a girl friend or perhaps one other member. But these were not stable friendships. The group served the function of a sounding board for their common but individualistic interests— of moral support for a way of life.

Finally, we may describe briefly the most clearly criminal group of boys we were able to locate, a clique of eight boys in a larger number of loosely related "hanging groups" who coalesced sporadically and in widely varying numbers for activities such as drinking, athletic contests, occasional drug use, driving around in cars, general "roughnecking" and "hell raising," and once in a great while, a fight of major proportions. According to the leader of the criminal clique, these boys had joined together specifically and exclusively for the purpose of promoting theft activities.[15]

. . . They were engaged in extensive auto stripping, burglary, and shoplifting—no "heavy stuff" such as strong-arming, robbery, or shakedown. The boys hung on the corner with the larger group, and when they did so were in no way distinguishable from this larger group. They were a clique only when they met away from the larger group, usually in each other's homes, to discuss and plan their theft activi-

ties. According to the worker assigned to these boys, "Bobby and his guys talk about what they are doing in one room, while Bobby's old man, who used to be some sort of wheel in the syndicate, talks to his friends about the 'old days' in the next room." The boys made it a point not to "clique-up" visibly on the street, and apparently their chief motivation for association with one another was the success of their predatory activities. In this way they were quite successful for a period of approximately two years. There is testimony that Bobby, in particular, enjoyed a considerable degree of police immunity.

In each of these instances, representing extremes of "specialization" in delinquency orientation, I believe the term "delinquent subculture," or some variant, is appropriate, but not sufficient to explain the behavior of the members of the groups. Similarly, for less specialized but highly involved groups, I believe their behavior is more easily understood in terms of subcultural participation. Norms are generated by the group, and there are many shared activities and attitudes among participants which, so far as group members are concerned, are the unique possession of the carriers of a particular subculture, though the boundaries of participation often transcend a particular group. Characteristically, the group effectively constrains individual members from expression of conventional "middle class" values, by derision of such attempts as may be made, and by espousing alternative (rather than "anti") values such as toughness, sexual prowess, being "sharp" or "cool," and so forth. Specific examples from our data include the merciless kidding of youngsters who attempt serious discussion of such matters as responsible family relations and future aspirations in this regard,[16] occupational and educational hopes and problems.[17] Yet these boys remain troubled and ambivalent about many of these problems, and their mention does not always meet with derisive or invidious comment relative to other goals and activities. Even when

[15] Short and Strodtbeck, *Group Process*, Chap. 9.

[16] Short, Strodtbeck, and Cartwright.
[17] Short and Strodtbeck, *Group Process*, Chap. 13.

serious comment is entertained, however, it is not likely to be helpful to the youngsters, for their experiences, individually and in common, rarely are such as to provide a basis for solutions or realistic hopes. Delinquent subcultures do not minister directly to these concerns. Instead they deal with alternatives in the search for gratifications of association and status in many dimensions, and in some measure, we believe, as compensation for rebuffs in more conventional institutional contexts and perhaps for relatively poor prospects of future achievement in the conventional world.

I do not believe these and perhaps other characteristics of the groups can be portrayed adequately without the subculture concept. Yet these characteristics are not adequate to explain the behavior of the boys unless other processes are incorporated into the notion of subcultures, chief among them the characteristics of individual gang boys, group mechanisms such as are discussed above, and the nature of lower class "institutions" which we now examine briefly.

LOWER CLASS INSTITUTIONS AS A GENERATING MILIEU OF GANG DELINQUENCY

In thus paraphrasing Walter Miller's rich and provocative treatment of lower class culture in relation to delinquency, the intention is to focus on organizational forms of association within lower class communities and the manner in which they are related to delinquency causation.[18] The nature of this relation goes beyond, but is intimately related to gang delinquency.

William Foote Whyte's brilliant depiction of significant features of *organization* in the slum which was Cornerville dispelled many false notions that blighted areas lacked organization.[19] From Doc and the Nortons, through the police and the racket, politics, the church, and "old country" ties, Whyte

demonstrated that Cornerville was organized by means of "a hierarchy of personal relations based upon a system of reciprocal obligations."[20] In the treatment which follows we will focus on organizational forms which are even less formally structured, and less "conventional" in orientation, than are those suggested by Whyte. Even in Cornerville it is clear that social organization was conducive to some types of behavior considered "deviant" by conventional standards—police and political corruption, gambling, exploitation of sexually available girls. The "institutions" to which I shall direct attention appear to lack the commitment to ethnic values and to community welfare which characterized Cornerville and the constraining features which are entailed in such commitments. They appear instead to be motivated by more "elemental," personal, and immediate goals, perhaps in part because the future holds little promie. The rewards they provide in many cases are shortlived but concrete, unstable but compelling and available. The contrast with Whyte's classic treatment is important, for I will be discussing institutions characteristic of a different ethnic subculture (I will focus on lower class Negro communities), and of persons more deeply embedded in poverty than were the residents of Cornerville. As was the case in Cornerville, however, these forms of association are recurrent, they have structure, and they are functional in a variety of ways to clientele. The variety of their functions provides an added dimension to youth problems, inasmuch as both youth and adults often are involved. Although the literature contains no systematic treatment of lower class institutions, as such, there are descriptions of various lower class ethnic communities which are rich and suggestive in this regard.[21] Since our concern is with juvenile delinquency, we will omit discus-

---

[18] Cf. Miller.
[19] Whyte.

[20] Whyte, p. 272; he was not the first to call attention to these forms of organization. See, e.g., the volumes by Shaw and McKay.
[21] St. Clair Drake and Horace R. Cayton, *Black Metropolis*, New York: Harcourt, Brace & World, Inc., 1945.

sion of institutions in which the clientele is primarily adult, such as store-front churches.

The type of institution with which we are primarily concerned is cogently revealed by the response of a detached worker to a question posed by the Director of the YMCA program with which the Chicago study of "Street Corner Groups and Patterns of Delinquency" was associated. The director (R. W. Boone) posed this question to the staff: "What are the most significant institutions for your boys [members of gangs with which the program was in contact]?" He had explained briefly the concept of institutions as recurrent forms of association which satisfy important needs of participants and which have recognizable structure. The detached worker who first answered the question deliberated briefly, then said slowly:

I guess I'd have to say the gang, the hangouts, drinking, parties in the area, and the police.

The other workers nodded assent, though a few thought they might want to add the boys' families. Certainly this list is not definitive, but it is instructive. The only reference to a conventional institution is the police, and this was clearly a negative association, an antagonistic link with the conventional world of social control associated with political and economic institutions. No reference was made to the school or the church, and the family received only halfhearted acknowledgment. The "institutions" listed, with the exception of the police, have much in common, for adults as well as adolescents. They call to mind Drake and Cayton's description of "The World of the Lower Class":

Lower-class people will *publicly* drink and play cards in places where people of higher status would lose their "reputations"—in the rear of poolrooms, in the backrooms of taverns, in "buffet-flats," and sometimes on street corners and in alleys. They will "dance on the dime" and "grind" around the juke-box in taverns and joints, or "cut a rug" at the larger public dance halls. They will "clown" on a street corner or in public parks.[22]

It is in such settings that much illicit behavior is encouraged:

These centers of lower-class congregation and festivity often become points of contact between the purveyors of pleasure "on the illegit" and their clientele—casual prostitutes, bootleggers, reefer peddlers, "pimps," and "freaks." Some of these places are merely "fronts" and "blinds" for the organized underworld.

The relation between institutions of this sort and delinquent behavior goes much beyond the contact they afford between illegitimate "purveyors of pleasure" and their potential clientele, however. It is in such settings that much behavior occurs which is disruptive of both the larger social order and the local community because of threats to basic values of life and property. Of particular concern are episodes of violence which result in serious injury, death, or property destruction, the threat of which is ever present in situations ranging from the shifting liaisons of common-law marriage to more elaborate but even less formally structured quarter parties, pool halls, and street corners. Drake and Cayton provide an apt example of the former in their portrayal of the trials and tribulations of Baby Chile and Ben which, for them, provided such a beautiful vehicle for contrasting styles of life among lower and middle (professional) class Negroes in "Black Metropolis."[23]

The latter are the subject of more extended treatment in *Group Process*.[24] For the present I will limit myself to discussion of "quarter parties," as revealed by detached workers from the Chicago project. The case materials presented are particularly instructive concerning the structure and functions of such gatherings in a lower class Negro community, home of the King Rattlers, a tough Negro group known throughout the city for their prowess as gang fighters, strong-

22 Drake and Cayton, p. 610.
23 Drake and Cayton, pp. 567–570.
24 Short and Strodtbeck, *Group Process*, Chap. 5.

armers, and purse snatchers. "Quarter parties" are regular events in this and in many other such communities. While there are variations in format and in composition of participants, there are common objectives to all such varieties. Typically, an adult will hold the party in his or her (usually her) home, for adults, teens, and usually some of both. The objective of the hostess is to make money. (In Seattle, I am told, such gatherings are called "rent parties.") Party goers pay a quarter to get into the party, and a quarter per drink after they are in. The parties are boisterous, loud, and crowded. Fights are not unusual—often they involve members of rival gangs. Two examples, one of the type of "body punching" which is so common among these lower class groups, and one of relations with girls, suffice to illustrate the manner in which these gatherings may precipitate serious gang conflict. In both instances, intervention by a detached worker appears to have averted serious consequences.[25]

A. . . . This teenage party that was held at this girl's house on 10th and Harwood. Her mother and father were there, although they stayed out of the way. There was friction. The Rattlers were there, and then there were some boys from the projects just west of the area [members of a rival gang known as Navahoes]. They weren't in the Rattlers. David and Donald, Duke's brother, took me down. It was a pay-at-the-door party. Pay a quarter at the door. Right away when I got in I knew there was friction because there was this one group of boys in one room and another group in another. I saw several bumpings as they came through the door and looks, "Stay out of my way." They were trying to see how much each group would take. They had three rooms occupied. Living room, dining room, and kitchen. I was in the dining room around 10:00, I guess. I heard this noise in the living room. Right away everyone started running for the living room. There's a fight out there. I started out and tried to get through the crowd to get into the living room, and just as I was fighting my way through the crowd I saw one of my boys, Bill, he's

16—very big though for his age. . . . He and this other fellow from the projects— it started out as these things usually do —they had started out boxing at a party. Bill had hit the other fellow a little too hard and he had hit back, and it led to that. This other fellow was much smaller than Bill but he was older, and he hit Bill and knocked him into this huge window, and *plang*, the window went out. By this time I saw my way through the crowd and I stopped them. . . . David helped me break it up. They respect him. . . . He grabbed the other fellow. Nobody bothers him. I just got between them and told Bill to stop. Bill said, okay. . . . He was coming back for the boy, though, after he broke the window, and he's a big boy. The other fellow stopped right away.

Q. Party go on?
A. No, the lady said this was it. But I thought there might be a little trouble 'cause some of the other boys from the projects were waiting outside, so I told Bill to stick close to me and we would leave together. Bill, myself, and Donald. This we did. The other boys were standing outside. They made a few remarks but they didn't do anything.

Two weeks later this same worker provided a more elaborate picture of a similar party in which adults played a major role. Here the objectives of various classes of party goers is commented on.[26]

This woman who is called "Ma" was giving the party. . . . There was a lot of drinking— inside, outside, in the cars, in the alleys, everywhere. There were Rattlers and a bunch of boys from the (housing) projects. They had two rooms, neither of them very large. There was some friction going on when I got there— boys bumping each other, and stuff like this.

There were a lot of girls there. Must have been about 50 to 75 people in these two rooms, plus another 20 or 25 outside. There were some older fellows there, too—mainly to try and grab one of these younger girls. The girls were doing a lot of drinking—young girls, 12- and 13-year-olds. This one girl, shortly after I got there, had passed out. I took her home. Nobody there, but two of the other girls stayed with her.

The age group in this party amazed me—

25 Interview, 1/13/61 (Dillard).

26 This case is reported in Short and Strodtbeck, *Group Process*, Chap. 5.

must have been from about 11 to the 30's. There were girls there as young as 11, but no boys younger than about 15. The girls are there as a sex attraction, and with the older boys and men around, you know the younger boys aren't going to do any good.

We had one real fight. One of David's sisters was talking to one of these boys from the projects—a good sized boy, bigger than me. I guess she promised to go out to the car with him. . . . To get outside you had to go out this door and down this hall, and then out on the porch and down the stairs. She went as far as the porch. As she got out there, I guess she changed her mind. By this time the guy wasn't standing for any "changing the mind" business, and he started to pull on her—to try and get her in the car. She yelled for David, and he came running out. All he could see was his sister and a guy he didn't know was pulling on her. David plowed right into the guy. I guess he hit him about 15 times and knocked him down and across the street, and by the time I got there the guy was lying in the gutter. David was just about to level a foot at him. I yelled at David to stop and he did. I took him off to the side and told Gary to get the guy out of there.

The worker walked down the street with David, trying to cool him down. What happened next very nearly precipitated a major gang conflict:

Duke, Red, and Mac were standing eight or ten feet away, sort of watching these project boys. This one boy goes up the street on the other side and comes up *behind* David and me. We don't see him. All of a sudden Duke runs right past me. I was wondering what's going on and he plows into this guy— crashed the side of his mouth and the guy fell flat. Duke was about to really work the guy over. . . .

Duke said, "Well look, man, the guy was sneaking up behind you. I wasn't gonna have him hit you from behind! I did it to protect you."

I got the guy up and he said, "I wasn't going to hit you—I just wanted to see what was going on," and this bit.

By now Duke says, "Well, the heck with it. Let's run all these project guys out."

They banded together and were ready to move, but I talked them out of it. I said,

"Look, don't you think you've done enough? The police aren't here yet, but if you start anything else they'll be here. Somebody is bound to call them. The party is still going on so why don't we all just go back inside. No sense in breaking up a good thing—you paid your quarter."

I finally got them all back inside, but Duke says, "We've been laying off fighting for the last year or so. Looks like we'll have to start again."

Other examples could be given involving explicitly many forms of behavior considered delinquent by the larger society, such as fighting, extensive property damage, excessive drinking, illicit sex (violent and nonviolent), drug use, disturbing the peace, and at times various forms of theft. Other settings such as pool halls and the street itself could be similarly described, but perhaps the point is sufficiently made.

I must comment very briefly concerning community-level *differences* confronted by our Negro and white lower class youngsters. Conventional ecological data indicate clearly that the white areas were not as disadvantaged economically as were the Negro areas. In the white areas our observers and workers reported the distinct impression that life tended to revolve around more conventional institutions such as the Catholic church, local political and "improvement" associations, ethnic and extended kinship organizations, unions and such formally organized recreational patterns as bowling leagues, social and athletic clubs. The research of Kobrin and his associates in largely white communities in Chicago is particularly instructive in this regard.[27]

Finally, with regard to community level problems, our data suggest that relations with adults differ for gang and for nongang boys. Thus, while gang boys rate local adult

[27] See Solomon Kobrin, "Sociological Aspects of the Development of a Street Corner Group: An Exploratory Study," *American Journal of Orthopsychiatry* (October 1951), pp. 685–702; and Solomon Kobrin, Joseph Puntil, and Emil Peluso, "Criteria of Status among Street Gangs," paper read at the annual meetings of the American Sociological Association, 1963.

incumbents of a variety of roles higher on their interest in teen-agers, and more as "right guys" than "reaction formation" or "adolescent protest" theories would suggest, nongang boys tend to rate these adults still higher.[28] Nongang boys also report more contact with these adults, and among Negroes, the nongang youngsters report that the adults have more "clout." When the boys were asked to nominate adults with whom they have the most contact (they were probed for four names), gang boys gave fewer names than the other boys, and their nominees had significantly lower occupations than did the nominees of the nongang boys. When samples of these "high contact" adults were interviewed, far more nongang nominees reported that they had been consulted about problems at school than did gang nominees. In other respects, nongang nominees appeared more "middle class" in their aspirations for their nominators, their attitudes toward juvenile misbehavior, and their conceptions of "a good life" for these youngsters.[29] Contrary to expectations based on the Cloward and Ohlin position concerning adult-adolescent relations in "integrated" as contrasted with "unintegrated" communities, and the impact which these differences have on adolescent behavior, however, there was at least as much consensus concerning such misbehavior among nominees from a conflict gang area as there was in an area characterized by a high degree of "integration" of the carriers of criminal and noncriminal values.[30] Negro lower class boys, both gang and nongang, had more multiple nominees than did their white counterparts. The conception of

conflict gang boys' relations with adults as being especially "weak" appears to call for some revision on the basis of findings such as these.

SOCIAL DISABILITY AND GANG DELINQUENCY

In this final section I should like to discuss some of the evidence concerning individual characteristics of the boys which appear to be related to the nature of their behavior in the group context. In so doing I will draw heavily from earlier work with Gordon and Strodtbeck.[31]

A "lack of social assurance" more serious in its implications for their social adjustment than that observed by Whyte for his corner boys was apparent almost from the beginning of our contact with the gang boys, and, as proved to be the case for so many types of observations, it was especially aggravated among Negro gang boys. Workers reported frequently that their boys did not feel comfortable outside "the area" and that they were ill at ease in most social situations outside the gang context. It was a surprise in semantic differential data gathered from these boys, however, which directed our attention to an apparent lack of gratification even of gang membership and interaction, and hence to a hypothesis concerning a fundamental lack of social skills on the part of gang boys which seems even more crucial to an understanding of their behavior than does lack of social assurance.

Gang boys were found to rate "someone who sticks with his buddies in a fight" less highly than "someone who stays cool and keeps to himself," while both lower class and middle class nongang boys (Negro and white) reversed these ratings. Gang boys *evaluated themselves* higher than they did *fellow gang members*, while these evaluations were more nearly equal for the other boys, and white middle class boys rated

[28] The data are discussed in James F. Short, Jr., Ramon Rivera, and Harvey Marshall, "Adult-Adolescent Relations and Gang Delinquency," *Pacific Sociological Review* 7 (Fall 1964), pp. 59–65.

[29] See James F. Short, Jr., Harvey Marshall, and Ramon Rivera, "Significant Adults and Adolescent Adjustment," revision of a paper read at the annual meetings of the Pacific Sociological Association, 1964 (mimeographed).

[30] See Harvey Marshall, "Slum Community Organization: Analysis of a Concept," unpublished M. A. thesis, Washington State University, 1964.

[31] The following treatment is based largely on Chaps. 10 and 12 in Short and Strodtbeck, *Group Process*.

their friends as "better" than themselves. Further evidence of ambivalence with respect to peer associations was found in a motivational opinionnaire administered to the boys. Gang boys more often than the other boys endorsed such statements as "Friends are generally more trouble than they are worth," and "Time spent with the guys is time wasted." And they agreed less often with the statement, "A guy should spend as much time with friends as he possibly can." Yet they also agreed more often than the other boys that "You can only be really alive when you are with friends," and less often that "People can have too many friends for their own good." We believe there is an implication here of dissatisfaction with present associates and perhaps an expression of things as they might be more ideally.

The range of Negro gang boys' physical movements is especially restricted, and only to a minor degree because of fear they may infringe on a rival gang's territory. More importantly, for both Negro and white gang boys, there is a reluctance to expose themselves to situations demanding skills which they lack, and so the development of role-playing abilities and sensitivities and the sensitivity to normative requirements of varying situations are further retarded.[32]

There is evidence that even with respect to activities which are inherently gratifying, and for which the gang provides opportunity for achieving such gratifications, such as sexual intercourse, gang boys (and girls) come off with less than satisfying experiences, particularly in terms of interpersonal relations. It is true that our gang youngsters were a good deal more sexually active than were their nongang counterparts, either lower or middle class, but most of these boys and girls are neither knowledgeable nor skilled in sexual matters or in interpersonal relations.[33] Relations with persons of the opposite sex tend to be characterized by the same sorts of aggressive expression as do many other interpersonal relations. Add the norm among males of sexual exploitation of females, and among females of economic exploitation of males, and the resulting combination has a high potential for tension and frustration, and very little likelihood of mutual and lasting gratification.

The gangs we have studied lack stability in membership and in attendance; hence the rate of social interaction is lower than was the case with the Nortons.[34] Mutual obligations tend to be tenuous among most gang members and in many instances, as is the case with the requirements of group norms, to be situationally specific. Hence, according to the argument, group cohesion is low. It seems likely, however, that gang boys are dependent upon one another for a large measure of interpersonal gratification, and so the gang achieves a high relative value for the boys. According to this interpretation, the gang is for its members a reasonably realistic solution to the boys' problems—problems which derive in part from the fact that these boys are adolescents, and in part from the peculiar situations in which these boys find themselves, lacking in interpersonal skills and in conventional institutional experiences which provide the context for interpersonal gratifications and achievement. Given the gratifications of gang membership and the lack of apparent alternatives which are available to these boys, for whatever reasons, it seems likely that the gang will be highly valued, especially by those boys who have experienced the most gratification and/or those whose interpersonal skills and perhaps other abilities are most impaired. When a boy is caught up in the group process, however, he may become involved in delinquency, regardless of his personal skills or even of the amount of gratification which he derives from gang

---

[32] See Erving Goffman's discussion of *Behavior in Public Places*, New York: The Free Press of Glencoe, 1963.

[33] Cf., the perceptive reports in Robert Rice, "The Persian Queens," *New Yorker* (October 19,

1963), pp. 153 ff.; and Harrison E. Salisbury, *The Shook-Up Generation*, New York: Harper & Row, Publishers, 1958, Chap. 4.

[34] Whyte.

membership. Jansyn's research in Chicago is relevant at this point.[35] Jansyn recorded daily the "attendance" and time spent with the group of members of a white gang with whom he was in contact for more than a year. A "solidarity index" constructed on the basis of these data was related to measures of individual and group behavior during this period. Delinquent acts, by individuals and with other group members, and nondelinquent group activities, were found to occur most frequently following low points of the index of group solidarity. The index characteristically arose following these behaviors. Jansyn's interpretation was that the boys were responding to low solidarity by creating situations which would bring the gang together, thus raising group solidarity. This was done, he believes, because solidarity of the gang was a primary value for these youngsters. Our interpretation is similar. Symbols, such as group names and individual nicknames, styles of dress and other behavioral affectation, provide a basis for group identity. But why delinquency? Aside from certain inherent gratifications, delinquent activities provide opportunities for the expression of dependency needs, and they create instrumental problems demanding cooperative enterprise.[36] This, for youngsters lacking in basic social skills, can be very important. Expression of dependency needs by lower class youngsters is likely to be difficult because of the persistent concern with toughness.[37] The problem is aggravated for

gang boys whose experiences in conventional institutional contexts are less than satisfactory in this respect and whose gang norms interpret dependency, except under special circumstances, as weakness. Among the excepted circumstances are protecting and caring for one another when under attack, or taking care of a buddy who may be in danger as a result of excessive consumption of alcohol or drugs. In effect, such activities represent contrived opportunities for realization of important gang functions. It is our hypothesis, therefore, that *social disabilities* contribute both to group norms and to group processes which involve these norms. The hypothesis is important, for by extension it provides a possible linkage between early family socialization, later experience, and gang behavior. Space does not permit this extension except to suggest that it seems likely to involve as important elements identity problems in early childhood, the inculcation of role-playing abilities and flexibility in this regard, and the cultivation of sensitivity to situational requirements for behavior. The aggressive posture and rigidity of response which is found among many gang youngsters cannot be explained by cultural themes alone. Observations from Strodtbeck's experimental nursery school for lower class Negro children in Chicago are appropriate. Strodtbeck and his associates find that at the age of four and one half these children are less able to maintain nonaggressive close physical bodily contact with their age mates than are children from middle class homes. The early development of these children appears to be a product of a combination of harsh socialization practices, frequent cautions about a threatening environment, and little cognitive development or verbal skill. The latter seems attributable in some measure to the almost complete absence of stimulation from reading materials and of any type of constructive play opportunities.[38] Data from our own per-

[35] See Leon Jansyn, "Solidarity and Delinquency in a Street Corner Group: A Study of the Relationship between Changes in Specified Aspects of Group Structure and Variations in the Frequency of Delinquent Activity," unpublished M.A. thesis, University of Chicago, 1960. Similar findings are also reported in Muzafer Sherif and Carolyn W. Sherif, *Reference Groups: Exploration into Conformity and Deviation of Adolescents*, New York: Harper & Row, Publishers, 1964.

[36] See Floyd H. Allport, "A Structuronomic Conception of Behavior: Individual and Collective. I. Structural Theory and the Master Problem of Social Psychology," *Journal of Abnormal and Social Psychology*, 64 (No. 1, 1962), pp. 1–30; and George C. Homans, *The Human Group*, New York: Harcourt, Brace & World, Inc.,

[37] See Miller.

[38] See Fred L. Strodtbeck, "The Reading Readiness Nursery: Short-Term Social Intervention Technique," Progress Report to the Social Security Administration (Project 124), The Social Psy-

sonality testing program indicate that gang boys are more reactive to false signals than their nongang controls, they are less self-assertive (in this conventional test like situation), they are slightly more anxious, neurotic, and narcissistic, and less gregarious. As we have noted elsewhere, "the possible cumulative effect of these differences is more impressive than are the individual findings, for they add up to boys who have less self-assurance and fewer of the qualities which engender confidence and nurturant relations with others."[39]

The social disability hypothesis is important, also, because it differs from "all for one, one for all" explanations of gang behavior, resting upon group solidarity and rigid conformity to group norms as the chief determinants of the behavior of gang members. The carefree image of "that old gang of mine" is hardly recognizable. Its functions and imperatives are seen quite differently.

The Sherifs offer the hypothesis that "the adolescent living in a setting where opportunities for peer contacts are available, either formally or informally, turns more and more to others caught up in similar dilemmas—to his age mates who can really understand him."[40] The "social disability" and "status threats" hypotheses suggest that one of the major problems of our gang youngsters is that "understanding" of their problems by fellow gang members occurs at a very superficial level—extending little beyond freedom to participate in "adult" activities, such as sex intercourse and drinking, and support for the achievement of freedom from adult control. The gang gives scant attention to, and in some instances acts as a deterrent to, the expression of interest and to the achievement of stable adult goals such as are involved, for example, in employment, family life, and civic participa-

tion, or to the expression of dependency needs. Gang experience is hardly conducive to stable adjustment in these areas, in terms of those "virtues" of modern industrial society—punctuality, discipline, and consistency on the job, the acceptance of authority relations, dependability concerning organizational commitments and interpersonal relations. It seems unlikely that gang experience, with its constant challenge to prove oneself tough, adept with the girls, "smart," "cool," "sharp," and so on, alleviates status insecurities or related social disabilities except for the few who are most successful in the gang, and then chiefly in terms of ability to respond to gang challenges. The extent to which these skills enhance one's prospects for status or achievement outside the gang is questionable, at best.

I would suggest that the failure of the gang to deal satisfactorily with these very real concerns and problems of its members contributes to the instability of most gangs. It contributes also to the fact that gang norms appear to be limited in direct influence on gang boys' behavior in situations directly involving other gang boys. That is, to paraphrase the Sherifs' recent work, "the attitudes (stands) the individual upholds and cherishes, the rules that he considers binding for regulating his behavior," are those defined by the gang only under special circumstances in which other gang boys are directly involved. When, in instances not involving other gang boys they nevertheless behave as gang boys, I suggest it is not gang norms, but other features of the situation and of gang boys' abilities to cope with them which accounts for this fact. Much latitude is given individual boys even when they are in the company of other gang boys, sometimes under circumstances most provocative of aggression and other forms of delinquent behavior. It seems a good hypothesis that the degree of such latitude for a given boy depends upon his own investment in the gang, his role in the gang and in the situation, and the importance of the situation to the gang. We can cite instances in which

---

chology Laboratory, University of Chicago, August, 1963.

[39] Short and Strodtbeck, *Group Process*, Chap. 13.

[40] Sherif and Sherif, p. 51.

each of these elements seem clearly related to the behavior of boys in a given situation.

CONCLUSION

Collaborators in this symposium are engaged in a common cause. We seek to describe and to understand reality, and more than this, to explain by general theoretical statements. In terms of the latter criterion, the work reported in this paper is largely exploratory, hypothesis-generating rather than -testing. Our *data* are drawn chiefly from Negro gangs, and the implications of the social disability hypothesis, in particular, appear to be more characteristic of the Negro gangs we have studied, than of the white. Preliminary observations from a study of Negro gangs in Los Angeles suggest that social disabilities of these boys are a good deal less serious than is the case with our boys.[41] The area in which these Los Angeles boys live looks very much like the community settings of our Negro *middle* rather than our lower class boys. The institutional setting in the Los Angeles communities is more conventional and less like the lower class varieties we have described.

If the hypothesis is to be theoretically significant, however, it must be the case that *to the extent that* a group is characterized by social disabilities such as those to which we have drawn attention, it will be characterized by attempts on the part of its members, individually and collectively, to create symbols and situations which will allow for—perhaps even demand—the expression of dependency needs and the achievement of interpersonal gratifications which for these youngsters are so difficult of realization. Friendships and loyalties which derive from this process are no less real, and they may prove to be quite as binding and lasting as any. To the extent that they must continue to exist in an unstable gang con-

text serving as an arena in which the consequences of status threats are played out, they are likely to be undermined and, therefore, shorter-lived and less binding. Certainly it cannot be denied that friendships exist among our gangs and that their gratifications are an important source of stability and continuity. Indeed, the ability of some—but not all—of our gangs to survive despite lack of support from conventional institutions, and often with considerable pressure against their continued existence, is remarkable. Derivation of the social disability and status threats hypotheses from our material should not obscure these facts. It has been our purpose to draw attention to processes which might account for behavior among our gangs which is specifically delinquent. We have attempted, on the one hand, to account for the delinquent content of group norms, and, on the other, for the circumstances under which delinquent norms are invoked. It may prove to be the case that empirical differences of this nature between the groups studied by the Sherifs and those to which we have had access in Chicago may account for differences in interpretation of the two studies. If so, it should be possible to resolve our differences by further empirical inquiry and theoretical synthesis.

In his summary of problems and prospects concerning "Personality and Social Structure," Inkeles argues strongly that the translation of social structural variables into behavior must include an explicit theory of human personality.[42] Thus, to the sociological S–R (State of society–Rate of behavior) proposition should be added P (Personality). "The simplest formula $(S)(P) = R$, although probably far from adequate, would be greatly superior to the S–R formula, since it provides for the simultaneous effect of two elements influencing action." The social disability hypothesis is hardly a theory of

[41] The study is under the direction of Malcolm W. Klein, Youth Studies Center, University of Southern California. Helen E. Shimota is senior research Associate for the study.

[42] Alex Inkeles, "Personality and Social Structure," chapter in Robert K. Merton, Leonard Broom, and Leonard S. Cottrell (eds.), *Sociology Today*, New York: Basic Books, Inc., 1959.

personality, but it is a step in this direction. It represents the introduction of a personality level variable which may provide an important link between social structure, early and later socialization, and behavior. If our observations concerning institutional relations, subcultural participation, and group process are correct, the equation may be further refined and a significant variable added. Experiences in conventional institutions and in lower class, ethnic, and peer group "institutional" or subcultural patterns of association may be viewed as refinements of S, social structure, or more specifically, the state of society so far as a particular individual is concerned. Group process, on the other hand, represents yet another *level*

of variable in the equation, in addition to S, P, and R. It should be clear that no simple linear relation exists between these variables. P, in our terms social disability, interacts with institutional and subcultural experience and with group process, and each of these with the others. It seems likely that social disability is a factor both in selection for gang membership and in within-gang participation, and therefore in group process involvement. The precise nature of these relationships, and of other parameters and other variables, is not well established, either theoretically or empirically. In their specification may be the resolution of fundamental differences in perspective among and within disciplines.

DELINQUENT SUBCULTURES: SOCIOLOGICAL INTERPRETATIONS OF GANG DELINQUENCY*

David J. Bordua

Presented here is a critique of current theoretical interpretations of lower class, urban, male subcultural delinquency. The theories of Cohen, Miller, and Cloward and Ohlin are discussed. The author concludes that there have been profound changes in the way social theorists view gang delinquency. These changes are only partially the result of actual changes in gang delinquency. In terms of recent theories of gang delinquency, it does not seem like much fun any more to be a gang delinquent.

The problem of group delinquency has been a subject of theoretical interest for American sociologists and other social observers for well over a half century. In the course of that period, the group nature of delinquency has come to be a central starting point for many theories of delinquency, and delinquency causation has been seen by

some sociologists as pre-eminently a process whereby the individual becomes associated with a group which devotes some or all of its time to planning, committing, or celebrating delinquencies and which has elaborated a set of lifeways—a subculture which encourages and justifies behavior defined as delinquent by the larger society.

* Reprinted from *The Annals of the American Academy of Political and Social Science*, 338 (November 1961), pp. 119–136, by permission of the author and the publisher.

In addition to the processes whereby an individual takes on the beliefs and norms of a pre-existing group and thereby becomes delinquent—a process mysterious enough in itself in many cases—there is the more basic, and in many respects more complex, problem of how such groups begin in the first place. What are the social conditions that facilitate or cause the rise of delinquency-carrying groups? What are the varying needs and motives satisfied in individuals by such groups? What processes of planned social control might be usable in preventing the rise of such groups or in redirecting the behavior and moral systems of groups already in existence? All these questions and many others have been asked for at least two generations. Within the limits of this brief paper, it is impossible to present and analyze in detail the many answers to these questions which have been put forward by social scientists. What I can do is single out a few of the major viewpoints and concentrate on them.

In its more well-developed and extreme forms, gang or subcultural delinquency has been heavily concentrated in the low status areas of our large cities. The theoretical interpretations I will discuss all confine themselves to gang delinquency of this sort.

THE CLASSICAL VIEW

Still the best book on gangs, gang delinquency, and—though he did not use the term—delinquent subcultures is *The Gang* by Frederick M. Thrasher, and his formulations are the ones that I have labeled "the classical view." Not that he originated the basic interpretative framework, far from it, but his application of the theoretical materials available at the time plus his sensitivity to the effects of social environment and his willingness to consider processes at all behavioral levels from the basic needs of the child to the significance of the saloon, from the nature of city government to the crucial importance of the junk dealer, from the consequences of poverty to the nature of

leadership in the gang still distinguish his book.[1]

Briefly, Thrasher's analysis may be characterized as operating on the following levels. The ecological processes which determine the structure of the city create the interstitial area characterized by a variety of indices of conflict, disorganization, weak family and neighborhood controls, and so on. In these interstitial areas, in response to universal childhood needs, spontaneous play groups develop. Because of the relatively uncontrolled nature of these groups—or of many of them at least—and because of the presence of many attractive and exciting opportunities for fun and adventure, these groups engage in a variety of activities, legal and illegal, which are determined, defined, and directed by the play group itself rather than by conventional adult supervision.

The crowded, exciting slum streets teem with such groups. Inevitably, in a situation of high population density, limited resources, and weak social control, they come into conflict with each other for space, playground facilities, reputation. Since many of their activities, even at an early age, are illegal, although often not feloniously so— they swipe fruit from peddlers, turn over garbage cans, stay away from home all night and steal milk and cakes for breakfast, play truant from school—they also come into conflict with adult authority. Parents, teachers, merchants, police, and others become the natural enemies of this kind of group and attempt to control it or to convert it to more conventional activities. With some groups they succeed, with some they do not.

If the group continues, it becomes part of a network of similar groups, increasingly freed from adult restraint, increasingly involved in intergroup conflict and fighting, increasingly engaged in illegal activities to support itself and to continue to receive the satisfactions of the "free" life of the streets. Conflict, especially with other groups, transforms the play group into the gang. Its

[1] Frederick M. Thrasher, *The Gang* (Chicago: University of Chicago Press, 1927).

illegal activities become more serious, its values hardened, its structure more determined by the necessity to maintain eternal vigilance in a hostile environment.

By middle adolescence, the group is a gang, often with a name, usually identified with a particular ethnic or racial group, and usually with an elaborate technology of theft and other means of self-support. Gradually, the gang may move in the direction of adult crime, armed robbery, perhaps, or other serious crimes.

Prior to that time, however, it is likely to have engaged in much stealing from stores, railroad cars, empty houses, parents, drunks, almost anywhere money or goods are available. The ready access to outlets for stolen goods is of major importance here. The junk dealer, especially the junk wagon peddler, the convenient no-questions-asked attitudes of large numbers of local adults who buy "hot" merchandise, and the early knowledge that customers are available all help to make theft easy and profitable as well as morally acceptable.[2]

Nonutilitarian? It is appropriate at this point to deal with a matter that has become important in the discussion of more recent theories of group delinquency. This is Albert K. Cohen's famous characterization of the delinquent subculture as nonutilitarian, by which he seems to mean that activities, especially theft, are not oriented to calculated economic ends.[3]

Thrasher makes a great point of the play and adventure quality of many illegal acts, especially in the pregang stages of a group's

development, but he also describes many cases where theft has a quite rational and instrumental nature, even at a fairly early age.

The theft activities and the disposition of the loot make instrumental sense in the context of Thrasher's description of the nature of the group or gang. Much theft is essentially for the purpose of maintaining the group in a state of freedom from adult authority. If a group of boys lives days or even weeks away from home, then the theft of food or of things which are sold to buy food is hardly nonutilitarian. If such a group steals from freight cars, peddles the merchandise to the neighbors for movie money, and so on, this can hardly be considered nonutilitarian. The behavior makes sense as instrumental behavior, however, only after one has a picture of the general life led by the group. Boys who feed themselves by duplicating keys to bakery delivery boxes, creep out of their club rooms right after delivery, steal the pastry, pick up a quart of milk from a doorstep, and then have breakfast may not have a highly developed sense of nutritional values, but this is not nonutilitarian.

Such youngsters may, of course, spend the two dollars gained from selling stolen goods entirely on doughnuts and gorge themselves and throw much of the food away. I think this largely indicates that they are children, not that they are nonutilitarian.[4]

[4] The examples cited above are all in Thrasher along with many others of a similar nature. In general, views of the nature of gang activity have shifted quite fundamentally toward a more irrationalist position. Thus, the gang's behavior seems to make no sense. Underlying this shift is a tendency to deal almost entirely with the gang's subculture, its values, beliefs, and the like, to deal with the relationships between this subculture and presumed motivational states which exist in the potential gang members before the gang or protogang is formed, and to deal very little with the developmental processes involved in the formation of gangs. Things which make no sense without consideration of the motivational consequences of gang membership are not necessarily so mysterious given Thrasher's highly sensitive analysis of the ways in which the nature of the gang as a group

[2] One of the charms of Thrasher's old-time sociology is the fashion in which fact intrudes itself upon the theorizing. For example, he tells us that there were an estimated 1,700 to 1,800 junk wagon men in Chicago, most of whom were suspected of being less than rigid in inquiring about the source of "junk." *Ibid.*, p. 148. He also does some other things that seem to have gone out of style, such as presenting information on the age and ethnic composition of as many of the 1,313 gangs as possible. *Ibid.*, pp. 73–74, 191–193.
[3] Albert K. Cohen, *Delinquent Boys: The Culture of the Gang* (Glencoe: The Free Press, 1955), pp. 25–26.

Let us look a little more systematically at the Thrasher formulations, however, since an examination can be instructive in dealing with the more recent theories. The analysis proceeds at several levels, as I have mentioned.

Levels of Analysis.   At the level of the local adult community, we may say that the social structure is permissive, attractive, facilitative, morally supportive of the gang development process.

It is permissive because control over children is weak; attractive because many enjoyable activities are available, some of which are illegal, like stealing fruit, but all of which can be enjoyed only if the child manages to evade whatever conventional controls do exist.

In another sense, the local environment is attractive because of the presence of adult crime of a variety of kinds ranging from organized vice to older adolescents and adults making a living by theft. The attraction lies, of course, in the fact that these adults may have a lot of money and live the carefree life and have high status in the neighborhood.

The local environment is facilitative in a number of ways. There are things readily available to steal, people to buy them, and places to hide without adult supervision.

The environment is morally supportive because of the presence of adult crime, as previously mentioned, but also for several additional reasons. One is the readiness of conventional adults to buy stolen goods. Even parents were discovered at this occasionally. The prevalence of political pull, which not only objectively protected adult crime but tended to undercut the norms

against crime, must be mentioned then as now. The often bitter poverty which turned many situations into matters of desperate competition also contributed.

Additionally, many gang activities, especially in the protogang stage, are not seriously delinquent and receive adult approval. These activities include such things as playing baseball for "side money" and much minor gambling such as penny pitching. Within limits, fighting lies well within the local community's zone of tolerance, especially when it is directed against members of another ethnic group.

At the level of the adolescent and pre-adolescent groups themselves, the environment is essentially coercive of gang formation. The presence of large numbers of groups competing for limited resources leads to conflict, and the full-fledged adolescent gang is pre-eminently a conflict group with a high valuation of fighting skill, courage, and similar qualities. Thus, the transition from spontaneous group to gang is largely a matter of participating in the struggle for life of the adolescent world under the peculiar conditions of the slum.

At the level of the individual, Thrasher assumes a set of basic needs common to all children. He leans heavily on the famous four wishes of W. I. Thomas, security, response, recognition, and new experience, especially the last two. Gang boys and boys in gang areas are, in this sense, no different from other boys. They come to choose different ways of satisfying these needs. What determines which boys form gangs is the differential success of the agencies of socialization and social control in channeling these needs into conventional paths. Thus, due to family inadequacy or breakdown or school difficulties, coupled with the ever present temptations of the exciting, adventurous street as compared to the drab, dull, and unsatisfying family and school, some boys are more available for street life than others.

Finally, it should be pointed out that the gang engages in many activities of a

---

led to the development—in relation to the local environment—of the gang culture. Current theory focuses so heavily on motive and culture to the exclusion of group process that some essential points are underemphasized. It would not be too much of a distortion to say that Thrasher saw the delinquent subculture as the way of life that would be developed by a group becoming a gang and that some recent theorists look at the gang as the kind of group that would develop if boys set about creating a delinquent subculture.

quite ordinary sort. Athletics are very common and highly regarded at all age levels. Much time is spent simply talking and being with the gang. The gang's repertory is diverse—baseball, football, dice, poker, holding dances, shooting the breeze, shoplifting, rolling drunks, stealing cars.

This is more than enough to give the tenor of Thrasher's formulations. I have purposely attempted to convey the distinctive flavor of essentially healthy boys satisfying universal needs in a weakly controlled and highly seductive environment. Compared to the deprived and driven boys of more recent formulations with their status problems, blocked opportunities (or psychopathologies if one takes a more psychiatric view), Thrasher describes an age of innocence indeed.

This is, perhaps, the most important single difference between Thrasher and some—not all—of the recent views. Delinquency and crime were attractive, being a "good boy" was dull. They were attractive because they were fun and were profitable and because one could be a hero in a fight. Fun, profit, glory, and freedom is a combination hard to beat, particularly for the inadequate conventional institutions that formed the competition.

WORKING CLASS BOY AND MIDDLE CLASS MEASURING ROD

If Thrasher saw the gang as being formed over time through the attractiveness of the free street life and the unattractiveness and moral weakness of the agencies of social control, Albert K. Cohen sees many working class boys as being driven to develop the delinquent subculture as a way of recouping the self-esteem destroyed by middle-class-dominated institutions.

Rather than focusing on the gang and its development over time, Cohen's theory focuses on the way of life of the gang— the delinquent subculture. A collective way of life, a subculture, develops when a number of people with a common problem of

adjustment are in effective interaction, according to Cohen. The bulk of his basic viewpoint is the attempted demonstration that the common problem of adjustment of the lower class gang boys who are the carriers of the delinquent subculture derives from their socialization in lower class families and their consequent lack of preparation to function successfully in middle class institutions such as the school.

The institutions within which the working class boy must function reward and punish him for acceptable or unacceptable performance according to the child-assessing version of middle class values. The middle class value pattern places great emphasis on ambition as a cardinal virtue, individual responsibility (as opposed to extreme emphasis on shared kin obligations, for example), the cultivation and possession of skills, the ability to postpone gratification, rationality, the rational cultivation of manners, the control of physical aggression and violence, the wholesome and constructive use of leisure, and respect for property (especially respect for the abstract rules defining rights of access to material things).[5]

The application of these values adapted to the judgment of children constitutes the "middle class measuring rod" by which all children are judged in institutions run by middle class personnel—the school, the settlement house, and the like. The fact that working class children must compete according to these standards is a consequence of what Cohen, in a most felicitous phrase, refers to as the "democratic status universe" characteristic of American society. Everyone is expected to strive, and everyone is measured against the same standard. Not everyone is equally prepared, however, and the working class boy is, with greater statistical frequency than the middle class boy, ill prepared through previous socialization.

Cultural Setting. Social class for Cohen is not simply economic position but, much more importantly, a set of more or less ver-

5 Albert K. Cohen, *op. cit.*, pp. 88–93.

tically layered cultural settings which differ in the likelihood that boys will be taught the aspirations, ambitions, and psychological skills necessary to adjust to the demands of the larger institutions.

Cohen goes on to describe this predominantly lower working class cultural setting as more likely to show restricted aspirations, a live-for-today orientation toward consumption, a moral view which emphasizes reciprocity within the kin and other primary groups and correlatively less concern with abstract rules which apply across or outside of such particularistic circumstances. In addition, the working class child is less likely to be surrounded with educational toys, less likely to be trained in a family regimen of order, neatness, and punctuality. Of particular importance is the fact that physical aggression is more prevalent and more valued in the working class milieu.

When a working class boy thus equipped for life's struggle begins to function in the school, the settlement, and other middle-class-controlled institutions and encounters the middle class measuring rod, he inevitably receives a great deal of disapproval, rejection, and punishment. In short, in the eyes of the middle class evaluator, he does not measure up. This is what Cohen refers to as the problem of status deprivation which constitutes the fundamental problem of adjustment to which the delinquent subculture is a solution.

Self-derogation. But this deprivation derives not only from the negative evaluations of others but also from self-derogation. The working class boy shares in this evaluation of himself to some degree for a variety of reasons.[6] The first of these is the previ-

ously mentioned democratic status universe wherein the dominant culture requires everyone to compete against all comers. Second, the parents of working class boys, no matter how adjusted they seem to be to their low status position, are likely to project their frustrated aspirations onto their children. They may do little effective socialization to aid the child, but they are, nevertheless, likely at least to want their children to be better off than they are. Third, there is the effect of the mass media which spread the middle class life style. And, of course, there is the effect of the fact of upward mobility as visible evidence that at least some people can make the grade.

In short, the working class boy is subjected to many social influences which emphasize the fact that the way to respect, status, and success lies in conforming to the demands of middle class society. Even more importantly, he very likely has partly accepted the middle class measuring rod as a legitimate, even superior, set of values. The profound ambivalence that this may lead to in the individual is simply a reflection of the fact that the larger culture penetrates the lower working class world in many ways.

Thus, to the external status problem posed by devaluations by middle class functionaries is added the internal status problem of low self-esteem.

This, then, is the common problem of adjustment. Given the availability of many boys similarly situated, a collective solution evolves, the delinquent subculture. This subculture is characterized by Cohen as non-utilitarian, malicious, and negativistic, characterized by versatility, short-run hedonism, and an emphasis on group autonomy, that is, freedom from adult restraint.

These are, of course, the direct antitheses of the components of the middle class measuring rod. The delinquent subculture functions simultaneously to combat the enemy without and the enemy within, both the hated agents of the middle class and the

---

[6] In presenting the theoretical work of someone else, it is often the case that the views of the original author are simplified to his disadvantage. I have tried to guard against this. At this point in Cohen's formulation, however, I may be oversimplifying to his benefit. In view of the considerable struggle over the matter of just what the working class boy is sensitive to, I should point out that Cohen is less than absolutely clear. He is not as unclear, however, as some of his critics

have maintained. For the best statement in Cohen's work, see *Delinquent Boys,* pp. 121–128.

gnawing internal sense of inadequacy and low self-esteem. It does so by erecting a counterculture, an alternative set of status criteria.

Guilt. This subculture must do more than deal with the middle-class-dominated institutions on the one hand and the feelings of low self-esteem on the other. It must also deal with the feelings of guilt over aggression, theft, and the like that will inevitably arise. It must deal with the fact that the collective solution to the common problem of adjustment is an illicit one in the eyes of the larger society and, certainly, also in the eyes of the law-abiding elements of the local area.

It must deal, also, with the increasing opposition which the solution arouses in the police and other agencies of the conventional order. Over time, the subculture comes to contain a variety of definitions of these agents of conventionality which see them as the aggressors, thus legitimating the group's deviant activities.

Because of this requirement that the delinquent subculture constitute a solution to internal, psychological problems of self-esteem and guilt, Cohen sees the group behavior pattern as being over-determined in the psychological sense and as linking up with the mechanism of reaction formation.

Thus, the reason for the seeming irrationality of the delinquent subculture lies in the deeply rooted fears and anxieties of the status deprived boy. I have already discussed the shift from Thrasher's view of delinquency as attractive in a situation of weak social control to the views of it as more reactive held by some modern theorists. Cohen, of course, is prominent among these latter, the irrationalists. It is extremely difficult to bring these viewpoints together at all well except to point out that Cohen's position accords well with much research on school failure and its consequences in damaged self-esteem. It does seem unlikely, as I will point out later in another connection, that the failure of family, school, and

neighborhood to control the behavior of Thrasher's boys would result in their simple withdrawal from such conventional contexts without hostility and loss of self-regard.

Cohen emphasizes that not all members of an ongoing delinquent group are motivated by this same problem of adjustment. Like any other protest movement, the motives which draw new members at different phases of its development will vary. It is sufficient that a core of members share the problem.

The analysis of the delinquent subculture of urban working class boys set forth in *Delinquent Boys* has been elaborated and supplemented in a later article by Cohen and James F. Short.[7]

Other Delinquent Subcultures. Responding to the criticism that there seemed a variety of kinds of delinquent subcultures, even among lower class urban youth, Cohen and Short distinguish the parent-male subculture, the conflict-oriented subculture, the drug addict subculture, and a subculture focused around semiprofessional theft.[8]

The parent subculture is the now familiar subculture described in *Delinquent Boys.* Cohen and Short describe it as the most common form.[9]

We refer to it as the parent sub-culture because it is probably the most common variety in this country—indeed, it might be called the "garden variety" of delinquent sub-culture —and because the characteristics listed above seem to constitute a common core shared by other important variants.

In discussing the conditions under which these different subcultures arise, Cohen and Short rely on a pivotal paper published in

[7] Albert K. Cohen and James F. Short, Jr., "Research in Delinquent Sub-Cultures," *Journal of Social Issues,* Vol. 14 (1958), No. 3, pp. 20–36.

[8] For criticism in this vein as well as for the most searching general analysis of material from *Delinquent Boys,* see Harold L. Wilensky and Charles N. Lebeaux, *Industrial Society and Social Welfare* (New York: Russell Sage Foundation, 1958), Chap. 9.

[9] Cohen and Short, *op. cit.,* p. 24. The characteristics are those of maliciousness and so on that I have listed previously.

1951 by Solomon Kobrin.[10] Dealing with the differential location of the conflict-oriented versus the semiprofessional theft subculture, Kobrin pointed out that delinquency areas vary in the degree to which conventional and criminal value systems are mutually integrated. In the integrated area, adult criminal activity is stable and organized, and adult criminals are integral parts of the local social structure—active in politics, fraternal orders, providers of employment. Here delinquency can form a kind of apprenticeship for adult criminal careers with such careers being relatively indistinct from conventional careers. More importantly, the interests of organized criminal groups in order and a lack of police attention would lead to attempts to prevent the wilder and more untrammeled forms of juvenile violence. This would mean, of course, that crime in these areas was largely of the stable, profitable sort ordinarily associated with the rackets.

LOWER CLASS BOY AND LOWER CLASS CULTURE

The interpretation of the delinquent subculture associated with Albert Cohen that I have just described contrasts sharply in its main features with what has come to be called the lower class culture view associated with Walter B. Miller.[11] Miller disagrees with the Cohen position concerning the reactive nature of lower class gang culture.[12]

In the case of "gang" delinquency, the cultural system which exerts the most direct influences on behavior is that of the lower class community itself—a long-established, distinctively patterned tradition with an integrity of its own—rather than a so-called "delinquent subculture" which has arisen through conflict with middle class culture and is oriented to the deliberate violation of middle class norms.

What, then, is the lower class culture Miller speaks of and where is it located? Essentially, Miller describes a culture which he sees as emerging from the shaking-down processes of immigration, internal migration, and vertical mobility. Several population and cultural streams feed this process, but, primarily, lower class culture represents the emerging common adaptation of unsuccessful immigrants and Negroes.

It is the thesis of this paper that from these extremely diverse and heterogeneous origins (with, however, certain common features), there is emerging a relatively homogeneous and stabilized native-American lower class culture; however, in many communities the process of fusion is as yet in its earlier phases, and evidences of the original ethnic or locality culture are still strong.[13]

In his analysis, Miller is primarily concerned with what he calls the hard core group in the lower class—the same very bottom group referred to by Cohen as the lower-lower class. The properties of this emerging lower class culture as described by Miller may be divided into a series of social

[10] Solomon Kobrin, "The Conflict of Values in Delinquency Areas," *American Sociological Review*, Vol. 16 (October 1951), No. 5, pp. 653–661.

[11] See the following papers, all by Walter B. Miller: "Lower Class Culture as a Generating Milieu of Gang Delinquency," *Journal of Social Issues*, Vol. 14 (1958), No. 3, pp. 5–19; "Preventive Work with Street Corner Groups: Boston Delinquency Project," *The Annals of the American Academy of Political and Social Science*, Vol. 322 (March 1959), pp. 97–106; "Implications of Urban Lower Class Culture for Social Work," *The Social Service Review*, Vol. 33 (September 1959), No. 3, pp. 219–236.

[12] Walter B. Miller, "Lower Class Culture as a Generating Milieu of Gang Delinquency," *op. cit.*, pp. 5, 6.

[13] Walter B. Miller, "Implications of Urban Lower Class Culture for Social Work," *op. cit.*, p. 225. Miller seems to be saying that the processes of sorting and segregating which characterized American industrial cities in the period referred to by Thrasher are beginning to show a product at the lower end of the status order. In this, as in several other ways, Miller is much more the inheritor of the classical view, as I have called it, than are Cohen or Cloward and Ohlin. Miller shows much the same concern for relatively wholistic description of the local community setting and much the same sensitivity to group process over time. Whether his tendency to see lower class culture in terms of a relatively closed system derives from differences in fact due to historical change or primarily to differences in theoretical perspective is hard to say.

structural elements and a complex pattern of what Miller calls focal concerns.

Focal Concerns. The first of the structural elements is what Miller calls the female-based household, that is, a family form wherein the key relationships are those among mature females (especially those of different generations but, perhaps, also sisters or cousins) and between these females and their children. The children may be by different men, and the biological fathers may play a very inconsistent and unpredictable role in the family. Most essentially, the family is not organized around the expectation of stable economic support provided by an adult male.

The relationship between adult females and males is characterized as one of serial mating, with the female finding it necessary repeatedly to go through a cycle of roles of mate-seeker, mother, and employee.

Closely related to and supportive of this form of household is the elaboration of a system of one-sex peer groups which, according to Miller, become emotional havens and major sources of psychic investment and support for both sexes and for both adolescents and adults. The family, then, is not the central focus of primary, intimate ties that it is in middle class circles.

In what is surely a masterpiece of cogent description, Miller presents the focal concerns of lower class culture as trouble, toughness, smartness, excitement, fate, and autonomy. His description of the complexly interwoven patterns assumed by these focal concerns cannot be repeated here, but a brief discussion seems appropriate.[14]

Trouble is what life gets you into—especially trouble with the agents of the larger society. The central aspect of this focal concern is the distinction between law-abiding and law-violating behavior, and where an individual stands along the im-

plied dimension either by behavior, reputation, or commitment is crucial in the evaluation of him by others. Toughness refers to physical prowess, skill, masculinity, fearlessness, bravery, daring. It includes an almost compulsive opposition to things seen as soft and feminine, including much middle class behavior, and is related, on the one hand, to sex-role identification problems which flow from the young boy's growing up in the female-based household and, on the other hand, to the occupational demands of the lower class world. Toughness, along with the emphasis on excitement and autonomy, is one of the ways one gets into trouble.

Smartness refers to the ability to "con," outwit, dupe, that is, to manipulate things and people to one's own advantage with a minimum of conventional work. Excitement, both as an activity and as an ambivalently held goal, is best manifested in the patterned cycle of the week end night-on-the-town complete with much drink and sexual escapades, thereby creating the risk of fighting and trouble. Between week ends, life is dull and passive. Fate refers to the perception by many lower class individuals that their lives are determined by events and forces over which they have little or no control. It manifests itself in widespread gambling and fantasies of "when things break for me." Gambling serves multiple functions in the areas of fate, toughness, smartness, and excitement.

The last focal concern described by Miller is that of autonomy—concern over the amount, source, and severity of control by others. Miller describes the carrier of lower class culture as being highly ambivalent about such control by others. Overtly, he may protest bitterly about restraint and arbitrary interference while, covertly, he tends to equate coercion with care and unconsciously to seek situations where strong controls will satisfy nurturance needs.

14 This description of the focal concern is taken from Walter B. Miller, "Lower Class Culture as a Generating Milieu of Gang Delinquency," *op. cit.*, especially Chart 1, p. 7. In this case especially, the original should be read.

Growing Up. What is it like to grow up in lower class culture? A boy spends the major part of the first twelve years in the company of and under the domination of women. He learns during that time that women are the people who count, that men are despicable, dangerous, and desirable. He also learns that a "real man" is hated for his irresponsibility and considered very attractive on Saturday night. He learns, too, that, if he really loves his mother, he will not grow up to be "just like all men" but that, despite her best efforts, his mother's pride and joy will very likely turn out to be as much a "rogue male" as the rest. In short, he has sex-role problems.

The adolescent street group is the social mechanism which enables the maturing boy to cope with a basic problem of feminine identification coupled with the necessity of somehow growing up to be an appropriately hated and admired male in a culture which maximizes the necessity to fit into all male society as an adult. The seeking of adult status during adolescence, then, has a particular intensity, so that manifestations of the adult culture's focal concerns tend to be overdone. In addition, the street group displays an exaggerated concern with status and belongingness which is common in all adolescent groups but becomes unusually severe for the lower class boy.

The street group, then, is an essential transition mechanism and training ground for the lower class boy. Some of the behavior involved is delinquent, but the degree to which the group engages in specifically delinquent acts, that is, constructs its internal status criteria around the law-violating end of the trouble continuum, may vary greatly depending on local circumstances. These include such things as the presence and salience of police, professional criminals, clergy, functioning recreational and settlement programs, and the like.

Like Thrasher, Miller emphasizes the wide range of activities of a nondelinquent nature that the gang members engage in, although unlike Thrasher's boys, they do not do so because of poor social control, but because of the desire to be "real men."

Participation in the lower class street group may produce delinquency in several ways:[15]

1. Following cultural practices which comprise essential elements of the total pattern of lower class culture automatically violates certain legal norms.
2. In instances where alternative avenues to similar objectives are available, the non-law-abiding avenue frequently provides a greater and more immediate return for a relatively smaller investment of energy.
3. The "demanded" response to certain situations recurrently engendered within lower class culture involves the commission of illegal acts.

Impact of Middle Class Values. Miller's approach, like the approaches of Thrasher and Cohen, has its strengths and weaknesses. Miller has not been very successful in refuting Cohen's insistence on the clash between middle class and lower class standards as it affects the sources of self-esteem. To be sure, Cohen's own presentation of just what the lower class boy has or has not internalized is considerably confused. As I have remarked elsewhere, Cohen seems to be saying that a little internalization is a dangerous thing.[16] Miller seems to be saying that the involvements in lower class culture are so deep and exclusive that contacts with agents of middle-class-dominated institutions, especially the schools, have no impact.

Actually, resolution of this problem does not seem so terribly difficult. In handling Cohen's formulations, I would suggest that previous internalization of middle class values is not particularly necessary, because the lower class boys will be told about them at the very time they are being status-deprived by their teachers and others. They will likely hate it and them (teachers and values), and the process is started. On the other hand, it

---

15 Walter B. Miller, "Lower Class Culture as a Generating Milieu of Gang Delinquency," *op. cit.*, p. 18.
16 David J. Bordua, *Sociological Theories and Their Implications for Juvenile Delinquency* (Children's Bureau, Juvenile Delinquency; Facts and Facets, No. 2; Washington, D.C.: U.S. Government Printing Office, 1960), pp. 9–11.

seems unlikely that Miller's lower class boys can spend ten years in school without some serious outcomes. They should either come to accept middle class values or become even more antagonistic or both, and this should drive them further into the arms of lower class culture.

This would be especially the case because of the prevailing definition of school work as girlish, an attitude not at all limited to Miller's lower class culture. With the sex-role identification problems Miller quite reasonably poses for his boys, the demands of the middle class school teacher that he be neat and clean and well-behaved must be especially galling.[17] In short, it seems to me inconceivable that the objective conflict between the boys and the school, as the most crucial example, could end in a simple turning away.

Miller also seems to be weak when he insists upon seeing what he calls the hard core of lower class culture as a distinctive form and, at the same time, must posit varieties of lower class culture to account for variations in behavior and values. This is not necessarily a factually untrue position, but it would seem to underemphasize the fluidity and variability of American urban life. It is necessary for him to point out that objectively low status urban groups vary in the degree to which they display the core features of lower class culture, with Negroes and Irish groups among those he has studied displaying it more and Italians less.

Validity of Female Base. Miller seems so concerned that the features of lower class culture, especially the female-based household, not be seen as the disorganization of the more conventional system or as signs of social pathology that he seems to overdo it rather drastically. He is very concerned to show that lower class culture is of ancient lineage and is or was functional in American society. Yet, at the same time, he says that lower class culture is only now emerging at the bottom of the urban heap. He also forgets that none of the low status groups in the society, with the possible exception of low status Negroes, has any history of his female-based household, at least not in the extreme form that he describes it.[18]

A closely related problem is posed by Miller's citation of cross-cultural evidence, for example, "The female-based household is a stabilized form in many societies—frequently associated with polygamy—and is found in 21 per cent of world societies."[19] I do not doubt the figure, but I question the implication that the female-based household as the household form, legitimated and normatively supported in societies practicing polygamy, can be very directly equated with a superficially similar system existing on the margins of a larger society and clearly seen as deviant by that larger society. Surely, in primitive societies, the household can count on the stable economic and judicial base provided by an adult male. The very fact that such a household in the United States is under continuous and heavy pressure from the law, the Aid to Dependent Children worker and nearly all other agents of the conventional order must make for a very different situation than in societies where it is the accepted form. In such societies, would mothers generally regard men as "unreliable and untrustworthy" and would the statement "all men are no good" be common?[20] Surely, such an attitude implies some awareness that things should be otherwise.

All this is not to argue that tendencies of the sort Miller describes are not present nor to underestimate the value of his insistence that we look at this way of life in its

[17] For evidence that lower class Negro girls seem to do much better than boys in adjusting to at least one middle class institution, see Martin Deutsch, Minority Group and Class Status as Related to Social and Personality Factors in School Achievement (Monograph No. 2, The Society for Applied Anthropology; Ithaca, New York: The Society, 1960).

[18] E. Franklin Frazier, The Negro Family in the United States (Chicago: University of Chicago Press, 1939).
[19] Walter B. Miller, "Implications of Urban Lower Class Culture for Social Work," op. cit., p. 225 fn.
[20] Ibid., p. 226.

own terms—a valuable contribution indeed —but only to ask for somewhat greater awareness of the larger social dynamics that produce his lower class culture.

Danger of Tautology. Finally, a last criticism of Miller's formulations aims at the use of the focal concerns material. There seems more than a little danger of tautology here if the focal concerns are derived from observing behavior and then used to explain the same behavior. One would be on much safer ground to deal in much greater detail with the structural roots and reality situations to which lower class culture may be a response. Thus, for example, Miller makes no real use of the vast literature on the consequences of prolonged instability of employment, which seems to me the root of the matter.

These criticisms should not blind us to very real contributions in Miller's position. Most importantly, he tells us what the lower class street boys are for, rather than just what they are against. In addition, he deals provocatively and originally with the nature of the adult culture which serves as the context for adolescent behavior. Finally, he alerts us to a possible historical development that has received relatively little attention—the emergence of something like a stable American lower class. This possibility seems to have been largely neglected in studies of our increasingly middle class society.

SUCCESS GOALS AND OPPORTUNITY STRUCTURES

The last of the major approaches to the problem of lower class group delinquency to be considered here is associated with Richard A. Cloward and Lloyd E. Ohlin.[21] Stated in its briefest form, the theory is as follows: American culture makes morally mandatory the seeking of success goals but differentially distributes the morally acceptable means to these success goals, the legitimate opportunities that loom so large in the approach.[22]

This gap between culturally universalized goals and structurally limited means creates strain among lower class youths who aspire to economic advancement. Such strain and alienation leads to the formation of delinquent subcultures, that is, normative and belief systems that specifically support and legitimate delinquency, among those boys who blame the system rather than themselves for their impending or actual failure. The particular form of delinquent subculture—conflict, criminal, or retreatist (drug-using)—which results depends on the nature of the local neighborhood and, especially, on the availability of illegitimate opportunities, such as stable crime careers as models and training grounds.

The criminal subculture develops in stable neighborhoods with much regularized crime present; the conflict form develops in really disorganized neighborhoods where not even illegitimate opportunities are available; the retreatist, or drug-use, subculture develops among persons who are double failures due either to internalized prohibitions against violence or theft or to the objective unavailability of these solutions.

Intervening between the stress due to blocked aspirations and the creation of the full-fledged subculture of whatever type is a process of collectively supported "withdrawal of attributions of legitimacy from established social norms."

This process, coupled with the collective development of the relevant delinquent norms, serves to allay whatever guilt might have been felt over the illegal acts involved in following the delinquent norms.

Since the argument in *Delinquency and Opportunity* is, in many ways, even more

---

21 The full statement of the approach is in Richard A. Cloward and Lloyd E. Ohlin, *Delinquency and Opportunity* (Glencoe: The Free Press, 1960); see also Richard A. Cloward "Illegitimate Means, Anomie and Deviant Behavior," *American Sociological Review*, Vol. 24 (April 1959), No. 2, pp. 164–176.

22 For the original version of this formulation, see Robert K. Merton, *Social Theory and Social Structure* (rev. and enl.; Glencoe: The Free Press, 1951), Chaps. 4, 5.

complicated than those associated with Cohen, Short, and Miller, I will discuss only a few highlights.[23]

Potential Delinquents.   On the question of who aspires to what, which is so involved in the disagreements between Cohen and Miller, Cloward and Ohlin take the position that it is not the boys who aspire to middle class status—and, therefore, have presumably partially internalized the middle class measuring rod—who form the raw material for delinquent subculture, but those who wish only to improve their economic status without any change in class membership. Thus, it is appropriate in their argument to say that the genitors of the delinquent subcultures are not dealing so much with an internal problem of self-esteem as with an external problem of injustice. Cohen says, in effect, that the delinquent subculture prevents self-blame for failure from breaking through, the reaction formation function of the delinquent subculture. Cloward and Ohlin say that the delinquent norm systems are generated by boys who have already determined that their failures, actual or impending, are the fault of the larger social order.[24]

This insistence that it is the "system blamers" who form the grist for the subcultural mill leads Cloward and Ohlin into something of an impasse, it seems to me. They must, of course, then deal with the determinants of the two types of blame and choose to say that two factors are primarily relevant. First, the larger culture engenders expectations, not just aspirations, of success which are not met, and, second, there exist highly visible barriers to the fulfillment of these expectations, such as racial prejudice, which are defined as unjust.

These do not seem unreasonable, and, in fact, in the case of Negro youth, perhaps, largely fit the case. Cloward and Ohlin, however, are forced for what seems overwhelmingly polemical reasons into a position that the feeling of injustice must be objectively correct. Therefore, they say (1) that it is among those actually fitted for success where the sense of injustice will flourish and (2) that delinquent subcultures are formed by boys who do not essentially differ in their capacity to cope with the larger institutions from other boys. This point deserves some attention since it is so diametrically opposed to the Cohen position which states that some working class boys, especially lower working class boys, are unable to meet the demands of middle-class-dominated institutions.

It is our impression that a sense of being unjustly deprived of access to opportunities to which one is entitled is common among those who become participants in delinquent subcultures. Delinquents tend to be persons who have been led to expect opportunities because of their potential ability to meet the formal, institutionally-established criteria of evaluation. Their sense of injustice arises from the failure of the system to fulfill these expectations. Their criticism is not directed inward since they regard themselves in comparison with their fellows as capable of meeting the formal requirements of the system. It has frequently been noted that delinquents take special delight in discovering hypocrisy in the operation of the established social order. They like to point out that it's "who you know, not what you know" that enables one to advance or gain coveted social rewards. They become convinced that bribery, blackmail, fear-inspiring pressure, special influence, and similar factors are more important than the publicly avowed criteria of merit.[25]

Delinquents and Nondelinquent Peers.   On the same page in a footnote, the authors go

[23] Large segments of *Delinquency and Opportunity* are devoted to refutations of other positions, especially those of Cohen and Miller. I felt that, at least for the present paper, criticizing in detail other people's refutations of third parties might be carrying the matter too far. It should be pointed out, however, that the tendency to take extreme positions as a consequence of involvement in a polemic which is apparent in Miller's work seems even more apparent in the Cloward and Ohlin book.

[24] Richard A. Cloward and Lloyd E. Ohlin, *Delinquency and Opportunity, op. cit.* For the problem of types of aspiration and their consequences, see, especially, pp. 86–97. For the matter of self-blame and their system blame for failure, see pp. 110–126.

[25] *Ibid.,* p. 117.

on to say that the research evidence indicates "the basic endowments of delinquents, such as intelligence, physical strength, and agility, are the equal of or greater than those of their non-delinquent peers."

The material in these quotations is so riddled with ambiguities it is difficult to know where to begin criticism, but we can at least point out the following. First, Cloward and Ohlin seem to be confusing the justificatory function of delinquent subcultures with their causation. All of these beliefs on the part of gang delinquents have been repeatedly reported in the literature, but, by the very argument of *Delinquency and Opportunity*, it is impossible to tell whether they constitute compensatory ideology or descriptions of objective reality.

Second, Cloward and Ohlin seem to be victims of their very general tendency to ignore the life histories of their delinquents.[26] Thus, there is no way of knowing really what these subcultural beliefs may reflect in the experience of the boys. Third, and closely related to the ignoring of life history material, is the problem of assessing the degree to which these gang boys are in fact prepared to meet the formal criteria for success. To say that they are intelligent, strong, and agile is to parody the criteria for advancement. Perhaps Cohen would point out that intelligent, agile, strong boys who begin the first grade using foul language, fighting among themselves, and using the school property as arts and crafts materials do not meet the criteria for advancement.

It is quite true that members of highly sophisticated delinquent gangs often find

themselves blocked from whatever occupational opportunities there are, but this seems, often, the end product of a long history of their progressively cutting off opportunity and destroying their own capacities which may begin in the lower class family, as described by either Cohen or Miller, and continue through school failure and similar events. By the age of eighteen, many gang boys are, for all practical purposes, unemployable or need the support, instruction, and sponsorship of trained street-gang workers. Participation in gang delinquency in itself diminishes the fitness of many boys for effective functioning in the conventional world.[27]

If, indeed, Cloward and Ohlin mean to include the more attitudinal and characterological criteria for advancement, then it seems highly unlikely that any large number of boys trained and prepared to meet these demands of the occupational world could interpret failure exclusively in terms which blame the system. They would have been too well socialized, and, if they did form a delinquent subculture, it would have to perform the psychological function of mitigating the sense of internal blame. This, of course, would make them look much like Cohen's boys.

In short, Cloward and Ohlin run the risk of confusing justification and causation and of equating the end with the beginning.

All of this is not to deny that there are real obstacles to opportunity for lower class boys. There are. These blocks on both the performance and learning sides are a major structural feature in accounting for much of the adaptation of lower class populations. But they do not operate solely or even primarily on the level of the adolescent. They

---

26 This is the most fundamental weakness in the book. The delinquents in Thrasher, Cohen, and Miller were, in varying degrees, once recognizably children. Cloward and Ohlin's delinquents seem suddenly to appear on the scene sometime in adolescence, to look at the world, and to discover, "Man, there's no opportunity in my structure." It is instructive in this connection to note that the index to *Delinquency and Opportunity* contains only two references to the family. One says that the family no longer conducts occupational training; the other criticizes Miller's ideas on the female-based household.

27 Here, again, Thrasher seems superior to some of the modern theorists. He stressed the fact that long-term involvement in the "free, undisciplined" street life with money at hand from petty theft and with the days devoted to play was not exactly ideal preparation for the humdrum life of the job. Again, Thrasher's sensitivity to the attitudinal and subcultural consequences of the gang formation and maintenance process truly needs reintroduction.

create a social world in which he comes of age, and, by the time he reaches adolescence, he may find himself cut off from the larger society. Much of the Cloward and Ohlin approach seems better as a theory of the origins of Miller's lower class culture. Each generation does not meet and solve anew the problems of class structure barriers to opportunity but begins with the solution of its forebears.[28] This is why reform efforts can be so slow to succeed.

Some Insights. The positive contributions of the Cloward-Ohlin approach seem to me to lie less on the side of the motivational sources of subcultural delinquency, where I feel their attempts to clarify the ambiguities in Cohen have merely led to new ambiguities, but more on the side of the factors in local social structure that determine the type of subcultural delinquency.

The major innovation here is the concept of illegitimate opportunities which serves to augment Kobrin's almost exclusive emphasis on the differentially controlling impact of different slum environments. I do think that Cloward and Ohlin may make too much of the necessity for systematic, organized criminal careers in order for the illegitimate opportunity structure to have an effect, but the general argument has great merit.

In addition to the concept of illegitimate opportunities and closely related to it is the description, or speculation, concerning historical changes in the social organization of slums. Changes in urban life in the United States may have truly produced the disorganized slum devoid of the social links between young and old, between children and older adolescents which characterized the slums described by Thrasher. Certainly, the new conditions of life seem to have created new problems of growing up, though our knowledge of their precise impact leaves much to be desired.

CONCLUSION

This paper should not, I hope, give the impression that current theoretical interpretations of lower class, urban, male subcultural delinquency are without value. Such is far from the case. Many of my comments have been negative since each of the theorists quite ably presents his own defense, which should be read in any case. In fact, I think that this problem has led to some of the most exciting and provocative intellectual interchange in all of sociology in recent years. I do believe, however, that this interchange has often been marred by unnecessary polemic and, even more, by a lack of relevant data.

As I have indicated, there have been some profound changes in the way social theorists view the processes of gang formation and persistence. These, I believe, derive only partially, perhaps even unimportantly, from changes in the facts to be explained. Indeed, we must wait for a study of gangs which will approach Thrasher's in thoroughness before we can know if there are new facts to be explained. Nor do I believe that the changes in viewpoint have come about entirely because old theories were shown to be inadequate to old facts. Both Cohen and Cloward and Ohlin feel that older theorists did not deal with the problem of the origins of delinquent subcultures, but only with the transmission of the subculture once developed.[29] A careful reading of Thrasher indicates that such is not the case.

All in all, though, it does not seem like much fun any more to be a gang delinquent. Thrasher's boys enjoyed themselves being

[28] Parenthetically, the Cloward and Ohlin position has great difficulty in accounting for the fact that lower class delinquent subculture carriers do not avail themselves of opportunities that do exist. The mixed success of vocational school training, for example, indicates that some fairly clear avenues of opportunity are forgone by many delinquent boys. For Negro boys, where avenues to the skilled trades may indeed be blocked, their argument seems reasonable. For white boys, I have serious question. In fact, the only really convincing case they make on the aspiration-blockage, system-blame side is for Negroes.

[29] Albert K. Cohen, *Delinquent Boys, op. cit.,* p. 18; Richard A. Cloward and Lloyd E. Ohlin, *Delinquency and Opportunity, op. cit.,* p. 42.

chased by the police, shooting dice, skipping school, rolling drunks. It was fun. Miller's boys do have a little fun, with their excitement focal concern, but it seems so desperate somehow. Cohen's boys and Cloward and Ohlin's boys are driven by grim economic and psychic necessity into rebellion. It seems peculiar that modern analysts have

stopped assuming that "evil" can be fun and see gang delinquency as arising only when boys are driven away from "good."[30]

[30] For a more thorough commentary on changes in the view of human nature which, I think, partly underlie the decline of fun in theories of the gang, see Dennis Wrong, "The Oversocialized View of Man," *American Sociological Review*, Vol. 26 (April 1961), No. 3, pp. 183–193.

THE NEGRO ARMED ROBBER AS A CRIMINAL TYPE: THE CONSTRUCTION AND APPLICATION OF A TYPOLOGY*

Julian B. Roebuck and Mervyn L. Cadwallader

In a larger study, Roebuck collected arrest histories of a sample of 400 Negro cases at the District of Columbia Reformatory. On the basis of the arrest histories, a typology of criminal behavior was constructed. The relationship between the types and a number of social and personal background factors was then investigated. Reported below are the characteristics of the armed robbers in comparison to the characteristics of the other offenders. Significant differences exist between the two groups. The authors suggest that the findings demonstrate the utility of a typology based upon arrest histories of offenders.

The present state and future prospects of sociological and behavioral theory must appear dim to all except the most sanguine of social scientists. The scientist who seeks to study society and human behavior is confronted by a welter of competing theoretical systems, uncodified generalizations, propositions and concepts. The criminologist does not escape this contemporary Babel by virtue of his specialized interests. In his research on the causes of criminal behavior he may choose from among any of the following: differential association, cultural, class conflict, ecological, psychodynamic, consti-

tutional, containment, anomie, and subculture theory. All of these theories, and many others, have been rejected by articulate critics who can always point to negative cases or exceptions that cannot be covered by a particular explanation. Criminologists appear to delight in the destruction of each other's theories.[1] Moreover, efforts to create a synthesis of elements from contending

[1] For an example of recent jousting over differential association theory see: *Social Problems*, 8 (Summer, 1960), pp. 2–37. For a discussion of the nihilistic state of criminology see: Frank E. Hartung, "A Critique of the Sociological Approach to Crime and Correction," *Law and Contemporary Problems*, 23 (Autumn, 1958), pp. 703–734.

* Reprinted from *Pacific Sociological Review*, 4 (Spring 1961), pp. 21–26, by permission of the authors and the publisher.

theories so far has done little more than add another to the ranks. The scientist cannot but be dissatisfied with such a state of explanatory chaos.

A review of current criminological theory reveals that the majority of these theoretical systems and propositions are general rather than special. It may be that this is the source of the difficulty. Any general theory of criminal behavior, given the current definitions of crime that include such different kinds of activity as drug addiction, murder, embezzlement, rape and treason, can hardly escape the necessity of being a general theory of human behavior. Perhaps without realizing it, the specialist in crime has been embarked upon the larger task of creating a universal theory for the whole of behavioral science. Actually, his special interest would seem to require a strictly circumscribed theoretical schema. Of course, any limited or "middle-range" theory must ultimately take its place as a subset of propositions within an acceptable general theory. This is the optimum strategy of any scientific discipline. But what does the criminologist do in the meantime?

Perhaps the difficulty encountered in the construction of a satisfactory and powerful general theory of criminal behavior could be overcome if the criminologist were to work first on middle-range theories designed to explain as fully as possible the origins, development, and dynamics of specific categories of such behavior. Instead of striving for the general theory at this time the investigator might well turn to the development and testing of a number of special theories.[2] The special theories could then serve in the construction of even more general theory. If this strategy for criminological research is accepted, the first step to be taken is the construction of a workable typology which would provide the means for isolating the specific categories of criminal behavior to be explained by the special theories.

The typology and research described below seeks to stimulate interest and research on specific types of crime and criminals. It is a tentative step in the direction of providing some of the facts needed for a theory of the etiology of armed robbery as a distinct criminal behavior pattern.

AN ARREST HISTORY TYPOLOGY

Several criminal typologies have already been constructed and a critical literature is growing up around the issue. We offer another typology because no typology has as yet proved satisfactory enough to gain acceptance throughout the discipline. Until some single classification scheme proves superior, through repeated application in research, criminologists will have to try first one and then another in a process of trial, elaboration, and modification. The typology employed in the research reported in this paper has certain advantages over the other classification systems already in existence. It has some disadvantages. The measure of its superiority, if any, can only be settled in the field. Because the typology is both new and basic to our research we must first turn to a brief discussion of the general problem of typology construction in criminology and a description of the actual typology used.

At the start of any such effort in the construction of a criminal typology a decision must be made in regard to the use of legal offense categories. The advantages and disadvantages of using legal categories cannot be discussed at length here. In a recent article Don C. Gibbons and Donald L. Garrity take a strong stand against the use of legal terminology.[3] They advocate instead the construction of behavioral categories which cut across the legal categories. In the same paper they give recognition to the sig-

[2] Walter C. Reckless, *The Crime Problem*, 3rd ed., New York: Appleton-Century-Crofts Inc., 1961, pp. 324, 325, among others, has called for special explanations. Examples of excellent work along this line are the studies by Donald R. Cressey on financial trust violators, and that of Edwin M. Lemert on systematic check forgers.

[3] Don C. Gibbons and Donald L. Garrity, "Some Suggestions for the Development of Etiological and Treatment Theory in Criminology," *Social Forces*, 38 (October, 1959), pp. 51–58.

nificance of the career dimension in the establishment of criminal types but do not pursue the matter further. The typology we advocate makes explicit use of legal terms and gives special emphasis to the criminal career. Two reasons are to be given for the use of legal terms: first, the accessible official data concerned with the official criminal histories exist in terms of the legal nomenclature, that is, arrests by criminal charges; and second, the criminal code contains more specific, hence operational, definitions of criminal behavior than any set of non-legal categories.[4] The use of legal terms in the construction of a typology does not necessarily mean that the offense for which the inmate is serving, or has served, his sentence must be taken as the basis for a criminal typology. This was the case in the classification scheme proposed by, among others, John Lewis Gillin.[5] The most serious disadvantage in the use of such a base is that many criminals serve time for offenses other than those for which they were arrested. This problem can be solved if the typology is based upon the configuration of total known arrests for the various criminal offenses. The arrest history has the advantage of being taken over a period of time and hence is longitudinal. This improves the likelihood of its indicating a fixed pattern of criminality. The case of an offender whose official arrest history shows nine robbery charges out of a total of twelve arrests may be taken as a hypothetical case. This approach makes it possible to classify individual criminals in *criminal-pattern* categories. Of course this index, because it is a product of official records, does not account for all the crimes committed by the subject in his criminal career. No offender is apprehended and charged for every crime he commits. However, the principal advantage in the use of arrest records stems from the fact, as

Sutherland and Cressey have noted, that the further one gets away from a criminal's arrest history the more obscure and distorted become the facts of his criminal activities.[6]

One of the basic assumptions underlying the construction of this typology and the research that flowed from it was that arrest patterns would indicate a particular scheme of behavior or criminal career. If non-criminals manifest a gestalt in their legally approved activities, then, the logic of contemporary behavioral theory leads us to assume that the illegal activities of the criminal similarly must manifest an identifiable pattern. Our typology is designed to classify criminals in terms of illegal careers as revealed in cumulative arrest histories. The basis for classification is the most frequent charge or charges in the total arrest history of the subject with the charges appearing in the later phases of the criminal's arrest history being given greater weight. It is reasoned that the later entries in an offender's arrest history more accurately reflect the current stage in his criminal development than those entries occurring earlier.[7]

The actual construction of the typology involved an extended analysis of a sample of 400 arrest histories selected from 1155 current Negro cases who entered the District of Columbia Reformatory, Lorton, Virginia, between the dates January 5, 1954 and November 8, 1955.[8] A tabulation of the frequency with which given criminal charges occurred in each history permitted

[4] Paul W. Tappan, *Crime, Justice and Correction*, New York: McGraw-Hill Book Co., 1960, pp. 4–22.
[5] John Lewis Gillin, *The Wisconsin Prisoner: Studies in Crimogenesis*, Madison, Wisconsin: University of Wisconsin Press, 1946.
[6] Edwin H. Sutherland and Donald R. Cressey, *Principles of Criminology*, 5th ed., Philadelphia: J. B. Lippincott Co., 1955, pp. 25–26.
[7] In addition to the question of frequency of charge, consideration was given to the role that time intervals between charges might play. A preliminary investigation of the sample revealed a remarkable homogeneity in the length of time intervals between charges. Only ten out of the total of 400 arrest histories exhibited an interval of five or more years between arrests (omitting, of course, time spent in incarceration).
[8] The Reformatory was actually a penitentiary and housed a heterogeneous group of felons who were serving sentences of various lengths ranging to life imprisonment.

the grouping of all cases into the following four general classes:[9] (1) *Single Pattern*—An arrest history which showed a high frequency of one kind of criminal charge; (2) *Multiple Pattern*—An arrest history of two or more single patterns; (3) *Mixed Pattern*—An arrest history in which the charges do not form a frequency pattern as defined above (jack of all trades); and (4) *No Pattern*—A residual category of those with less than three arrests which were judged too few to support analysis. By identifying the specific patterns within each of the four general classes a final typology of thirteen criminal patterns was produced, eleven of which correspond to distinct legal categories. These patterns were: (1) single pattern of robbery; (2) single pattern of narcotic drug laws; (3) single pattern of gambling; (4) single pattern of burglary; (5) single pattern of sex offenses; (6) single pattern of auto theft; (7) single pattern of confidence games; (8) single pattern of check forgery; (9) triple pattern of drunkenness, assault, and larceny; (10) double pattern of larceny and burglary; (11) double pattern of assault and drunkenness; (12) mixed pattern; and (13) no pattern.

Given the above typology, the next step was to investigate the relationship between the several classes of criminals and those social and personal background factors generally held to be among the significant determinants of human behavior whether legal or illegal. These characteristics, taken from the life-history or total career of each offender, included family and community background, peer and reference group relations, and indices of personal disorganization and juvenile delinquency.

It should be noted that the typology suggested by Gibbons and Garrity is in one sense exactly a photographic negative of the one described here. They start with social and personal background factors as the classificatory criteria in their typology and then proceed toward etiological research focused upon the time-serving offender. We start with the offender, classify him according to his arrest history, and then proceed to etiological research making use of similar social and personality variables.

The remainder of the present paper reports the findings of a study in which the Negro armed robber ($N = 32$), is compared with the rest of the sample ($N = 368$), that is, all other Negro offender types with reference to thirty social and personal characteristics.

COMPARISON OF NEGRO ARMED ROBBERS WITH OTHER CRIMINAL TYPES

The statistical analysis showed that the thirty-two subjects, characterized by a pattern of arrests for armed robbery, differed widely from the other three hundred and sixty-eight offenders in twenty-two of the thirty social and personal characteristics studied. These differences were significant at the .01 level. An additional four were significant at the .05 level, making a total of twenty-six characteristics in which the differences were deemed significant when measured by chi-square.[10]

The robbers were a comparatively young group of offenders with a median age of 30. All grew up in urban areas. They approached average intelligence; the median I.Q. was 90, and the Stanford Achievement Test grade median was 5.0, while for the remainder of the sample the median age was 33, the S.A.T. grade median was 5.0, and the median I.Q. was 86.

The armed robbers were reared in slum neighborhoods where unfavorable home and

---

[9] In determining criminal patterns (arrest-history patterns) a chronological arrest history on each of the 400 cases was derived from the official arrest records. Legal nomenclature was adhered to, including the offense categories found in the criminal codes of the District of Columbia, the various states, and the U.S. Code.

[10] The data were obtained from institutional records and from interviews. The records included social case workers' admission summaries, case histories and clinical psychologists' personality profiles based on clinical interviews and Minnesota Multiphasic Personality Inventories.

Table 1.

PER CENT OF OFFENDERS EXHIBITING SELECTED SOCIAL
AND PERSONAL ATTRIBUTES BY SINGLE PATTERN OF ARMED
ROBBERY OFFENDERS AND ALL OTHER OFFENDERS

SELECTED SOCIAL AND PERSONAL ATTRIBUTES	ARMED ROBBERS $(N = 32)$ *(per cent)*	ALL OTHERS $(N = 368)$ *(per cent)*	X^2
Reared in more than one home	78	37	0.01
Mother figure southern migrant	91	39	0.01
Mother figure domestic servant	97	73	0.01
Dependent family	94	72	0.01
Family broken by desertion	47	34	0.05
Demoralized family	84	46	0.01
Criminality in family	78	40	0.01
Mother figure dominant	81	52	0.01
Inadequate supervision-father	97	73	0.01
Inadequate supervision-mother	91	69	0.05
Conflict in family	59	58	0.00
Hostility toward father	94	38	0.01
Hostility toward mother	19	20	0.00
Disciplinary problem at home	56	27	0.01
History of running away	84	42	0.01
Weak parental family structure	87	50	0.01
No parental family ties	78	70	0.01
Reared in urban area	100	82	0.00
Reared in slum area	100	59	0.01
Living in slum when arrested	94	74	0.05
History of school truancy	91	47	0.01
Disciplinary problem at school	94	43	0.01
Street trades as juvenile	87	47	0.01
No marital ties	91	70	0.05
Juvenile delinquent companions	97	56	0.01
Member delinquent gang	97	30	0.01
Adjudicated juvenile delinquent	94	40	0.01
Committed as juvenile	91	32	0.01
Police contact prior to 18	100	51	0.01
Criminal companions as juvenile	97	36	0.01

area conditions prevailed more frequently than for the men in the rest of the sample. They grew up more frequently in several homes which were marked by criminality, conflict, and inadequate parental supervision. Public assistance was the rule, their families being known to several social agencies over long periods of time. Their childhood experiences were unsettled as a consequence of frequent moves to foster homes and to the homes of relatives. Their mothers entertained various paramours in the home situation and their sisters were often prostitutes. Their fathers were generally heavy drinkers who displayed little interest in them. Frequently their parents and siblings had misdemeanor as well as felony-sentence records. More frequently the mother figure was the dominant parental figure, a migrant from the South, and a domestic servant. In a home marked by conflict, parental supervision by either parent was at a minimum. A pattern of unadjustment since early childhood was easily discernible in their home, school, and community backgrounds. They more frequently expressed hostility to their father figures. They were more often disciplinary problems at home and school, and a higher proportion of them were truants and "home run-aways." They worked more frequently at street trades during childhood and adolescence, and more of them had had delinquent companions. Moreover, more of them were juvenile delinquents and juvenile delinquent gang leaders. A larger proportion of them had associated with adult criminal companions as adolescents.

The interviews revealed a disorganized home background shot through with conflict, economic, and emotional deprivation.[11] Their responses indicated qualitative as well as quantitative differences in their homes when compared with the other men in the sample. The robbers talked more about such physical violence in the home as corporal punishment, fights with brothers, sisters, and the father, than did the men in the other criminal patterns. One of the robbers commented:

There was always a battle going on. My younger brother wanted everything. I had to fight him every week to keep him in place. The old man would come home drunk as hell and start kicking people around. When I got fourteen, I poked him once or twice. The nothing used to smack my mother too.

They had run away from home frequently and found what they felt to be more satisfying group attachments in "street corner society." Upon reaching their middle teens, they generally left home and shifted for themselves, usually living in rented rooms in cheap boarding houses. These remarks were typical:

With all the hell at home and half hungry too, I stayed on the street most of the time. I run with a bunch of boys, who I had fun with.

[11] In addition to the statistical findings reported here considerable qualitative evidence was gathered from interviews to support and extend the quantitative study. This material is summarized below.

We shot pool and run up and down, you know. We got money too, you know; we had our ways.

An early patterning of stealing from their parents, from school, and on the street; truancy, and suspension or expulsion from school; street fighting, association with older delinquents, and juvenile delinquent gang memberships, all were usually evident in their social backgrounds. When compared with the men in the other criminal categories it was found that there was more destruction of property in their delinquent activities, and there were more frequent fights with schoolmates, male teachers, and delinquent companions. There was a higher incidence of "mugging" and purse snatching. They had more often been the leaders of delinquent gangs, and they claimed they were leaders because of their superior size and physical strength. This quotation from one of the robbers was typical:

I soon found out the man who was boss got the most bread (money). Well, I was the biggest and strongest, so I just knocked off the top boy and took over. If they didn't go my way, I clipped them, that's all.

These men more frequently carried and used weapons of violence as juvenile delinquents.

Sometimes you gotta carry some heat to put the pressure on. Some people won't get up off that money less they see you are ready. The studs I ran with, Jack, had to have some kind of heat . . . knife, gun, blackjack or something.

Criminal progression appeared to occur at a more rapid rate with an early trend toward crimes of violence—from petty thefts and playground fights, to the rolling of drunks and homosexuals, and on to holdups with such weapons as pistols and knives.

Of the thirty-two armed robbers studied only seven maintained strong ties with their family. Only three had conjugal ties and twenty had never married. In discussing their criminal companions these offenders indicated a broad knowledge of the organized underworld but without close ties with that underworld.[12] Their close affiliations were with former juvenile delinquent companions with whom they had served time as juveniles and as adults. These companions were usually robbers and were referred to as "rap partners."

> I never did nothing with no pimps . . . dudes with no heart. I run with the studs I know from way back, studs I had done a bit with. We know what we want, and we know how to get it. We learned the hard way but we was ready.

They scoffed at their criminal acquaintances who were nonviolent property offenders, particularly check forgers and confidence men. These offenders lacked nerve, physical courage and strength, according to the robbers. They represented themselves as brave, daring men who took what they wanted in a straightforward way.

> You got heart, you can get that bread in a hurry! Course you got to figure the angles. These pimps and con men ain't nothing. Those suckers are punks on the street just like they are here. Holler at one and see him keep getting up.

The arrest histories of these offenders showed a mean of 18.2 arrests. Sprinkled through the arrest histories were a scattered assortment of assault and sex charges, and occasionally charges for drunkenness and disorderly [conduct]; however, the pattern of robbery was clear-cut. Most of the nonproperty arrest charges were for crimes against the person.

The District Attorney's reports on all crimes for which these offenders had served under felony sentence revealed a robbery *modus operandi* at various levels of operation. Fifteen of the thirty-two incorporated at least five of the following procedures in their *modus operandi*: (1) There was a definite target of operations where there was reasonable assurance that a large sum of cash

was available; (2) the target was carefully "cased" at least three weeks in advance; (3) at least one practice run was made; (4) a careful and detailed timetable was established; (5) there was a getaway car and a special driver; (6) there was a "gun man" and an accomplice for the inside job; (7) there was a look-out man; (8) there was a definite leader; (9) there was a prearranged agreement for the division of the money and a definite time and place were planned for this part of the operation; (10) there was a plan of escape to follow the robbery. Six of the thirty-two operated as "loners" holding up individuals at the point of a gun or knife. Six operated with one accomplice. Two simply knocked the victim down and relieved him of his money by physical force.[13]

As a group the robbers appeared to be physically strong and in very good health. They gave the impression of being five to ten years younger than their chronological age and they made very few somatic complaints.[14] They seemed to be repressing a great deal of restless, physical energy. They verbalized well in a glib, aggressive, and breezy fashion. Their vocabularies revealed them to be a group of street-wise toughs who were quite familiar with the criminal argot. At times during the interviews they gave the impression of being friendly, gay, and cooperative. At other times they reacted in an aggressive and hostile manner. This was particularly the case when the interview probed in the area of their relationships with their parents. They were extremely self-centered and nearly every sentence uttered made use of the first person singular. Generally they were sharply critical of other people including relatives and friends. They

---

[12] They knew by name and criminal specialty the numbers operators, the heads of the gambling houses, the operators of the afterhours clubs, the operators of the houses of prostitution, and the bootleggers. They did not associate with nor did they engage in such criminal activity.

[13] Everett Debaun, "The Heist: The Theory and Practice of Armed Robbery," *Harper's*, 200 (February, 1950), pp. 69–77. This article, by an armed robber, gives an extended description of the *modus operandi* of this type of criminal that agrees in every detail with our own findings.

[14] All of these thirty-two men were found to be organically sound and in general good health by an examining physician of the District of Columbia Department of Corrections.

criticized established social institutions: the family, marriage, the church, the economic system, the courts, and law enforcement machinery. They took great pride in their individualism.

The robbers expressed no clear-cut long-term goals, and their remarks indicated a preoccupation with the immediate present. The plans they did mention in regard to the future were vague and whimsical. They rationalized away their past difficulties by placing the "blame" for their mistakes on others. They expressed bitterness toward police and the courts for their present sentence. Most of them insisted that they were not technically guilty of their present charge and over one-half of them asked the interviewer questions about the legal writs which they were working on. They demonstrated little insight into the nature of their past difficulties and expressed little desire for any modification of their own personality. Throughout the interviews they spoke of physical violence as the best possible means to settle any and all difficulties.[15]

In summary, the armed robbers were a group of hardened, anti-social recidivists, the products of disorganized homes and slum neighbors where they came in contact with criminal norms and activities at an early age. Rejected and ill-supervised in homes charged with emotional conflict, they entered street corner society early—between the ages of six and nine. Case histories showed a pattern of unadjustment at home, school, and in the community. They had usually been gang leaders prone to violence and the destruction of property. Perhaps their size, physical strength, and excess energy had something to do with their leadership role as juveniles. Twenty of them had been amateur boxers. As adults they

[15] The Admission Summaries in their official dossiers showed that during past and present incarcerations twenty-five of these men had been diagnosed as psychopathic personalities by psychiatrists and clinical psychologists. All of them had been disciplinary problems at one time or another in a correctional institution.

sought out criminal companions of a similar type, that is, other robbers. They took real pride in their criminal style—the taking of property by force or threat of force. Most of them had developed some skills and a *modus operandi* in their criminal activities. Criminal progression was accelerated in the careers of the robbers. As a group these offenders comprised a more homogeneous category personality-wise than did any other criminal-pattern group with perhaps the exception of the drug laws offenders. All of them exhibited a clearly delineated pattern of armed robbery.

SUMMARY AND CONCLUSION

The writers believe that the present study demonstrates the utility of a typology based upon criminal careers as established by legal arrest histories. The use of the typology in the study reported here (and in research on narcotic drug laws offenders reported elsewhere) permitted the delineation of clear-cut and relatively homogeneous criminal categories. It should be made clear that the writers do not mean to suggest that this is the only useful typology nor, for that matter, that this is the only means of constructing a criminal careers typology.

Rather, the essential point is that the criminal population as currently defined is not sufficiently homogeneous to permit the construction and testing of a satisfactory general theory of crime and criminal behavior, given the present state of sociological and psychological theory.

The comparative research reported here constitutes a first step in the necessarily complex task of formulating and testing special etiological principles for specific types of criminal behavior. The empirical data, both quantitative and qualitative, demonstrate clearly that the armed robbers differ in kind and degree from other criminal types in terms of theoretically relevant social and psychological background factors.

CHAPTER 8

Organized
Crime

Organized crime, as understood by criminologists today, refers to business enterprises organized for the purpose of making economic gain through illegal activities.[1] Currently, organized crime is one of the major forms of crime in American society, although numerically it does not involve a large proportion of criminal offenders. Large-scale organized crime did not exist in the United States prior to this century.[2] At an earlier time, during the frontier period in American history, a number of outlawed activities had been carried out on a modest scale by roving criminal groups. Later, in villages and in developing cities, various groups were formed to make money by illegal means. Neighborhood gangs were able to gain control of illegal activities in their localities, such as gambling, prostitution, distribu-

---

[1] See Thorsten Sellin, "Organized Crime: A Business Entreprise," *The Annuals*, 347 (May 1963), pp. 12–19.

[2] See Virgil W. Peterson, *Barbarians in Our Midst*, Boston: Little, Brown & Company, 1952; Harry Elmer Barnes and Negley K. Teeters, *New Horizons in Criminology*, 3d ed., Englewood Cliffs, N.J.: Prentice-Hall, Inc., 1959, Chap. 2; Ruth Shonle Cavan, *Criminology*, 3d ed., New York: Thomas Y. Crowell Company, 1962, Chap. 6.

tion of beer and liquor, and various rackets. These gangs prospered because of the desired, although illegal, services they provided for the public and because of their connection with local politics.

After the turn of the century organized crime expanded into a wider range of activities and extended over larger geographical areas. The single event which brought about the greatest change in organized crime was Prohibition, forbidding by law the sale and distribution of alcoholic beverages. Because of the Eighteenth Amendment, adopted in 1920, and the supporting Volstead Act, organized crime was able to provide the illegal services and commodities which were demanded by millions of citizens. Conflict between organized adult gangs and widespread use of violence were inevitable as rival groups competed to serve the public. A number of the strongest gangs finally dominated the scene. These organized groups, because of the large sums of money they amassed and the elaborate organization they achieved, continued in illegal activity after Prohibition was repealed.[3]

The modern era of organized crime is represented by the crime syndicate. Organized crime has been expanded to the point where leaders have been able to coordinate illegal activities over state and regional boundaries. The new era of organized crime is also represented by the extension of organized crime into an increasing number of legitimate businesses and occupational activities. The characteristic features of modern organized crime can be summarized as follows:

1. Hierarchical structure involving a system of specifically defined relationships with mutual obligations and privileges
2. Monopolistic control or establishment of spheres of influence among different organizations and over geographic areas
3. Dependence upon the use of force and violence to maintain internal discipline and restrain competition
4. Maintenance of permanent immunity from interference from law enforcement and other agencies of government
5. Large financial gains secured through specialization in one or more combinations of enterprises

CRIMINAL CAREER OF THE OFFENDER

As with any large-scale enterprise, organized crime requires a structure of positions with an accompanying hierarchy of command. It has been noted by Burgess that the hierarchical structure of organized crime represents a feudal system.[4] At the top of the pyramid are powerful leaders, the "lords" of the underworld, who make the important decisions and run the organization. These leaders maintain a master-serf relationship over other persons in the feudal structure. A middle echelon of gangsters, henchmen, and lieutenants carry out the demands of the leaders. At the bottom of the structure are persons marginally associated with organized crime—narcotics peddlers, prostitutes, bookies, runners—who deal directly with the public. The structure is held together by a chain of command, per-

[3] Andrew Sinclair, *Era of Excess: A Social History of the Prohibition Movement*, New York: Harper & Row, Publishers, 1964, especially Chaps. 10 and 11.
[4] Ernest W. Burgess, "Summary and Recommendations," *Illinois Crime Survey*, Chicago: Illinois Association for Criminal Justice, 1929, pp. 1092–1094. Also see Marshall B. Clinard, *Sociology of Deviant Behavior*, rev. ed., New York: Holt, Rinehart and Winston, Inc., 1963, pp. 273–284; and Russell R. Dynes, Alfred C. Clarke, Simon Dinitz, and Iwao Ishino, *Social Problems*, New York: Oxford University Press, 1964, pp. 558–564.

sonal loyalties, a moral code, alliances with rival groups, and hostility toward conventional society.

The hierarchical structure of organized crime makes generalization about the careers of its members difficult. Many organized criminals, especially those lower in the hierarchy, have careers similar to the conventional offender, in which there is association with young gang members and a long series of delinquencies and crimes. Instead of ending their careers in their early twenties, however, they have continued their criminal activities in association with organized criminals.

The delinquent gang of the slum produces the adult "gangster" who uses strong-arm methods and is employed for this purpose by organized criminal groups. Gangsters usually come from large cities, frequently have long criminal records of armed robberies, and have a conception of themselves as "tough." Those who are successful in organized crime sometimes become its leaders.

> In many instances organized criminal machines have called upon the services of gangsters for protective or offensive operations only to have the gangsters take over the operations themselves. In other instances gangsters have been content to be on the payroll of a prosperous organization and to get a considerable cut of the profits without assuming full control. Gangsters are usually recruited from the slums of American cities. They have come up though the sand lots of crime and have made crime their career. Most of them have been members of small boys' gangs and have graduated to larger boys' gangs and later to affiliation with organized crime and political machines. They have made themselves useful to both political machines and organized crime. The gangster is the toughest of American criminals, and invariably his is a blatant career of criminal activity.[5]

Organized crime may thus provide a person with the opportunity for a lifetime career in crime. Selection of a career in organized crime, rather than one of the other criminal careers, is apparently dependent upon the existing social conditions of the area in which the person lives.[6] Little is known, however, of the specific mobility of the criminal from one position to another once he is a part of the hierarchy of organized crime. The career histories of organized criminals are not usually available because of the immunity of these persons from detection and imprisonment.

Progression into organized crime usually represents for the offender an increasing isolation from conventional society. While there are undoubtedly variations according to the location of the person within the hierarchy of organized crime, most organized criminals are committed to the world of crime. Their commitment to the larger society is concentrated on the goal of pecuniary success. The means of achieving such success are illegal. There is little or no interest on the part of organized criminals for the welfare of the larger society.

A number of social conditions and forces in American society are conducive to the separation of the organized criminal from the larger society. In coming up

[5] Walter C. Reckless, *The Crime Problem*, 3d ed., New York: Appleton-Century-Crofts, Inc., 1961, p. 203.
[6] Solomon Kobrin, "The Conflict of Values in Delinquency Areas," *American Sociological Review*, 16 (October 1951), pp. 653–661.

through the ranks of street gangs, organized criminals have been nominally separated from the dominant culture.

> The juvenile gang, then, develops as a culture within our culture. The first great "civilizing force" directed by the total society at taming this unruly group—namely, the school—is of minimum value. Truancy becomes for many youths the first crime. If attendance is compelled, the school becomes a blackboard jungle. The second great "civilizer," the reform school, becomes a place of criminal learning. The settlement house is an avenue of entry to the outer world for the boys who want to go "social," but it is an object of scorn for those who proclaim their own status and status symbols.
> The delinquent culture becomes an inner frontier, raising barbarians in our midst, strange and hostile to our larger civilization. Out of this culture comes the young gang that in adulthood becomes part of organized crime, either by absorption or by conquest.
> Organized crime . . . is a powerful, ever renewed social force with which America will have to contend for many years to come.[7]

The leaders in organized crime are involved in activities which are in continuous conflict with the law. A philosophy of justification allows them to carry out their illegal activities appropriately. They have contempt for the government, its officials, and the general public. Underworld leaders may, however, choose to live segmented lives, retiring to the seclusion of respectability.[8] Their commitment, nevertheless, remains with the world of crime, where in detachment from the values of the larger society they receive their prestige, power, and a life style of luxury.

GROUP SUPPORT OF CRIMINAL BEHAVIOR

Persons involved in most levels of organized crime associate regularly with other criminals and receive group support for their criminal behavior. Since most persons in organized crime associate with a particular group of criminals, support and prescription of behavior come from a specific group of criminals. These groups are organized for the purpose of gaining monopolistic control over a sphere of activity. During Prohibition in the United States, for example, specific organized criminal groups competed in an attempt to control the manufacture and distribution of liquor. More recently organized criminal groups have attempted to gain monopolistic control of gambling, prostitution, drug traffic, and various rackets.

Monopolistic control of a criminal activity by criminal groups often entails an interlocking control over other illegal activities. Interlocking interests are found in organized crime in patterns similar to those in corporate business. Furthermore, in achieving monopolies, organized crime is not restricted by traditional political and geographical boundaries.

[7] Gus Tyler, "The Roots of Organized Crime," *Crime and Delinquency*, 8 (October 1962), p. 338.

[8] Compare Virgil W. Peterson, "The Career of a Syndicate Boss," *Crime and Delinquency*, 8 (October 1962), pp. 339–354.

FORCE AND VIOLENCE. Organized crime depends upon the use or threat of force and violence, plus intimidation and bribery, as methods of operation to ensure large economic gains, to control illegal activities, and to survive in competition with other criminal groups. The "gangster," who is usually associated with organized criminal enterprises, actually performs the violent acts. Continued slaying of rival gang members marks the existence of gangland warfare. Because of underground tactics, such killings are not usually cleared by arrest.

The St. Valentine's Day massacre of 1929 stands out as the archetype of gangland warfare. Al Capone and his gang had acquired control of the illegal liquor field in the Chicago area during the Prohibition era. Eventually other rivals attempted to "muscle in" in the field and compete for the large profits. Capone eventually exhibited superiority over his principal rival gang with summary dispatch. On St. Valentine's Day, Capone's gunmen, disguised as police officers, lined seven members of the Bugs Moran gang against the wall of a garage and mowed them down with submachine guns. Although such a mass killing in organized crime has never been equaled, hundreds of slayings have occurred in the course of economic competition in organized crime.

A more recent use of violence in organized crime has been employed in racketeering. Since the 1930s organized crime has found a fertile field in "protecting" businessmen from possible harm. By means of intimidation organized criminals have been able to extort large sums of money from legitimate businesses. A classic illustration of how the racket works can be found in the laundry business. Laundry proprietors in particular cities have been visited by gang representatives who inform the proprietors that the laundry business is in "danger" and that protection will be provided. Failure on the part of laundrymen to subscribe to the protection plan has resulted in destruction of laundry equipment or personal violence. Such demonstrations of force, provided of course by those who would otherwise provide "protection," usually convinces laundry proprietors and other businessmen that protection is worth the money demanded for it.

PERMANENT IMMUNITY. The existence of organized crime is dependent on the maintenance of permanent immunity from interference of law enforcement agencies. Permanent immunity is achieved in several ways. First, the leaders of organized crime are not usually arrested and prosecuted because they stay behind the scenes of operation. Gangland activity cannot be readily traced to its leaders. Second, persons lower in the hierarchy of organized crime, if arrested, are likely to be released by action from their superiors. Such release and avoidance of prosecution and punishment are assured through what is popularly known as the "fix." For various reasons, persons not directly involved in criminal activity contribute to the protection of organized criminals. Law enforcement officials, judges, doctors, businessmen, and others may at times provide needed services for the protection of organized criminals.

A third way in which organized crime may acquire immunity is by gaining political power through contributions to political organizations. Elected officials may owe their election to organized criminals. Furthermore, regular "payoffs" to officials provide protection for organized crime. Thus, on a permanent basis, organized crime may be immune to law enforcement through political graft and corruption. Fourth, because organized crime provides the public with illicit and desired services, such as prostitution, gambling, and narcotics, a certain amount of immunity from arrest and prosecution results from public toleration of organized crime.

A fifth means of immunity is found in the functioning of the law itself. Existing laws and enforcement procedures have not been especially successful in coping with organized crime. The survival and continuance of organized crime is possible because legal action is kept at a minimum. Lack of effective legislation and weak law enforcement are, in turn, a reflection of public toleration of organized crime in the United States.

Finally, through the infiltration of legitimate business, organized crime is able to evade the law. Organized crime today often operates behind the façade of legitimate business, obscuring its operation and making its detection difficult. Also, in the case of racketeering, organized crime escapes the law because intimidated businessmen must contend with reprisal if a report is made. In addition, organized crime and legitimate business may mutually assist one another, as in the regulation of prices of given commodities or through the enforcement of labor contracts. As Vold has commented, the interdependence of the underworld of crime and the upperworld of business assures the maintenance of both systems.[9] Mutual assistance, accompanied by public espousal of the profit motive under almost any arrangement, provides considerable assurance of immunity for organized crime.

CRIME SYNDICATES. From an organizational standpoint, all of organized crime operates on a syndicated basis. That is, skilled persons with considerable capital resources are organized to establish and maintain a large-scale business enterprise devoted to the coordination and control of products or services. Illegal activity is involved in that the nature of the coordination and control may be illegal, and, also, the products and services may be illegal. However, given the syndicated pattern of organized crime, there are questions regarding the pervasiveness and geographical extensiveness of the organization of illegal activity. For example, in the United States are there a great number of criminal groups on a syndicated basis? Are some groups interlocked according to a plan? Or, is there a single crime syndicate in the United States which coordinates all the activities of organized crime?

There is considerable disagreement concerning the nature of crime syndicates in the United States. There have been exponents of the idea that there exists in the United States a nation-wide crime syndicate dominated by the Mafia, the Mafia being an imported secret terrorist organization from Sicily.[10] In 1950 the Kefauver Committee, a Senate crime investigating committee, while admitting that it had no direct evidence of a national crime syndicate, suggested that there was in fact a nation-wide crime syndicate with two centers of operation, in the east (New York) and in the midwest (Chicago).[11] There have been others who have denied that the Mafia ever existed in the United States.[12]

Recent evidence throws some light on the structure of organized crime in this

[9] George B. Vold, *Theoretical Criminology*, New York: Oxford University Press, 1958, pp. 237–240.

[10] A strong case for the Mafia is presented in Ed Reid, *Mafia*, New York: Random House, Inc., 1952.

[11] U.S. Senate Special Committee to Investigate Organized Crime in Interstate Commerce, *Third Interim Report*, Senate Report No. 307, 83d Cong., 1st Sess., Washington, D.C.: Government Printing Office, 1951. An abridgment of the investigation is found in Estes Kefauver, *Crime in America*, New York: Doubleday & Company, Inc., 1951.

[12] Most recently in Givanni Schiavo, *The Truth about the Mafia*, New York: Vigo Press, 1962.

country. The meeting of over sixty known gang leaders in upstate New York in 1957, the so-called Appalachian Conference, suggests a periodic gathering of leaders in organized crime to discuss problems of mutual interest and concern.[13] The meeting also indicates the existence of a complex and differentiated system consisting of a number of criminal groups engaged in the business of organized crime. The 1963 testimony of Joseph Valachi, former organized criminal turned informer, before the McClellan Committee provides further clues to the syndicated nature of organized crime in the United States.[14] He named the Cosa Nostra as a group of "families" engaged in illegal economic gain. At the top of the "family" system is a commission which serves as a court to settle disputes and inflict punishments. The Cosa Nostra apparently provides for the autonomous functioning of several organized criminal groups.

A full description of the organizational aspects of organized crime was recently reported by the President's Commission on Law Enforcement and Administration of Justice, published under the title *The Challenge of Crime in a Free Society*.[15] According to the report, the core of organized crime today consists of twenty-four groups (or families) which operate as criminal cartels in large cities across the country. While the scope and effect of the organized criminal operations vary from one area to another, the wealthiest and most influential groups operate in New York, New Jersey, Illinois, Florida, Louisiana, Nevada, Michigan, and Rhode Island. In terms of the internal structure of each of the twenty-four core groups membership varies from as many as 700 men to as few as twenty. Each family is headed by one man, the "boss," who maintains order and maximizes profits. Beneath each boss is an "underboss," who collects information for the boss, relays messages to him, and passes instructions down to underlings. On the same level as the underboss is the *consigliere*, who is a counselor or adviser to the boss. Below the level of the underboss are the *caporegime*, some of whom serve as buffers between upper and lower level personnel while others serve as chiefs of operating units. The lowest-level members are the *soldati*, the soldiers or "button" men who report to the *caporegime*. Outside the structure of the family are the large number of employees and agents who do most of the actual work in the various criminal enterprises. Finally, the President's Commission notes, the twenty-four families or criminal cartels are ruled by a "commission." This body is a combination legislature, supreme court, board of directors, and arbitration board but functions primarily as a judicial body. The commission is composed of the bosses of the most powerful families and varies from nine to twelve men. The balance of power of this nation-wide council currently rests with the leaders of the five families of New York, which is considered the unofficial headquarters of the entire operation of organized crime in the United States.

From a historical perspective, it appears that organized crime has been underlying organizational change in recent years. Thus, the old Mafia of Sicily, as a traditional type of organization, has developed into a highly complex organization

[13] U.S. Senate Select Committee on Improper Activities in the Labor or Management Field, *Final Report, Part 3*.

[14] U.S. Senate Permanent Subcommittee on Investigations, *Organized Crime and Illicit Traffic in Narcotics, Part I*, 88th Cong., 1st Sess., Washington, D.C.: Government Printing Office, 1963.

[15] President's Commission on Law Enforcement and Administration of Justice, *The Challenge of Crime in a Free Society*, Washington, D.C.: United States Government Printing Office, 1967, pp. 191–196.

in America. As the Cosa Nostra, it operates as a modern bureaucracy in terms of hierarchy of authority, specialization, a system of rules, and impersonality.[16]

CORRESPONDENCE BETWEEN CRIMINAL BEHAVIOR AND LEGITIMATE BEHAVIOR PATTERNS

Even as a type of crime, organized crime itself actually consists of a number of different types. Various writers have suggested forms of organized crime. The forms may be distinguished according to the correspondence between the criminal behavior involved and legitimate behavior patterns, with special attention to the mode of operation and the product or service which is being controlled. The following general classification can be used to include most forms of organized crime: (1) control of illegal activities, (2) control of legitimate business, and (3) racketeering.

CONTROL OF ILLEGAL ACTIVITIES. Much of organized crime traditionally has been found in areas of behavior which are illicit, such as gambling, prostitution, and narcotics. In these areas public sentiment is divided over the actual immorality of such behavior. Organized crime, thus, finds limited opposition from the public when it controls these illegal activities. Furthermore, organized crime provides a service for some of the public when it assures access to these activities.

CONTROL OF LEGITIMATE BUSINESS. In addition to the control of illegal activities, organized crime has infiltrated legitimate kinds of activity. This has been accomplished by employing illegal means and by investing large financial resources. Organized crime has at times, of course, used legitimate business as a front for other criminal activities. More recently, however, organized crime has used legitimate business as a major source of income.

The Kefauver Committee found that organized crime had infiltrated approximately fifty areas of legitimate business, including advertising, the amusement industry, the automobile industry, banking insurance, juke box distribution, the liquor industry, loan business, the oil industry, radio stations, real estate, and scrap surplus sales.[17] Organized crime has thus found a lucrative source of income in the operation of legitimate businesses which have been purchased through profits obtained from the operation of illegal activities.

Somewhat related to the control of legitimate business is the infiltration of organized crime into politics. Political graft and corruption are usually mentioned as forms of organized crime. Few groups of organized criminals, however, become involved in politics for the sole purpose of economic gain. Such infiltration is usually for the purpose of protection from legal interference in other criminal activities of organized crime. The liaison with public officials is actually a method for achieving immunity from the law, and should be so considered rather than regarded as a separate type of organized crime.

RACKETEERING. The third and final general type of organized crime is racketeering,

16 Robert T. Anderson, "From Mafia to Cosa Nostra," *American Journal of Sociology,* 71 (November 1965), pp. 302–310.
17 U.S. Senate Special Committee to Investigate Organized Crime in Interstate Commerce, *Third Interim Report,* p. 171.

the systematic extortion of money from persons or organizations. Its purpose is financial gain on a regularized basis.

Racketeering operations are, of course, infinitely varied in terms of the methods of operation and the kinds of organizations victimized. Mention of a few forms of racketeering which exist in the United States today will indicate the varied possibilities of this type of organized crime. For the most part, racketeering in the United States has concentrated on organizations which are engaged in the distribution of services and commodities. These organizations are especially vulnerable to the operation of rackets.

One of the simplest forms of racketeering is the *protection* racket in which persons or organizations are "protected," by payment of regular fees, for the privilege of operating without being destroyed by the organized criminals themselves. This kind of operation is not exclusive of other forms of racketeering, but may be used as one of the means of maintaining control over various services and commodities.

Racketeering has operated successfully for a number of years in the control of some groups of organized labor. Various schemes are employed today. Laborers may be forced to pay high fees and dues in order to find and hold jobs. Union leadership may be taken over by organized criminals. A considerable portion of the operating funds of unions may go to organized crime. Furthermore, money may be extorted from employers. Strikes are often threatened as a means of controlling employers. The building trades are particularly vulnerable to racketeering because of the importance of purchasing materials at crucial times and the need to complete projects by a certain date.

The wholesaling of perishable products, such as fruit, vegetables, and fish, is another field for racketeering operations. Racketeering is also prevalent in laundry businesses, cleaning establishments, trucking, loading businesses, and among such workers as motion picture operators, bartenders, waiters, truck drivers, and retail clerks. Powerful organized criminal groups may extend their operations to the control of many kinds of products and services.

SOCIETAL REACTION

As already indicated, there are a number of characteristics of American society which give support to organized crime. In fact, it may be argued that organized crime is a result of the particular structure of our society. To begin with, the motives for organized crime are largely the same as those valued so highly in the free enterprise system.[18] Organized crime, like legitimate business, attempts to achieve maximum returns, with a minimum of expenditure, through efficient organization and skilled management. The difference is that legitimate business operates within the law (most of the time) and organized crime operates outside the law.

Gambling itself, as a major area of operation for organized crime, is a deeply ingrained aspect of American culture. As Bloch has pointed out, gambling is a natural consequence of a culture which encourages success, skill, competition, and diversion.[19] The element of chance and the tendency to speculate in certain risks

[18] See Donald R. Taft and Ralph W. England, Jr., *Criminology*, 4th ed., New York: Crowell-Collier and Macmillan, Inc., 1964 Chaps. 12 and 16.

[19] Herbert A. Bloch, "The Gambling Business: An American Paradox," *Crime and Delinquency*, 8 (October 1962), pp. 355–364.

not only are found in illegal gambling but are a major aspect of investment and finance in the legitimate business world. It is little wonder that a large-scale business has developed in America to satisfy the demand for gambling.

In one of the early writings on organized crime, Lindesmith stressed the social context of organized crime when he noted that organized crime is an integral part of our total culture.[20] He observed that such factors as the profit motive, indifference to public affairs, general disregard for law, laissez-faire economics, and questionable political practices have produced a fertile place for organized crime in our large cities. Similarly, Bell has indicated that the development of organized crime, and gambling in particular, is related to immigration patterns, ethnic groups, neighborhood politics, and the American economy.[21]

Organized crime receives a great deal of public toleration in the United States because of its close relation to legitimate business. As Vold concluded:

> One basic fact stands out from the details of this discussion, namely, that organized crime must be thought of as a natural growth, or as a developmental adjunct to our general system of private profit economy. Business, industry, and finance all are competitive enterprises within the area of legal operations. But there is also an area of genuine economic demand for things and services not permitted under our legal and social codes. Organized crime is the system of business functioning in the area. It, too, is competitive, and hence must organize for its self-protection and for control of the market.[22]

Organized crime thus provides illegal services and products to business and the public. It continues to exist without a great deal of public action against it because of a hypocrisy in which citizens try to prohibit illegal practices in which they often indulge. In this clash of values and interests, organized crime provides the illegal services that the public desires. This paradox has been described as follows:

> It would seem that the vast majority of Americans today would like to have their proverbial cake and eat it, too, by theoretically affirming values which they hold dear, and, at the same time, reserving for themselves a certain leeway in realizing wishes which may not always correspond to these values. As a result, law and a high degree of lawlessness exist side by side, and moralists and gangsters complement each other.[23]

While creation of more effective laws and an attempt at better law enforcement may assist in the control of organized crime, the structured paradox of public indignation of illegal behavior, on the one hand, and toleration and approval of

---

[20] Alfred R. Lindesmith, "Organized Crime," *The Annals*, 217 (September 1941), pp. 76–83.
[21] Daniel Bell, "Crime as an American Way of Life," *Antioch Review*, 13 (June 1953). pp. 131–154.
[22] Vold, p. 240. Also see Daniel P. Moynihan, "The Private Government of Crime," *Reporter*, (July 6, 1961), pp. 14–20.
[23] Robert K. Woetzel, "An Overview of Organized Crime: Mores Versus Morality," *The Annals*, 347 (May 1963), p. 8.

illegal behavior, on the other, provides American society with its most serious handicap in the control and prevention of organized crime. The absence of a strong public reaction to organized crime has been crucial to its growth in America. With this in mind, the President's Commission on Law Enforcement and Administration of Justice concluded that one of the major problems in combatting organized crime is the lack of public and political commitment to its control.

> The public demands action only sporadically, as intermittent, sensational disclosures reveal intolerable violence and corruption caused by organized crime. Without sustained public pressure, political office seekers and office holders have little incentive to address themselves to combatting organized crime. A drive against organized crime usually uncovers political corruption; this means that a crusading mayor or district attorney makes many political enemies. The vicious cycle perpetuates itself. Politicians will not act unless the public so demands; but much of the urban public wants the services provided by organized crime and does not wish to disrupt the system that provides those services. And much of the public does not see or understand the effects of organized crime in society.[24]

SELECTED BIBLIOGRAPHY

1. Anderson, Robert T., "From Mafia to Cosa Nostra, *American Journal of Sociology,* 71 (November 1965), pp. 302–310.
2. Barnes, Harry Elmer, and Negley K. Teeters, *New Horizons in Criminology,* 3d ed., Englewood Cliffs, N.J.: Prentice-Hall, Inc., 1959, Chap. 2.
3. Bill, J. F., "Corruption and Union Racketeering," *Current History* 36 (June 1959), pp. 343–346.
4. Bloch, Herbert A., "The Dilemma of American Gambling: Crime or Pasttime?" in Herbert A. Bloch (ed.), *Crime in America: Controversial Issues in Twentieth Century Criminology,* New York: Philosophical Library, Inc., 1961, pp. 333–351.
5. ———, "The Gambling Business: An American Paradox," *Crime and Delinquency,* 8 (October 1962), pp. 355–364.
6. ———, and Gilbert Geis, *Man, Crime and Society,* New York: Random House, Inc., 1962, Chap. 9.
7. Cavan, Ruth Shonle, *Criminology,* 3d ed., New York: Thomas Y. Crowell Company, 1962, Chap. 6.
8. Clinard, Marshall B., *Sociology of Deviant Behavior,* rev. ed., New York: Holt, Rinehart and Winston, Inc., 1963, Chap. 10.
9. Johnson, Earl, Jr., "Organized Crime: Challenge to the American Legal System, Part I," *Journal of Criminal Law, Criminology and Police Science,* 53 (December 1962), pp. 399–425.
10. Kefauver, Estes, *Crime in America,* New York: Doubleday & Company, Inc., 1951.

[24] President's Commission on Law Enforcement and Administration of Justice, p. 200.

11. Lawrence, Louis A., "Bookmaking," *The Annals*, 269 (May 1950), pp. 46–54.

12. Lewis, Norman, *The Honored Society*, New York: Dell Publishing Company, Inc., 1964.

13. Lindesmith, Alfred R., "Organized Crime," *The Annals*, 217 (September 1941), pp. 76–83.

14. Moynihan, Daniel P., "The Private Government of Crime," *Reporter*, (July 6, 1961), pp. 14–20.

15. Peterson, Virgil W., "The Career of a Syndicate Boss," *Crime and Delinquency*, 8 (October 1962), pp. 339–354.

16. ———, "Rackets in America," *Journal of Criminal Law, Criminology and Police Science*, 49 (March–April 1959), pp. 583–589.

17. Ploscowe, Morris, "The Law of Gambling," *The Annals*, 269 (May 1950), pp. 1–8.

18. President's Commission on Law Enforcement and Administration of Justice, *The Challenge of Crime in a Free Society*, Washington, D.C.: United States Government Printing Office, 1967.

19. Reckless, Walter C., *The Crime Problem*, 3d ed., New York: Appleton-Century-Crofts, Inc., 1961, Chap. 10.

20. Schiavo, Giovanni, *The Truth about the Mafia*, New York: Vigo Press, 1962.

21. Sellin, Thorsten, "Organized Crime: A Business Enterprise," *The Annals*, 347 (May 1963), pp. 12–19.

22. Thornton, Robert Y., "Organized Crime in the Field of Prostitution," *Journal of Criminal Law, Criminology and Police Science*, 46 (March–April 1956), pp. 775–779.

23. Tyler, Gus, *Organized Crime in America: A Book of Readings*, Ann Arbor: University of Michigan Press, 1962.

24. ———, "The Roots of Organized Crime," *Crime and Delinquency*, 8 (October 1962), pp. 325–338.

25. Vold, George B., *Theoretical Criminology*, New York: Oxford University Press, 1958, Chap. 12.

26. Woetzel, Robert K., "An Overview of Organized Crime: Mores Versus Morality," *The Annals*, 347 (May 1963), pp. 1–11.

THE ORGANIZATION OF CRIMINALS
FOR PROFIT AND POWER*

George B. Vold

*The implications of organized crime for criminological theory
are pointed out by Vold in a selection from his book* Theoretical
Criminology. *Organized crime is seen as a natural adjunct to the
American system of private profit economy. Two parallel*

systems of competitive business activities—legitimate and criminal—go on at the same time in the same community. Organized crime is in a constant competitive struggle for favor and position in the economy.

A colorful, more or less common-sense vocabulary has come into existence during the last half century or so as a result of newspaper writers' and other interpreters' of the current scene trying to convey to their readers some understanding of certain specialized kinds of criminal activity. Well-written, hard-hitting books like Martin Mooney's *Crime Incorporated* (1935), Courtney Ryley Cooper's *Ten Thousand Public Enemies* (1935), and J. Edgar Hoover's *Persons in Hiding* (1938) not only documented many of the lurid details of specific instances of gangster control of crime, but they also contributed a strong influence to the general acceptance of the idea of crime as an organized business, conducted for business profit.[1] Words and phrases such as the professional criminal, organized crime, the syndicate, the mob, the gang, the brain, the fix, the fence, and so on, run through these accounts with considerable consistency of meaning and implication. What is this activity? If it is illegal, why is it not promptly suppressed? What brings it about?

These and many other questions have been discussed in numerous books and articles dealing with various aspects of this relatively commonplace yet subtle and elusive side of the general crime problem.[2] This activity will be the focus of attention in this discussion. Primary concern will be with the relation of this kind of collective behavior to criminological theory rather than with any extended discussion of the activity as such.

1. THE PROFIT MOTIVE IN CRIME

In normal society nearly everyone works with someone else in order to earn a living. Everywhere men have been interested in getting a maximum return for a minimum expenditure of effort and energy. It is axiomatic that this urge has been a useful spur to self-improvement and to the realization of a more abundant life. This drive is said to be a basic reason for the organization of business and the co-ordination of specialized effort to achieve a higher level of industrial production.

The incentive reward of a greater return for the more intelligently co-ordinated effort of many individuals is one of the essential considerations underlying the so-called 'profit motive' in business and industry. Organization, specialization of effort, co-ordination of activity to eliminate duplication and waste, all these are but a few of the commonplace virtues associated with organization and skillful management of business and industry. The result is increased production, greater earnings for everyone; in short, increased profits for everyone connected with the activity.

The incentive appeal of a more effective and profitable return for effort expended is also the keystone to the understanding of organization in the field of crime.[3] Organized crime always deals with efforts to obtain

---

[1] Martin Mooney, *Crime Incorporated*, McGraw-Hill, New York, 1935; Courtney Ryley Cooper, *Ten Thousand Public Enemies*, Little, Brown, Boston, 1935; J. Edgar Hoover, *Persons in Hiding*, Little, Brown, Boston, 1938.

[2] Charles Hamilton, ed., *Men of the Underworld: The Professional Criminal's Own Story*, Macmillan, New York, 1952, gives a bibliography of over 100 titles of books and magazine articles appearing since 1900, the overwhelming majority of which are accounts and interpretations of various kinds of organized crime. There is also a seven-page 'glossary of underworld terms' that includes approximately 225 different words or phrases.

[3] See J. R. C. MacDonald, *Crime Is a Business*, Stanford University Press, Palo Alto, Cal., 1940, and Ernest D. MacDougal, ed., *Crime for Profit: A Symposium on Mercenary Crime*, Stratford Company, Boston, 1933, for elaboration of this fact.

more money easily and with a minimum of effort. It is a particularly virulent form of the common economic drive to 'get rich quick.' The motivation, in this general sense, is largely the same as that of legitimate business, except that organized crime operates frankly 'outside the law' rather than 'within the law' as business generally tries to do.

2. DESCRIPTIVE TERMINOLOGY

The terminology used in describing the organization of criminal activity is not very uniform or precise. In general, however, the words used as terms or technical phrases reflect something of the degree of complexity of organization involved and something of the magnitude of the operations performed. The minimum unit of co-operative effort is the *partnership* of two or three working together to 'pull' a particular 'job.' At the other extreme is the large circle of influence and subordination that operates somewhat as any business organization and is often referred to as the *syndicate* or the *combination*.

Organized crime must be distinguished from the efforts of the large number of individual operators, petty thieves, drunks, disorderly persons, and others of this type who try their hand at crime but without much effective accomplishment. Part of their difficulty stems from their wasteful, inefficient, and unsystematic way of going about their criminal activity. Organization brings with it planning, leadership, division of labor, co-operation, and a form of social structure that gives personal status and a place where the individual belongs in the world of his associates. Loyalty to his group and the sharing of responsibility for action of large-scale magnitude, involving many other individuals and careful attention to timing and the details of a special task, become the individual's bond of communality with his fellow criminals in a normal action-pattern type of group. This is the social-psychological reality of the organized group in crime. It is evidence of the 'structure of social action' to

apply a phrase that has become popular as the title of a well-known book in theoretical sociology.[4]

The individual operator, in committing crime, is severely limited both as to the type of 'job' he may attempt and as to the skills and services he can bring to bear on any situation. He needs lookouts and decoys as well as someone to alibi for him. Hence, there are relatively only a very few criminals who really work alone. They form *partnerships* of two or three who work together sharing risks and dividing profits. Some kinds of crime, such as picking pockets, call for a *team* of two or three, each with specialized and definite duties. Such teams often become *mobs;* that is, small groups, often several teams, working together with co-ordination of activities and co-operation in arranging for *fixes,* and in dealing with *fences* to dispose of the loot.

Such combinations of individual criminals occur generally as varied forms of intimacy groupings, where all individuals working together are personally known to one another. As these groups become larger and more clearly fused and identified as specialty groups devoted to crime as a way of life, with sufficient manpower and skill to take care of all contingencies that may arise in the course of any job undertaken, they take on the characteristics of criminal *gangs.* The gang specializes in violence, intimidation, and fast profits. There is great emphasis on loyalty to the group, much identification 'with the boys,' and generally a concern with specialized types of crime calling for extensive manpower, great mobility of all personnel, and a significant line of 'connections' to help protect and cover up all necessary incidental activity. Burglary, large-scale bank robbery, kidnapping for ransom, and so on, are some of the common crimes typically carried out by gangs. A gang usually does not involve itself in small-time or petty crimes, but goes after the bigger 'jobs' where

[4] Cf. Talcott Parsons, *The Structure of Social Action,* New York, 1937; reprinted 1949 by Free Press, Glencoe, Ill.

the 'take' may be expected to be worth the risk and yield enough return for everyone to get something in the 'pay-off.'[5]

The criminal gang is characteristically an action group. It operates as a group. Its form of organization is therefore generally not unlike that of any simple, small-scale military unit. There must be a recognized head or leader (commanding officer) with a cadre of subordinate officers (lieutenants, sergeants, corporals) and a working force of individuals (privates) who are expected to carry out the several and varied assignments made by the leader. As in a military unit in battle, everyone has a specific assignment or job to do, including the leader, and everyone participates in the active combat, but only the commanding officer may give orders or make major decisions about the course of action to be followed.

The individual for whom crime has become the regular and accepted way of earning a living is sometimes called a professional. To be really applicable, the term implies some degree of skill and competence in criminality beyond that of the beginner, and especially beyond that of the stupid dolt who may try to live by crime but has no talent for it. Being professional means not only earning a living by crime but the following of a way of life with a full set of attitudes and rationalizations in support of such activity. With the idea of professionalization in any field goes the notion of training in the required skills, the instilling of 'professional attitudes,' the subscription to a 'code of conduct' or 'ethics,' the violation of which leads to disgrace and expulsion from the profession. Any worthwhile

professional man is proud of the profession he practices and is loyal to the code of conduct required of him.

The same basic ideas should apply when the term professionalization is used in connection with crime and the criminal. The professional criminal must be distinguished from the merely habitual one whose activity, while repetitive and habitual, has no other element of a profession. A lawyer 'habitually' practices law; a doctor is in the habit of practicing medicine. We do not, however, speak of them as habitual lawyers or doctors, but as professional men of law or medicine. Similarly, the term 'habitual criminal' is descriptive of a less specific and less meaningful vocational identification with crime than is true of the professional. Such a person is often a repeater in crime, but essentially a failure in the practice of crime as a vocation and a way of life. He frequently gets caught, yet wants to work at crime and associate with other criminals, but often is not good enough to be trusted with any significant assignments. Consequently, he sometimes has to work at legitimate employment between 'jobs' and prison sentences. The merely habitual criminal, whose only accomplishment is that he has been caught several times, has no place and no status among truly professional criminals. Shoplifters, picking pockets, and 'con' men, together with an upper crust of thieves specializing in very expensive diamonds and the like, are among the more clearly skilled and well-established 'professionals' in crime.[6]

3. CRIME AS BUSINESS: SYNDICATES, RACKETS, AND POLITICAL GRAFT AND CORRUPTION

In contrast to the criminal gang, which is an active, mobile group directly involved in crime activity, the *criminal syndicate* is a rel-

[5] There are systematic discussions of organized crime in many contemporary textbooks in criminology. See, for example, Ruth Shonle Cavan, *Criminology*, 2nd ed., Crowell, New York, 1955, chs. 5 and 6, pp. 125–79; W. C. Reckless, *The Crime Problem*, 2nd ed., Appleton-Century-Crofts, New York, 1955, chs. 9 and 10, pp. 160–203; D. E. Taft, *Criminology*, 3rd ed., Macmillan, New York, 1956, ch. 13, pp. 233–57; H. E. Barnes and N. K. Teeters, *New Horizons in Criminology*, 2nd ed., Prentice-Hall, New York, 1951, ch. 1, pp. 3–57.

[6] The interpretation of terminology given in this discussion is the writer's formulation, but is drawn from many sources and experiences in the United States and elsewhere.

atively stable type of business organization. Its business is to integrate and co-ordinate existing crime opportunities, practices, and personnel into a smoothly functioning, large-scale enterprise devoted to the assurance of a high level of profits for the organization. The term 'syndicate' is taken directly from the language of legitimate business. Webster defines a syndicate as 'an association of persons who combine to carry out a financial or industrial project.'[7] The large Oxford dictionary says it is 'a combination of capitalists or financiers, entered into for the purpose of prosecuting a scheme requiring large resources of capital, especially one having the object of obtaining control of the market of a particular commodity.'[8] The significance of the term in the present context lies in the fact that it represents an important, large-scale combination of capital and skilled personnel devoted to criminal activity. This may make it a very powerful influence in the local community, or in the state, and sometimes even in the nation. Like the truly 'big business' corporation on which it is patterned, it can afford to buy the best talent available in services and in technical skill that it may need but may happen not to be able to furnish directly from within the organization.

The syndicate is in the business of providing forbidden and illegal services or commodities desired by customers who are able and willing to pay for what they want. Prostitution, drugs, alcohol, and gambling are the main staples sold to willing customers at prices high enough to give a substantial profit to management after meeting all costs of carrying on the business. War-time rationing of food, gasoline, rubber tires, and other scarce commodities offered brief opportunities for the syndicates during World War II, but the time span was too short and the controls too uncertain to bring about the kind of extensive organization of activity devoted to the violation of food rationing that there had been in connection with the violation of prohibition legislation and the Eighteenth Amendment.[9]

The crime syndicate flourishes only because people with money in their pockets are willing to pay the price asked for the service or the commodity being sold. No one is forced to patronize a crime syndicate and there no compulsion on the customer to contribute to its profits. In this sense, it is a business organization functioning on merit, and profitable only as it can give the customer what he wants at a price he is willing to pay. He may be asked to pay an outrageous price for what he wishes to buy, but that is equally true of many commodities on the market in legitimate business. The syndicate must keep the customer willing to pay without the support of the advertising ballyhoo in mass-communication media so familiar in connection with many kinds of legitimate business activity.

Testimony before the Senate Crime Investigating Committee, the so-called Kefauver Committee,[10] in 1950 led that group to conclude that there was then in the United States a nation-wide crime syndicate built around two general axes or centers of organization. One was an eastern combine led by Frank Costello, Joe Adonis, and Meyer Lansky with headquarters in New York City and in general control of the East Coast crime business. The other axis was a Chicago group (a revamped Al Ca-

[7] Webster's *Collegiate Dictionary*, 2nd ed. G. & C. Merriam, 1947, p. 1012.
[8] *The Oxford Universal Dictionary*, 3rd ed., 1944, rev. with addenda, 1955. The Oxford University Press, printed in the U.S.A. by the Conkey Division of Rand McNally, p. 2112.

[9] See Marshall B. Clinard, *The Black Market*, Rinehart, New York, 1952, for a book-length analysis of criminality in connection with war-time rationing experiences in the United States.
[10] The official title of the committee was 'Special Committee to Investigate Organized Crime in Interstate Commerce' of the United States Senate, 81st Congress, 2nd Session. The membership of the committee consisted of the following senators; O'Conor (Md.), Hunt (Wyo.), Tobey (N.H.), Wiley (Wis.), with Kefauver (Tenn.) as chairman. It was established May 3, 1950, and filed its final report May 1, 1951. An authoritative digest and summary of the voluminous detail of the main report is available in the modest little book by Estes Kefauver, *Crime in America*, Doubleday, New York, 1951.

pone syndicate) led by Anthony Accardo, Jacob Guzik, and Rocco Frischetti, which handled the business in the Midwest and West Coast.[11] There were thought to be many interrelations, mutual investments, exchange of services, and other involvements cutting across many state lines. This gave the entire business of crime a nation-wide character analogous to other large-scale business corporations, such as those merchandising automobiles, home appliances, or other commodities with a national market. Many of these variously assorted underworld characters, the 'big shots' of the business and their not quite so big lieutenants, apparently were in the habit of meeting in something like regular crime conventions (even as other business groups) in resort places like Hot Springs or Miami Beach, in order to coordinate better their activities and come to necessary agreements on territories, percentages of 'cuts' or 'commissions,' and various exchanges of services.[12]

The *racket* in crime is the systematic practice of extortion under threat of some kind, usually of personal injury or of property damage. Typically, the racketeer insists on being 'cut in' for a percentage of the returns from some existing, profitable enterprise under threat of some penalty for refusal. If the business is illegal, or only marginally within the law, the opportunities for the racketeer are normally greatly increased, since no appeal for redress can then be made to police or other public authorities.

The details of racket operations are almost infinitely varied and extensive as to the kind of business enterprise that may be vulnerable.[13] An illustration of one of its simplest forms is the so-called 'protective association' which forces retail business establishments to pay high dues and regular 'fees' for the privilege of operating without molestation. The 'hazards' against which the merchant is 'protected' are supposed to be interference by 'enemy' gangsters, but in actuality are mostly those originating with and under the control of the racketeers themselves. Should the retailer refuse to go along with the demands made on him, he may find his windows broken, or his shop bombed, or his goods damaged. In case of continuing obstinacy on his part, personal violence, beatings, eye-gouging, and so on, may be used as more effective arguments of persuasion. The 'sales talk' of the racketeer may include the suggestion that the added costs of 'protection' be passed on to the customers, thus making it a more profitable business both for the merchant and for the protective association.

The so-called 'labor racketeer' has become relatively well known in the area of union-employer relations. Waterfront racketeering in great port cities like New York or San Francisco has become widely recognized and has been actively investigated for many years. For example, according to Johnson's *Crime on the Labor Front* (1950),[14] the port of New York has a floating labor force of over 20,000 men, each of whom is only occasionally and irregularly employed in the loading or unloading of ships' cargoes. There are no permanent jobs, only a succession of different jobs as ships come and go. This puts the hiring-hall boss in a strategic position to say who shall work and who shall not. Also, he is in a favorable position to play favorites and give the jobs to those who will 'kick back' part of their pay to him and keep their mouths shut.

An investigating committee in 1951 found non-existent employees carried on the

11 Estes Kefauver, *op. cit.*, pp. 20–21.

12 *Ibid.*, pp. 21–2.

13 For detailed accounts of specific racket and syndicate operations and for interpretations of 'who worked what racket,' see especially accounts like those of J. Edgar Hoover, *Persons in Hiding*, *op. cit.*; Edward Dean Sullivan, *Rattling the Cup on Chicago Crime*, Vanguard Press, New York, 1929; Philip S. Van Cise, *Fighting the Underworld*, Houghton Mifflin, Boston, 1936;

Courtney Terrett, *Only Saps Work*, Vanguard Press, New York, 1930; and Estes Kefauver, *op. cit.*

14 Malcolm Johnson, *Crime on the Labor Front*, McGraw-Hill, New York, 1950.

payroll and their pay collected by 'stooges' who turned it over to the racketeers in charge of the union hiring halls.[15] Much attention has been given to 'cleaning up' the whole waterfront situation, both from the inside by leaders of organized labor and on the part of governmental units with some jurisdiction. However, at the end of 1954 *The New York Times* news follow-up report on the situation in New York found evidence of continuing racketeer influence.[16]

Political graft and corruption are always intimately related to effective organization of crime.[17] The political machine, especially in the anonymity of city life, easily becomes corrupt and a ready and willing partner with various organized criminal elements. Thus, for a consideration (graft) 'protection' against undue police interference can be arranged for the syndicate that specializes in the business of peddling sex, liquor, drugs, or what have you, all of which may be in considerable economic demand but cannot be merchandised legally. Then it becomes true that what is good and profitable for the syndicate likewise becomes profitable for the political party machine.

The syndicate knows well on which side of the bread the butter is, and contributes generously to the re-election of its friends, and helps actively to 'get out the vote' for the party thus favored. Since the syndicate has control of considerable personal power, and since it can afford to pay well for the services performed, it may arrange for vari-

ous kinds of election frauds and irregularities to help keep in office those politicians willing to grant the favors necessary to the continued profitable operation of the illegal business that is the source of income for the syndicate. It also controls naked force through organized gangs of criminals who may be either ordered to or paid to 'do the job' (i.e. intimidate through use of physical violence, beating, torture, acid throwing, even killing when necessary) on a dangerous opponent or preferably on some of his supporters and helpers.

One of the older forms of election dishonesty in the United States, now largely eliminated through the general adoption of systems of permanent voter registration, consisted of rounding up numerous transients and 'skid-row' unfortunates, taking them to the nearby polling places, and paying them a stipulated sum after they had voted. Sometimes the same group of more or less dependable transients would be taken around to several polling places to repeat their performance. This is what the one-time Chicago philanthropist and reformer, Raymond Robbins, used to describe as 'voting early and often.'[18] That kind of easy and simple ballot box stuffing has been curbed to a great extent, though it would be naïve to assume that all possibilities of 'vote buying' have been entirely eliminated from modern elections. That intimidation through physical attack, bombing, acid throwing, and so on is still a factor to be reckoned with is clearly evident in the 1956 attack on the anti-racketeering television commentator, Victor Riesel.[19]

This, in brief, is the general nature of the unholy alliance between the corrupt political machine and organized crime that

[15] *Ibid.*, p. 107.
[16] *New York Times*, December 9, 1954, Section E, p. 8.
[17] Classical studies of American politics and crime include accounts such as the following: Lincoln Steffens, *The Shame of the Cities*, McClure, Philips, New York, 1904; R. C. Brooks, *Corruption in American Politics and Life*, Dodd, Mead, New York, 1910; F. C. Howe, *Privilege and Democracy in America*, Scribner, New York, 1910; Frank R. Kent, *The Great Game of Politics*, Doubleday, New York, 1923; Herbert Asbury, *The Gangs of New York*, Knopf, New York, 1928; David Loth, *Public Plunder: A History of Graft in America*, Carrick & Evans, New York, 1938; J. T. Salter, *Boss Rule: Portraits in City Politics*, McGraw-Hill, New York, 1935.

[18] In a campaign speech on behalf of William Dever for Mayor, at the Garrick Theatre, Chicago, as reported in the *Chicago Tribune*, April 3, 1923.
[19] A news story review of the case of acid blinding of anti-racketeering, labor columnist and television commentator Victor Riesel, may be found in *Time*, April 16, 1956. There is a follow-up account in the issue for August 27, 1956.

all too often has characterized local, city, and county government in the United States.[20] The problem must not be confused with that of the occasional personal dishonesty among individual politicians in their dealings with other individuals, ostensibly businessmen, but who also have connections with criminal gangs and syndicates. The crux of the matter lies in the widespread diffusion (almost collective action) of corruption and favoritism among a group of politicians who are accustomed to working together and who maintain contacts with organized crime syndicates that can well afford to pay for special services or for special immunities. The co-ordinated co-operation of numerous individuals is usually involved in obtaining approvals and signatures necessary for government action of any kind, and therefore corruption and graft involving public officials is seldom a matter of an isolated individual or two. The question of individual or personal dishonesty is not usually so much directly involved as is the fact of chicanery, double-dealing, and general dishonesty on the part of a whole clique or group of government officials— the essential fact back of the phrase 'corrupt government'—joining the criminal syndicate in the exploitation of a relatively inarticulate and essentially helpless general public.[21] Any sense of personal wrongdoing on the part of individual public officials in these situations seems to have been blunted in the psychological support of the group situation, whereby they have the acceptance and assurance of support of fellow officials. What so many others do without self-incrimination cannot be really so very bad is the commonplace self-justification of ordinary individuals involved in these situations.

4. UNDERWORLD COMPETITION AND GANG WARS

It is usually only certain spectacular aspects of organized crime that come to public attention. Such an incident was the sensational St. Valentine's Day 'massacre' in Chicago in 1929 in which seven members of a North-side criminal gang were lined up against the inside brick wall of a garage and executed by machine gun fire at the hands of gunmen from a rival South-side gang. Before this there had been many other incidents and killings, including that of the notorious Dion O'Banion whose funeral, even now thirty years later, is still considered to have been the most sumptuous and extravagant gangster funeral ever seen in Chicago or elsewhere. It presented an incongruous mixture of highly placed city and county government officials sharing the limelight with all the better-known 'big shots' of the underworld. In New York, also, there was obviously method and organization in the activities of the much-publicized 'Legs' Diamond, 'Lucky' Luciano, and the 'combination' which came to be known as Murder Incorporated. Detroit had its Purple Gang and the sensational murder of Jerry Buckley, a radio anti-racketeering crusader who was alleged to have been 'in' on the shakedown rackets connected with the bootlegging of alcohol during the prohibition period.[22]

Descriptive details of these bloody affairs are of no particular significance in seeking to understand why these battles took place. The explanation of the violence is to be found in the fact that the businesses involved were both illegal and enormously profitable. It is a commonplace of any business activity that where there are good

---

[20] For some detailed specifications on the contemporary linkage of crime and politics in American cities, big and small, see the summary of the Kefauver committee hearings by Estes Kefauver, op. cit., pp. 50–81.

[21] See Kefauver, op. cit., p. 79, for an account of a price mark-up on bakery supplies brought on through corruption and a promoter's racketeering.

[22] Details of these and many other notorious instances of sensational crimes having probable linkage with government officials as partners and sharers of the profits may be found in the accounts of J. Edgar Hoover, op. cit.; Courtney Ryley Cooper, op. cit.; Arthur B. Reeve, The Golden Age of Crime, New York, 1931; and Philip S. Van Cise, op. cit.

profits to be earned there will be competitors trying to get in on the return. Our system of private profit economy, therefore, has had a long history of dealing with the problem of the proper control of the conditions of competition. How avoid monopoly and yet not suffer from 'cutthroat' competition?

Within the area of legitimate enterprise, there are always law, government, and the opportunity for court litigation, acting as supervisors and umpires to restrain the impetuous and to guide and control the competitive process. But under the law, we do permit 'successful' combinations in industry, business, and finance to 'eliminate' and to 'wipe out' their competitors. This is clearly an important aspect of why 'big business' is big rather than continuing to develop as many independent small businesses. Thus, in the story of the automobile industry in the United States, numerous competitors have disappeared in the consolidations and mergers that have resulted in today's mammoth Big Three. There is still competition in the automobile field, but it is controlled and regulated in many ways. For example, Buick, Oldsmobile, and Chevrolet, onetime independent competitive companies, are now competitive units within the General Motors 'empire.' The competition that remains now never becomes 'cutthroat,' because all three units are under a common general management with a genuine pooling of resources and engineering skills that was impossible on the independent, small-scale company basis.

The situation is strikingly similar in the case of the underworld 'combination' or 'syndicate.' This same element of order and control is precisely what these forms of organization bring to the system of underworld business enterprises. Since the profits from these activities are enormous, really of 'big time' proportions, involving over $20,600,000,000 annually in gambling alone, according to a writer in *Pageant* in 1950,[23]

there will inevitably be competitors trying to 'muscle in' on the lush take. Yet the activities are illegal and under cover, so no appeal can be made to recognized channels for redress or protection against unfair methods of competition. The needed 'police protection' therefore must be informal, private, and supplied by the underworld itself. Competitors are brought into line by direct interference and intimidation. The 'goon squads' of mobile gunmen employed for this work are better understood as the 'enforcers' of underworld decrees and decisions. There are always critical questions, in this world of shadowy existence, of where the orders come from, who has authority to give orders, and whether or not orders need to be obeyed. Uncertainties about the answers to these critical questions are resolved through direct battle—gang war—and through 'peace conferences' that here, as in the world of nations, follow after wars.[24]

It is as an incident in the battle between underworld business organizations in competition that the sensational and bloody St. Valentine's Day 'massacre' becomes understandable. As the story now has come to light, it seems that in the Chicago of that day the sale of illicit alcohol and the control of brothels and of the 'dope trade' had developed two principal underworld groups or gangs with numerous more or less independent operators affiliated with each. There was a South-side organization that had come under the control of the notorious Al Capone (after a whole series of mysterious but convenient killings and disappearances of other leaders like 'Big Jim' Colosimo and Johnny Torrio) and a North-side group, the so-called 'Bugs' Moran mob. There was really 'big money' in the profits from the various enterprises, and the Capone syndicate proceeded to establish monopoly control. This was resisted by the

---

[23] From detailed estimates by Murray Teigh Bloom in 'Gambling: America's Ugly Child,' *Pageant*, April 1950, pp. 12 ff.

[24] Cf. Alfred R. Lindesmith, 'Organized Crime,' *The Annals of the American Academy of Political and Social Science*, 217:76–83, September 1941.

Moran group through a long series of battles and killings, on both sides, but resistance collapsed when seven of the principal gunmen and 'organizers' for the Moran group were so summarily executed on St. Valentine's Day in 1929. The power of the 'Bugs' Moran mob declined rapidly after that significant defeat, and it was soon merged with and became part of the larger Capone 'empire.' Both 'Bugs' Moran and other prominent members of his gang were thus reduced from the status of independent businessmen to that of employees of a larger combine in which they took only their permitted 'percentage' or 'commission' while passing on the major share of the profits to the top command of the Capone syndicate.[25]

Other cities besides Chicago had their underworld mergers and consolidations. The stories are all more or less the same except for local names and details.[26] The basic reason for the whole sorry mess was the solid economic fact of big money in profits and the need to establish tighter monopoly control over an illegal enterprise in order to enlarge the profits and to see that only the right people got a share of the easy money.

This is where the Kefauver Committee picked up the story in 1950–51. With legalization of the trade in alcoholic beverages, underworld activities had concentrated on gambling, narcotics, and sex vice. These were still illegal and continued to be enormously profitable. Thus the Committee heard of certain so-called 'policy wheels' (interrelated and controlled gambling establishments) that were returning net profits of from $50,000 to $200,000 per year for each 'partner' in their control. 'Forced mergers' and 'muscling in' as techniques for controlling business competition in the underworld had not changed much by 1950 from the

earlier story of the 'roaring twenties.'[27] Organized crime was still competitive, it still provided its own brand of 'private law enforcement,' and most important of all, the profits were still great enough to make the necessary risks and dangers seem worthwhile.[28]

5. INTERRELATION OF UNDERWORLD AND UPPERWORLD

As social structures, the underworld of crime and the upperworld of business and politics are, as the terms imply, in many ways essentially two sides of the same coin. The nature and character of the underworld, in any given city or county, is clearly a reflection of the kind of business integrity and political morality that is characteristic of the dominant elements of the community. When community leaders ask few questions about the nature of the practices followed in connection with their own sources of profits, it may be expected that there will be considerable tolerance for various kinds of political favoritism that would be rejected by the leaders of another community. It is a well-established truism of social interaction, referred to by Park and Burgess in Introduction to the Science of Sociology (1924), that one of the more corrupting influences in government is that of personal friendships and primary group contacts.[29] The behavior of friends, or behavior tolerated by friends, somehow seems less reprehensible than it might otherwise seem to be. This thin line between what is proper behavior, what is frowned upon, and what is wrong, in the interrelations of private and public morality, has been subjected to book-length discussion and analysis by E. S. Atiyah, The Thin Line (1952).[30] This 'thin line' appears to be one of the vulnerable

[25] For a succinct account of the Capone story see Arthur B. Reeve, op. cit. 'The King of the Rackets,' pp. 52–66.

[26] For a Western version of the story of underworld organization and operation see the account of the activities of the notorious Lou Blonger of Denver in Philip S. Van Cise, op. cit.

[27] Kefauver, op. cit. p. 51.

[28] Ibid. pp. 52–3.

[29] Park and Burgess, op. cit. pp. 330–31.

[30] E. S. Atiyah, The Thin Line, Harper, New York, 1952.

chinks in the armor of public morality in the North America of today.

Because business is competitive and because profits increase when there is opportunity to eliminate competition, there is normally a continuous struggle between the various economic units for power and for a more favorable place in the world of everyday business activity. This competition may become a desperate struggle for survival. Help from questionable sources may then be welcomed, provided the competitive position of the business is improved. Such assistance is likely to be on an exchange of favors basis: help will be given provided non-interference with the operation of the racket is promised. If the promise is broken there will be trouble; there may be threats, beatings, and even murder. No tears are ever shed for the competitor who loses his business, be he in the upperworld of legitimate activities but forced to the wall, or be he in the underworld situation of having his territory taken over by a stronger mob.

An early formulation of the idea of a basic structural relationship between business activity (with its supporting world of government and politics) and criminality came out of the empirical researches of Enrico Ferri and Fillipo Poletti . . . that were carried out on French and Italian data nearly three-quarters of a century ago.[31] Poletti's basic proposition that increase in legitimate activity gives increased opportunity for and increased incentives for criminal activity carries with it the implication that both kinds of activities (legitimate business and criminality) are mutually interdependent and interrelated parts of the normal structure of society. It would follow from this theoretical orientation that the same general conditions that are useful in understanding and explaining one are similarly the explanation of the other. This view also makes clear the reason for the high degree of similiarity in the structural organization and functioning of organized crime and of organized business.

A more recent as well as more down-to-earth formulation of the nature of the interrelationship of upperworld and underworld may be found in the words of Jacob G. Grossberg, a Chicago lawyer, describing the relation between crime and the political party machine in *Crime for Profit:*[32]

Professional crime is an integral part of politics, is a major factor in it, and its share of the spoils is immunity to ply its trade. . . . Politics is the business of the party organization; party organization is the business of the mercenary criminal, the racketeer. The political boss is usually the well paid agent or manager for the latter; and the men he puts in office are usually puppets. . . . The policeman on the beat or the plain clothes man dares not 'bring in' the 'Big Shot,' whose gang controls his ward committeeman, who controls his captain, who controls him. . . . It is the party organization which furnishes the governor, the judge, the prosecutor, and which gives orders to the police. In other words, it furnishes the law enforcing organization. It is manifest that that organism suffers paralysis . . . and a paralyzed body cannot function properly.

This seemingly extreme statement of conditions that may operate to tie political party machines and business rackets into an unholy alliance of protection and money-making for everybody on the 'inside' at the expense of the exploited public, nevertheless had dramatic corroboration in the investigations of the Kefauver committee. Testimony before it dealing with the tie-in of politics and organized crime in Kansas City, Missouri, spelled out a picture in clear outline with names, dates, and places, of the interrelations of crime bosses and politicians in

[31] Fillipo Poletti published his formulation in book form in 1882 after several years of work and discussion in several shorter papers. See his *Del sentimento nella scienza del diritto penale*, Undine, 1882. This work is cited and interpreted with quotations translated into English by Morris Ploscowe, 'Some Causative Factors in Criminality,' *Report on the Causes of Crime*, vol. 1, pt. 1, pp. 5–161 (especially pp. 113–15) of no. 13, Report on National Commission on Law Observance and Law Enforcement, Washington, D.C., June 26, 1931.

[32] Jacob G. Grossberg, 'Mercenary Crime and Politics,' in *Crime for Profit*, ed. by Ernest D. Mac-Dougall, Stratford Co., Boston, 1933, pp. 156–7.

that community. The need to have the 'right people' in government positions led finally to the outrageous vote frauds in Jackson County, Missouri, in 1948 with its aftermath of violence and murder as between rival gangster elements.[33] Instances and illustrations from other cities could be multiplied in endless detail.[34]

6. IMPLICATIONS FOR THEORY AND FOR CONTROL

One basic fact stands out from the details of this discussion, namely, that organized crime must be thought of as a natural growth, or as a developmental adjunct to our general system of private profit economy. Business, industry, and finance all are competitive enterprises within the area of legal operations. But there is also an area of genuine economic demand for things and services not permitted under our legal and social codes. Organized crime is the system of business functioning in this area. It, too, is competitive, and hence must organize for its self-protection and for control of the market.

With two parallel systems of competitive business activities going on at the same time, in the same community, there are obviously many opportunities for profitable interchange of services in meeting the threat of specific competitors. Thus, for example, a legitimate business enterprise in competition with another may utilize the services of a labor-boss racketeer to call a strike in a competitor's establishment in order to gain a business advantage. Such collaboration obviously becomes mutually advantageous to the racketeer as well as to the business unit profiting from the misfortunes of the competitor.

The whole area of organized crime is clearly one in which the factors of individual differences can be written off as of little theoretical significance. This kind of criminal activity, and its organization as a system of economy, seems clearly to be an aspect of the competitive struggle for favor and position in the economy. Many of the more violent competitive struggles are between elements of the underworld, one gang against a competing one rather than between underworld and upperworld groups. In the struggle of one business unit with another, it may, and apparently often does, seek the assistance of available underworld elements. As long as they are mutually useful to one another, their interdependence continues and both become established aspects or fixtures in the normally functioning social structure.

There is an underlying fact of mutual trust and confidence, both in the business ability and in the personal integrity of fellow operators, that appears to be the principal cohesive factor in underworld organization. There can be no legal 'incorporation' or other binding contract; there can only be the code of the gentleman whose word is as good as his bond. In this the parallel is strikingly similar to that of the legitimate business world. A California executive may telephone a New York broker or wholesaler negotiating an important business transaction. There will be no hesitancy about arrangements provided there is mutual trust and confidence. This is the heart and core of legitimate business activity, even more than written agreements and court orders.

In the underworld it is even more explicitly true that reliance must be placed on a man's reputation for keeping his promises. He must be dependable. This was dramatically pointed out to the Kefauver committee by the well-educated lawyer-gambler, Sidney Brodson of Milwaukee.[35] The somewhat emotional, self-righteous indignation that was the committee's reaction to this testimony[36] overlooked entirely the essential truth of Brodson's contention that the most

[33] Kefauver, op. cit. pp. 82–90, especially pp. 82–3.

[34] For an excellent short factual account of the details of racketeering and white collar crime in America, with numerous explanations of specific instances, see Barnes and Teeters, op. cit. ch. 1, pp. 3–57.

[35] Kefauver, op. cit. p. 164.

[36] Ibid., p. 165.

valuable asset a bookmaker has is his reputation for integrity and honesty in covering all bets. With that reputation, he can accept bets over the telephone from coast to coast, and his business will grow and prosper. If he welches on his obligations, he is as much out of business as would be the legitimate business merchant who balked at meeting obligations incurred orally over the telephone.

From the standpoint of the problem of control, organized crime seems to be more significantly affected by economic facts of supply and demand, and the fads and foibles in consumer habits, than by much legisla-tion and sporadic attempts at formal control.[37] It must always be remembered that underworld businesses are as capable of failure (as businesses) as are those of the upperworld. There is the same obligation to 'keep up with the times' as there is for business and industry in general. In the long run, this may turn out to be a more fundamental and a more significant control factor than explicit legislation and the customary sporadic police drives.

[37] See the discussion in D. R. Taft, *Criminology*, 3rd ed., 1956, pp. 304–11, and pp. 316–25 as this applies to the traffic in drugs and to the possible control of prostitution.

ORGANIZED CRIME:
A BUSINESS ENTERPRISE*

Thorsten Sellin

Organized crime, as discussed by Professor Sellin, is synonymous with economic enterprise organized for the purpose of conducting illegal activities and which, when in pursuit of legitimate ventures, uses illegal methods. Financial profit is the goal of these illegal businesses, which subscribe to the tenets of American entre-preneurship. Findings from the investigation of numbers and gambling in Buffalo indicate that the numbers racket, among syndicated underworld operations, is one of the most highly organized, staffed, and disciplined. Playing the numbers and gambling in general, like participation in other vices, survive because large portions of the population enjoy them, see no harm in them, and do not regard them as immoral, even when they are illegal.

If we take a closer look at the term "organized crime," it becomes apparent that, as used today, it is not a very precise term. The word "crime" creates no difficulty, for it means, in this connection, conduct that violates the criminal law and can subject the offender to punishments prescribed by that law. It is the word "organized" that proves a stumbling block, because it could have more than one implication or interpretation.

* Reprinted from *The Annals of the American Academy of Political and Social Science*, 347 (May 1963), pp. 12–19, by permission of the author and the publisher.

We assume that it does not describe the behavior of an individual, who carefully plots and carries out a crime, which is to bring him some personal gratification, without the aid or co-operation of others, no matter how systematically he may organize his plan of action. When he needs the co-operation of others to carry on his criminal activity and gain the benefits from it, we can begin to talk of "organization." A team of jewel thieves or pickpockets is one example; its members must have leadership and carry out specific and perhaps diverse tasks, stolen goods must be disposed of through a "fence," and, if they are caught, there may be an attorney, who knows them, who will handle their case. All these functions and relationships are parts of a pattern of organization.

This is not the kind of operation, however, that is covered by the term "organized crime" as it is commonly used today. It has come to be synonymous with economic enterprises organized for the purpose of conducting illegal activities and which, when they operate legitimate ventures, do so by illegal methods. They have arisen for the chief purpose of catering to our vices—gambling, drinking, sex, narcotics—which our laws do not tolerate, and they have found many other collateral ways of gaining illegitimate profits. Whatever form they take, financial profit is the goal, which they share with the entrepreneurs of legitimate business. Indeed, in their perverted way, they subscribe to the tenets of American entrepreneurship, in a system of free enterprise, as described by Sawyer:[1]

individualism; competitive economic activity within an impersonal market; mobility, social and geographical; achieved as against ascribed status, with economic achievement the main ladder of advancement; emphasis on "success" in a competitive occupational system as the almost universally prescribed goal; money income as a primary reward and symbol of success; the institutionalization of innovation, risk-taking, change and growth.

These illegal enterprises also resemble the legal ones in other respects. An illegal liquor business, for instance, must own or have access to distilleries, means of transporting the wares, warehouses, outlets in saloons, clubs, restaurants, or private establishments. This requires capital, managerial personnel, and employees of various kinds. An illegal gambling enterprise faces the same problems of organization as a legitimate banking chain. The basic difference between the illegal enterprise and a legal one devoted to similar but approved functions is not in the hierarchical structure, the table of organization, or the distribution of the duties of its components, for they are essentially alike. It lies in the fact that the illegal nature of the business has created problems that have to be solved in ways that a legal firm does not have to employ. Both have in common a hope for continuity and survival. "Unlike most criminal groups but like most business enterprises, a criminal organization contemplates a continuous life-span."[2]

THE NUMBERS BUSINESS

To illustrate the continuity just mentioned as well as the manner in which an illegal business must operate to survive, only one such business will be discussed, the one commonly referred to as the "numbers racket." Most people probably know what it consists of, for newspapers, magazines, and television have often described it. Briefly, "numbers" is an illegal lottery in which the player bets that a certain number or combination of numbers will win in a drawing. It is frequently assumed that it is of recent origin. "The origins of the game are somewhat obscure, but some believe that it was brought to this country from the

[1] John E. Sawyer, "The Entrepreneur and the Social Order," Chap. 1 in William B. Miller (ed.), *Men in Business: Essays on the Historical Role of the Entrepreneur* (New York and Evanston: Harper & Row, 1962).

[2] Earl Johnson, Jr., "Organized Crime: Challenge to the American Legal System, Part I," *Journal of Criminal Law, Criminology and Police Science,* Vol. 53 (December 1962), p. 401.

Caribbean area early in this century and operated in various cities on a small-time basis"—according to an official New York report.[3] The same source calls the game either "policy" or "numbers," as though these words were interchangeable. In fact, they represent quite different ways of conducting the lottery, policy being an older form. The specific way of drawing the winners in numbers may not be very old and is bound up with the demise of legal lotteries in the United States, but the illegal lottery of which numbers is the most representative today may be nearly as old as the legal ones. It has survived all efforts to eliminate it, by law or law enforcement.

Evolution of the Genoese Lottery. The number lottery, or lotto, is said to have originated in Genoa early in the seventeenth century; it simulated the election of five political candidates from among a large number—rarely over 110 and finally fixed at 90—all identified by a number from 1 to 90. Printed lists of the names of the candidates and their numbers were distributed and bets were placed that one, two, or three numbers would appear among the five drawn in a public drawing from an urn. A bet on two numbers was called an *ambo*, on three a *terno*.

Lotteries based on the Genoese practice were organized in many American states during the last century. Although prohibited by law in New York in 1834, an author writing in 1868 claimed that New York City was the headquarters for lotteries in Kentucky and Missouri, where public drawings were held at noon and at night, respectively, the winning numbers being telegraphed to New York. These lotteries were known as ternary ones, based on numbers from 1 to 78, in which a lottery ticket with any three of the up to fourteen numbers drawn won the highest prize, and those with but two or one of the numbers won less.

It is a by-product of these lotteries, however, that is of special interest to us. According to Martin, writing in 1868:[4]

Together with the sale of [lottery] tickets is carried on an extensive game of gambling known as "policy." To "policy" is to bet on certain numbers coming out in the [lottery] drawing, for either morning or evening. Thus, if I believe 4, 11, 44 will be drawn, I stake a dollar at the lottery office, or any sum I see fit, up to five hundred dollars, and if all three of the numbers make their appearance on the drawing, the liberal managers will give me two hundred dollars for my one . . . the three numbers taken are called a "gig"; two numbers a "saddle"; four numbers a "horse."

"Policy"—a Variation. Martin claimed that there were some 600 places in the city, known as exchanges, where lottery tickets could be bought and, presumably, "policy" played.

The Negroes of the city are great "policy" players. . . . [One old woman] says she dreams her numbers. The sale of lottery dream-books is really immense. One firm on Ann Street sells several thousand a month of these books, wherein every possible dream is described and the proper "policy" attached to it.[5]

Essentially the same picture of "the lottery business, closely connected with which is 'policy dealing'," was described fourteen years later by McCabe[6] and in 1891 by Colonel Knox, who had this to say about it:[7]

"Playing policy" is a cheap way of gambling. . . . The play is upon numbers . . . drawn daily, usually in Kentucky or Louisiana, and sent by telegraph. The numbers are from 1 to 78; the room where the game is played is, like those of other cheap gambling dens, usually at the rear of a cigar store, barroom or other place, where it does not arouse suspicion if many persons are seen entering. A long

[3] Temporary Commission of Investigation of the State of New York, *An Investigation of Law Enforcement in Buffalo* (New York, January 1961).

[4] Edward Winslow Martin, *The Secrets of the Great City* (Philadelphia, 1868), pp. 513–514.
[5] *Ibid.,* p. 517.
[6] James D. McCabe, *New York by Sunlight and Gaslight* (Philadelphia, 1882), p. 549.
[7] Helen Campbell, Thomas W. Knox, and Thomas Byrnes, *Darkness and Daylight; or Lights and Shadows of New York Life* (Hartford, Conn., 1891), p. 639.

counter extends the entire length of the room, and behind this counter, near its center, sits the man who keeps the game and is called the "writer." He is not the proprietor, but simply a clerk on salary, and his duties are to copy the slips handed up by the players, mark them with the amount paid, and watch to see that no fraud is practiced. There are twenty-five plays every morning and the same number in the evening at the regular shops, and they all get their winning numbers from a central office in Broad Street. Near the writer is an iron spike or hook on which are the policy slips; each slip contains the winning numbers and is placed face downwards so that nobody can see what it is.

A player, said Colonel Knox, might take a slip on the counter, write, let us say, five pairs of numbers and bet a sum on five "gigs." When the other players in the room have filed their bets, the writer picks up the top slip from the iron spike, writes the numbers he finds on it, in two columns of twelve each, on a slate and hangs it up for all to see. If the player has guessed two of the numbers in either column in one of the gigs he has won ten times the amount on his bet.[8]

Policy has survived and is still played in much the same manner as it was done a century ago. It flourishes in Chicago, according to recent descriptions. In 1945 Drake and Cayton wrote:[9]

Almost as numerous as the churches (and more evenly distributed) are Bronzeville's [Chicago's South Side Negro district] 500-odd "policy stations," in any one of which a person may place a bet that certain numbers will be announced as lucky by one of 15 or 16 "policy companies" . . . In order to keep up a semblance of respect for the law, about half the stations are "fronted" by legitimate businesses. Most of the others can be easily recog-

nized by the initiated . . . by a sign on a window or door: "Open"—"4–11–44"— "Doing Business"—"All Books" . . . Winning numbers are listed three times daily, after selection at a public "drawing." The places where the drawings are made are known as "wheels" . . . scattered about the community. . . . The drawings are made from a small drum-shaped container in which 78 capsules or balls, numbered consecutively, are placed. After each turn of the drum, a ball is pulled and its number read aloud. As they are called, a printer sets the numbers into a special printing press. As soon as the last number is drawn, the press rolls out the policy slips, which are then distributed all over Bronzeville. . . . Indispensable for the inveterate policy player is his "dream book," valuable for translating both dreams and "significant" occurrences into "gigs." . . . The policy station is simply a brokerage office for the players. . . . Station owners are allowed to keep 25 percent of the gross business they write, and so lucrative is the business that the 500 stations employ some 2000 porters, writers, and other employees. . . . Some legitimate businessmen have turned to it as their major enterprise and use their other business merely as a front. The station is simply the most visible expression of a complex machine, employing over 5000 persons, which in 1938 had a weekly payroll of over twenty-five thousand dollars and an annual gross turnover of at least $18 million. This business is organized as a cartel with a syndicate of 15 men . . . in control of the game. On the syndicate payroll were 125 clerks, more than 100 pickup and delivery men, a dozen or so accountants, including several CPA's, and over 100 miscellaneous employees—doormen, floormen, janitors, stampers, bookkeepers, and "bouncers."

The Modern Numbers Game. In most of our large cities today, the old policy lottery has been displaced by or transformed into what people know as the numbers game. This has made it possible to dispense with public drawings, eliminate the paraphernalia and operations needed for them, and substitute an ingenious method of selecting the winning numbers, which enables the players to determine for themselves whether or not they have won at the end of the day, because newspapers will—inadvertently—give them the information. The operation of this variant of the Genoese lottery has necessitated

[8] *Ibid.*, p. 640.
[9] Herbert L. Marx, Jr. (ed.), *Gambling in America* (New York: H. W. Wilson Co., 1952), pp. 74–77, quoting St. Clair Drake and Horace R. Cayton, *Black Metropolis* (New York: Harcourt, Brace, 1945). A slightly more recent account, including illustrative photographs of the drum used in drawings and of a policy ticket, is found in W. T. Brannon's "Chicago—Penny Ante Paradise," *U.S. Crime*, Vol. 1 (December 1951), pp. 76–83.

a change in the technique of betting. The player places a bet with a writer that, let us say, a certain number containing three digits, from 000 to 999, will be the winning one. He knows or is told how to find out the results of the "drawing." In some cities, the last figures in the number of (a) stocks that advanced, (b) stocks that declined, and (c) stocks that remained unchanged on the stock market would furnish the answer; in others, certain figures, perhaps the last three digits, in the total sum of money passing through the New York Clearinghouse; in still others, certain digits in the daily balance of the United States Treasury or in the total amount of money wagered by the pari-mutuel method on certain combinations of races at some predetermined track. Whoever invented the system, it is reasonable to believe that, when the Louisiana State Lottery collapsed in 1890 and Congress the same year prohibited the mailing of lottery tickets or material and, in 1895, the interstate transportation of tickets, somebody figured out this substitute for the ternary system that had relied on the results of the drawings in the southern lotteries as the source of the winning numbers. This may also explain the belief that numbers originated about the turn of the century.

THE BUFFALO INVESTIGATION

In 1959, as a result of prior extensive investigations made in Buffalo by the New York State Commission of Investigation, wholesale raids were made on numbers and other gambling operations. The raids and subsequent hearings provided much information about the nature of the illegal lotteries and the circumstances and conditions that permitted them to flourish. Thirteen numbers "banks" and "drops" (key collection points) were caught in the raids, which netted forty-six policy operators ("numbers" is still called "policy" in New York, in spite of the differences previously explained); they "included many key figures in the highest echelons of the policy racket,

some of whom had never been arrested by the Buffalo Police Department, although they had operated for years. Voluminous books and records, policy slips, collectors' slips, bank tally sheets, and miscellaneous paraphernalia were seized."[10] The knowledge thus acquired by the Commission confirmed the belief that the numbers racket "is one of the most highly organized, fully staffed and disciplined of all underworld syndicated gambling operations."[11]

Organization and Operation. In Buffalo, bets could be placed with one of many hundreds of writers on the street or in many business establishments, even with some policemen. Investigators for the Commission made repeated bets in more than forty locations. The bets were recorded on specially printed slips called "B/R" slips or "Bond-Race" slips because they could be used either for bets on the outcome of New York Stock Exchange deals or on race-track wagering. The slips were made out in triplicate from bound pads, the original going to the bank and the copies retained by the writer and the player. The pads were supplied by the I. and M. Sufrin Company of Pittsburgh, Pennsylvania, whose records showed that in 1958 and 1959 some 200,000 pads had been shipped by common carrier to five "banks," or a total of five million sets of slips per year. In many instances, the supplier received payment in cash sent in packages by parcel post.

The bankers assigned specific territories to various members of their organizations in order to avoid conflict and to insure maximum efficiency.

[Because] the nature of the operation requires that money and betting slips be deposited at the bank or in the hands of trusted members of the conspiracy prior to "post time" [at the race track] or the closing hour for wagers . . . control points known as "drops" were set up where writers turned in their slips and money. Pick-up men were employed to collect num-

[10] *An Investigation of Law Enforcement in Buffalo,* op. cit., p. 23.
[11] *Ibid.*, p. 38.

bers and money from the drops and writers and to deposit them in the hands of controllers. From the drops, pick-up men and controllers would return winnings, if any, on the following day. All of these individuals, each essential to successful operation of the racket, were under the strictest discipline and control. Any deviation from fixed procedures or time deadlines could only be authorized by the top banker himself . . . unflinching obedience to orders was required.[12]

The "banks" or headquarters . . . where all management functions of the racket take place, in some instances were located in fully equipped offices containing furniture, telephones and calculating machines. A staff of clerical help assisted the bankers and controllers in the rapid calculations necessary to record and conduct the day's business.[13]

The Commission estimated, on the basis of information gained by the raids, that seven banks were managed by sixteen bankers. The net annual profits of these banks were estimated at close to two million dollars. This was achieved due to the favorable conditions under which the operations were carried on. One of the special investigators for the Commission

was directed by a uniformed Buffalo policeman to a location where numbers could be played . . . this advice proved to be correct, as shortly after he actually placed numbers bets at the address. In many stores and business establishments in certain areas of Buffalo, numbers were played openly with slips and money freely displayed on store counters. Lines of people waiting to place their numbers bets were a common occurrence.[14]

The business was run quite openly.

The same pick-up men and controllers, using the same vehicles and generally following the same designated routes, made their rounds every day at almost exactly the same times in carrying out their functions without displaying any appreciable concern over the possibility that their activities were being observed.[15]

Law-Enforcement Deficiencies. In New York, persons who contrive a lottery or own,

12 *Ibid.*, p. 39.
13 *Ibid.*, p. 37.
14 *Ibid.*, p. 14.
15 *Ibid.*, p. 37.

direct, and manage numbers operations are committing a felony, and persons found in possession of numbers slips are guilty of a misdemeanor. What, then, were the police of Buffalo doing about these violations under their very noses? Departmental instructions require police officers to make periodical reports of "suspected premises," but, during 1958, 1959, and the first two months of 1960, not a single such report was turned in concerning numbers operations. What of arrests? In the two years 1958–1959, a total of 195 persons were arrested for all kinds of gambling offenses, of which 131 were clearly identifiable as involving numbers.

Comparing the total policy arrests for 1959 with the total number of policy racket violators . . . again demonstrates the complete inadequacy of this performance. . . . Commission accounts have estimated that 3,560 persons were engaged in acts constituting policy misdemeanors and 182 persons . . . in acts constituting policy felonies, on any given day in 1959. Yet only 72 persons were arrested for policy violations during the entire year, *and all of them for policy misdemeanors*.[16]

What happened to those arrested? One served a jail sentence of thirty days, two received suspended sentences, and a total of 4100 dollars was collected in fines from all those arrested.

During the hearing held by the Commission, a police captain with thirty years of service in the department expressed his belief that no gambler operated in his bailiwick, although some of the top racket figures in the city had been doing so for years. Other police officers testified that they knew that numbers operations existed and who directed them, but they failed to account for the lack of law enforcement. In other words, official tolerance of the illegal lotteries was, one might say, complete. How such tolerance was purchased is another matter. An illegal business, unlicensed because prohibited, is forced to resort to bribery and corruption of law-enforcement personnel and politicians in order to operate. Their illegal

16 *Ibid.*, p. 72.

character also makes them vulnerable to extortion by persons who can in return offer immunity from arrest.

DEMAND AND SUPPLY

Buffalo has been used as an example, but its counterparts are numerous in all sections of the United States. It is claimed that, during the last decade or more, strong efforts by federal, state, and some local governments—stimulated by the findings of highly publicized congressional investigations—to combat organized crime of all kinds have met with some success. However, so far as the illegal lottery business is concerned, history suggests that this particular business is not likely to suffer more than temporary reverses. Like other businesses, it has its ups and downs, its recessions and recoveries, but, as long as it can count on a sizable market for its services, it will survive them all. In the last analysis, they continue to thrive because a large section of the population enjoys betting—betting on horses, football games, boxing matches, basketball games, and on numbers—sees no harm in it, and does not regard it as immoral even when it is illegal. As long as this public attitude persists and is shared by or exerts an influence on candidates for elective office or servants of the law, no effective enforcement of law is conceivable. We are, in fact, caught on the horns of a dilemma, for under these circumstances our gambling laws, passed in a noble hope that they would rescue the citizen from his own evil appetites or protect him against exploitation, have also inadvertently helped to create an entrenched source of bribery and political corruption, an undesired and undesirable effect of our high-mindedness.

THE GAMBLING BUSINESS:
AN AMERICAN PARADOX*

Herbert A. Bloch

What makes gambling, in spite of its ancient history, a special type of problem to Americans is the peculiar combination of contradictory attitudes with which it is regarded in this country. The ambivalent public attitude toward gambling is revealed in the legally sanctioned tolerance of certain forms of gambling, such as parimutuel wagering on racetrack premises and church-sponsored bingo games, while the line is drawn at more extensive and popular forms of "poor man's gambling." Where to draw the line separating governmentally sanctioned forms of gambling from illegal forms is a difficult and subtle problem, and frequently the attitudes determining it are without sufficient rational and empirical support. The gambling racketeer capitalizes with large profit on the deep-rooted compulsions which encourage Americans to gamble.

* Reprinted from *Crime and Delinquency*, 8 (October 1962), pp. 355–364, by permission of the author and the publisher.

A long-standing embarrassment of the American social and economic scene is the incapacity of the public and its officialdom to make up their minds.

OUR CONTRADICTORY ATTITUDES

Much of this dilemma arises from the peculiarly American ambivalent penchant for moral disapproval of a variety of publicly enjoyed practices. The Volstead experiment was agony because it outlawed what people wanted—America is a drinking nation —and boosted, in exchange, a historic though unrealistic craving for a moral rectitude which most of them neither understood nor were willing to make sacrifices for. This peculiar inner dialogue of the American public conscience is expressed as well in American sexual patterns, as the Kinsey reports of recent memory so amply testify, and in the subject of this discussion —the gambling business. In affirming the ironic American ambivalence toward values which are neither fully understood nor desired, we are mindful of Norman Douglas' perceptive statement in *South Wind:* "The country . . . is full of half-tones, not only in nature. Because a thing seems good, there must be some bad in it. It seems bad to us —therefore it must be good for us. Bedlamites! I like clean values. They make for clean living." In the vast penumbra of American interests—of which gambling constitutes a large share—it may hardly be said that we enjoy "clean values." Our concern here, as elsewhere, appears to deny in principle what we enjoy in practice.

The most painful part of this hard truth, perhaps, is that there may actually be inestimable wisdom in the attempt to achieve a high-minded purpose despite repeated disavowal in practice. In making this statement, however, we should be mindful of the distinction between the pious and hortatory sentiments with which we like to associate ourselves and to which we pay lip-service, and those realities of choice which determine and *reflect* our actual moral values.

Moral and ethical values, to serve a significant and legitimate purpose in organized society, must be reinforced by historic need and necessity. Further, such values must provide a reasonable chance of successful functioning in the determination of widespread objectives for the society as a whole and in the light of existent social reality. The sociologist has long recognized the distinction between, to use his terms, *manifest* and *latent* functions of the social order— those functions to which the society officially subscribes and, in contrast, those which are fashioned by the exigencies and realities of social living. Acknowledgment of a latent function in no way incurs the necessity for its moral endorsement. Further, recognition of the disparity between our public views and our actual practices insures an honest perspective upon reality and provides a means of preserving a semblance of social sanity.

CONFUSED VIEWS
TOWARD GAMBLING

Within our historic culture there has never been a clearcut conception of the immorality or the so-called evils of gambling. Indeed, in the early history of the Republic, some of our most worthy educational institutions were financed through public lotteries.[1] Further, certain compulsive factors that lead to pervasive gambling are deeply imbedded within the American social structure itself. It is important to recognize also that in a country as socially and culturally heterogeneous as our own, stemming from national and ethnic backgrounds which have frequently been congenial to public forms of gambling, it becomes extremely difficult to lay down a basis for a universal proscription against it.

The rationales which have frequently

[1] Among the institutions of higher learning financed in part by public lotteries, common from early colonial times until the 1830's, were Columbia, Harvard, and Yale. See Herbert A. Bloch and Gilbert Geis, *Man, Crime, and Society* (New York: Random House, 1962), p. 230.

been advanced against gambling in any form, ordinarily by religious denominations of fundamentalist persuasion, are based upon quasi-theological views, themselves open to serious question and limited in their conception of practices which satisfy utilitarian objectives. Virgil Peterson notes that "even when fraud and manipulation are absent," the gambling business "operates on a one-sided percentage basis that makes it impossible for the patrons as a class to derive any benefit."[2] That the "sucker" hardly ever gets a fair break in most forms of organized gambling today cannot be denied, but whether or not the individual gambler derives any benefit from the activity as seen from his own standpoint is a different matter. How can we assess the kinds of recreational satisfaction, for example, that large masses of the public derive from gambling? How is one to assess the recreational "benefit" derived from observing, or following, a horse race (on which one has placed a bet), or a boxing contest, or a baseball game, and what is the difference, as far as recreational "benefit" is concerned, between these activities and watching television or spending time in a local barroom? These questions should not be construed as a brief for large-scale public gambling.

The argument that gambling produces no tangible "benefits" offers the supplementary view that it is essentially a sterile activity; gambling, according to this position, does not add to the total wealth of the community and can hardly be conceived, in the traditional Calvinistic view, as contributing to the productive use of capital. The flaw in this argument is that the charge of nonproductivity is equally applicable to a number of current economic practices regarded as eminently respectable.

It may be depressing that large masses of Americans, Britons, Frenchmen, Spaniards, Italians, and other nationalities engage in various forms of public gambling, but the

fact remains that they do so despite the charge that such activity is nonproductive. For that matter, it can be argued, so is a sunny afternoon spent on the golf links.

SOME MORAL DILEMMAS

To argue against all forms of gambling activity on the grounds of their so-called social sterility is to overlook far more significant activities whose utility is likewise open to serious question. For example, economists are sharply divided as to the value of a large volume of speculative trading on the stock exchange; the question is whether such trading actually contributes to national economic vitality and productive growth. If we require a reminder about this, we have simply to recall the recent Black Monday, during the last week of May of this year, when the stock market collapsed as a result of a sustained trend in speculative trading. From the standpoint of the psychological motivations involved, the difference between such speculative trading and ordinary gambling risks is one of degree rather than of kind. A study was conducted under the auspices of the Board of Governors of the New York Stock Exchange shortly after this debacle to discover the reason for the unanticipated collapse; it concluded that the cause was largely the average speculators' desire for short-run profits and rapid turnovers, and consequently the abandonment of sound investment in the so-called long-range "growth" stocks. It can be reasonably argued that such speculative risk-taking, coupled especially with extensive buying on margin, constitutes a particularly ominous form of "making book" with partially solvent claims. The glaringly speculative basis of the debacle may be clearly seen in the fact that the fall in security prices had little relevance to the state of the economy itself.

While it is certainly not our intention in this analysis to suggest that all stock investments are akin to sheer gambling speculation, the tendency to speculate in certain forms of risk stocks and commodity prices

[2] Virgil W. Peterson, "Gambling—Should It Be Legalized?" Journal of Criminal Law and Criminology, Sept.–Oct., 1949, p. 322.

undoubtedly does constitute part of a broad spectrum of national interest in gambling. In contrast to outright gambling, such speculation can have a sinister effect on the economy and even, at times, on our survival, as may be seen in the report issued by the Commodity Exchange Authority of the United States Department of Agriculture in August, 1950, a few weeks after the outbreak of hostilities in Korea. According to this report, up to 85 or 90 percent of the dealings in soybeans on July 21, 1950, for example, was pure speculation—betting that the market would go up as a result of the crisis —with potentially dangerous effects upon our economy during a period of national crisis.

A speculator who purchased just before the Korean episode and deposited the minimum margin could have "cashed in" five weeks later, on July 28, with an approximate 450 percent profit on lard, 300 percent on cotton-seed oil, 300 percent on soybeans, 150 percent on cotton or wool tops, and a comparatively modest 100 percent on the relatively sluggish wheat futures.[3]

THE SOCIAL PRESSURE TO GAMBLE

The motivation to gamble very likely constitutes a deeply ingrained aspect of our national culture. Indeed, it appears quite likely —and this is something ordinarily not appreciated by the public and its political leaders—that the cultural system itself has built-in characteristics which tend to encourage expression of gambling interests. As in any widespread demand for a consumer commodity or service, institutional arrangements of supply invariably emerge to satisfy an extensive functional demand. Such arrangements may be licit or illicit; that they will emerge is as inevitable as the age-old law of supply and demand. What has been true of liquor and is presently true of narcotics is even more true of gambling.

[3] U.S. Department of Agriculture, *Report of the Commodity Exchange Authority* (Washington, D.C.: Government Printing Office, August, 1950).

It is within this peculiar socio-economic and cultural context that the unique American ambivalence toward gambling must be examined. The public conscience is in turmoil not so much because of the gambling itself but rather because of two correlative problems created by our ambivalent attitudes. The first is our justified concern over underworld control of certain broad, consumer-based forms of gambling, with all the ramifications into many legitimate phases of American public life which large-scale enterprise, whether licit or illicit, automatically introduces. Secondly, in an age of easy familiarity with the neurotically inspired social disorder, we are concerned with the phenomenon of the compulsive gambler. The first is a problem of effective law enforcement or some form of feasible state control, or a combination of both; the second is a problem for the psychiatrist.

Gambling is a big business—indeed it is one of the leading business enterprises in the United States. It has all the institutional characteristics and drives of large-scale economic enterprises, including trends toward monopolistic control and limited competition, control of auxiliary services and supply, and development of insurance safeguards as a means of market control and protection of mammoth investments. An example of security safeguards paralleling those of legitimate enterprises is the way in which underworld gambling syndicates have sought to control the network of wire services in the country. It should be noted that legitimate enterprises have also profited from this association. In St. Louis, for example, the Kefauver Committee found that the relaying of gambling information accounted for approximately $100,000 a month profit to a national telegraph agency. As part of its findings, the Committee declared:

It is quite clear that . . . [the agency] aided and abetted the violation of the gambling laws of the state because it was profitable to do so. . . . One wonders whether [its] obliviousness to its public responsibility not to permit its facilities to be used in violation of state laws was in part due to the fact . . . a well-known gambler is one of its outstanding stockholders.

Before examining the extensiveness of the gambling business itself, we might profit by glancing at some of the "built-in" components of the social system which establish a climate congenial to gambling.

The essential basis for all gambling inheres in the chance factor of success for its participants, irrespective of the type of device or game which is employed. The chance element, however, always varies. Gambling may call for skill, as in certain card games and athletic competitions, or it may simply depend on the chance throw of a pair of dice or the draw of a card, as in stud poker. In any event, the element of chance is always present. It is an indispensable aspect of its universal appeal.

Certain social and cultural systems, particularly those where status largely depends on competitive pecuniary standards, seem to foster and exploit the element of chance in human life. This is notably true in the United States, where rapid commercial expansion and industrial development conspire to make economic success dependent on sharp competitive practice and, at times to a considerable degree, on precarious and speculative enterprise. In the United States, as we have already noted, the distinction between certain forms of approved and legitimate stock market speculation and the cultivation of the gambling interest is largely a matter of degree, yet one is approved and the other condemned.

Operating against chance, however, are the stabilizing and routinized mechanisms which are the bases of the social order. Every society, to achieve security and insure its own continuance, strives to reduce ignorance and the unpredictable. Nevertheless, a certain degree of ignorance concerning the operation of both physical and human events must, of necessity, always exist. Ignorance of events, therefore, and of their outcome serves as a dynamic function

in all societies.[4] Where knowledge of the outcome of a given series of human events is certain, there is no incentive toward competition and other forms of social striving. Von Neumann and Morgenstern have demonstrated this point of view in their analysis of economic behavior as compared to the "sporting" chance present in playing games.[5]

A society such as our own—complex, impersonal, and yet highly competitive—places a great premium on conformity and routine. At the same time, there is great pressure to break the routine—to initiate, to promote, and to experiment in order to bring about the dynamic growth of a continuously expanding social economy. For large masses of individuals, this is difficult, if not impossible. Hedged in by increasingly stereotyped employments, the fear of insecurity, the pressures of family, and the opinions of others, the average person is afraid or unable to "take a chance" that may mean riches and prestige, despite the traditional assurance that the country's growth has come from people who did exactly that.

WORKING-CLASS FAMILIES AND GAMBLING

Moreover, as Allison Davis, E. W. Bakke, and others have shown in their studies of working-class families, lower socio-economic class members frequently feel that they are trapped and that neither opportunity nor incentive exists for further advancement.[6] It is equally instructive to understand, as Walter Miller, the anthropologist, has

[4] See Robert K. Merton, "The Unanticipated Consequences of Purposive Social Action," *American Sociological Review*, Dec., 1936, pp. 894–904.

[5] John von Neumann and Oskar Morgenstern, *Theory of Games and Economic Behavior*, 2nd Edition (Princeton: Princeton University Press, 1947).

[6] See, for example, Allison Davis, "The Motivation of the Underprivileged Worker," *ETC: A Review of General Semantics*, Summer, 1946, pp. 243–253.

shown in his study of the culture of working-class families, that the belief in luck and
fate is virtually endemic within such groups.
For many, the chances of success in making
a "killing"—by betting on a number or on
the Irish Sweepstakes or by winning the
giant jackpot on some television "giveaway"
program—appear to be favorable; the odds
are hardly ever taken into consideration.
Further, the rewards are immediate; unlike
the course of "turning an honest penny,"
there is no lengthy and painful deferment
and no risk of uncertain achievement. The
types of strain induced by the lack of opportunity among working-class youths have
been studied from different vantage-points
among delinquents and young offenders
by Albert K. Cohen, Richard Cloward and
Lloyd Ohlin, and the writer, all of whom
recognize the pressures toward immediate
gratification of wants among certain segments of working-class families.

There can be little doubt that this lack
of opportunity is fertile soil for the flourishing numbers and policy games. In fact,
among economically depressed urban families, to "play the numbers" is more than a
gambling venture; the players constitute, in
fact, a cult, as Drake and Cayton have
noted in their *Black Metropolis*. One of
William F. Whyte's informants in *Street
Corner Society*, a study of youth in a Boston
slum, tells him: "I'm batted out. I'm so
batted out that I don't have a nickel to
put on the numbers today. When a Cornerville fellow doesn't have the money to put
on a number, then you know he's really
batted out."[7] This has been underscored in
the study of the Black Belt in Chicago by
Drake and Cayton, where the authors found
many residents defending the pervasive
numbers game as crucial to the economic
survival of the community because of the
jobs it provided.[8] When Cornerville women

send their children to the grocery store for
staples, they give them an extra coin to put
on a number. "Dream books," sold openly,
claim to provide clues to winning numbers.
A numbers operation in an East Harlem
apartment raided by New York City police
last June 14 was reported to have handled
500,000 bets a day, with a total annual volume of business estimated in excess of
$35,000,000. This single operation main-
tained 60 controllers and 400 collectors to
carry on its business.

The conditions of class and cultural associations, opportunity, and the large blocks
of unplanned leisure produced by our highly
mobile society play an important part in
encouraging certain forms of gambling
which can be readily capitalized upon by
the commercial purveyors of gambling enterprise. Games of chance are traditionally found, and even nurtured, in the
play of children in modern society, ranging
from traditional guessing and matching
games to early imitation of adult gambling
and card games. In many families, on all
class levels, card-playing and other forms
of gambling have become deeply entrenched. There are ethnic, class, and even
sex differentials in these common forms of
recreation, recognized as a diversified market by the entrepreneurs of organized gambling. Bridge-playing is largely a middle-
class diversion, while poker is traditionally
considered a "man's game," and the casting
of dice, aside from professional gambling
interest, has been especially common among
Negroes. For many young men of the lower
and middle classes, learning to play cards
is part of the process of growing up and becoming identified with adults and their
standards. For the person who has few inner
resources, whose tedious and boring employment offers little opportunity for progressive
challenge and advancement, and whose
early experience included gambling in some
form, learning to gamble is as commonplace
and natural as becoming an ardent baseball
fan or a television addict.

[7] William F. Whyte, *Street Corner Society* (Chicago: University of Chicago Press, 1955), p. 115.
[8] St. Clair Drake and Horace R. Cayton, *Black
Metropolis* (New York: Harcourt, Brace, 1945),
Ch. 17.

GAMBLING AS BIG BUSINESS

To satisfy this enormous demand for gambling activity, there has developed in this country a gargantuan gambling enterprise, which comprises not only the actual gambling interests, both legitimate and illegitimate, but also a wide variety of thriving auxiliary and fringe industries. For example, at least 4,000 pinball machines are manufactured every week, according to the estimate by the California Crime Commission in its 1949 report. While the public may generally tend to regard the pinball operation as innocuous, such a rate of manufacture means that more than 200,000 new machines are placed in various establishments each year, and it also means that the Commission's estimate of 250,000 to 300,000 machines in operation at any given time is very likely a highly conservative figure. As Teeters has pointed out, the United States Treasury receives taxes from only a negligible number of establishments where such machines are placed. And, as the McClellan Senate Committee revealed in 1957 in disclosures concerning the operation of pinball machines in Oregon, large sums of money are paid out to control the concessions where the machines are located.

To determine with any degree of precision the extent of gambling in the United States, in terms of the amount of money expended and the number of persons involved in different types of gambling enterprises throughout the country, is extremely hazardous. At best, we must depend on what the research student refers to as quantitative indexes, or indicators. These suggest that the volume of gambling is greater than the estimates at the time of the Kefauver investigation over a decade ago. At that time, it was estimated that approximately 50,000,000 adult Americans participated in some form of syndicated or professional gambling, all of which involved an annual sum of approximately $30,000,000,000 and yielded an annual profit to the gambling entrepreneurs of about $6,000,000,000,[9] greater than the combined annual profits of the United States Steel Corporation, General Motors, and the General Electric Corporation. We have reason to question the accuracy of such estimates, especially when we recognize that, as the California Crime Commission disclosed in its survey, slot machines alone take in approximately $20,000,000,000 each year.

Ernest R. Mowrer has shown that the incidence of gambling rises in war, postwar, and inflationary periods.[10] Undoubtedly the total volume of gambling through expanded facilities offered by professional gambling groups and syndicates has risen sharply since the Kefauver hearings. Estimates offered by several reporters lead to the conclusion that about 70 percent of the annual volume of gambling consists of bets illegally placed with bookmakers and "numbers" runners. One well-known authority in the field estimates that as many as 112,000,000 persons participate annually in some form of gambling, ranging from bingo, lottery, dice, and card games to bets on horse races.[11] According to this estimate, approximately 43 percent of gambling participation occurs in various forms of lotteries, football and baseball pools, and playing cards and dice for money. It should be kept in mind, however, that the composite figure affords us, at best, an unreliable index. For example, we have no way of knowing how large a part of this total—and it must be considerable—is made up of persons who engage in more than one type of gambling. Further, in view of regional disclosures of police data, the estimated total annual volume of 8,000,000 "numbers" players appears conservative, as does the annual estimate of 8,000,000 persons placing bets on horse races. The metro-

---

[9] Second Interim Report of the Kefauver Committee (Washington, D.C.: Government Printing Office, 1951).

[10] Ernest R. Mowrer, "Social Crises and Social Disorganization," *American Sociological Review*, Feb. 1950, p. 64.

[11] Ernest E. Blanche, "Gambling Odds Are Gimmicked!" *The Annals*, May, 1950, pp. 77–80.

politan area of New York City, for example, is believed to have as many as 20,000 bookmakers distributed throughout the district.[12]

As noted above, much of this information, clandestine by nature, is based on indicators whose reliability is questioned, but evidence of the extensiveness of gambling and its inroads into conventional life can be found in other sources—for example, periodic disclosures of involvement of respectable citizens in various phases of the gambling business. Certain organizations with extensive business interests, some of them legitimate, have been used to conceal even more extensive and profitable gambling activity. Thus, the Kefauver Committee's previously mentioned disclosure of a telegraph service's large monthly profits in St. Louis and the 1950 conviction of eight officials of the Guarantee Finance Company of Los Angeles on charges of criminal conspiracy with a vast bookmaking enterprise are deeply revealing. Such facts provide a significant index to the wide range of public participation and expenditures in gambling. They point to a public interest which, judged by the volume of participation, is big enough to qualify as a national pastime—possibly the public's favorite pastime.

SOCIAL CONTROL OF GAMBLING

The history of the attempt to control gambling in the United States is a record of contiguous cycles. In the initial stage of the cycle, the more flagrant abuses of public tolerance lead to imposition of controls on the more egregious aspects of public gambling enterprise. This, in turn, frequently leads to further efforts to extend control, occasionally ranging from rigid prohibition of off-track betting to the curbing of bingo games. Attempts at such broad control have invariably led in the past to widespread public tolerance of syndicated underworld control, to syndicate absorption or domination of legitimate enterprises, and, more

disastrously, to deals with and pay-offs to corrupt law enforcement officials. Usually the next stage is indignant public recoil and an attempt at new approaches and appraisals, leading to greater relaxation of existent standards or more feasible legal control. This, in turn, often leads to further relaxation until excesses and abuse of public tolerance once again give birth to efforts to impose rigid restrictions, and thus the cycle is reintroduced.

Our British cousins appear to have been somewhat more rational about this problem, as they are about other forms of social ills ordinarily resistant to legal control. Even before licensing of premises for off-track wagers—a system introduced in April, 1961 —bookmaking by telephone had long been legal in Great Britain. A state-operated pool on soccer games is so popular that it accounts for about 10 percent of domestic mail during the nine months of its operation each year.

In 1951, after a two-year study, the Parliamentary Commission on gambling recommended that the person of modest circumstances with a little money to gamble be afforded the same opportunity for placing bets as his more affluent fellow citizen who might be able to spend his time at the race track or place his bets through other arrangements. It was this report that led to the present British practice of licensing off-track betting establishments, under rigid governmental control of hours and mode of operation.

The Parliamentary Commission came to the following conclusion: "We can find no support for the belief that gambling, provided that it is kept within reasonable bounds, does serious harm to the character of those who take part . . . their family circle, [or] the community generally."

So far as we know, the British character has not degenerated since that famous pronouncement. Even if it had, it would be presumptuous to attribute the decline to a more tolerant public view of gambling.

[12] See, for example, Louis A. Lawrence, "Bookmaking," *The Annals*, May, 1950, pp. 46–54.

FROM MAFIA TO COSA NOSTRA*

Robert T. Anderson

The old Mafia of Sicily was a preindustrial peasant institution. Its organization was intimate and diffuse. It now operates in the highly urbanized and industrialized milieu of the United States. As an urban, industrial institution it has evolved into a different kind of organization. The real and fictive kinship ties of the old Mafia are still utilized among fellow Sicilians and Italians. But these ties are now subordinate to bureaucratic ones as defined in terms of specialization, a hierarchy of authority, a system of rules, and impersonality.

Sicily has known centuries of inept and corrupt governments that have always seemed unconcerned about the enormous gap between the very rich minority and the incredibly poor majority. Whether from disinterest or from simple incapacity, governments have failed to maintain public order. Under these circumstances, local strong men beyond reach of the government, or in collusion with it, have repeatedly grouped together to seek out their own interests. They have formed, in effect, little extra-legal principalities. A code of conduct, the code of omertà, justified and supported these unofficial regimes by linking compliance with a fabric of tradition that may be characterized as chivalrous. By this code, an "honorable" Sicilian maintained unbreakable silence concerning all illegal activities. To correct abuse, he might resort to feud and vendetta. But never would he avail himself of a governmental agency. Sanctioned both by hoary tradition and the threat of brutal reprisal, this code in support of strong men was obeyed by the whole populace. The private domains thus established are old. After the 1860's they became known as "Mafias."[1]

As an institution, the Mafia was originally at home in peasant communities as well as in pre-industrial towns and cities. (Sicilian peasants are notable for urban rather than village residence.) The Mafia built upon traditional forms of social interaction common to all Sicilians. Its functions were appropriate to face-to-face communities. Mafias persist and adapt in contemporary Sicily, which, to some extent, is industrializing and urbanizing. Mafias also took root in the United States, where industrialization and urbanization have

[1] Giuseppe Pitrè, *La famiglia, la casa, la vita del popolo siciliano* (Palermo: Stabilimento Tipografico virzi, 1913), I, 289–91; George Wermert, *Die Insel Sicilien in volkswirtschaftlicher, kultureller und sozialer Beziehung* (Berlin: Dietrich Reimer [Ernest Vohsen], 1905), pp. 397–402, 437; Gaetano Mosca, "Mafia," *Encyclopaedia of the Social Sciences* (London: Macmillan & Co., 1933), X, 36; Margaret Carlyle, *The Awakening of Southern Italy* (London: Oxford Press, 1962), pp. 111–12; Jerre Mangione, *Reunion in Sicily* (Boston: Houghton Mifflin Co., 1950), p. 74; Francis M. Guercio, *Sicily, the Garden of the Mediterranean: The Country and Its People* (London: Faber & Faber, 1954), p. 69; *Time* (August 15, 1960), p. 25; E. J. Hobsbawm, *Primitive Rebels. Studies in Archaic Forms of Social Movement in the 19th and 20th Centuries* (Manchester: Manchester University Press, 1959), p. 40; Antonino Cutrera, *La Mafia e i mafiosi: origini e manifestazioni, studio di sociologia criminale* (Palermo: Alberto Reber, 1900), p. 177; Norman Lewis, "The Honored Society," *New Yorker* (February 8, 15, 22, 1964).

* Reprinted from the *American Journal of Sociology*, 71 (November 1965), pp. 302–310, by permission of the author and of the publisher.

created a new kind of society, and here, too, they have persisted and adapted. But can a pre-industrial peasant institution survive unchanged in an urban, industrial milieu? May we not anticipate major modifications of structure and function under such circumstances? The available evidence on secret organizations, though regrettably incomplete, inconsistent and inaccurate,[2] suggests an affirmative answer. The Mafia has bureaucratized.

Formal organizations of a traditional type, whether castes in India, harvesting co-operatives in Korea, monasteries in Europe or other comparable groups, normally change as they increase the scale of their operations and as their milieu urbanizes.[3] They often simply disappear, and their surviving activities are taken over by other institutions. In the Japanese village of Suye Mura, for example, Ushijima finds that work formerly done by co-operative exchange is now done by wage labor.[4] Alternatively, however, these traditional associations may survive by being reconstituted as rational-legal associations or by being displaced or overlain by such associations, as castes in India, traditionally led by headmen and councils (panchayats), are now being reconstituted by the formation of caste associations.[5] The substitution of

rational-legal for traditional organization is of world-wide occurrence today.[6] Because models of rational-legal organization are almost universally known, and because modern states provide the possibility of regulating organizations by law, bureaucratization rarely occurs now by simple evolution. The Mafia is one of the few exceptions. Because it is secret and illegal, it cannot reorganize by reconstituting itself as a rational-legal organization. Yet it has changed as it has grown in size and shifted to an urban environment. Analysis of this change assumes unusual importance, because the Mafia is a significant force in modern life and because, as a rare contemporary example of the reorganization of a traditional type of association without recourse to legal sanctions, it provides a basis for comparison with potential other examples. Much of the present controversy about the Mafia, particularly about whether such an organization exists in the United States, is the result of confusing a modern, bureaucratic organization with the traditional institution from which it evolved.

THE TRADITIONAL MAFIA

A Mafia is not necessarily predatory. It provides law and order where the official government fails or is malfeasant. It collects assessments within its territory much as a legal government supports itself. While citizens everywhere often complain about taxation, these Mafia exactions have been defended as reasonable payment for peace. The underlying principle of Mafia rule is that it protects the community from all other strong men in return for regularized tribute.[7]

To illustrate, the Grisafi band of the Agrigento countryside, led by a young, very large man called "Little Mark" (Marcuzzo Grisafi) formed a stable, though illicit, gov-

[2] As Hobsbawm has pointed out, information about the Mafia, and especially quantitative and detailed information, does not meet standards normally set for institutional analysis. It is, after all, a secretive criminal organization. But while one cannot speak as authoritatively as one would like, this type of organization does need to be considered by social theorists, both as an important kind of institution and as a powerful force in Sicily and elsewhere. Hobsbawm, op. cit., p. 40.

[3] Peter M. Blau, Bureaucracy in Modern Society (New York: Random House, 1956), p. 36; Robert T. Anderson, "Studies in Peasant Life," Biennial Review of Anthropology (1965), ed. Bernard J. Spiegel (Stanford, Calif.: Stanford University Press) (in press).

[4] M. Ushijima, "Katari in Suye Mura—Its Social Function and Process of Change," Japanese Journal of Ethnology, XXVI (1962), 14–22.

[5] Robert T. Anderson, "Preliminary Report on the Associational Redefinition of Castes in Hyderabad-Secunderabad," Kroeber Anthropological Society Papers, No. 29 (Fall, 1963), 25–42.

[6] Anderson, op. cit.

[7] Cutrera, op. cit., p. 116; Gavin Maxwell, Bandit (New York: Harper & Row, 1956), pp. 31–33; Mangione, op. cit., p. 73.

ernment that oversaw every event in his area for a dozen years (1904–16). An excellent marksman, he was able by his strength and with the aid of four to eight gunmen to guarantee freedom from roving bandit and village sneak alike.

On a larger scale, between approximately 1895 and 1924, a group of eleven villages in the Madonie Mountains were also ruled by a Mafia. The head and his assistants had a private police force of as many as 130 armed men. A heavy tax resembling official annual taxes was imposed upon all landowners. As with the Grisafi band, this Mafia was not a roving body of terrorists. Their leaders, at least, were well-established citizens, landowners, and farmers. While they might mount up as a body to enforce their tax collections, they stayed for the most part in their homes or on their farms. They assumed supervision of all aspects of local life, including agricultural and economic activities, family relations, and public administration. As elsewhere, the will of the Mafia was the law. The head, in fact, was known locally as the "prefect" ("U Prefetto").[8]

Although not necessarily predatory, Mafias seem always to be so, despotisms possessed of absolute local power. Many in the band or collaborating with it may find it a welcome and necessary institution in an otherwise lawless land. But multitudes suffer gross injustice at its hands. No one dares offend the Mafia chief's sense of what is right. The lines between tax and extortion, between peace enforcement and murder, blur under absolutism. Many would claim that the Agrigento and Madonie mafiosi were mostly involved in blackmail, robbery, and murder. An over-all inventory of Mafia activities leaves no doubt that it is a criminal institution, serving the interests of its membership at the expense of the larger population.[9]

In organizational terms, the Mafia is a social group that combines the advantages of family solidarity with the membership flexibility of a voluntary association.

The most enduring and significant social bond in Sicily is that of the family.[10] Its cohesiveness is reinforced by a strong tendency to village endogamy. Only along the coast, where communication was easier, was it common to marry outside of the locality. The tendency to family endogamy further included some cross-cousin marriage.[11] Family bonds are not necessarily closely affectionate ones, but the tie has been the strongest social relationship known. It is the basic organizational group both economically and socially, functioning as a unit of production as well as of consumption.[12]

Family ties often bind members of the Mafia together. The Mafia of the Madonie included two sets of brothers, as did the core membership of the Grisafi group. Not only are members of the Mafia frequently concealed and aided by their families, but their relatives commonly speculate on their activities and profit from them so that a clear line cannot be drawn between the

8 Cesare Mori, The Last Struggle with the Mafia, trans. Orlo Williams (London: Putnam & Co., 1933), pp. 113–33, 165–67, 179.

9 Mori, op. cit., 130–33; Cutrera, op. cit., p. 116;

August Schneegans, La Sicilia nella natura, nella storia e nella vita (Florence: G. Barbera, 1890), p. 291.

10 Pitrè, op. cit., p. 30; William Foote Whyte, "Sicilian Peasant Society," American Anthropologist, XLVI (1944), 66; Giovanni Lorenzoni, Inchiesta parlamentare sulle condizioni dei contadini nelle provincie meridionali e nella Sicilia, Vol. VI: Sicilia (Rome: Tipografia nazionale di Giovanni Berlero, 1910), p. 462.

11 At the turn of the century an explicit preference existed for cross-cousin marriage. Such marriages, forbidden both by secular and canon law, were actually rare. But more remote consanguineous relatives did marry, and more commonly (one marriage in a hundred) than in most other parts of Italy. Figures for marriages between affinal kin are not available (Lorenzoni, op. cit., pp. 464, 467; Whyte, op. cit., p. 66; Vincenzo Petrullo, "A Note on Sicilian Cross-Cousin Marriage," Primitive Man, X, No. 1 [1937], 8–9).

12 Pitrè, op. cit., pp. 38–39; Salvatore Salomone-Marino, Costumi ed usanze dei contadini di Sicilia (Palermo: Remo Sandron, 1897), pp. 5–10; Lorenzoni, op. cit., pp. 462, 469–73.

criminal band on the one hand and the circle of kinsmen on the other.[13]

Family ties have a certain utility for organizing social action. Brothers are accustomed to work together. They possess a complex network of mutual rights and obligations to cement their partnership. The father-son and uncle-nephew relationships, equally enduring and diffuse, possess in addition a well-established leader-follower relationship. Cousins and nephews may be part of the intimate family, and it has been suggested that the children of brothers are especially close as indicated by their designations as *fratelli-cugini* (brother-cousins) or *fratelli-carnale* (brothers of the flesh).[14]

The family has one major drawback as a functioning group: its membership is relatively inflexible. Typically, family members vary in interests, capabilities, and temperaments. While this may be of little consequence for running a farm, it can constitute a serious handicap for the successful operation of a gang. Some offspring may be completely devoid of criminal capacity, while good potential *mafiosi* may belong to other families. To a certain degree this drawback is countered by the extension of ties through marriage. But often a desirable working alliance cannot be arranged through a suitable wedding.

Throughout Europe a technique is available for the artificial extension of kinship ties. The technique is that of fictive or ritual kinship. Godparenthood, child adoption, and blood brotherhood make it possible to extend kin ties with ease. These fictive bonds are especially notable for the establishment of kinlike dyadic relationships. Larger social groups have not commonly been formed in this way in Europe except as brotherhoods, the latter with variable, sometimes minimal, success. The Mafia constitutes an unusual social unit of this general type in that the fictive bond is that of godparenthood, elsewhere used for

allying individuals, but only rarely for forming groups.[15]

The godparenthood tie has had a variable history in Europe. In the Scandinavian countries it is a momentary thing, with few implications for future interaction. But in the Mediterranean area, and especially in Sicily, it is usually taken very seriously. An indissoluble lifetime bond, it is often claimed to be equal or even superior to the bond of true kinship.[16] While the godparenthood (*comparatico*) union may cross class lines to link the high and the low in a powerful but formal relationship, it is more often a tie of friends, affective in an overt way that contrasts with the lesser open affection of the domestic family.[17] Above all, the relationship is characterized by mutual trust.

Sicilians in general, then, live with greatest security and ease in the atmosphere of the family with its fictive extensions. The Mafia is a common-interest group whose members are recruited for their special interests in and talents for the maintenance

[15] Friedrich notes for the Tarascans that "every man strongly needs a certain number of intimates, many of whom are usually his ceremonial co-parents, or compadres—the fathers of his godchildren and the godfathers of his children." (Paul Friedrich, "Assumptions Underlying Tarascan Political Homicide," *Psychiatry: Journal for the Study of Interpersonal Processes*, XXV, No. 4 [November, 1962], 316). The Mexican-Americans of Salsipuedes, California, normally feel insecure until they have established godparenthood ties with neighbors (Margaret Clark, personal communication). These Mexican and Mexican-American groups appear to be ego-oriented, however, and not well-defined corporate bodies. Eugene Hammel is presently studying godparenthood groups in Yuogoslavia (personal communication).

[16] Various ways of contracting godparenthood ties are known to the Sicilians. See Whyte, *op. cit.*, pp. 66–67; Henry Festing Jones, *Castellinaria and other Sicilian Diversions* (Plymouth, England: William Brendon, 1911), pp. 131–34; Giuseppe Pitrè, *Usi e costumi credenze e pregiudizi del popolo siciliano* (hereinafter cited as "Usi e costumi"), "Biblioteca delle tradizioni popolari siciliane," Vol. XV (Florence: G. Barbera Editore, n.d.), 255.

[17] This utility of fictive kinship for psychological release is a striking feature that merits further attention but cannot be dealt with here. See Cutrera, *op. cit.*, pp. 58–59; Pitrè, *Usi e costumi*.

[13] Mori, *op. cit.*, pp. 130, 166, 172, 218; Wermert, *op. cit.*, 398; Gaston Vuillier, *La Sicile, impressions du présent et du passé* (Paris: Hachette, 1896), p. 165; Maxwell, *op. cit.*, p. 160.

[14] Petrullo, *op. cit.*, p. 8.

of a predatory satrapy. As noted above, this tie of shared interest often originates within a kinship parameter. When it does not, a kinlike tie is applied by the practice of becoming co-godparents. Although the Mafia *setta* (cell) may or may not be characterized by other structural features, it always builds upon real and fictive kinship.[18]

The Mafia of nineteenth-century Sicily practiced a formal rite of initiation into the fictive-kin relationship.[19] Joseph Valachi underwent the same rite in 1930 in New York.[20] In addition to the "baptism of blood," the chief at the first opportunity normally arranges to become the baptismal godfather of the tyro's newborn child. Lacking that opportunity, he establishes a comparable tie in one of the numerous other *comparatico* relationships. The members among themselves are equally active, so that the passing years see a member more and more bound to the group by such ties.

Ritual ties seem to function in part as a temporizing device. Although efficacious in themselves, they are usually the basis for the later arrangement of marriages between sons and daughters, and thus ultimately for the establishment of affinal and consanguineous bonds. The resultant group is therefore very fluid. It utilizes to the utmost its potentialities for bringing in originally unrelated individuals. Yet it possesses the organizational advantages of a lasting body of kin.[21]

Mafia family culture supports member-

ship flexibility additionally by providing for the withdrawal of born members. The criminal family passes on Mafia tradition just as the farming family passes on farming traditions. Boys are taught requisite skills and attitudes. Girls are brought up to be inconspicuous, loyal, and above all silent. The problems of in-family recruitment are not greatly different from those of non-criminal groups. Just as a son without agricultural propensities or the chance to inherit land leaves the countryside to take up a trade or profession, the Mafia son lacking criminal interests or talents takes up a different profession. Indeed, sometimes Mafia family pride comes to focus upon a son who has left the fold to distinguish himself as a physician or professor. But while such an individual might not himself take up an illegal occupation, he is trained never to repudiate it for his kindred. In the Amoroso family, who controlled Porta Montalto near Palermo for many years in the nineteenth century, Gaspare Amoroso, a young cousin of the chief, degraded himself by joining the police force (*carabiniere*). When the youth was discharged and returned to his family home, the Amoroso leaders removed this dishonor by having him killed in cold blood.[22]

The headship of a Mafia is well defined. Referred to as *capo* ("head") or *capomafia* ("Mafia head"), and addressed honorifically as *don*, the chief is clearly identified as the man in charge. Succession to this post, however, is not a matter of clearcut procedure. In some cases family considerations may result in the replacement of a *capo* by his son or nephew. Commonly, an heir apparent, who may or may not be related consanguineously, is chosen on an essentially pragmatic basis and succeeds by co-optation. Generally, promotion is by intrigue and strength. It must be won by the most powerful and ruthless candidate with or without the blessing of family designation or co-optation. Only the *capo*, in any case, is formally recognized. The appoint-

---

[18] Cutrera, op. cit., p. 59.

[19] Alexander Rumpelt, *Sicilien und die Sicilianer* (2d ed.; Berlin: Allgemeiner Verein für Deutsche Literatur, 1902), pp. 141–42.

[20] *Organized Crime and Illicit Traffic in Narcotics: Report of the Committee on Government Operations, United States Senate, Made by Its Permanent Subcommittee on Investigations, together with Additional Combined Views and Individual Views* (hereinafter cited as "Organized Crime and Illicit Traffic in Narcotics") (Report 72, Senate, 89th Cong. 1st Sess [Washington, D.C.: Government Printing Office, 1965]), p. 12.

[21] Frederic Sondern, Jr., *Brotherhood of Evil: The Mafia* (New York: Farrar, Straus & Cudahy, 1959), pp. 5, 242–43. *Organized Crime and Illicit Traffic in Narcotics*, pp. 39–43.

[22] Cutrera, op. cit., pp. 152–60; Sondern, op. cit., pp. 5–6, 24; Maxwell, op. cit., p. 34.

ment of secondary leaders and ranking within the membership are informal.[23]

In sum, the traditional Mafia may be described as family-like. It would not be considered a bureaucratic organization. Of the four basic characteristics of a bureaucracy (according to Blau), the Mafia lacked three—a hierarchy of authority, specialization, and a system of rules.[24] Impartiality, the fourth characteristic, requires a special note. Impartiality requires that promotion, reward, and job assignment ideally be uninfluenced by the pervasive ties of a primary group and determined solely by individual performance-achievement. The Mafia is a kind of kin group. The individual, once a member, belongs for life with a family member's ineluctable rights to group prerogatives. Yet, the Mafia seems always to have been ruthlessly impersonal when it mattered. A criminal association survives by making its best marksmen assassins, its best organizers leaders, and by punishing those who are disloyal or not observant of *omertà*. Impartiality in the Mafia is not fully developed, but bureaucracy in this sense has no doubt always been present. The Amoroso murder of the *capo-mafia*'s cousin, for example, illustrates extreme impartiality for a family group.

BUREAUCRATIZATION OF THE MAFIA

Though still seriously underdeveloped, Sicily seems poised for industrialization with its concomitant changes. To the extent that change has already occurred, the Mafia has adapted and expanded its techniques of exploitation. Claire Sterling writes of the intensification of urban activities: "Today there is not only a Mafia of the *feudo* (agriculture) but also Mafias of truck gardens, wholesale fruit and vegetable markets, water supply, meat, fishing fleets, flowers, funerals, beer, *carrozze* (hacks), garages,

and construction. Indeed, there is hardly a businessman in western Sicily who doesn't pay for the Mafia's 'protection' in the form of '*u pizzu.*' "[25]

Mafia formal organization seems at a turning point. The Mafia so far has remained essentially a hodgepodge of independent local units confined to the western part of the island, although cells have been established outside of Sicily. Co-operation among localities in Sicily has an old history. The more successful *capi* have at times established hegemony over wider areas. But it appears that large-scale groupings could not endure in an underdeveloped milieu with notoriously poor communication systems.[26] Modernization, however, is breaking down this local isolation. The scale of operations is expanding. The face-to-face, family-like group in which relationships on the whole are diffuse, affective, and particularistic is changing into a bureaucratic organization.

The best-documented example of early bureaucratization concerns the Mafia of Monreale. Known generally as the *Stoppaglieri*, or facetiously as a mutual-aid society (*società di mutuo soccorso*), and world famous later for the criminal success of some members who migrated to America, the group first formed in the 1870's, when one of Monreale's political factions, in danger of losing local power, formed a Mafia that succeeded in wresting control from the older Mafia of the area. The basic group consisted of 150 members in the city itself. As they prospered they expanded into the surrounding area. Affiliated chapters were established in Parco, San Giuseppe Iato, Santa Cristina, Montelepre, Borgetto, Piana dei Greci, and Misilmeri. A hierarchy of authority was created by the formal recognition of three ranked leadership roles rather than only one. The head of the whole organization was designated *capo*, but each area, including the various quarters of Mon-

[23] Guerico, *op. cit.*, p. 69; Sondern, *op. cit.*, p. 6; Burton B. Turkus and Sid Feder, *Murder, Inc.: The Story of "The Syndicate"* (New York: Farrar, Straus & Young, 1951), pp. 78–87.
[24] See Blau, *op. cit.*, p. 19.

[25] Claire Sterling, "Shots in Sicily, Echoes in Rome," *Reporter* (August 4, 1960), pp. 35–36. See Danilo Dolci, *Outlaws*, trans. R. Munroe (New York: Orion Press, 1961), p. 319.
[26] Hobsbawm, *op. cit.*, p. 33.

reale, was placed under the direct jurisdiction of a subhead or *sottocapo*. Each subhead in turn had an assistant, the *consiglio directtivo*. The rules of the association were made somewhat more explicit than those of other Mafias in providing for the convocation of membership councils to judge members charged with breaking the regulations of the group. And these regulations, completely traditional in character, were very precise, binding members:

1. To help one another and avenge every injury of a fellow member;
2. To work with all means for the defense and freeing of any fellow member who had fallen into the hands of the judiciary;
3. To divide the proceeds of thievery, robbery, and extortion with certain considerations for the needy as determined by the *capo*;
4. To keep the oath and maintain secrecy on pain of death within twenty-four hours.

Group intimacy among the *Stoppaglieri* appears to have been less than that of a smaller Mafia. The whole membership could not be easily convoked as they grew in size and territory. Patterns of universalism intruded upon those of particularism so that, according to some reports, a secret recognition sign was devised. On the whole, however, third-party introductions were more common than secret recognition signs.[27]

This, then, is what we know of one Mafia that bureaucratized to some extent at a relatively early date. Other and recent Mafias in Sicily display similar bureaucratization when they expand their operations.[28] Whatever the terminology—it tends

to vary—these larger organizations are all characterized by an embryonic hierarchy of authority. They also continue a degree of impartiality and operate in terms of the traditional, explicitly elaborated, though unwritten rules. Specialization and departmentalization do not appear much developed. The problem of succession to authority continues to be troublesome. Journalists tend to designate one or another chief as the head for all of Sicily. A high command on this level does not seem to have developed beyond irregular councils of autonomous *capi*.

One may observe further bureaucratization of the Mafia in the United States. Mafias were first established in America in the latter part of the nineteenth century. During the prohibition era they proliferated and prospered. Throughout this period these groups continued to function essentially like the small traditional Mafia of western Sicily.

Recent decades in the United States have witnessed acceleration of all aspects of modernization. Here, if anywhere, the forces of urbanization impinge upon group life. But while American criminals have always been quick to capitalize upon technological advances, no significant organizational innovation occurred until the repeal of prohibition in 1932, an event that abruptly ended much of the lucrative business of the underworld. Small face-to-face associations gave way over subsequent decades to the formation of regional, national, and international combines, a change in which American *mafiosi* participated.[29]

As always, information is incomplete

27 Cutrera, *op. cit.*, pp. 118–22, 132–41; Ed Reid, *Mafia* (New York: New American Library of World Literature, 1952), p. 100; Albert Falcionelli, *Les Sociétés secrètes italiennes* ("Bibliothèque historique" [Paris: Payot, 1936]), p. 208; "Mafia," *Encyclopaedia Britannica* (1951), XIV, 622; Hobsbawm, *op. cit.*, pp. 41–42; Peter Maas, "Mafia: The Inside Story," *Saturday Evening Post* (August 10, 1963), p. 21.
28 Cutrera, *op. cit.*, pp. 165–75; F. Lestingi, *La Fratellanza nella provincia di Girgenti* (Archivo di Psichiatria, Scienze penali ed antropologia criminale), V, No. iv; Salvo di Pietraganzili, *Rivoluzione siciliane dei 1848 a 1860* (Palermo: Bondi, 1898), II, 59. See Pasquale Villari, *Le lettere meridionali ed altri scritti sulla questione*

sociale in Italia (2d ed.; Turin: Fratelli Bocca, 1885), p. 28; Pitrè, *La famiglia, la casa, la vitadel popolo siciliano*, p. 292; Jones, *op. cit.*, p. 163; Vuillier, *op. cit.*, p. 84.
29 Walter C. Reckless, *Criminal Behavior* (New York: McGraw-Hill Book Co., 1940), p. 135; Donald R. Taft, *Criminology* (3d ed.; New York: Macmillan Co., 1956), p. 233; Robert G. Caldwell, *Criminology* (New York: Ronald Press Co., 1956), pp. 77–82, 86; *Life* (February 23, 1959), p. 19; Estes Kefauver, *Crime in America* (New York: Doubleday & Co., 1951), p. 14; Daniel P. Moynihan, "The Private Government of Crime," *Reporter* (July 6, 1961), p. 15.

and conflicting. Bureaucratization, however, seems to have increased significantly beyond that even of bureaucratized Sicilian groups. Specialization, generally undeveloped in Sicily, became prominent. Personnel now regularly specialize as professional gunmen, runners, executives, or adepts in other particular operations. Departmentalization was introduced and now includes an organizational breakdown into subgroups such as narcotics operations; gambling; the rackets; prostitution; and an enforcement department, the infamous Murder, Inc., with its more recent descendants.[30]

The hierarchy of authority has developed beyond that of bureaucratized Sicilian Mafias. Bill Davidson describes a highly elaborated hierarchy of the Chicago Cosa Nostra, which he compares to the authority structure of a large business corporation. He points to the equivalent of a three-man board of directors, a president of the corporation, and four vice-presidents in charge of operations. He also notes a breakdown into three geographical areas, each headed by a district manager. District managers have executive assistants, who in turn have aides. Finally, at the lowest level are the so-called soldiers.[31] National councils of the more important capi apparently meet from time to time to set up territories, co-ordinate tangential activities, and adjudicate disputes. They serve to minimize internecine strife rather than to administer co-operative undertakings. The problem of succession has still not been solved. The Valachi hearings revealed an equally complex hierarchy for the state of New York.[32]

A written system of rules has not developed, although custom has changed. Modern mafiosi avoid the use of force as much as possible, and thus differ strikingly from old Sicilian practice. The old "mustachios" are being replaced by dapper gentlemen clothed in conservative business suits. But as a criminal organization, the Mafia cannot risk systematizing its rules in written statutes.

A major element of bureaucratization is the further development of impartiality. Mafiosi now freely collaborate on all levels with non-Sicilians and non-Italians. The Chicago association includes non-Italians from its "board of directors" down. In these relationships, consanguineous and affinal ties are normally absent and co-godparenthood absent or insignificant. Familistic organization, the structural characteristic that made for the combination of organizational flexibility with group stability in the traditional associations of Sicily—and that goes far to explain the success of Mafias there—apparently proved inadaptive in urban America. When it became desirable and necessary to collaborate with individuals of different criminal traditions, it sufficed to rely for group cohesion on the possibility of force and a business-like awareness of the profits to be derived from co-operation.[33] Family and ritual ties still function among Sicilian-American criminals to foster co-operation and mutual support within cliques, but pragmatic considerations rather than familistic Mafia loyalties now largely determine organizational arrangements.[34]

[30] Sidney Lens, "Labor Rackets, Inc.," Nation (March 2, 1957), pp. 179–83; Martin Mooney, Crime Incorporated (New York: McGraw-Hill Book Co., 1935), pp. 5–6; Harry Elmer Barnes and Negley K. Teeters, New Horizons in Criminology (Englewood Cliffs, N.J.: Prentice-Hall, Inc., 1959), pp. 24–28.

[31] Bill Davidson, "How the Mob Controls Chicago," Saturday Evening Post (November 9, 1963), pp. 22–25.

[32] Organized Crime and Illicit Traffic in Narcotics, pp. 19–32.

[33] Lens, loc. cit.; Mooney, op. cit.; Barnes and Teeters, op. cit.; Paul W. Tappan, Crime, Justice and Correction (New York: McGraw-Hill Book Co., 1960), p. 232; Kefauver, op. cit., pp. 24–25 et passim; Turkus and Feder, op. cit., pp. xiii-xiv, 6, 44, 85–87, 426, 431; Sondern, op. cit., pp. 104–6; L. McLain, "Mafia: A Secret Empire of Evil," Coronet (November, 1958), pp. 60, 62. See Reckless, op. cit.; Sondern, op. cit., p. 181; Joseph N. Bell, "Exploding the Mafia Myth," Pageant (May, 1960), p. 52.

[34] Organized Crime and Illicit Traffic in Narcotics, pp. 37–38, 43.

CONCLUSION

The Mafia as a traditional type of formal organization has disappeared in America. Modern criminals refer to its successor as *Cosa Nostra*, "Our Thing." The Cosa Nostra is a lineal descendant of the Mafia, but it is a different kind of organization. Its goals are much broader as it exploits modern cities and an industrialized nation. The real and fictive kinship ties of the old Mafia still operate among fellow Sicilians and Italians, but these ties now coexist with bureaucratic ones. The Cosa Nostra operates above all in new and different terms. This new type of organization includes elaboration of the hierarchy of authority; the specialization and departmentalization of activities; new and more pragmatic, but still unwritten, rules; and a more developed impartiality. In America, the traditional Mafia has evolved into a relatively complex organization which perpetuates selected features of the older peasant organization but subordinates them to the requirements of a bureaucracy.

CHAPTER 9

Professional Crime

Professional crime consists of a variety of specialized criminal activities. Conceivably, professional criminal activity can be found in any of the crimes of economic gain. It is not the legal definition of the crime, but the skill with which the crime is performed that determines the professional aspect of the behavior.[1]

Consequently, conventional crimes like robbery and burglary could be performed in a professional way. As an example, one observer of armed robbery has indicated that a professionalized form of armed robbery ("the heist") is emerging in the United States. It involves finding a mark (the location for the holdup), getting together a team of specialists, planning the holdup, and executing the job.[2]

Traditionally, however, professional crime has been limited to nonviolent forms of behavior and activities that do not require the use of strong-arm tactics. In this

[1] Walter C. Reckless, *The Crime Problem*, 3d ed., New York: Appleton-Century-Crofts, Inc., 1961, p. 170.
[2] Everett DeBaum, "The Heist: The Theory and Practice of Armed Robbery," *Harper's Magazine*, 200 (February 1950), pp. 69–77.

sense, criminal activity which involves the theft of large sums of money through the use of skillful, nonviolent methods best represents professional crime. The varieties of professional theft have been divided by one professional thief into the following categories:

1. Picking pockets (cannon).
2. Sneak thieving from stores, banks, and offices (the heel).
3. Shoplifting (the boost).
4. Stealing from jewelry stores by substituting inferior jewelry for valuable jewelry (pennyweighting).
5. Stealing from hotel rooms (hotel prowling).
6. Confidence game (the con).
7. Miscellaneous rackets such as passing illegal checks, money orders, and other papers (hanging paper).
8. Extorting money from others engaged in or about to engage in illegal acts (the shake).[3]

Except for Sutherland's study of professional theft cited above and Maurer's work on the confidence game,[4] there has been little empirical research on the various types of professional crime. The research that does exist includes Cameron's study of professional (and nonprofessional) shoplifters in a Chicago department store, Maurer's research on professional pickpockets, Roebuck and Johnson's study of the "short con" man, Polsky's observations on the pool hustler, and Lemert's study of the systematic check forger.[5]

CRIMINAL CAREER OF THE OFFENDER

Of all the criminal offenders, the professional criminal has the most highly developed criminal career. As the word implies, professional criminals are accorded great prestige by other criminals. They engage in a variety of highly specialized crimes, all of which are directed toward economic gain. By means of skill and elaborate techniques, professional criminals through various forms of professional thievery or fraud are often able to acquire considerable sums of money without being detected. In the unusual cases when they are apprehended, professional criminals are able generally to find ways to have the charge dropped.

Professional criminals differ from other criminals in still other ways. In addition to being more skilled in their criminal activity, professional criminals are able to operate without the use of violence and strong-arm tactics. Professional criminals recognize their own talents and status in crime. Regarding themselves as professionals, they avoid other types of criminals and associate primarily with one another. Professional criminals, in being committed to a life of crime, avoid contact with much of the larger society.

Professional criminals tend to come from better economic backgrounds than do

[3] "Chic Conwell" in Edwin H. Sutherland, The Professional Thief, Chicago: University of Chicago Press, 1937, Chap. 3.
[4] David W. Maurer, The Big Con, New York: Signet Books, 1962.
[5] Mary Owen Cameron, The Booster and the Snitch, New York: The Free Press of Glencoe, 1964; David W. Maurer, Whiz Mob, New Haven, Conn.: College and University Press, 1964; Julian B. Roebuck and Ronald C. Johnson, "The 'Short Con' Man," Crime and Delinquency, 10 (July 1964), pp. 235–248; Ned Polsky, "The Hustler," Social Problems, 12 (Summer 1964), pp. 3–15; and Edwin M. Lemert, "The Behavior of the Systematic Check Forger," Social Problems, 6 (Fall 1958), pp. 141–149.

conventional and organized criminals. Many, according to one professional thief, start in legitimate employment as salesmen, hotel clerks, waiters, or bellboys.[6] Few of them come from the slums and the ranks of amateur thieves. A person entering professional crime may continue to engage in his legitimate employment until he is successful in crime.

The professional criminal is likely to begin his career in crime at a relatively late age. Furthermore, once in professional crime, he tends to continue in it for the rest of his life. Lemert has summarized the life career of the confidence man (con man) as follows:

> The con man begins his special career at a much older age than other criminals, or perhaps it is better said that he continues his criminal career at a time when others may be relinquishing theirs. Unemployment occasioned by old age does not seem to be a problem of con men; age ripens their skills, insights, and wit, and it also increases the confidence they inspire in their victims. With age the con man may give up the position of the roper and shift to being an inside man, but even this may not be absolutely necessary. It is possible that cultural changes outmode the particular con games older men have been accustomed to playing and thereby decrease their earnings somewhat, but this seems unlikely. We know of one con man who is seventy years of age and has a bad heart, but he is still as effective as he ever was.[7]

The longevity in crime is attributable in part, of course, to the fact that very few professional criminals are ever arrested, brought to trial, convicted, or serve time in prison.

A significant characteristic of professional criminals is the philosophy of life they develop to justify their criminal careers. But, as Tannenbaum has noted, "the philosophy of criminals does not differ from that of any other group. So far as other men believe in a set of assumptions and use them to explain their conduct, so far they do no more and no less than the criminal does. Each uses his philosophy of life as a means of making his activities seem reasonable."[8] In his relations with persons of similar interest, the professional criminal acquires a philosophy which gives him answers to questions related to the worth of his activity and to his own self-image.

Basic to the professional criminal's philosophy of life is the belief that all men are actually dishonest and that the criminal is engaging in activity similar to that of other businessmen. The professional criminal also justifies his behavior by the belief that all noncriminals would commit crime if they could. As one successful confidence man, Joseph "Yellow Kid" Weil, said of himself:

> The men I fleeced were basically no more honest than I was. One of the motivating factors in my action was, of course, the desire to acquire money. The other motive was a lust for adven-

6 Sutherland, pp. 21–25.
7 Edwin M. Lemert, *Social Pathology*, New York: McGraw-Hill, Book Company, Inc., 1951, pp. 323–324.
8 Frank Tannenbaum, *Crime and the Community*, New York: Columbia University Press, 1938, p. 177. Also see Elmer Hubert Johnson, *Crime, Correction, and Society*, Homewood, Ill.: Richard D. Irwin, Inc., 1964, p. 243.

ture. The men I swindled were also motivated by a desire to acquire money, and they didn't care at whose expense they got it. I was particular. I took money only from those who could afford it and were willing to go in with me in schemes they fancied would fleece others.[9]

The victim of the con game, after all, has been willing to participate in a crime in order to make money. The professional criminal can justify his own crime in terms of the behavior of the victim. Such justifications are, of course, shared and supported by professional criminals in their associations with one another.

GROUP SUPPORT OF CRIMINAL BEHAVIOR

The social characteristics of professional crime have perhaps been best summarized by Sutherland in his interpretation of an extensive document written by a professional thief.[10] Sutherland observed that professional crime is characterized by (1) *skill*—a complex of techniques exists for committing crime; (2) *status*—professional criminals have a position of high prestige in the world of crime; (3) *consensus*—professional criminals share common values, beliefs, and attitudes, with an *esprit de corps* among members; (4) *differential association*—association is with other professional criminals to the exclusion of law-abiding persons and other criminals; and (5) *organization*—activities are pursued in terms of common knowledge and through an informal information and assistance system. Related to these characteristics are several others which are also associated with the group support which underlies professional crime.

SELECTION AND TRAINING. The recruitment of personnel into professional crime is regulated by established professional criminals. Recognition by other professional thieves, as Sutherland has noted, is the absolutely necessary and definitive characteristic of the professional thief.[11] Without such recognition, no amount of knowledge and experience can provide the criminal with the requirements for a successful career in professional crime.

Included in the process of acquiring recognition as a professional criminal are the two necessary elements of selection and tutelage.[12] A person cannot acquire recognition until he has had tutelage or the necessary training, and tutelage is granted only to a few selected persons. Selection and tutelage are interrelated and continuous processes. A person is tentatively recognized and selected for limited training and in the course of tutelage advances to more certain stages of recognition.

Contact is, of course, a necessary requisite for selection and tutelage. Professional criminals may come in contact with prospective professionals through their limited association with other criminals (amateur thieves, burglars), with persons on the fringes of criminal activity (pimps, "fences"), or with persons engaged in legitimate occupations. The contacts may be made in places where professional

[9] Joseph R. Weil and W. T. Brannon, *"Yellow Kid"* Weil, Chicago: Ziff-Davis Publishing Company, 1948, p. 293.
[10] Sutherland, Chap. 9.
[11] Sutherland, p. 211.
[12] Sutherland, pp. 211–215.

criminals are working, in jails, or in places of leisure-time activities. Selection is reciprocal in that both professional thieves and prospective candidates must be in mutual agreement regarding the arrangement.

Tutelage involves the learning of skills, techniques, attitudes, and values through informal means. The neophyte, rather than receiving formal verbal instruction, learns while engaging in criminal activity. During the probationary period the neophyte assimilates standards of group morality, such as honesty among thieves and not informing on others, learns methods of stealing and disposing of goods, and becomes acquainted with other professional criminals. Gradually he is accepted as a professional criminal. As long as the recognition continues, whether he continues in criminal activity or not, he is regarded as a professional criminal.

LANGUAGE PATTERN.   While many criminals tend to use a distinctive language, professional criminals probably have the most extensive and colorful argot. The hundreds of terms used by professional criminals have developed over a considerable period of time; many were common in the seventeenth century. The language has grown out of the specialized activity of the professional criminal. The argot used reflects the attitudes of the professional toward the law, toward himself, toward the victim, toward other criminals, and toward society in general. As an example of this argot, Maurer, in an extensive analysis of the argot of the professional pickpocket, quotes a professional pickpocket who gave the following account of what happened to him in police court:

> *Judge:* Now you just tell the Court in your own way what you were doing.
> *Me:* Well, Judge, your honor, I was out gandering around for a soft mark and made a tip that was going to cop a short. I eased myself into the tip and just topped a leather in Mr. Bates' left prat when I blowed I was getting a jacket from these two honest bulls. So I kick the okus back in his kick and I'm clean. Just then this flatfoot nails me, so here I am on a bum rap. All I crave is justice, and I hope she ain't blind.[13]

Within professional crime, there are distinctive argots according to the various types of criminal activity. Some of the argots are closely related, while others are widely divergent. All real professionals are able to speak the one argot that is associated with their particular crime. Extensive knowledge of the argot is truly the mark of the professional; many years are required to use it effectively.

Why do argots develop? According to Maurer there are several reasons.[14] First, because professional criminals work outside the law, there are strong pressures to consolidate the criminal subculture. A common argot serves to develop group solidarity and provides a sense of camaraderie among members of the subculture. Second, specialized work requires and fosters the creation of a special language. Professional criminals within a particular racket, as craftsmen, are faced with identical problems which must be solved with certain known techniques. Third, many concepts exist for professional criminals for which there are no terms in the vocabulary of the ordinary citizen. It is necessary that professional criminals create,

[13] Maurer, *Whiz Mob,* p. 55.
[14] Maurer, *The Big Con,* pp. 228–229.

borrow, or adapt words to meet their unique needs. Finally, Maurer discredits the usually assumed reason for criminal argot, that is, that criminals develop a special language to confuse and deceive their victims. Maurer believes this form of argot usage is minimal and limited. Most professionals speak argot only among themselves, not in the presence of outsiders. It appears that secrecy and deception are very minor reasons for the formation and use of argot among professional criminals. The specialized language serves, rather, as a means of social support for the way of life of the professional criminal.

CORRESPONDENCE BETWEEN CRIMINAL BEHAVIOR AND LEGITIMATE BEHAVIOR PATTERNS

A similarity exists between professional criminal behavior and the legitimate behavior patterns of conventional society in that the professional criminal is engaged in a full-time pursuit; he is self-employed. Also, normally law-abiding persons must serve as "accomplices" in order for some forms of professional crime to exist. The confidence game perhaps best illustrates the correspondence between professional criminal behavior and legitimate behavior patterns.

Of the types of professional theft, the confidence game is the most sophisticated and respected form. Furthermore, the "big con" is the aristocrat of professional crime and is granted the greatest prestige in the world of crime. Confidence men receive this deference not only because of their ability to gain large sums of money through skill, without the use of guns and violence, but also because of their cultural backgrounds, their dress and manners, and their general style of life.

Confidence games are generally divided roughly into big con and short con games. Short con games require only a short period of time to carry out and are limited to small amounts of money. Big con games require a longer period of time and involve larger sums of money. Short con games take place between one or two con men and their victim. Big con games generally require the abilities and planning of a number of persons. Big con games proceed through a series of steps. Maurer, who has extensively studied forms of the big con, such as the "wire" and the "pay-off" (racing swindles), and the "rag" (involving stocks and bonds), lists the following steps in a big con swindle:
1. Locating and investigating a well-to-do victim. (Putting the mark up.)
2. Gaining the victim's confidence. (Playing the con for him.)
3. Steering him to meet the insideman. (Roping the mark.)
4. Permitting the insideman to show him how he can make a large amount of money dishonestly. (Telling him the tale.)
5. Allowing the victim to make a substantial profit. (Giving him the convincer.)
6. Determining exactly how much he will invest. (Giving him the breakdown.)
7. Sending him home for this amount of money. (Putting him on the send.)
8. Playing him against a big store and fleecing him. (Taking off the touch.)
9. Getting him out of the way as quickly as possible. (Blowing him off.)
10. Forestalling action by the law. (Putting in the fix.)[15]

15 Maurer, The Big Con, pp. 15–16.

Thus, the first requirement for the operation of a con game is the willing participation of an accomplice. A prospective victim, the "mark," must be found who will enter into an illegal scheme. Such an alliance assures the con man a degree of protection and makes the victim a partner in the proceedings. The legitimate behavior patterns of our society are suggestive of, or at least neutral toward, participation in the confidence scheme. This is illustrated in a comment by one professional con man who noted the following: "It is hard to con an honest man, but there are so few truly honest men that the so-called con game can be successfully worked on the average person. A professional con man works on the assumption that 99 out of every 100 people are suckers."[16]

In his work on the big con, Maurer has observed that most marks come from the upper strata of society.[17] Included among marks are bankers, wealthy farmers, police officials, and professional men, especially doctors, lawyers, dentists, and an occasional college professor. Even respectable church trustees on occasion use church funds in order to play the con game. One church trustee, who was sentenced to prison for misappropriating church funds, received the following wry comment from his con man, ironically, who was acquitted: "He was a very religious man, but I guess the temptation for the dough was too much for his scruples." But, according to Maurer, it is the businessman that makes the best mark.

> Businessmen, active or retired, make fine marks for big-con games. In fact, probably the majority of marks fleeced by the big-time confidence men are businessmen. Their instincts are sound for the confidence game, they respond well to the magnetic personalities of roper and inside-man, and they have or can raise the necessary capital with which to plunge heavily.[18]

The extent of confidence game activities in the United States is difficult to determine. There are a number of reasons for lack of knowledge about the confidence game. First, the laws often are not clear as to what constitutes illegal confidence activity. Second, in some cases the victim does not realize he has been victimized. Third, the victim hesitates to inform on confidence men because of his own humiliation or because he himself has been an accomplice in the crime. Finally, confidence men, because of the "fix," are usually able to escape conviction.

The confidence game, thus, can be best understood as a sociological phenomenon in relation to legitimate behavior patterns. As Schur has indicated, the confidence game appeals to the playful, sporting, and manipulative aspects of our society.[19] Confidence games, much like the games of the young, represent a form of pleasurable activity. Confidence game activity also appeals to the American value of successful salesmanship. The con man, as a successful businessman, is able to outwit members of the public who are willing to participate in illegal activity.

[16] See Robert Louis Gasser, "The Confidence Game," *Federal Probation*, 27 (December 1963), p. 47.
[17] Maurer, *The Big Con*, Chap. 4.
[18] Maurer, *The Big Con*, p. 94.
[19] Edwin H. Schur, "Sociological Analysis of Confidence Swindling," *Journal of Criminal Law, Criminology and Police Science*, 48 (September–October 1957), pp. 296–304.

SOCIETAL REACTION

The high status of professional criminals is indicated not only by the attitudes of other criminals but by the special treatment usually accorded professional criminals by the police, court officials, and others. Because of their favored position in crime, professional criminals are able to make arrangements with public officials which allow them to avoid conviction and punishment. The professional criminal may even be able to avoid arrest by regular payments to certain officials.

The professional criminal has the ability to fix cases because of the cooperation of certain members of society. One professional criminal described the involvement of others in the fix as follows:

> In order to send a thief to the penitentiary, it is necessary to have the cooperation of the victim, witnesses, police, bailiffs, clerks, grand jury, jury, prosecutor, judge, and perhaps others. A weak link in this chain can practically always be found, and any of the links can be broken if you have pressure enough. There is no one who cannot be influenced if you go at it right and have sufficient backing, financially and politically. It is difficult if the victim is rich or important; it is more difficult in some places than in others. But it can practically always be done. It is just a question, if you have the backing, of using your head until you find the right way.[20]

In other words, the professional criminal is able to escape conviction because of certain informal processes that operate in the administration of the law, or to put it more directly, "no criminal subculture can operate continuously and professionally without the connivance of the law."[21]

Public toleration of professional crime results from a combination of factors, including the correspondence between some forms of professional crime and some legitimate behavior patterns, the involvement of the public as victims in illegal arrangements, and public apathy toward crimes which do not affect each person directly and concretely. Maurer has suggested also that the public tolerates professional crime because of a naïveness about crime and the relationship between the criminal and the law.

> The man in the street sees crime something like this: if a confidence man trims someone, he should be indicted and punished; first he must be caught; then he must be tried; then, if convicted, he should be sent to prison to serve his full term. The average citizen—if we ignore his tendency to wax sentimental about all criminals—can be generally counted upon to adopt the following assumptions: that the victim of the swindle is both honest and unfortunate; that the officers of the law want to catch the con men; that the court wishes to convict the criminals; that if the court frees the con men, they are *ipso facto* innocent; that if

[20] Sutherland, pp. 82–83.
[21] Maurer, *Whiz Mob*, p. 129.

they are convicted, they will be put in the penitentiary where they belong to serve out their time at hard labor. If these assumptions even approximated fact, confidence men would have long ago found it impossible to operate.[22]

The myth that surrounds the operation of the legal process no doubt serves as a device for the public toleration of much crime.

Finally, there is some indication that professional crime may be changing as other changes are taking place in society. At the end of the last century, persons and organizations that were the victims of professional crime, especially of forgery, established as a reaction to professional crime a number of schemes which subsequently brought about a change in the organization and operation of professional crime.[23] The establishment of the bankers' associations, the creation of merchants' protective agencies, and improvements in police methods made the risks of organized professional forgery exceedingly great. Also important to the decline of professional forgery has been the increasingly widespread use of business and payroll checks as well as personal checks. Because of these reactions the systematic check forger no longer has to resort to criminal associates or to employ the more complex procedures used in past decades. Thus, it can be seen that professional crime, as is true of other types of crime, is related to the structure of society. As society and the reaction to crime change, so do the organization and operation of the types of crime.

SELECTED BIBLIOGRAPHY

1. Bloch, Herbert A., and Gilbert Geis, *Man, Crime, and Society*, New York: Random House, Inc., Chap. 8.
2. Cameron, Mary Owen, *The Booster and the Snitch: Department Store Shoplifting*, New York: The Free Press of Glencoe, 1964.
3. Gasser, Robert Louis, "The Confidence Game," *Federal Probation*, 27 (December 1963), pp. 27–54.
4. Jahoda, Gustav, " 'Money-Doubling' in the Gold Coast: With Some Comparisons," *British Journal of Delinquency*, 8 (April 1958), pp. 266–276.
5. Lemert, Edwin M., "The Behavior of the Systematic Check Forger," *Social Problems*, 6 (Fall 1958), pp. 141–149.
6. Maurer, David W., *The Big Con*, New York: Signet Books, 1962.
7. ——, *Whiz Mob*, New Haven, Conn.: College and University Press, 1964.
8. Polsky, Ned, "The Hustler," *Social Problems*, 12 (Summer 1964), pp. 3–15.
9. Reckless, Walter C., *The Crime Problem*, 3d ed., New York: Appleton-Century-Crofts, Inc., 1961, Chap. 9.
10. Roebuck, Julian B., "The Negro Numbers Man as a Criminal Type: The Construction and Application of a Typology," *Journal of Criminal Law, Criminology and Police Science*, 54 (March 1963), pp. 48–60.
11. ——, and Ronald C. Johnson, "The 'Short Con' Man," *Crime and Delinquency*, 10 (July 1964), pp. 235–248.

[22] Maurer, *The Big Con*, p. 176.
[23] Lemert, "The Behavior of the Systematic Check Forger," *Social Problems*, 6 (Fall 1958), pp. 146–147.

12. Schur, Edwin M., "Sociological Analysis of Confidence Swindling," *Journal of Criminal Law, Criminology and Police Science*, 48 (September–October 1957), pp. 296–304.
13. Sutherland, Edwin H., *The Professional Thief*, Chicago: University of Chicago Press, 1937.

SOCIOLOGICAL ANALYSIS OF CONFIDENCE SWINDLING*

Edwin M. Schur

Below is an analysis of confidence swindling in terms of its relation to modern American society. Schur calls attention to the fact that fraud is a game, involving chance and playful activity. The confidence game is related to socially sanctioned attributes associated with successful salesmanship. Confidence swindling is viewed by Schur as being functional to our prevailing value system.

INTRODUCTION

Almost twenty years ago L. L. Bernard, noting the prevalence of various types of fraud in American society, stated: "We have reached the fraud stage of social control in the evolution of succession of forms in social control."[1] There seems little doubt that today we are still in what Bernard terms the fraud stage of development. Swindling appears to be a strongly entrenched national phenomenon, many instances of which are reported daily in newspapers throughout the country.

Though fraud of course takes on a wide variety of forms, from a sociological view almost all fraud can be seen to contain the kernel of the "confidence game" procedure —the creation, by one means or another, of a relation of confidence, through which a

swindle is effected. All types of con games fall into a general pattern which may be described briefly as follows. The swindler (or swindlers, for several racketeers often band together to form a "con mob") selects a person who appears likely to be a good "sucker" (or, in the argot of the con man, "mark"). After establishing some degree of rapport with the mark, and once he sees that the mark will trust him, the con man tells the mark of a dishonest scheme by which they can make some money. The mark gives the swindler his money, which he never again sees. Because he has placed his confidence in the con man, it never occurs to the mark (until it is too late) that he is the object rather than the co-perpetrator of the swindle.

Unfortunately there is no way to accurately gauge the extent of criminal fraud in the United States today. Victims of con games (who, themselves, sought to gain

[1] Bernard, L. L., *Social Control*, New York: Macmillan, 1939, p. 36.

* Reprinted by special permission of the author and the *Journal of Criminal Law, Criminology and Police Science*, Copyright © 1957 by the Northwestern University School of Law, Volume 48, Number 3, September–October, 1957, pp. 296–304.

dishonestly) rarely report their losses; many victims of related types of fraud never fully realize they were "taken." And where the loss is small, the victim often prefers not to bother getting involved with the police. Thus especially in the realm of fraud, "crimes known to the police" fall far short of crimes actually committed.

Despite the uncertainty, experts agree on the magnitude of the fraud problem. According to Maurer, it may well be that "the three big-con games, the wire, the rag, and the pay-off, have in some forty years of their existence. . . . produced more illicit profit for the operators and for the law than all other forms of professional crime (excepting violations of prohibition law) over the same period of time."[2] And the most recent edition of the late Professor Sutherland's competent text reports: "It is probable . . . that fraud is the most prevalent crime in America."[3]

Current efforts to curb fraud are typically ineffectual. As noted above, the reporting of fraudulent crimes is minimal. Then too, the variety of statutes relevant to various kinds of fraud is, in many jurisdictions, close to chaotic: "Enact, as Colorado has done, some two dozen statutes on the general topic of obtaining property illegally and confusion is bound to result."[4] In some states, there are separate statutes covering larceny, embezzlement, false pretenses, confidence game, and forgery. This may enable a defendant to play one provision off against another—against a larceny charge raising a defense that the evidence shows embezzlement, then reversing his stand in a subsequent embezzlement trial. Composite larceny statutes in New York and California undoubtedly simplify the law-enforcement-prosecution task. New York's law is particularly well-drafted in that it makes irrelevant the thorny questions of possession as against title which plague prosecutors in many states.[5]

Another difficulty for prosecutors arises because of the general rule of criminal law that a false pretense or representation, to be indictable, must be an untrue statement regarding a past or present fact. While a leading California decision recently held that false promises are false pretenses,[6] the outdated common law doctrine is still the majority rule. Exacting evidenciary requirements under specific statutes, together with the possibilities of professional swindlers "fixing" cases, further inhibit successful prosecution of fraud.

Even where statutes have been simplified so that the required proof would not hinder prosecution, law-enforcement authorities and courts seem reluctant to give fraud laws a broad application, particularly where a segment of the business community might be imperiled. For instance, under the Federal Mail Fraud Act, there need be no showing that anyone is in fact defrauded and promissory fraud as well as misrepresentation of past and present fact is indictable; yet the government has relied largely on the noncriminal "fraud order" technique, rather than using the criminal sanctions also provided by the Act. An important element seems to be the "reluctance to stigmatize the overzealous advertiser as a criminal."[7]

Where sanctions are imposed in swindling cases, they are rarely stringent; prison statistics show that, generally, sentences imposed in this country for fraud are relatively light. Fraud offenders, then, are rarely uncovered and even more rarely prosecuted; of those who are prosecuted, most are at least able to avoid serious punishment. The

[2] Maurer, David, *The Big Con*, Indianapolis: Bobbs-Merrill, 1940, p. 17.
[3] Sutherland, Edwin H., *Principles of Criminology*, Philadelphia: Lippincott, 5th ed. rev. Cressey, 1955, p. 42.
[4] Hegarty, James E., "False Pretenses, Confidence Game and Short Check in Colorado," 25 *Rocky Mtn. L. Rev.* 325 (1953).

[5] *New York Penal Law*, Sec. 1290 (Clevenger-Gilbert, 1951).
[6] *People v. Ashley*, 267 P2d 271 (1954), cert den. 348 U.S. 900 (1954); Note, "False Promises as False Pretenses," 43 *Cal. L. Rev.* 719 (1955).
[7] Note, "The Regulation of Advertising," 56 *Col. L. Rev.* 1018,1041 (1956).

con game, perhaps the nucleus of much American fraud, is particularly untouchable because of the victim's equivocal position.

The extent to which particular criminal statutes are unenforceable should not be attributed to chance factors. If the law's efforts to curb fraud seem of no avail, the answer lies not merely in the cleverness of the swindler and the inadequacy of current police techniques for fraud-detection. To understand the real meaning of the fraud problem in America, one must turn to an analysis of the social dynamics of fraud and the con game within the modern American social system.

SWINDLING AS INTERACTION

An important element in an analysis of fraud (particularly in the confidence game situation) centers around the fact that the con game is, in a very real sense, a game. Though the term con game probably originated with the situations in which a swindler would induce his victim to compete in a "game of chance" (from which the swindler had carefully eliminated the chance element), it has been carried over to cover quite (superficially) different situations. Perhaps too little attention has been paid the interesting fact that confidence rackets are called "games," while most other criminal offenses receive (even from their practitioners) far less playful appellations.

Sociology has long recognized the great significance, for understanding human action, of play and games. Georg Simmel wrote:

All the forms of interaction or sociation among men—the wish to outdo, exchange, formation of parties, the desire to wrest something from the other, the hazards of accidental meetings and separations, the change between enmity and cooperation, the overpowering by ruse and revenge—in the seriousness of reality, all of these are imbued with purposive contents. In the game, they lead their own lives; they are propelled exclusively by their own attraction. For even where the game involves a monetary stake. . . . to the person who really enjoys

it, its attraction rather lies in the dynamics and hazards of the sociologically significant forms of activity themselves. The more profound, double sense of "social game" is that not only the game is played in a society (as its external medium) but that, with its help, people actually "play" "society."[8]

As George H. Mead suggested, the development of the human "self" may be illustrated by the child's participation first in play and later in the organized game. In the earlier stage of pure play the child typically "takes on" the roles of particular persons he sees about him; he plays at being other people. In the organized game stage, there is more complex role-playing, the self emerges through the creation of a "generalized other," and the game has rules which must be followed.[9] Interestingly enough, the confidence game would seem to embody aspects of both these stages. Certainly the "taking on" of another's role, the playing at being someone else, so characteristic of Mead's pure-play stage, is a prime factor in confidence swindling. At the same time there is little doubt that, at least from the swindler's standpoint, the con game has rules which must be followed and is the sort of game where "taking the attitude of the other" (one of Mead's favorite phrases) may be vitally necessary. Maurer notes, "Big-time confidence games are in reality only carefully rehearsed plays in which every member of the cast except the mark knows his part perfectly."[10]

Traditionally, criminology has studied crime and the criminal. Little attention has been paid the victim of criminal offenses; in many instances this is a grave shortcoming. Hans von Hentig pointed out an important but typically ignored fact when he wrote that, "in a sense the victim shapes and moulds the criminal."[11] This holds particu-

---

[8] Wolff, Kurt H. (ed. and tr.), *The Sociology of Georg Simmel*, Glencoe: The Free Press, 1950, pp. 49–50.
[9] Mead, George H. *Mind, Self and Society*, Chicago: Univ. of Chicago Press, 1934, 1950, pp. 152–164.
[10] Maurer, *op. cit.*, p. 108.
[11] Von Hentig, Hans, *The Criminal and His Victim*, New Haven: Yale Univ. Press, 1948, p. 384.

larly true for most fraud situations. As
Maurer explains:

A confidence man prospers only because of
the fundamental dishonesty of his victim.
. . . As the lust for large and easy profits is
fanned into a hot flame, the mark puts all his
scruples behind him. . . . In the mad frenzy of
cheating someone else, he is unaware of the
fact that he is the real victim, carefully selected
and fatted for the kill. Thus arises the trite,
but none the less sage maxim: "You can't
cheat an honest man."[12]

Similarly, Professor Sutherland quotes one
professional con man as follows: " 'A confidence game will fail absolutely unless the
sucker has got larceny in his soul.' "[13] And
as Sutherland went on to note, there is no
known case of a prospect declining to continue with a scheme once he learned it was
dishonest.

One writer has argued that the victim's
state of mind is completely irrelevant to the
question of whether the crime of false pretenses is committed in a particular case:

Whether the swindler obtains the confidence
of his victim seems entirely unimportant if in
fact the swindler intended to defraud and
actually does defraud his victim. . . . the
fraudulent trick or device is undoubtedly what
causes the unwary citizen to lose his property.
. . . To reason otherwise would seem almost
to promote dishonesty, and cheating, and to
reward artful treachery.[14]

While this approach might make it easier
for prosecutors to proceed under false pretenses laws, it clearly fails to do justice to
the actual dynamics of the fraud situation.
Is it really the trick or device which "undoubtedly . . . causes" the citizen to lose his
property? At best, that is only part of the
true picture.

Confidence swindlers are generally recognized to be the elite of the underworld.
Proceeds from such fraud can be exceptionally large, the con man tends to be his own

boss (even where several swindlers form a
mob), and unlike the "heavy rackets" swindling involves no violence. While factors
such as these help to account for the swindler's high status in the underworld, there
are satisfactions still more basic to the
swindling process which accrue not only to
the polished professional confidence man
but all the way down the line to the small-
time sharper.

One writer comments, for example, that
"above all, every deception, every impos-
ture is an assumption of power. The person
deceived is reduced in stature, symbolically
nullified, while the impostor is temporarily
powerful, even greater than if he were the
real thing."[15] It may well be that from the
psychodynamic standpoint, the assertion of
power over the victim is as important to the
swindler (though perhaps not on the conscious level) as is obtaining the sought-after
money or property.

Indeed the concepts of power and power
relations seem quite appropriate to an analysis of defrauding. To some extent at least,
we may even apply to the fraud situation a
few of the ideas currently used in the analysis of small group interaction processes. For
in a sense rivalry, coalition and strategy are
of the very essence of the confidence game.
(It is interesting to note in this regard that
the term "payoff," which features significantly in the analytic scheme developed by
von Neumann and Morgenstern,[16] is also
the label given by professional criminals to
several of the more ambitious of the traditional confidence games.)

We have seen that the victim has an
active role to play in bringing about his own
downfall. Invariably, the swindler convinces
the victim that together they can swindle a
third party; this third party, too, must be
reckoned with in studying the structure of

12 Maurer, op. cit., p. 16.
13 Sutherland, Edwin H., The Professional Thief,
   Chicago: Phoenix Books, 1937, 1956, p. 69.
14 Attwell, Joseph J., "The Confidence Game in
   Illinois," 49 Northwestern Univ. L. Rev. 737,
   751 (1955).
15 Klein, Alexander (ed.), Grand Deception: The
   World's Most Spectacular and Successful Hoaxes,
   Impostures, Ruses and Frauds, Philadelphia: Lippincott, 1955, p. 13.
16 Von Neumann, John and Oskar Morgenstern,
   Theory of Games and Economic Behavior,
   Princeton: Princeton Univ. Press, 1947.

power relations inherent in the confidence game situation. One way of picturing such a *triad* would be to say that the victim enters into a spurious coalition with the swindler against an imaginary third party. The would-be alliance between the con man and his victim is, of course, based wholly on a lie. But as Simmel aptly stated: "However often a lie may destroy a given relationship, as long as the relationship existed, the lie was an integral element of it. The ethically negative value of the lie must not blind us to its sociologically quite positive significance for the formation of certain concrete relations."[17] Though the victim's alliance with his swindler is indeed, as he will eventually discover, a spurious one, it is his belief in the lie and his confidence in the coalition which induces him to act as he does.

Basic to the widespread willingness to play the role of victim in such dramas would seem to be the desire to get "something for nothing." Again there may be the power element; the attempt to best a third party may underlie the victim's eagerness. But it is also interesting to note that potential victims do not seem to learn from their own or others' past experiences; indeed awareness of the widespread existence of swindling seems to help little in putting a swindle-prone public on its guard. This may suggest the presence of a desire (conscious or unconscious) to be victimized. Modern psychology has stressed the need for punishment which plays an important role in unconscious life, particularly among criminal offenders; this need is often illustrated by the frequency with which offenders betray themselves by leaving some telltale clue at the scene of the crime. A similar mechanism may operate to promote a willingness to be defrauded.

The potential victim is probably quite aware that the plan of action his confidant proposes is "wrong." Under such circumstances, he may harbor a strong ambivalence about winning; he may almost sense that he is to be swindled, but may unconsciously

17 Wolff, *op. cit.,* p. 316.

desire to be punished for his own wrongdoing. The question whether such self-defeating mechanisms should be attributed to a basic "death wish" or masochism must be left to the psychoanalysts.

A STRUCTURAL IMMORALITY

Most American studies of fraud and related offenses have been oriented to the individual offender, whose depredations are usually explained in terms of what may be called a "situational approach." Thus the conclusion of Lottier, based on firsthand study of embezzlers in a court's psychopathic clinic: "In every case, without exception, a critical tension situation of one kind or another invariably preceded the embezzlement behavior."[18] Similarly Cressey, in his recent book, *Other People's Money,* developed a modified situational theory of trust violation:

Trusted persons become trust violators when they conceive of themselves as having a financial problem which is non-shareable, are aware that this problem can be secretly resolved by violation of the position of financial trust, and are able to apply to their own conduct in that situation verbalizations which enable them to adjust their conceptions of themselves as users of the entrusted funds or property.[19]

Such theories may have validity with reference to the "chance offender" (assuming for the moment that the "chance" offender is not merely a persistent offender who got caught early in the game); to explain the persistent swindler we need a theory which transcends the situational approach. In any case, since various types of fraud abound in modern American society, we must look to our present social system for clues to explain the great drawing-power the roles of swindler and victim currently display.

C. Wright Mills, who has perhaps sensed the crux of the problem, states:

18 Lottier, Stuart, "A Tension Theory of Criminal Behavior," 7 *Amer. Sociol. Rev.* 840 (1942).
19 Cressey, Donald R., *Other People's Money: A Study in the Social Psychology of Embezzlement,* Glencoe: The Free Press, 1953, p. 30.

Many of the problems of "white-collar crime" and of relaxed public morality, of high-priced vice and of fading personal integrity, are problems of *structural* immorality. They are not merely the problem of the small character twisted by the bad milieu. And many people are at least vaguely aware that this is so. As news of higher immoralities breaks, they often say, "Well, another one got caught today," thereby implying that the cases disclosed are not odd events involving occasional characters but symptoms of a widespread condition. There is good probative evidence that they are right.[20]

In attempting to understand how such a "widespread condition" influences crime patterns, we should perhaps take for a lead the notion of the French sociologist Gabriel Tarde that "all the important acts of social life are carried out under the domination of example." Tarde asserted that "criminality always being . . . a phenomenon of imitative propagation . . . the aim is to discover . . . which among these various spreadings of example which are called instruction, religion, politics, commerce, industry, are the ones that foster, and which the ones that impede, the expansion of crime."[21]

One system of values which may foster crime, and particularly fraud, in our society, is that relating to the phenomenon of salesmanship. As Sutherland notes, "The confidence games are based essentially on salesmanship. . . ."[22] To a great extent our society is built on salesmanship, and the term implies much more than the mere sale of material goods. In an era when an increased premium is being put on "idea men," the ability to "sell a bill of goods" (in the figurative sense as well as the literal) takes on added importance. It is just this ability which the successful con man must demonstrate. Closely related to "selling a bill of goods" is the cultural stress on "putting across" one's "personality." We are all quite familiar with the importance in modern American society of being "well liked," of getting along and of being a "good mixer." These socially sanctioned attributes are the

very hallmark of the experienced swindler. Maurer notes that con men ". . . have cultivated the social side more than any other criminal group. They are able to fit in unobtrusively on any social level. . . . Although their culture is not very deep, it is surprisingly wide and versatile."[23]

Though women frequently act as lures or accomplices in certain con games, full-fledged confidence swindling seems to be primarily a male offense in this country. Since nothing is required for the commission of fraudulent acts which would be beyond the physiological capacities or social opportunities of women, the fact that swindlers are predominantly male tends to underscore the influence of general social values in shaping patterns of fraud. The specific attributes of the swindler tend to be typically male attributes under our present social system. This is generally true of the ability to sell things and of having a successful "personality"; certainly, "coming up with an idea," "putting an idea across" and convincing others are held to be almost exclusively within the masculine domain. It may be interesting also to note that the role of confidant (which the swindler usually takes on, often with great success), be it in the form of priest, lawyer, doctor or psychoanalyst, is characteristically taken by a male in our society. Quite likely, we should expect an increase in female fraud in the future. Otto Pollak has noted that ". . . an increase in female crimes against property is a concomitant of the social emancipation of women."[24] As the "idea woman" comes more and more into vogue, the "confidence woman" may cease to be a rarity. What effect this will have on the total extent of fraudulent crime remains to be seen.

Reinforcing the rationalizations which the social system provides the swindler, and further inciting his depredations, is the seemingly unlimited supply of victims. Businessmen seem particularly likely marks; as

20 Mills, C. Wright, *The Power Elite*, New York: Oxford Univ. Press, 1956, pp. 343–344.
21 Tarde, Gabriel, *Penal Philosophy*, tr. Howell, Boston: Little, Brown, 1912, p. 362.
22 Sutherland, *Principles of Criminology*, p. 233.
23 Maurer, *op. cit.*, p. 186.
24 Pollak, Otto, *The Criminality of Women*, Philadelphia: Univ. of Pennsylvania Press, 1950, p. 75.

von Hentig has noted, "There is . . . general consensus that businessmen are excellent victims in all respects."[25] This must be at least partly attributed to certain values of the business community which seem to underlie the trend to what Mills terms a "structural immorality." As Donald Taft comments:

. . . success is based somewhat increasingly upon financial gain similar to that of the banker or speculator rather than upon that of the old-fashioned industrialist whose fun was in the day's work. Whatever the economists may say, speculative gains look more like luck than hard work, and more nearly approximate the something-for-nothing philosophy of the pickpocket.[26]

Similarly, a probable influence on victim behavior is risk-taking, a generally approved activity which appears in numerous forms throughout our social life. The high value placed on risk-taking underlies the characteristic zeal for success which has played an integral part in shaping patterns of American social mobility. As Geoffrey Gorer has observed, "Gambling is . . . a respected and important component in many business ventures. . . . Like the gambler 'for fun' the American businessman is generally prepared to take proportionately far greater risks than his European equivalent."[27]

The victim, then, like the swindler, can easily take advantage of conflicting and overlapping patterns of expected behavior to justify his participation in fraudulent schemes. And in the swindler, who is the idea man, the convincer (and who thus in part typifies the leader), the victim may see something of his own (real or hoped-for) image; it may be this image to which he responds.

IMPLICATIONS
FOR THE SOCIOLOGY
OF CRIME

According to Professor Sutherland's "differential association" theory, "A person be-

comes delinquent because of an excess of definitions favorable to violation of law over definitions unfavorable to violation of law."[28] While the impact of such "definitions" is evident in much of what I have suggested above, it may be more useful to view value orientation on the social-system level, rather than membership in particular social groups within that system, as the prime vehicle for assimilation of the definitions. Furthermore, at least insofar as it is offered as a general theory of all crime, the differential association theory is negligent in limiting the subject matter of criminology to the understanding of the individual offender. As Clarence Jeffery has remarked in his highly valuable article, "Crime must be studied as an aspect of institutional systems. Institutions, not individual offenders, should be the subject matter of criminology." Under such an approach, "The concept of cause is replaced by one of function."[29]

"Structural-functional" sociology indeed offers much that is fruitful for analysis of the sociology of crime. According to this view, "deviance is always relative to a given institutionalized value-pattern system. . . ."[30] Sutherland at least sensed this basic unity of legality and illegality, as evidenced by his thesis that essentially the same sort of processes which result in lawful behavior also result in unlawful behavior.

Structural-functional analysis makes clear that a given item may have "diverse consequences, functional and dysfunctional, for individuals, for subgroups, and for the more inclusive social structure and culture."[31] Thus crime, usually thought of as negative and disorganizing, can serve positive as well as negative functions within the social system. While there has been some recogni-

[25] Von Hentig, op. cit., p. 435.
[26] Taft, Donald R., Criminology, New York: Macmillan, rev. ed. 1950, p. 231.
[27] Gorer, Geoffrey, The American People, New York: Norton, 1948, p. 178.
[28] Sutherland, Principles of Criminology, p. 78.
[29] Jeffery, Clarence R., "Crime, Law and Social Structure. Part I: Methodology," 47 J. Crim. Law, Criminol. & Police Sci. 423 (1956).
[30] Parsons, Talcott, The Social System, Glencoe: The Free Press, 1951, p. 283.
[31] Merton, Robert, Social Theory and Social Structure, Glencoe: The Free Press, 1949, 1951, p. 32.

tion of possible economic functions of crime,[32] other social functions of crime are less frequently recognized.

The distinction between "manifest" and "latent" functions "aids the sociological interpretation of many social practices which persist even though their manifest purpose is clearly not achieved."[33] This idea may be particularly useful in analysis of seemingly unenforceable criminal laws; I have elsewhere tried to apply such an analysis to our current laws against abortion.[34] Since our fraud laws are rarely applied, and when applied do not seem effective, why do we maintain them in their present form? The answer may lie in the important functions served by the practices nominally sought to be outlawed; we might well ask ourselves —could we really afford to effectively curtail fraud?

Structural-functional analysis has underscored the fact that in order to eliminate an existing social structure one must first provide the necessary "functional alternatives." This should make evident the futility of attempting to curb fraud by merely increasing penalties. Rusche and Kirchheimer have quite rightly stressed this "uselessness of shifting penal policies as a weapon against

socially determined variations in the crime rate."[35] Just what sort of adjustment in the social system must be made is uncertain, but the idea that radical changes are needed is not new. Sutherland, for example, recognized that "adequate control of professional crime cannot be attained by proceeding against thieves one at a time either by punitive or by reformative policies. Control calls, in addition, for modifications in the general social order out of which professional theft grows."[36] Perhaps the only real hope for a major reduction of fraud lies in such changes as may gradually result from an informed questioning of some of our prevailing social value systems.

Criminology has been seriously hampered in the past by its refusal to abandon the "social welfare approach" in favor of a truly sociological orientation. The former, as Kingsley Davis suggests, labors under the like-causes-like fallacy, here the idea that evil causes evil. To adopt a genuinely sociological mode of analysis, criminology must first of all recognize that "the contramoral is always functionally related to the moral. . . ."[37] With such recognition as a starting point, the phrase "sociology of crime" begins to take on real meaning.

[32] Hawkins, E. R. and Willard Waller, "Critical Notes on the Cost of Crime," 26 J. Crim. Law and Criminol. 684 (1936).

[33] Merton, op. cit., p. 64.

[34] Schur, E. M., Abortion and the Social System, 3 Social Problems 94 (1955).

[35] Rusche, George and Otto Kirchheimer, Punishment and Social Structure, New York: Columbia Univ. Press, 1939, p. 201.

[36] Sutherland, The Professional Thief, p. 229.

[37] Davis, Kingsley, Illegitimacy and the Social Structure, 45 Amer. J. Sociol. 215 (1939).

THE BEHAVIOR OF THE SYSTEMATIC CHECK FORGER*

Edwin M. Lemert

Projected against Sutherland's analysis of professional theft, Lemert describes the behavior of the systematic check forger.

* Reprinted from Social Problems, 6 (Fall 1958), pp. 141–149, by permission of the author and the publisher.

Although forgery behavior can be described as systematic, *it lacks the characteristics of professional theft. The author concludes that* present-day *check forgery, in contrast to nineteenth- and early twentieth-century forgery, does not appear to be a professional behavior system. Check forgers of today tend to avoid intimate association with other criminals.*

The concept of behavior systems in crime was first approximated in this country in Hall's analysis of several types of larceny in terms of their historical, legal, and social contexts.[1] Later the concept was made explicit and formulated into a typology by Sutherland and by Sutherland and Cressey.[2] Although this has hitherto inspired only a few monographic studies, there seems to be a growing consensus that focusing attention on specific orders of crime or making behavior systems the unit of study holds considerable promise for criminological research.

Because this paper proposes to assess the usefulness of Sutherland's formulation of the behavior system in analyzing or understanding the behavior of the systematic check forger, the typology outlined in his study of the professional thief will be employed. The five elements of the behavior system of the thief are as follows: (1) stealing is made a regular business; (2) every act is carefully planned, including the use of the "fix"; (3) technical skills are used, chiefly those of manipulating people; this differentiates the thief from other professional criminals; (4) the thief is migratory but uses a specific city as a headquarters; (5) the thief has criminal associations involving acquaintances, congeniality, sympathy, understandings, rules, codes of behavior, and a special language.

Altogether seventy-two persons currently serving sentences for check forgery and writing checks with insufficient funds were studied. Three additional check offenders

were contacted and interviewed outside of prison. The sample included eight women and sixty-seven men, all of whom served time in California correctional institutions.

Thirty of the seventy-five check criminals could be classified as systematic in the sense that they (1) thought of themselves as check men; (2) had worked out or regularly employed a special technique of passing checks; (3) had more or less organized their lives around the exigencies or imperatives of living by means of fraudulent checks. The remaining forty-five cases represented a wide variety of contexts in which bogus check passing was interspersed with periods of stable employment and family life, or was simply an aspect of alcoholism, gambling, or one of a series of criminal offenses having little or no consistency.

FINDINGS

Projected against the typology of professional theft, the behavior of the persons falling into the systematic check forgery category qualified only in a very general way as professional crime. In other words, although it is possible to describe these forgeries as *systematic*, it is questionable whether more than a small portion of them can be subsumed as *professional* under the more general classification of professional theft. A point-by-point comparison will serve to bring out the numerous significant differences between systematic forgery and professional theft.

1. *Forgery as a "regular business."* It is questionable whether check men look upon their crimes as a "regular business" in the same way as do members of "other occupational groups" who "wish to make money in safety." In virtually all cases the motiva-

[1] Jerome Hall, *Theft, Law and Society*, 2nd ed., Indianapolis: Bobbs-Merrill, 1952.
[2] E. H. Sutherland, *The Professional Thief*, Chicago: University of Chicago Press, 1937; E. H. Sutherland and D. R. Cressey, *Principles of Criminology*, 5th ed., Philadelphia: Lippincott, 1955.

tion proved to be exceedingly complex. This fact was self-consciously recognized and expressed in different ways but all informants revealed an essential perplexity or conflict about their criminal behavior. The following statement may be taken as illustrative:

Nine out of ten check men are lone wolves. Those men who work in gangs are not real check men. They do it for money; we do it for something else. It gives us something we need. Maybe we're crazy. . . .

The conflicts expressed involved not merely the rightness or wrongness of behavior; they also disclosed a confusion and uncertainty as to the possibility of living successfully or safely by issuing false checks. All of the cases, even the few who had a history of professional thieving, admitted that arrest and imprisonment are inevitable. None knew of exceptions to this, although one case speculated that "it might be done by an otherwise respected business man who made one big spread and then quit and retired."

The case records of the systematic check forgers gave clear testimony of this. Generally they had but short-lived periods of freedom, ranging from a few months to a year or two at the most, followed by imprisonment. Many of the cases since beginning their forgery careers had spent less total time outside prisons than within, a fact corroborated by the various law-enforcement officers queried on the point.

Many of the check men depicted their periods of check writing as continuous sprees during which they lived "fast" and luxuriously. Many spoke of experiencing considerable tension during these periods, and two cases developed stomach ulcers which caused them to "lay off at resorts." A number gambled and drank heavily, assertedly to escape their internal stress and sense of inevitable arrest. A number spoke of gradual build-up of strain and a critical point just before their arrest at which they became demoralized and after which they "just didn't care any more" or "got tired of running." The arrests of several men having a very long experience with checks resulted

from blunders in technique of which they were aware at the time they made them. Some of the men gave themselves up to detectives or F.B.I. agents at this point.

In general the picture of the cool, calculating professional with prosaic, matter-of-fact attitudes towards his crimes as a trade or occupation supported by rationalizations of a subculture was not valid for the cases in question.

2. *Planning as an aspect of forgery.* In regard to the second element of professional theft—planning—the behavior of check forgers is again divergent. Actually the present techniques of check passing either preclude precise planning or make it unnecessary. Although systematic check passers undeniably pay careful attention to such things as banking hours, the places at which checks are presented, and the kinds of "fronts" they employ, these considerations serve only as generalized guides for their crimes. Most informants held that situations have to be *exploited as they arise*, with variation and flexibility being the key to success. What stands out in the behavior of systematic check forgers is the rapid tempo —almost impulsiveness—with which they work.

The cases seemed to agree that check forgers seldom attempt to use the "fix" in order to escape the consequences of their crimes. The reason for this is that although one or a small number of checks might be made good, the systematic forger has too many bad checks outstanding and too many victims to mollify by offering restitution. Although the forger may be prosecuted on the basis of only one or two checks, ordinarily the prosecuting attorney will have a choice of a large number of complaints upon which to act. About the best the check forger can hope for through fixing activities is a short sentence or a sentence to jail rather than to prison.

3. *Technical skills.* Although the systematic check man relies upon technical skills—those of manipulating others—these are usually not of a high order, nor do they require a long learning period to master.

From the standpoint of the appearance of the check or the behavior involved at the time of its passing, there need, of course, be no great difference between passing a bad check and passing a good check. This is particularly true of personal checks, which are at least as favored as payroll checks by check men.

When check men impersonate others or when they assume fictitious roles, acting ability is required. To the extent that elaborate impersonations are relied upon by the forger, his check passing takes on qualities of a confidence game. Most of the check men showed strong preference, however, for simple, fast-moving techniques. A number expressed definite dislike for staged arrangements such as that of the "out of town real estate buyer" or for setting up a fictitious business in a community, then waiting several weeks or a month before making a "spread" of checks. As they put it, they "dislike the slow build-up involved."

4. *Mobility.* Like the thief, the systematic forger is migratory. Only one check man interviewed spoke of identifying himself with one community, and even he was reluctant to call it a headquarters. Generally check men are migratory within regions.

5. *Associations.* The sharpest and most categorical difference between professional theft and systematic forgery lies in the realm of associations. In contrast to pickpockets, shoplifters, and con men, whose criminal techniques are implicitly cooperative, most check men with highly developed systems work alone, carefully avoiding contacts and interaction with other criminals. Moreover, their preference for solitude and their secretiveness give every appearance of a highly generalized reaction; they avoid not only cooperative crime but also any other kinds of association with criminals. They are equally selective and cautious in their contacts and associations with the noncriminal population, preferring not to become involved in any enduring personal relationships.

A descriptive breakdown of the thirty check forgers classified as systematic bears out this point. Only four of the thirty had worked in check passing gangs. Two of these had acted as "fences" who organized the operations. Both were close to seventy years old and had long prison records, one having been a receiver of stolen property, the other having worked as a forger. Both had turned to using gangs of passers because they were too well known to detectives either to pass checks themselves or to permit their handwriting to appear on the checks. The other two forgers who had worked in gangs were female drug addicts who had teamed up with other female addicts.

Three other systematic check forgers did not work directly with other criminals but had criminal associations of a *contractual* nature. One oldtime forger familiar with the now little-used methods for forging signatures and raising checks usually sold checks to passers but never had uttered (passed) any of his own forgeries. Two men were passers who purchased either payroll checks from a "hot printer" or stolen checks from burglars. Apart from the minimal contacts necessary to sell or obtain a supply of checks, all three men were lone operators and very seclusive in their behavior.

Six of the thirty systematic forgers worked exclusively with one other person, usually a girl or "broad." The check men seemed to agree that working with a girl was equivalent to working alone. These pairs ordinarily consisted of the check man and some girl not ordinarily of criminal background with whom he had struck up a living arrangement and for whom he felt genuine affection. The girl was used either to make out the checks or to pass them. In some cases she was simply used as a front to distract attention. Some men picked up girls in bars or hotels and employed them as fronts without their knowledge.

The remaining seventeen of the thirty systematic check forgers operated on a solitary basis. The majority of these argued that contact with others is unnecessary to obtain and pass a supply of checks. Most of them uttered personal checks. However, even where they made use of payroll or corporation checks they contrived to manufacture or obtain them without resorting to interaction with criminal associates or intermediaries. For example, one Nisei check man arranged with a printer to make up checks for a fraternal organization of which he represented himself as secretary-treasurer. Another man frequented business offices at noon time, and when the clerk left the office, helped himself to a supply of company checks, in one instance stealing a check writing machine for his purposes.

It was difficult to find evidence of anything more than rudimentary congeniality, sympathy, understandings, and shared rules of behavior among the check forgers, including those who had worked in gangs. Rather the opposite seemed true, suspicion and distrust marking their relationships with one another. One organizer of a gang, for example, kept careful account of all the checks he issued to his passers and made them return torn off corners of checks in case they were in danger of arrest and had to get rid of them. Only two of the thirty forgers indicated that they had at times engaged in recreational activities with other criminals. Both of these men were lone wolves in their work. One other lone wolf stated that he had on occasion had dinner with another check man he happened to know well and that he had once or twice entered into a rivalry with him to see who could pass a check in the most difficult place.

The two men who had organized gangs of check passers worked with a set of rules, but they were largely improvised and laid down by the fence rather than voluntarily recognized and obeyed by the passers. The other check men with varying degrees of explicitness recognized rules for passing checks —rules learned almost entirely on an individual trial-and-error basis. The informants insisted that "you learn as you go" and that one of the rules was "never use another man's stunt."

Such special morality as was recognized proved to be largely functional in derivation.

Thus attitudes toward drinking and toward picking up women for sexual purposes were pretty much the result of individual perceptions of what was likely to facilitate or hamper the passing of checks or lead to arrest. Many of the men stated that since they were dealing primarily with business, professional, and clerical persons, their appearance and behavior had to be acceptable to these people. "Middle class" is probably the best term to describe their morality in most areas.

Careful inquiries were made to discover the extent to which the check men were familiar with and spoke an argot. Findings proved meager. Many of the men had a superficial acquaintance with general prison slang, but only four men could measurably identify and reproduce the argot of check forgery or that of thieves. Three more could be presumed to have some familiarity with it. Only one of these spoke the argot in the prison setting. Another said that he never used the argot either in prison or on the outside, except years previously when once in a great while he had "let down at a thieves' party." There were only two men who spoke of themselves as being "on the scratch."

INTERPRETATION

How can these findings be reconciled with the specific statement of Sutherland's informant[3] that "laying paper" is a form of professional theft most often worked in mobs? The answer to this apparent contradiction requires that a distinction be made between forgery of *the nineteenth and early twentieth centuries and that of the present day.* In the past forgery was a much more complex procedure in which a variety of false instruments such as bank notes, drafts, bills of exchange, letters of credit, registered bonds, and post office money orders as well as checks were manufactured or altered and foisted off. A knowledge of chemicals, papers, inks, engraving, etching, lithography, and penmanship as well as detailed knowledge of bank operations were prime req-

[3] E. H. Sutherland, p. 77.

uisites for success. The amounts of money sought were comparatively large, and often they had to be obtained through complex monetary transactions.[4] The technological characteristics of this kind of forgery made planning, timing, specialization, differentiation of roles, morale, and organization imperative. Capital was necessary for living expenses during the period when preparations for the forgeries were being made. Intermediates between the skilled forger and the passers were necessary so that the latter could swear that the handwriting on the false negotiable instruments was not theirs and so that the forger himself was not exposed to arrest. A "shadow" was often used for protection against the passer's temptation to abscond with the money and in order to alert the others of trouble at the bank. "Fall" money was accumulated and supplied to assist the passer when arrested. Inasmuch as forgery gangs worked together for a considerable length of time, understandings, congeniality, and rules of behavior, especially with regard to the division of money, could and did develop. In short, professional forgery was based upon the technology of the period.

Although precise dating is difficult, the heyday of professional forgery in this country probably began after the Civil War and lasted through the 1920's. It seems to have corresponded with the early phases of industrialization and commercial development before business and law-enforcement agencies developed methods and organization for preventing forgery and apprehending the offenders. Gradually technological developments in inks, papers, protectographs, and check-writing machines made the forging of signatures and the manufacture of false negotiable instruments more difficult. According to one source, for example, raised drafts have been virtually nonexistent since 1905.[5] Similarly, at the present time raising of checks is quite rare. The establishment of a protective committee by the American Bankers Association in 1894, related merchants' protective agencies, and improvements in police methods have made the risks of organized professional forgery exceedingly great.

Check gangs have always been vulnerable to arrest but this vulnerability has been multiplied many times by the large amounts of evidence left behind them in the form of countless payroll checks. Vulnerability is also heightened by the swiftness of communication today. If one person of a check-passing gang is arrested and identifies his associates, it becomes a relatively simple matter for police to secure their arrest. A sexually exploited and angered female companion may easily do the same to the check man. This goes far to explain the extreme seclusiveness of systematic check forgers and their almost abnormal fear of stool pigeons or of being "fingered." The type of persons who can be engaged as passers—unattached women, bar waitresses, drug addicts, alcoholics, petty thieves, and transient unemployed persons—also magnifies the probabilities that mistakes will be made and precludes the growth of a morale which might prevent informing to the police. These conditions also explain the fact that when the forger does work with someone it is likely to be one other person upon whom he feels he can rely with implicit confidence. Hence the man-woman teams in which the woman is in love with the man.

. . .

Further evidence that organized forgery is a hazardous type of crime, difficult to professionalize under modern conditions, is indicated by the fact that the organizer or fence is apt to be an older criminal with a long record, whose handwriting methods are so well known that he has no choice other than to work through passers. Even then he does it with recognition that arrest is inevitable.

A factor of equal importance in explaining the decline of professional organized forgery has been the increasingly widespread

[4] G. Dilnet, *The Bank of England Forgery*, New York: Scribners, 1929.
[5] J. W. Speare, *Protecting the Nation's Money*, Rochester: Todd Protectograph Co., 1927.

use of business and payroll checks as well as personal checks. Whereas in the past the use of checks was confined to certain kinds of business transactions, mostly involving banks, today it is ubiquitous. Attitudes of business people and their clerical employees have undergone great change, and only the most perfunctory identification is necessary to cash many kinds of checks. Check men recognize this in frequent unsolicited comments that passing checks is "easy." Some argue that the form of the check is now relatively unimportant to passing it, that "you can pass a candy bar wrapper now days with the right front and story." It is for this reason that the systematic check man does not have to resort to criminal associates or employ the more complex professional procedures used in decades past.

These facts may also account for the presence among lone-wolf check forgers of occasional persons with the identification, orientation, skills, codes, and argot of the thief. Case histories as well as the observations of informants show that older professional criminals in recent decades have turned to check passing because they face long sentences for additional crimes or sentencing under habitual criminal legislation. They regard checks as an "easy racket" because in many states conviction makes them subject to jail sentences rather than imprisonment. Check passing may be a last resort for the older criminal.

The presence of the occasional older professional thief in the ranks of check forgers may actually token a general decline and slow disappearance of professional thieving. One professional thief turned check passer had this to say:

I'm a thief—a burglar—but I turned to checks because it's getting too hard to operate. Police are a lot smarter now, and they have better methods. Police are different nowadays too; they report things more. It's hard to trust anyone now. Once you could trust cab drivers; now you can't. We live in a different world today.

THE CHECK FORGER AS AN ISOLATE

The preference of many systematic check forgers for solitary lives and their avoidance of primary-group associations among criminals may also be explicable in terms of their educational characteristics and class origins. The history of forgery reveals that in medieval times it was considered to be the special crime of the clerical class, as indeed it had to be inasmuch as the members of this class monopolized writing skills.[6] It also seems to be true from the later history of the crime that it has held a special attraction for more highly educated persons, for those of higher socioeconomic status and those of "refined" or artistic tastes. The basic method of organized forgery is stated to have been invented and perfected in England, not by criminals but by a practicing barrister of established reputation in 1840. An early gang of forgers organized by a practicing physician is also described by Felstead.[7] A number of studies directed to the differentiating characteristics of check criminals point to an "above average" intelligence and formal education. This refers to the general population as well as to the criminal populations with which they have been compared.

All of this is not to say that less-educated persons do not frequently pass bad checks but rather that the persons who persist in the behavior and develop behavior systems of forgery seem much more likely than other criminals to be drawn from a segment of the population distinguished by a higher socioeconomic status. Generally this was true of the systematic forgers in this study. Eight of the thirty had completed two or more years of college. Fourteen of the thirty had fathers who were or had been in the professions and business, including a juvenile court judge, a minister, a postmaster

6 T. F. Tout, *Medieval Forgers and Forgeries,* Bulletin of the John Rylands Library, 5, 3, 4, 1919, pp. 5–31.
7 T. S. Felstead, in *Famous Criminals and Their Trials,* New York: Doran, 1926.

of a large city, and three very wealthy ranch owners. One woman came from a nationally famous family of farm implement manufacturers. Four others had siblings well established in business and the professions, one of whom was an attorney general in another state. Two of the men had been successful businessmen themselves before becoming check men.

The most important implication of these data is that systematic check forgers do not seem to have had criminal antecedents or early criminal associations. For this reason, as well as for technical reasons, they are not likely to seek out or to be comfortable in informal associations with other criminals who have been products of early and lengthy socialization and learning in a criminal subculture. It also follows that their morality and values remain essentially "middle" or "upper" class and that they seldom integrate these with the morality of the professional criminal. This is reflected in self-attitudes in which many refer to themselves as "black sheep" or as a kind of Dr. Jekyll–Mr. Hyde person. Further support for this interpretation comes from their status in prison where, according to observations of themselves and others, they are marginal so far as participation in the primary groups of the prison is concerned.

CONCLUSION

The cases and data presented suggest that present-day check forgery exists in systematic form but does not appear to be a professional behavior system acquired or maintained through associations with other criminals. The technical demands of contemporary check forgery preclude efficient operation on an organized, cooperative basis. In addition to these factors, the class characteristics and backgrounds of systematic forgers incline them to avoid intimate association with other criminals.

WHIZ MOB*

David W. Maurer

Some of the most perceptive observations of professional criminals have come from the work of David W. Maurer. In the selection below, from his larger study of professional pickpockets, the author describes the patterns of activity associated with the act of theft among pickpockets. The analysis is concerned primarily with the technical argot and its use in connection with pickpocketing, especially as the argot is related to the teamwork ("mob work") of specialists following a sharp division of labor.

THE MOB AND THE MARK

Theft from the person is a highly specialized act which has preoccupied a certain class of thieves throughout the ages. While these thieves have never distinguished themselves by spectacular acts, they have built a prosperous illicit profession (perhaps sec-

---

* Reprinted from David W. Maurer, Whiz Mob, New Haven, Conn.: College and University Press, 1964, Chap. 5, by permission of the author and the publisher.

ond only to prostitution in venerability) which has survived a multiplicity of social changes and innumerable efforts to stamp it out. As has been suggested earlier, thievery is more than an illegal act; when practiced professionally and consistently, it becomes a way of life, a parasitic subculture.

In order to observe this act of theft more closely—along with the argot which translates it from a complex of body movement into symbolic articulation—it will be necessary to break it down into the several stages through which all thefts from the person must theoretically pass, individual exceptions to the contrary notwithstanding. The act is usually perpetrated against a representative of the dominant culture, and within range of the hazards which attend such an act. It must be shown happening within the considerable variety of situations under which professionals are known to work. In short, we must observe various types of pickpockets at work and consider some of the variations in their pattern of activity.

While a few pickpockets develop other types of lucrative operation, the pickpocket's subsistence comes almost exclusively from the act of theft. Probably this is why theft from the person occupies so much of the pickpocket's thinking and conversation, and why it looms so large in the factors which characterize this subculture; since there is little or no diversity of occupation, the tendency is to refine, insofar as possible, on this one source of subsistence, the result being that the entire subculture becomes what we might call craft-directed. Shop talk dominates; in fact, few pickpockets see much point in discussing anything else; hence every act of theft is hashed and rehashed by all concerned.

In order to avoid confusing the reader, the act of theft from the person will be presented three times in the course of this discussion. First, immediately following, it will be described in a paragraph or two so that the reader may get a quick review of what the act is. Second, in the section on *mob work*, it will be expanded and treated

in some detail in order to illustrate how the mob achieves the act. Last, in the sections on *The Tool* and *The Stall* it is described in very intimate detail.

First, however, let us oversimplify the act of theft and describe it in terms which can be well understood by persons not familiar with the profession. Initially, of course, the thief must want to steal someone's pocketbook. He must have anticipated a great variety of disasters, both legal and nonlegal, which may befall him during or after this act of theft. He must have taken what seem to him adequate precautions against these disasters, or at least be prepared to meet them offhand as they arise, if and when they do. We are right if we presume that most of these disasters will stem either from the victim who is being robbed, or from the law, which is supposed to prevent this very sort of thing. We will assume that this particular thief is sufficiently astute and skillful to avoid detection except by the most exceptional victim—and we will not let him operate on this type of victim at this time. Let us take it for granted that he has cleared with the law to the tune of a hundred dollars a day for the privilege of working unimpeded, except under certain circumstances which will be described later on. Unless this pickpocket is exceptional, he will have one or more partners; we will give him only one in this instance, just to keep the action as simple as possible. The thief will not think of these elements as we have stated them, but will image them in terms of his rich and vivid argot.

When this pair appear on the streets, their first concern is to find a potential victim. Unless they are very primitive in their methods, they will want to have some assurance that they are robbing someone who has enough money to make the theft worthwhile. Professionals become quite adept at selecting such victims by sight, then following up their selection with a rapid and deft manual exploration of the person to ascertain where the money or wallet may be carried. They are right a high percentage of the time. This act is performed by the tool, whose action of *fanning* the victim is covered or *shaded* by his stall. Once the loot is located, the stall rapidly and unobtrusively maneuvers the victim (called a *mark*) into position so that the tool can work. The stall, working from signals given by the tool, or simply so familiar with the tool's technique that he automatically functions in a variety of situations, then holds the victim in position with his body, using his upper arms, his back, his elbows, or his legs to block any movement the mark may make, and to keep the mark's hands clear of the pocket to be picked; this is called *framing the mark*, or *putting up for the mark*, who is held, unawares of course, in position for the few seconds necessary for a good tool to take his money. "You have to wait till they frame for him." "Well, you can't frame with a singlehanded gun." "The idea is the frame, the way a man is framed for. If he walks out natural to get in a train or a bus or a taxicab—he has to be going somewhere, in other words, he has to be moving. But then it's up to the stall to maneuver that man, to put that man in a position so that he can be worked on, so that you can handle the mark in the proper way, and when you handle the mark, naturally I mean clip him."

When the theft is complete, the tool signals the stall, who takes the wallet, and they move on to another spot and locate another victim. The stall usually carries the wallets until they call a halt, when the wallets are thoroughly searched, the money divided, and the wallets disposed of. This last step may vary with different types of mob.

The act described above in an oversimplified form is basic to all theft from the person by professional pickpockets. The entire profession is built around it, although it may be extended, expanded, or varied in a score of different ways. Some pickpockets work by themselves, without a partner or other support; some work *two handed, three handed*, or even *four handed*. In Europe

some mobs may work as many as eight or ten *strong*. "Everybody's a tool over there. Everybody's a hook, except them four guys on the points of the compass. They are eight or ten strong over there." But all professional pickpockets, however expert or however clumsy, operate on the basis of the situation just outlined.

From here on, this study will be concerned with the technical argot and its use in connection with the act of theft in all its ramifications, but especially as it concerns *mob work*, or the teamwork of specialists following a sharp division of labor.

The reader should be reminded that the pickpocket is strictly nonviolent; that he is set apart from the *heavy rackets* in that he does not use violence to take money, but lets a victim—even a well-heeled one—go rather than excite his suspicions, or call attention to the fact that thievery is being committed; and that this psychology is diametrically opposed to the behavior of professionals on the *heavy rackets*, who do not hesitate to use any amount of force necessary—even unto the shooting of the victim —to take his valuables. The act of theft from the person by stealth is essentially what is referred to as a *sneak job*, which implies the successful robbery without the victim's knowledge. The pickpocket differs from other operators on the *grift* in that he steals directly from the person, and in that he cannot capitalize on the cupidity of the victim, as do those who use the numerous *short con* and *big con* rackets.

The pickpocket uses psychology in his work, but it is rather the psychology of bodily contact, of tactilism, of strategy in maneuvering his victim into position, of misdirection which distracts the victim's attention so as to take his mind off his money. The pickpocket likes to perform successive acts of thievery in the same locality without attracting attention; he then likes to move on to a new locality before his victims discover their losses and call upon the law. He moves softly and melts into any crowd with great skill. If he is really good, he dresses so unobtrusively that he is difficult to observe and remember; but at the same time his clothes are of good quality, and, once singled out, it is difficult for the average person—and even the law—to imagine that a man of such substantial appearance could be guilty of trying to steal a pocketbook.

It will also be noted that *the argot hardly reflects this gentle art, but rather evokes images of violence and aggression far beyond those elements actually involved.*

MOB WORK

When a mob is active professionally, they are *working* and the same verb is applied in a secondary sense to stealing in certain localities or from certain people, as *working a tip, working a get on, working right spots,* etc. "On this occasion there happened to be quite a little tip in there. So we root right in and work it." For purposes of illustration, we will use a *road mob* which is *working* racetrack crowds in various cities. The terms *hustle* and *grift* are also used in some senses as the equivalents of *work.* Let us expand the simple *two handed mob* just briefly described and say that this mob is *hustling three handed.* This means that they have two stalls and one tool. One of the stalls is the *steer* for the mob.

Pickpockets over the centuries have established a sharp division of labor. The tool selects the mark to be robbed, and actually takes the score. "The first five scores was cold." The stalls work within a short radius of the tool as he prospects about in the crowd for marks. It is their responsibility to watch the tool closely at all times and to follow his cues. They must close in rapidly, unobtrusively, and almost automatically to *make the frame.* They often sight the mark as soon as the tool does; if not, they can tell from the direction of his movement where the *chump* is; when the *hook* ("A hook is a britch tool who actually hooks his finger onto the poke instead of pinching the poke") steps in behind a man,

they know definitely that this is the mark. The tool makes the decision in selecting the victim; the stalls work under his guidance somewhat like bird dogs working with a hunter. And like bird dogs, they must know a great deal about the habits of the game as well as the habits of the hunter. They close in smoothly, without appearing to do so. "The frame seems natural to the sucker, but it really isn't. A smart dick will notice that." The exception to this is, of course, the rare tool who works entirely by himself; he will be considered separately later on. Normally the tool has the constant support of one or more stalls.

When the tool sees a potential victim, he falls in behind him to *locate,* that is to *fan* the *chump* to see whether or not he has a fat wallet or a roll of money worth taking, and if so where he carries it. "I went up to this guy and fan him, and he's got on a pair of jeans underneath those overalls." Around racetracks, where our theoretical mob is working, much of the *locating* is done by sight, for people there are notoriously careless about handling money. However this information is gathered, it is communicated by sign, signal, or actual argot terms, such as for instance, *left bridge impression,* which means that the man has a good bankroll in his left-hand side pants pocket. Some stalls work so closely with their tools that they do not need to receive specific manual signals or to say anything; they read the tool's body-stance and attitude so automatically that they know as soon as he does what the situation is. Rarely stalls *locate* for the tool, but usually not in *organized mobs.* Routinely they depend on the tool to *locate* as he makes bodily contact with the victim.

Usually, as the tool makes the first contact with the mark, he *locates* immediately and communicates with the stalls so that they may put the mark into position for whatever type of *score* the situation demands. That is, he may say to the stalls, who have closed in as soon as they see from his movements that he is making contact and is *locating* with a mark, such a phrase as *turn him in for a pit* or *pit*, meaning that the mark is carrying his wallet in his inside coat pocket and that the tool wants the stalls to maneuver the mark so that he is in position for the tool to take this type of *score*, which in this instance will probably be taken from the side. "So I said 'pit' to Mickey. And of course he came through." Good stalls read the body movements of their tool just as readily as he reads theirs, and automatically sense the type of *score* that is to be taken. "When the tool says, 'Turn John in for a pit,' the sucker wouldn't associate that with himself at all. After hustling for a number of years, they won't need many words. A clever cannon talks as little as possible." "Sometimes in a police line-up, the sucker will say, 'Have him say something' and those few words might make a lot of difference."

Pickpockets operate cautiously and so unobtrusively that only a trained observer can tell that they are *working* in a crowd, or anywhere else for that matter, for, contrary to general belief, they do not necessarily work in crowds at all. They are, however, very aggressive, within the limits which mark their profession; they study the victim rapidly but with great care; they size him up from several angles; they project any of several possible approaches to him, thinking in terms of bodily movement; they are (unconsciously) highly sensitive to his rhythms of stride, his size and weight, the problems presented by his clothes or by the *location* previously mentioned, and the presence of onlookers who might see the *touch* come off from certain angles; they register firearms, knives, or other weapons on his person; they note the fabric of his clothes, his necktie, his stance and build, the very complexion of the back of his neck, which some tools retain with photographic clarity.

It is important to sense immediately and with great precision not only whom to rob and how, but even more important whom not to rob and why. It is better to refrain from picking the pockets of FBI

men, for instance, though some would do it; and it is also good to avoid *rumbling* marks who have just previously been taken. The nature of the mark will be discussed in detail in a later chapter.

In order to clarify the phase of the act of theft now being discussed, suffice it to say that within a matter of seconds after a mark is spotted and his money *located*, the mob has closed in and the stalls are preparing him for the safest and most effective type of kill that this particular mob is capable of executing. This continuum of spotting a victim and closing in on him, with the tool in a position to *work*, or actually *working*, is known as *playing for a mark*, or *playing*, or *making a play*. "I spotted the guy. At Columbia I want to make a play for him, see." The presence of marks who are worth robbing with the consequent natural action of *mob work* is known as *play*. When the mob is working smoothly and profitably together, they say that they are *digging in, rooting in* or *batting away*. "And they never seen anybody like us. And we're rooting in and they don't savvy."

To summarize, then, we have the situation for an act of theft from the person when one or more stalls puts a victim into a position so that the tool can rob him. The act of the tool is the climax and takes place within a very few seconds. Let us see how this division of labor works out.

THE STALL

Although it might at first appear that the most difficult part of the act of theft is the removal of the wallet from the victim's pocket (and indeed this is a key act), a good stall makes it much easier than it could otherwise be. Men who have done both seem to agree that stalling is more demanding than *hooking*, or playing the part of the tool. "I learned both. I learned to stall and I learned to hook too, and I broke in many a stall. A lot of stalls won't break in, you see, because they're thieves and they won't be told. That's the reason they are thieves. They don't want people to tell them what to do. So if you can't tell a man what to do, then he can't stall."

The stall's work is diverse and intuitive, compared to the tool's. He must have a fine eye for marks which the tool wants to *fan* and be able to cover much ground when necessary in a crowd without attracting attention. While he may use his entire body, including his hands and feet, to maneuver and hold a mark, he uses his back as much or more than any other part of his body. He refers to his back as his *hump*, and speaks of its use in stalling as *throwing a hump* or *putting his hump up* (for someone). "So Frenchy said, 'Come on, Conk, and put your hump up for me.'" "I throwed a hump at him in the doorway." "I put my back up for him." The same phrase may be used with the "someone" indicating the victim rather than the tool, as "Slim, why don't you put your hump up for that mark in the white hat?" It also occurs as *to put up for*. "We put up for him at the get on."

This focus on the back is functional, since much of the time the stall works with his back to the victim, expertly using his body to control him. However, a good stall uses the upper part of his back also, including his shoulders, and especially his elbows. "The buttocks are seldom, if ever, used by a male stall. Broads plant their kiester against the mark, but just for an instant. The upper part of the back and the elbows is used to keep the mark in position."

When a stall is *working* in front of the mark, he is called the *front man* and said to be *fronting the mark*. "Yeah, Al got that score, but I was fronting for him." This is seldom a permanent position from which he operates, since a mob is a versatile group, and the stalls should be able to work in any position desired by the tool. Either stall should be able to work in this position, but one may be more effective than the other. "The tool might have a preference in some instances, because one stall has more moxie, so he'll say, 'Louie, you front this mark.'"

Usually it works out so that whichever stall gets into the front position is, for the time being, *front man*. In fact, the stalls may change positions several times if they have to give the tool more than one *slant* at the mark. This term also occurs as a verb with the meaning varying according to who is the subject. If a stall says, "I was fronting the mark," it means that he was in position as described above. But if the tool says, "I'll front the mark," or "I'll be front man," it means that the tool wants to take the *score* from the front (not a very safe practice, which will be discussed further under *The Tool*), and the stalls immediately fall to a position beside and behind the mark, to hold him in the proper position. The stall who then works directly behind the mark is called a *backstop*, especially in the Chicago area. "John O'Keefe lost more backstops on the dip than Sherman lost men marching to the sea." "Old Windy Dick could take it out of your eyes. Always singlehanded. Didn't need no backstops for him."

Stalls must also be expert at maneuvering a mark about in a crowd so as to get him into a good position for the tool, or to hold him in a given position until the tool gets to him. This is called *pratting in* or *pratting out*, as the case may be. "That String Kid was a bang-up tool. He could nail them as fast as two stalls could prat them in." This is called *pratting* because of the way in which the hips are used to move a man one way or another—though, of course, all parts of the body are used in order to keep the action from attracting attention. For instance, suppose a tool has spotted two *fat* marks in a *tip* boarding a train. One is just about to go up the steps, but the other one is far back in the crowd. So the tool may say, "Prat that big mark out and we'll beat him." The stalls then get in front of the big mark indicated and rapidly *prat him out of the tip*, that is, work him backward so that he cannot board the train until the tool has robbed him; the stalls then *prat him back into the tip*, so that he will get on the train immediately and be gone before he *blows*. "Some mobs put a stall on the mark's tail to see if he blows before he gets on the rattler." Meanwhile, if the second mark the tool selected has not already moved up into the *tip*, the tool will get the stalls to *prat him in* so that he can be robbed unobtrusively just before he boards. Or the stalls might simply *prat* the first mark *out* in order to delay his progress until the second mark could be *beaten*; then the tool could step in behind the first mark. *Pratting out* may also refer to moving a man out of the way so that the tool can get at the mark. "This John just stood there and I like to broke a leg trying to prat him out."

This type of action by stalls is not easy to describe because there is so little to see; if any of their moves attract attention either from the mark or from anyone else in the crowd, they are not *bang up* stalls. "Good stalls are few and far between. There ain't any good ones turning out any more. Stalls are at a premium." Every move they make must be slight enough and natural enough to be inconspicuous, but at the same time definitely calculated to move the mark in the direction and into the position desired. When they work in pairs, their movements are beautifully synchronized, and they get results with incredible swiftness. They use their bodies with the surety and timing of professional dancers, at the same time disguising each move as a natural one.

When the stall is a woman, the technique may be the same; she uses her back and elbows like a man. She also knows, however, how to use her buttocks in a very different and much more effective way. The male stall must never attract the attention of the mark as he maneuvers him in or out; the woman, on the other hand, may be skilled in doing just the opposite. She uses her buttocks against the genitals of the victim in such a way that he is startled, flattered, and perhaps confused or embarrassed. This is usually done just as the tool is ready to *get his duke down*, or rob the victim, and must be perfectly timed. "She knew exactly how long to put her prat against a mark and then take it away. It was just enough to lead him on, to give him an idea that there might be some chance for a make, and then take her prat away from the mark because it's liable to be in the way at any time. She uses her back and elbows just the same as a male stall, but even more so than a man, because a woman can get away with more in a crowd at any time."

Of course, this sexual approach is extremely brief and no opportunity is given the victim to follow through, even should he so desire; many of the more alert marks are said to seize the girl's buttocks in both hands, throwing all caution to the winds, and counting on the closeness of the crowd to conceal their movements; as they clutch at elusive sex appeal, they become completely vulnerable to the tool who works from behind or from the side, as conditions demand. The girl remains in contact with the victim only for a matter of seconds, then eludes his ardor by swiftly *pratting out* other persons who block her way and *pratting in* persons who may block the path of her recent admirer. The girls used as stalls of this sort are sharp, attractive girls, very well dressed and in no way resembling prostitutes. Their effect on upper middle-class men is immediate and disastrous.

Stalls of both sexes also perform other coöperative services for the tool. At the command "*come through*" they know how to reverse position, or turn to the right or left, holding the victim in position and blocking his hands from possible access to the pocket being picked by the tool. "The stall comes through so as to put the mark into position for the wire. You [the stall] come through when there is a little squeeze in the crack at the top of the kick and the poke is tight there. It's to distract the mark's attention for just a split second. The wire is careful not to let the mark bump into him when you [the stall] come through."

The stall *comes through* on the side

where the *score* is *coming off*; that is, he will reverse position from immediately in front of or to the side of a mark and double back toward the tool. The contact between the stall and the mark is slight, not enough to attract much attention but strong enough to make the mark conscious that someone wants to pass him going the other way. The stalls usually *come through* for *left* or *right britch* or *pit scores*.

They may be required to *raust* a victim, that is, by bodily contact or specific movement cause him to respond to what the professional magician calls "misdirection" and take his hands off his money or move into a more favorable position. "The office 'raust and come through' means that you [the stall] actually bump the mark as you come back. But there isn't much bumping done by a class mob. Root-and-toot mobs—maybe yes. It's the business of the whiz to be as inconspicuous as possible, for anything that attracts attention may be recalled later on." Some tools like to use a very gentle *raust* when taking a *pit score* (*insider*) from the side. The less *rausting* the better, however, if the mark is not to be *rumbled*. "Say, 'Raust . . . come through . . . raust.' That would mean in order to raust him, you know how to raust a mark? Just take his hat like that." [Informant pushes my hat forward over my eyes with a gentle touch from the back.] "Now that is a raust. Well, then, the first thing he does is he takes both his hands. Did you ever see a man straighten his hat with one hand? He'll come up with both hands and straighten his hat and [the informant chirps the office for 'it's off'] that's all she wrote."

The stall may be required to *stick* the victim (hold him firmly) for the tool. "Jigs, they work a lot different from us. I mean, you stick one for me and I'll stick one for you." "I was sticking this mark down for Bradley and I got my own mitt down on another mark in front of me." The latter quotation shows a very unorthodox act on the part of the stall, who was also trying to act as a tool, a diversity which is never practiced in well-organized mobs. "The tool is the only member of the mob who steals. The stall isn't even allowed to fan a man unless it's an accident. That sort of thing will really get him hurt." Or he may receive an office or an argot communication from the tool like "*stick and split me out*," which means to hold the victim firmly until the theft is complete, then move in instantaneously between the victim and the tool so that there is no chance for the victim to catch or see the tool, even if he becomes aware of the theft. This act of *splitting the tool out* is not habitually used by smooth operators, but in the event of an emergency every stall must be prepared to *split out* the tool for the protection of the mob. Stalls also *shade the duke* for their tools; that is, they cover the hand of the tool with a coat, a newspaper, or their own bodies so that his actions in *fanning* or *locating* are not visible to onlookers. "I shaded her duke with my raincoat, my tog." Coats used for this purpose are carried over the arm, and are called *togs*; sometimes the stall wears the coat and expertly spreads the front of it to complete the *shade*; newspapers carried for this purpose are called *stiffs* or *sheets* or, by old-timers, *blutes*.

In mobs which have more than one stall, whichever one covers the tool's hand and takes his position on the side of the victim where the money is located is called a *duke man*. He also usually takes the *score* from the tool as soon as the theft is complete, so that the tool will not have it in his possession in the event of trouble. A *duke man* is not a specialist; he simply happens to be in that position at the tool's direction.

In *road mobs*, such as the one we are using for this example, the stall also is the *steer* or *steer man* for the mob; that is, he plans the itinerary so as to catch various races at conveniently related locations, and attempts to work in any other fairs, athletic games, or celebrations which might make the trip more profitable. "A good steer man has to know all the doin's and the right spots." He often also has an encyclopedic knowledge of how the fix operates in each community, what territory is worked by which other pickpocket mobs, what the best transportation is between cities, and a good deal more besides. "A good stall can always get filled in, especially if he reads the papers and can steer."

A stall who does this specialized work is also called a *folder man* (because he handles the *folders* or time-tables), a *finder* (because he "finds" the best places and times to work) or an *advance man* (because he plans the work in advance for the mob). "Ninety percent of the racket is having a perfect folder man." Of course so-called *local mobs* do not need and do not use a specialized *steer*, but *road mobs* would be handicapped without one.

While we are speaking of stalls, a concept commonly misunderstood by the public—and often by the police apparently—should be mentioned. This is the concept of *jostling*. It is commonly believed that a stall *jostles* the victim, that is shoulders into him roughly, elbows him, throws him off balance, etc. "Now if that man is jostled, if you knock into the mark, or brush into him roughly, you're liable to knock the tool off balance." (Detective showing use of this term): "It was rough work, so about that time the Kid threw him the jostle." (Class *cannon* commenting on the illustration): "Whoever told you that wasn't no pickpocket. That's a dick's term." Another *cannon* comments: "When you're working in a guy's britch, your hand . . . it's a suspended animation. You're in his kick, and yet you're not in his . . . you understand what I mean? And if you, if your stall knocks into that man, he's liable to cause your hand to hit him, and that's all of it. So that's a dick's term strictly, that 'jostle'."

This concept is so firmly established, however, that the police use it all the time and in some states like New York there are laws designed to enable officers to arrest pickpockets even though they are not caught stealing, or to arrest the stall even though he has stolen nothing. These statutes refer to *jostling* and the participation of the stall is commonly referred to as *jostling*. Actually, except amongst mobs who operate so crudely that we could hardly call them pickpockets, the victim is never *jostled*, nor is he conscious of the stall's work at any time. Skilled pickpockets do not use the concept or the term to refer to their own work. "I want my mark to behave and step along like a little gentleman. I don't want nobody stomping on his toes or bumping into him, or knocking him around or jostling him. That will wake a sucker up." Rough stalls (with *hit and run* mobs) sometimes push the mark around if they think they can get away with it. "If they grab a sucker and shove him on the train, that would be a snatch score. Good mobs don't do this. It's only in New York."

The work of the stalls is called *framing* or *framing for the mark*; the situation at the moment when the tool takes the *score* is called the *frame*. This concept applies even if there is only one stall, but of course is not present technically, at least, when a pickpocket is working singlehanded—a situation which will be discussed in detail later on. When a *four handed mob* are working, they use a *double duke frame*—that is, one stall on the right, one on the left, and one in front. The tool *works* behind. Should the tool want to *front the mark*, he changes places with a stall who goes to the rear.

THE TOOL

The tool, as we have shown in the early portion of this chapter, does the actual stealing. He is also called a *hook, wire, mechanic,* etc. Old-timers or Britishers may call him the *claw*. There are also various kinds of tools, such as *careful tools*, ("Some careful tools reef every score." "Little Midge was a careful tool. He didn't take so many scores, but he'd go for weeks without a rumble."), *cautious tools, rough tools* (those who work without finesse; those who are not too careful about *rumbling* the victim), *wild tools* (those who will try anything), *buggy tools* (those who are unpredictable), and *hungry tools* (those who are on the hustle day and night because they are money hungry).

While the division of labor between stalls and tools is sharp, and is usually observed in so-called *organized mobs*, some professionals can work equally well in either position, or can *fill in* as stalls, even though they are properly tools, and vice versa. It is important during the act of theft that each mob member observe the division of labor agreed upon by that particular mob in advance, for a stall who suddenly decided to turn tool and take an *easy score* might well jeopardize the safety of the entire mob. However, among *makeshift* or *pickup* mobs, and often among Negro or Latin-American pickpockets, there is very loose mob-organization. "Among Jigs, it's 'You put your back up for me, and I'll put my back up for you. If you get caught, you're in jail.'"

The tool may be so versatile that he can take money or wallets from any pocket, provided he can get into position and depend upon his stalls. "If I can get that hook in, it don't make no difference whether it's a left britch, right britch, or left prat, right prat." Some, however, are not so versatile, or have definite limitations regarding certain types of *work*. For instance, many tools cannot go in successfully under overcoats; these are called *summertime tools* or *summer cannons*. They are often glad to get work as stalls in the winter if they do not go to a warmer climate. Others specialize in hip pocket work and are called *prat diggers*. "There's a lot of guns I know specialize strictly in prat pokes." Sometimes these tools who specialize in the hip pocket are really superior at taking *prat scores*; others are just not very good tools. "Some tools have something in one line. Some like prat kicks, others like insiders and coat pits, and some play for britch kicks." Most American tools like to work from behind the victim, or from the side; part of this is tradition, part of it the dislike which they

have for *giving up their kisser*, or allowing the victim to see their faces.

I like to take a top britch from the side, if the mark doesn't look at me. If a man looks at me, that's the end of it. Anytime a guy points me out in a line-up and says, "There—that's the guy that stole my pocketbook," he's telling a damn lie, because if he even so much as wrinkles them little muscles on the back of his neck, and acts like he's going to look around, I let him go, because there's a lot of people in the world, there's a lot of pockets, and a lot of pants. There's always another guy right behind him, you know what I mean. It ain't worth while jeopardizing your liberty, the most valuable thing in the world to a thief. There ain't no use in jeopardizing that unnecessarily and that's what you do any time you let a sucker look at you.

Some Americans, however, are *front workers* or *front men*; that is, they can and do work facing the victim. "A jug score is easy for a front worker, because it's usually a pit or an insider." Most of the European tools, especially the old-timers, are *front workers*, probably because of the custom, generally more prevalent in Europe than in America, of cutting men's side pants pockets with the opening parallel to and just below the waistband, instead of with the opening following the line of the outside trouser seam, which runs at right angles to the waistband. Thus a European tool will *take* this type of pocket, called a *top britch* or *top bridge*, while facing the victim, and he *takes* it exactly as an American tool would *take* a hip pocket when standing behind the victim. Trousers cut with *top britches*, while worn in this country by a certain class of people, are now not common in standard business suits, but are frequently found in work clothes. European tools, however, often continue to *work* from the front, even after they have been in America for years. Most American tools avoid *working* directly facing the mark by taking *pit scores* or *insiders* from the side, approaching the mark diagonally or at an angle. For working the hip pockets or the side pants pockets, they like to be behind the mark, or slightly to the right or left as the case may be, facing the same way as the mark but well out of his line of vision.

Whatever the specialty of the tool, if indeed he has any, it is well known to the mob, and his stalls play to that specialty. Generally, however, he does more than just lift a pocketbook from a helpless mark held firmly but unconsciously in the *frame*. He does all the *locating* with *organized mobs*. He must have a good knowledge of people, so as to select victims who are carrying large amounts of money rather than those who are well-dressed but who have little cash. He must be very observant of small details which, added up, lead him to the consistently satisfactory *scores*. He must have a very fine sense of timing and strong *grift sense*. He directs all operations while the mob is *working*; the stalls follow his directions meticulously.

In other words, the tool is a practical psychologist. He listens to conversations in the crowd, and from them pieces together information he can use. He sees every move where money is involved. He notes the build, stance, dress, and manner of everyone he can see. He almost automatically separates local citizens from travelers; if he is in a *road mob*, he will take the travelers by preference (other things being equal) because they are likely to carry more money; if he is a *local* operator, he will want to avoid robbing local residents, since they may upset his arrangements with the police. He knows how to smell an officer of the law; some types he avoids religiously, other types he robs with pleasure. He recognizes other thieves, even though he has never seen them before, with uncanny precision. "Mobs recognize a frame anywhere they see it in a tip. Also, there are damned few who wouldn't recognize each other on sight." He registers any attention whatever from onlookers as he *works*. He knows how to be unobtrusive and almost a nonentity in a crowd or on a street-corner; he also realizes that he must be prepared to melt away into a crowd if he sees anyone who is looking too closely.

He is always alert, always under tension, though of a different kind, even when he is not *working*, for he is well aware that someone may tap him on the shoulder at any moment. Perhaps this perpetual tension is one of the reasons why a very high percentage of pickpockets are narcotic addicts— a higher percentage than has been encountered in any other *racket*.

There is a lot of nervous tension during the time you're stealing. I guess that is why there is a lot of junkies, because it releases that tension after the grifting is over. A lot of whiz that don't use junk will do outlandish things for the same reason. They have to blow off steam. Sex is one outlet. You can mark this down, too, as soon as the grift is over, they can't get along with each other.

However, as the tool we were using as a laboratory specimen *works* on the street, in a railway station, or at a racetrack, all these things are in the back of his mind. Principally, he is looking for *scores*. In this case, he sees a man leaving the betting window at the track. It is the $50 window. He knows that the man must either have made a bet or collected one. He catches a *flash* of green in the man's hand as it goes to his pants pocket, then the man moves into the crowd. Immediately he knows that this a *fat* mark, possibly very *fat*. The chances are that this tool knows exactly the prices that all three horses paid in the last race, and he can figure instantaneously what a $50 ticket would pay on any one of them; besides, if the man is buying a $50 ticket, he must have enough money on him to make him worth while; in that case, the *flash* was not winnings, but the remainder of the roll from which he is betting. If he was cashing a $50 ticket, that would be all right too. And if he has bought one or more $50 tickets, the thief can cash them as easily as the purchaser can.

The tool catches the eye of the nearest stall, who may also have spotted this sucker. It is better not to *clip* him right here near the window, for such spots are often *covered* by track detectives, by Pinkerton men, or, at big races, by out-of-town detectives who may not be averse to shake-down tactics. Besides, the man is striding off toward the stands. The second stall senses that the wind is up as soon as he observes the actions of the tool and the first stall, and even if he has not seen the mark, he knows that there will be *action* shortly. All three of them follow the mark separately but as swiftly as possible without attracting attention. The tool steps up behind his man, which act serves as an *office* to the stalls, who are walking just in front of the tool, one on each side. The mark suddenly stops to talk to someone. That might bring the entire party to a standstill. The stalls still have to get abreast of the mark in order to *make a frame*.

Of course, it would be quite possible for the three of them to *split the man out* from his friend momentarily and rob him in the flurry, or to rob the friend as well, but to do so smacks too much of the *hit and run* or *clout and lam* tactics or reckless *guns*. They slow their pace, the stalls actually blocking the progress of the tool if necessary, so that all three are walking, but not getting anywhere, especially if the crowd is thick. The mark leaves his friend and turns toward a ramp leading to the grandstand. They all sense this and the tool *offices* that they will *clip* him as he enters the ramp. They are now right *on his tail*, although no one except an experienced observer could tell this as they move through the crowd, which is a little heavier about the entrance to the ramp. We have slowed the *action* down abnormally in order to get some of the details in.

All this has taken perhaps a minute and a half or two minutes from the time the tool first caught the *flash* of money at the $50 window. The stalls have moved slightly in front of the victim, almost touching him with their elbows now, and the tool is directly behind him. The mark is entering the *frame*, but it has not closed yet, for the tool must *locate*. The stalls are already *shading* for him. In twenty seconds it will

be *off*, if all goes well. The tool moves very close to the mark, *cutting into him* (making bodily contact) in such a way that the victim is not alerted; in fact, he probably is unaware of the contact. The stalls *shade his duke* with their *togs* while he runs deft, sensitive fingertips over the right pants pocket, then the left. There is the *impression* in the left side pocket, just as he thought, and some loose silver in the right. He wonders about the ticket, and checks both side coat pockets. There it is (probably), a thin piece of cardboard in the change-pocket just under the flap of the right *coat tail*.

He checks the *insider* and the *pit* too, for this is a substantial mark, and he might have a long, flat wallet *stashed* there. These pockets contain only what feel like letters or envelopes. Both *prat kicks* are checked; the right has some keys in it and the left a wallet. The reserve may be in that. The procedure of *locating* has taken about five seconds, and the stalls are watching the tool as they walk, slowing imperceptibly so that the mark comes against them, rather than their coming against him, but all four walking in what appears to be a normal fashion. The tool *offices* for a *left bridge* and a *left prat*, and the *frame* closes. Ten seconds more to go.

The stalls know that there will be a roll of cash in the left pants pocket even if the tool does not *office* for *scratch*, which he is not likely to do since he works closely with the stalls and since they would expect anything coming from the *left bridge* to be cash, anything from the *left prat* to be a *leather*. As they close the *frame* they block off the mark's hands (in case he should feel something and reach for his money) and the tool, coming behind and very slightly to the right, *gets his duke down* very fast under the *shade* which the *duke man* provides to the left. He goes for the left pants pocket first, for he knows there is considerable folding money there. Hooking his index finger just within the *crack* of the pocket, he takes up a pleat in the lining, then makes a dozen or so tiny pleats, folding the lining with great dexterity between his fingers. This is called reefing or reefing a kick. "I was taught to reef a britch from the bottom so a tweezer-poke would end up in the palm of your hand." His hand does not go into the pocket at any time, but the shortening pocket-lining moves the roll of bills upward so that it emerges at the mouth of the pocket. In fact, if the reader could see this take place, it would appear that the bills rise rapidly of their own volition and emerge from the pocket into the thief's hand. As the roll rises toward his hand, he offices "come through," then gives the signal for "it's off." "Cop," he says, and the duke man has the roll.

The stalls then rapidly set up the mark for a prat score, shading the duke again, and the tool unsloughs (rhymes with plows) the button on the victim's hip pocket; then, without breaking stride, he moves slightly to the right and forks the wallet from the left hip pocket with his middle and index finger, using his left hand. No need to come through on the prat. Another office that "it's off," and the duke man has the wallet; he is careful to shade it, lest its passing to his hand give an onlooker a flash which might reveal the theft.

Now for the ducket, and the tool offices the stalls for a right coat tail, moves his right hand deftly under the mark's right elbow, which is blocked, lifts the pocket-flap and pinches the race-ticket between his thumb and index finger. He comes away with it swiftly, palming it himself without duking it to the stall. The entire act of theft has taken less than fifteen seconds. The duke man moves off to the left with the scores in his pocket. Simultaneously, the other stall splits out the tool from the victim, and all three are rapidly lost in the crowd.

For purposes of illustration, a standard, uncomplicated touch was used, in which everything went off according to schedule, the mark behaved like a little gentleman, and no emergencies developed. Even so, the action was still oversimplified because it is impossible to describe the simultaneous actions of three thieves and a sucker without becoming very complicated. Of course, this score could have been taken in several different ways, and any pickpockets who might discuss it would probably become involved in heavy argument whether it should have been done this way or that, whether or not the tool was left-handed (most good tools are ambidextrous), or whether or not the tool should have let the race-ticket go since he already had the money and wasn't even sure he was getting a race-ticket anyway. And perhaps some tools would have pocketed the scratch instead of passing it to the duke man. Also, we have used two stalls because we had them; in actual practice, one might have stuck the mark quite as effectively, though it might have taken longer and been more risky. Many mobs would have done it differently.

Actually, there is no such thing as a stereotyped touch. Every one is different, with many variables involved, some of which are the personalities and techniques of the mob which makes the touch, the nature of the victim, the degree and security of the fix, and the physical conditions under which the theft takes place. The important point is that each good mob is a fluid, adaptable unit of thievery, capable of scenting the quarry instantaneously, and of cooperating with a high degree of teamwork, feeling their way as they go and shaping their activities to fit the situation with great speed and cunning. This knowledge that they can beat a man, together with what appears to be an almost uncanny foreknowledge of how to do it, is what is known as grift sense or grift know. "A tool has to have grift sense, but he doesn't get grift sense until after he grifts. He has got to take a lot of pinches. It's not so much a question of dexterity, but he knows when to steal the poke and when to let it go." "Sometimes you get a feeling a mark might burn you. Then, even if you had the guy's poke topped, and were a smart tool, you'd let it go. That's grift know."

In the case of pickpockets, the sense of touch is an important adjunct to this *grift sense*, for the pickpocket receives and sends a constant set of signals to and from the victim by means of manual contact and bodily contact during the entire act of theft; some of these the victim responds to although he does not know their meaning; others he reacts to without being aware that he has received them. Likewise, a set of signals is constantly being exchanged by the mob members, some oral and verbal, some oral and nonverbal, some kinesic, some tactile, and some unconsciously sent or received; this aspect of highly developed tactilism and nonverbal communication among thieves has not been previously reported. It should be studied further by someone with special facilities for analyzing it; it might well throw some new light on the peripheral aspects of communication. Among thieves it is a vital part of communication, since the success of the theft depends upon it. Besides being heavily functional, it is so thoroughly integrated with ostensibly natural physical movement and verbal communication that it is difficult to isolate. The speed and accuracy by which communication takes place on this level are phenomenal.

PERIPHERAL AND INCIDENTAL DETAILS OF THE ACT OF THEFT

It might be of value to go back to the theft just described for a moment to see a few of the possibilities or variants in the pattern which such a mob as we are describing might have encountered. For example, when the tool *located* the *okus* or *leather*, we assume that it was a conventional-type billfold; "She had the okus topped, but she didn't pull it, as she made the fuzz and didn't even rumble the mark." It might well have been any one of a number of other types of pocketbook. . . . But it turned out to be a common *leather*, so we have no problem here. However, was it *on its feet* or was it *lying down* (or *laying down*)? If it was *on its feet*, it was standing in the pocket with

the fold at the top or the bottom, and in a good position to *fork* or *spear*. If it was *lying down* or *on its side*, it was crosswise or on edge in the pocket, and the tool would have to *top it* or *top it up* before he *forked it*. The *sting* we described involved a wallet obviously *on its feet*, a situation which might make it easier for some tools, especially inexpert ones. "On its feet, it's pretty easy. It's when it's lying down that it's tough." A good tool, however, has only to *top it up* and thinks little of this maneuver.

Not for a pickpocket, and I'm talking about people in my class, it don't make no difference if it's laying down, on edge, on its side, upside down, or how it's laying, as long as he's in position and he's got the proper support, all of them are alike. As long as it ain't chained, as long as it ain't latched down, it don't make any difference whether it's standing up, laying down, on edge, upside down, or whatnot.

Or this *skin* could have been carelessly put into the hip pocket, or the pocket itself could have been shallow enough that the wallet was protruding from the *crack* of the pocket. The tool would think of this as a *pop up*, a *hanger*, a *kick out*, or a *kick in the ass*, the implication being that any slight disturbance of equilibrium would be sufficient to dislodge it. "Vulgarity in class mobs is just as taboo as it would be in front of your wife, or in my own home. I'd say 'kick out' or 'easy score.'" (This informant refused to verify *kick in the ass* in the presence of a lady.)

The reader may recall, however, that our mark was an orderly fellow who buttoned or *sloughed* his wallet snugly into his hip pocket and that consequently the tool had to *unslough* the flap of the pocket before he could take the score.

At them tobacco auctions now, there's where you get a workout. Them hoosiers with overalls on over their pants . . . new overalls. And you got to unslough them two buttons on the side so you can get at any of their pants pockets. They slough them up and them new overalls are terrible, so stiff and slick. But you step up behind the right hoosier and unslough them two buttons and you got yourself a tobacco crop.

He does this, incidentally, with a quick, gentle upward flip of the first joint of the index finger, assisted in stubborn cases by the ball of the thumb.

Perhaps he couldn't *nail* this *hide* easily, but had some trouble *bringing* it (that is, getting it out) either because the pocket was tight or because, blessed be any saints who patronize thieves, the wallet was too fat to *come* easily. It is also possible that an inexpert or *rough* tool might *rumble* the *come on*, or mark, at the *come off*, or point when the wallet can be taken out. This would be more likely to happen on the *left britch score* when the tool is *reefing* the *scratch*. "He works it up and works it up, and right at the come off the sucker grabs for him."

When the tool goes after something in a pocket, he says that he *gets his mitt down* or *gets his duke down*. "I must have stalled for fifty mobs, but I never did get my duke down." When he gets what he is after, he says that he *comes up with it* or *comes away with it*. Some tools say that they *swing* or *swing with it*; this latter phrase is most often used by tools who have had experience with other types of thieving, especially shoplifting; women thieves use the phrase *swing underneath with it* or simply *swinging underneath* (the ultimate reference being to concealing an object under the skirt), and male thieves sometimes use the same phrase referring to concealing an object beneath an overcoat or topcoat.

Some tools, in thinking about a *score* or talking about it afterward, refer to themselves as *owning* it after a certain point in the theft, and show resentment if something happens to deny them the *score* at that point. "After I had it topped I figured I owned it." Even though the wallet is still in the victim's possession these tools behave as if it *belongs* to them, and are not likely to relinquish it unless the danger is acute. "I don't agree with this. That's not the psychological moment for him to say he owns it. I've topped a poke many times and had to let it go. A good tool would not say that

when it was topped it belonged to him." An interesting case in point is the story told about a mob operating in depression days, when it was not unusual for a mob to board a streetcar or bus without fare, depending upon being able to steal it as they got on, or by the time it was needed; pockets were actually picked for metal coins—*ridge* or *smash*.

Back in depression days when I turned out, you'd get on a short car and fan a mark to see if you could find scratch. It takes a lot more dexterity to steal a small amount of smash than a lot of scratch. But during the depression you'd take what you could get. For nine cents at least you could eat. When you got on a short car the first thing you had to do was get the money for the kayducer. Many's the time we had to make it before we worked up to the center of the car where the kayducer stood.

This particular tool *fanned* a nondescript mark and *located* a paper bill in his side pants pocket. This was big game, for it might be a five or a ten. The mark wore an overcoat, and under that a long sweater which came down over his pants pockets. The tool *reefed the kick* and got the bill between his finger-tips; the mark sensed that something was amiss, and reached down on the outside, under his overcoat but outside the sweater, to check his bill. He took hold of it through the sweater and the pants, and felt the tool moving it away. "I had a death-grip on the scratch. The sucker had hold of it on the outside, but I had it on the inside . . ." There ensued an amusing miniature tug of war, which the mark lost since the tool actually had hold of the bill and the victim could not hold to it through his clothing; while the tool got the bill, the mark was not only *rumbled*, but he *blew* and caused the mob a little trouble, though they escaped by dropping off the car after the mark *beefed gun*, or announced publicly that he had been robbed. There are tales of this sort of incident ad infinitum amongst the *whiz*.

As a matter of fact, objects often leave the pockets in which they are carried with some reluctance. For instance, large rolls of paper money sometimes fit so tightly inside pants pockets that the tool has difficulty removing them. Sometimes he tries it one way and must *let it go* because he is not in exactly the right position, or because of circumstances he had not taken into consideration, like the cut or tightness of clothes, the build of the man, etc. "If a mark looks like he's going to rumble, a careful tool lets him go. There is a lot of people in the world and a lot of pockets, so he lets him go if he seems like he's going to look around."

In such cases, he may *office the stall* or stalls to *let him gee*, and then *put up for him* again so that the tool gets a different *crack* or *slant* at the mark. If the tool who *gets his mitt down* is a competent *mechanic*, he will find a way to take it, even if several tries are necessary. Sometimes very large rolls of bills are taken from very tight pockets without the victim being even slightly aware that he is being robbed. For instance, one informant recounts an incident which involves the removal of a large roll from a man's pocket under quite different circumstances. The roll had been secured with a rubber band, which became disengaged as the tool was working on the roll, which then began to swell. As he brought it up in the pocket, it became larger and larger, and consequently more difficult to move upward. When it emerged, all pressures were off it, and it expanded suddenly, filling the tool's hands to overflowing. The tool *officed* "*cop in your hat*," to the astonishment of the stalls, who had never heard such an *office*. One of the stalls subsequently covered it with his hat until it could be removed from the immediate scene of the theft. "If this ain't nothing but one-dollar bills," he said, "we've got all the money in the world."

There are, too, cases where objects other than money or wallets are mistaken for valuables, and time and energy wasted before the pickpockets discover their mistake; American pickpockets working in England and the Colonies where pipes are very commonly smoked always note the difficulty they have in mistaking tobacco pouches for wallets—and fat ones too.

Right-handed people usually carry their money on the left side. But in areas under the British flag this don't run true to form. I think it is because they are great pipe-smokers and carry their tobacco in the most convenient place and carry their dough in the right britch or in a couple of extra pockets they have, with the flaps buttoned down. I must have had a split-basket full of them tobacco pokes. We were hustling four handed—two guys and two twists—and all you have to do in a case like that is fan the mark and take the leather. But nine chances out of ten them tobacco pokes was made out of leather and very fat, and were standing on their feet right in the left prat. I took off a basket full before we found out that they had tobacco in them. Then we had to go back and look for tweezer pokes, and we usually found them in the right britch.

Money, too, sometimes comes in large packages; I have a record of one *touch* which netted several thousand dollars which were being carried to a bank; the money was wrapped in newspaper and fitted tightly into the owner's overcoat pocket; he was accompanied by a guard. The theft, while not easy, came off without trouble, and the owner never realized how he lost the money. One of his employees (suspected of carrying on an affair with the owner's wife) was accused of taking the money from the coat before the owner departed for the bank, was tried for the theft, and was acquitted. The mob attended the trial with considerable interest and one of them, now dead, told me—for what it may be worth—that if an innocent man had been convicted, he would have found a way to clear the employee by mail without endangering the mob; this would have been quite possible, since he could have shown an intimate knowledge of the movements of the victim and his guard which no one but the people who stole the money could have had. Note that this thief, with considerable character, albeit unappreciated by the dominant culture, had no sympathy whatever for the victim, but did not want an innocent man to suffer for something he did not do. . . .

The stalls performed smoothly and effectively in the *trick* at the racetrack, which we described in detail above; in fact, any self-respecting tool could probably have *handled* the mark we picked with half as many stalls. But we had them, so we used them. We put the mark in a *vise* and held him there so that the *action* could be properly described. However, had one of the stalls *turned the mark into* the tool a bit roughly, or in such a way as to arouse his suspicion or even his attention, he might well fear that he had *crumbed the play*. "I came through too soon and crumbed the play." If the mark had become suspicious, that is, if he thought of his wallet or perhaps checked it with his hand, or if he showed any sign of being annoyed or specifically aware of the presence of pickpockets, the tool would cease operations or postpone them, because the sucker had been *rumbled*. If the mark showed definite symptoms of suspecting theft from his person, the mob would realize that he had *tumbled*, or that he had been *ranked*, a term used mainly on the West Coast. "He ranked that move." "I don't think that is right. It's from the point of view of the mob—it's one of the mob that ranks him." "We framed for that sucker and I was about to beat him for his poke when some broad ranked him." In such a case the mob would probably *let him go* (or *let him gee*) unless he was known to carry enough money to make it worth while to *tail* him until the tool could get another *slant* at him. Sometimes the sucker is not *rumbled*, but an onlooker is *ranked* (usually the fault of the stall for not properly *shading the duke* of the tool) with the result that there are witnesses who may report the theft and support the mark if he *beefs gun*. In such cases, when it is possible, the tool returns the money or wallet to the pocket of the victim, who will then be easier to *cool out*.

Perhaps the mark only *rounds*, or turns to look at the tool, although he is unaware of the theft; this can be serious if the theft is completed, for the victim then can possibly identify, or *make*, the tool if he is arrested; good tools never *give up their kis-*

ser to a mark who *rounds*, and are reluctant to go back for a second *crack* at a mark who may have seen them clearly enough to make identification. However, if the *frame* is properly set up, the tool knows that the mark is never going to see the man who robbed him. Stalls, of course, do not have the same problem, for they do not get into the victim's pockets, although they seem to be arrested as often as tools, if not oftener; also, they are very likely to have the wallet which has been passed to them.

While the tool is most likely to sense suspicion on the part of a mark, or the realization of a bystander that theft is in progress, the stalls too are always alert for this; when they sense it, they try to ascertain whether or not the tool has also sensed it and, if not, they alert him by an *office* or signal, which may vary from mob to mob. The tool himself, however, must make the decision whether or not to go through with the *touch*, and the stalls accede to his judgment; if they sense that he is going right ahead, they perform their work even though they may think he is making a mistake; while they relay to him any information which may indicate a *rumble*, they must have confidence in his judgment.

An experienced tool makes these decisions in a split second, and his accuracy in making them is easily checked by the amount of time he spends in the clink. The tools with *class mobs* are usually most conservative, or as *safe as kelsey*, for they know that there are always plenty more pocketbooks to be taken, but that one false move may put them behind bars. One of the informants who contributed to this study had his last *square pinch* (an arrest for a theft he was caught in the act of committing) in 1939. Good tools become supersensitive to any reaction by the mark which may indicate suspicion; often they concentrate on the back of the victim's neck (when they are working from behind, as they usually are) and one informant says he photographs the back of the victim's neck in his mind, never to forget it; certainly he remembers it during the time he is working in a given crowd on a given day; how much longer he can recall it is, of course, a matter of opinion. Some thieves have phenomenal memory for people, comparable to the ability of those few detectives who merit the name of *camera eye*. Some pickpockets register the build, the stance, and other physical characteristics of the victim so perfectly that they automatically avoid him after he has been robbed. Some memorize one detail, such as the pattern of the man's necktie, and register that automatically whenever they may see it again in the crowd. Both stalls and tools have need to be sensitive to identification, but the decision to rob a man is, in the last analysis, made by the tool, and he must be able to avoid repeating on a mark, even though the stalls should be so stupid as to put the man in the *frame* without realizing that he has already been robbed.

THE HUSTLER*

Ned Polsky

The poolroom hustler is a special kind of con man. He continually engages in deception and in the manipulation of other people's impressions of reality within the context of a game. The observations below are derived in part from the author's personal involvement with the poolroom world. Polsky describes the work situation of the poolroom hustler, including the hustler's skills, his associates on the job, methods of deception, the betting relationship, and the setting of the poolroom.

"Such and such a man spends all his life playing every day for a small stake. Give him every morning the money that he may gain during the day, on condition that he does not play—you will make him unhappy. It will perhaps be said that what he seeks is the amusement of play, not gain. Let him play then for nothing; he will lose interest and be wearied."
—Blaise Pascal

"They talk about me not being on the legitimate. Why, lady, nobody's on the legit when it comes down to cases; you know that."—Al Capone[1]

[1] The Pascal quotation is from *Pensées*, V. Al Capone's remark is quoted in Paul Sann, *The Lawless Decade* (New York: Crown Publishers, 1957), p. 214.

The poolroom hustler makes his living, or tries to do so, by betting his opponents in various types of pool or billiard games; and as part of the playing and betting process he engages in various deceitful practices. The terms "hustler" for such a person and "hustling" for his occupation have been in poolroom argot for decades, antedating their application to prostitutes. Usually the hustler plays with his own money, but often he makes use of a "backer." In the latter event the standard arrangement is that the backer, in return for assuming all risk of loss, receives half of the hustler's winnings.

As a necessary and regular part of their

* Reprinted from *Social Problems*, 12 (Summer 1964), pp. 3–15, by permission of the author and the publisher.

work, hustlers break certain of America's generally agreed-upon moral rules, and because of this they are stigmatized by respectable outsiders. More knowledgeable outsiders see the hustler as one who violates an ethic of fair dealing, as a quasi-criminal who systematically "victimizes" people. Less knowledgeable outsiders (the large majority of outsiders) regard hustlers as persons who, whatever they may actually do, certainly do not hold down respectable jobs; therefore this group also stigmatizes hustlers—"poolroom bums" is the classic phrase—and believes that society would be better off without the hustler. Hustling, to the degree that it is known to the larger society at all, is classed with that large group of social problems composed of morally deviant occupations.

However, in what follows I try to present hustlers and hustling on their own terms. Insofar as I treat of problems they are not the problems posed by the hustler but for him; not the difficulties he creates for others, but the difficulties that others create for him.

My approach is basically that of Everett Hughes to occupational sociology. In this paper I deal chiefly with questions about the work situation: How is the hustler's work structured? What skills are required of him? Whom does he interact with on the job? What does he want from them, and how does he try to get it? How do they make it easy or hard for him?[2]

PREVIOUS RESEARCH

A bibliographic check reveals no decent research on poolroom hustling, sociological or otherwise. Apart from an occasional work of fiction in which hustling figures, there are merely a few impressionistic accounts in newspapers and popular magazines. With a couple of exceptions, each article is based on interviews with only one or two hustlers. No article analyzes hustling on any but the most superficial level, or even provides a well-rounded description of hustling. The fullest survey of the subject not only omits much that is vital, but contains numerous errors of fact and of interpretation.[3]

The desirability of a study of hustling first struck me upon hearing comments of people who saw the movie The Hustler (1961, re-released spring 1964). Audience members who are not poolroom habitués regard the movie as an accurate portrait of the contemporary hustling "scene." Now, the movie does indeed truly depict some social characteristics of pool and billiard hustlers and some basic techniques of hustling. But it neglects others of crucial importance. Moreover, the movie scarcely begins to take proper account of the social structure within which hustling techniques are used and which radically affects their use. The Hustler is a reasonably good but highly selective index of the poolroom hustling scene as it existed not later than 30 years ago. And as a guide to today's hustling scene—the terms on which it presents itself

[2] See Ned Polsky, Hustlers, Beats, and Others, (Chicago: Aldine Publishing Co., 1965) for the rest of the study, which focuses on: the hustler's career line (e.g., recruitment and induction, colleagueship, career crises, retirement); his moonlighting, especially in more forthrightly criminal (felony) jobs; the relation of his work situation and career to larger social structures and to social change; and implications of the data for occupational theory and criminological theory.

[3] The compendium of misinformation and cockeyed interpretation is Jack Olsen's "The Pool Hustlers," Sports Illustrated, 14 (March 20, 1961), pp. 71–77. Jack Richardson's "The Noblest Hustlers," Esquire, IX (September, 1963), pp. 94, 96, 98, contains a few worthwhile observations; but it is sketchy, ill-balanced, and suffers from editorial garbling—all of which make it both confusing and misleading for the uninitiated. One article conveys quite well the lifestyle of a particular hustler: Dale Shaw, "Anatomy of a Pool Hustler," Saga: The Magazine for Men, 23 (November, 1961), pp. 52–55, 91–93. Useful historical data are in Edward John Vogeler's "The Passing of the Pool Shark," American Mercury, 48 (November, 1939), pp. 346–351. For hustling as viewed within the context of the history of pool in America, see Robert Coughlan's "Pool: Its Players and Its Sharks," Life, 31 (October 8, 1951), pp. 159 ff.; though Coughlan's account of the game's history contains errors and his specific consideration of hustling is brief (p. 166), the latter is accurate.

and on which the audience takes it—the movie is quite misleading.

METHOD AND SAMPLE

My study of poolroom hustling extended over eight months. It proceeded by a combination of: (a) direct observation of hustlers as they hustled; (b) informal talks, sometimes hours long, with hustlers; (c) participant observation—as hustler's opponent, as hustler's backer, and as hustler. Since methods (b) and (c) drew heavily on my personal involvement with the poolroom world, indeed are inseparable from it, I summarize aspects of that involvement below.

Billiard playing is my chief recreation. I have frequented poolrooms for over 20 years, and at one poolroom game, three-cushion billiards, am considered a far better than average player. In recent years I have played an average of more than six hours per week in various New York poolrooms, and played as much in the poolrooms of Chicago for most of the eight years I lived there. In the course of traveling I have played occasionally in the major rooms of other cities, such as the poolrooms on Market Street in San Francisco, on West 25th Street in Cleveland, and the room on 4th and Main in Los Angeles.

My social background is different from that of the overwhelming majority of adult poolroom players. The latter are of lower-class origin. As with many American sports (e.g., baseball), pool and billiards are played by teenagers from all classes but only the players of lower-class background tend to continue far into adulthood. (And as far as poolroom games are concerned, even at the teenage level the lower class contributes a disproportionately large share of players.) But such differences—the fact that I went to college, do highbrow work, etc.—create no problems of acceptance. In most good-sized poolrooms the adult regulars usually include a few people like myself who are in the poolroom world but not of it. They are there because they like to play, and are readily accepted because they like to play.

The poolroom I play in most regularly is the principal "action room" in New York and probably in the country, the room in which heavy betting on games occurs most often; sometimes, particularly after 1:00 A.M., the hustlers in the room well outnumber the non-hustlers. Frequently I play hustlers for money (nearly always on a handicap basis) and occasionally I hustle some non-hustlers, undertaking the latter activity primarily to recoup losses on the former. I have been a backer for two hustlers.

I know six hustlers well and during the eight months of the study I talked or played with over 50 more. All are now usually based in New York, except for two in Chicago, two in Cleveland, one in Philadelphia, one itinerant hustler whose home base is Boston and another whose home base is in North Carolina. However, the hustlers based in New York are of diverse regional origins; almost a third grew up in other states and started their hustling careers in other states.

It is not possible to demonstrate the representativeness of this sample because the universe (all U.S. pool and billiard hustlers) is not known exactly. But the hustlers I asked about the number of real hustlers in America, i.e., the number of people whose exclusive or primary occupation is hustling, generally agree that today the number is quite small. In response to my queries about the total number of poolroom hustlers, one hustler said "thousands" and another said "there must be a thousand," but the next highest estimate was "maybe 400" and somewhat lesser estimates were made by 19 hustlers. Moreover, the three hustlers making the highest estimates have rarely been out of New York, whereas over half the others either come from other parts of the country or have made several road trips. It seems safe to assume that the sample is at least representative of big-city hustlers. Also, it is highly probable that it includes the majority of part-time hustlers in New York, and certain that it includes a good majority of the full-time hustlers in New York.

POOLROOM BETTING:
THE STRUCTURE OF "ACTION"

Hustling involves betting one's opponent, by definition. But the converse is not true. The majority of poolroom games on which opponents bet do not involve any element of hustling. In order to understand how hustling enters the picture, one must first establish a perspective that encompasses all betting on poolroom games, hustled or not.

In pool or billiard games, the betting relationship has three possible modes: (1) player bets against player; (2) player(s) against spectator(s); (3) spectator(s) against spectator(s). In most games only the first mode occurs, but combinations of the first and second are frequent, and slightly less so are combinations of the first and third. Combinations of all three are uncommon, but do occur when there is more "ready action" offered to the player(s) by the spectator(s) than the player(s) can, or wish(es) to, absorb. I have never seen the second mode occur alone, nor a combination of second and third. I have seen the third mode occur alone only twice—at professional tournaments. The betting relationship, then, involves the mode player-vs.-player, whatever additional modes there may be.

If two mediocre players are betting, say, upwards of $15 per game, and at another table two excellent players are playing for only a token amount, the first table will invariably draw many more people around it. The great majority of spectators, whether or not they bet much and whatever their own degree of playing skill, are attracted more by the size of the action than the quality of the performance. (A visiting Danish billiardist tells me this is not so in Europe, and also that betting on poolroom games is far less frequent than in America.)

There is an old American poolroom tradition that players should make some kind of bet with each other, if only a small one. This tradition remains strong in every public poolroom I know. (It is weak in the pool or billiard rooms of private men's clubs and YMCAs, weaker still in student unions, and virtually nonexistent in faculty clubs.) When one player says to another, "Let's just play sociable," as often as not he means that they should play for only a dollar or two, and at the very least means that they should play "for the time" (the loser paying the check). It is only some of the newer and least skilled players who refuse to bet at all (want to "split the time"), and nearly always they rapidly become socialized to the betting tradition by a carrot-and-stick process—the stick being that it is often hard to get a game oherwise, the carrot that better players are always willing to give poorer ones a handicap (a "spot"). Most of the regular players will not even play for the check only, but insist on a little money changing hands "just to make the game interesting." The player who claims that just playing the game is interesting enough in itself is regarded as something of a freak.

Although few serious bettors (hustlers excepted) care for big action, nearly all (including hustlers) want fast action. They may not want to bet much per game, but they want the cash to change hands fairly quickly. Consequently, in an action room the standard games are redesigned for this purpose. Some are simply shortened: players gambling at snooker will remove all the red balls but one; or three-cushion billiard players will play games of 15, 20, or 25 points instead of the usual 30, 40, or 50. In straight pool (pocket billiards), where the standard game is 125 or 150 points, good players are usually reluctant to play a much shorter game because scoring is so easy—any good player can occasionally run more than 50 points—that shortening the game makes it too much a matter of chance. Therefore, in an action room one finds most of the pool players playing some variant of the game that requires high skill and minimizes luck, and that therefore can be short (take only 5 to 20 minutes per game). Today the chief of these variants are "nine ball" and "one pocket" (also called "pocket apiece").

Every poolroom has at least one "No Gambling" sign on display, but no poolroom enforces it. The sign is merely a formal gesture for the eyes of the law (and in some cities required by law). It is enforced only in that the proprietor sometimes may ask players to keep payoffs out of sight—not to toss the money on the table after the game—if the room is currently heaty, e.g., if an arrest has recently been made there. Police are never really concerned to stop the gambling on poolroom games, and everyone knows it. (But police sometimes check to see that the minimum age law is observed, so proprietors will often ask youths for identification.) Betting is so taken for granted that in most poolrooms the proprietor—the very man who displays a "No Gambling" sign over his desk—will on request hold the players' stake money.

However, in no poolroom does the house take a cut of the action; i.e., the proprietor gets no fee for permitting gambling or holding stake money, and wouldn't dream of asking for one. His payment from bettors is simply that they comprise most of his custom (in equipment rental).[4] And hustlers, as he and they well know, count in this regard far beyond their numbers, for they play much oftener and longer than other customers; indeed, they virtually live in the poolroom.

NON-HUSTLED POOLROOM GAMBLING

Hustling is not involved when the games played for money are any of the following:

(a) Non-hustler vs. non-hustler. A "sociable" game in which the bet is a token one. The only betting is player vs. player.

(b) Non-hustler vs. non-hustler. A game for significantly more than a token amount. The players play even-up if they are fairly equal. If they are aware of a significant difference in skill levels, the weaker player is given an appropriate handicap. Usually the betting is just between players; rarely, one or both players will bet spectators; spectators do not bet each other.

(c) Hustler vs. non-hustler. The players are aware of the difference in skills, and this is properly taken into account via an appropriate spot. Usually the betting is only player vs. player, though sometimes spectators bet players or each other. The hustler tries to avoid this type of game, and agrees to it only when he has nothing better to do.

(d) Hustler vs. hustler. Each player knows the other's mettle, if only by reputation ("Minnesota Fats" vs. "Fast Eddy" in The Hustler, for example). The hustler, contrary to the impression given by the movie, does not prefer this type of game (though he does prefer it to the foregoing type) and does not regard it as hustling. But he plays it often because he often can't get the kind of game he wants (a true "hustle") and this alternative does offer him excitement—not only the greatest challenge to his playing skill, but the most action. The average bet between two hustlers is much higher than in any other type of poolroom contest.[5] And the betting modes 2 and 3 (player vs. spectator, spectator vs. spectator) occur much more often.

Be that as it may, the hustler much prefers to hustle, which means to be in a game set up so as to be pretty much a sure thing for him, a game that "you're not allowed to lose" as the hustler puts it. In order to achieve this, to truly hustle, he engages in

---

[4] The only non-bettor whose payment is somewhat related to the size of the action is the rack boy (if one is used), the person who racks up the balls for the players after each frame. The bigger the action, the larger the tip he can expect, and if one player comes out very much ahead he tips the rack boy lavishly. The rack boy's position is thus analogous to that of the golf caddie, except that a rack boy is used in only about half of hustler-vs.-hustler contests and in but a tiny fraction of other contests. Sometimes he is an employee (sweeper, etc.) of the poolroom, but more often is a spectator performing as rack boy on an ad hoc basis.

[5] When two high-betting hustlers agree to play each other there is often a real race among poorer spectators to offer rack-boy services because, as previously indicated, if one is engaged for such a session he can expect a good tip. I witnessed one six-hour session between hustlers in which the winning hustler came out $800 ahead and tipped the rack boy $50.

deception. The centrality of deception in pool or billiard hustling is perhaps best indicated by the fact that the poolroom hustlers' argot originated that widespread American slang dictum, "never give a sucker an even break."[6]

THE HUSTLER'S METHODS
OF DECEPTION

The structure of a gambling game determines what methods of deception, if any, may be used in it. In many games (dice, cards, etc.) one can deceive one's opponent by various techniques of cheating. Pool and billiard games, though, are so structured that this method is virtually impossible. (Once in a great while, against a particularly unalert opponent, one can surreptitiously add a point or two to one's score—but such opportunity is rare, usually involves risk of discovery that is judged to be too great, and seldom means the difference between winning and losing anyway; so no player counts on it.) One's every move and play is completely visible, easily watched by one's opponent and by spectators; nor is it possible to achieve anything via previous tampering with the equipment.

However, one structural feature of pool

or billiards readily lends itself to deceit; on each shot, the difference between success and failure is a matter of a small fraction of an inch. In pool or billiards it is peculiarly easy, even for the average player, to miss one's shot deliberately and still look good (unlike, say, nearly all card games, where if one does not play one's cards correctly this is soon apparent). On all shots except the easiest ones, it is impossible to tell if a player is deliberately not trying his best.

The hustler exploits this fact, so as to deceive his opponent as to his (the hustler's) true level of skill (true "speed"). It is so easily exploited that, when playing good opponents, usually the better hustlers even disdain it, pocket nearly every shot they have (intentionally miss only some very difficult shots), and rely chiefly on related but subtler techniques of failure beyond the remotest suspicion of most players. For example, such a hustler may strike his cue ball hard and with too much spin ("english"), so that the spin is transferred to the object ball and the object ball goes into the pocket but jumps out again; or he may scratch (losing a point and his turn), either by "accidentally" caroming his cue ball into a pocket or by hitting his cue ball hard and with too much top-spin so that it jumps off the table; or, most commonly, he pockets his shot but, by striking his cue ball just a wee bit too hard or too softly or with too much spin, he leaves himself "safe" (ends up with his cue ball out of position, so that he hasn't another shot). In such wise the hustler feigns less competence than he has.

Hustling, then, involves not merely the ability to play well, but the use of a kind of "short con." Sometimes the hustler doesn't need to employ any con to get his opponent to the table, sometimes he does; but he always employs it in attempting to keep his opponent there.

The best hustler is not necessarily the best player among the hustlers. He has to be a very good player, true, but beyond a certain point his playing ability is not nearly so important as his skill at various kinds of

---

[6] Its pool-hustler origin is noted by Vogeler (op. cit., p. 347), a reliable observer. It is recorded in none of the slang sourcebooks (Mencken, Mathews, Berrey and Van den Bark, et al.) except Harold Wentworth and Stuart Berg Flexner's Dictionary of American Slang (New York: T. Y. Crowell, 1960), p. 527. Wentworth and Flexner do not attempt to account for the phrase's origin. They claim that it dates to ca. 1835, but this seems impossibly early. The only source they cite is its use as the title of a 1941 W. C. Fields movie.
    Actually, Fields used the phrase earlier in his Poppy (1936), where it is his exit line and the last line of the movie. Fields' partiality to the phrase is quite in keeping with Vogeler's account of its origin, as Fields was the son of a Philadelphia poolroom owner, spent much of his boyhood in his father's poolroom, was an excellent player, and built his funniest vaudeville act around his pool-playing skill (at the act's climax he sank 15 balls with one shot). Cf. Douglas Gilbert, American Vaudeville (New York: Whittlesey House, 1940), pp. 273-274.

conning. Also, he has to possess personality traits that make him "rocklike," able to exploit fully his various skills—playing, conning, other—in the face of assorted pressures and temptations not to exploit them fully.

THE HUSTLER'S CARDINAL RULE

As the foregoing indicates, the hustler's cardinal rule is: *don't show your real speed.* Of course, an exception is permitted if by some miracle the hustler finds himself hustled, finds himself in a game with someone he thought would be easy but who turns out to be tough. But this is not supposed to happen, and it rarely does. For one thing, hustlers generally know each other, or of each other, and their respective skill levels. Secondly, any pool or billiard game is overwhelmingly a game of skill rather than luck —even in the chanciest type of poolroom game the element of skill counts for much more than in any card game whatsoever— and this means it is possible to rate the skill levels of various players (to "handicap" them) along small gradations with a high degree of accuracy. For example, if one has seen the three-cushion billiard players X and Y play various people over a period of time, it is possible to arrive at the judgment "On a 30-point game, X is 2 or 3 points better than Y" and to be dead right about it in at least 8 out of 10 contests between them.

The corollaries of the hustler's chief rule are: (a) The hustler must restrain himself from making many of the extremely difficult shots. Such restraint is not easy, because the thrill of making a fancy shot that brings applause from the audience is hard to resist. But the hustler must resist, or else it would make less believable his misses on more ordinary shots. (b) He must play so that the games he wins are won by only a small margin. (c) He must let his opponent win an occasional game.

It may be thought that once a hustler has engaged an opponent, a bet has been agreed upon and the stake money put up, and the game has started, the hustler might safely let out all the stops. This would be terribly short-sighted.

In the first place, as noted earlier, the typical non-hustler bets only a small amount on the game. The hustler's only hope of making real money, therefore, is to extend the first game into a series of games, entice his opponent into doubling up when he is behind, etc. If the hustler does this well, the opponent will hang on for a long time, may even come back after the first session to play him on another day, turn into a real "fish" (the poolroom term for an inferior opponent who doesn't catch on that he's outclassed, and keeps coming back for more). And when the opponent starts demanding a spot, as sooner or later he will, the hustler can offer him his (the hustler's) average winning margin, or even a little better, and still have a safe game.

Secondly, there are spectators to take into account. Some of them will bet the hustler if he offers the non-hustler a seemingly fair spot. More importantly, some of them are potential opponents. Nearly all poolroom spectators are also players (except for the inevitable contingent of poor and lonely old men, who use the poolroom as a poor man's club). The hustler doesn't want to look too good to spectators either.

He knows that as he beats various opponents his reputation will rise, and that increasingly he'll have to offer spots to people, but he wants to keep his reputation as low as possible as long as possible with as many people as possible. He also knows that he has to play superbly on occasion—that he will play fellow hustlers when there's no other action around, and that then he must show more skill—but he wants to keep these occasions few. (It helps considerably, by the way, that because hustler-vs.-hustler games occur when hustlers give up hope of finding other action, these games usually take place after midnight when there aren't so many non-hustler potential victims around to watch.)

The sooner everyone in the poolroom knows the hustler's true speed, the sooner he exhausts the real hustling possibilities among the room's regular players. Then, either he must move on to a room where he's less known or, if he stays in the room, has to take games he shouldn't take or else restrict his pickings to strangers who wander in.

JOB-RELATED SKILLS AND TRAITS

Although the hallmarks of the good hustler are playing skill and the temperamental ability to consistently look poorer than he is, there are other skills and traits that aid him in hustling. Some are related to deceiving his opponent, some not.

Chief of these is argumentative skill in arranging the terms of the match, the ability to "make a game." The prospective opponent, if he has seen the hustler play, may when approached claim that the hustler is too good for him, or ask for too high a spot, i.e., one that is fair or even better than that. The hustler, just like the salesman, is supposed to be familiar with standard objections and with ways of overcoming them.

Another side of the ability to make a game reveals itself when the prospective opponent simply can't be argued out of demanding a spot that is unfair to the hustler, or can be convinced to play only if the hustler offers such a spot. At that point the hustler should of course refuse to play. There is often a temptation to do otherwise, not only because the hustler is proud of his skill but because action is his lifeblood (which is why he plays other hustlers when he can't find a hustle), and there may be no other action around. He must resist the temptation. In the good hustler's view, no matter how badly you want action, it is better not to play at all than to play when you are disadvantaged; otherwise you are just hustling yourself. (But the hustler often will, albeit with much argument and the greatest reluctance, agree to give a fair spot if that's the only way he can get action.)

The hustler, when faced, as he very often is, with an opponent who knows him as such, of course finds that his ability to make a game assumes greater importance than his ability to feign lack of skill. In such situations, indeed, his game-making ability is just as important as his actual playing ability.

On the other hand, the hustler must have "heart" (courage). The *sine qua non* is that he is a good "money player," can play his best when heavy action is riding on the game (as many non-hustlers can't). Also, he is not supposed to let a bad break or distractions in the audience upset him. (He may pretend to get rattled on such occasions, but that's just part of his con.) Nor should the quality of his game deteriorate when, whether by miscalculation on his part or otherwise, he finds himself much further behind than he would like to be. Finally, if it is necessary to get action, he should not be afraid to tackle an opponent whom he knows to be just about as good as he is.

A trait often working for the hustler is stamina. As a result of thousands of hours of play, all the right muscles are toughened up. He is used to playing many hours at a time, certainly much more used to it than the non-hustler is. This is valuable because sometimes, if the hustler works it right, he can make his opponent forget about quitting for such a "silly" reason as being tired, can extend their session through the night and into the next day. In such sessions it is most often in the last couple of hours, when the betting per game is usually highest, that the hustler makes his biggest killing.

Additional short-con techniques are sometimes used. One hustler, for example, entices opponents by the ancient device of pretending to be sloppy-drunk. Other techniques show more imagination. For example, a hustler preparing for a road trip mentioned to me that before leaving town he was going to buy a soldier's uniform: "I walk into a strange room in uniform and I've got it made. Everybody likes to grab a soldier."

Finally, the hustler—the superior hustler

at any rate—has enough flexibility and good sense to break the "rules" when the occasion demands it, will modify standard techniques when he encounters non-standard situations. An example: Once I entered a poolroom just as a hustler I know, X, was finishing a game with non-hustler Y. X beat Y soundly, by a higher margin than a hustler should beat anyone, and at that for only $3. Y went to the bathroom, whereupon I admonished X, "What's the matter with you? You know you're not allowed to win that big." X replied: "Yeah, sure, but you see that bastard S . . . over there? [nodding discreetly in the direction of one of the spectators]. Well, about an hour ago when I came in he and Y were talking, and when S . . . saw me he whispered something to Y. So I had a hunch he was giving him the wire [tipping him off] that I was pretty good. And then in his middle game it looked like Y was stalling a little [missing deliberately] to see what I would do, so then I was sure he got the wire on me. I had to beat him big so he'll think he knows my top speed. But naturally I didn't beat him as big as I *could* beat him. Now he'll come back cryin' for a spot and bigger action, and I'll nail him." And he did nail him.[7]

THE ART OF DUMPING

As we saw, the structure of a pool or billiard game makes it virtually impossible for the hustler to cheat his opponent. By "stalling" (deliberately missing some shots, leaving himself out of position, etc.) and by "lemoning" or "lemonading" an occasional game in the session (winning in a deliberately sloppy and seemingly lucky manner, or de-

[7] This sort of situation is unusual. One part of the poolroom code, adhered to by virtually all regular players, holds that a player is supposed to watch out for himself in the matches he gets into, find out for himself whom he can and cannot beat. Ordinarily one does not warn a player about who is superior or who the hustlers are, unless one is a close friend of that player. (And even if one is a friend, the code demands that such warning be given only before any match is in prospect; that is, once a player has started to "make a game" with another, third parties are supposed to stay out.)

liberately losing the game), the hustler keeps his opponent on the hook and entices him into heavier action, but such deception falls short of outright cheating. However, in examining betting we saw that there is considerable variation in the interpersonal superstructure of the game, i.e., that there are several possible types of betting relationships between and among players and spectators. One of these varieties does lead to outright cheating by the hustler—not cheating of his opponent, but cheating some spectators.

When two hustlers play each other, not only is the betting between players relatively heavy, but the betting of spectators against players is also, typically, at its height. Therefore, two hustlers sometimes will agree before their session that if, on any game, there is a good disparity between the amounts of action that each gets from spectators, the player with the most to gain from side bets with spectators will win the game and the players will later share the profits. The amount that spectators bet each other is of course irrelevant to such calculations; and in such circumstances the amount that the players bet each other automatically becomes a phony bet, strictly for deluding the spectators.

For example, one such game I know of went as follows: Hustler A played hustler B for $70. A's side bets with spectators totaled $100 and B's side bets with spectators totaled $380. Therefore A deliberately lost to B, paying him $70 and paying $100 to spectators, with B collecting $70 from A and $380 from spectators. Later, in private B gave A $310 (the $70 that A had "lost" to B, the $100 that A had paid to the audience, plus $140 or one-half the overall amount won from the audience). Each player thus made $140 on the deal.

Sometimes the hustlers will set up the audience for such disparity in side betting, via previous games in the session. An example: Hustler X played hustler Y for $20 per game. By pre-arrangement, both players refused to make side bets with spectators on the first three games and player Y deliberately lost the first three games. At the end of the third game Y became enraged, claiming that bad breaks had beat him, that X was just lucky, etc.; he raised his bet with X to $50 and also offered to bet spectators. Naturally, he got lots of action from spectators—and just as naturally he won the fourth game.

More commonly, however, such setting up does not occur. Rather, the hustlers will agree before their session that they will play each other in earnest and the bets between them will be real, but that if there is a disparity in side betting with spectators on a given game and one player gives the other a prearranged signal (gives him "the office" as the hustler's argot has it), the player with the most side action will win.

In the hustler's argot, the above type of deliberate losing is called "dumping." It is always distinguished from "lemoning" (where deliberate losing is strictly a means of conning one's opposing player). Though all hustlers use the verb "to dump" in referring to a game that the hustler deliberately loses for the purpose of cheating spectators, hustlers vary in the object they attach to the verb. Some hustlers would say that the hustler who lost "dumped the game," others that he "dumped to" his opponent, and others that he (or both players in collaboration) "dumped the bettors." Some hustlers on occasion prefer a nominal use: "the game was a dump."

Because dumping involves outright cheating and could lead to serious, in fact violent, reprisals if discovered, it is the aspect of hustling that hustlers are most evasive about. A profession not merely has "open secrets" which only novices and outsiders don't know about, but, as Erving Goffman noted, also has "strategic secrets" which professionals often talk about among themselves but try to keep from outsiders, and "dark secrets" which professionals not only try to keep from outsiders but seldom talk about even with each other. Dumping falls in the "dark secret" category. No hustler likes to own up to dumping, even in talk with other hustlers. One learns about dumping indirectly, via hustlers' comments on other hustlers, hardly ever via a hustler's

direct admission that he has engaged in it. It is my impression that such reticence is always pragmatic rather than moral, i.e., that no hustler has strong compunctions about dumping and that every long-time hustler has dumped at least on occasion.

Although dumping is a possibility whenever two hustlers playing each other make unequal amounts of side bets with spectators,[8] it actually occurs in only a minority of such situations, perhaps a sixth of them. For dumping is risky even when it is not literally discovered, i.e., sometimes the spectators' suspicions are aroused even though nothing can be proven; and hustlers can't afford to have this happen often, because it would kill their chances of side betting.

In this regard there are two kinds of spectator-bettors that the hustler distinguishes and takes account of: First, there are the ignorant majority of spectators who don't know about dumping; the hustler doesn't want talk, much less actual knowledge, of dumping to reach their ears. Second —and equally important to the hustler because, though they are in the minority, they bet more—there are some knowledgeable spectators (including other hustlers) who know about dumping but also know that it occurs in only a minority of hustler-vs.-hustler contests and therefore will often risk a bet. That is to say, just as some horse players assume that at certain tracks there probably will be one race per day that is fixed (one race "for the boys") and are willing to discount this because it's only one race out of eight or nine, similarly there are poolroom spectators who will bet on one hustler against another because they know that dumping occurs but seldom. (Among the knowledgeable spectators there are also, of course, some cautious types who refuse to make such bets because of a possible dump, even though they know the odds are against it.)

In sum, the fact that spectators will bet players in hustler-vs.-hustler games not only

8 Under certain special circumstances dumping can also occur when there are no bets with spectators or such bets are approximately equal on both sides. See below.

permits dumping but at the same time restrains the extent of it. Hustlers must severely limit their dumping, both to prevent it becoming known to the ignorant and, just as importantly, to prevent knowledgeable spectators from feeling that hustlers *generally* dump when they play each other. No hustler wants to get a reputation as a dumper; therefore he cautiously picks his spots. As a result, dumping provides only a small portion of his true hustling income, i.e., his "sure-thing" income. The great bulk of such income derives from his games with non-hustler opponents.

THE HUSTLER AND HIS BACKER

The hustler frequently uses a backer, who pays the losses if the hustler loses and receives 50% of any winnings. A backer hardly ever assumes any managerial function. All he does is put up the hustler's stake money in return for a half share in the profits.

Once in a very great while, a hustler will work out a standing agreement for backing, i.e., have someone agree to back him regularly. There is no time limit specified for such an arrangement; the deal lasts only as long as both parties consent to it.

But almost always the hustler has no standing agreement with a backer. Rather, he looks for backing on an *ad hoc* basis as the occasion for backing arises. The "occasion" is not that the hustler decides, in the abstract, to play on someone else's risk capital; it is a specific match with a particular opponent, whose handicap terms (if any) the hustler has already arranged or knows he can get. Indeed, even a topnotch hustler rarely can get backing without being able to tell the backer who the prospective opponent is and what the terms of the game are; the hustler has to convince the backer that the particular deal is a good one.

After tentatively arranging a game with his opponent, the hustler asks one of his acquaintances in the room to back him, and if he can't find backing in the room he phones a potential backer to hurry on down with some cash. Sometimes the hustler enters the poolroom with his backer in tow.

The backer specifies the maximum amount per game that he is willing to invest, but makes no guarantee about a total investment. That is, if the hustler starts to lose, the backer can pull out after any game. And if the hustler starts winning, he cannot then bet only his "own" money and dispense with the backer; the backer is in for 50% of the profit made on the entire session.

Under what conditions does the hustler seek a backer? The obvious answer is that when the hustler is broke or nearly broke (as he very often is), he looks for backing, and when he has his own money to invest he plays with that. This is indeed how the average hustler operates. The superior hustler, however, figures more angles than that. As one of the most intelligent hustlers explained to me: "If you've got lockup action [a game impossible to lose] and you're broke or maybe you need a bigger stake, you should first try like hell to *borrow* the dough. It's crazy to cut somebody in on action like that unless you have to. The other big thing—what some of these jerks don't understand—is that when you have a real tough game you should *always* look for a backer, even if you've got the dough. You should take out insurance."

The backer, then, should not assume he is being approached for backing because the hustler can raise stake money no other way (though this is usually the case), but has to consider the possibility that it's because the hustler has a very difficult game he wants to "insure."

Also, the backer must consider the possibility that he may be dumped by the hustler: If the hustler is playing a colleague, they may have agreed that one of them will win the good majority of games and that they will later split the profits. (When both hustlers making such an agreement are using backers, the decision as to which hustler will lose is more or less arbitrary. If one hustler is using a backer and the other is not, it is of course the former who agrees to lose.) Or, if the hustler is playing a non-hustler with whom no such collusion is possible, he may deliberately lose on the backer's money until the backer quits, and then, after the backer has left the room or on some other occasion, the hustler, playing with his own money, will slaughter the opponent he has set up on the backer's money.

All in all, it takes as much sophistication to be a good backer as to be a good hustler.

THE HUSTLER AS CON MAN

As several parts of this study illustrate in detail, hustling demands a continuous and complicated concern with how one is seen by others. Attention to this matter is an ineluctably pervasive requirement of the hustler's trade, and is beset with risks and contradictions. The hustler has not only the concerns that one ordinarily has about being esteemed for one's skills, but develops, in addition to and partly in conflict with such concerns, a complex set of special needs or desires about how others should evaluate him, reactions to their evaluations, and behaviors designed to manipulate such evaluating.

The hustler is a certain kind of con man. And conning, by definition, involves extraordinary manipulation of other people's impressions of reality and especially of one's self, creating "false impressions."[9] Now, if one compares the hustler with the more usual sorts of con men described by David Maurer in *The Big Con*, part of the hustler's specialness is seen to lie in this: the structural contexts within which he operates— the game, the setting of the game within the poolroom, the setting of the poolroom within the larger social structure—are not only more predetermined but more constraining. Structures do not "work for" the poolroom hustler to anywhere near the extent that they often do for other con men, and hence he must involve himself in more personal ways with active, continuous conning.

The point is not simply that the hustler can't find an ideal structural context, but that much less than the ordinary con man is able to bend a structure toward the ideal or create one *ab ovo* (come up with an analogue of the con man's "store"). That is, the hustler is far less able to be a "producer" or "director" of ideal social "scenes." To a much greater degree he must work in poor settings, and to a correspondingly greater degree he must depend on being a continuously self-aware "actor."[10] (In this connection, note the ease with which many passages of this essay could be restated in dramaturgical or Goffmaniacal terms.)

The nature and degree of the hustler's concern about the evaluation of him by another person varies, of course, with the specific kind of "other" that the person represents. For the hustler the three main types of significant others are: outsiders, intended or actual victims, and colleagues. His shifting concerns about each group relate not only to particular work situations but to his general lifestyle and career line.

---

[9] Of course conning is only a matter of degree, in that all of us are concerned in many ways to manipulate others' impressions of us; and so one can, if one wishes, take the view that every man is at bottom a con man. This form of "disenchantment of the world" is central to Herman Melville's *The Confidence Man* (perhaps the bitterest novel in all of American literature) and to the sociological writings of Erving Goffman. Its principal corollary is the view expressed by hustlers, by professional criminals, and by Thorstein Veblen, that all businessmen are thieves.

[10] The kinds of structural problems faced today by the pool or billiard hustler are by no means all endemic. Some are the result of recent social change (see Polsky, *op. cit.*).

On the other hand, such change does not create structural problems for all types of hustling. Today the golf hustler, for example, finds that with precious little "acting" he can (a) get heavy action from non-hustlers, (b) lose the majority of the 18 holes and still clean up, and at the same time (c) not be suspected as a hustler. The structure of the game of golf itself, the peculiar structurally predetermined variations in the betting relationship as one makes the round of the course ("presses," etc.), and the present setting of the game within the larger society—all these combine to create a situation that is tailor-made for hustling. But that is another story.

AUTHOR INDEX

SUBJECT INDEX